英語フィロロジーと
コーパス研究
English Philology
and Corpus Studies

今井光規教授
古希記念論文集
A Festschrift in Honour of
Mitsunori Imai to Celebrate
His Seventieth Birthday

Edited by
渡部眞一郎
細谷行輝 編
Shinichiro Watanabe
and
Yukiteru Hosoya

松柏社
SHOHAKUSHA

First published 2009
by Shohakusha Publishing Co.,Ltd.,Tokyo
1-6-1 Iidabashi
Chiyoda-ku,Tokyo 102-0072   Japan

©2009 Shinichiro Watanabe and Yukiteru Hosoya

ALL RIGHTS RESERVED. No part of this book may be reproduced or utilized in any form or by any electronic, mechanical, or other means, now known or hereafter invented, including photocopying and recording, or in any information storage or retrieval system, without permission in writing from the publishers.

Printed in Japan

今井光規教授近影

Foreword

With these few lines I would like to express my warmest congratulations to Professor Mitsunori Imai on the occasion of his seventieth birthday.

Over the years Professor Imai has made constant efforts to promote the academic and non-academic relationship between Denmark and Japan. Since his first visit to Copenhagen on a Danish Government Scholarship in 1982 he has established firm bonds with scholars and people in Denmark. Furthermore, his effort has developed into the promotion of increased academic relations between the Nordic countries and Japan.

Professor Imai is the first Japanese member of the Nordic Association for English Studies, and he has a wide circle of friends and acquaintances at the universities in the Nordic countries. All these relationships originated from his academic life in Denmark.

Professor Imai has also contributed extensively to the promotion of the academic exchange between Denmark and Japan. For instance, the exchange programme between the University of Copenhagen and Osaka University was initiated into its full-fledged present form by Professor Imai. During his time as President for the Japan Society for Medieval English Studies and for the Japan Association for English Corpus Studies he also invited many Nordic Scholars to Japan.

Professor Imai is one of the pillars in the history of academic cooperation between Denmark and Japan and the Danish Embassy will continue its support for his invaluable work.

February 20, 2009   Franz-Michael Skjold Mellbin
                     Ambassador of Denmark to Japan

Preface

It is our great pleasure to dedicate this Festschrift to Professor Mitsunori Imai to celebrate his seventieth birthday, December 4, 2008.

Over the past forty-three years, Professor Imai has contributed at home and abroad to the academic field of English studies, which includes English philology, English corpus studies, and English language teaching. He has published numerous academic works in this field. Yet, his primary concern is English philology, and some of his important works are concerned with syntax and style in Middle English Romances. He has been an active member of the Medieval English Romance Research Group since 1976. He has dedicated his life to the study of English philology and is without doubt one of the greatest philologists in Japan.

In Japan, Professor Imai has played an important role in several academic societies: he acted as President of the Japan Society for Medieval English Studies for the two academic years of 2003 and 2004, and he also acted as President of Japan Association for English Corpus Studies for three academic years from 2001 to 2004. He has made a great contribution to English language teaching in Japan. He has taught English, full time or part time, at many universities: he taught full time at Hiroshima University, and he gained his full professorship at Osaka University, where he assumed the position of Dean from 1997 till 2001. At his retirement from Osaka University in 2002, he was appointed Professor Emeritus of Osaka University. Currently, he is Professor and President of Setsunan University.

We are pleased to say that we have thirty-five contributors for this Festschrift: twenty-five from Japan and ten from abroad. Let us here and now record our deep gratitude to all those concerned for their generous support, and special thanks are due to Professor Jiro Yoshioka, Professor Masatomo Ukaji, Professor Matsuji Tajima, and Professor Junsaku Nakamura for their contributions.

One most notable feature of Professor Imai's academic life is his Nordic connections. Since his first visit to the University of Copenhagen on a Scholarship from the Danish Government during 1982-83 he has, as we understand, visited Denmark more than twenty times and established close and firm relationships with scholars and people there and in other Nordic countries. It is our great pleasure and honour to have ten contributors from abroad. We would like to express our sincere gratitude for their contributions to Professor Karin Aijmer (University of Gothenburg, Sweden), Professor Graham D. Caie (University of Glasgow, UK), Professors Arne Zettersten and Dorrit Einersen (University of Copenhagen, Denmark), Professors Risto Hiltunen and Päivi Pietilä (University of Turku, Finland), Professor Maldwyn Mills (University of Wales, UK), Professor Young-Bae Park (Kookmin University, Korea), Professor Matti Rissanen (University of Helsinki, Finland), and Dr. Mogens Magnusson from Denmark. Thus, in this Festschrift we have many contributions from the world-acclaimed scholars from Nordic countries, Scotland, Wales and Korea as well as from Japan.

Lastly, we would like to tender our heartfelt gratitude to Ms. Atsuko Yamamoto, who has devoted herself to compiling all the papers by using the TEX/LATEXsystem and helping solve many technical problems we encountered in editing the volume . We would also like to thank our publisher, Mr. Nobuhisa Mori, the president of the Shohakusha Publishing Company.

March 10, 2009   Shinichiro Watanabe
                                                Yukiteru Hosoya

CONTENTS

Foreword .... Franz-Michael Skjold MELLBIN i
                             Ambassador of Denmark to Japan

Preface .... Shinichiro WATANABE & Yukiteru HOSOYA iii

I

Then – A Temporal Adverb and a Discourse Marker
.... Karin AIJMER   3

Chaucer's *Man of Law's Tale*:
 A Case of Medieval Pathos or Just Pathetic? ... Graham D. CAIE   23

Jeanette Winterson and Medieval Romance Making It New
.... Dorrit EINERSEN   41

On Promotional Discourse in Caxton's Prologues
 *"[E]very man naturally desireth to know
 and to con newe thynges"* .... Risto HILTUNEN   59

The Percy Folio Text of *Lybius Disconius* ... Maldwyn MILLS   79

Some Aspects of Chaucer's Religious
 and Philosophic World in his *Canterbury Tales*
.... Young-Bae PARK   93

Grammatical vs. Lexical Competence
of Advanced Foreign Language Learners .... Päivi PIETILÄ 115

Grammaticalisation, Contact and Adverbial Connectives:
The Rise and Decline of *Save* .... Matti RISSANEN 135

Great Strides forward in Ancrene Wisse Research
To be or not to be AB? .... Arne ZETTERSTEN 153

The Verb *Pray* in Different Letters of the Paston Family
with Special Reference to its Pragmatic Use .... Yoko IYEIRI 169

A Historical Approach to Variant Word Forms in English
.... Akiyuki JIMURA 185

Dynamics of Repetition:
Subversion and Resistance in Two Dramas .... Sei KOSUGI 195

How does the Computer Look at the Shakespearian Sonnets?
A Quantitative Observation by Means of
Quantification of Contingency Table ..... Junsaku NAKAMURA 211

The *Cunningest, Rummest, Superlativest Old Fox:*
A Multivariate Approach to Superlatives in Dickens and Smollett
.... Tomoji TABATA 227

On the Concept of Habitual Style in the BNC
.... Kaoru TAKAHASHI 243

Gentleman in *Oliver Twist*:
A Linguistic Approach to Literature .... Shinichiro WATANABE 259

Translating Julian of Norwich's Politeness into Japanese
.... Fumiko YOSHIKAWA 273

Mitsunori Imai – Spredte Indtryk af en Japansk Ven
.... Mogens MAGNUSSON　289

II

Paston Letters and Papers における否定接続詞 ne
.... 宇賀治　正　朋　301

BNC の自然会話資料
　― 乳幼児とテープレコーダの「いる」日常 ― 内　田　充　美　317

1600 年代イギリス文学作品における過去形と現在完了形の交替
　― 散文と演劇を比較して ― .... 大　津　智　彦　331

キャクストン訳『イソップ』における軽動詞表現
　― 中仏語による原典との比較 ― .... 尾　崎　久　男　345

中世文学とテクスト校訂
　― 『梟とナイティンゲール』二つのテクスト校訂 ―
.... 菊　池　清　明　357

West Saxon Gospels マルコ伝翻訳者の統語上の一特徴
　― 等位主節における VO/OV の選択に関して ―
.... 小　塚　良　孝　371

ガウェイン詩群における「人物」を表す絶対形容詞
.... 田　島　松　二　381

Caxton の翻訳技法としての Word Pairs
　― *Paris and Vienne* ― .... 谷　　　明　信　397

Chaucer の言語とメトニミー 　—*Troilus and Criseyde* の場合 — .... 中　尾　佳　行	413
PPCME2, PPCEME に見る強意副詞 .... 西　村　秀　夫	427
Dafydd ap Gwilym の詩注解 .... 吉　岡　治　郎	439
芸術作品の擁護 　—『ベーオウルフ』「グレンデルのヘオロット襲撃」の 　文章構造と詩人の技法 — .... 渡　辺　秀　樹	455
『ユリシーズ』第 8 挿話を読む — 不完全なる完全 　..................................... 今　井　安　美	475
メタファーに見る感情のプロトタイプ特性 .. 大　森　文　子	489
語彙概念構造の潜在項と多義性 　—「つく」と「つける」を中心に — ...... 板　東　美智子	503
デジタル時代における言語研究 .... 細　谷　行　輝	519
エッダ神話詩動詞出現形と作品形式との関係 堀　井　祐　介	529
日本の友人今井光規氏の折々の印象 　.............. モーンス・マグヌッソン　堀井　祐介　訳	541
今井光規教授略歴................................	551
今井光規教授研究業績............................	553
あとがき..	563
CONTRIBUTORS 執筆者一覧.......................	565

I

Then – A Temporal Adverb and a Discourse Marker[1]

Karin Aijmer

1 Introduction

At first sight the meaning of *then* seems to be unproblematic. It is a deictic temporal adverb with the meaning to signal that something will take place 'after something has happened': *First the passengers and then the stewards jumped from the wreckage* (Longman). A closer look at the adverb shows that it can have additional meanings and uses where it is best described as a discourse marker.

Schiffrin in her influential monograph on discourse markers (1987) has taken an interest in 'markers whose deictic meanings influence their use on several different discourse planes' (Schiffrin 1987: 228). *Now* and *then* are deictic since they 'convey a relationship between the time at which a proposition is assumed to be true, and the time at which it is presented in an utterance' (Schiffrin, ibidem) at the same time as they have developed a number of non-deictic or discourse uses (cf Levinson 1983:66). Deixis is illustrated in sentences such as

I can now see the hill

where the reading of *now* depends on who the speaker is and the time at which it is presented in the utterance. In

I could then see the hill

then refers to a time in the past in relation to the time of the utterance. Both *now* and *then* have developed textual and interpersonal functions which go beyond reference to the temporal location. *Then* as a marker is non-temporal: it refers to discourse time (the order in which a speaker presents utterances in a discourse; Schiffrin 1987: 298) rather than reference time (the time of utterance): its function is to 'create a bridge to a prior discourse time created by an utterance from either the speaker him/herself or from the other' (Schiffrin 1987: 266). *Then* connects units of discourse and is related to other discourse markers such as *moreover, besides, well, consequently* in utterance-initial position (cf Levinson 183: 96; Fraser 1996).

The present article wants to contribute to the discussion of the relation between context and meaning by studying how the different meanings and contextual values of *then* are reflected in the translations into another language. Translators have to be sensitive to the context in order to make judgements about meanings and their appropriate translations. Translations can therefore provide the semantic raw material enabling us to analyze different functions of multifunctional elements. When *then* is translated as a temporal adverb (eg as Swedish *sedan* specifying that an event takes place later than another event) it is a temporal adverb with deictic meaning. *Then* is of interest since it can also be anaphoric. In Swedish the deictic and anaphoric uses of *then* are distinguished by different translations.

2 The uses of deixis

What makes *then* difficult to analyze as a deictic is that it can belong to several deictic systems involving time, closeness to the speaker, and discourse. *Now* and *then* have to with temporal deixis which we have described above as the relationship between a proposition and the time of the utterance. Discourse deixis concerns the different ways in which utterance signals its relation to the surrounding text (Levinson 1983: 85). *Then* can for instance relate units of discourse. The properties of *now* and *then* can also be understood on the deictic axis proximal/distal. Elements which are proximal (eg *now*) are ego-centred while *then* is distal and more remote from the speaker. Another deictic dimension is needed to explain that *now* focuses on the speaker and upcoming talk, while *then* points backwards to what has been said in prior discourse (Schiffrin 1987: 240. 246). The problems of describing different usages of deictic terms are summarised by Levinson as follows:

> Clearly the proliferation of different kinds of usage of deictic terms is a source of considerable confusion to the analyst. The following summary of distinctions may help to keep them clear:
>
> *Different usages of deictic terms*
> 1. deictic: a. *gestural*
>   b. *symbolic*
> 2. non-deictic: c. *non-anaphoric*
>   d. *anaphoric*
>
> (Levinson 1983: 67-68)

The three-fold distinction (gestural, symbolic, non-deictic) can be illustrated with *now*. In the following three examples from Levinson (1983: 66), the first example is gestural, the second is symbolic and the third is non-deictic:

    a. Push not *now*, but *now*

    b. Let's go *now* rather than tomorrow

    c. *Now,* that's not what I said

In the gestural usage *now* is interpreted in reference to the physical monitoring of the speech act (Levinson 1983: 65). In b. on the other hand *now* makes reference to the temporal information available to the speakers in the speech situation.

    Both *now* and *then* have deictic and non-deictic usages. However it is difficult to think of gestural examples of *then*. The symbolic use is illustrated in 'then the stewards jumped from the wreckage' where *then* can only be interpreted with reference to the speech situation. Non-deictic uses would be those where *then* has primarily the textual or discourse-organizing function. Moreover *then* is both deictic and anaphoric. I will return to a discussion of the anaphoric *then* in Section 6.

3 Parallel corpora

Corpora are essential to get a picture of what *then* means in different contexts. The meaning of *then* needs to be studied from several points of view such as position in the utterance, collocations, and occurrence in different types of sentences (declarative sentences, imperatives and questions). However we can still be left with some uncertainty about what *then* means in different contexts. We can confirm or disconfirm the hypotheses from other approaches by using a parallel or translation corpus to study how the different meanings of *then* are reflected or paraphrased in another language. This method has the advantage that meanings become more tangible than if the linguist relies on his or her intuition or observation to study multifunctionality. Moreover by studying a large number of translations of *then* in different contexts we can capture meanings which may escape the linguist's intuitions because they are not frequent or salient.

The corpus which I have used to extract examples is the English-Swedish Parallel Corpus (ESPC) (Altenberg and Aijmer 2001). The English-Swedish Parallel Corpus contains almost 2 million words of fiction and non-fiction texts in equal proportions (40 texts of each category). It is a bidirectional corpus containing English original texts and their translations into Swedish as well as the Swedish texts and their translations into English. However only the translations from English into Swedish have been used for this study (c 1 million words). *Then* has been excerpted from the English source texts and the translations noted (with their Swedish glosses) (see Section 4, Table 1). As a first step I will use the data from the corpus to establish what the translations can reveal about the meanings of *then*.

4 *Then* in translation

The table below shows that *then* has several translations.

Table 1. Translations of *then* into Swedish

sedan (sen) 'later than'	378
då 'at that time'	157
så 'so'	55
vid det laget 'by that time'	14
(men) i så fall 'but in such a case'	9
alltså 'thus', 'consequently'	5
därefter, därpå 'after that', efter ett tag 'after a while'	5
men ju 'but of course'	4
nu 'now'	4
från den dagen (stunden) 'from that time', sedan dess 'since then'	4
på den tiden 'at that time'	3
också 'also'	2
förstås 'of course'	2
i det ögonblicket 'at that moment'	2
men (fast) å andra sidan 'but on the other hand'	2
men väl 'but surely'	2
till dess, fram till denna tidpunkt 'up till then'	2
genast, på en gång 'at once'	2
i alla fall, ändå 'anyhow'	2
och (samtidigt) 'and at the same time'	2
ø	41
other	40
Total	737

The translations are intended as a spring-board to explaining different meanings and nuances of *then* which are difficult to pinpoint otherwise. The translations serve as paraphrases of different source meanings but need to be further explained.

We notice that three lexical items make up the bulk of the translations. *Sedan (sen)* is the most frequent translation (51%). *Då* occurred in 21% of the examples and *så* represented 7%. Other translations are also of interest even if they are not frequent since they may make a meaning more explicit. In many examples *then* had not been translated (41 examples) suggesting that the temporal meaning can be redundant.[2] The examples marked 'other' were reformulations giving little information about the meaning of *then*.

The main feature determining the interpretation of *then* is whether it is deictic or anaphoric. I shall therefore discuss these uses separately.

5 Deictic *then*

5.1 *Then* translated as 'sedan' ('sen')

Whenever *then* is translated as 'sedan' it can have the deictic meaning of pointing to what is happening next, after something else has happened (cf Longman *then* 2). *Then* is typically found in thematic position to bring the discourse forwards. Initial position (including *and then, but then*) is therefore potentially a typical discourse marker function (cf Schiffrin 1987: 248). The following example illustrates the meaning of *then* to signal a succession of events or actions:

(1) There was a silence, then Andrew said: " No, I don't think it's strange at all (AH1)

Det blev tyst, sedan sade Andrew: Nej jag tycker inte det är underligt alls.

Examples of more explicit lexical alternatives to *sedan* specifying temporal succession are *därefter, därpå* 'after that'. In (1) I would regard *then* as a time adverb (time adjunct). In other cases *sedan* functions more like a connective relating units in discourse although it retains some temporal meaning. 'Since discourse unfolds in time, it seems natural that time-deictic words can be used to refer to portions of the discourse' (Levinson 1983: 85).

The close relationship between temporal succession in the real world and the succession or organization of events in the unfolding discourse is reflected in the following example. The girl gives a list of things she knows about the speaker (as arguments for approaching him for her purposes).

> (2) This unusual girl, he thought, had many facets. He asked, "What *do* you know?" "Well, for one thing you were at the top of your medical school class at Johns Hopkins. For another, you did your internship and residency at Massachusetts General – I know only the best get in there. Then Dr. Townsend chose you out of fifty applicants and took you into his practice because he knew you were good. (AH1)
>
> Den här märkliga flickan, tänkte han, har många sidor. Han frågade: "Vad *vet* du?" "Nja, för det första var du etta i din kurs på Johns Hopkins. För det andra hade du din allmäntjänstgöring och fick din specialistutbildning på Massachusetts General Hospital – jag vet att bara de bästa kommer in där. Sedan valde doktor Townsend ut dig bland femtio sökande och tog dig till medarbetare för att han visste att du var bra.

The translator's use of *sedan* suggests that the temporal meaning has not disappeared but that the time reference is relative to the discourse. *Then* introduces the last (and the strongest) argument.

5.2 *Then* translated as 'så'

When *then* signals a change from one stage of the discourse to another I would analyze it as a discourse marker rather than a temporal adverb. However many examples can be interpreted in either way as for example (2) above. On the other hand, when the translator has chosen *(och) så* this suggests that the temporal meaning has weakened and *then* functions as a discourse marker rather than as a temporal adverb. *Then* as a discourse marker can for instance signal a subtopic or an episode in a narrative; it can precede a point in an argument, add things to a list, etc. In the following example *and then* introduces some order into the speaker's recollections which is not temporal:

(3) 'It's one of my most vivid memories,' he says.'I don't often long back, but this is one thing I'll never forget. Writing in front of an open window at night. The large moths, the flying beetles. Crickets outside. And <u>then</u> this smell: there's grass in it, bruised green grass, but dry stalks too. (BR1)

"Det är ett av mina livligaste minnen", säger han. "Det är inte ofta jag längtar tillbaka, men det här är någonting som jag aldrig kommer att glömma. Att sitta och skriva vid ett öppet fönster på natten. De stora nattflyna, de flygande skalbaggarna. Syrsor utanför. <u>Och så</u> den här lukten: det är gräs i den, sönderhackat grönt gräs, men torra stjälkar också.

In the following example the topics are unordered although they are forced into what looks like temporal sequencing in the discourse:

(4) The narrow quiver of the plane. Provence. London. Foggy mornings in Hyde Park. Paris –) <u>Then</u> as she looks straight back at him: 'You won't find out by asking.' (BR1)

Flygplanet, trångt som ett pilkoger. Provence. London. Dimmiga morgnar i Hyde Park. Paris –) <u>Så</u>, medan hon möter hans blick utan att väja undan: "Det får du inte reda på genom att fråga."

The plane, Provence, London, Hyde Park, Paris are associated in the speaker's memory. *Then* both marks the end of the list and a continuation of the narrative.

Further evidence for the weakening of the temporal meaning comes from translations of *then* with a discourse marker having additive meaning (an additive conjunct). The following example is interesting because the translation marks the meaning as additive (*then* = *dessutom* 'besides').

(5) He needed, he felt, to live in it alone for a week or two before finally making up his mind whether to keep it for occasional holidays, sell, or pass it over at a nominal price to the Norfolk Windmill Trust who were, he knew, always anxious to restore old windmills to working order. And then there were family papers and his aunt's books, particularly her comprehensive library of ornithology, to be looked at and sorted and their disposal decided upon. (PDJ1)

Han kände att han behövde bo där ensam i en eller ett par veckor innan han slutgiltig bestämde sig för om han skulle behålla den för att tillbringa en och annan semester där, om han skulle sälja den eller om han för en symbolisk summa skulle överlåta den till Stiftelsen för Norfolks väderkvarnar, vilken, det visste han, alltid var angelägen om att restaurera gamla väderkvarnar så att de kunde sättas i drift igen. Dessutom fanns där en hel del släktpapper och hans fasters böcker, särskilt hennes omfattande ornitologiska samling, att gå igenom och sortera och sedan måste han besluta sig för vad han skulle göra med dem.

The old windmill, family papers, ornithology books are things which have been left by the main character's deceased aunt. They do not share any property which can explain that they are presented in a special order. Instead the order found reflects the fact that the speaker has to present the things in a linear order (cf Schiffrin 1987: 262). The distinction can sometimes be neutralized namely if discourse time directly reflects the temporal order. However the discourse-marking function to express relations between portions of the discourse is an important function of *then* which should not be confused with the temporal adverb functions. Ideas, topics, events, actions can be ordered in many different ways which do not imply temporal sequencing. They can be associated in the speaker's mind, they can be part of a list, reasons for an argument, etc.

In the function illustrated *then* is no longer a temporal adverb but a discourse marker, a category of items which can express a number of different relationships between an utterance and the prior discourse. Cf Levinson (1983: 87), "there are many words and phrases in English, and no doubt most languages, that indicate the relationship between an utterance and the prior discourse. Examples are utterance-initial usages of *but, therefore, in conclusion, to the contrary, still, however, anyway, well, besides, actually, all in all, so, after all,* and so on.

What they seem to indicate, often in very complex ways, just how the utterance that contains them is a response to, or a continuation of, some portion of the prior discourse."

Notice finally that it is important to look at the markers in a larger discourse context. The following example illustrates the switching from one type of marker to another reflecting whether the focus is on the temporal ordering of events or their importance for the narrative:

(6) Then, suddenly, to our astonishment, the woman lifted him up by the pants and threw him to the ground. The crowd yelled. The man flailed, got up, shouted and huffed. Then he pounced on her, lashing at her face.Dad started towards him, but his rescue attempt was cut short.The madame grabbed the bad loser's crotch and he screamed so loud that the crowd fell silent.Then, with a practised grunt, she lifted him on her shoulders, turned him round once, showing his mightiness to the sky, and dumped him savagely on the hard earth. He stayed unconscious for a while, his mouth open. She then proceeded to turn him upside-down, emptying out all the money in his pockets. (BO1)

Och så plötsligt, till vår stora förvåning, lyfte kvinnan upp honom i byxorna och kastade honom på marken. Hopen jublade.Mannen fäktade med armarna, reste sig, skrek och gormade.Så rusade han mot henne och gjorde ett utfall mot ansiktet på henne.Pappa sprang emot honom, men hans räddningsförsök kom av sig. Kvinnan grep tag i skrevet på den dålige förloraren, och han skrek så högt att hopen förstummades. Sedan lyfte hon honom, med ett inövat stönande, upp på axlarna, snurrade runt med honom en gång för att visa himlen hur mycket han var värd och slängde häftigt ner honom på marken.En stund låg han medvetslös med öppen mun. Hon fortsatte då med att vända upp och ner på honom och tömma ut alla pengar han hade i fickorna.

Och så (plötsligt) marks the unit as part of a series of events while *sedan* focuses more on temporal succession. *Då* is anaphoric (cf the following section).

To sum up, the translations (into Swedish) seem to indicate that the temporal meaning of the deictic *then* can be weakened and that it can become a marker of the succession of topics or arguments, etc in discourse. When *sedan* was chosen as a translation *(and) then* focuses on the temporal succession of events. *Så,* on the other hand, is used more broadly about events associated with each other in a person's memory, reasons underlying an explanation, an unordered list of things a person knows, temporally ordered events, actions, episodes.

6 Anaphoric *then*

6.1 *Then* translated as *då*

The translational approach is most successful when a lexical item in the source language is monosemous and corresponds to several different lexical items in the target language. However *då* as a translation of *then* can have several different interpretations. When translations give insufficient clues I will look more closely at the context in which *then* occurs. Even when *då* is a possible translation the translator sometimes uses a more explicit translation giving a clue to the translation. Such examples are therefore of particular interest and will be included in the discussion below.

Another major meaning of *then* is illustrated when it is translated by *då*.

(7) But his nights were terrible. It wasn't that he had trouble getting to sleep in the first place. That was easy. He'd watch TV till his eyes burned; then he'd climb the stairs. (AT1)

Men nätterna var förfärliga. Inte så att han hade svårt att somna. Det var en enkel sak. Han brukade titta på TV tills det sved i ögonen, och då gick han upp i övre våningen.

Then is anaphoric when it 'indicates a temporal relationship between two linguistic events' (Schiffrin 1987: 248) with reference to Reichenbach (1947). The translation with *då* shows that *then* has the anaphoric reading to relate an event (he climbed the stairs) to the preceding event that he used to watch TV. Compare *then* = 'sedan' which would have indicated temporal succession between two events rather than 'relating units internal to the context' (Schiffrin 1987: 249).

The anaphoric use can be described as a reorientation from the time of the speech situation to 'a distinct reality' in the prior discourse (following Hansen's analysis of the anaphoric use of the French *alors*):

> By thus anaphorically referring to a 'distinct reality' established in the preceding clause, one which sets the stage for the information conveyed by its host utterance, *alors* may be said to have a re-perspectivizing or reorienting effect. (Hansen 1998: 334)

The anaphoric meaning of *då* can be made explicit in the translation of *then* by a phrase containing a demonstrative pronoun pointing to the prior context (vid <u>det</u> laget 'at that time', på <u>den</u> tiden 'at that time', i <u>det</u> ögonblicket 'at that moment'):

(8) That medieval cottage someone had forgotten to list, vanished overnight. Too late for protest, then; every ancient brick not so much dumped as sold, gone, vanished. (FW1)

det där lilla femtonhundratalshuset som man hade glömt att föra upp på listan över kulturminnesmärkta byggnader och som bara försvann över en natt. Och <u>vid det laget</u> var det för sent för protester: alla de uråldriga tegelstenarna var borta, och inte låg de på soptippen heller, utan sålda var de, försvunna, förlorade.

The discourse marker uses of *then* can be related both to its deictic and anaphoric use. We have shown that *then* can point backwards in the discourse and express temporal succession or express relations between discourse units (translations as *sedan* or *så*). When it is translated as *då*, it can have other pragmatic functions as illustrated in A-F below. *Then* in these examples enables us to make inferences about what the hearer knows, what is shared knowledge or what has gone on in the preceding discourse. *Then* can be used to to solicit agreement from the hearer (as in meaning A). It can also be used to to draw a conclusion from preceding talk as in (B). Other uses of *then* =*då* are found in requests and in questions. The translation is *då* or a more explicit translation.

A. Soliciting agreement from the hearer:

(9) He hesitated. "She's gone into a coma." "Then she is dying?" (AH1)
Han tvekade. "Hon ligger i koma." "Då är hon alltså döende."

The view that she is dying is treated as information known to the hearer. *Då ... alltså* marks a tentative conclusion by the current speaker and can therefore come to solicit agreement.

B. Result or conclusion based on preceding talk

Då has the meaning 'in that case' (i så fall) signalling result or conclusion warranted by previous talk. In (10) it is used in the collocation *but then*.

(10) All right, it might even be possible for the two of us to go together − but then only with special permission, with a permit, with official sanction, a document branding us as exceptions to the rule, outcasts, deviants in their society, like paraplegics or monsters with five legs or two heads.(BR1)

Nåja, det kanske till och med kunde vara möjligt för oss att återvända tillsammans, men då bara på särskilt tillstånd, på en licens, med myndigheternas godkännande, ett dokument som stämplade oss som undantag från regeln, parias, avvikande i deras samhälle, som svårt handikappade eller monster med fem ben eller två

(11) I wish I was − then I could see a way out of this dismal place.(FW1)

Jag önskar att jag vore det − då skulle jag kunna se en väg bort från denna dystra plats.

In (12) the more explicit form ('i så fall') has been chosen in the translation to mark inference:

(12) "Can't. I'm too happy."
"Then I'll be serious for both of us."(AH1)
"Det går inte. Jag är alldeles för lycklig."
"I så fall ska jag vara allvarlig för oss båda."

The following question can be paraphrased with an *if*-clause indicating that the meaning is no longer (only) deictic or temporal: 'If it was horrible why would you not have lunch with him':

(13) "It was." I said. "It was horrible." "Then why would you want to have lunch with him?" (MA1)
"Det var det", sade jag. "Det var förfärligt." "Varför skulle du i så fall vilja äta lunch med honom?"

Then should be regarded as modal in such examples rather than as an inferential discourse marker since *then* brings in a speaker and hearer perspective (cf Hasselgård 2006 on *now* and the Norwegian *nå* as modal particles).

C. Acknowledgement of what has preceded in the discourse
In the collocation *well then, then* is never deictic but we have a marker with a backwards-looking function translated as *då så* (= i alla fall 'in that case'). *Då så* is used to acknowledge information in the answer to a preceding question. The translation indicates the speaker's positive or reserved attitude (*OK then*).

(14) "Didn't I read in the paper that you're on the injured list but hope to be back racing well before Christmas?" "You did read that, yes." "Well, then."(DF1)
"Läste jag inte i tidningen att ni står på skadelistan men hoppas kunna vara tillbaka gott och väl före jul?" "Jaså, ni läste det? Jodå." "Då så."

D. Using the preceding discourse for the argumentation
Then in the combination *but then* can be part of the argumentation. In the example below the translator could not have used *då*. The translation (*men ju* 'but as we both know') marks a return to the shared knowledge of how the hearer used to be. The effect of taking up a stance towards something which is implicit in the preceding context may be that it is treated as less important:

(15) "I liked the way you were. You were worried about your patient and you didn't care about anything else. Your caring showed. But then you're always that way." (AH1)

"Jag uppskattade ditt sätt. Du var orolig för din patient, och du struntade i allt annat. Det märktes att du tänkte på henne. Men du är ju alltid sådan."

E. Making a request by referring to the preceding context
The discourse marker pointing backwards to prior discourse is used in particular contexts. When *then* is used before an imperative it signals that the request is obvious from what has preceded in the discourse. *Då* conveys that both speaker and hearer agree to do something:

(16) The head night nurse, an elderly R.N. who worked part time, had prepared a tray with a hypodermic. She opened a refrigerator and added a clear glass drug container which the Felding-Roth saleswoman had brought. "Yes, it is." "Then let's go." (AH1)

Nattöversköterskan, en äldre deltidsarbetande dam, hade ställt fram en bricka med en injektionsspruta. Hon öppnade ett kylskåp och tog fram en genomskinlig glasflaska som representanten för Felding-Roth haft med sig."Ja, det är klart." "Då sätter vi igång."

F. Questions which originate in the preceding context
In questions *then* suggests that an inference is made from the preceding context:

(17) He saw me across the acreage, came to within ten feet, and said, "Shall I fetch the car, <u>then</u>?" and when I nodded, wheeled away and departed. (DF1)

Han såg mig tvärs över lokalen, och sa när han var några meter ifrån mig: "Ska jag hämta bilen <u>då</u>?" När jag nickade, vände han sig om och gick.

Similarly in (18), *then* is used as a marker signalling that the question is warranted in the prior discourse (cf Schiffrin 1987: 258). "'Could we have saved her then" can be paraphrased "could we have saved her if we had thought about where she was last Sunday.'" *Then* conveys that the hearer's opinion is asked for:

(18) "And you didn't wonder where she was on Sunday?" Violet dabbed at her eyes."Oh, dear," she whispered, "could we have saved her <u>then</u>? (MW1)

"Och ni undrade inte var hon höll hus i söndags?" Violet torkade sig i ögonen. "Åh kära nån", viskade hon, "hade vi kunnat rädda henne <u>då</u>?

The translation with 'kanske' (perhaps) which can replace *då* makes explicit the contextual meaning of *then* to make a suggestion (something which can be inferred from the context is presented as a possibility):

(19) "I don't find you boring." "Depressing, <u>then</u>?"(MD1)

"Jag tycker inte du är trist." "Deprimerande <u>kanske</u>?"

To sum up, *då* as a translation is used in different contexts from *sedan* which can be explained by its anaphoric use to refer to prior time. It can also be used as a discourse marker which suggests that it can refer both to the discourse and to the hearer. As a discourse marker *then* is oriented to what the hearer knows, shared knowledge and to prior talk. This explains that it can have meanings such as soliciting agreement, suggestion, acknowledgement of an answer, a request (on the basis of the agreement to do something), a question asking for an opinion. *Då* has at least the following meanings depending on the context:

- with anaphoric meaning to refer to an earlier period of time ('at that point of time')
- with the inferential meaning to draw a conclusion based on the prior discourse ('in that case'). Translation: *i så fall* 'in that case'
- with the meaning to request confirmation. Translation *alltså* 'in other words'
- in questions originating in or inferred from the earlier context 'warranted questions'. Translation: *i så fall* 'in that case'
- in imperatives originating in or inferred from the earlier context to strengthen a request
- in reluctant acknowledgements of information in the preceding discourse. Translation *då så*.

7 Conclusion

In this paper I have not dealt with the larger issues raised by deixis. The aim of this paper has instead been to show that translations and parallel corpora can be used in addition to monolingual corpora to say something about the meanings and functions of lexical items with deictic properties. The data used are from Swedish but hopefully they can be used to illustrate some points about *then* even to readers who are not speakers of Swedish. In particular I have wanted to make the point that translations (and parallel corpora) can be used to get a better picture of what *then* means when it is deictic, non-deictic (discourse marker function), anaphoric, or non-anaphoric (with modal or interpersonal functions). These meanings are not distinguished when *then* is used in English although position (initial or final) and collocations may be help to show what meaning it has. *Well then* was for instance always a marker with discourse function. *And then* could have the textual function to relate topics or arguments with a weakening of the temporal meaning of *then*. In *but then* I could sometimes interpret *then* as a temporal adverb but it could also be a discourse marker derived from the anaphoric meaning.

Swedish uses different lexical items for the deictic and anaphoric use which makes translations an interesting starting-point for discussing the meanings of *then* as well as larger questions such as the difference between temporal adverbs, discourse markers with a connective function and modal or interpersonal markers. The translation can for instance distinguish between temporal and non-temporal discourse-organizing uses. When the translations have shown that the function of *then* has been to indicate a time in the past or a temporal succession of events (Swedish *sedan* 'after that') *then* has been regarded as a temporal adverb. When translated as *så* 'so' the function is not temporal only but *then* is used to organize a list or reasons for an explanation.

The translations can also help us to show how the meanings and functions are related. *Sedan* (deictic) and *då* (anaphoric) correspond to core temporal meanings of *then* from which new meanings can be developed by means of processes such as implicature. *Then* can for instance have additive or discourse marker meanings (ordering topics, arguments, objects in a list, recollections) which are closely associated with the deictic meaning. The modal or interpersonal meanings (drawing a conclusion, acknowledgement, seeking agreement with the previous speaker or making a suggestion, etc) are more closely related to the anaphoric meaning. These developments would be interesting to study diachronically. However such a study would require a different type of data and corpora.

Notes

1   Many thanks to Göan Kjellmer for reading an earlier version of the text.
2   The following translations occurred only once and have therefore been disregarded in the table:
    innan dess 'before this', *dittills* 'so far', *i sista minuten* 'at the last minute', *kanske* 'perhaps', *där* 'there', *och dessutom* 'and furthermore'.

References

Altenberg, Bengt and Karin Aijmer (2001) "The English-Swedish Parallel Corpus: A Resource for Contrastive Research and Translation Studies." In Mair, Christian and Marianne Hundt (eds.) *Corpus Linguistics and Linguistic Theory. Papers from the 20th International Conference on English Language Research on Computerized Corpora (ICAME 20) Freiburg im Breisgau 1999*. Amsterdam & Philadelphia: Rodopi. 15-33.

Fraser, Bruce (1996) "Pragmatic Markers." *Pragmatics* 6(2): 167-190.

Hansen Mosegaard, Maj-Britt (1998) *The Function of Discourse Particles*. Amsterdam/Philadelphia: John Benjamins.

Hasselgård, Hilde (2006) "'Not now'– On non-correspondence between the cognate adverbs *now* and *nå*." In Aijmer, Karin and Anne-Marie Simon-Vandenbergen (eds.) *Pragmatic Markers in Contrast*. Amsterdam: Elsevier. 93-113.

Levinson, Stephen C. (1983) *Pragmatics*. Cambridge: CUP.

Longman Dictionary of Contemporary English. 1995 (1978). [Longman]

Reichenbach, Hans (1947) *Elements of Symbolic Logic*. London: Macmillan.

Schiffrin, D. (1987) *Discourse Markers*. Cambridge: Cambridge University Press.

Chaucer's *Man of Law's Tale*:
A Case of Medieval Pathos or Just Pathetic?

Graham D. Caie

Many Middle English romances deal with the emotion of pity, appealing to the reader's emotions, while pathos is a common rhetorical mode of persuasion. The hero or heroine is often of noble birth, separated from his or her home and loved ones and suffers greatly before being reunited in a happy ending. An example is *Havelok the Dane*, a romance which Professor Imai has closely researched. This traditional tale concerns a wicked uncle usurping the kingdom which rightfully belongs to the young Havelok of Denmark. A kindly fisherman, Grim, takes him to England where he flourishes, and, after many adventures, he returns to claim his rightful throne. The legend of the banished heir, whose virtues are instinctively reflected in his or her nobility of spirit, no matter how lowly they become, is one of the most common themes in medieval literature and a version of it is found in Chaucer's *Man of Law's Tale* (hereafter *MLT*) in *The Canterbury Tales*. Sources for the *MLT* include Nicholas Trevet's *Chronicle* and the redaction of the Constance-story in John Gower's *Confessio Amantis*, which was completed sometime before 1390. There has been much debate concerning Chaucer's debt to Gower, though more recently scholars have suggested that Chaucer did indeed know Gower's work before he wrote *MLT*.[1]

Trevet's fourteenth-century Anglo-Norman *Chronicle* covers the period of 1135 and 1307 and is intended to trace the history of the Angevin kings, while into this narrative he introduces the tale of Constance, the persecuted and banished queen.² Chaucer, however, reworks the tale, adding his own material and giving it a totally different interpretation than that of Trevet. One of the major differences is that of mood and in particular pathos throughout the tale. The political aspects which Trevet introduces, such as the Scottish wars undertaken by Alla, are only briefly alluded to Chaucer, and are simply a reason for the king's absence from his wife. The romance elements in Chaucer's work create a more attractive heroine than Trevet's, but one cannot call this tale a romance as such.

This Tale has received less attention by scholars than other tales, largely because of what is thought by many to be too strong an element of pathos and too great a stress on the emotional for contemporary readers. Many are repelled by the sweet and thick layer of pathos or 'tear-jerking' that is liberally applied. A.S.G Edwards states in the introduction to "Critical Approaches to The Man of Law's Tale" (1990, 85) that "most critics have found it easier to avoid the *Tale* than attempt even an apologetic defence." Martin Stevens (1979, 72) writes of its "brilliant satire of dullness", while Baum (1958, 115) deplores the "crudity of the story", which he finds "preposterously improbable." Morton Bloomfield (1972, 384-8) comes closer to expressing why we are not attracted to this tale, as it "cannot fully engage our sympathies or even sometimes our interest '[because of] the stylization of emotion." The key to understanding the tale, he suggests, is the tradition of *contemptus mundi*, 'contempt of the world', a philosophy also alien to our modern sensibilities. Perhaps the problem lies with a major change in attitudes and emotional responses since the fourteenth century, and what was acceptable then may be embarrassing today. David Benson in his Introduction to *Chaucer's Religious Tales* (1990, 4) asks:

> what could be more damning of Chaucer than to imagine that he would deliberately write over a thousand lines of dullness. Such critics are judging (and none too subtly) the Man of Law and not his tale, which deserves to be treated more sympathetically, if only because it enlarged

the possibilities of English poetry by introducing a level of learning and rhetorical elaboration not previously achieved by native religious verse.

However, can it be classed as religious verse? Edwards (1990, 87) notes: "the Tale resists precise generic placement and seems to have done so from the beginning of the history of its reception", and so we judge it by labelling it a romance, a religious tale, a saint's life or a folk tale and this influences our interpretation. In BL Harley 1239 *MLT* is in a collection of tales which are generally classed as romances along with the tales of the Knight, Wife of Bath, Clerk and Franklin, while in CUL Ee.2.15 it is placed with saints' lives. Paul Clogan (1977, 217-33) analyses the significance of the convergence of hagiography and romance in *MLT* and calls it "hagiographical romance". In fact it is nearly impossible to put this tale into one of the traditional genre boxes – it would appear that Chaucer has created a new genre by mixing many elements of other genres. The motifs, such as the accused queen and structural repetitions are characteristic of folk-tale, yet it is perhaps nearer a religious exemplum than a folktale. Yunck (1960, 250-8) claims it combines folktale with homily, calling it "romantic homily on the virtues of complete submission to divine providence, worked out against the harshest vicissitudes which folktale could provide". Although the tale has many hagiographical elements, and at times Custance displays the dogged self-righteousness of many saints, it is not a saint's life. By the constant pathos evoked this tale also belongs to the literature of sensibility, akin to penitential literature, as it makes us aware of mutability, the fragile nature of human existence and thus prepares us for penance. It is significant that in the sixteenth century the *Man of Law's Tale* was the first of the *Canterbury Tales* to be singled out from the others and printed separately in Alsop's 1520 edition, as it was seen to have a specific didactic function as penitential literature works, which pricked the conscience and prepared one for confession.

Before going any further, I should perhaps summarise the Tale, as it is not so well known, for the reasons given above. The Tale begins in Rome where the Christian Roman emperor in his wisdom, or lack of it, marries off his beautiful daughter Custaunce – and the name Constance is of course symbolic – to a pagan sultan. The sultan is willing to convert to Christianity for the sake of his beautiful new wife, yet Custaunce is not happy about this marriage and we first see her in the depressed mode which will dominate her throughout the Tale:

> Custance, that was with sorwe al overcome,
> Ful pale arist, and dresseth hir to wende
> For wel she seeth ther is noon oother ende.
> Allas, what wonder is it thogh she wepte.[3] (264-7)

The Sultan's mother is furious about her son's conversion to Christianity, and, as the stereotypical evil mother-in-law, she has her son and all those who converted killed. With melodramatic effect the mother-in-law is vilified by the narrator:

> O Sowdanesse, roote of iniquitee!
> Virage, thou Semyrame the secounde!
> O serpent under femynyntee,
> Lik to the serpent depe in helle ybounde!
> O feyned womman, al that may confounde
> Vertu and innocence thurgh thy malice
> Is bred in thee, as nest of every vice! (358-64)

There is no sympathy for the Christian martyrs, as the camera is strictly on Custaunce who escapes in a small boat, laden with her entire dowry and all the food and clothes she needs for her travels. This close detail to material goods has often been used as a comment on the worldliness of the narrator and is discussed below.

Custaunce lands up in Northumbria and communicates in "a maner Latyn corrupt" with the warden and his wife, Dame Hermengild, who are good to her and, after constant preaching by Custaunce, both convert to Christianity. An evil knight who is spurned by the self-righteous Custaunce has a fiendish plot to get his revenge and stabs Hermengild who is in the same bed as Custaunce, leaving the knife in Custaunce's hand. The king of Northumbria, Alla, however, on his return from war, immediately knows, by looking at the sad face of Custaunce, that this saintly woman is innocent.

> This Alla kyng hath swich compassioun,
> As gentil herte is fulfild of pitee,
> That from his eyen ran the water doun. (659-61)

The knight is struck down by a divine hand and all problems seem to disappear when King Alla marries Custaunce and they have a child. Unfortunately Custaunce finds herself with a second wicked mother-in-law, Donegild, who hates her. When the king goes off to war again, Donegild, Alla's mother, exchanges her son's letters so that Custaunce receives a forged missive which falsely accuses her and leads to her and her son's banishment. Much weeping and wailing resume, and the pathetic Custaunce sets out once more on her travels.

> Wepen bothe yonge and olde in al that place,
> Whan that the kyng this cursed lettre sente,
> And Custance, with a deedly pale face,
> The ferthe day toward the ship she wente. (820-4)

Pathos dominates this scene as she cries bitterly, while protecting her son:

> Hir litel child lay wepyng in hir arm,
> And knelynge, pitously to hym she seyde,
> "Pees, litel sone, I wol do thee noon harm."
> With that hir coverchief on hir heed she breyde,
> And over his litel eyen she it leyde,
> And in hir arm she lulleth it ful faste,
> And into hevene hire eyen up she caste. (833-41)

Such a scene is reminiscent of the Pieta image, with mother and child weeping in deep sorrow. Her following prayer to the Virgin makes the link even more obvious:

> Thow sawe thy child yslayn bifore thyne yen,
> And yet now lyveth my litel child, parfay!
> Now, lady bright, to whom alle woful cryen,
> Thow glorie of wommanhede, thow faire may,
> Thow haven of refut, brighte sterre of day,
> Rewe on my child, that of thy gentillesse,
> Rewest on every reweful in distresse.
> O litel child, allas! what is thy gilt,
> That nevere wroghtest synne as yet, pardee? (848-56)

Once more she sets out by ship with no destination, but the ship is miraculously washed up back home near Rome. She is saved by a Roman senator who turns out to be married to her aunt and then, again miraculously, her husband King Alla also appears in Rome to do penance for killing all involved in the plot against Custaunce. So a happy ending is achieved with Custaunce, her son Maurice, father and husband all reunited, but not before much grief, pathos and wailing:

> Whan Alla saugh his wyf, faire he hire grette,
> And weep, that it was routhe for to see.
> . . . .
> Long was the sobbyng and the bitter peyne,
> Er that hir woful hertes myghte cesse;
> Greet was the pitee for to heere hem pleyne,
> Thurgh whiche pleintes gan hir wo encresse.
> I pray yow alle my labour to relesse;
> I may nat telle hir wo until to-morwe,
> I am so wery for to speke of sorwe. (1051-2; 1066-71)

As can be seen from the above quotations, the mood of pathos dominates this tale. One wonders what other hardship the ever-weeping Custaunce could possibly suffer. The major question is whether the pathos and the melodramatic rhetoric are deliberately manipulated by the teller, the Man of Law, to get his audience to sob their way into voting him the best story teller, which, after all, is the aim of the pilgrims. One might also ask if this is Chaucer's way of telling us about the dangers of false rhetoric which this lawyer-narrator applies to create the sense of pathos? If one were to equate the Sergeant of the Lawe in the *General Prologue* with this character, then one might be excused for thinking that the Man of Law is superficial, worried about worldly goods ("Of fees and robes hadde he many oon": *General Prologue*, 317), but with no spiritual depth. The Sergeant has been called a *bourgeois parvenu*, pretentious, concerned only with worldly prosperity and appearances, and indeed the word 'seems' recurs in the Portrait and the Tale: "Nowher so bisy a man as he ther nas,/ And yet he semed bisier than he was" (*General Prologue* 321-2). *Bisy* here could have the modern meaning of 'occupied', often in a negative sense as in ' a busybody', but it also had the sense in Middle English of 'caring', 'solicitous, 'anxious', or 'devoted', referring to mental faculties and emotions. In the context of the *General Prologue* portrait, these lines might be interpreted as meaning that the Sergeant "seemed more caring than he was." There is no suggestion that he is sensitive or with any moral depth either, so one might well think that he substitutes rhetoric for moral substance in his tale. But *is* he the worldly Sergeant of the Lawe in the *General Prologue*? The narrator of the Tale is also frequently worried about financial details. The Tale begins with rich merchants with "clothes of gold, and satyns riche of hewe" (136) and the narrator spends much time describing Custaunce's dowry and worries that she has enough supplies of food and money on her trips.

Chauncey Wood (1970, 242), who sees the whole tale as a satire on lawyers, suggests that the initial bargain between Host and teller is a contract and the pervading legal language marks acceptance of the rule of law. The Syrian marriage, for example, is presented in terms of legal formalities and strict observance of property. However, such an interpretation which depends on the character of the teller and of the dubious link between Sergeant and the narrator of the tale is problematic. If it is a satire, then the rhetorical devices in the Tale have to be seen as only an extravagant show by the narrator. Derek Pearsall (1985, 257) criticises the tendency of critics to concentrate too heavily on the narrator and to view the Tale as a means of commenting on him; in Pearsall's opinion, the narrator "falls into the role simply of a person who has to tell a story, and there is nothing that can be discerned in the Introduction, or the Prologue, or the Tale, that has specifically to do with a lawyer" (257). So if the extravagant rhetoric is not a ploy to satirize the teller and lawyers in general, then we must look elsewhere for a solution.

I would, therefore, like to consider the possibility that Chaucer's audience did not consider the rhetoric out of place or exaggerated. It could be that we are dealing with a genre much loved and respected in the Middle Ages, but which is now misunderstood. If that were the case, then the Man of Law might be a gifted story-teller whose tale reflected the sensibilities of the fourteenth century. It would mean that this tale functioned perfectly well in Chaucer's time, that it was not meant to reflect defects in the teller, or to parody second-rate religious romances. The problem is with us, the readers, who are hardened to suffering and whose culture does not look favourably on outer signs of pathos, weeping, or demonstrable emotions. We see in our television screens daily images of women, children and men screaming and crying out their despair at bereavement, tearing their clothes and mourning in a demonstrative fashion which is frowned upon by the 'British stiff upper lip' which allows no sign of emotion – except perhaps at football matches. The British queen was shocked to hear that her typically British attitude and dry-eyed expression in public at the news of Princess Diana's death was considered unfeeling and insensitive. She was just being British!

Naturally the *Man of Law's Tale* is not unique when it comes to the rhetoric of pathos; we have the Clerk's tale of patient Griselda, the Prioress's tale of the pathetic Christian boy whose tongue is cut out by the Jews, and, to a lesser extent, the Monk's and Second Nun's tales. These works have the following in common: they have simple plots and morally black or white characters; the cruel and dominating characters punish and torment the good; the reader is meant to sympathise with the suffering of the good character, who shows patience and constancy; and the overall effect is one of strong emotion, pity, compassion leading to tears. The central figure is invariably the innocent victim, passive, powerless and accepting all that is thrown at him or, more usually, her. This leads to pain, distress and tragedy, but the ending is always happy, albeit with tears of joy.

Another common denominator in these tales is that of heightened rhetoric, and it is this that alienates the modern reader as much as the tears. The laments, apostrophes, exclamations, all appear over-the-top, melodramatic, as in the "O Sowdanesse" outburst above (358), or this:

> O sodeyn wo, that evere art successour
> To worldly blisse, spreynd with bitternesse!
> The ende of the joye of oure worldly labour! (421-3)

or:

> O donegild, I ne have noon englissh digne
> Unto thy malice and thy tirannye!
> And therfore to the feend I thee resigne;
> Lat hym enditen of thy traitorie!
> Fy, mannysh, fy! – o nay, by God, I lye –
> Fy, feendlych spirit, for I dar wel telle. (778-83)

In such an apostrophe the narrator turns from his narrative to address us, his audience, with heightened emotions, presumably to reinforce the dramatic nature of the scene and to solicit our outrage.

The Tale is indeed a "masterpiece of eloquentia", as Kittredge (1915, 11) noted, possibly the most elaborately rhetorical of all Chaucer's works. Edward Block (1953, 572-6) demonstrates how Chaucer's rhetorical skills "materially changed the form and content" of Trevet's version in order to create pathos. I believe that it is a modern failing to consider the Man of Law's application of amplification as being excessive, undermining the seriousness of his tale, and thereby demonstrating a weakness in the teller. The tale's self-conscious and colourful rhetoric, which includes repetition, apostrophe, sententia, occupatio, comparatio, exclamatio, and learned quotations, is a device which heightens pathos, and is often found in hagiographical works. There is then created by this formal language a tension between the audience's emotional, sympathetic and personal response to the dilemma of the central figure, and the didactic, Christian or philosophical message which the narrator intends to impart. Alfred David (1967, 140) suggests that this ornate rhetoric "brings something new to Middle English religious poetry and produces a tale that is unequalled as an elevated, learned celebration of the triumph of Christian values." It is significant to note that many of Chaucer's tales written in rhyme royal are saints' lives and hagiographies such as the Second Nun's, Prioress's, and Man of Law's tales, where divine justice is finally demonstrated. Charles Muscatine has called rhyme royal "an implement of seriousness" (1986, 192). All these tales evoke a strong, emotional response which is counterbalanced by both the rhetoric and the formal verse form.

Another significant influence on Chaucer's retelling and absent in Trevet are his paraphrases of Innocent III's *De Miseria* (*De contemptu mundi*); the only other tale to have references to Innocent III is the Pardoner's. In Prologue G of the Legend of Good Women Chaucer states that:

> He hath in prose translated Boece
> And of the Wrechede Engendrynge of Mankynde,
> As man in pope Innocent ifynde. (413-5)

The five passages in this tale from Innocent III are almost literal translations; there are also many marginalia in the manuscript margins which quote from what might be Chaucer non-extant translation of this most influential and widely read of medieval texts (Caie 1999b, 175-85). Lewis (1966, 25-26) notes how closely Chaucer's paraphrase of Innocent's text matches the Latin gloss, and suggests that Chaucer uses his own translation when paraphrasing *De Miseria* in his poem, so this is a work, like Boethius's *De consolatione philosophiae*, that is very close to Chaucer's own philosophy. Its central tenet was one of the contempt or disdain of this world, the wretchedness of man's condition in life, a view which is probably as unfashionable today as the pathos in the Tale. The *De Miseria* passages, such as the one quoted above (lines 421-3), stress the central principle of the alternation of "wo after gladnesse" and "joye after wo", and create the roller-coaster of emotions that permeates the Tale. As soon as Custaunce has found happiness and stability then something outside her influence opens the door for more suffering, yet the conclusion brings closure with joy after woe. It is significant that a paraphrase from *De Miseria* is the opening line of the Prologue: "O hateful harm, condicioun of poverte" and thus unites the introductory material with the tale of Constance, stressing the moral, philosophical and serious intentions of the narrator. Innocent III's world view may find disfavour in our modern world, just as the rhetoric of pathos and the public display of tears. And so Custaunce becomes unattractive today, as someone who accepts her fate, laments her condition and never questions the divine plan. Just like Griselda, she allows herself to be acted upon rather than acting and this passivity makes many readers irritated; she is too perfect, distant from real people's reactions, almost allegorical, and at times one wants to shake her into rebellion! Yet her vulnerability, humanity and pathos do make us sympathise with her, especially when she is banished with her child. The reader's problem here may be akin to that Milton's Satan, namely that activity is more attractive than passive goodness. Like Griselda, she teaches us that all things work together for good, to those who love God and that prayer is a better answer to one's predicament than physical action.

So how would Chaucer and his contemporaries have viewed such a character as Custaunce and would they too have had the same reaction to visible demonstrations of the pathetic? It has often been said that the face of Christ in any era reflects the spirit of the age. The regal, triumphant Christ on the Cross of the early Middle Ages, exemplified by the Aaby Crucifix in the National Museum of Denmark, is replaced in the later Middle Ages by a pitifully suffering image of a Christ dying, covered in blood and emasculated. The horrific punishment and cruelty inflicted on Christ is dramatically seen in the presentation of the Crucifixion in the York Mystery Plays, for example. Similarly, the pathetic suffering of the weeping Mary as the Pieta takes central stage in this period. In contemporary lyrics, the pathos of the Crucifixion is frequently shown through the eyes of the distressed Mary, even at the Nativity, when she senses the tragic end of her child.

Such scenes of suffering were common in the all-important literature of penance which encouraged mankind to meditate on sins in preparation for confession, contrition and penance; thus the penitent is made to feel part of the suffering, to empathize with Mary and experience her deep sorrow which was caused by mankind's sin. Books of Hours portray the patron, often a lady, within the scene of the Advent or the Crucifixion, kneeling, crying, associating with the events which are thus taken out of time and made universal and omnipresent. This affected piety is present in many contemporary medieval lyrics in which the sufferings of Christ and Mary are made immediate and in the eternal present. An example is the well-known Corpus Christi lyric in which the present tense verbs stress the immediacy of the scene:

> And in that bed ther lith a knight,
> His woundes bleding day and night.
> By that bede side ther kneleth a may,
> And she wepeth both night and day.[4]

In this humanistic tradition Mary hold the central position, the mother both of Christ and all mankind. One can see the way in which Custaunce is modelled on this tradition with her humility, compassion, and unquestioning obedience, suffering as a mother, as seen, for example in lines 848-56, quoted above.

If one is still thinking that Chaucer is mocking a contemporary tradition of sickly-sweet pathos, then one should remember that Chaucer chose to translate the acrostic *La Priere a Nostre Dame* in his work *Of Our Lady An ABC* and portrayed Mary in this manner:

> Ladi, thi sorwe kan I nat purtreye
> Under the crois, ne his greevous penaunce.
> But for youre bothe peynes, I yow preye,
> . . . .
> Contynue on us thy pitous eyen cleere. (81-3 and 88)

In the *Prologue to Second Nun's Tale* there is a similar Invocation to the Virgin (lines 29-84).

Tears of compassion were considered an outward expression of inner spirituality, as they cleansed the soul; this was expressed in English literature as early as the Old English *Judgement Day II* in which Christ is the divine Physician, advocating the shedding of tears. Tears are an important prelude to penance, a gift that comes from the love of God, states Jean Leclerq in *The Love of Learning and the Desire for God*: "the desire for Heaven inspires many texts on tears. The tears of desire [are] born of the compunction of love."[5] St Jerome has an entire treatise on the function of tears, while St Francis, sometimes called the patron saint of pathos, also advocates tears of compassion. The church father Smaragdus in *On the Grace of Tears* lists occasions in the bible and church fathers when tears are mentioned, and so an entire literature of *suspiria* 'sighing' emerged. John of Fecamp in *Confessio theologica* states that the soul, desirous of God, will sigh and find nothing sweeter than to groan and weep. Arguably Marjory Kemp must take the prize as the best example of someone in the late Middle Ages who thrives on tears and who would launch into sobbing at the slightest provocation.

The Virgin's *planctus* became a stereotype to be imitated, as it reflected the most blessed and innocent of states and a necessary preparation for meditation and confession. Pearsall (1985, 262) suggests that this image is central to the

Tale and that the prayers which Custance offers up turns it "into an extended exemplum of God's grace granted to patience and constant faith", while Muscatine (1986, 107) suggests that "one can isolate, somewhere between realism and convention, a Chaucerian 'pathetic' style, composed with simple characterisation, plain diction, spare and humble setting, and reaching great idealising power."

Most of the tears in the Tale are naturally associated with Custance, but she also inspires others to weep, for example, when the constable first meets her he "hath of hir so greet pitee / And eek his wife that they wepen for routhe" (528-9). Later, her husband weeps at the reunion: "Whan Alla saugh his wyf, faire he hire grette, / And weep that it was routhe for to see" (1051-52). "Long was the sobbyng and the bitter peyne" (1065) in the final scenes, when there might not be a dry eye amongst Chaucer's audience.

Pathos may well be a convention, but Chaucer here and in his other religious tales, makes it much more than a convention and uses it to shape the meaning of the tale. The pathos is controlled, the melodrama not over-the-top and the audience would have accepted it as a fitting way of conveying the mood of suffering and patience. If we accept that Chaucer is not being satirical or parodying contemporary hagiographies, then we see a dimension to Chaucer that is hidden in the more worldly fabliaux and romances. Far from being cycnical about life, he appears here a deeply religious man, one who can clearly empathise with human suffering.

The Tale is summed up in the Epilogue by Harry Bailey as "thrifty" – "This was a thrifty tale for the nones!" (line 1165). 'Thrifty" means 'useful', 'profitable', 'worthy', or 'decorous'. He does not say that it was tragic or sad, but concentrates on the moral and practical results. It is a tale that we *should* find profitable. In so doing the Man of Law, who modestly starts his tale in the Prologue by stating: "I kan right now no thrifty tale seyn" (46), finally shows that he can indeed produce a work that is worthy and useful to his audience. I believe it would have been accepted by his audience as such, namely that he intended to tell a serious, austere, didactic work, and that it is we, the post-medieval audience, who search for satire, irony and deception. Perhaps we too need to learn to express our emotions more openly?

Notes

*It is a great privilege to be invited to contribute to this volume of essays in honour of Mitsunori Imai. As much of his research has been on Middle English romances, it is only fitting to choose this genre as a tribute to him.

1 See Peter Nicholson (1991, 153). Nicholson stressed the debt Chaucer owes to Gower.
2 See Schlauch (1950, 402), also Block (1953, 574), Frank (1990, 46) and Pratt (1969, 308) for the origins of the story and how Chaucer reworked the legend. Hibbard (1924, 3-80) and Hornstein (1967, 120-32) discuss analogous Middle English romances of trial and faith in which families are exiled and separated until the recognition scene and happy reunion.
3 All quotations from Chaucer's works are taken from the Riverside Chaucer.
4 From *Early English Lyrics,* eds. F. Sidgwick and E.K.Chambers, London: Sidgwick and Jackson, 1966, p. 148.
5 Leclerq (1977, 58). He also states: "The ultimate role of compunction is to bring to the soul a longing for Heaven, and it is understandable that this theme is related to the theme of tears" (p. 30) and "Let our eyes stream constantly with tears toward the joys which are promised us" (p. 66).

References

Baum, Paul (1958) *Chaucer: A Critical Appreciation.* Durham, N.C. Duke University Press.

Block, Edward A. (1953) "Originality, Controlling Purpose, and Craftmanship in Chaucer's *Man of Law's Tale*." *PMLA* 68: 572-616.

Bloomfield, Morton (1972) "*The Man of Law's Tale*: A Tragedy of Victimization and a Christian Comedy." *PMLA* 87: 384-90.

Caie, Graham D. (1999a) "'This was a thrifty tale for the nones': Chaucer's Man of Law." In G. Lester (ed.) *Chaucer in Perspective: Middle English Essays in Honour of Norman Blake.* Sheffield Academic Press: Sheffield, pp. 47-60.

Caie, Graham D. (1999b) "Innocent III's *De Miseria* as a gloss on the Man of Law's Prologue and Tale." *Neuphilologische Mitteilungen* 100: 175-85.

Cloggan, Paul (1977) "The Narrative Style of The Man of Law's Tale." *Medievalia et Humanistica* n.s. 8: 217-33.

David, Alfred (1967) "The Man of Law vs. Chaucer: A Case in Poetics." *PMLA* 82: 217-25.

Edwards, A.S.G. (1990) "Critical Approaches to The Man of Law's Tale." In D. Benson and E. Robertson (eds.) *Chaucer's Religious Tales*. Cambridge: Brewer, pp.85-94.

Frank, Jr., Robert W. (1990) "Pathos in Chaucer's Religious Tales." In Benson and Robertson, pp. 39-52.

Hibbard, Laura (1924) *Mediaeval Romance in England*. London: Oxford University Press.

Hornstein, Lillian (1967) "Eustace, Constance-Florence-Griselda Legends." In J. B. Severs (ed.) *A Manual of the Writings in Middle English* Fasc. 1, pp. 120-32; 278-91.

Kittredge, G.L. (1915) *Chaucer and His Poetry*. Cambridge, Mass.: Harvard University Press.

Leclerq, Jean (1977) *The Love of Learning and the Desire for God*. New York: Fordham University Press, 1977.

Lewis, Robert E. (1966) "Chaucer's Artistic Use of Pope Innocent III's *De Miseria Humane Conditionis* in *The Man of Law's Prologue and Tale*." *PMLA* 81: 485-96.

Muscatine, Charles (1986) *Chaucer and the French Tradition*. Berkeley: University of California Press.

Nicholson, Peter (1991) "Chaucer Borrows from Gower: The Sources of the *Man of Law's Tale*." In Yeager (ed.) 1991, pp. 85-99.

Pearsall, Derek A. (ed.) (1985) *The Canterbury Tales*. London: George Allen and Unwin.

Pratt, Alfred (1969) "Chaucer and Les Cronicles of Nicholas Trevet. In E. Atwood and A. Hill (eds.) *Studies in Language, Literature, and Culture of the Middle Ages and Later in honor of Rudolph Willard*." Austin: University of Texas Press, pp. 303-11.

Schlauch, Margaret (1950) "Historical Precursors of Chaucer's Constance." *Philological Quarterly* 29: 402-12.

Stevens, Martin (1979) "The Royal Stanza in Early English Literature." *PMLA* 94: 62-76.

Wood, Chauncey (1970) *Chaucer and the Country of the Stars: Poetic Uses of Astrological Imagery*. Princeton, N.J.: Princeton University Press.

Yunck, John A. (1960) "Religious Elements in Chaucer's Man of Law's Tale." *English Literary History* 27: 249-61.

Jeanette Winterson and Medieval Romance Making It New

Dorrit Einersen

My paper takes as its subject the revival of medieval romance in selected texts by Jeanette Winterson, primarily *Oranges are not the only Fruit* (1985), *The PowerBook* (2000) and *Lighthousekeeping* (2004).

It is motivated by a wish to show continuities and connections between themes in medieval romances, which are of lifelong interest to professor Imai, and my favourite contemporary writer, Jeanette Winterson.

Although Winterson is usually classified as a postmodernist, experimental writer who frequently uses intertextual references in a playful way it seems to me that her reverence for her predecessors, for instance Dante, T.S. Eliot, Virginia Woolf, is deep and when she revives and revises medieval and modernist texts she makes them integral parts of her own work.

Medieval writers frequently emphasize their reverence for earlier writers. One example of this would be Chaucer's *Troilus and Criseyde* where near the end of the poem he mentions classical writers: Virgil, Ovid, Homer, Lucan and Statius. The source Chaucer claims to be following, one Latin writer, Lollius, is non-existent and he is definitely not just translating as he claims but writing his own original version of the story of Troilus and Criseyde, so we find a mixture of playfulness and reverence which can be compared to Winterson's use of intertextuality.

Malory's *Morte d'Arthur* shows a less subtle but also somewhat misleading use of the concept of authority. He claims as his source "the French book" but never specifies which French book he is thinking of whereas the Arthurian romances he retells in his own way are based on a number of English and French romances.

In her collection of essays *Art Objects* Winterson states "the calling of the artist, in any medium, is to make it new. I do not mean that in new work the past is repudiated, quite the opposite, the past is reclaimed. It is not lost to authority, it is not absorbed at a level of familiarity. It is re-stated and re-instated in its original vigour" (*Art Objects* p. 12).

In **Oranges are not the only Fruit** (1985) the fundamental subtext is the Old Testament, which forms the basis of Jeanette's quest story. *Oranges* is fundamentally a subversion of a patriarchal narrative in which women, Jeanette, her mother, Melanie and other female figures are central. Fairytales are scattered in the text, the well known, traditional fairytale "Beauty and the Beast", and new ones: that of the princess who learns practical skills and how to teach and that of the prince who seeks a perfect woman and is told by her that perfection does not exist, only balance. He does not accept this and has her head chopped off.

In "Judges", the penultimate chapter of the novel, we find the beginning of the story of Perceval:

> Sir Perceval, the youngest of Arthur's knights, at last set forth from Camelot. The king had begged him not to go; he knew this was no ordinary quest. Since the visit of the Holy Grail one feast day, the mood had changed. They were brothers, they laughed at Sir Gawain and his exploits in the land of the green knight. (*Oranges* p. 127)

Winterson's Perceval story has no counterpart in Malory but is a new version with parallels, I think, to *Sir Gawain and the Green Knight* which is only referred to this once and very briefly.

Winterson's quest story seems to conflate Perceval and Gawain and calls to mind Gawain's leaving Arthur's court and going on his lonely journey north to find the green knight. The emphasis is on Gawain's loneliness, far from his friends and the comforts of the court: "All alone must he lodge through many a long night / Where the food that he fancied was far from his plate" (*Norton I, Part II*, l. 693-694) and "Many a cliff must he climb in country wild; / Far off from all his friends, forlorn must he ride" (l. 713-714). The resolution of the story of Gawain, when he returns to king Arthur and they all laugh at him in relief that he is still alive, is less important in Winterson's version than the knight's loneliness, which is mirrored in Arthur's own nostalgia and longing for the past. "Arthur thinks of before, when there were lights and smiles" (*Oranges* p. 127).

After leaving Arthur Sir Perceval goes to the wood, where other knights have lost their way and despaired and one has died. "He has heard tell of a ruined chapel, or an old church, no one is sure, only sure that it lies disused and holy" (*Oranges* p. 132). Sir Perceval's uncertainty here mirrors Sir Gawain's when he is seeking the Green Knight's Chapel. He "sought on every side for a sight of the Chapel, / But no such place appeared, which puzzled him sore, / Yet he saw some way off what seemed like a mound" (*Norton I, Part IV,* l. 2169-2171). Gawain now fears that the Green Knight is the fiend himself who has lured him to "this Chapel of mischance" (l. 2196), "As accursed a country church as I came upon ever!" (l. 2196).

Sir Perceval, alone in the wood, dreams of Arthur sitting on a wide stone step, holding his head in his hands in sorrow. "Sir Perceval falls to his knees to clasp his lord, but his lord is a tree covered in ivy. He wakes, his face bright with tears" (*Oranges* p. 133). This description may call to mind the Old English elegy "The Wanderer" where the wanderer or exile thinks with longing of the lord and friends he has lost. The wanderer dreams "that he is embracing and kissing his liege lord and laying his hands and his head on his knee" (*Norton I*, p. 112). Sir Perceval is alone in the wood whereas the wanderer is surrounded by frost and snow mingled with hail. The difference between the two situations is that in Winterson's version the closeness between Arthur and Perceval is stressed, they miss each other, whereas the wanderer's longing is described as one-sided.

Sir Perceval's quest takes him to a glorious castle built of mountain rock and set upon the side of a hill (*Oranges* p. 161). This is reminiscent of the castle Gawain finds after being alone for many months in the wilderness. The castle is "built of stone blocks to the battlements' height" (*Norton I, Part II*, l. 789). Instead of a porter welcoming Gawain, in Winterson's version there are two dwarves, fully armed. But the greeting of welcome is the same just as the encouragement to rest occurs in both texts. Perceval thinks with longing of king Arthur and reflects that he might have gone back to him. "On the first day and the second day and the third day, Perceval could have turned back, he was still within the sphere of Merlin." But "on the fourth day, the woods were wild and forlorn, and he did not know where he was" (*Oranges* p. 161). Perceval thinks back to the fateful days where the knights were sitting in the hall and the Holy Grail had appeared to them and they had all vowed to seek it. To Perceval the Grail symbolizes perfect heroism and peace. "He sought it again, to balance him. He was a warrior who longed to grow herbs" (*Oranges* p 161). After having been a knight and warrior Sir Perceval needs to cultivate his female nurturing side.

The final episode in Winterson's Perceval story shows Perceval studying his two hands: "One hand was curious, sure and firm. His gentle, thoughtful hand. The hand for feeding a dog or strangling a demon. The other hand looked underfed. A stark, questioning, blank, uncomfortable hand. A scared hand but the hand for balancing" (*Oranges* p. 168). The emphasis is on balance and wholeness which is the real aim of the quest for full humanity.

Perceval at this point feels frustrated and angry. "His journey seemed fruitless, and himself misguided. His host had asked him why he had left, not really wanting to hear, presuming reasons of his own, that the king was mad, or the

Round Table ruined" (*Oranges* p. 168), which is, of course, the well-known end of the story of Arthur's court. Perceval thinks that he had gone for his own sake, for the sake of his own quest. "He had thought that day of returning. He felt himself being pulled like a bobbin of cotton, so that he was dizzy and wanted to give in to the pull and wake up round familiar things" (*Oranges* p. 168). The story ends inconclusively with Perceval still in doubt whether to go back just as Jeanette near the end of the novel wonders whether she will have to go back to her mother (*Oranges* p. 155). Jeanette's doubt whether to go back is phrased as follows: "Going back after a long time will make you mad, because the people you left behind do not like to think of you changed, will treat you as they always did" (*Oranges* p. 156). This proves true when Jeanette begins to wonder if she has ever been anywhere. "My mother was treating me like she always had; had she noticed my absence? Did she even remember why I'd left?" (*Oranges* p. 164). The momentous choice Jeanette made not to repent of her "unnatural passion" for Melanie and not to become a missionary as her mother had wished seems to have made little or no impact on her fundamentalist mother, who stills lives in her own world although she has, in fact, moved with the times and bought an electronic organ to supplant her old piano (*Oranges* p. 159). Jeanette's own change is far-reaching and she reflects:

> I could have been a priest instead of a prophet. The priest has a book with the words set out. Old words, known words, words of power. Words that are always on the surface. Words for every occasion. The words work. They do what they're supposed to do; comfort and discipline. The prophet has no book. The prophet is a voice that cries in the wilderness, full of sounds that do not always set into meaning. The prophets cry out because they are troubled by demons.
>
> (*Oranges* p. 156)

The contrast between having one book, the Bible, and not having one fixed text but many different ones that do not have one meaning but multiple meanings, is fundamental to Winterson's art. The writer who is troubled by demons will not try to or wish to find the absolute truth.

Parallel to the invented story of Sir Perceval Winterson creates the story of Winnet Stonejar, which is pure invention with no counterpart in existing stories but with elements from Arthurian literature. Winnet is a female hero on a quest who first appears in the chapter called "Ruth", which seems to suggest the significance of a close relationship between women. In the Old Testament (The Book of Ruth 1,16) Ruth bonds with her mother-in-law, Naomi, and tells her "Where you go I will go, where you lodge I will lodge, your people shall be my people, and your God my God." It can be argued that the fact that Jeanette goes back to her mother indicates a close relationship between the two, but it is emphasized that she just comes to visit her mother for Christmas and will leave her again.

The Winnet story begins with Winnet seeing a black bird with huge wings and after that a sorcerer or wizard opposite her, on the other side of a stream. He helps her cross the water and draws a chalk circle round her to protect her. He wants her to become his apprentice and learn magic from him. After one wrong guess he guesses her name and so gains power over her. Winnet asks him "How long have you been a sorcerer?" and he replies: "Oh, I can't say ... you see I am one in the future too, it's all the same to me" (*Oranges* p. 141). So like Merlin and Arthur he lives in the past, present and future at the same time. Winnet discovers the sorcerer's enormous embossed ear trumpet and asks him what he uses it for. He replies: "Well, I'm not always as old as I am now, and when I'm older, I can get a bit deaf" (*Oranges* p. 141).

Winnet stays with the sorcerer at his castle and forgets how she had come there and what she had done before. "She believed she had always been in the castle, and that she was the sorcerer's daughter. He told her she was. That she had no mother, but had been specially entrusted to his care by a powerful spirit." (*Oranges* p. 141). It is a common feature in medieval romance that an enchanted castle will make you forget your past and make you lose your sense of time. It is significant that the sorcerer is male and that the power relationship Jeanette has experienced in real life between her strong mother and weak father is reversed here. The sorcerer is a powerful male figure and when Jeanette strikes up a friendship with a boy the sorcerer thinks the boy spoils her and he has him bound and thrown into the darkest room in the deepest part of the castle (*Oranges* p. 143). Just as Jeanette's mother and the church locked her up for loving a girl and tried to exorcise her demon the sorcerer here tries to punish the boy, but Winnet has learned magic arts and releases him. The sorcerer now forces her to leave him and she goes through the forest and crosses the river. She feels homesick and is unable to walk for many days but is revived by a woman by means of herbs with magic healing power. She hears about a beautiful city, a long way off, with buildings that run op to the sky. The city is guarded by tigers and difficult to get into. The city dwellers do not sow or toil but think about the world (*Oranges* p. 149).

To get to the city she has to learn how to sail a boat and is taught by a blind man (*Oranges* p. 154). It is said: "The need for the city fastens her heart to her mind" (*Oranges* p. 155). It gives her one settled purpose. She is surrounded by water and there is no possibility of turning back. So Winnet learns practical things like setting sail to achieve her ultimate purpose, to find the city of contemplation, which can be interpreted as fulfilling the role of the prophet who has time to meditate and can express his or her thoughts in many unforeseeable ways.

The heroic tale of Winnet can thus be seen as having a happy ending although the novel itself has an open ending. "I knew a woman in another place. Perhaps she would save me. But what if she were asleep? What if she sleepwalked beside me and I never knew?" (*Oranges* p. 171).

At the end Jeanette has lost her fixed belief in God. She says:

> I don't even know if God exists, but I do know that if God is your emotional role model, very few human relationships will match up to it … As it is, I can't settle, I want someone who is fierce and will love

me until death and know that love is as strong as death, and be on my side for ever and ever. (*Oranges* p. 165)

Both her mother and Melanie have betrayed Jeanette so the quest for such a love remains unfulfilled.

The two romance intertexts, the Perceval story and the Winnet story, are both invented by Winterson but inspired by medieval romances. The male quest story is dominated by loneliness and sadness, the female story is dominated by courage and resourcefulness, so they both subvert traditional ideas of maleness and femaleness. They also mirror Jeanette's quest which is dominated by sadness and loneliness after her mother has thrown her out as well as by her courage and ability to fend for herself and find her own place and role in life.

Although there are a few references in *Oranges are not the only Fruit* to the 1960's in which the novel takes place it gives the impression of taking place in a timeless universe where the Old Testament, fairytales and medieval romance coexist.

The PowerBook (2000) takes place in the twenty-first century where virtual reality has given possibilities for playing with multiple identities but where the central subject is love and passion.

In sections 67 to 74 entitled "Search" we find a retelling of the story of Lancelot and Guinevere which was not part of the Arthurian quest story in *Oranges are not the only Fruit*. Lancelot states here "That you were married to someone else meant nothing to me. Which is more important – a dead marriage or a living love?" Triangular stories are common in medieval times and they almost invariably end in tragedy.

Section 70 runs:

> The rumours increased. There was a plot. Mordred and Agravaine warned the King against us and set to trap me in your room. I killed all twelve of those cowards who lusted after our bravery, and it is brave to

love, for love is the mortal enemy of death. Love is death's twin, born in the same moment, each fighting for mastery, and if death takes all, love would do the same. Yet it is easier to die than to love.

Lancelot's courage and heroism are seen as less important than the strength of his love. Lancelot also states "Death will not separate us. Love is as strong as death."

After the lovers have been found together Guinevere does penance for their illicit love in a nunnery and Lancelot becomes a hermit and does penance for seven years. He then dreams that the queen is dead and when he gets to her she has died half an hour before.

In sections 73 and 74 he says:

> You are closed and shuttered to me now, a room without doors or windows, and I cannot enter. But I fell in love with you under the open sky and death cannot change that.
>
> Death can change the body but not the heart.

The focus in this retelling is on the man, Lancelot, and his emotions.

The subsection in this part of *The PowerBook* is called "great and ruinous lovers". Half of these great lovers are medieval: Lancelot and Guinevere, Tristan and Isolde, Siegfried and Brunnhilde, Abelard and Heloïse, Paolo and Francesca, and the narrator states: "There are three possible endings: Revenge, Tragedy, Forgiveness."

Section 79 which ends the chapter says "Love is worth death. Love is worth life. My search for you, your search for me, goes beyond life and death into one long call in the wilderness. I do not know if what I hear is an answer or an echo. Perhaps I will hear nothing. It doesn't matter. The journey must be made."

Although this is in the form of an e-mail it is more like a timeless and universal love letter.

The next section is entitled "View". It is situated in Capri where the narrator sees a beautiful woman with a man, slightly sinister, who has iron-grey hair. A triangular situation but with two women and one man, the husband, just as in *The Passion* (1987) where Vilanelle falls in love with the Queen of Spades and in *Written on the Body* where the protagonist, probably but not quite certainly, a woman, falls in love with Louise. In *The PowerBook* the narrator asks the beautiful woman:

> 'Is he your husband?'
> She nodded.
> 'How about tomorrow then – lunch?'
> She shook her head.
> 'You choose a time then'.
> 'How about the Middle Ages?'
> 'The food isn't that good.'

Here the reference to the Middle Ages is playful but it also suggests that the relationship may end in revenge or tragedy.

The next very brief section is entitled "night screen". It runs "I keep telling this story – different people, different places, different times – but always you, always me, always this story, because a story is a tightrope between two worlds." The story is the same although the situations may vary. The world of comfort is contrasted with the world of love and passion.

In the section "View as Icon" the narrator says "This is the story of Francesca da Rimini and her lover Paolo. You can find it in Boccaccio. You can find it in Dante. You can find it here" stressing the lines of connection between the Middle Ages and our time. Again it is a triangular story as Francesca is married to a small man with a twisted body and a cruel disposition. "He cared for nothing but hunting and women, and he lashed his dogs and his whores with the same strap" (section 127). Together Francesca and Paolo, her husband's brother, read the story of Lancelot and Guinevere, as they do in Dante's *Inferno*.

Francesca who is the central figure speaks here "Paolo, your love for me was a clear single happiness, and I would not give it up to save my soul."

This story ends in the husband's revenge. He finds the lovers together and kills them both. Francesca says:

> He was dead then, and I dead under him, and hand in hand our souls flew down the corridors and out of his brother's place as easily as our bodies had done when we left my father's house. I have never let go of his hand. We are as light now as our happiness was, lighter than birds. The wind carries us where it will, but our love is secure. No one can separate us now. Not even God (section 128).

This section becomes a universal story of true love.

In the section called "own hero" it is stated:

> In this life you have to be your own hero.
> By that I mean you have to win whatever it is that matters to you by your own strength and in your own way.
> Like it or not, you are alone in the forest, just like all those fairy tales that begin with a hero who's usually stupid but somehow brave, or who might be clever, but weak as straw, and away he goes (don't worry about the gender), cheered on by nobody, via the castles and the bears, and the old witch and the enchanted stream, and by and by (we hope) he'll find the treasure (section 155).

This heroic quest story might be a fairytale or a romance and the hero may be male or female.

The section entitled "Help" takes place in London. Here we are told that "Love's exquisite happiness is also love's exquisite pain", a common medieval idea found for instance in Andreas Capellanus *De Arte Honeste Amandi*. In this section the Lancelot story turns up again.

"In the Grail legends Lancelot, the best knight in the world, never does see the Grail because he cannot give up his love for Guinevere." His son by Elaine,

Galahad, is the perfect, chaste knight who finds the grail and is taken up into heaven by angels, whereas Lancelot is the flawed knight who betrays his King.

And the section concludes with the narrator's words "So when you ask me why I cannot love you more calmly, I answer that to love you calmly is not to love you at all" (section 189).

The last section is entitled "Save" which means keep the love story in the computer, which will make it possible to change the ending indefinitely.

"You can change the story. You are the story", you can make and remake your story and make it end in revenge, tragedy or forgiveness. Near the end, in section 237, we are told: "The rain was thick as glass. For many days I had eaten, drunk, slept, walked, cased in glass. I felt like the relic of a saint", one of love's martyrs or saints.

The PowerBook ends:

> Your face, your hands, the movement of your body ...
> Your body is my Book of Hours.
> Open it. Read it.
> This is the true history of the world.

A medieval book of hours contains everything, the passing of time, the sequence of the seasons, love and labour, pain and suffering.

As long as the narrator keeps writing and rewriting she has power over her own story – the power to make it end happily – at least in her imagination. At one point she tries to leave the choice to her beloved, saying:

"The train is leaving, leaving now, and you won't meet my eyes. I can't come with you. You're not coming with me. The whistle blows. I have to jump up, forcing apart the closing doors. Then I'm outside again, walking down the platform, walking faster and faster, miming at you to pull the emergency cord. Just pull it. The train will stop. You can get off, leave your bag, and come with me. I'm running now. There's still time, still time. Then there's a moment when time is so still it stops and the train moves ahead for ever" (section 205).

One moment's choice can lead to a happy or unhappy ending.

In *The PowerBook* the two main romances, Lancelot and Guinevere and Paolo and Francesca, are medieval triangular stories with a jealous husband who is forced to punish his favourite knight and his queen and a jealous husband who kills his wife and her lover, and both stories may mirror the narrator's situation of being in love with a married woman.

Connections and continuities are central in *The PowerBook*. But are the narrator and her beloved real or imagined? Do they exist only in virtual reality? We as readers cannot be sure.

In *Lighthousekeeping* (2004) the main story of the little girl, Silver, whose mother is lost in a storm and who is adopted by the blind lighthousekeeper, Pew, is interwoven with the story of the clergyman, Babel Dark, who in the 19th century marries a woman who is "as dull as a day at sea with no wind" (*Lighthousekeeping* p. 54). The love of his life is Molly with whom he spends two months a year. Babel Dark beats and rapes his wife and at one point he beats Molly out of mistaken jealousy so that her daughter is born blind. Babel Dark is compared to Stevenson's Dr Jekyll and Mr Hyde.

The story of Arthur is mirrored in Babel Dark's thoughts of Pentecost:

> He loved the story of the Grail coming to the Court of King Arthur at the Feast of Pentecost. He loved it, and it made him sad, because that day every knight had pledged to find the Grail again, and most lost their way, and even the best were destroyed. The Court was broken. Civilisation was ruined. And why? For a dream-vision that had no use in the world of men. (*Lighthousekeeping* p. 115)

Here the ruin of Camelot is caused not by Lancelot's betrayal of the King but by the impossible vision of the Holy Grail and Galahad is not mentioned. Babel Dark's pessimism is too great for there to be any hope and his dog's fateful name is Tristan. When Molly comes to make Babel go with her to France and start a new life together with her he refuses and seeking his own death by drowning he feels that he finds Molly again and they die together, a "Liebestod".

The main medieval story to be retold in *Lighthousekeeping* is the story of Tristan and Isolde, which is contrasted with Darwin's *The Origin of Species*. Where Darwin is "objective, scientific, empirical, quantifiable", Wagner is "subjective, poetic, intuitive, mysterious" (*Lighthousekeeping* p. 169).

> In Tristan the world shrinks to a boat, a bed, a lantern, a love-potion, a wound. The world is contained within a world – Isolde.
> The Romantic solipsism that nothing exists but the two of us, could not be farther from the multiplicity and variety of Darwin's theory of the natural world. Here, the world and everything in it forms and is re-formed, tirelessly and unceasingly. Nature's vitality is amoral and unsentimental; the weak die, the strong survive.
> Tristan, weak and wounded, should have died. Love healed him. Love is not part of natural selection.
> Where did love begin? What human being looked at another and saw in their face the forests and the sea? (*Lighthouskeeping* p. 169-170).

According to C.S. Lewis in *The Allegory of Love* romantic love originated in the Middle Ages with the troubadours in the 11. century.

In Winterson's version as in many medieval versions there is no literal love-potion. Isolde says, "Tristan, I didn't drink it either. There was no love-potion, only love. It was you I drank" and "Death frees us from the torment of parting. I cannot part with you. I am you" (*Lighthousekeeping* p. 182).

In Greece Silver sees a woman kneeling in prayer and relates:

> You smiled, stood up, and came out into the sunshine. Perhaps it was the light on your face, but I thought I recognised you from somewhere a long way down, somewhere at the bottom of the sea. Somewhere in me. (*Lighthousekeeping* p. 200-201)

Love is recognition, and forms a link between Silver's father who "came out of the sea and went back that way" (*Lighthousekeeping* p. 3), Babel Dark drowning and Tristan feeling "Already the world is fading, returning to the sea" (*Lighthousekeeping* p. 182).

In spite of the connections between Tristan and Isolde's "Liebestod" and Babel Dark's illusory union with Molly at the moment of drowning which is another "Liebestod", Silver's love for the unnamed woman ends hopefully. "You are the carved low door into the Chapel of the Grail. You are the door at the edge of the world. You are the door that opens onto a sea of stars" (*Lighthousekeeping* p. 219). The final words are:

> I love you.
> The three most difficult words in the World.
> But what else can I say? (*Lighthousekeeping* p. 232)

The story of Tristan and Isolde is primarily used in *Lighthousekeeping* as an illustration of the ultimate value of love as against the rational, objective view of the world represented by science. The narrator states:

> I think of love as a force of nature – as strong as the sun, as necessary, as impersonal, as gigantic, as impossible, as scorching as it is warming, as drought-making as it is life-giving. And when it burns out, the planet dies. (*Lighthousekeeping* p. 199)

In an interview with Louise Tucker "From Innocence to Experience" in an appendix to the text Winterson says:

> I've always liked to work with existing texts. I like to do cover versions of stories that we know very well, whether it's Lancelot and Guinevere or Tristan and Isolde. It's a way of rewriting what we know, but in the rewriting we find new angles, new possibilities, and the rewriting itself demands an injection of fresh material into what already exists, so the story changes. The thing is kept alive by the retelling, by the changing. It's a way of making an oral tradition out of a literary tradition so that the thing is continuously in the mouth.
>
> (*Lighthousekeeping* appendix p. 2-3)

Winterson's aim is to recreate an oral tradition in which storytelling is more important than written literature – just as it was in the Middle Ages.

In *The Prophetic Writer and the Redemptive World in the Work of Jeanette Winterson* Cindie Maagaard notes that "biblical references, medieval romance, folk and fairy tale, high modernism and numerous other modes of writing are woven into her own texts in varying degrees of explicitness and recognizability" (*The Prophetic Writer* p. 20).

Where medieval writers will sometimes explicitly bow down to earlier authorities and acknowledge their debt to them Winterson appropriates earlier texts, incorporates them, rewrites them, makes them new, makes them universal as well as relevant to the world we live in now. This is in line with T.S. Eliot's statement in "Tradition and the Individual Talent" (1919) that the writer should write "with a feeling that the whole of the literature of Europe from Homer and within it the whole of the literature of his own country has a simultaneous existence and composes a simultaneous order" (*Selected Essays* p. 14).

Finally I should like to quote an often-quoted passage from *Oranges are not the only Fruit*:

> On the banks of the Euphrates find a secret garden cunningly walled. There is an entrance, but the entrance is guarded. There is no way in for you. Inside you will find every plant that grows growing circular-wise like a target. Close to the heart is a sundial and at the heart an orange tree. This fruit had tripped up athletes while others have healed their wounds. All true quests end in this garden, where the split fruit pours forth blood and the halved fruit is a full bowl for travellers and pilgrims. To eat of the fruit means to leave the garden because the fruit speaks of other things, other longings. So at dusk you say goodbye to the place you love, not knowing if you can ever return, knowing you can never return by the same way as this. It may be, some other day, that you will open a gate by chance, and find yourself again on the other side of the wall. (*Oranges* p. 120)

Marianne Børch calls this a myth spoken in a quiet but authoritative tone. (*The Return of Romance and Rise of Narratology* p. 2). The phrase "All true quests" makes a universal statement and it links the medieval quest, the quest for the holy grail and wholeness, to the garden in *Le Roman de la Rose* in which the lover seeks his rosebud but with a new emphasis on the quest as never completed but perpetually renewed. The passage is apparently unconnected with the story of Jeanette's quest for individuality and sexuality and it is ungendered. It has an evocative and suggestive power which calls to mind medieval romance while not being tied to a specific time.

References

Børch, Marianne (2006) *The Return of Romance and Rise of Narratology*. Pre-Publications of the English Department of Odense University (The University of Southern Denmark) No. 145, August-September.

Capellanus, Andreas *De Arte Honeste Amandi* (c. 1185) translated into English by J.J. Parry (1941) *The Art of Courtly Love*. New York: Columbia University Press.

Chaucer "Troilus and Criseyde" (ca. 1385) in *The Riverside Chaucer* Larry D. Benson (ed.) (1987) Oxford University Press.

Dante *The Inferno* (c.1307) translated by Ciaran Carson (2002). Belfast: Belfast University Press 2002.

Darwin *The Origin of Species* (1859) Oxford World's Classics (1996). Oxford University Press.

Eliot, T.S. (1919) "Tradition and the Individual Talent" in *Selected Essays*. (1932) London: Faber and Faber.

Greenblatt, Stephen (ed.) (2006) *The Norton Anthology of English Literature* Volume I, Eighth Edition.

Le Roman de la Rose by Guillaume de Lorris (c. 1230) and Jean de Meun (c. 1275) translated into English by C. Dahlberg (1971). New York: Princeton University Press.

Lewis, C.S. (1936) *The Allegory of Love. A Study in Medieval Tradition*. London: Oxford University Press.

Maagaard, Cindie (2003) *The Prophetic Writer and the Redemptive World in the Work of Jeanette Winterson*. Pre-Publications of the English Department of Odense University (The University of Southern Denmark) No 125, April.

Malory, Thomas (c. 1469) "Morte d'Arthur" in Malory *Works* (1971). London: Oxford University Press.

"Sir Gawain and the Green Knight" (c. 1385) translated by Marie Borroff (1967) in *The Norton Anthology of English Literature* Volume I, Eighth Edition 2006.

Winterson, Jeanette (1995) *Art Objects. Essays on Ecstasy and Effrontery.* Vintage 1996.

Winterson, Jeanette (2004) *Lighthousekeeping.* Harper Perennial 2005.

Winterson, Jeanette (1985) *Oranges are not the only Fruit.* Vintage 1991.

Winterson, Jeanette (1987) *The Passion.* Vintage 1996.

Winterson, Jeanette (2000) *The PowerBook.* Jonathan Cape.

Winterson, Jeanette (1992) *Written on the Body.* Vintage 1993.

On Promotional Discourse in Caxton's Prologues [1]
"[E]very man naturally desireth to know and to con newe thynges"

Risto Hiltunen

1 Introduction

Having learned the art of printing on the Continent, in Bruges and Cologne, William Caxton moved back to England in 1476 and set up his printing press in Westminster, in the precincts of Westminster Abbey, close to the court. The site was very well chosen, for in the years to follow the court, court circles, and major institutions of the society came to form the core of his clientele (cf. Blake 1969: 80). Caxton printed books that would appeal to members of the court, and it was also court circles that he turned to when he was looking for patrons for his books. In addition to large quantities of ephemera of various kinds, including documents of an ecclesiastical and administrative nature, his press produced literary texts of more lasting importance. Caxton's output as translator and printer of literary texts in the period up to about 1490 comprises a remarkable variety of works that he published in English for the English market (cf. Blake 1969: 224-239; 1973: 11-12).

In terms of English book production and literary culture, the establishment of the press signalled the beginning of a new era. With his printing press, William Caxton may be said to stand at the crossroads of the Middle Ages and the Renaissance. As suggested by Jenny Adams (2005: 133), Caxton's double identity as author and printer challenges the conventional boundary dividing the medieval and early modern worlds. His role as printer marks him as a contributor to the English Renaissance, while many of the texts that came out from his press echo earlier literary forms.

One of the traditions of book production that Caxton carried forward was the adding of prologues and epilogues to his volumes.[2] In this paper, the focus will be specifically on the prologues. Several of Caxton's books, including his "own prose" (Blake 1973), i.e. his prologues and epilogues, have been examined in a number of publications, most notably in those by Norman Blake (see Bibliography). Interestingly, this material has also been addressed in several studies that have appeared in the last few years.[3] In a number of contexts, Blake draws attention to Caxton's businesslike attitude towards his work as publisher (see e.g. Blake 1991: 56, 106), maintaining that he was a publisher and entrepreneur rather than a printer in the strict sense of the word: he provided the capital, chose the books and distributed them, leaving the printing to others (*ibid.* 59). The aspect of Caxton's entrepreneurial attitude to be followed up in the present study concerns his awareness of the importance of promoting his books, as seen in the prologues.

2 Functional elements of the prologues

Prologues may be said to constitute a genre of their own, if by the term we mean "a class of communicative events, the members of which share some set of communicative purposes" (Swales 1990: 58). The communicative purpose of a prologue is primarily to introduce the text to the reader by providing relevant information about it. The precise nature of this information may vary depending on the context, but there are several communicative events that may be conventionally associated with prologues. This aspect of the notion is emphasized in the formulation of Bhatia (2004:23), according to which genre refers essentially to "language use in a conventionalized communicative setting in order to give expression to a specific set of communicative goals." These communicative goals in turn "give rise to stable structural forms by imposing constraints on the use of lexico-grammatical as well as discoursal resources" (*ibid.*).

Prologues typically introduce the book to the reader from the perspective of the writer, but in such as way as to involve the reader. Normally, the writer is also the author of the book, but in the present case the author of the prologue is usually the translator of the book. In both instances, however, the perspective of the author is similarly highlighted. Caxton's prologues usually convey information not only about the content of the book but also about the translator-printer himself, often with a personal tone of voice. In the process of doing so, the prologues frequently draw attention to features of the books that the writer must have thought of as particularly attractive and interesting in the eyes of the potential readership.

While the genre of the prologue consists of texts sharing a common communicative purpose, individual prologues characteristically share a range of recurrent elements of the kind called "moves" by Swales (1990) and Bhatia (2004). According to Bhatia (1993:30), "[j]ust as each genre has a communicative purpose that it tends to serve, similarly, each genre also serves a typical communicative intention which is always subservient to the overall communicative purpose of the genre." Texts belonging to the same genre are thus characterized by having the same moves, sometimes occurring in a fixed order. To realize a particular communicative intention at the level of a move, different rhetorical strategies may be used by individual writers. Thus, Caxton's prologues, for example, usually provide an account of what the book is about and why it was deemed important to provide an English translation of it. Almost always there is also an acknowledgment of the patron of the work. Naturally, such elements are likely to be presented in ways that are expected to arouse the interest of readers. On the other hand, there does not appear to be any fixed order in which the various moves are introduced in the text. Rather, it seems to have been the case that on each occasion the text was put together using familiar building blocks in an order that was individually determined for the text at hand. This impression is supported by an observation according to which Caxton did not have any particular regular system of text presentation in his writings (cf. Blake 1991:106).

3 Promotional discourse

3.1 *Background*

One aspect of Caxton's personality that Blake emphasizes time and again in his in-depth work on Caxton's career and his impact on English literary culture is his pragmatism. According to him, it has not always been understood, or at least not sufficiently appreciated by scholars, that as a printer Caxton was "a shrewd businessman, who would have made careful plans to ensure the successful completion of his project" (Blake 1969:56). Blake further points out that although Caxton went abroad to learn the trade of printing, and although he later became an administrator, negotiator, arbitrator, translator and printer, he remained basically a buyer and seller of goods for the rest of his life. There is thus no need to see a sharp dividing line between Caxton's career as merchant-adventurer and as scholar-printer: in the latter part of his career he remained a merchant selling wares, even if those wares were his books (Blake 1969: 34).

3.2 *Purpose*

In examining how Caxton's pragmatism is reflected in his prologues, my aim will be to identify elements that carry a market-oriented message to the projected readership, and to discuss the techniques employed for this purpose. The manifestations range from openly promotional statements to implied references. The latter constitute a more heterogeneous group, involving references for example to the audience, purpose, and content of the book in question. That

Caxton was aware of the need of promotion is not in doubt. An early "Advertisement", printed c. 1477 (Blake 1969: 223; 1973: 55), encourages "ony man spirituel or temporel to bye ony pyes of two and thre comemoracions of Salisburi Use enpryntid after the forme of this present lettre" and "com to Westmonester into the Almonesrye at the Reed Pale and he shall have them good chepe." According to Blake (1976: 115), the advertisement indicates Caxton's awareness of the fact that the introduction of a distinctive feature or mark would set his volumes apart and perhaps guarantee a certain standard.

3.3 Material and method

For the present pilot study of promotional features in Caxton's prologues the following ten texts were chosen for closer examination, using Blake (1973) as primary data: 1. *History of Troy* (c. 1473), 2. *Game of Chess* (1st ed., 1474), 3. *Caton* (c. 1484), 4. *Knight of the Tower* (1484), 5. *King Arthur* (1485), 6. *Book of Good Manners* (1487), 7. *Blanchardin and Eglantine* (c. 1489), 8. *Four Sons of Aymon* (c. 1489), 9. *Doctrinal of Sapience* (1489), and 10. *Eneydos* (c. 1490).[4]

Chronologically, the material extends from Caxton's first printed translation, *History of Troy* (1475), which he prepared and printed while still on the Continent, to his last translation, *Eneydos* (1490). The prologues represent a wide variety of books, but their subject matter falls broadly speaking into three groups: (a) chivalry and romance (1, 5, 7, 8, 10); (b) manners and proper behaviour (4, 6), and (c) wisdom and morality (2, 3, 9). On the other hand, the selection does not include any prologues which are, or are likely to be, translations of prologues in the French originals. These were excluded on the grounds that they might not reflect Caxton's own introduction of promotional discourse into the prologues. As Blake explains (1969:154), "when the book he was publishing already had a prologue, he never omitted it, but either modified it and made it his own, or left it substantially intact, but added something to it." The picture is more complicated when there is only one undivided prologue, for which the original has not survived. Using the *Mirror of the World* as an example, for which the original French prologue has survived, Blake demonstrates how Caxton followed it only in part, omitting certain sections and inserting his own comments, so that his version is much longer than the original (cf. Blake 1969: 155-157).

4 Analysis of promotional moves

The prologues contain a variety of elements that have, or may be interpreted as having, a promotional motive. Altogether ten such moves have been identified in the present sample, falling into three main groups. The identification is based on the function of particular statements about the book conveying a promotional move. Such moves typically contain keywords foregrounding the relevance of some aspect of the book for the reader. In examples (1)-(3) below, the superiority of the text is described by means of adjectives like *best*, *synguler*, *noble* and *virtuous*. In the following discussion, the promotional moves have been divided into three groups. The first group consists of statements that foreground the text of the book itself (text-specific moves); those of the second group foreground the translation (translation-specific moves), while those in the third group focus on the printing press (press-specific moves). Some of the moves in these categories may naturally be multifunctional.

4.1 Text-specific moves

4.1.1 *Pre-eminence of the text*

The prologue to *Caton* is unique in the present material in containing moves that stress the excellence of the book. The text is a translation from French into English of an original Latin text "by the noble Catho" (Blake 1973: 65/30). The original Latin manuscript, however, has not been identified (Blake 1976:

117). Examples of how Caxton's prologue singles out *Caton* from among other comparable works include the following:

(1) And as in my jugement it is the beste book for to be taught to yonge children in scole (*Caton* 64/34)[5]

(2) For among all other bookes this is a synguler book and may well be callyd 'The Regyment or Governaunce of the Body and Sowle'. (*Caton* 64/58)

(3) ... this is a noble booke, and a vertuous, and suche one that a man may eschewe alle vyces and ensiewe vertue. (*Caton* 64/70)

4.1.2   *Authority of the text*

A feature related to the previous one concerns the representation of the book as an authoritative text. This authoritativeness may be signalled by stating the translator's own opinion, as in (1)-(3) above, or by appealing to established authorities, such as those invoked in favour of Arthur as a historical figure in the prologue to *King Arthur* (Blake 1973: 108/55-73). The move of authoritativeness is usually introduced after the translator has first explained why and how he came to translate the text, as in (4):

(4) ... a lytel book named the *Book of Good Maners*, whiche book is of auctoryte for as moche as there is nothyng sayd therin but for the moost parte it is aledged by scrypture of the Byble or ellis by sayeng of holy sayntes, doctours, philosophers and poetes ... (*Book of Good Manners* 60/11-15)

4.1.3   *Content of the text*

Seven out of the ten prologues examined contain a content-based account of the book, of varying length. Sometimes the content is introduced only in passing (e.g. in *Eneydos* 78/7-14), sometimes it takes the form of a fairly detailed summary of the entire table of contents (e.g. *Caton* 65/87-116, *King Arthur* 109/137-176). Merely listing the table of contents is not an indication of a particular market orientation as such, except perhaps in the most general sense. It is the accounts of the content that are presented in a manner that is clearly meant to arouse the reader's interest by highlighting some aspects of it. In the present material such examples occur above all in the prologues to the romances, as for instance in (5):

(5) Whiche booke specyfyeth of the noble actes and fayttes of warre achyeved by a noble and victorious prynce named Blanchardin ... for the love of a noble pryncesse callyd Eglantyne ... and of the grete adventures, labours, anguysshes and many other grete dyseases of theym bothe tofore they myghte atteyne for to come to the fynall conclusion of their desired love ... (*Blanchardin and Eglantine* 58/29-38)

This is a typical example in containing a lively narrative of the main storyline. It is riddled with the vocabulary of adventure and romantic excitement, including *noble, prynce, pryncesse, adventures, anguysshes,* and *desired love.*

4.2 Translation-specific moves

4.2.1 *Justifying the translation*

There are three kinds of moves that promote the translation. First of all, Caxton's prologues typically contain statements justifying the translation: by making the text available in English, it is made accessible to the readers in England. In such instances it is not always easy to draw a line between 'text-specific' and 'translation-specific' considerations, since the translator is naturally also speaking indirectly of the significance of original text at the same time. Here I attempt to group those instances separately where the role of the translation is clearly emphasized. A discourse focused on the translation is assumed to be geared towards arousing an interest in the prospective reader for buying the book. The prologue to the *Book of Good Manners* provides an example of this. The translator first states how he has observed "the condycions and maners of the comyn people" to be "rude and not manerd" (60/1, 2), and "that every man shold have knowleche of good maners" (60/6). Against this background and on the suggestion of his mercer friend, William Pratt, Caxton decided to translate the *Book of Good Manners* "into Englyssh, our maternal tonge, to th'ende that it myght be had and used emonge the people for th'amendement of their maners to to th'encreace of vertuous lyvyng" (60/15).

4.2.2 *Stating benefits for the reader*

Another apparent promotional move in the prologues involves making explicit to potential readers the benefits of buying the book and reading it. These benefits are described as essentially spiritual, concerned with achieving a better life, both in one's lifetime and in the world to come, cf. examples (6)-(8):

(6) In whiche I doubte not, and yf they wylle rede it [= this sayd *Book of Cathon*] and understande, they shal moche the better conne rewle themself therby. (*Caton* 64/56)

(7) Thenne to th'ende [i.e. that a man may eschewe alle vyces and ensiewe vertue] that this sayd book may prouffyte unto the herars of it, I byseche Almyghty God that I may ach[y]eve and accomplysshe it unto this laude and glorye, and to the th'erudicion and lernynge of them that ben ygnoraunt that they maye thereby prouffyte and be the better. (*Caton* 64/72)

(8) And I beseche Almyghty God ... that al they that shal rede or here it that they may the better lyve in this present lyf that after this lyf they and I may come to the everlastyng lyf in heven where as is joye and blysse perdurable. (*Book of Good Manners* 61/29)

Such spiritually edifying objectives are characteristic of groups (b) and (c) of the texts (cf. above), i.e. those concerned with manners and proper behaviour and with wisdom and morality. The yield for the reader of texts concerned with chivalry and romance, in contrast, has more to do with their function as entertainment. Good stories will be not only morally instructive but also entertaining:

(9) I thought in myself hit shold be a good besynes to translate hyt into oure Englissh to th'ende that hyt myght be had as well in the royame of Englond as in other landes, and also for to passe therewyth the tyme ... (*History of Troy* 97/13)

(10) Whiche booke, as me semed, sholde be moche requysyte to noble men to see as wel for the eloquence as the historyes ... (*Eneydos* 79/17)

(11) ... wherein they shalle fynde many joyous and playsaunt hystoryes and noble and renomed actes of humanyte, gentylnesse and chyvalryes (*King Arthur* 109/108).

4.2.3 *Audience*

In accordance with Caxton's awareness of the significance of marketing, we should expect to find references to the presumed audience(s) of his books. As noted above, Caxton was probably thinking above all of the nobility as his principal clientele (cf. example 10), since this was the class with the highest proportion of both literacy and wealth. References to the nobility would probably have worked in both directions, in accordance with what Leech (1983: 135) has called the approbation maxim.[6] The publisher expresses appreciation towards his potential readers by implying that they belong to a prestigious group. For the potential readers, on the other hand, such recognition of group solidarity might have been an incentive to act as desired and purchase the book.

Caxton makes an effort to be specific about his projected audience. There are very few examples of collective references to the public at large. When such reference is made, as in describing the merits of chess "unto the moralite of the publique wele as well of the nobles as of the comyn peple" (*Game of Chess* 85/19),[7] or referring to *Caton* as "a short and prouffitable doctryne for all maner of peple" (65/81), or to "al they that shal rede or here it" in example (8) above from the *Book of Good Manners*, it may not have been intended as recognition of the primary audience. In these instances too the audience is likely to have been understood to consist of those higher up on the social scale. In one instance, *Doctrinal of Sapience*, the text is first introduced as intended for a restricted audience (*prestes*), later extended to include also "symple prestes that understonde not the scriptures" (77/3). Still further on, the writer says that the intention of the text is "to styre and moeve the symple peple to devocion" (78/37).

The gender-specific references show an interesting pattern in that there are only a few specific references to "noble men" as the target audience; cf. example (10) above. In spite of this, however, it is the male audience that is to be taken as the default, unless otherwise indicated. Caxton translated most of his books primarily for noble and educated gentlemen to read. When women are included in the audience, they are explicitly mentioned:

(12) ... and knewe wel that the storye of hit was honeste and joyefull to all vertuouse yong noble gentylmen and wymmen for to rede therin, as for their passe-tyme. (*Blanchardin and Eglantine* 57/12)

As the example indicates, it is in the romances that female audiences are most frequently invoked. One of the texts in the present selection, *Knight of the Tower*, is the prologue to a book specifically aimed at instructing "al yong gentylwymen" (111/8) about proper conduct. However, the prologue also advises "every gentilman or woman havyng such children ... to gete and have this book" (112/35), in order to be able to educate their daughters properly.

4.3 Press-specific moves

With regard to advertisements (see section 3.2. above), where the work of the press is openly publicised, it will be relevant to ask whether the same thing happens in the prologues. Here this kind of promotion is generally indirect in nature. A number of elements might be seen to bear on this function indirectly, but the relevant moves are not formulated explicitly as promotional statements. Rather, the press is promoted by bringing the role of the translator-printer-publisher himself into focus. Here I address three aspects of this issue.

4.3.1 *Patronage*

Patrons were essential for Caxton, not only for financial reasons but also – and perhaps more importantly – for promotional ones. The higher up the patron was in the social hierarchy, the more he or she was likely to contribute financially to the project and the better his or her name for the publicity of the press. In actual fact, the patrons did not always contribute very much financially. In the prologue to *Four Sons of Aymon* (84/30), for example, Caxton complains that he had to print the volume entirely at his own expense, his patron, the Earl of Oxford, having failed to support him. On the other hand, the promotional function of many of the patrons was also truly significant for the press. This can be inferred from the generous space allotted to the presentation of patrons in the prologues. The fact that such moves are expressed in an elevated style and usually placed early in the prologues further reinforces the impression of the importance of the patrons. For example, Margaret, Duchess of Somerset, is introduced as "the right noble, puyssaunt and excellent pryncesse, my redoubted lady, my Lady Margarete, Duchesse of Somercete, moder unto our naturel and soverayn lord and most Crysten kynge, Henry the Seventh, by the grace of God Kyng of Englonde and of Fraunce, Lord of Yrelond etc." at the beginning of the prologue to *Blanchardin and Eglantine* (57/2). The patron is usually presented as the instigator of the translation, and the finished work is presented to the patron. In the present sample the patrons that supported Caxton's work include members of the royalty and nobility (prologues 1, 2, 7, 8, 10), anonymous (noble) persons (4, 5), a merchant friend (6), and the City of

London (3). Only in one instance (9) is no patron mentioned.

4.3.2 *The translator-printer*

In this section we come to Caxton's own role in the process as translator and printer. These roles are differently represented in the texts. Caxton's dual role as both translator and printer appears most typically in the colophons and epilogues at the end of the books.[8] Examples typically include variations of "translated", "printed", "finished", "achieved" and "ended" (for a discussion of the interpretation of these verbs, see Blake 1973: 12ff.). In the prologues Caxton refers to himself by name on four occasions (prologues 1, 2, 3, 7). The name is mentioned in connection with the presentation of the volume to the patron, where it immediately follows the formulaic introduction of the patron's name. In this context Caxton presents himself as a humble servant of the patron. In two instances (prologues 1 and 3) he mentions, in addition, that the patron is a mercer in the City of London. In prologue 3 (*Caton*) this is of special importance, since the volume is dedicated not to any noble patron but to the City of London; see (13) below. Blake (1969: 92) suggests that Caxton was hereby stressing his connection with the merchants. It is possible that the special praise he affords to the volume (cf. 4.1.1. above) is connected with the purpose of marketing the book to the mercer community.

(13) Unto the noble, auncyent and renommed cyte, the Cyte of London in Englond, I William Caxton, cytezeyn and conjurye of the same and of the fraternyte and felauship of the mercerye, owe ... (*Caton* 63/12)

The prologues typically contain first-person accounts of the how the translation project originated. This narrative is usually geared to expressing the translator's humility in view of the daunting task of turning the original text, written in ornate and admirable discourse in French, into the "rude" diction of the English language. In the famous prologue to *Eneydos*, the concern about making correct linguistic choices is elaborated on in considerable detail in the form of a lengthy narrative. The pattern whereby the translator expresses his modesty about the work is called "humility formula" by Blake (e.g. 1969: 153). The following passage is a typical example:

(14) Besechynge my sayd ladyes bountyuous grace to receyve this lityll boke in gree of me, her humble servaunt, and to pardoune me of the rude and comyn Englyshe, where as shall be found faulte; for I confesse me not lerned ne knowynge the arte of rethoryk ne of suche gaye termes as now be sayd in these dayes and used. (*Blanchardin and Eglantine* 58/39)

The humility formula is absent only in one instance, *King Arthur*, a book for which Caxton was not the translator. In another instance, *Caton*, the translation is mentioned without the usual epithet of "rude" English. This is interesting in that here Caxton was in a difficult situation, having been without a patron for some time (Blake 1969: 92). Perhaps he felt that in such a situation he had less reason to feel apologetic about his translation.

The humility formula coupled with references to the imperfections of the English tongue can hardly be seen as reflexes of promotional discourse, unless we look upon them as patterns of discourse characteristic of the period. Such formulaic expressions were traditionally used to downplay the role of the translator in search of ways of dealing with the inadequate medium his native language. On the other hand, what the humility formula may in essence be claiming is that the translator has done everything humanly possible to overcome the limitations of the English language, and has despite those limitations managed to produce a readable version of the original. The communicative intention may thus have been to intimate to the reader that he or she, having enjoyed the book in translation, will appreciate the good work of the translator and be interested in acquiring further titles by him. Seen in such a light, the formula turns into yet another item of promotional discourse in the prologues, along with safeguarding the translator against the detection of potential errors and against criticism on the part of readers.[9]

5 Concluding remarks

Ten out of the twenty-four texts in Blake's edition (1973) were examined to identify features of promotional discourse in Caxton's prologues. The relevant moves were classified into three main categories: those promoting the text, the translation, and the printing press. The presence of the individual promotional moves in the material is set out in Table 1.

The presence of the types of moves in the material indicates that promotional discourse, as understood here, is a common feature of the prologues. All texts show traces of it. Thus for example an account of the content of the text is part of every prologue, while all but one contain a dedication to the patron(s) and a reference to the audience, either generic or gender-specific. Justifying the translation and mentioning the benefit(s) of the text for reader(s), along with the humility formula, are present in eight of the ten prologues. The least common moves are those drawing attention to the pre-eminence of the text (one instance), the quality of English (four instances), the authority of the text (five instances) and the name of the translator-printer (five instances).

None of the prologues contain all ten moves, but eight of them contain seven or eight moves.[10] The *Game of Chess* and *Doctrinal of Sapience* have fewer promotional moves than the other prologues. The distribution of the moves in terms of the grouping of the texts into (1) chivalry and romance, (2) manners and conduct, and (3) wisdom and morality (cf. 3.3. above) does not show any difference between groups (1) and (2), the average being 7.5 moves per text in both categories. The ratio for group (3) is somewhat lower, 5.7 per prologue. Overall, the result indicates that the features of promotional discourse highlighted in the prologues tend to remain fairly stable elements in most of the texts studied. In terms of type of promotion, the prologues contain on average 8.6 moves promoting the press. The corresponding figure for moves promoting the translation is 8.3. For moves promoting the text of the book, the ratio, at 5.3 per prologue, is the lowest of the three categories.

Table 1. Distribution of promotional moves in the prologues

PROMOTION		PROLOGUE										Total
		1	2	3	4	5	6	7	8	9	10	
1 Text	Pre-eminence of text			+								1
	Authority of text		+	+	+	+	+			+		5
	Content of text	+	+	+	+	+	+	+	+	+	+	10
2 Translation	Justification of translation	+	+	+	+	+	+	+	+		+	8
	Benefit(s) for the reader(s)	+		+	+	+	+	+	+	+	+	8
	Audience reference: generic	+										1
	male				+	+	+	+	+	+	+	7
	female			+	+			+				3
3 Press	Patronage	+	+	+	+	+	+	+	+		+	9
	Translator-printer named	+	+	+		+		+				5
	Humility formula	+			+		+	+	+		+	8
	Quality of English	+			+		+		+			4
	Total	8	4	8	7	7	7	7	7	5	7	

Key to the prologues: 1= *History of Troy*, 2= *Game of Chess*, 3= *Caton*, 4= *Knight of the Tower*, 5= *King Arthur*, 6= *Book of Good Manners*, 7= *Blanchardin and Eglantine*, 8= *Four Sons of Aymon*, 9= *Doctrinal of Sapience*, 10= *Eneydos*

These findings show that promotion was considered such an important element that a number of moves to that effect were consistently incorporated into the prologues. Different prologues nevertheless have somewhat different profiles in terms of the distribution of the moves. Further work will be needed to gain a more precise understanding of the structure of promotional discourse in the individual prologues, taking into account the length of the prologues and the frequency of the moves per prologue, as well as examining a more representative range of prologues. Still, the significant proportion of promotional moves in the present pilot sample bears evidence of the emerging importance of market awareness in the early printing and publishing business, which was part and parcel of the new culture of book-making.

Notes

1 I am grateful to Professor Shinichiro Watanabe for his valuable help and cooperation during the preparation of this paper. I would also like to thank Dr Matti Peikola for a very stimulating discussion of early English prologues and epilogues and his comments on the present study. My thanks are also due to Dr Ellen Valle for her comments on the style of the paper. For any shortcomings I am naturally alone responsible. – The quotation in the title is from Caxton's prologue to his translation of *Four Sons of Aymon* (Blake 1973:83).
2 For the medieval background of prologues see Wogan-Browne, Watson, Taylor and Evans (1999: *passim*) and Galloway (2005:288-305).
3 For example Nelson (1998), following the model of Gérard Genette, discusses Caxton's prologues and epilogues as "paratexts", surrounding the text proper. Jenny Adams examines Caxton's interest in political models, as reflected in his translation of the *Game and Playe of Chesse*, a text that uses chess as an elaborate allegory of an ideal political order (Adams, J. 2005), while Carole Weinberg focuses on Caxton, Anthony Woodville, and the prologue to the *Morte Darthur* (Weinberg 2005), and Tracy Adams on the construction of a specifically merchant readership for some of Caxton's books, especially his conduct books (Adams, T. 2005).
4 In Blake's edition (1973) the prologues are numbered as follows; 6, 45, 15, 73, 72, 9, 6, 44, 34, and 36.
5 The references following the examples refer to the page/line number in Blake (1973).
6 What is at stake here is actually an act of flattery on the part of the publisher. The

perlocutionary act (Austin 1962:101) of the buyer consists of recognizing the flattery and acting upon it, as desired. Leech, however, prefers the term 'approbation' instead of flattery, since flattery is normally understood as an insincere approbation . In full, the approbation maxim states "Minimize dispraise of other; maximize praise of other" (Leech, *ibid.*).

7   In the prologue to the second edition of the *Game of Chess*, which is not part of the sample examined, the reference has been changed to read: "Wherefore bycause thys sayd book is ful of holsom wysedom and requysyte unto every astate and degree, I have purposed to enprynte it, shewyng therein the figures of suche persons as longen to the playe, in whom al astates and degrees ben comprysed." (88/25)

8   Cf. Blake (1976: 114-115). In one instance (*King Arthur*), Caxton is not the translator of the book but only the printer. He explains this as follows, "Thenne to procede forth in thys sayd book ... I Wyllyam Caxton, symple persone, present thys book folowyng whyche I have enprysed t'enprynte ..." (109/124). In one instance (*Four Sons of Aymon*), the printer is Wynkyn de Worde (cf. 84/3).

9   An interesting example in this vein is provided by the prologue to the *Game of Chess* (85/33), where Caxton, in presenting the book to his patron, asks him "not to disdaygne to resseyve this lityll sayd book in gree and thanke as well of me your humble and unknowen servant as of a better and gretter man than I am, for the right good wylle that I have had to make this lityll werk in the best wyse I can ought to be reputed for the fayte and dede."

10 The three variants of "Audience reference" (generic, male, female) have been counted as one per prologue.

References

Primary source

Blake, N.F. (1973) *Caxton's Own Prose*. London: André Deutch.

Secondary source

Adams, Jenny (2005) "'Longene to the Playe': Caxton, Chess, and the Boundaries of Political Order." *Essays in Medieval Studies* 21: 133-166.

Adams, Tracy (2005) "'Noble, wyse and grete lordes, gentilmen and marchauntes': Caxton's Prologues as Conduct Books for Merchants." *Parergon* 22: 53-76.

Austin, J.L. (1962) *How to Do Things with Words*. Cambridge, MA: Harvard University Press.

Bhatia, Vijay K. 1993. *Analysing Genre: Language Use in Professional Settings*. London: Longman.

Blake, N.F. (1976) *Caxton and his World*. London: André Deutsch.

Blake, N.F. (1976) *Caxton: England's First Publisher*. London: Osprey.

Blake, N.F. (1979) "Continuity and change in Caxton's prologues and epilogues: the Bruges period." *Gutenberg-Jahrbuch*, vol. 1979:72-77.

Blake, N.F. (1991) *William Caxton and English Literary Culture*. London and Rio Grande: The Hambledon Press.

Galloway, Andrew (1995) *Readings in Medieval Texts: Interpreting Old and Middle English Literature*. Oxford. Oxford University Press.

Leech, Geoffrey N. (1983) *Principles of Pragmatics*. London and New York: Longman.

Nelson, Kristopher (1998) "A Pretext for Writing: Prologues, Epilogues, and the Notion of Paratext." Available at: http://www.ekris.org/eng599.html

Swales, John M. (1990) *Genre Analysis: English in Academic and Research Settings*. Cambridge: Cambridge University Press.

Weinberg, Carole S. (2005) "Caxton, Anthony Woodville, and the Prologue to the *Morte Darthur*. *Studies in Philology* 102 (1): 45-65.

Wogan-Browne, Jocelyn; Watson, Nicholas; Taylor, Andrew; Evans, Ruth (eds.) (1999) *The Idea of the Vernacular: An Anthology of Middle English Literary Theory, 1280-1520*. Exeter: Exeter University Press.

The Percy Folio Text of *Lybius Disconius*

Maldwyn Mills

The text of *Lybius Disconius* that is contained in the mid-seventeenth century MS British Library Additional 27879 (the Percy Folio MS: henceforth P) is not one that is much esteemed by students of the Middle English romances. For one thing – and it was the one that particularly offended its editors, J. W. Hales and F. J. Furnivall[1] – it breaks off before celebrating the marriage of the hero and heroine that had provided the climax of the story in all of the medieval copies;[2] for another – as might have been expected in so late a text – many of its readings are more commonplace than their medieval counterparts.[3] All of which makes this *Lybius* seem very much the poor relation of these last, and even to represent – as the Percy *Sir Degree* has been said to represent – the terminal decline of the story that it tells.[4] But there is also a more positive side to it. Not all of the new readings of P are weaker than their medieval equivalents; some offer valid alternatives to them, make clearer sense than they do, or even supply necessary detail that all of them had left out.[5] In what follows we shall be most concerned with four of the larger-scale of its unique readings, but we shall first note examples of some shorter ones, classified under five headings (which sometimes overlap). These readings will throughout be set against their closest equivalents in the medieval copies of *Lybius*, but in all cases line-references will be given to one or other of the texts contained in British Library MS Cotton Caligula a. ii (C) and Lambeth Palace Library MS 306 (L), since these are the most accessible as well as (usually) the most authentic of those that have survived.

(1) **Nonsensical readings**

These are relatively rare, but one striking example is P 1263 *And vnder a chest of tree* ('wooden box') which replaces L 1217 *Vnder a chesteyne tree* to denote the place at which Sir Otes de Lile surrenders to the hero after their battle in the forest.

(2) **Weaker readings**

These, by contrast, are relatively common, and one appears near the very beginning of the romance, as part of the description of the hero, when P 10 *without ffable* replaces the *profytable* (= 'worthy', 'deserving') of C 10 and the other medieval versions (and does so again in P 1639 (for C 1531)). Weaker too is the replacement of C 396 *deray* ('lamentation') by P 438 *array* ('pomp') to describe the reactions of the nephews of William de la Braunche to their uncle's bloody state after his combat with the hero.

(3) **Translated readings**

These will substitute more up-to-date equivalents for the medieval originals, and will sometimes denote weapons or equipment: C 1120 *arblaste* becomes P 1192 *crossebowes*. Also (minimally) translated are two of the locations of the hero's combats when L 199-200 *At Poynte Perilowse, / Besyde the Chapell of Awntrous* become P 205-6 *Att the Bridge of Perrill, / Beside the Aduenturous Chappell.*[6]

(4) **Alternative readings**

Elsewhere quite distinct (but still perhaps more comprehensible) words will be used to denote items of dress and armour. In P 394 *coyfe* ('hood of mail') replaces L 372 *barbe* ('armour protecting the chin'); in P 265 and 1491 *hawberke* replaces C 224 and 1383 *gypell* ('tunic'), while in P 1382 *paytrill* and *crouper* ('armour protecting the breast and hindquarters of a horse') and P 1682 *paytrell* and *armoure* replace *lyngell* and *trappure* ('harness straps ... horse cloths') in C 1274 and 1574.

(5) **More meaningful readings**

One such is the name given one of the opponents of the hero. In C he is, rather obscurely, named *Gyffroun le Flowdous,* ~ *Fludous* (C 751, 772, 904);[7] in P the second element of the name becomes ~ *Fraudeus* (P 802, 823, 967), which is not only more meaningful in itself, but brings to mind allusions to the knight's use of trickery in fighting (P 803-4 and 810 (the first also in C 752-3)). And while in C 1295 the lords and ladies of the Yle d'Or had watched the fight of Lybius and Mangys from the rather puzzling *pomet tours* of that castle, in P 1403 it is from its less obscure *pount tornere* ('drawbridge').

Not all the above types of variant readings are clearly present in the four longer passages that we shall be looking at. None of these last seems either wholly nonsensical (though the first comes fairly close to being so), or wholly the translation of something similar but not identical. On the other hand, their larger scale makes possible alterations of kinds that have not yet been mentioned, and in particular, changes to the versification. In the most reliable of the medieval texts of *Lybius* both the metre and the rhyme-pattern of the stanza were relatively uncommon, with the couplet- as well as the tail-lines generally of three main stresses, and with the first two of these couplets rhyming together to give *aabaabccbddb* as the pattern of the stanza as a whole.[8] In P however this pattern is frequently altered to the more usual *aabccbddbeeb*, while a large number of the couplet-lines (and even some of the tail-lines) are given an extra main stress. Compare, for example, these excerpts from the hero's fight with the nephews of William de la Braunche:

Þo was Lybeaus agreued Whan he feld on hedde Þat sword wyth egre mode. His brond abowte he weuede: All þat he hyt he cleuede, As werrour wyld and wode. 'Allas,' he seyde þo, 'Oon aȝens two, To fyȝte þat ys good!' Wel faste þey smyte to hym, And he, wyth strokes grym, Well harde aȝens hem stode. (C 502-13)	Sir Lybius was served in þat stead When hee felled on his head Þat the sword had drawen blood. About his head the sword he waued: All that hee hitt, ffor soothe, hee cleeued, As warryour wight and good. Sir Lybius said swithe thoe, 'One to ffight against two Is nothing good!' Fast they hewed then on him: With stroakes great and grim, Against them he stifflye stood. (P 547-58)

More important still were the results of altering the rhyme-words in tail-rhyme position, since this would often create stanzas both larger and smaller than the twelve-line norm. Most common of all are stanzas of six lines,[9] as in the following excerpt from the hero's climactic battle at Sinadone with the enchanters Mabam and Iron; here and in our next two comparisons, the tail-rhyme words are set in bold face:

As they togedyr gan hewe, Maboune, the more shrewe, In ffelde vp **aroos**; He herde and well knewe That Irayne yaue dyntis fewe: Therof hym sore **agroos**. To hym he went full right To helpe to fellen in fight Lybeous of noble **loose**; But Lybeous faught with bothe, Though they weren wrothe, And kepte hymselffe **close**. (L 1953-64)	Then together gan they hew; Mabam, the more shrew, Up he ros **againe**; He heard, and alsoe knew Iron gaue strokes ffew: Therof he was not **ffaine**; But to him he went ffull right For to helpe Iron to ffight And auenge him on his **enemye**; Tho he were neuer soe wroth, Sir Lybius fought against them both, And kept himselfe **manlye**. (P 1999-2010)

(1) In the first of the four passages of larger scale alteration in P, an odd number of new lines have been inserted into a regular twelve-line stanza in a way that dislocates, not only its own rhyme-structure, but also that of no fewer than eleven of the stanzas that follow it. The crucial stanza is the second of two describing the dwarf who, in company with Maid Hellen, has come to Arthur's court to find a champion for their mistress, the Queen of Sinadone, now the prisoner of Mabam and Iron:

Wyndeleyn was his name:	Teddelyne was his name:
Wyde sprong his fame,	Wide sprang of him the [f]ame,
Est, west, northe, and **southe**.	East, west, north, and **southe**.
Myche he couthe of game:	Much he cold of game and glee:
S[y]tell, sawtre in same;	Ffiddle, crowde and sowtrye:
	He was a merry man of **mouth**.
Herpe, fidyll þan wele he **couthe**.[10]	Harpe, ribble and sautrye:
	He cold much of minstrelsye:
He was a gode gestoure	He was a good **jestour**
	(There was none such in noe country);
	A jolly man forsooth was he
Wiþ ladys in þeir bowre	With ladyes in their **bower**.
A mery man of **mouthe**.	
He seyd to þe meyd, 'I wene,	Then he bade maid Hellen
To tell þ[y] tale bedene	Fforto tell her tale bydeene
Tyme it is **forsothe**.'	And kneele before the **king**.
(A 145-56 (C 133-44))	(P 145-59)

For all its amplification and rearrangement of earlier detail, this offers virtually nothing really new or significant. More interesting than its content are the questions that it prompts about how it came into being. Since almost every word in the earlier version of the stanza is kept, we cannot say that its immediate source was so difficult to read that the redactor of P, or of one of its sources, was forced to draw upon his (unremarkable) powers of invention to produce his own version of it. It would seem more likely that at this point he for some reason abandoned the direct copying of his exemplar, to rely, very briefly, upon his confused memories of it.[11] But what is beyond dispute are the effects that this inflation of the stanza had upon the ones following. It set in motion a chain-reaction of alteration in the words in the tail-lines, since if the stanzas containing them were to be made of even (and acceptable) length – that is, of six, twelve, or eighteen lines –[12] then either the first or the last of the 3-line units in the original stanzas would have, like P 157-9, to be given a new tail-rhyme word. One important consequence of this upsetting of the original stanza-limits is that form and content will often fall out of step, since closely-related tail- and couplet-lines that were originally juxtaposed within a single stanza may now become the last unit of one stanza, and the first unit of the next.[13] The original boundaries of the stanzas are not restored until the very end of the scene at Arthur's court, by simply extending the king's valedictory blessing of Lybius from three lines to six:

And seyd, 'God gyffe þe grace	And said, 'God þat is of might
T[o] hafe spede and space	And his mother Marry bright
Thorow þat lady **hende**.'	Þat is flowre of all **women**
(A 286-8 (C 250-2))	Giue thee gracce fforto gone
	Forto gett the ouerhand of thy fone
	And speed thee in thy journey. **Amen**
	(P 289-94)

(2) Our second passage is at once less disruptive and more inventive. Less disruptive, because the number of lines inserted was this time an even one, and so did not make necessary any alteration in the boundaries of the stanzas that followed; more inventive, because the extra material here is more than a tangle of repetitive (and mostly familiar) detail, and instead presents a character who has just appeared in the story in more detail and from a different point of view than in the medieval texts. This character is Sir Otes de Lile, a knight identified by the dwarf (from his horn call) as a former vassal of the Queen of Sinadone, who had abandoned her when she was taken prisoner, had fled into the forests of the Wirral, and become more of a huntsman than a knight. As

such, his dearest possession is the multi-coloured hound which had only a little earlier been caught and given to Hellen by Lybius; this act of gallantry will later compel him to fight with Otes, and two groups of his vassals. The new material in P comes between the theft of the dog, and this battle.

They houyd vnder a lynde	The[y] hunted still vnder the lind
To se þe course of þe hynde,	To se the course of þat hind
Sir Libeus and hys fere;	Vnder the fforrest side.
	There beside dwelled þat knight
	Þat Sir Otes de Lile hight,
	A man of much pride.
Than comme after þe hynde	He was cladd all in inde
A knyȝht clothyd in jnde	& ffast pursued after the hind
Vpon a bay deyster;	Vpon a bay distere.
Hys bugyll gan he blaw	Loude he gan his horne blow
For þat his men schuld knaw	For the hunters shold itt know
Jn what sted þat they were.	& know where he were.
	As he rode by þat wood right,
	There he saw þat younge knight
	And alsoe þat ffaire may;
	The dwarffe rode by his side.
	Sir Otes bade they shold abyde –
	They ledd his ratch away.
	'Freinds,' he said, 'why doe you soe?
	Let my ratch ffrom you goe –
	Good for you itt were!
He seyd, 'Be seynt Mertyne!	J say to you without lye,
That ilke rache was myne	This ratch has beene my
Not fully gon a ȝere.'	All out this 7 yeere.'
(A 1092-1103 (C 1039-50))	(P 1099-1122)

Here again some of the new material suggests the redactor-scribe's recall of earlier detail in the story, but this time at much longer range than in our first passage. P 1102-4 recall moments in earlier episodes in which Ellen (and not the narrator) had given advance warning of an enemy that would have to be fought with,[14] while P 1112-13 recall at least one earlier point in which just such an enemy first catches sight of the hero.[15] But this time there is no confusion of any of the detail from the earlier versions. The new material simply shifts the reader's attention from Lybius to his new adversary, who now has a rather larger part to play than before, and is also made to seem more reasonable. The narrative technique becomes more explicit and less dramatically surprising, but presents us with nothing really new. In this respect the passage contrasts sharply with our remaining two examples, both of which provide information that is genuinely new and arguably necessary.

(3) The first of them comes when Lybius, having killed Mabam, the more dangerous of the two enchanters, turns to deal with Iron, who is already badly wounded, only to find that he has been mysteriously carried off (C 1969-71, P 2089-91).[16] He is quite unable to find him after extensive searching, and is greatly worried by this (L 2046-57, P 2092-100). Despite the later assurances of the queen, his fears continue to trouble him, and are not set at rest in any of the medieval copies until further on in the story, and then only confusedly.[17] In P, however, there is no delay and no ambiguity, since matters are at once set right by inserting a run of six-line stanzas within an original one of twelve:

And whan he fonde him noughte,
He helde him selfe bekaughte
And byganne to syke sore;
And seide, in word and thought,   As he stood & him bethought
'This will be dere bought –   Þat itt wold be deere bought
That he is fro me fare!   Þat he was ffrom him ffare
He will with sorcerye   (For he wold with sorcerye
Do me tormentrye: Doe much tormentrye
Þat is my moste care.'   And þat was much care!)

                                        He tooke his sword hastilye
                                        And rode vpon a hill hye
                                        And looked round about;

> Then he was ware of [a] valley –
> Thitherward he tooke the way
> As a sterne knight and stout.
>
> As he rode by a riuer side,
> He was ware of him þat tyde
> Vpon the riuer brimm;
> He rode to him ffull hott
> And of his head he smote,
> Fast by the chinn.
>
> And when he had him slaine,
> Fast hee tooke the way againe
> Forto haue þat lady gent;
> As soone as he did thither come,
> Of his horsse he light downe
> And into the hall hee went
>
> And sought þat ladye ffaire and hend,
> But he cold her not find –
> Therfor he sighed full sore;
> Still he sate mourni[n]g
> For þat ladye ffaire & young –
> For her was all his care!

Sore he sate and sighte –	He ne wist what he doe might,
He nuste whate do he myght,	But still he sate and sore he sight –
He was of blysse all bare.	Of joy hee was fful bare.
(L 2049-60)	(P 2095-127)

The beheading of Iron in P 2111-12 serves both to recall and fulfil the promise that the hero had made before the combat with the enchanters: '*And Mabam and Iron / Smite of there anon / Theire heads in þat stoure*' (P 1837-9). At one point the present passage is less explicit than might have been expected, since Iron is not actually named in P 2108; only the 'him' tells us that Lybius has found the man he is looking for. But the new stanzas are quite neatly fitted into their inherited context by making the last of them tell of his failure to find not Iron, but the Queen of Sinadone (not a cause of concern at this point in the medieval versions) as the cause of his despair.

(4) As it happens, the lady appears on the scene almost immediately, in the form of a serpent, and – as in all the earlier versions – is soon changed back into human shape after kissing Lybius. But this too has consequences which are not immediately set right in these texts, and which give rise to the last of the major interpolations in P. For the transformation from serpent to human shape has left the lady naked, which grieves the hero greatly (C 2014-6, P 2158-60), but his immediate action (after she has expressed her gratitude and promised future rewards) is, in the earlier versions, to dash back to Sinadone to report his success to Lambard, the queen's steward. In all of the texts, the clothing necessary for her triumphal return into her city is indeed sent to her, but only after two further stanzas (C 2044-67) in which Lybius gives an account first, of his victory, and then of the lady's transformation, and her assurances that both of the enchanters have been killed. The first of these stanzas is kept as P 2200-11, but the second is not, since assurances that Iron has been killed are no longer needed in P, after the insertion of the passage considered above.

This apparent lack of real concern for the lady's predicament had implications for the hero's status as a model of chivalry that clearly worried the redactor of P, and led to the interpolation of yet another short run of six-line stanzas in which Lybius, before dashing off to Sinadone, expresses his devotion (and submission) to the lady, as well as his determination to find clothes for her:

Lybeauus was glad and blyþe And lepte to horse swyþe And lefte þat lady stylle;	Then was he glad and blythe
	And thanked God often sythe, That him þat grace had sent; And sayd, 'My L[ady] faire & ffree, All my loue I leaue with thee, By God omnipotent.

> But euer he dradde Yrayn,
> For he was naȝt y-slayn:
> Wyth speche he wold hym spylle.
> (C 2038-43)

> I will goe, my Lady bright,
> To the castle gate ffull right,
> Thither ffor to wend
> Forto feitch your geere
> Þat yee were wont to weare,
> And them I will you send.
>
> Alsoe if itt be your will,
> I pray you to abyde still
> Till I co[m]e againe.'
> 'Sir,' shee said, 'I you pray,
> Wend fforth [on] your [w]ay—
> Therof I am ffaine.'
> (P 2182-99)

The new material at once fills a gap in the narrative logic of the story, and securely establishes the claims of Lybius to be considered a true hero of romance.

How far does the above material suggest for P a coherent approach both to tail-rhyme narrative and to romance in general? At first sight, the innovations of this text seem as diverse in their implications as they are in their scale; what is new in the first and second of the major passages relates chiefly to style (or, in the case of the first, to the lack of it), while the third and fourth (together with some of the shorter passages) introduce new material that is of functional importance to the story itself. But, taken together, they suggest an approach to tail-rhyme narrative that is both fairly coherent, and significantly different from that of the earlier versions of the story. In these last the narrative manner, like the versification, was relatively concentrated, dramatic, and sometimes surprising; in P it is more often loose-limbed, explanatory, and reasonable. Even the favourite six-line stanza, for all its brevity, fits in quite well with this approach.

One further point may be made. It has more than once been noted that a number of the distinctive features of P may in fact derive from a printed text of *Lybius*, now lost. But whether they appeared first in a sixteenth-century print, or appeared in the seventeenth-century manuscript that we have, they belong to a context of private reading,[18] in which the oral dimension of the original text, while not wholly absent, seems much diminished, and with it a sensitivity to metre and rhyme. Sound has become less important than sense – which is appropriate to a text in which the major alterations are so concerned with meaning.

Notes

1 'It is so very wrong of the copier or translator to have broken off the story without giving the wedding between Lybius and his love, that I add it here from the three unprinted MSS. as well as the Cotton one,' (J. W. Hales and F. J. Furnivall, *Bishop Percy's Folio Manuscript*, II, London, 1868, p. 497).

2 There are five in all: British Library MS Cotton Caligula a. ii (C); Lambeth Palace Library MS 306 (L); Lincoln's Inn Library, MS Hale 150 (H); Bodleian Library Oxford MS Ashmole 61 (A), and Bibliotheca Nazionale, Naples, MS xiii. B. 29 (N): the Lincoln's Inn copy gives only half of the text. Full texts of the first two (and full variants from all the others, and from the Percy Folio copy) are given in M. Mills, *Lybeaus Desconus* (EETS 261), 1969; an edited text of all six versions, (also with complete variants) in M. Kaluza, *Libeaus Desconus* (Altenglische Bibliothek, V), Leipzig, 1890. Of the medieval manuscripts A is, in its first half; the one that has most in common with P: see Kaluza, p. xxxv-viii.

3 In marked contrast to the Folio texts of *Triamoure*, *Eglamoure* and *Degree*, not even the fragment of a printed text of *Lybius* has survived, although the existence of one is attested by allusions in Skelton (see Kaluza p. x). Because of this we have no means of knowing whether these alterations of the earlier text were created by the Percy scribe, or simply copied by him from a print. For a full list of the variant readings of P, see Mills, *Lybeaus*, pp. 291-302; a complete text of it is given on pp. 415-97 of Hales and Furnivall, II.

4 See Nicolas Jacobs, *The Later Versions of Sir Degarre*, Medium Ævum Monographs. N. S. xviii (1996), pp. 88-124. Since in this case a number of prints of this romance have survived, their individual readings can be precisely distinguished from those of P. A classified account of them is given in Chapter 2 '*Sir Degore*: A romance revised for a sixteenth-century printer', on pp. 65-87.

5 On one occasion, P even preserves the readings of the archetype of the romance

better than any other text; see note 13 below.

6   The same translations occur (in reverse order) in P 321 and 324 (= L 302 and 305). Sometimes, however, the same word may be sometimes translated, sometimes kept: *arsoun* in C 623, 1172 and 1181 becomes 'saddle' in P 674, 'saddle bow' in P 1244, and 'sadle crest' in P 1253 but is kept (in both of the first two of these senses) in P 363, 516, 1430 and 1722 (= C 321, 483, 1322 and 1614).

7   The name is a corruption of *Giflés li fius Do*, his opponent at the same point in Renaut de Beaujeu's, *Le Bel Inconnu* the twelfth-century French version of the story (ed. G. P. Williams, (*CFMA* 38, Paris, 1929, 1983). The other texts of *Lybius* give the name as *Jeffron le Freudys* (L 789), ~ *le Fredieus* (N 809), ~ *le Frendys* (A 816). Some kind of fraudulent practice is suggested in the lines that immediately follow the naming of Giffron in all the versions; in P 803-4 these read: 'in ffighting he hath an vse, / Knights fforto beguile.'

8   This 'four-rhyme' version of the tail-rhyme stanza is especially common in the romances of the Auchinleck MS, being used throughout *The King of Tars*, *Amis and Amiloun*, and *Horn Childe*, and in parts of *Rouland and Vernagu* and the tail-line continuation of *Guy of Warwick*.

9   Tail-rhyme stanzas of six lines were fairly common in medieval manuscript copies of romances. For their use in *Sir Isumbras* in both these and in later prints see my '*Sir Isumbras* and the Styles of the Tail-Rhyme Romance' in *Readings in Medieval English Romance*, ed. Carol M. Meale, Cambridge, 1994, pp. 1-24. Of the texts of *Lybius* they occur with particular frequency in the later parts of A and P, but hardly ever at exactly the same points.

10 The A reading here is a distortion of the *Harpe, fydele & croupe* found in C 138 and in all the other medieval texts. If this was indeed in the text used by our redactor at this point he must have guessed that the name of a third musical instrument was needed in this line.

11 For another suggestion of memorial provenance in P, see below pp. 83-4.

12 Within the part of the text affected, the stanzas, as defined by their tail-rhymes are, in sequence, of 6, 12, 6, 18, 12, 12, 12, 12, 12, 6, 18 and 12 lines.

13 Thus in the dwarf's verbal attack on Lybius, P 222 *Whosoe lookith on thee may know* and 223 *Thou ne durste, for thy berde*, which were originally the third and fourth lines of the same stanza, become the final line of one, and the first line of the next. Near the end of the story, form and content even get out of step in this way in C: see especially C 2046/2047 and C 2070/2071. Ironically, at the first of these two points P (in lines 2202/3) is not only superior to C in keeping the proper division into stanzas, but to all the other medieval copies as well: see Kaluza, op. cit., pp. xxxv-xxxvi and 121-2.

14 Notably in the references to William de la Braunche in P 304-6 '*This way keepeth a knight / Þat with euery man will ffight: / His name springeth wyde*', and to Giffroun

la Fraudeus in P 769-71 *Then laughed þat maiden bright* / *& sayd, 'Here dwelleth a knight,* / *The best þat here is about'*. When the dwarf had identified Sir Otes by his horn call, he had not yet become a threat to the hero (P 1066-74).

15 As when Gffroun first notices Lybius in P 827-8 (*Then he was ware of Sir Lybius* / *As a prince of much pryde*).

16 Presumably by the devil, since the transformed queen tells him in P 2166 (L 2099), after she has assured him that he has slain both of the enchanters, that they '*wrought by the ffeende*'.

17 He is still worrying that Iron may be alive, and so capable of destroying him, when he rides back to Sinadone in C 2041-3, and tells the queen's steward Lambard no more than that '*Maboun was yslayn* / *And* wondede *was Yrayn*' (C 2053-4), even if he also, a little later, goes on to repeat to him the Queen's words of reassurance ('*And seyde, "Now y am sure* / *My fomen beþ yslayn* / *Maboun & Yrayn* / *In pes now may we dure*"' (C 2064-7)). None of this is kept in P, since no doubts about Iron's fate were possible after the passage interpolated in that text after L 2057. A very different attempt to put Iron's fate beyond doubt was inserted after C 2041-3 in the Ashmole and Naples texts, in the form of a single tail-rhyme stanza in which Lybius finds the vanished enchanter within the castle, and cuts off his head. But since the equivalent of C 2053-4 was allowed to remain, the hero's doubts must still persist. For a fuller account of the revisions in A and N, see M. Mills, 'A Mediæval Reviser at Work', *Medium Ævum* 32(1963), 11-23.

18 It also may be worth noting that the Percy *Lybius*, like some other romances of the Folio MS, is divided into parts, and that the dividing lines between them, while generally placed where we might have expected them (that is, between separate episodes) are sometimes not. The first and second adventures met with by Lybius after leaving court are grouped together to give the second part (which has a kind of logic, since this unites the combat with William de la Braunche with the one with the nephews who would avenge his defeat), but the climactic battle with the enchanters is split, to give the eighth and ninth parts, just before the disappearance of Iron (which has no logic at all).

Some Aspects of Chaucer's Religious and Philosophic World in his *Canterbury Tales*

Young-Bae Park

> Chaucer followed nature everywhere, but was never so bold as to go beyond her. — J. Dryden

I

In this paper we shall limit our discussion to Chaucer's religious and philosophic world through the heterogeneous nature of some of the characters in *Canterbury Tales* to find out what the Middle Ages was indeed and what the hierarchy of the medieval Church really was and how Chaucer observes the "degrees" of his characters by the order in which he presents them in the *General Prologue*.[1]

We shall first review Chaucer's use of the hierarchy of the medieval Church which was a complicated structure at those times, and need not be considered here except insofar as Chaucer implicitly treats of it. And then we shall proceed to discuss the topic of the paper in which theoretically a pilgrimage is religious in character and consequently the subject belongs in any investigation of Chaucer's religious world and review furthermore the philosophic aspect of the *Canterbury Tales* in which Chaucer is mainly concerned with two of Destiny's agents: the force of the stars and the force of Fortune. The philosophers of the Middle Ages conceived of the universe as a finality and according to medieval belief, the stars as agents of Destiny combined with Fortune as powerful determinants for a man's life. This can be clearly seen in the *Knight's Tale* and illustrated elsewhere in the *Canterbury Tales*. If we examine the description of the Physician in the *General Prologue*, we observe a marriage of philosophy and science. The belief that stars are agents of Destiny joins the Physician's portrait to the practical aspects of his profession as the stars played a large part in the professional life of many physicians, particularly the so-called fashionable ones.

And finally we shall describe the so-called "degrees" by the order of some of the main characters in the *General Prologue* in which Chaucer presents them. Thus the Prioress and the Monk stand at the top, for each is the head of a subordinate House of some parent Order. Next comes the Friar, followed by the Clerk, then the Parson and finally there is that pair of arch-rascals, the Summoner and the Pardoner, who are presumably on ecclesiastical business.

II

To understand fully Chaucer's religious and philosophic world in one of his great works, *Canterbury Tales,* we should at first glance briefly at the temper of the late Middle Ages in a more general sense. What sort of world was this, peopled by what sort of men and women? Today man understands his physical surroundings more fully than did his medieval ancestor. In striking contrast, medieval man lived in the unending fear of "battle, murder, sudden death," of monstrous devils lying in wait for him around every corner, of a material and terrible hell, of storms and convulsions of nature, of the rigors of every winter, and of the horrors of pestilence and famine. Fears of that sort, exceedingly violent in themselves, bred a species of violence in the medieval mind, so that the average man of intelligence saw nearly everything in the light of exaggerated contrast: human beings were deemed to be either extremely good or extremely bad, they were either Fortune's favorites, or Fortune's victims, they were either brilliantly happy or bowed down in black despair; statements had to be wholly true or wholly false, decisions had to be based on the most literal and stern interpretation of justice or on completely unthinking "mercy."

Besides, in medieval England, everyone who could read (or who could listen to another's reading) was able to find a book telling him how to behave in his particular estate; ethic and etiquette were one, and politeness, which had at first sprung from religion, now became a complicated and self-justifying set of formalities. Hence the setting up of the ideal pattern – a pattern, which if we are to believe the evidence of narratives and sermons, was rarely followed in actual life – became a virtue in itself, for it brought preservation to the ideal and assurance – even a sort of insurance – to mankind. The fears, the extremes, the rituals thus all played a general part in forming the mind of "any man" living in the late Middle Ages. But what about Geoffrey Chaucer, who is both "any man" and a great genius, living in his particular circumstances?

We know that much (if not all) of Chaucer's early boyhood must have been spent in London where his father, John Chaucer, resided and conducted his business. Thus, fourteenth-century London at mid-century was enjoying a few rare years of optimism. England may be said to have come of age as a unified nation by the year 1350. The great victory over the French at Crécy in 1346, followed by a series of other military successes, encouraged Englishmen for at least a decade to think of themselves as a closely knit, invincible force, and – truly medieval – they were as extravagant in their feeling that all was materially well as they were soon to feel that all was materially ill. Chaucer, in his early boyhood, imbued with imaginative power, must have walked each day through the excitements of London's narrow, crooked streets – streets lined with open-fronted shops displaying their tempting wares, the shops interrupted here and there by one of London's many churches, or by the stately façade of a merchant's house, or by an imposing hall of one of the Gilds. There could scarcely have been a noisier city in the whole medieval world than London, and we may confidently add that at the middle of the fourteenth century no other city in England could surpass London in sights and sounds provocative to the imagination of a poet. Thus, Chaucer, a thoroughly and urban individual of his time, dwelling in relative comfort over the Aldgate entrance to London during the first part of this quarter century, could and did observe life both within and without his city, noisy London from one window, and the long road leading to Mile End and East Anglia from an opposite window. London was undoubtedly an environmental influence upon the poet. As a busy civil servant, Chaucer had to be daily in touch with men of affairs, constantly aware of all walks of fast-paced life. Further, London was the intellectual centre of England, Chaucer's native many-sided interests – in human nature and in the ways men act, in philosophy and in religion among others – widened and deepened inevitably because of his residence there.

Then, what was the religious culture of the late Middle Ages in England, the age in which Chaucer lived and the context in which his poetry was written?[2] It is clear that what characterises religion in the fourteenth century, and what distinguishes it most from our present era, is the omnipresence of ecclesiastical rites and institutions in the rhythms of everyday life. Religion was not an activity set aside for worship on a single day of the week; it was an integral part of work, play, and significant events in the calendar year.[3] In the late Middle Ages, the Church did everything in its power to 'bind, contain, or tie securely' everyone who adhered to its system into a single moral community. Accordingly, religious rituals attended the most commonplace of events: birthdays, marriages, anniversaries, celebrations of every imaginable kind, sicknesses, and burials. At those times, nearly everyday was a saint's day and the stories associated with the particular saint made the events in the liturgy more meaningful to the laity and enabled them to link religious activity more fully with the social and the communal. To be sure, the Church exercised considerable power and authority over the laity and had control over many instruments of culture, but in the fourteenth century it lacked the homogeneity associated with it today.[4]

It might be said of Chaucer that religion is both nowhere and everywhere in his poetry. It is nowhere if we look for a sustained or coherent religious vision of the kind we find in several of his contemporaries. But that does not mean that Chaucer is any less committed to engaging contemporary religious issues and problems. Even a casual review of his poetry reveals that Chaucer appreciates how religion is tightly woven into the fabric of everyday life. Nearly all of the *Canterbury Tales* deals directly or indirectly with a religious issue. The Reeve and the Shipman, for example, give stinging accounts of Church corruption at the local level. The Wife of Bath challenges the sexual politics of the Church and exposes how deeply misogyny is embedded in clerkly discourse. What we learn when we look closely is that Chaucer's poetry does indeed take us 'deep into the practice of religion among the common people.' We can see this practice clearly in the portraits of the Parson and the Plowman in the *General Prologue* which will be dealt with later in this paper.[5]

Many of present-day man's religious beliefs and concepts existed in the Middle Ages, of course, but at the same time some of us find a few of the medieval ideas to be strange. Chaucer expresses a number of such religious and ethical concepts of the fourteenth century in the course of the *Canterbury Tales*, usually without "taking sides"; the poet allows the actors to state in appropriate terms what they themselves think of the ideas. For example, the poet uses satire and humour in having the *Wife of Bath* "argue" the relative merits of the married state and virginity. Dame Alisoun is aware that the Church teaching of her day claims virginity to be a greater good than the most virtuous of marriages. Consequently, Alisoun sets about to refute that claim as soon as she can in her "long preamble of a tale," by quoting in fine apposition from Scripture: there are no actual comments against marriage, she says, for God "putte it in oure owene juggement." St. Paul, she continues, only wished "that every wighte were swich as he." We cannot all be perfect – not every dish in the household is of gold, and surely, God meant some women to marry.

Theoretically, a pilgrimage is religious in character and consequently the subject belongs in any investigation of Chaucer's religious world. By the time Chaucer was writing, however, the journey to a shrine had become the liveliest and most sought-after pleasure for the majority of English citizens, both lay and cleric, and a visit to St. Thomas' shrine in Canterbury – internationally venerated and marked by the Church as one of the places of "greater pilgrimage" – was especially popular.[6] Thomas à Becket met his martyr's death in Canterbury Cathedral some two hundred years before Chaucer's day and that he became a saint almost as soon as he became a martyr was largely because of the curative powers thought to be in his miraculously preserved blood and in the presence of his now sacred body; but as time passed, pilgrimage to St. Thomas' shrine was claimed to bring about many other blessings besides the healing of ailments. As has been suggested, Chaucer's Knight may be making his journey to Canterbury to offer prayers of thanksgiving for a successful campaign. On the whole, however, the many among the pilgrims asked for St. Thomas' help "whan that they were seeke."

It has been said by some modern critics that Chaucer's basis for the *Canterbury Tales* may come from the idea that life is a "pilgrimage" which mankind makes to the shrine of Heaven. Certainly the idea is not one which would have been unfamiliar to Chaucer, but the flesh-and-blood character the poet gives to his pilgrims on their gay and noisy journey to Canterbury seems to nullify any figurative suggestion. It is impossible to believe that Chaucer had never been on a pilgrimage himself or that he had not fully observed the behaviour or actual wayfarers – their loudness in laughter, in quarrels, in the music they played, and in the stories with which they regaled each other – as they rode along the dusty or muddy roads on their journeys to a shrine. The "ful devout corage" would not be manifest until the shrine was reached and the *Canterbury Tales* – at least, as we know the work – concerns actualities of a "real" journey.

A good place to start to take us 'deep into the practice of religion among the common people' is with the portraits of the Parson and the Plowman in the *General Prologue*. Individually, each leads us to think about what kinds of things ordinary Christians were expected to know and how they were to learn it. Together they reflect some of the conceptual changes that were taking place in religion and society, especially the greater consciousness of social morality and the new emphasis on charity, or *caritas*, that resulted in the formation of a new kind of layperson.

The Parson in the *Canterbury Tales* is described [I (A) 477-528] as rich in "hooly thought and werk," and as devoutly teaching his parishioners. He is "lerned," for he has been a university student. Many times he has proved himself to be patient, diligent and benign. Chaucer's Parson knows, however, that it is his duty to collect the tithes. This good man is not lazy or given to idle pleasure. On the contrary, in all kinds of weather, and even if he is troubled or ill, he visits on foot the members of his parish in their houses "fer asonder," not caring whether those he calls upon are rich or poor. But perhaps his most striking characteristic as a priest is his setting of an example before asking others to follow it. He holds to two figures: if gold rusts, iron will do far worse; and if the shepherd is soiled, the sheep cannot be clean. We hope that Chaucer knew the Parson in actual life, and that the character is not a mere reversal of the "bad" priests whom everyone apparently knew in fourteenth-century England.

Chaucer's Parson obviously sets a high standard in the fulfillment of his office. He visits the sick and needy in his parish, and his refusal to overreact to those who did not pay their tithes (GP 486) coincides with his Christ-like poverty and sensitivity to the limited means of his parishioners. Abuses of tithes and taxes was an issue that aroused the ire and resentment of the laity towards venal priests in Chaucer's day. The Parson's primary goal is one appropriate to his station: to teach Christ's lessons, to preach the Word, and to lead his people to heaven by his own good example.

Meanwhile, the Plowman sets an excellent example for all laypeople. To achieve salvation laypeople were obliged to attend Mass, receive the sacraments, and pay tithes. They were also expected to avoid sin and to lead a moral existence; that is, they were expected to practice charity. Charity, or *caritas*, was a medieval imperative, fundamental to defining one's Christianity. The programme of instruction discussed above brought pressure on the laity to adopt an active Christianity and to acquire a sense of social responsibility, transforming *caritas* from a spiritual obligation to an act of social consciousness. R. N. Swanson (1995: 19) neatly summarises the place of charity or *caritas* in the whole Christian scheme of the late Middle Ages as follows:

> The emphasis on *caritas* is crucial, for while Christianity focused on Christ, it could be argued that it centred on Mankind. It was, essentially, an attempt to provide the means whereby a defective creature could achieve perfection ... Whoever, was to blame, Mankind had fallen, had lost Eden. Christianity held out the prospect of its recovery, but not in this world. To that end, the penalties of original sin, latently expunged by Christ's Incarnation and Crucifixion, were actually expunged by baptism. Thereafter, it was for individuals, following the precepts of Christ and the church, to live out the pilgrimage of this earthly life, hoping to merit eternal presence with God after the final judgement.

In keeping with this ideal, Chaucer's Plowman is described as loving God best with his whole heart and then his neighbour as himself, thus honouring Christ's two commandments. He also pays his tithes without complaint and he lends his labour to the poor:

> He wolde thresshe, and thereto dyke and delve,
> For Cristes sake, for every povre wight,
> Withouten hire, if it lay in his myght. (GP 536-8)

His charity is a sign of the inwardness of his faith, and is linked to his community and to attaining salvation by action. What ordinary laypersons like the Plowman needed to enhance the interiority of their religious devotions and activities, especially during the Mass, which was celebrated in Latin, were written materials like those afforded the parish priests which would allow them to become participants in the ceremony and be able to express their prayers to God in their own language. In the course of the fourteenth century, manuals and devotional texts were produced that taught them how to conduct themselves in church, how to adore the Eucharist, and how to recite the appropriate prayers during the Mass.

Chaucer's Summoner is basically wicked. The poet writes that if the Summoner find anywhere some "good felawe" who is sinning, he will teach him to have no awe of the "ercedekenes curs" unless his soul is in his purse. "Purs is the ercedekenes helle," claims the Summoner, implying that money will set everything right. Meanwhile, the Pardoner, who is "freend" and "compeer" to the Summoner, is a fitting companion for a rogue, for he himself is also a wicked man and, like a summoner, he is tempted to sin by the nature of his calling, for he deals largely with the helpless poor and ignorant. The literature of complaint is much more vehement about pardoners than about summoners, however, probably because the pardoners did much greater harm to the soul than the summoners.[7] The Middle Ages would, of course, consider damaging a man in his future life a far greater sin than cheating or blackmailing him in this life, a belief shared by some people today, but no longer a belief of universal acceptance.

III

The Middle Ages was indeed an Age of Faith, in spite of the skepticism which began early and reached a culmination in the fourteenth century. That skepticism, however, was confined in England to the philosophic thinker, rather than to the average man, no matter what his class, and may be said to be agnostic instead of atheistic in character. The medieval proverb, "where there are three physicians, there are two atheists," probably grew out of the physician's disregard of the medieval Church's hostility to certain aspects of medical research. When Chaucer complains about ecclesiastical abuses in medieval church, he does so in apparent deep regret that the guardians of the Faith are sometimes unworthy of their trust, never attacking faith itself. In fact, the hierarchy of the medieval Church was a complicated structure and in the same way that secular nobles are omitted from the pilgrimage in the *Canterbury Tales*, so, too, the princes of the Church are omitted, as in actual life they would find their way to Canterbury with their own retinues. But less important ecclesiastical figures are on the pilgrimage, and Chaucer observes their "degrees" by the order in which he presents in the *General Prologue*. The Prioress and the Monk stand at the top, and next comes the Friar, followed by the Clerk (a university student in Minor Orders), then the Parson (a parish priest, rich in good works, but humble in degree), and finally there is that pair of arch-rascals, the Summoner and the Pardoner.

To understand the Prioress first in the *General Prologue*, we should know something about nuns in general in the Middle Ages. In actual life, nuns were nearly always of gentle birth for a reason that was largely economic. Nearly every woman of the Middle Ages had her social "place" fixed from birth. As a young girl, the lady herself had probably been schooled by gentle nuns who had taught her all the polite accomplishments, as well as the practical arts belonging to her station. In fact, the life of the schoolgirl in the convent was often more exciting and could be far more opulent than in her own home. Further, the nuns being medieval women, reared in the tradition of the medieval Church, would indicate the Church's tenet that virginal life was the "best," the one most surely to be rewarded everlastingly in the life to come.

With all those facts in mind, we are sure that Chaucer created his Prioress straight from his own world. True to type, she is essentially well-bred. But, paradoxically, that very fact also individualises her for us as Madame Eglantine: her apparent memory of and sustained interest in her early life of refinement has led her to indulge in particular foibles and vanities which are distinctly hers, and yet which certainly belonged, either wholly or in part, to many nuns of Chaucer's time. Madame Eglantine is not always careful about obeying the injunctions of the bishop who inspects her convent: nuns were forbidden to go on pilgrimage by fourteenth century bishops, yet they frequently did so, and here is our Prioress, albeit she is properly accompanied by another nun and a priest. But even though Chaucer does censure Madame Eglantine for her vanities and for her disregard of the bishop's injunctions, the blame is extremely mild. The poet makes the lady charming, but sometimes her graceful femininity is too strong for the strictly religious. Harry Bailly recognises the Prioress' aristocratic bearing by toning down his customary rude exuberance, when he addresses her before she begins her Tale. He politely says:

> My lady Prioresse, by youre leve,
> So that I wiste I sholde yow nat greve,
> I wolde demen that ye tellen sholde
> A tale next, if so were that ye wolde.
> Now wol ye vouches auf, my lady deere?
> (VII (B^2 1636-1641) 446-451)

Thus, the *Prioress' Tale* is by its nature appropriate to the teller, for the story primarily concerns a miracle wrought by the Virgin. From Madame Eglantine's own point of views, the miracle would be the only matter of importance in the Tale: mere nvention provides the source for casting the Jews as villains in the plot.

The medieval monk, not unlike the medieval nun, was most usually a man of the gentry or noble class; if he came from a lower class, he would need a generous patron to provide him with an expensive education, for monks had to be learned men. The monk's calling was "an ancient and honourable" one, and many of the great princes of the medieval Church – popes, cardinals, archbishops and bishops – were chosen from the monastic Orders. The widely accepted picture of a monk in the *Canterbury Tales* is reflected in Chaucer's portrait of Daun Piers, who is frequently an "outridere," that is, he leaves his cloister – and Chaucer reminds us that a monk outside the cloister is like a fish out of water; he owns greyhounds which are as swift as birds in flight, and in his stables are many valuable horses. Thus, Chaucer's Monk is a lively representative of a class. On the other hand, however, Chaucer gives the portrait added vitality and strength by a few individual touches. Daun Piers has large, prominent eyes and a glistening, ruddy countenance, he is bald and stout; and his pomposity and implied resentment against the world are manifest.

Chaucer also writes about such a monk in the *Shipman's Tale*, the monk of the *fabliaux* which is by definition coarsely cynical, its "realism" consisting largely in true-to-life dialogue and objective description – situations in a *fabliau* therefore sometimes go beyond the factual aspect of life in an author's desire to titillate his audience. The monk of the *Shipman's Tale* could be brother to Daun Piers in that he is also an outrider, a lover of pleasure and of rich food; that he is lecherous in no way serves to identify him as a member of a monastic Order, but is added to give the conventionally burlesque "entertainment" expected in the *fabliau*. Although Daun Piers as a typical monk is no longer interested in books, he has had an education proper to his calling: he is able to give a learned definition of tragedy to the company, and he informs them that he has a hundred tragedies in his "celle" – he is quite capable of instructing lesser folk. He says:

> I wol biwaille, in manere of tragedie,
> The harm of hem that stood in heigh degree,
> And fillen so that ther nas no remedie
> To brynge hem out of hir adversitee.
> For certein, whan that Fortune list to flee
> Ther may no man the cours of hire withholde.
> Lat no man truste on blynd prosperitee;
> Be war by thise ensamples trewe and olde.
> (VII (B^2 3181-3188) 1991-1998)

The Monk is here partially reverting to a type of an earlier age: he is now the didactic teacher, explaining the vicissitudes of Fortune to the uninformed laity; but he also remains the man who has himself suffered disappointment and who therefore thoroughly enjoys recounting the woes of those who have fallen from "heigh degree."

The monks, as has been observed, were often scorned by the laity because of the immense wealth of their orders and the luxury and idleness of the lives of many of the individual brothers, but, as historians have pointed out, the individual monk was nearly always looked upon with some degree of respect. The typical medieval friar, in contrast, seems to have met with no respect anywhere. Gower writes of him as pretending to be poor but, in actuality, as being as rich as a king. Friars are hypocrites, Gower continues, for they talk publicly against sin but condone it privately both in themselves and others. They will have nothing to do with anyone who will not advance them; and they wait for the husband to be absent and then have illicit relations with the wife. Friars usurp the function of others in the Church; and they are everywhere.

Popular literature of the fourteenth century – the so-called political songs – all condemn friars as imbued with wickedness. When Chaucer was writing, there were four major Orders of Friars in England and although there were some small differences among them, the four major Orders had become, by the fourteenth century, essentially the same; consequently, if we trace the fall from grace of one Order, we have traced the fall of all. The medieval friar had other opportunities for illicit gain. Friars were not cloistered, yet they belonged to religious Orders; hence they could be employed as ecclesiastical taxgatherers and they could be licensed to hear confessions. Chaucer's Friar has further faults, not as grave as the "selling" of absolution, but serious enough. He will have nothing to do with lepers, or with the poor in the towns he passes through; he will deal only with people who can advance him in some way: the wealthy, the sellers of food, the barmaids in the taverns. In that respect, Chaucer's Brother Hubert is in striking contrast to St. Francis. Is Hubert a Franciscan? We cannot say; but when the Summoner tells his Tale to spite Hubert, the friar in that Tale is described as a Franciscan, and it is unlikely that Chaucer would have the pilgrim Summoner step out of character by telling a story against a friar of an Order different from Hubert's. In fact, we suspect that the friar of the *Summoner's Tale* is intended by the Summoner to be Hubert himself or, at least, that the Summoner would have the company of pilgrims make such an identification.

The Summoner states that his friar is a "lymytour," and continues the picture as follows:

> In every hous he gan to pour and prye,
> And beggeth mele and chese, or elles corn,
> His felawe hadde a staf tipped with horn,
> A peyre of tables al of yvory,
> And a poyntel polysshed fetisly,
> And wroot the names alwey, as he stood,
> Of alle folk that yaf him any good,
> Ascaunces that he wolde for hem preye.
> 'Yif us a bushel whete, malt, or reye,
> A Goddes kechyl, or a trype of chese
> Or elles what yow lyst, we may nat cheese;
> A Goddes halfpenny, or a masse peny,
> Or yif us of youre brawn, if ye have eny;
> A dagon of youre blanke, leeve dame,
> Oure suster deere, - lo! heere I write youre name, −
> Bacon or beef, or swich thing as ye fynde.' (III (D) 1738-1753)

Chaucer's Clerk is a university student who is in Minor Orders, for he is a candidate for a benefice. The word *clerk* in the Middle Ages always indicated a university student who, having received the tonsure, was entitled to certain ecclesiastical privileges; the clerk might or might not be in Minor Orders. Chaucer's Clerk is probably typical of the "good" students of the fourteenth century. The life of the "bad" student on the other hand, is fully documented in legal records and in fiction: such a student is uniformly depicted as quarrelsome, lawless, frivolous and licentious. For evidence of the loose living of the medieval clerk, we must turn to fiction, and here Chaucer himself supplies us with sufficient example. First we should note that in none of the most conspicuous analogues to the *Miller's Tale* are the wife's lovers stated to be clerks, but Chaucer elected to cast university students for the parts of the lovers. "Hende Nicholas" of the *Miller's Tale* is described as "sleigh and ful privee"; he has a private income, unlike Chaucer's impoverished Clerk, and hence he is able to afford a relatively luxurious room all to himself at the carpenter's house, where he can be free much of the time from university rules.

Absalom, the other clerk in the *Miller's Tale* and of much the same nature as Nicholas, also makes no bones about coveting the pert young wife; indeed, he would have pounced upon her immediately "if she hadde been a mous and he a cat," and he loses no time in attempting to win her favours. If we place Chaucer's Clerk beside Nicholas and Absalom – or beside the two Cambridge clerks of the Reeve's Tale, who have no qualms about casually seducing Simkin's wife and daughter – the contrast is striking. Unlike Absalom of the *Miller's Tale*, the Clerk never displays unseemly levity in behaviour; he does not speak one word more than is necessary, and when he does speak, he is brief, to the point and always noble in his meaning. Chaucer's final line of description for his scholar – "And gladly wolde he lerne and gladly teche" – epitomizes the Clerk for us today, and perhaps provides us with a brief summing-up of what all good teaching has meant in the past and will mean in years to come.

Exactly as it is necessary to contrast the Clerk with someone he in no way resembles, so is it necessary to contrast the Parson; for the good priest, like the good student, has no documented history. Chaucer's "povre Persoun of a Toun" furnishes us with the antithesis of the bad priest as we have already mentioned above. The Parson is described as rich in "hooly thought and werk," and as devoutly teaching his parishioners. Chaucer's Parson knows, however, that it is his duty to collect the tithes; consequently in cases of need, he will make up the deficit out of his own small "substaunce," or even out of the "offryng," the voluntary contributions – meager, we feel sure – which, by rights, he should spend upon his own needs. The ending of the narrative of the Clerk's Tale is the high point of Chaucer's religious poetry. It is a moment soon dissipated in gestures of withdrawal, concessions, high clowning, as Chaucer characteristically encloses the tale in a network of ambiguities and interpretative paradoxes. Only in the *Parson's Tale*, however, can he be said to speak unequivocally from and of the truth of faith, and it is penitential treatise with a lengthy account of the Seven Deadly Sins and their remedies. It is the ground-plan of salvation. The *Parson's Tale* is a work of considerable care and skill, much the best piece of writing of its kind in English, and it is the expression of a deep and orthodox piety; or, at least, it accepts the necessity of contracting in to the comprehensive, all-pervading, non-negotiable system of belief which is called the Christian faith.

There is an extraordinarily large quantity of reference in the *Canterbury Tales* to religion and religious practice. Apart from the half-dozen or so tales that have as their ostensible motive the demonstration and promotion of the Christian faith, there are a large number of others which have officers of the church as their tellers or principal characters, or which are otherwise full of religious allusion. Furthermore, six of the longest and most detailed portraits in the *General Prologue* are devoted ecclesiastics (Prioress, Monk, Friar, Parson, Summoner, Pardoner), in the proportion of five bad (one not so bad) to one good, so that the principal memory of reading the *General Prologue* is of the detailed and minute revelation of ecclesiastical malpractice.

The ubiquity of the Christian faith and its practices in the *Canterbury Tales* mentioned above is not a sign that they are to be interpreted allegorically as witnesses to the higher law of charity. There would otherwise be no tales 'that sownen into synne' for Chaucer to retract at the end of the *Canterbury Tales* (X. 1086). But religion is nevertheless important: the fun and audacity of these tales, the delighted outrage of the reader, would be the less if we really thought that religion were as irrelevant to the important business of life as the characters seem to think it is.

IV

As we know, the philosophers of the Middle Ages conceived of the universe as a finality: there could be no change in it. The perfected and all-embracing plan, existing with neither beginning nor end, had its being in the mind of God, that aspect of God which was called "Providence." God, however, was an indivisible unit, infinitely remote from man, so that the carrying out of the decrees of Providence was believed to be delegated to a force called 'Destiny'; without "will" of its own, Destiny merely followed the divine will. As a force, Destiny was divisible into different powers: powers of angelic (and demonic) spirits, of the configurations of the planets and the stars, of nature, and of – most commonly – a mysterious force, usually personified, called 'Fortune', which capriciously controlled each man's personal life so that his successes and disasters often had the appearance of the illogical and the cruel. In fact, medieval man believed that God's love was what held in place the physical universe – the earth and the Ptolemic spheres – and which ordinarily, in the last analysis, controlled the orderly cycles in this world, the cycles of the seasons and the tides and animate birth, growth and death.

In the philosophic aspect of the *Canterbury Tales*, Chaucer is mainly concerned with two of Destiny's agents: the force of the stars and the force of Fortune. Early in the *Knight's Tale* when he mistakenly supposes that Palamon is lamenting their imprisonment, Arcite addresses his companion as follows:

> For Goddes love, taak al in pacience
> Oure prisoun, for it may noon oother be.
> Fortune hath yeven us this adversitee.
> Som wikke aspect or disposicioun
> Of Saturne, by som constellacioun
> Hath yeven us this, although we hadde it sworn;
> So stood the hevene whan that we were born.
> We moste endure it; this is the short and playn. (I (A) 1084-1091)

We should especially note here that the power of the planet Saturn, the planet considered to be the bringer of the greatest misfortune to man, is emphasised. Saturn, personified as the heathen god, speaks himself later in the *Knight's Tale* (I (A) 1454-2469). Arcite when he hears that he is to be ransomed, tells Palamon that Fortune has "yturned thee the dys," and speaks again of God's will (I (A) 1251-1258; 1266-1267). After Arcite's departure, Palamon also reflects in similar fashion, addressing Fortune as a "goddess":

> O crueel goddes that governe
> This world with byndyng of youre word eterne,
> And written in the table of atthamaunt
> Youre parlement and youre eterne graunt,
> What is mankynde moore unto you holde
> Than is the sheep that rouketh in the folde?
> . . .
> But man after his deeth moot wepe and playne,
> Though in this world he have care and wo. (I (A) 1303-1321)

Some scholars, notably Walter C. Curry(1960), have pointed out that the kings who support Palamon and Arcite, Emetreus and Lycurgus, are respectively personifications of the planets Mars and Saturn. Chaucer's mind is apparently running on Saturn's influence on mankind throughout the *Knight's Tale*. At the close of the Knight's Tale, Theseus comments in his speech to Emily and Palamon on the wisdom of Providence, the "Firste Moevere." He says:

> The Firste Moevere of the cause above,
> Whan he first made the faire cheyne of love,
> Greet was th'effect, and heigh was his entente.
> Wel wiste he why, and what thereof he mente; (I (A) 2987-2990)

Man never escapes from the ultimate plan of God but virtue – and virtue alone – could sometimes modify the machinations of Destiny's agents. In the

Man of Law's Tale Constance's life is spared after her marriage to the Sultan because of her prayers to Christ. She is worthy of the intervention of a higher power.

The *Monk's Tale*, since it is a series of tragedies, is "philosophical" almost by definition. The Monk himself somewhat condescendingly informs the company what the *tragedy* means: "A tragedy," he says in his Prologue, "is a story of a man who stood in great prosperity and then falls out of his high position into misery, and so ends wretchedly." The Monk adds in the first stanza of his tale:

> For certein, whan that Fortune list to flee,
> Ther may no man the cours of hire withholde. (VII (B^2) 1995-1996)

In each of the seventeen tales which the Monk tells the company before being interrupted in his dolorous progress, Fortune does bring about a disaster.

According to medieval belief, the starts as agents of Destiny combined with Fortune as powerful determinants for a man's life. We have seen that brought out in the *Knight's Tale* and it is elsewhere illustrated in the *Canterbury Tales*. The Wife of Bath in the Prologue to her Tale blames her "constellacioun," meaning her horoscope, or the aspect of the stars at the moment of her birth, for her very nature. She was born, she explains, under the influence of three planets – Mercury, Venus and Mars – which appear in her zodiacal sign of Taurus, and these planets are scarcely at peace with each other:

> Mercurie loveth wysdom and science,
> And Venus loveth ryot and dispence.
> And, for hire divrse dissposicious,
> Ech falleth in otheres exaltacioun.
> And thus, God woot, Mercurie is desolate
> In Pisces, wher Venus is exaltat,
> And Venus falleth ther Mercurie is reysed. (III (D) 699-705)

Mars has also intensified and debased the influence of Venus so, although the

Wife could have loved in more ladylike fashion if solely under Venus' influence, she is, because of Mars, coarse and frankly animal in her desires. Because of Mercury, she is extremely efficient and intelligent, but the sign of Taurus brings her passions to the fore. Consequently, it is not only Fortune, but the stars as well, which have, through shaping her nature, brought her the five husbands and "oother compaignye in youthe."

Finally, if we examine the description of the Physician in the *General Prologue*, we observe a marriage of philosophy and science. The belief that stars are agents of Destiny joins the Physician's portrait to the practical aspects of his profession. Many physicians in the Middle Ages were, like Chaucer's Doctor of Physic, "grounded in astronomye," although such knowledge was scoffed at by some of the more advanced practitioners. Each of the twelve signs of the zodiac was thought to control a different part of the human body; further, the physical characteristics and the temperament of each person were determined at his birth by his horoscope. Here we have the origin of the four medieval "humours," concepts which lasted well into the seventeenth century and which have left their traces in the speech of today – we still speak of someone being in a "good humour" or in a "bad humour," of a "sanguine" or a "phlegmatic" person, and so on.

The stars played a large part in the professional life of many physicians particularly the so-called fashionable ones. It was the custom of those physicians always to cast the horoscope of the patient; they then thought it necessary to know the positions of the stars at the time of the outset of the illness, and at the time of the physician's visit to the patient. In the Middle Ages the purely medical school of the physicians was aided by the philosophical belief in the influence of the stars, those agents of Destiny, and, hence indirectly of the Divine.

Notes

1 Quotations from Chaucer in this paper are made from L. D. Benson's text (New York, 1987) based on *The Works of Geoffrey Chaucer* edited by F. N. Robinson.
2 Ellis (2005) discusses three formidable problems of the rich and varied religious culture of the late Middle Ages in England: the first is the difficulty of reducing the vast body of complex material that constitutes late medieval Christianity without omitting or slighting something that is vital or substantial to one's understanding of the subject. The second problem involves gauging the relationship between the sacred and the secular. The third problem is the modern tendency to assume that the masses of people were naïve, superstitious, and unquestioning in their faith. For the details, see Ellis (2005: 81-83).
3 Etymologically, 'religion' is derived from the Latin *ligo* or *lego*, and more directly from *religo*, which has the sense of 'to bind or to tie securely.'
4 In an age lacking in mass communication it might have been technically impossible to expect or to enforce a uniformity of belief or practice. Besides, at that time the Church had hundreds of divisions and subdivisions, ranging from the Church of the Lateran in Rome to the remote village parishes of rural England, which meant that a wide variety of beliefs and practices was able to flourish, and dissent and calls for reform were commonplace.
5 Although their portraits are highly idealised, they do represent the vast majority of ordinary Christians who in Chaucer's time lived and worked in parishes throughout England. Perhaps Chaucer makes his Parson and Plowman brothers to suggest the kind of mutuality and interdependence that could and should exist between the laity and its priests, whereas the ideal nature of their portraits may indicate how much reform would be needed if a true Christian society were to be found.
6 In one year alone in the early fifteenth century, more than one hundred thousand persons from all over the Europe are said to have made the Canterbury Pilgrimage. See Bowden (1964: 75) for details.
7 The fourteenth-century pardoner added two other activities, as a rule, to the selling of pardons: the selling of saints' relics – often not relics at all, but bones and bits of rags which the pardoner himself collected from refuse heaps – and preaching. The preaching, however, even if insincere, probably was generally eloquent, for most swindlers need to cultivate silver tongues.

References

Allen, Mark and John H. Fisher (1987) *The Essential Chaucer: An Annotated Bibliography of Major Modern Studies*. Boston, Mass.: G. K. Hall & Co.

Andrew, Malcolm (ed.) (1991) *Critical Essays on Chaucer's Canterbury Tales*. Toronto

& Buffalo: University of Toronto Press.

Ashton, Gail (1998) *Chaucer: The Canterbury Tales*. Analyzing texts. New York: St. Martin's Press.

Benson, Larry D (ed.) (1987) *The Riverside Chaucer*. Third Edition. New York: Houghton Mifflin Company.

Boitani, Piero & Jill Mann (eds.) (1986) *The Cambridge Chaucer Companion*. Cambridge: Cambridge University Press.

Bowden, Muriel (1964) *A Reader's Guide to Geoffrey Chaucer*. London: Thames and Hudson.

Brewer, D. S. (1973) *Chaucer*. (1973) 3rd edition. Longman.

Brewer, D. S. (1984) *An Introduction to Chaucer*. Longman.

Brown, Peter (ed.) (2002) *A Companion to Chaucer*. Oxford: Blackwell Publishers.

Cooper, Helen (1983) *The Structure of the Canterbury Tales*. London: Gerald Duckworth & Co. Ltd.

Curry, Walter Clyde (1960) *Chaucer and the Mediaeval Sciences*. revised edition. New York: Barnes and Noble.

Ellis, Steve (2005) *Chaucer: An Oxford Guide*. Oxford: Oxford University Press.

McGerr, Rosemarie P. (1998) *Chaucer's Open Books: Resistance to Closure in Medieval Discourse*. Gainsville: University Press of Florida.

Mehl, Dieter (2001) *English Literature in the Age of Chaucer. Longman Literature in English Series*. Longman.

Park, Y. – B. (2007) *Rereading Chaucer's Canterbury Tales: The Ordering Debate of the Fragments*. In Mayumi Sawada, Larry Walker, and Shizuya Tara. (eds.) *Language and Beyond. A Festshrift for Hiroshi Yonekura on the Occasion of His 65th Birthday*. Tokyo: Eichosha, 57-71.

Pearsall, Derek (1992) *The Life of Geoffrey Chaucer*. Oxford: Blackwell.

Rudd, Gillian (2001) *The Complete Critical Guide to Geoffrey Chaucer*. London and New York: Routledge.

Swanson, R. N. (1995) *Religion and Devotion in Europe c. 1215- c. 1515*. Cambridge: Cambridge University Press.

Ussery, Huling E. (1971) *Chaucer's Physician: Medicine and Literature in Fourteenth-Century England*. New Orleans: Tulane University Press.

Grammatical vs. Lexical Competence of Advanced Foreign Language Learners

Päivi Pietilä

1 Introduction

The relationship between grammatical competence and lexical competence in a foreign, or second, language is intriguing for many different reasons. Indeed, it has been examined from various standpoints, although the exact nature of it still remains unclear, and research continues. Some researchers are interested in this issue from a neurolinguistic or psycholinguistic point of view, while others have a more practical perspective with a view to ultimately benefiting language learning and teaching.

The present article is a report on a study which was carried out to investigate the lexical and grammatical skills of advanced learners of English. In addition to a desire to explore the relationship between these two skills, or areas of competence, it was hoped that the study would reveal those areas of language competence in which advanced language students would need instruction and practice in spite of their generally high proficiency. Before taking a look at the study, let us consider some issues concerning the relationship between lexis and grammar.

2 Grammar and lexis in the brain

From the neurolinguistic point of view, it seems that grammar and lexis are located in different areas of the human brain, which would imply that they are separate entities which develop independently of one another. It has been known for a long time that, while the language areas are primarily localised in the left hemisphere for most right-handed individuals, there are distinct areas within the left hemisphere dedicated to morphology, syntax, and language production (the frontal lobe, the so-called Broca's area) on the one hand, and to lexis, semantics, and language comprehension (the temporal lobe, the so-called Wernicke's area) on the other hand (Hatch 1983: 201-204). Evidence for this has been found in studies on aphasia: patients suffering from Broca's aphasia (impairment of grammatical ability) have been able to preserve their ability to use lexical semantic information (Kempler, Curtiss & Jackson 1987: 343). On the other hand, several studies on demented patients with language impairments have shown that it is more common to suffer from the loss of semantic and pragmatic ability than syntactic ability. In other words, in cases of dementia, L1 grammar tends to be preserved better than vocabulary (ibid.).

A study by Indefrey *et al.* (2001) revealed that syntactic processing is indeed independent of semantic processing. The authors used meaningless sentences to investigate the detection of grammatical errors and found that the semantic content of the items had no bearing on the subjects' decisions. However, a rather different conclusion was drawn in a study by Barcroft (2007), who found that native-speaker grammaticality judgments were strongly dependent on whether the sentences used contained unreal words or only real words.

In addition to pointing to different localization of grammatical and lexical operations, most neurolinguistic findings also suggest that the two operations are different in nature: there is a difference in the degree of automaticity between grammatical and lexical competence. L1 syntax, once acquired, is automatic and does not require conscious attention. Lexical selection, on the other hand, is a control process which requires the attention of the speaker. What is more, the range of lexical alternatives is basically unlimited and unpredictable, which is radically different compared with syntax. Syntactic choices are more limited in number, and each structure occurs more frequently than individual lexical words.

In second language acquisition, a similar distinction can be postulated: L2 syntax, acquired to varying degrees (and probably fossilized) may have become automatized, so that it no longer requires conscious reflection. Therefore, it may seem to be used rather fluently, although it may still contain errors. In speech, the automatization of grammar can best be seen (or heard) as a lack of hesitations (pauses, corrections etc.), which are particularly common in connection with lexical searches. This is understandable, as lexical choices are conscious, controlled processes and often have to be accompanied by pauses, repetitions, corrections and other time-saving devices. In L2 writing, the amount of hesitation is more difficult to detect, as we usually examine the product and not the process of writing (unless we have access to a computer program such as *ScriptLog*, which analyses the writing process in real time and records everything the writer does).

As the study reported on in this article concentrated on written translations in an examination situation, it was not possible to examine the ongoing translation process. Instead, the main emphasis was on an examination of lexical and grammatical errors in the translated texts.

3 The multilingual lexicon

The question how a bilingual / multilingual person's grammars and lexicons are located in the brain has evoked a great deal of research and discussion, but there do not seem to be any definite answers as yet. In fact, research results are rather contradictory. A fair amount of research has been carried out specifically to explore a multilingual person's mental lexicon. Some researchers argue for an integrated multilingual mental lexicon, based on neuroimaging studies which show that lexical-semantic aspects of language processing are localized in the same areas of the brain, regardless of the number of languages known to the person (Franceschini, Zappatore & Nitsch 2003: 163). This would suggest a high degree of interconnectivity between the lexicons. Moreover, other studies have discovered that in word recognition tasks not just the target word but a range of similar word forms from other languages known to the individual are also activated (Singleton 2003: 172). This would also seem to indicate that the various lexicons are if not completely integrated, at least closely connected. The same would apply to instances of codeswitching: in bilingual communities people switch from one language to the other in midspeech. This would hardly be possible if the two languages were completely separate.

According to Libben's *Homogeneity Hypothesis*, there are no language-specific mental lexicons at all, but multilinguals possess a single lexical store (Libben 2000). By introducing his hypothesis, Libben has taken a rather extreme stand on the issue, but he bases his views on earlier models of lexical representation, which seem to reflect a steady progression towards a more and more integrative understanding of the multilingual mental lexicon.

However, it is also evident that multilingual people can keep their languages apart if they want to. In Grosjean's words, they have then chosen a monolingual speech mode and restrict themselves to just one language (Grosjean 1989: 8). Other evidence for the separation of a multilingual's languages can be found in studies of aphasia. In some cases, only one of an individual's languages has been affected. In cases of language loss e.g. due to a head injury, it is possible that a multilingual patient recovers one or two languages but not his/her mother tongue (Singleton 2003: 166-167). In view of this, the existence of a single mental lexicon, or "a homogeneous lexical architecture" (Libben 2000: 230) does not seem very likely.

It has been suggested that the brain of the same bilingual individual may possess different types of L1 – L2 relationships. Concrete words and cognates are probably stored together, in a compound manner (connected at the meaning level), whereas abstract words and noncognates are stored separately, in a coordinate manner. Moreover, low levels of proficiency in the second language seem to be associated with subordinate bilingualism (originally a term introduced by Weinreich in 1953), where L2 words and their meanings are mediated by L1 words (Singleton 2007: 8-9). Translation from the mother tongue constitutes a special case of second language use, as the starting point is a native language word and not a concept to be expressed.

4 Grammar and lexis in language learning

Language learners tend to think of grammar and vocabulary as two separate and very different things. Most learners probably feel that what constitutes the most useful component of language competence is the vocabulary. After all, it is the lexical words that carry the meaning of the utterance, and as we know, people take dictionaries with them when they travel, not grammar books.

In the traditional model of communicative competence introduced by Canale and Swain in 1980, vocabulary was seen as belonging to grammatical competence, together with word formation, sentence formation, pronunciation, spelling and linguistic semantics (Canale 1983: 7). Only fairly recently has vocabulary gained a more independent status, as second language researchers have started to pay more attention to lexical matters. As Henriksen states, "[w]e have witnessed a shift of attention to lexical competence and an increase in lexical studies in second language acquisition research over the last two decades (Henriksen 2006: 13). At the same time, some researchers have emphasized the role of lexis to the extent of claiming that it is the very basis of language. The advocates of the **lexical approach** to language teaching talk about "grammaticalised lexis, rather than lexicalised grammar" (Lewis 1993), and say that by learning lexical items and collocations, the learner will also internalise the grammar of the language.

The Common European Framework of Reference for Languages (*CEFR*), which was published by the Council of Europe to provide a common basis for the development of language teaching in Europe, divides communicative language competences into three components: linguistic competences, sociolinguistic competences and pragmatic competences. **Linguistic competences** include both lexical and grammatical competences (in addition to four other competences which are semantic, phonological, orthographic, and orthoepic competence) (*CEFR* 2001: 108-109). Within lexical competence, the *CEFR* distinguishes between lexical elements and grammatical elements, which means that the division into lexis and grammar is not that clear-cut. Lexical elements include *single word forms* and *fixed expressions* (such as greetings, proverbs, fixed phrases of various kinds, fixed collocations etc.), whereas grammatical elements include e.g. articles, quantifiers, demonstratives, pronouns, and conjunctions (*CEFR* 2001: 111), in other words, elements which could just as well be regarded as belonging to grammar altogether. Grammatical competence, according to the CEFR, refers to the ability to produce and recognise well-formed phrases and sentences in accordance with a set of principles "as opposed to memorising and reproducing them as fixed formulae" (*CEFR* 2001: 113). Among the various grammatical phenomena, the *CEFR* lists e.g. **categories** such as number, case, gender, active/passive voice, tenses, and aspect, **processes** such as nominalisation and affixation, **structures** such as phrases, clauses and sentences, and **relations** such as concord and valency (*CEFR* 2001: 113).

According to some SLA researchers, it would, indeed, be advisable to talk about lexico-grammar, rather than about grammar and lexis separately. Larsen-Freeman takes the phrasal verb as an example of a unit which has a grammatical structure but which has to be learned more as a lexical entity. As far as grammar is concerned, Larsen-Freeman sees it as a skill, and emphasizes its dynamic nature by calling the skill grammaring. For her, grammaring is the fifth skill which needs to be taught, just like the other four - reading, writing, speaking and listening (Pérez-Llantada 2007: 158-159).

As regards the relationship between lexis and grammar, a study by Salem (2007) also revealed a continuum, rather than two discrete phenomena. This made her conclude that "lexis and grammar should be considered as interdependent, rather than as two separate entities" (Salem 2007: 211). Salem's study investigated the gravity of errors in student compositions. Instead of dividing the errors into lexical and grammatical ones, the author found that they fell into three overlapping categories: **lexical**, **word-dependent**, and what she called '**pure-grammar**' errors. Both lexical and word-dependent errors were word-sensitive to various degrees, which meant that the erroneousness in them was derived from a lexical word and was not inherently grammatical. Thus Salem's lexical errors included collocations, word choices, and word forms, whereas an example of a word-dependent error was 'a car injured her', where "[t]he verb 'injure' has the inherent quality of sounding strange when used with 'car' as a subject, and is rather uncommon in the active voice" (Salem 2007: 216). The pure-grammar group consisted of syntactic slips ('A close friend it is very good') and taught grammar rules ('that doesn't call a good friendship'). Salem seems to have a good case for claiming that lexis and grammar are indeed interconnected and form a continuum, but the fact remains that error classification is always a subjective process. Salem's **word form** errors (a subcategory of lexical errors), as in 'beautifully cakes' instead of 'beautiful cakes', could be categorized as grammatical errors just as well. As will be seen in the next section, the criteria for error classification in the present study were rather different.

5 Grammar and lexis in student translations

The purpose of the study reported on here was to find out about the relationship between the lexical and grammatical competence of advanced learners of English. Would the analysis show greater mastery of one of these areas compared with the other? Given the unlimited nature of lexical choices in the language, would the students' lexical competence prove to be in greater need of improvement than their grammatical competence? If that was the case, we would have to start planning some remedial measures to help our students improve their skills.

5.1 *Subjects and data*

The subjects in the present study were young students (about 19-20 years of age) who were taking the entrance examination to be able to study English Philology at the University of Turku. All the subjects had successfully completed highschool before taking the university entrance examination, and they had about ten years of school English behind them. Their level of English ability could be described as low advanced or advanced, corresponding to B2 or C1 on the CEFR proficiency scales (*CEFR* 2001: 24). Only the best applicants were included in the present study, i.e. those 61 who were accepted (40 female and 21 male students). The majority of the applicants were accepted as English majors (the quota being 40) and the rest as English minors. As the entrance examination was exactly the same for all applicants, the subjects will be treated here as one group of English students.

The data consisted of translations from Finnish into English. In addition to the translation task, the examination also included a test in linguistics and an essay to be written on the basis of a novel. The translation task was chosen for this analysis, as it was expected to reveal differences in linguistic ability in a more systematic way than the other two tasks, in which the applicants were free to write whatever they saw fit, and by the same token, to avoid difficult concepts and expressions. The same source text provided a good basis for a comparison of the students' productions. As pointed out earlier, translation from the mother tongue into a foreign language constitutes a special kind of language use. In most communicative situations, the speaker has an idea which he or she wants to express, whereas in a translation task, the language users are given an idea in one language and they are required to express it in another. That is clearly a task of linguistic manipulation and has nothing to do with genuine communication. Moreover, not surprisingly, translating from L1 has been found to produce more L1 interference than spontaneous language use (Ellis & Barkhuizen 2005: 38).

Comparing the translations of all the applicants (279; 197 females, 82 males) would undoubtedly have given even more intriguing results, but my primary goal was to see whether the group of the very best applicants would show any discrepancies in terms of lexical and grammatical competence. It is my intention to expand my analysis to include also the unsuccessful applicants, at a later date, in order to explore the differences caused by variation in second language proficiency.

The translation task was a text of about 170 Finnish words, which rendered an average of 220 words in the English version. The difference is due to the fact that, as a synthetic language, Finnish has e.g. a great number of compound words, and uses case endings instead of prepositions. The text was about the economic development of India (*India Strides into the Future* being one possible English translation of the title), and it had been taken from a magazine which focused on scientific and scholarly issues but was aimed at the general public. The students had one hour to complete the translation task.

5.2 *Identification of errors*

As mentioned earlier, the classification of errors in this study was not done in the same way as in Salem's research described in Section 4. Three main error categories could be distinguished in the present data: lexical, syntactic, and spelling errors.

Lexical errors were identified primarily on semantic grounds, and they were restricted to content words (nouns, verbs, adjectives, and adverbs). In most cases, they were the result of a wrong word choice, as in example 1:

(1) one third of the population is ***illicit*** (target word: *illiterate*)

Here the writer is clearly on the right track, and the result could even be a mere slip, but it was definitely a lexical error. In example 2, we can again see a word which exists in English, but as it is not exactly the equivalent of the word in the source text, it has to be counted as erroneous:

(2) the cities choke with ***pollution*** (target word: *exhaust fumes*)

In my third example, the word ***new*** is erroneous, as it does not convey all of the semantic information of the target word ***renewable:***

(3) for ***new*** energy sources (target word: *renewable*)

As the above examples demonstrate, many of the lexical errors in the present data do not look like errors at all, and in other circumstances the language user would not be punished for producing them – quite on the contrary. Simply from the communicative point of view, the words in examples 2 and 3 would probably work well enough, and the message would be fairly successful. In fact, language learners should be encouraged to say at least something even if they do not know a particular word or expression. That is what communication (or compensatory) strategies are all about: using e.g. a paraphrase or a circumlocution, coining a word, or possibly reducing the intended meaning slightly to be able to express oneself (see e.g. Kasper & Kellerman 1997). However, this was a test situation, and the translations were expected to mirror the original Finnish source text as faithfully as possible.

As far as error gravity is concerned, the lexical error in example 1 above (*illicit* instead or *illiterate*) is more serious than the errors in examples 2 and 3. In example 1, the message is changed completely, whereas in 2 and 3 the message is somewhat reduced but still fairly close to the original. The lexical errors in the present data have, indeed, been divided further into the following types:

near-synonyms (as in examples 2 and 3), **existing but completely wrong words** (hereafter abbreviated as **ex-but**s; as in example 1), **blanks** (where a student has not even tried to produce a word but has left a blank instead), and **vague expressions** (which are correct English but do not convey the precise meaning of the original Finnish expression). Admittedly, the difference between near-synonyms and vague expressions may not always be very clear, and they probably represent slightly different degrees of the same phenomenon: partial coverage of the intended message. Examples 4, 5 and 6 contain vague expressions where common, high frequency words are used instead of the more precise ones:

(4) there are *poor villages* (target: *slum dwellings*)

(5) the cities *are full of* exhaust fumes (target: *choke with, are suffocating in*)

(6) in *ponds filled with dirty water* (target: *the gutter*)

Grammatical errors included errors in function words (articles, prepositions and conjunctions) and in syntax. One type of syntactic error found in the data involved subject – verb concord, as in example 7:

(7) The problems brought on by the differences of the member states *is* the current cause of concern ...

Another grammatical difficulty experienced by some applicants manifested itself in an overuse of the progressive aspect, as in example 8:

(8) but compared to India, our problems *are fading* (target: *seem trivial; fade*)

As far as **spelling errors** were concerned, they were easy and straightforward to identify. In the following, the proportion of spelling errors will be discussed briefly, but the main focus will be on lexical and grammatical errors.

5.3 Errors in the data

An error analysis was carried out on the English translations of the 61 students. Table 1 shows the absolute numbers and percentages of the different error types in the data, as well as the frequency of errors per 100 words.

Table 1. Distribution of error types in the student translations

Error types	Occurrences	%	No. / 100 words	No. / Student
Lexical	482	50	4	7.9
Syntactic	295	30	2	4.8
Spelling	188	20	1	3.1
All errors	964	100	7	15.8

As can be seen in Table 1, half of the errors in the present data were lexical in nature, while the other half was divided between syntactic errors (30 %) and errors in spelling (20 %). The total number of errors is fairly low, as can be expected in the English of successful applicants (only the average of 7 per 100 words, or 15.8 errors per student, on an average).

The 482 **lexical errors** were further divided into the four subcategories described above: near-synonyms, ex-buts, blanks, and vague expressions. Their frequencies are given in Table 2.

Table 2. Distribution of lexical error types in the student translations

Error types	Frequency	%
Near-synonyms	77	16
Ex-buts	108	22
Blanks	8	2
Vague expressions	289	60
All lexical errors	482	100

As Table 2 shows, the proportion of vague expressions is quite considerable in the data (60 %). If vague expressions and near-synonyms are counted together, the number of translations which express the intended meaning partially is even greater (76 % of all lexical errors). This is an important finding, as it might well reflect a more general tendency to undermine the importance of accuracy and precision in second language production. As a further example of this phenomenon, let us examine one particular sentence taken from the present data. The English translation (9) is one of the model versions provided by one of our native-speaker lecturers:

(9) The country also manufactures effective vaccines and is developing methods of treatment for many of the **diseases which plague all humankind.**

The part given in bold type was translated, for example, in the following ways:

(10) ...plagues concerning the whole humanity.
(11) ...diseases that trouble the whole humankind.
(12) ...illnesses that are a nuisance for the whole mankind.
(13) ...diseases that cause trouble to all humankind.
(14) ...diseases that tease the whole humankind.
(15) ...things that bother all the humankind.

Compared with the model translation, the above versions are somewhat vague. They lack precision, as they contain words with rather general meanings (especially example 15). Some of these solutions can be traced back to the applicants' native language, Finnish, such as the use of the verb **tease**, the Finnish equivalent of which can also have the meaning 'to plague.'

Grammatical errors were much less frequent than lexical errors. It seems, then, that our applicants had learned English grammar fairly well. Of course, it is also possible that the text to be translated was structurally not challenging enough. However, the errors that did occur revealed problems especially in areas which are typically difficult for Finnish learners of English: the article system and prepositions. The third largest category of grammatical errors consisted of various oddities in syntactic structures which were rather difficult to give a straightforward and unambiguous title. Many of the instances in this category had to do with word order or the mixing of features from two structures. The result was often rather strange as in examples 16 and 17:

(16) ... but there live twice as many people.
(17) There are also produced efficient vaccines ...

For want of a better term, let us call errors illustrated in 16 and 17 mixed structures. As far as prepositional errors in the data were concerned, most of them consisted of erroneous choices of prepositions, as in examples 18 and 19:

(18) In India, cities suffocate **to** fumes ...
(19) ... develops treatments **to** disases ...

In some cases, a preposition was omitted (example 20) or a superfluous preposition was used (example 21):

(20) Indian economy is growing ___ no less than twice the speed ...
(21) Despite **of** all this ...

Finnish makes very little use of prepositions. Instead, some postpositions and especially various cases and case endings are used to indicate the kinds of relationships that English expresses with prepositions. What is more, a particular preposition does not correspond to a particular grammatical case, and vice versa, so it is rather challenging for Finns to learn the English system of prepositions.

As many studies have shown, for language learners with no articles in their mother tongue, the article system of the foreign language is also difficult to learn (see e.g. Ringbom 2007: 69; Butler 2002). Examples of sentences containing errors in the use of articles are 22 and 23, from the present data. In both sentences, the definite article has been omitted:

(22) ... the economy of India grows twice as fast as that of ___ European Union.

(23) ...the economy of India is growing twice as fast as that of ___ EU's.

In addition to the omission of the definite article, example 23 contains an error in the genitive construction: the final s is superfluous.

In examples 24 and 25, the indefinite article is missing:

(24) India is ___ country of contrasts.

(25) Even though ___ third of its citizens are illiterate, ...

Sometimes an article is used, but it is not the correct one, as in examples 26 and 27:

(26) India is **the** country of controversies.

(27) ...just over **an** Euro a day.

The error in 26 probably reflects the writer's uncertainty about the English articles, whereas the error in 27 is probably just a slip of the pen and would not have occurred in speech.

It is also possible to make a mistake by using an article where it is not required. The present data included a few instances of these superfluous articles, as in examples 28 and 29:

(28) A few kilometres from the mansions of **the** billionaires ...

(29) ...the cities are being toxicated by **the** exhaust fumes ...

In examples 28 and 29, *billionaires* and *exhaust fumes* have generic reference, so they should be accompanied by the zero article. Table 3 shows the distribution of grammatical errors in the present data.

Table 3. Distribution of grammatical errors in the student translations

Syntactic error types	Occurrences	%
Articles	110	37.3
Prepositions	69	23.4
Mixed structures	51	17.3
Number & Concord	36	12.2
Aspect	16	5.4
Other	13	4.4
Total	295	100

Examples of errors in concord and aspect were already given in section 5.1. The category 'Other' includes a mixture of erroneous expressions or, indeed, missing text. If a student had left out a piece of text longer than one lexical item, it was counted as a syntactic error and included in this category. The few instances of erroneous conjunctions were also contained in this group.

All in all, the grammatical competence of the students was quite good, as the number of grammatical errors was very low, only 2 per 100 words (see Table 1). As mentioned already, the relatively high number of article errors came as no surprise. It might well be that the use of English articles cannot really be mastered without a lengthy stay in an English-speaking country. Explicit instruction may simply never be enough.

6 Conclusion

The purpose of the study reported in this article was to see whether there are differences between the lexical and grammatical competences of advanced learners of English. Differences were, in fact, expected, as it seems to be an established fact that grammar and lexis are governed by different cognitive processes and behave differently in many ways. Indeed, the results of the present study showed that the grammatical competence of the students was clearly better than their lexical competence. At least, the translation task did not prove to be very difficult structurally, and the number of grammatical errors was only two per 100 words. As for lexical errors, they were more numerous (four per 100 words), and they were mostly caused by the student using a word which did not quite cover the intended meaning. In other words, most of the lexical errors involved a lack of precision. It could be speculated that this kind of vagueness might well be the result of a modern tendency to emphasize communicativeness, even at the expense of accuracy. On the other hand, if this had not been a test situation, some of the circumlocutions and near-synonyms the students used would have been accepted and even applauded. They would probably have conveyed the message sufficiently regardless of their vagueness compared with the target word.

It was also the aim of this study to find out what aspects of the language competence of our new students would need special attention. Given the small number of language skills classes that we offer in the English Department, the hours should be allocated in the most sensible way. The question now is whether we should start planning a course on English vocabulary skills, or whether we could integrate vocabulary acquisition more systematically in the rest of the course work. The language of instruction is English throughout our classes, so implicit vocabulary acquisition inevitably takes place to some extent anyway. Maybe a combination of implicit and explicit learning would be ideal.

References

Archibald, J. (ed.) (2000) *Second Language Acquisition and Linguistic Theory.* Malden, Mass.: Blackwell Publishers.

Barcroft, J. (2007) "When knowing grammar depends on knowing vocabulary: native-speaker grammaticality judgements of sentences with real and unreal words." *The Canadian Modern Language Review* 63/3: 313-343.

Butler, Y. G. (2002) "Second language learners' theories on the use of English articles. An analysis of the metalinguistic knowledge used by Japanese students in acquiring the English article system." *Studies in Second Language Acquisition* 24: 451-480.

Canale, M. (1983) "From communicative competence to communicative language pedagogy." In Richards & Schmidt (eds.): 2-26.

Canale, M. & M. Swain (1980) "Theoretical bases of communicative approaches to second language teaching and testing." *Applied Linguistics* 1/1: 1-47.

Cenoz, J., B. Hufeisen & U. Jessner (eds.) (2003) *The Multilingual Lexicon.* Dordrecht: Kluwer Academic Publishers.

CEFR = Council of Europe (2001) *Common European Framework of Reference for Languages.* Cambridge: Cambridge University Press.

Ellis, R. and G. Barkhuizen (2005) *Analysing Learner Language.* Oxford: Oxford University Press.

Franceschini, R., D. Zappatore & C. Nitsch. (2003) "Lexicon in the brain: what neurobiology has to say about languages." In Cenoz, Hufeisen & Jessner (eds.): 153-166.

Grosjean, F. (1989) "Neurolinguists, beware! The bilingual is not two monolinguals in one person." *Brain and Language* 36: 3-15.

Hatch, E. M. (1983) *Psycholinguistics, A Second Language Perspective.* Rowley, Mass.: Newbury House.

Henriksen, B. (2006) "Exploring the quality of lexical knowledge in the language learner's L1 and L2." In Pietilä, Lintunen & Järvinen (eds.): 13-36.

Indefrey, P., P. Hagoort, H. Herzog, R. J. Seitz & C. M. Brown (2001) "Syntactic processing in left prefrontal cortex is independent of lexical meaning." *NeuroImage* 14: 546-555.

Kasper, G. & E. Kellerman (eds.) (1997) *Communication Strategies. Psycholinguistic and Sociolinguistic Perspectives.* London: Longman.

Kempler, D., S. Curtiss & C. Jackson (1987) Syntactic preservation in Alzheimer's disease. *Journal of Speech and Hearing Research* 30: 343-350.

Lenguel, Z. & J. Navracsics (eds.) (2007) *Second Language Lexical Processes.* Clevedon: Multilingual Matters.

Lewis, M. (1993) *The Lexical Approach: The State of ELT and a Way Forward.* Hove: LTP.

Libben, G. (2000) "Representation and processing in the second language lexicon: the Homogeneity Hypothesis." In Archibald (ed.): 228-248.

Pérez-Llantada, M. C. (2007) "New trends in grammar teaching: issues and applications. An interview with Prof. Diane Larsen-Freeman." *ATLANTIS* 29/1: 157-163.

Pietilä, P., P. Lintunen & H.-M. Järvinen (eds.) (2006) *Kielenoppija tänään – Language Learners of Today*. AFinLA Yearbook 2006. Jyväskylä: The Finnish Association of Applied Linguistics.

Richards, J. C. & R.W. Schmidt (eds.) (1983) *Language and Communication*. New York: Longman.

Ringbom, H. (2007) *Cross-linguistic Similarity in Foreign Language Learning*. Clevedon: Multilingual Matters.

Salem, I. (2007) "The lexico-grammatical continuum viewed through student error." *ELT Journal* 61/3: 211-219.

Singleton, D. (2007) "How integrated is the integrated mental lexicon?" In Lenguel & Navracsics (eds.): 3-16.

Singleton, D. (2003) "Perspectives on the multilingual lexicon: a critical synthesis." In Cenoz, Hufeisen & Jessner (eds.): 167-176.

Weinreich, U. (1953) *Languages in Contact*. New York: Linguistic Circle of New York.

Grammaticalisation, Contact and Adverbial Connectives: The Rise and Decline of *Save*

Matti Rissanen

1 Introduction

Adverbial connectives form a fascinating group of items for the description and analysis of the development of the English language from Old to Present-Day English. From the historical point of view, this group of connectives includes adverbs, prepositions, and subordinating conjunctions, to use the names of traditional grammatical categories. At the earliest stages of hypotactic linking, most adverbial subordinators seem to have developed from linking adverbs, for example, the adverbial phrase *for þam* 'for that reason' (see (1a)) develops into the subordinator indicating 'for the reason that', 'for', 'because', exemplified by the hypothetical example (1b) and the attested Old English example (1c):

(1a) *Ic ondræde me **for ðam**: ic eom nacod.
  'I fear me for that: I am naked.'
  'I am afraid for that reason: I am naked.'

(1b) *Ic ondræde me **for ðam** ic eom nacod.
  'I fear me for that I am naked.'
  'I am afraid for that reason (that) I am naked.'

(1c) ic ondræde me **for ðam ðe** ic eom nacod,
(*Hept. Gen.* 3 AELFOLD HC)[1]
'I fear me for that [reason] that I am naked'

The relationship between prepositions and adverbial subordinators is also an obvious one. The categorization by Huddleston and Pullum (2002: 599ff), who treat adverbial subordinators as just a sub-category of prepositions, is particularly appropriate for the discussion of the early history of these connectives. Consider the Old English examples (2a) and (2b):

(2a) fela fortacna sculon geweorðan wide on worulde ... **ær ðam þe** se dom cume þe us eallum wyrð gemæne.
(*Wulfstan's Homilies* 123 WULF3 HC)

'many signs will appear widely in the world ... before the doom comes that will be common to all of us.'

(2b) nan man nys þe hyg wite **ær þam miclan dome**.
(*Prose Solomon and Saturn* 32 SOLOM HC)

'there is nobody who will know it before the great doom.'

In (2a) the preposition *ær* forms part of a prepositional subordinator introducing a temporal clause while in (2b) it is used as a preposition. Note also the translations 'before the doom comes' and 'before the great doom'.

Perhaps the most interesting and important aspect of the discussion of the rise and development of adverbial connectives pertains to grammaticalisation.[2] In Old English, grammaticalisation is mostly seen in the formation of subordinators from connecting adverbs and prepositions or prepositional phrases, as indicated by my examples (1) and (2). In Middle English, a new type of forming connectives gains ground: grammaticalised forms based on nouns, verbs and, occasionally, adjectives borrowed from French or Latin.

The preposition and subordinator *save*, which is the main topic of this paper, first appears in the Middle English period. In this paper, the rise, development and uses of this item will be traced from Middle to Present-Day English.

Particular attention will be drawn to three questions, which are also of general interest in the study of the grammaticalisation of the adverbial connectives in English:

> 1. What is the role of the grammaticalised forms in the source language in the grammaticalisation of connectives based on borrowed elements in Middle English? Does the connective *save* go back to the Middle English adjective *sauf* or the verb *saven*, or is it borrowed from the Old French grammaticalised connective *sauf*?
>
> 2. What are the roles of the various genres of Middle English texts, especially those using official language, in the establishment of borrowed connectives? In which genres was *save* popular, and was it avoided in some genres?
>
> 3. What is the role of layering, i.e., the relationship between the connective use and other uses of the same word, in the later development and present-day popularity of the connective? Why is *save* clearly less popular today than *except*? [3]

This survey is based on evidence collected from historical and Present-Day English corpora. These include *The Helsinki Corpus of English Texts* (HC), *The Penn-Helsinki Parsed Corpus of Middle English* (PPCME), *The Middle English Compendium* (MEC), the *Corpus of Middle English Medical Texts* (MEMT), *The Penn-Helsinki Parsed Corpus of Early Modern English* (PPCEME), *The Corpus of Early English Correspondence Sampler* (CEECS), *A Corpus of English Dialogues* (CED), *A Representative Corpus of Historical English Registers* (ARCHER), *The Corpus of Late Modern English Texts* (CLMET), and the most important twentieth-century English corpora.[4]

2 From Old to Middle English: new ways of forming connectives

Most Old English prepositions and connecting adverbs go back to common Germanic stock. A typical way of forming adverbial subordinators was by combining prepositions with oblique forms of the demonstrative pronoun *þæt*, as in (1c) and (2a), above. Some adverbs could be used as subordinators either by themselves, with the subordinating particle *þe* or *þæt* (*þeah, nu, siþþan,* etc.), or with *swa* (*swa lange swa, swa oft swa, swa feor swa,* etc.). *Gif* is probably the "most original" of the subordinators.[5] The only Old English subordinator which is formed from a noun and thus shows more thoroughgoing grammaticalisation than the types mentioned above is *þa hwile þe* 'while' (see Hopper and Traugott 2003: 90-92).

The Middle English period saw a radical change in the formation of adverbial connectives. A large number of new prepositions and adverbial subordinators emerge, mostly based on borrowed (Latin and/or French) nouns, verbs and even adjectives. The reasons for this are probably manifold. The increase in the number of texts composed in English in the Late Middle English period and the development of new genres of writing may have increased the need for new, more nuanced and more emphatic ways of indicating relationships between items and propositions. The language of the statutes and other official documents in the late fourteenth and fifteenth centuries in particular demanded accuracy and the avoidance of ambiguity. Such connectives as *because of/(that), in case of/(that), except (that),* and *according to/as* can be found from the fourteenth century onwards. Loan translations are represented by items such as *notwithstanding,* cf. L/F *non obstant(e)* (see, e.g., Rissanen (2002b)). In many cases, the grammaticalised connective use appears later than the earliest instances of the borrowed lexical item so that grammaticalisation can be said to have taken place in Middle English. In other cases, however, Latin and French offered models for the formation of grammaticalised connectives; the influence of these source language connectives is an interesting question which still needs a lot of research. Some connectives, e.g., *except (that)*, were probably borrowed in their grammaticalised form, cf. Latin *excepto quod* (see Rissanen 2002a).

3 The rise and early development of the connective *save*

3a. Origin

The earliest instances of the verb *saven*, which goes back to Old French *salver, sauver* (OED s.v. *save*, v.), are recorded in early thirteenth-century texts:

(3) He neodeles (= voluntarily) nom (= took) uppon him seoluen us for to **saluin** & maken us stronge.
(c1225 (?c1200) *St. Kath. (1)* (Roy 17. A. 27) 55/474 MED)

(4) **Sawuin** ow seoluen ne maten (= overcome) hem betere ne mahe (= may) ʒe o nane wise. (c1230 (?a1200) *Ancr.* (Corp-C 402) 52/14 MED)

The adjective *safe* is recorded somewhat later, in texts dating from c. 1300:

(5) Þe Quen a-non þoruʒh is bone (= prayer) deliuered was of childe..þe king i-say (= saw) þe Quene **sauf**, and þat child al-so.
(c1300 *SLeg.* (LdMisc 108) 458/51 MED)

(6) Þe king..bed him al **sauf** to him to gloucestre wende (= go) And Make him obligacion..Þat he ssolde to him come al **sauf** in ech ende.
(c1325 (c1300) *Glo. Chron. A* (Clg A.11) 8041, 8043 MED)

It is of considerable interest that the earliest instances of the connective *save* occur as early as the first decades of the fourteenth century:

(7) God ʒaf him [Adam] a gret maist[r]i Of al þat was in watir and londe.. **Saf** o tre he him forbede. (?a1325 Þe grace of god Hrl 913. 46 MED)

(8) For þat he was so hende (= beautiful) & gode, Men blisced him..**Saue** þe steward. (c1330 (?c1300) *Amis* (Auch) 346 MED)

(9) Swich bataile dede neuer non Cristene man..**Saue** sir Launcelet de Lake.
(c1330 (?c1300) *Bevis* (Auch) 122/260 MED)

(10) Al is pes þar ichaue (= I have) went, **Saue** in þe lond of Dabilent
(1330 (?c1300) *Bevis* (Auch) 110/2270 MED)

(11) Ithe (= in the) selve maner, mac the sise (= fluid) to goldfoyl, **save** tac a lutel radel (= red ochre) ant grynt to thin asise
(c1325 *Recipe Painting(1)* in *Archaeol. J. 1* (Hrl 2253) 65 MED)

The approximate times of the appearance of the verb and adjective, *saven* and *sauf*, in Middle English are confirmed by corpus evidence (HC, MED, MEC). Both the verb and the adjective are relatively frequent in early fourteenth-century texts, including *Robert of Gloucester, The South-English Legendary, Cursor Mundi* and *The Earliest English Prose Psalter*. Occurrences in thirteenth-century texts are uncommon, however: in addition to examples (3) and (4), there are only two instances, both in the *Kentish Sermons* (c. 1275). It is obvious that both the verb and the adjective were common at the time the first instances of the connective use appear, but not much earlier. Thus, it seems unlikely that the connective *save* was grammaticalised independently in Middle English, either from the verb or, especially, from the adjective. It is more likely that the connective was to a large extent based on the model offered by the connective use of *sauf* 'saving, except' in Old French (cf. OED s.v. **save** *quasi-prep*. and *conj.*) The OED statement that the connective *save* developed from the adjective *safe*, "in imitation of the similar development in the use of the equivalent F. *sauf*" may be basically correct, but is over-simplified. The same can be said about the MED statement that *save* derives "from **sauf** adj." (s.v. **sauf** prep.).

If the French connective use is regarded as the main source of the Middle English connective *save*, it can also be argued that the Early Middle English borrowed verb *saven* contributed to the appearance of this connective as much as did the adjective *sauf*, which appears somewhat later in Middle English texts. This suggestion is supported to some extent by the great variety of spellings of this connective in fourteenth-century Middle English texts: forms with medial <v> and/or final <e> are common, as can be seen in examples (8)-(11) above. In view of the inconsistency of Middle English spelling conventions, however, the value of this observation is minimal. More attention could be called to the fact that the verb form *saving* appears as a variant of the connective *save* from the late fourteenth century on (examples (12)-(15)) and gains ground in the fifteenth century (MED s.v. **saving(e** prep.)**.** The development of this form indicates that, in the minds of speakers, *save* was associated not only with the adjective, but also with the verb. Similar variation in the form can be seen in the connective *except/excepting/excepted* (Rissanen 2002a; 2007: 203-204).[6]

(12) Adam..welte (= ruled over) al paradys **sauyng** o tree.
(c1375 Chaucer *CT. Mk.* (Manly-Rickert) B. 3200 MED)

(13) No wight..wiste of this lone (= loan) **Sauyng** this marchant and daun Iohn allone. (c1390) Chaucer *CT. Sh.* (Manly-Rickert) B.1486 MED)

(14) For at þe first tyme when þou dost it, þou fyndest bot a derknes, and as it were a cloude of vnknowyng, þou wost (= know) neuer what, **sauyng** þat þou felist in þi wille a nakid entent vnto God.
(a1425 *Cloud of Unknowing* 16-17 CLOUD HC)

(15) and alle they that desired the kynges frendship were there / **sauyng** reynard the foxe / the rede false pilgrym whiche laye in a wayte to doo harme / (1481 *Reynard the Fox* 51 REYNARD HC)

The development of the form *saving* was no doubt supported by the grammaticalised use of *saving* in the sense 'with due respect, regard, or consideration for (someone's honor, wish, advice, etc.)' (MED s.v. **saving(e** prep. 2):

(16) Whan a brother or a suster schal be resceyued..þey schul be swore vpon a book to þe brotherhede for to holde vp & meyntene þe poyntz & the articles þat be write after folwynge, eche man to his power, **sauynge** his estat.
(1389 *Lond. Gild Ret.* in *Bk. Lond. E.* (PRO C 47/var.) 48/19 MED)

(17) He ys a worschyppull man, sers, **sauyng** yowr reuerens.
(c1475 *Mankind* (Folg V.a.354) 463 MED)

Note also the use of the adjective *sauf* in the sense 'preserving (sth.), (sth.) being preserved; without prejudice or harm to (sth.); with due regard for (sb. or sth.), without disrespect to' (MED s.v. **sauf** adj. 7) in examples (18)-(19). According to the MED, this use goes back to "a similar development of OF **sauf**, ult. from L **salvus**, used in abl.absol. constr."

(18) Alle þe lawes and þe costomes we shullen holde..Þat beothz to holde sire, **sauue** oure riȝte. (c1300 *SLeg. Becket* (LdMisc 108) 478 MED)

(19) A fals harlot, **sauf** your reuerens, one James Cook..diffamed me and my wif. (1454 *Paston* 2.88 MED)

3b. Establishment

In Late Middle English, the grammaticalised uses of the preposition and subordinator *save* and *saving* increase rapidly in frequency. Table 1 shows the frequencies in the sub-periods ME3 (1350-1420) and ME4 (1420-1500) in the *Helsinki Corpus*. For the sake of comparison, the corresponding figures for *except* are also given. All spellings and all grammaticalised forms of *save/saving* are included in the data, including those in which the word has the sense 'with due regard', etc.:

Table 1. *Save/saving* and *except(ing/ed)* in the Late Middle English sub-periods (ME3-ME4) of the *Helsinki Corpus*. Figures per 100,000 words in brackets.

	save/saving	except(ing/ed)
ME3 (1350-1420)	16 (8.7)	0
ME4 (1420-1500)	31 (14.5)	16 (7.5)

As can be seen from Table 1, the grammaticalised *save/saving* appears earlier than *except(ing/ed)* and is clearly more frequent than *except* forms even in the 1420-1500 sub-section.

An interesting difference between the fifteenth-century (1420-1500) uses of *save* and *except* is that, while *save* is common in all kinds of texts, *except* is largely restricted to statutes and other official documents. The distribution is shown in Table 2:

Table 2. The occurrences of *save/saving* and *except(ing/ed)* in statutes and other official documents (official) and other texts (other) in the sub-period ME4 in the *Helsinki Corpus*. Figures per 100,000 words in brackets.

	save/saving		except(ing/ed)	
	official	other	official	other
1420-1500	9 (37.4)	22 (11.4)	8 (39.7)	8 (4.1)

Table 2 indicates that both *save* and *except* are common in the officialese, but it is worth noting that, in five of the nine instances, the sense of *save/saving* is 'with respect to' and not 'except'.

Table 3. The occurrence of the grammaticalised forms of *save/saving* in various texts and genres of Late Middle English texts in the *Helsinki Corpus* (ME3 and ME4, 1350-1500). Absolute figures.

Statutes and documents	13
Astrolabe	1
Canterbury Tales	5
Early Planets	4
Cloud of Unknowing	1
Siege of Jerusalem	1
Reynes, *Commonplace*	3
Metham, *Days of Moon*	1
Serm. Innocents	1
Capgrave *Serm.*	2
Hilton	1
Capgrave *Chron.*	2
London Chron.	2
Reynard the Fox	3
York Plays	2
Towneley Plays	1
Private letters	3
Official letters	1
	47

A more significant difference, however, is the higher frequency of *save* in other types of texts in comparison to *except(ing/ed)* (11.4 vs. 4.1 occurrences per 100,000 words). Table 3, which lists the occurrences of *save/saving* in various texts dating in the period 1350-1500, illustrates this issue.

The figures for the *Helsinki Corpus* are fairly low for the comparison of the overall popularity of the use of *save* and *except* in Late Middle English. The figures taken from the *Corpus of Middle English Prose and Verse* in Table 4 confirm the overall trend.

Table 4. Grammaticalised uses of *save* and *except* in the *Corpus of Middle English Prose and Verse* (from Rissanen 2002a).

	save	except
1350-1400	100	4
1400-1500	261	177

The *Corpus of Middle English Medical Texts* shows that the connective *save* had also found its way into the language of early scientific language, soon after the vernacularisation of this genre. There are 23 instances in this corpus, 4.6 per 100,000 words.

3c. Early Modern English development

In view of its Late Middle English distribution, we might expect that even in Early Modern English *save* would remain the most popular connective indicating exception. However, the *Helsinki Corpus* figures in Table 5 show that this was not the case.

Table 5. Occurrences of *save/saving*, *except(ing/ed)* and *unless* in the Early Modern English part (1500-1710) of the *Helsinki Corpus*. Figures per 100,000 words in brackets.

	save/saving	except(ing/ed)	unless
EModE1 (1500-1570)	26 (13.7)	48 (25.2)	11 (5.8)
EModE2 (1570-1640)	10 (5.3)	40 (21.1)	18 (9.5)
EModE3 (1640-1710)	12 (7.0)	16 (9.4)	34 (19.9)

As can be seen from Table 5, *except(ing/ed)* supersedes *save/saving* in frequency as early as the sixteenth century. In the seventeenth century, the increasing popularity of *unless* as the subordinator indicating negative condition explains the decreasing frequency of *except(ing/ed)*.

These relationships are confirmed by the *Penn-Helsinki Parsed Corpus of Early Modern English* (Table 6):

Table 6. Occurrences of *save/saving, except(ing/ed)* and *unless* in the *Penn-Helsinki Parsed Corpus of Early Modern English*. Figures per 100,000 words in brackets.

	save/saving	except(ing/ed)	unless
EModE1 (1500-1570)	49 (8.5)	134 (23.3)	33 (5.7)
EModE2 (1570-1640)	36 (5.5)	152 (23.2)	65 (10.0)
EModE3 (1640-1710)	22 (3.9)	84 (14.9)	100 (18.8)

Furthermore, the waning of *save* over the course of the Early Modern period can clearly be seen in the figures from both CEECS and CED, which represent text-types approaching the spoken expression, i.e. informal correspondence and dialogue (Table 7). The almost complete absence of *save/saving* at the end of the seventeenth and in the eighteenth century is particularly remarkable.[7]

Table 7. Occurrences of *save/saving*, *except(ing/ed)* and *unless* in the *Corpus of Early English Correspondence Sampler* and the *Corpus of English Dialogues*. Figures per 100,000 words in brackets.

	save/saving	except(ing/ed)	unless
CEECS 1 (1418-1638)	35 (14.2)	34 (13.8)	19 (7.7)
CEECS 2 (1580-1680)	9 (4.4)	23 (11.3)	23 (11.3)
CED1 (1560-99)	9 (4.5)	35 (17.5)	34 (17.0)
CED2 (1600-39)	9 (4.4)	11 (5.3)	20 (9.8)
CED3 (1640-79)	6 (2.3)	8 (3.1)	37 (14.3)
CED4 (1680-1719)	2 (0.7)	14 (4.7)	51 (17.2)
CED5 (1720-1760)	0	21 (9.4)	29 (13.0)

One of the features connected with the grammaticalisation of *save* is the form of the personal pronoun governed by the prepositional *save*. With the subjective forms, i.e. *I, thou, ye, he, she, we,* and *they*, traces of the non-prepositional character of *save* may still exist and the grammaticalisation is not complete.

Unfortunately, the number of instances of *save* + personal pronoun is very small; however, the few instances in HC or PPCME all have the pronoun in the subjective form:

(20) *Baily* Your talke is such, I can scarse learne who shuld be most in fault
Ga~mer Yet shal ye find no other wight, **saue** she, by bred & salt
(1552-1563 Stevenson, *Gammer Gurtons* Nedle 60 STEVENSO HC)

(21) Not that eny man hath sene the father, **save** he which is of God:
(1534 *Tyndale New Testament* John 6:40 TYNDNEW HC)

(22) what their names be, none can tell, **saue** he whose eies doe behold the secret disposition of all mens harts
(1614 *Hooker* 17.108 PPCEME)

The OED (s.v. **save** *quasi-prep. and conj.* 1b) suggests that this was "app[arently] the normal construction".

4 *Save* as a connective in Late Modern and Present-Day English

In view of the evidence from Early Modern English corpora, it is obvious that *save* had lost the competition with *except* and *unless* by c. 1700. The Late Modern English corpora, ARCHER and CLMET confirm this development (Table 8):

Table 8. Occurrences of *save/saving*, *except(ing/ed)* [8] and *unless* in the *Corpus of Late Modern English Texts* and ARCHER. Figures per 100,000 words in brackets.

	save/saving	except(ing/ed)	unless
CLMET1 (1710-1780)	13 (0.6)	408 (20.0)	306 (14.6)
CLMET2 (1780-1850)	181 (4.9)	803 (21.5)	482 (12.9)
CLMET3 (1850-1920)	314 (7.9)	886 (22.2)	518 (13.0)
ARCHER (1700-1799)	3 (0.6)	107 (19.9)	62 (11.6)
ARCHER (1800-1899)	26 (4.8)	104 (19.3)	64 (11.9)
ARCHER (1900-1990)	9 (1.7)	140 (26.2)	44 (8.2)

The figures show how, after the very infrequent use in the eighteenth century, the connective *save* becomes fairly well established, a situation which continues right up to the present day. CLMET3 shows a relatively high frequency in the second half of the nineteenth and the early twentieth century, while the ARCHER figure for the twentieth century suggests a decreasing trend, possibly due to the increasing use of *except*. It should be mentioned that the forms *saving* and *excepting/excepted* become more and more infrequent over the course of the Late Modern English period: in the ARCHER texts dating from the nineteenth century there is one instance of the connective *saving* and seven of *excepted/excepting*, while in the twentieth-century texts there are no occurrences of *saving* or *excepted* and two of *excepting*.

The present-day pattern of the connective use of *save*, in relation to *except* and *unless*, is shown by the figures from the *Lancaster-Oslo/Bergen Corpus* and the *Brown Corpus*, along with their Freiburg counterparts *Freiburg-LOB* and *Freiburg-Brown* (Table 9):

Table 9. Occurrences of *save/saving*, *except(ing/ed)* and *unless* in the *Lancaster-Oslo/Bergen Corpus*, the *Brown Corpus*, the *Freiburg-Lancaster-Oslo/Bergen Corpus* and the *Freiburg-Brown Corpus*. The size of each corpus is c. one million words.

	save/saving	*except(ing)*	*unless*
LOB	19	204	154
Brown	7	180	101
F-LOB	6	121	111
Frown	7	138	90

The typical uses of *save* in present-day usage are prepositional (23), or governing a prepositional phrase (24). The combination *save for* is not uncommon (25). It can also govern a subordinate clause, when combined with *that* (26); the subordinator use of *save* is marked as archaic in Quirk *et al.* (1985: 1090). *Save* governing a subordinate clause can also be followed by another subordinator (27).Thus, we can say that the connective functions of *save* are still as varied as they were during its heyday in Late Middle and Early Modern English, although this connective has been overshadowed by *except* and, in subordinator use, by *unless*.

(23) To help him do so The Prince had conferred control of his land forces on a soldier who was different from him in almost every respect **save** one: (Brown G50:52)

(24) I never saw her **save** during the daytime (LOB K26:19)

(25) Herschel would have been happy to sign for Talbot as well **save for** his continuing protest against the Society). (Frown J60:1)

(26) **Save that** they are drawn from every part of the multiverse, they are very much of a type I left behind me long ago (F-LOB M02:40)

(27) broadcast from Deutchlandsender-Berlin in equally unbrokenstream **save when** the girl announcer would break in with air (LOB G05:16)

5 Discussion

The most important question about the long history of *save*, besides its origin and earliest grammaticalisation, is why, despite a very promising start and its favourable phonetic shape, it did not develop into the most common unmarked connective indicating exception. Ever since the seventeenth century, *except* and the subordinator *unless* have been clearly more frequent than *save*. At the beginning of the eighteenth century, the connective *save* seems to have veered close to complete extinction, but since then its position has been re-established. Nevertheless, even in recent decades it seems to be on the wane, as can be seen from the figures in LOB and F-LOB, which represent British English in the 1960s and the 1990s. Quirk *et al.* label the prepositional use formal (1985: 667, 707), and the *Collins Cobuild Dictionary* describes it as "a very formal use" (s.v. **save** 7). The subordinator use without a following *that* or another subordinator is archaic.

One important reason for the seventeenth-century development was probably the support given to *except* by its frequent use at the esteemed level of formal language. The language of administration most probably played an important role in the establishment of borrowed adverbial connectives in the emerging Southern standard (see Rissanen 2000; 2007). The same phenomenon can be seen in the early popularisation of *notwithstanding*, which was clearly more frequent than *in (de)spite of* or *despite* in Early Modern English (Rissanen 2002b). Nonetheless, while the shorter and less formal sounding *(de)spite* forms have become more common and less stylistically marked than *notwithstanding* in the course of the last few centuries, this never happened with *save* in comparison to *except*.

It seems that the grammaticalisation of *save* was never quite completed. Quirk *et al.* label *save* as a marginal preposition with verbal affinities and list it in the same group as *bar, barring, excepting, excluding, concerning, considering, regarding, respecting, given, granted,* etc. (1985: 667). Semantically important meanings of the verb *save* are by far more frequent than the connective use throughout the Modern English period (Table 10).

Table 10. The connective and other uses of *save/saving* in CLMET, ARCHER, LOB and F-LOB.

	Connective	Other
CLMET (1710-1780)	508	985
ARCHER (1700-1990)	38	145
LOB	19	152
Brown	7	147
F-LOB	6	132
FROWN	7	125

It seems, indeed, that this relationship between connective and other (mainly verbal) uses of *save* prevented the complete grammaticalisation of *save*, not to mention *saving*. With *except*, the proportions are completely the reverse. LOB and Brown do not show a single use of *except* as a verb, and even in earlier corpora the instances of this use are most infrequent. *Unless* is only used as a subordinator. By way of comparison, it is worth noting that in F-LOB and FROWN the various forms of *cause* (verb and noun) occur 576 times, while the connective *because* occurs 1899 times.

This does not mean, of course, that the avoidance of the connective use of *save* results from the speaker's or writer's conscious avoidance for fear of ambiguity. Polysemy or homonymy are in most cases highly doubtful explanations for the loss of lexical or grammatical items. The influence of the high frequency of non-grammaticalised uses on the popularity of a grammaticalised form must be sought at a much more basic cognitive level. Be that as it may, it seems that the details of layering deserve particular attention in the study of the paths of grammaticalisation of English connectives.

6 Final remarks

In this paper I have tried to describe the history of the preposition and subordinator *save* from its very beginning in the fourteenth century to our own days, making use of the richness of English corpora and databases. I have referred to the role played by the source language in the grammaticalisation of the Middle English connectives and the favouring of different connectives in different genres of texts. The question of layering, i.e. the co-occurrence of old non-grammaticalised and new grammaticalised forms, has been mentioned in the discussion of the development and frequency of *save*. Reference has been made to the long-diachrony developments of other connectives. I hope that this paper may raise questions that will contribute to the more general overall study of the grammaticalisation of English connectives.

Notes

1   See, e.g., Mitchell (1985: §2421-2432); Rissanen (2007: 177-178). The capitalised abbreviated titles used in the reference lines of the *Helsinki Corpus* (HC)

examples are explained in the *Manual* (Kytö 1996: 167-230) or
< http://khnt.hit.uib.no/icame/manuals/HC/>.

2 According to a recent definition, grammaticalisation is "the process whereby lexical material in highly constrained pragmatic and morphosyntactic contexts is assigned grammatical function, and once grammatical, is assigned increasingly grammatical, operator-like function"(Traugott 2003: 645). Cf. also Hopper and Traugott (2003: xv).

3 According to Hopper and Traugott (2003: 124), "layering" is "the persistence of older forms and meanings alongside newer forms and meanings." In the present context, "layering" refers to the coexistence of older and newer (grammaticalised) meanings of *save*.

4 Information on these corpora can be found at the following Internet sites:
http://khnt.hit.uib.no/icame/manuals/index.htm (HC, CEECS, present-day corpora),
http://www.ling.upenn.edu/hist-corpora/ (PPCME, PPCEME)
http://ets.umdl.umich.edu/m/mec/ (MEC)
http://www.benjamins.com/cgi-bin/t_bookview.cgi ? bookid= Z%2031 (MEMT)
http://www.engelska.uu.se/corpus.html (CED)
http://perswww.kuleuven.be/ ~u0044428/clmet.htm (CLMET)
For ARCHER, see, for example, Biber & Finegan (1997).

5 For lists of Old English subordinators, see Kortmann (1997: 292) and Mitchell (1985: 1232–1233). Mitchell does not separate adverbial subordinators from other clausal connectives, but he does distinguish prepositional from non-prepositional conjunctions. See also the grouping and discussion of the types of Old English adverbial subordinators in Rissanen (2007: 177-188).

6 Cf. OED (s.v. **save** *quasi-prep.* and *conj.*), "... the later exclusive form of *save* is probably due to the identification of the word with the imperative of the verb: cf. *except*, which appears to have been similarly apprehended as an imperative."

7 One of the two instances in CED4 comes from a trial record: *I think we have now proved it against everybody we design,* **save only** *against Mr.Deagle* (Trial of Pilkington 33). The other instance comes from a comedy: *I have a great pain in my back, and cannot make water,* **saving** *your presence* (Shadwell 37)

8 The figures for *except(ing/ed)* include the verbal uses of the word. However, the occurrences of these uses are so infrequent that they do not affect the comparison between the connectives.

References

Biber, Douglas and Edward Finegan (1997) "Diachronic relations among speech-based and written registers in English." In Terttu Nevalainen and Leena Kahlas-Tarkka (eds.) *To explain the present: Studies in the changing English language in hon-*

our of Matti Rissanen. Helsinki: Société Néophilologique. 253-275.

Hopper, Paul J. and Elizabeth Closs Traugott (2nd ed.) (2003) *Grammaticalization.* Cambridge: Cambridge University Press.

Huddleston, Rodney and Geoffrey K. Pullum (2002) *The Cambridge grammar of the English language.* Cambridge: Cambridge University Press.

Kortmann, Bernd (1997) *Adverbial subordination: A typology and history of adverbial subordinators based on European Languages.* Mouton de Gruyter: Berlin/New York.

Kytö, Merja (1996) [1991]. *Manual to the diachronic part of the Helsinki Corpus of English Texts: Coding conventions and lists of source texts.* (3rd ed.) Helsinki: Department of English, University of Helsinki.

Mitchell, Bruce (1985) *Old English Syntax* I-II. Oxford: Clarendon Press.

Rissanen, Matti (2000) "Standardisation and the language of early statutes." In Laura Wright (ed.) *The development of Standard English: Theories, descriptions, conflicts.* Cambridge: Cambridge University Press. 117–130.

Rissanen, Matti (2002a) "'Without except(ing) unless...': On the grammaticalisation of expressions indicating exception in English." In Katja Lenz and Ruth Möhlig (eds.) *Of dyuersite & chaunge of langage: Essays presented to Manfred Görlach on the occasion of his 65th birthday.* Heidelberg: C. Winter Universitätsverlag. 77–87.

Rissanen, Matti (2002b) "*Despite* or *notwithstanding*? On the development of concessive prepositions in English." In Andreas Fischer, Gunnel Tottie and Hans Martin Lehmann (eds.) *Text types and corpora: Studies in honour of Udo Fries.* Tübingen: Gunter Narr Verlag. 191–203.

Rissanen, Matti (2007) "The development of adverbial subordinators in early English." In Matti Rissanen, Marianna Hintikka, Leena Kahlas-Tarkka and Rod McConchie (eds.) *Change in meaning and the meaning of change: Studies in semantics and grammar from Old to Present-Day English.* Helsinki: Société Néophilologique. 173–210.

Traugott, Elizabeth Closs (2003) "Constructions in grammaticalization." In Brian D. Joseph and Richard D. Janda (eds.) *The Handbook of historical linguistics.* Oxford and Malden, MA: Blackwell. 624-647.

Great Strides forward in Ancrene Wisse Research
To be or not to be AB?

Arne Zettersten

Few scholarly editions of major works within English medieval literature have been anticipated with more interest than Bella Millett's *Ancrene Wisse: A Corrected Edition of the Text in Cambridge, Corpus Christi College, MS 402, with Variants from other Manuscripts, Vol. I-II,* published for the Early English Text Society by Oxford University Press in 2005-2006. Dr. Millett has also been responsible for another innovation in the new millennium, namely to present the beginning of a new edition of *Ancrene Wisse* (=*AW*) on the the World Wide Web as part of the EETS aim to publish editions of Old and Middle English texts in electronic form. It will be possible at any point in this electronic edition to access the original Middle English text with the translation into modern English or Millett's commentary based on E.J. Dobson's textual comments with additional notes by Richard Dance.

Bella Millett explains in her preface to volume I that the foundation of her work is the edition of *Ancrene Wisse* left unfinished by Dobson at his death in 1984. The first volume of her edition contains a Textual Introduction with a description of manuscripts and versions as well as an analysis of the relations of the manuscripts and a modified version of Dobson's stemma. There is also a presentation of the development of the *Ancrene Wisse* in subsequent centuries. Volume I further contains the critical apparatus after the edited text.

Volume II includes a General Introduction, a Textual Commentary, partly based on Dobson's work, and a glossary produced by Richard Dance. The General Introduction deals with important aspects of *Ancrene Wisse* scholarship, such as The *Ancrene Wisse* Group, Date, Localisation, Authorship, Audience, Institutional Context, Sources and Analogues, and Methods of composition.

One could say that Millett's edition of 2005-2006 constitutes the peak of a long tradition of editorial work on the 17 manuscripts of the *Ancrene Wisse*, starting as early as 1853, more than 150 years ago, with James Morton's edition of the Nero manuscript (with additional readings from the Corpus and Titus manuscripts). Due to the fact that this edition by Morton came out so early and was for nearly a hundred years the only manuscript of the *Ancrene Wisse* in print, the Nero manuscript was much more in focus among early scholars than its position in the tradition and quality justify. Most of the information on the *Ancrene Wisse* in handbooks, dictionaries, monographs and articles before the 1960s emanates from this manuscript, which may well be termed inferior to the Corpus MS.

The title *Ancrene Riwle* is not recorded as a phrase in any of the existing manuscripts, so one could point out that it has no medieval authority, as *Ancrene Wisse* (of the same meaning) has, being recorded on fol.1r of Corpus Christi College, Cambridge, MS 402. The former title was decided from the beginning to be used by the Early English Text Society. The tendency now is that more and more scholars prefer the latter title, the *Ancrene Wisse*, just as Bella Millett and Richard Dance. The work carried out by the Early English Text Society started in 1944 with the editions of the Latin and French versions. All the EETS editions of the *Ancrene Wisse* are diplomatic edtions and the Latin and French ones, usually semi-diplomatic. The principles followed by the Early English Text Society editors are best expressed in the prefatory note of the edition of MS Nero by Mabel Day (1946), p.1:

"The English manuscripts of the *Ancrene Riwle* are reproduced as they stand without emendation. Alterations made by the original scribe are enclosed in angular brackets; letters or words expuncted are so printed, alterations and additions by other hands are recorded in the footnotes. The capitalization, punctuation, and word division of the manuscript are retained; the ordinary hyphens used are those of the manuscript, being almost always at line-ends." Another point was that contractions were normally expanded without italics.

My own contacts with the Early English Text Society in Oxford reach back to 1961 when the President of the Society, Norman Davis, introduced me to J.R.R. Tolkien who had just submitted his edition of the Corpus Christi College, Cambridge, version of *AW* to the Society for printing. I had started to write to Tolkien in 1959 when I started to struggle with the AB language. This is how I realized that Tolkien had been allowed to change the rules of the Society for printing *AW* texts by preserving the lineation of the manuscript on the printed page. This meant that I was able to make references to the exact manuscript line, which would be identical with references to Tolkien's own edition, during my preparations of my doctoral thesis on the *Ancrene Wisse*, called *Studies in the Dialect and Vocabulary of the Ancrene* Riwle, printed in 1965.

Since I had been in touch with the owner of the Lanhydrock fragment of the *Ancrene Wisse*, Lord Robartes of Bodmin, Cornwall, who—to my great surprise—first asked me if my own department at the University of Lund was interested in buying the MS and then instead donated it to the Bodleian Library, it seemed natural that I was selected to edit the fragment for the Society (in 1963). Later in the 1960s I was asked to edit the Pepys MS as well (published in 1976) and after that the Vernon MS (published with Bernhard Diensberg) in 2000.

Some of my final editorial work on the edition of Vernon was carried out in the latter half of the 1990s, when I had the pleasure of visiting the University of Osaka several times as part of the new cooperation between the English Department at the University of Copenhagen and the Graduate School of Foreign Languages, University of Osaka. Professor Mitsunori Imai and I had taken the initiative in 1993 to propose a project which triggered various kinds of cooperation between Japan and the Nordic countries. Scholars from Osaka could participate in Nordic conferences and Nordic scholars were invited to lecture at universities in Japan. Two major areas of English studies were given priority, medieval and Early Modern English philology and corpus linguistics, areas where Imai's own competence and experience were great assets. The International Symposium, called "Reading the *Ancrene Riwle*", held on 25 January, 1997, at Osaka University became a great success with no less than 46 participants. The papers were published in 2000, edited by Mitsunori Imai and Hideki Watanabe.

It is easy to realize from the list of diplomatic and semi-diplpmatic editions of *AW* listed below that scholars had to wait for about a quarter of a century to see the final Vernon MS in published form and the subsequent new edition of the Corpus Christi College, MS 402, by Bella Millett.The manuscripts of the *Ancrene Wisse*, which were all edited by the Early English Text Society before Bella Millett's edition came out, will be listed below, including indications of the approximate datings:

A: Cambridge, Corpus Christi College, MS. 402

Tolkien, J.R.R. (ed.), *The English Text of the Ancrene Riwle, Ancrene Wisse, edited from MS. Corpus Christi College Cambridge 402,* EETS o.s. 249 (London, 1962). Date: second quarter of the 13th ct.

C: London, British Library, MS. Cotton Cleopatra C. vi

Dobson, E. J. (ed.), *The English Text of the Ancrene Riwle edited from B.M. Cotton MS. Cleopatra C. vi,* EETS o.s. 267 (London, 1972). Date: second quarter of the 13th ct.

F: London, British Library, MS. Cotton Vitellius F. vii

Herbert, J.A. (ed.), *The French Text of the Ancrene Riwle edited from British Museum MS. Cotton Vitellius F vii,* EETS o.s. 219 (London, 1944). Date: early 14th ct.

G: Cambridge, Gonville and Caius College, MS. 234/120

Wilson, R.M. (ed.), *The English Text of the Ancrene Riwle edited from Gonville and Caius College MS. 234/120,* EETS o.s. 229 (London, 1954). Date: second half of the 13th ct.

N: London, British Library, MS. Cotton Nero A. xiv

Day, Mabel (ed.), *The English Text of the Ancrene Riwle edited from Cotton Nero A. XIV,* EETS o.s. 225 (London, 1952). Date: second quarter of the 13th ct.

O: Bodleian Library, MS. Eng. th. c. 70 (The Lanhydrock Fragment)

Mack, Frances M. and A. Zettersten (eds.), *The English Text of the Ancrene Riwle edited from Cotton MS. Titus D. XVIII, together with the Lanhydrock Fragment, Bodleian MS. Eng. th.c. 70,* EETS o.s. 252 (London ,1963). Date: first half of the 14th ct.

P: Cambridge, Magdalene College, MS: Pepys 2498

Zettersten, Arne (ed.), *The English Text of the Ancrene Riwle edited from Magdalene College, Cambridge MS. Pepys 2498,* EETS o.s. 274 (London, 1976). Date: second half of the 14th ct.

R: London, British Library, MS. Royal 8. CI

Baugh, A.C. (ed.), *The English Text of the Ancrene Riwle edited from British Museum MS. Royal 8 C.I,* EETS o.s. 232 (London, 1956). Date: 15th ct.

T: London, British Library, MS. Cotton Titus D. cviii

Mack, Frances M. and A. Zettersten (eds.), *The English Text of the Ancrene Riwle edited from Cotton MS. Titus D. XVIII, together with the Lanhydrock Fragment, Bodleian MS. Eng. th. c. 70,* EETS o.s. 252 (London, 1963). Date: second quarter of the 13th ct.

L: Merton College, Oxford, MS. C. I. 5

d'Evelyn, Charlotte (ed.), *The Latin Text of the Ancrene Riwle,* EETS o.s. 216 (London, 1944).

Date: first half of the 14th ct. The edition contains variant readings from the following MSS:

Magdalen College, Oxford, Latin MS. 67
Date: late 14th or early 15th ct.

British Museum Cotton MS. Vitellius E. VII
Date: first half of the 14th ct.

British Museum MS. Royal 7 C.X.
Date: first half of the 16th ct.
S: Trethewey, W.H. (ed.), *The French Text of the Ancrene Riwle edited from Trinity College Cambridge MS. R. 14. 7*, EETS o.s. 240 (London, 1958).
V: Bodleian, MS. Eng. poet. a 1 (MS. Vernon)
Zettersten, Arne and B. Diensberg (eds.), *The English Text of the Ancrene Riwle edited from Oxford, Bodleian Library MS. Eng. Poet. a.1*, EETS o.s. 310 (London, 2000). Date: second half of the 14th ct.

The subsequently much discussed AB langage was identified by J.R.R. Tolkien in a famous essay published in *Essays and Studies*, 14, in 1929. Tolkien made a point of showing that the scribes of MS Corpus Christi College, Cambridge of the *Ancrene Riwle*, also called the *Ancrene Wisse* (=A) and MS Bodley 34 of the Katherine Group (=B) used a language and spelling nearly "as indistinguishable as that of two modern printed books". The *Katherine Group* is a closely related group of five prose texts, most fully preserved in MS Oxford, Bodleian Library, Bodley 34, namely, *St.Katherine, St. Margarete, St. Juliana, Hali Meidenhad* and *Sawles Warde*. The 'Wooing Group', also closely connected to the *Ancrene Wisse*, consists of *The Oreisun of Seinte Marie, On Lofsong of ure Louerde, On wel swude god Ureisun of God Almihti* and *The Wohunge of ure Lauerd*.

Tolkien had by his conclusion proposed the existence of a "new" variety of Middle English, which could be called a written literary standard. The connections between the manuscripts of the *Ancrene Riwle* and those of the *Katherine Group* had been touched on by some previous scholars, like G.C. Macaulay, J. Hall and K. Luick. It was, however, J.R.R. Tolkien who pointed out the close relationship in language and spelling, almost amounting to identity, between the *Ancrene Wisse* (A) and the Bodley MS of the *Katherine Group* (B). Nowhere else in Middle English literature do we find two different manuscripts of two different literary works copied by different scribes that show such obvious similarities. The immediate conclusion by Tolkien was that the two manuscripts must be connected in time and place.

These unique circumstances led Tolkien to suppose either (i) that A or B or both are originals, or (ii) that A and B are in whole or part accurate translations, or (iii) that the vanished originals of A and B were in this same language (AB), and so belonged to practically the same period and place as the copies we have. According to Tolkien, the first possibility can at once be dismissed. Neither A nor B could be originals. Further, Tolkien did not think that an accurate translation is credible. He firmly believed that the originals of A and B were written in the same language and spelling (AB) as the copies. He admitted that the spelling suggests obedience to some school or authority. This school would be the centre of learning where the AB language was taught, read and written.

Tolkien placed the AB language in the West Midlands, more specifically in Herefordshire. E.J. Dobson developed Tolkien's research even further and concluded that Wigmore Abbey in north-west Herefordshire was the place of origin of the *Ancrene Wisse*. He further suggested that the author was "Brian(us) of Lingen", a secular canon of Wigmore. Dobson proposed that the sentence 'Inoh medful Ich am, þe bidde se lutel' = 'I am moderate enough, who ask for so little' (fol. 117v) conceals a pun on Brian's name (Lat. *Bria* = 'moderate') and an anagram of Linthehum ('of Lingen'). See Dobson's *Origins of Ancrene Wisse*, 349-53. This type of conclusion based on a pun and an anagram would certainly have been to Tolkien's liking, had he still been alive when it was put forward (in 1976). Dobson's proposition — brilliant as it first sounds — has been criticized or doubted later on (see, for example, M. Black 1999, and the localization now regarded as the most credible is the one based on the data of the *Linguistic Atlas of Late Middle English*. According to Jeremy Smith, the localization based on the *Atlas* is North Herefordshire or the southern tip of Shropshire. See B. Millet, *et al, Ancrene Wisse, The Katherine Group, and the Wooing Group*, 11, n.7, and *Ancrene Wisse. A Corrected Edition of the Text in Cambridge, Corpus Christi, MS 402, with Variants from other Manuscripts*, vol.II (2006), xiii-xvi.

The *Ancrene Wisse* (meaning 'a rule or guide for female recluses') is considered by numerous critics as one of the finest pieces of prose from the early Middle English period. Its language is elegant and varied, rich in vocabulary and memorable phrases, full of wit and intricate allusions. It is the most cited text from medieval literature in the *Oxford English Dictionary* apart from Chaucer's *Canterbury Tales*, although it cannot pride itself by the same universal renown as Chaucer's masterpiece. It has been regarded by Derek Pearsall, Harvard and York, as the finest piece of prose work in English literature (personal communication).

In her lucid and erudite Textual Introduction to her edition, Bella Millett points out that Ian Doyle had referred to the "exceptionally dynamic character" of the *Ancrene Wisse* as early as 1954 (in his unpublished PhD. thesis). Over the years the EETS editions of the *Ancrene Wisse* have been often discussed and criticized for being too specialized and not intended for general scholarly use or for general readers. This became particularly clear on the background of the existence of the facsimile edition of the Vernon MS.

Bella Millets wrote in her excellent bibliography of the AB texts (Millett 1996, 36) that Dobson "was laying the foundation for a critical edition of *AW* in a series of publications dealing wholly or partly with its textual transmission ... and had reached the beginning of Part 3 before his death in 1984; his edition is currently being completed by Millett and Jack ... for a progress report, and a discussion of the theoretical and practical problems involved in producing a critical edition of a work of this kind." In the Introduction to her *AW* edition, lx, Millett explains her intentions in the following manner:
"In the textual tradition of this kind, the traditional aim of critical editing, the reconstruction of 'a single authorial intention', becomes problematic it is likely that what underlies the text of A is not a single authorial intention but a series of intensions, not all of them necessarily authorial. This edition, therefore, does not offer a 'critical' text of the *Ancrene Wisse* in the traditional sense. Instead, it provides a corrected version of one historical form of the work, the text in

A, removing mechanical errors and misunderstandings and supplying lacunae, but retaining other variations from the original version."

This is a most crucial statement by Millett and it explains why the text presented to the readers may be regarded as a usable, functional and readable text for all kinds of scholarly purposes. There is, however, one important question that does not seem to have been answered fully by Millett. She writes in the same Introduction, xlvl, that "Dobson's editorial principles have been modified, however, to take account both of recent developments in textual theory and of the textual transmissions of the work itself. Although the edited text probably differs very little in practise from the text that Dobson himself would have produced, it is not, as his would have been, a 'critical edition' in the traditional sense; ..."

I am not too sure that a finished edition by Dobson would have differed only "very little in practise" from the present functional edition by Millett. Just like Dobson, she naturally chooses as the base manuscript the MS Corpus Christi College (=A) for the obvious reasons that

1. ... it is "very consistently spelt and in a dialect which is not far removed from the original author"

2. ... "its text is relatively free from error, ... in general it requires very little emendations" and

3. ... "it contains substantial revisions and addition, some not found in any other manuscript, which are probably to be attributed to the original author."

Millett also explains that it is difficult to discuss problems connected with the editing of MS A in the langauage of traditional textual criticism. It is particularly important to analyse the role of the scribe, since classical textual criticism tended to set the 'author' and 'scribe' in binary opposition and to see textual transmission as a degenerative process overusing the term 'scribal error'. Since the whole *Ancrene Wisse* tradition in the Middle English period is filled with changes, revisions and adaptations, it is obvious that Millett's 'variants', 'variant readings' and 'modifications' are the proper concepts to be used here. It should also be observed that Bella Millett has explained thoroughly that the author of the *Ancrene Wisse* was probably a Dominican, not an Augustinian canon as Dobson advocated. See Millett, "The Origins of *Ancrene Wisse*" (1992), 206 ff.

The first scholar to analyse the stemma of the *Ancrene Riwle* in great detail was Eric Dobson in "Affiliations of the Manuscripts of *Ancrene Wisse*", published in the Festschrift for Professor Tolkien on the occasion of his seventieth birthday in 1962. Yoko Wada in her "Temptations from *Ancrene Wisse*" provides an "extended stemma," in which she illustrates Dobson's views of the influence of the revised text from a lost copy, being a parallel to A, on V, L and P.

As Wada rightly observes (p. 82), "No proper assessment of Dobson's textual history or of his extraordinary comprehension and precise account of the early history of *Ancrene Wisse* can be undertaken, however, until these have been studied in the cold light of variorum texts of those parts of the work which can be so treated." This turns out to be the case and Millett presents a new modified version of Dobson's stemma suggested by the full collation of the texts, indicating that all the manuscripts are descended from a single archetype, probably not the same as the author's holograph. There are a number of interesting and relevant modifications, for example, those regarding G, N and V. Millett is able to postulate a GNV group with NV as a sub-group.

In the course of the latter half of the 20th century, *Ancrene Wisse* studies were characterized by a large scholarly output, due to a great number of highly interesting unsolved problems conncected with authorship, provenance, sources, stemmatic relations, vocabulary, style, monastic tradition, audience, etc. Towards the end of the twentieth century many new research areas came into focus, such as feministic readings of several AB texts. This is made clear by Bella Millett's comprehensive annotated bibliography published in 1996 with the assistance of George B. Jack and Yoko Wada. This excellent bibliography is characterized by useful summaries as well as critical comments that may be extremely valuable to anybody who wants an overview of a difficult research area, about which a great deal has been written.

Additional bibliographic material is also provided by Roger Dahood in his article "The Current State of *Ancrene Wisse* Group Studies" in *Medieval English Studies Newsletter,* No. 36 (1997), 6-14, and by Robert Hasenfratz in *Ancrene Wisse*, 38-54. An excellent example of how clearly AB research has moved forward at the beginning of the new millennium, can be found in Yoko Wada's *A Compendium to Ancrene Wisse* (2002). Particularly the article by Richard Dance, called "The AB Language: the Recluse, the Gossip and the Language Historian" (57-82), provides new information on a number of issues connected with the AB language.

Besides Millett's edition there is one more major work which has contributed considerably to forwarding research on the AB language. Richard Dance published his impressive study of *Words Derived from Old Norse in Early Middle English* (2003), which clarifies the problem why there are so many Scandinavian words in many texts which seem to have been written in areas outside the original Scandinavian settlement. Dance concentrates his studies of Scandinavian words to the most important South West-Midland texts, *Ancrene Wisse*, The Katherine Group, The *Wohunge* Group, Layamons *Brut*, The "Lambeth Homilies", The "Worcester Fragments" and the glosses of the "Tremulous Worcester Hand". There is an impressive analysis of the phonology, morphology, word-formation, distribution, semantics and style of all these texts, including a most interesting section on etymological and textual difficulties. One overall question, which is discussed in detail by Dance, is the way in which Scandinavian words are used in competition with native synonyms or near-synonyms. This problem has not yet been fully solved, but Dance has certainly laid the foundation for a final solution.

In addition to these important steps forward in AB research, there are many new possibilities regarding textual analysis that have been brought to light with regard to the use of modern electronic techniques. One such innovation has been introduced by a Japanese reseach group headed by Tadao Kubouchi. The Tokyo Medieval Manuscript Reading Group launched in 1996 a project for an "Electronic Corpus of Diplomatic Parallel Manuscript Texts as a Tool for Historical Studies of English." The final version of their parallel *Ancrene Wisse* texts contains in computer-readable text-file form the four English manuscript texts of MSS Corpus, Cleopatra, Nero and Vernon. These parallel texts were edited by Tadao Kubouchi and Keiko Ikegami in two volumes, The *Ancrene Wisse. A Four-Manuscript Parallel Text.* [Vol.I: Preface and Parts 1-4; Vol.II: Parts 5-8 with wordlists].

It is of great interest to observe above that there are so many links between scholars in Japan, The United Kingdom and the Nordic countries, as concerns activities and achievments in *Ancrene Wisse* research. Some of these links emanate from Kikuo Miyabe, who died in 1981 but had started an edition of the Vernon manuscript as early as the end of the 1970s. Mitsunori Imai is one representative of the system of European-Japanese linkage with a connection to *AW* research, namely the Symposium, "Reading the Ancrene Riwle" with proceedings edited by Imai-Watanabe. Some links point forward to further research, namely the recent symposium in 2006 at Kyoto Sangyo University, called "The Linguistic and Literary Context of the *Acrene Wisse* Group" organized by the Tokyo Medieval Manuscript Reading Group. The Proceedings were published in 2007. I should like to confirm the hopeful tone of Tadao Kubouchi's conclusion of his foreword to the proceedings: "We are sure that the project will in the days to come further the textual and linguistic research being carried out in the *Ancrene Wisse* Group and related works not only in Japan but also in Britain, and lead to a new consideration of their cultural context, with concrete published results."

References

Benskin, Michael and Margaret Laing (1981) "Translations and *Mischsprachen* in Middle English manuscripts." *So meny people longages and tonges: philological essays in Scots and mediaeval English presented to Angus McIntosh*. Michael Benskin and M.L. Samuels (eds.) (1981) Edinburgh: 55-106.

Black, Merja Riitta (1999) "AB or Simply A? Reconsidering the Case for a Standard." *Neuphilologische Mitteilungen* 100, 155-74.

Cerquiglini, Bernard (1989) *Éloge de la variante: Histoire critique de la philologie*. Paris: Seuil.

Dahood, Roger. "*Ancrene Wisse*, the Katherine Group and the *Wohunge* Group." *Middle English Prose: A Critical Guide to Major Authors and Genres*. Ed. A.S.G. Edwards. New Brunswick, NJ: Rutgers UP.

Dahood, Roger (1997) "The Current State of *Ancrene Wisse* Group Studies." *Medieval English Studies Newsletter* 36 (June 1997), 6-14.

Dance, Richard (2003) *Words Derived from Old Norse in Early Middle English*. Studies in the Vocabulary of the South-West Midland Texts. Medieval and Renaissance Texts and Studies, 246. Tempe: Arizona Centre for Medieval and Renaissance Studies.

Dobson, E.J. (1962) "The affiliations of the manuscripts of *Ancrene Wisse*." *English and Medieval Studies presented to J.R.R. Tolkien on the Occasion of his Seventieth Birthday*. Norman Davis and C.L. Wrenn (eds.) (1962) London, 128-63.

Dobson, E.J. (1966) "The date and composition of *Ancrene Wisse*." *Proceedings of the British Academy* 52, 181-208.

Dobson, E.J. (1976) *The Origins of Ancrene Wisse*. Oxford: Clarendon Press.

Hasenfratz, Robert (ed.) (2000) *Ancrene Wisse*. Kalamazoo, MI.

Kubouchi, Tadao et al. (eds.) (1997) *Electronic Parallel Diplomatic Manuscript Texts of the Ancrene Wisse, Preface, Parts I & II*. Tokyo: Tokyo Medieval Manuscript Reading Group.

Kubouchi, Tadao, and Keiko Ikegami (eds.) (2003, 2005) The *Ancrene Wisse*: A Four-Manuscript Parallel Text, 2 vols. [vol. I: Preface and Parts 1-4, vol. II: Parts 5-8 with Wordlists], Studies in English Medieval Language and Literature 7, 11. Frankfurt am Main: Peter Lang.

Laing, Margaret (1993) *Catalogue of Sources for a Linguistic Atlas of Early Medieval English.* Cambridge: D.S.Brewer.

McIntosh, Angus, M.L. Samuels and Michael Benskin (1986) *A Linguistic Atlas of Late Mediaeval English.* 4 vols. Aberdeen: Aberdeen UP.

Millet, Bella, with the assistance of George B. Jack and Yoko Wada (1996) *Ancrene Wisse, The Katherine Group, and the Wooing Group. Annotated Bibliographies of Old and Middle English Literature.* Volume II. Cambridge: D.S.Brewer.

Millett, Bella (1992) "The Origins of *Ancrene Wisse*: New Answers, New Questions." *Medium Aevum* 61, 206-28.

Millett, Bella (1994) "*Mouvance* and the Medieval Author: Re-Editing *Ancrene Wisse.*" *Late-Medieval Religious Texts and their Transmission.* Ed. A.J. Minnis. Cambridge: Brewer, 1994, 9-20.

Miyabe, Kikuo (1979) "The Vernon Version of the *Ancrene Riwle.*" *Poetica* (Tokyo) 7, 80-107.

Miyabe, Kikuo (1982) "The Vernon Version of the *Ancrene Riwle.*" *Poetica* (Tokyo) 13, 1-14.

Morton, James (ed.) (1853) *The Ancren Riwle: A Treatise on the Rules and Duties of Monastic Life, Edited and Translated from a Semi-Saxon MS. of the Thirteenth Century.* Camden Society, first series 57. London.

Shippey, T.A. (1992) *The Road to Middle-Earth.* London: Grafton.

Smith, J.J. (1991) "Tradition and Innovation in South-West-Midland Middle English." *Regionalism in Late Medieval Manuscripts and Texts: Essays celebrating the publication of* A Linguistic Atlas of Late Mediaeval English. Ed. Felicity Riddy. Cambridge: Brewer, 53-65.

Smith, J.J. (1992) "A Linguistic Atlas of Early Middle English: tradition and typology." *History of Englishes: New Methods and Interpretations in Historical Linguistics.* Eds. Matti Rissanen et al. Topics in English Linguistics 10. Berlin: Mouton, 582-91.

Tolkien, J.R.R. (1929) "*Ancrene Wisse* and *Hali Meidhad.*" *Essays and Studies* 14, 104-26.

Wada, Yoko (ed.) (1994) *Temptations from Ancrene Wisse.* Vol. I. Kansai University Institute of Oriental and Occidental Studies. Sources and Materials Series 18. Osaka: Kansai UP, 1994. Cambridge: D.S. Brewer.

Wada, Yoko (ed.) (2003) *A Companion to Ancrene Wisse.* Cambridge: D.S. Brewer.

Zettersten, Arne (1965) *Studies in the Dialect and Vocabulary of the Ancrene Riwle.* Copenhagen & Lund: Ejnar Munksgaard & G.W.K. Gleerup.

Zettersten, Arne (1997) "Editing the *Ancrene Riwle* for the Early English Text Society: Past experienc and future prospects." *Studies in Medieval English Language and Literature.* 12, 1-28.

Zettersten, Arne (2006) "The AB Language Lives." *The Lord of the Rings 1954-2004. Scholarship in Honor of Richard E. Blackwelder*, edited by Wayne G. Hammond and Christina Scull. Milwaukee, Wisconsin: Marquette University, 13-24.

The Verb *Pray* in Different Letters of the Paston Family with Special Reference to its Pragmatic Use[1]

Yoko Iyeiri

1 Introduction

Under 8a-d of *pray* in *The Oxford English Dictionary* are listed examples where the same verb is used parenthetically:

(1) Maister yong-man, you *I praie you*, which is the waie to Maister Iewes? (1596 Shakes. *Merch. V.* ii. ii. 35)[2]

(2) *Pray thee* let me know it.   (1590 Marlowe *Edw.* II, ii. ii)

(3) *Pray* set it down, and rest you.   (1610 Shakes. *Temp.* iii. i. 18)

I praie you in (1) functions almost as a marker to introduce an interrogative sentence. Likewise, *pray* in (2) and (3) is used to introduce imperative sentences. *Pray* in these examples has a pragmatic function at the discourse level. When borrowed from French, however, it was used with the full lexical meanings of 'to beseech' and 'to ask' (*OED*, s.v. *pray*). It gradually developed pragmatic uses as illustrated by (1)-(3) in the history of English, and in this process experienced a gradual reduction of its physical forms. *Pray* in (3) is more reduced in form than *pray thee* in (2), which in turn is more reduced in form than *I praie you* in (1). In addition, Early Modern English records further reduced forms like *I prithee* and *prithee*, where the verb and its object are contracted (see Traugott and Dasher 2002: 254).

Since relevant citations in *The Oxford English Dictionary* are from the sixteenth century or later periods, the development of the pragmatic use of *pray* is often considered to be a feature of the Modern English period. Ukaji (1978: 131-143) and Akimoto (2000), however, suggest that later Middle English needs to be further studied in relation to this verb. Ukaji (1978: 135-136) gives a few Middle English examples of the pragmatic use of *pray*, stating that they are earlier than *The Oxford English Dictionary* citations. Akimoto (2000) also provides some relevant examples from late Middle English texts. Furthermore, a recent investigation by Hirayama (2001) also demonstrates that the development of the pragmatic use of *pray* is already visible in late Middle English.

The central concern of the present paper is to investigate the initial stage of the development of this use of *pray*, paying special attention to *The Paston Letters* in the fifteenth century. Although Akimoto (2000) and Hirayama (2001) have analysed the same text, their studies need to be widened. Akimoto (2000) explores the examples of *pray* with first person subjects only, perhaps because they are the ones related to the development of its pragmatic use. The development of *pray* with first person subjects will, however, be elucidated only when contrasted with *pray* with other types of subjects. Hirayama (2001) investigates all types of *pray*, but unfortunately, his analysis does not highlight sufficiently the distinction between first person and other subjects,[3] which is necesssary for the purpose of clarifying the development of its pragmatic use.

In the following discussion, I will investigate the family members who provide more than ten examples of *pray*: William I (letters and papers, 1425-1444), Agnes (letters and papers, 1440-1479), John I (letters and papers, 1444-1465), William II (letters and papers, 1452-1496), Clement (letters, 1461-1466), Margaret (letters and papers, 1441-1482), John II (letters and papers, 1461-1479), John III (letters and papers, 1461-1485), and Edmond II (letters and papers, 1471-1492). The examples under consideration are essentially those followed by complements such as *that*-clauses and infinitives. *Pray* followed by imperatives as illustrated by (2) and (3) above is also considered.[4]

2 First person subjects in the present tense

To observe the historical development of the pragmatic use of *pray*, it is necessary to delve into the relationship between the person of the subject and the tense of the verb, since its function can be pragmatic when it occurs with the first person subject and in the present tense. See Table 1, which reveals that many instances of *pray* already satisfy this condition:

Table 1. The subject and the tense of *pray* in *The Paston Letters*

Subjects	First person		Others	
Tense	Present tense	Others[5]	Present tense	Others
William I	8	3	0	0
Agnes	9	1	3	3
John I	28	2	1	5
William II	20	4	2	1
Clement	14	1	0	0
Margaret	138	25	24	11
John II	128	8	4	4
John III	142	11	8	5
Edmond II	19	1	2	0
Totals	506	56	44	29

As many as 506 examples (79.7%) of the total of 635 (506 + 56 + 44 + 29) are found with the first person subject and in the present tense,[6] as in:

(4) *I pray* you send me word yf ye haue it. (Margaret Paston, 303/41-42)[7]

It is feasible that the use of *pray* was increasingly restricted to this environment already in later Middle English. I have at hand the proportions of *pray* used with the first person subject and in the present tense in *The Canterbury*

Tales (64.3%) and in *Reynard the Fox* (51.2%). Thus, *pray* is more likely to appear in the marked environment in *The Paston Letters* than in *The Canterbury Tales* and *Reynard the Fox*, although all three texts go back to the later Middle English period.[8]

The situation differs to a certain extent, however, depending upon the author of the letters as Figure 1 shows. Here, I have calculated the proportions of the first column in Table 1 (i.e. first person subject and present tense) to the entire sample of *pray* (i.e. the totals of the four columns) for each member of the Paston family:

Figure 1. Proportions of *pray* used with the first person subject and in the present tense (%)

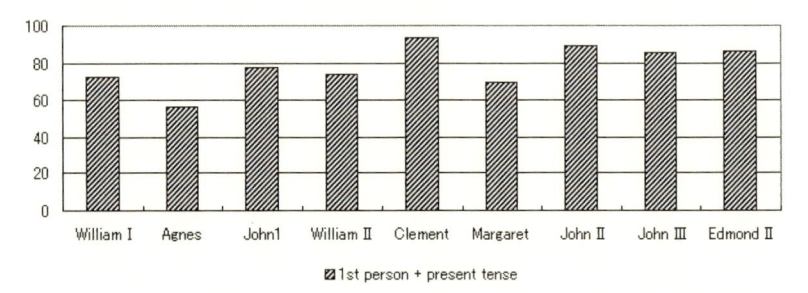

☒ 1st person + present tense

This graph displays to what extent the use of *pray* is restricted to the particular environment of the first person subject and the present tense. A close look at this graph reveals that the two female authors, i.e. Agnes and Margaret, present a slightly lower proportion than the other members of the family, probably illustrating their relatively conservative linguistic behaviours.[9] Supposing that the use of *pray* in letters was quite formulaic by this time,[10] female authors were probably slower in adopting formulas of this kind in their letters.

In the case of Margaret, however, there is a marked contrast between her earlier letters (Nos. 188-230) and later ones (Nos. 124-187), which the table below evinces:

Table 2. The subject and the tense of *pray* in Margaret's letters

Subjects	Firstst person		Others	
Tense	Present tense	Others	Present tense	Others
Letters 124-187	89	24	23	11
Letters 188-230	49	1	1	0

As Table 2 indicates, the use of *pray* with the first person subject and in the present tense is quite firmly established in her later letters, while this is not the case in her earlier ones. I am not certain as to whether this contrast is ascribable to the amanuenses involved in drafting her letters, but it is clear at least that her later letters display a further developed stage of *pray*. In other words, the conservative feature of Margaret as shown in Figure 1 is largely attributed to her earlier days.

3 Syntactic developments

The development of the pragmatic use of *pray* is a process by which it ceases to be the matrix verb. In other words, the same verb gradually undergoes the decline of *that*-clauses in its development and the original subordinate clause becomes the main clause. The present section intends to investigate this syntactic process. Here, the table provided by Akimoto (2000: 70-71), which is given below as Table 3, is noteworthy. He investigates how frequently imperatives, *that*-clauses, and *to*-infinitives are encountered after *I pray you/thee* in three Middle English texts from the fifteenth century:

Table 3. Frequencies of complements found with *I pray you/thee* in the fifteenth century

	Paston Letters	Margery Kempe	Thomas Malory
imperative	59	38	14
þat-clauses	56	1	3
to-infinitive	9	2	4

(From Akimoto 2000: 70)

Indeed, a dramatic decrease of *that*-clauses (*þat*-clauses in the table) takes place after *The Paston Letters* in this table. Now the question arises as to whether the decline of *that*-clauses is observed only after *The Paston Letters* or within. The following discussion gives further detailed analyses of different members of the Paston family to elucidate this point.

In Table 4 below, I have given the raw frequencies of various complement patterns of *pray* with the first person subject in the present tense. In the interest of consistency throughout the present paper, I have included here not only *I pray you/thee* (as investigated by Akimoto 2000) but also other forms like *I pray* (i.e. *I pray* without the object), *I pray God*, and *we pray you*. Incidentally, the category of "imperatives or bare infinitives" in the table includes examples like the following:

(5) And jn cas I come not hom within thre wekis, I pray yow *come* to me; ... (John Paston I, 135/1)

Come in this example is most likely imperative, but the bare infinitive interpretation cannot be eliminated. Mustanoja's (1960: 533) comment that "this verb [i.e. *pray*] usually requires *to*, but plain infinitive may also occur" in Middle English suggests that he takes the bare infinitive interpretation. By contrast, Akimoto (2000: 71), perhaps rightly, classifies examples like (5) under the category of "imperatives", since *pray* is most dominantly followed by imperatives once its pragmatic use is fully established.[11] I find it unnecessary at least at this stage, however, to clarify this matter, since the important point is that the decline of *that*-clauses leads to the increasing use of imperatives or complements which may be interpreted as imperatives, i.e. bare infinitives, when the subject of *pray* is the first person. *To*-infinitives or *for to*-infinitives are also available, but this is a separate issue, which I will discuss later.

Table 4. Complements after *pray* with the first person subject in the present tense

	that-clauses(incl. *that* unexpressed)	imperatives or bare infinitives	*to*-infinitives or *for to*-infinitives
William I	3	1	4
Agnes	3	5	1
John I	5	22	1
William II	4	14	2
Clement	0	14	0
Margaret	59	72	7
John II	13	99	16
John III	19	115	8
Edmond II	6	11	2
Totals	112	353	41

Table 4 shows that the extent to which the pragmatic use of *pray* has developed seems to differ depending upon the member of the family to a significant extent, which suggests that the development of the verb is in progress within the text. Members like John II and John III reveal a notable loss of *that*-clauses. By contrast, Margaret seems to retain the use of *that*-clauses to a large extent for her generation. To have a clearer view of the differences among the family members, I have calculated the proportions of "imperatives or bare infinitives" to the totals for each author and obtained the data as displayed in Figure 2:

Figure 2. The proportions of "imperatives or bare infinitives" in the case of the first person subject and the present tense (%)

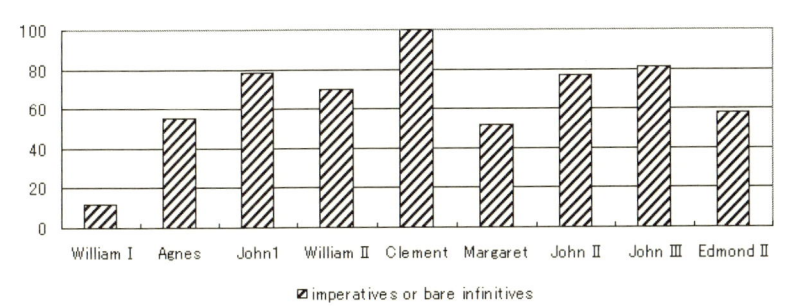

This graph needs to be handled carefully in two respects. First of all, some members present only a limited number of relevant examples, making the normalized statistical figures unstable. Secondly, examples of *to*-infinitives and *for to*-infinitives are involved, though not abundantly, in the totals. As I will discuss later, they are examples of a separate development. Still, Figure 2 presents the overall picture of the development of the pragmatic use of *pray* in *The Paston Letters*. William I, who belongs to the oldest generation and who is the only one born in the fourteenth century, does not really seem to present the pragmatic use of *pray*. The examples of "imperatives or bare infinitives" themselves are scarcely observed in his letters. Also fairly conservative are Agnes, Margaret, and perhaps Edmond II. As in the case of section 2 above, a sociolinguistic explanation may be possible for the two female authors, although Agnes's case may be related to the relatively early dates of her letters.

As for Margaret's letters, different tendencies are again observed depending upon when they were written. See Table 5, which exhibits the notable contrast between her earlier letters (Nos. 124-187) and her later ones (Nos. 188-230):

Table 5. Complements after *pray* with the first person subject in the present tense in Margaret's letters

	that-clauses (incl. *that* unexpressed)	imperatives or bare infinitives	*to*-infinitives or *for to*-infinitives
Letters 124-187	48	37	4
Letters 188-230	11	35	3

The extensive retention of *that*-clauses in Margaret's letters as shown in Figure 2 clearly reflects the feature of her earlier letters, which include more frequent use of *pray* than her later ones. The proportion of "imperatives or bare infinitives" to the total in her earlier letters is 41.6% while in her later ones it is 71.4%. Thus, her later letters reach the level of William II.

As the final point in the syntactic developments of *pray*, I would like to refer to the use of *to*-infinitives (and *for to*-infinitives), which has so far been ignored. In theory, the recession of *that*-clauses does not lead only to the development of the "imperatives or bare infinitives", but it can also lead to the expanded use of *to*-infinitives and/or *for to*-infinitives. This is, in my view, a different development from the development of the pragmatic use of *pray*, however, since the use of *to*-infinitives and/or *for to*-infinitives is a feature particularly well observed outside the context of the first person subject in the present tense. Table 6 gives the raw frequencies of different complement types of *pray* with the first person subject but not in the present tense, and Table 7 shows the same frequencies of second and third person subjects.

Table 6. Complements after *pray* with first person subjects (not in the present tense)

	that-clauses (incl. *that* unexpressed)	imperatives or bare infinitives	*to*-infinitives or *for to*-infinitives
William I	1	0	2
Agnes	0	0	1
John I	2	0	0
William II	0	0	4
Clement	0	0	1
Margaret	6	0	19
John II	3	0	5
John III	1	0	10
Edmond II	1	0	0
Totals	14	0	42

Table 7. Complements after *pray* with second and third person subjects (present tense as well as others)

	that-clauses (incl. *that* unexpressed)	imperatives or bare infinitives	*to*-infinitives or *for to*-infinitives
William I	0	0	0
Agnes	4	0	2
John I	1	0	5
William II	0	0	3
Clement	0	0	0
Margaret	27	0	8
John II	2	1	5
John III	5	0	8
Edmond II	1	0	1
Totals	40	1	32

Some illustrative examples are:

(6) And my moder prayd hym *for to gett* for hyr sum good mariage yf he knewe any. (Margaret Paston, 287/6-7)

(7) and than he answereth and prayeth me no more *to speke* of that mater ... (William Paston II, 161/56-57)

(8) She preyid yow *to get* hym an asygnement for it to som maner in Norffolk or in Lothynglond. (John Paston III, 576/41-43)

The most interesting point in Tables 6 and 7 is that "imperatives or bare infinitives" are extremely limited. The sole instance under this category runs as follows:

(9) and that ye preye God *make* an ende betwen vs, ...
                                                    (John Paston II, 414/56)[12]

The restricted occurrence of this type in Tables 6 and 7 strongly discourages the interpretation that *to*-infinitives and *for to*-infinitives are simple alternatives to what may be interpreted as bare infinitives. Thus, "imperatives or bare infinitives" are likely to be imperatives rather than bare infinitives, since different types of infinitives often alternated in Middle English.[13] All in all, I would surmise that the occurrences of *to*-infinitives or *for to*-infinitives in the above tables are most feasibly related to the general increase of non-finite forms such as infinitives and gerunds in place of *that*-clauses, which was taking place from later Middle English to early Modern English. Iyeiri (2003), for example, discusses the decline of *that*-clauses after the verb *forbid* and the subsequent development of *to*-infinitives in their place. Manabe (1979: 4-5) argues that this development is visible with a number of verbs from later Middle English onwards. *Pray* could simply be one of them. Thus, this is a separate development from the development of the pragmatic use of *pray*.

4 Intervening elements

Finally, I would like to discusse examples like (10), where there are intervening elements other than the object between *pray* and its complement:

(10) Therfor I pray you *wyth all myn herth* þat ye wyll don yowre part to haue hys godelordschep and his love jn ese of all the materis that ye haue to don, and jn esyng of myn hert also.
(Margaret Paston, 236/29-32)

In this example, the phrase *wyth all myn herth* intervenes between *I pray you* and the clause introduced by *that*. Examples like this are perhaps relevant in the context of what Rohdenburg (1996: 151) calls the Complexity Principle, which runs as follows:

> *Complexity Principle*: In the case of more or less explicit grammatical options, the more explicit one(s) will tend to be favoured in cognitively more complex environments.

Rohdenburg (1996: 166-168) demonstrates that *that*-clauses are more explicit and therefore more likely to be employed than non-finite forms like infinitives when complexities like the existence of intervening elements are involved.

The present investigation shows that the Complexity Principle is applicable to the development of *pray* in *The Paston Letters*. The existence of intervening elements indeed seems to delay the decline of *that*-clauses, and as a consequence to delay the development of the pragmatic use of *pray* in the case of the first person subject or the development of *to*-infinitives or *for to*-infinitives in all cases. The table below displays the proportions of *that*-clauses to the totals of the examples of *pray*, in the entire sample and in examples with intervening elements:

Table 8. The proportions of *that*-clauses after *pray* in *The Paston Letters*

	The entire sample	With intervening elements
Pray with first person subjects	126/562 (22.4%)	34/ 71 (47.9%)
Pray with other subjects	40/ 73 (54.8%)	13/ 16 (81.3%)

Table 8 makes it evident that the presence of intervening elements affects the choice of complements. *The Paston Letters* gives a total of 71 instances of *pray* with the first person subject and with intervening elements, of which 34 (47.9%) are followed by *that*-clauses. The proportion here is about twice as large as the corresponding proportion (22.4%) of the entire sample. The same applies to the other subjects, although examples with intervening elements are not as copious here. *The Paston Letters* provides a total of sixteen, of which twelve are followed by *that*-clauses and one by a clause with elliptical *that*. This gives the proportion of 81.3%, which is much larger than the 54.8% of the entire sample. Needless to say, elliptical *that* is less explicit than *that* expressed. Even after deducting this single example, however, *The Paston Letters* still gives the ratio of 75.0%, which is much larger than 54.8%.

5 Conclusion

The present paper has thus far discussed the development of the verb *pray* in *The Paston Letters*, paying particular attention to its pragmatic use. In this text, the use of the verb is increasingly restricted to the environment where its function can be pragmatic: with the first person subject and in the present tense. This tendency is observed in all the letters I have investigated, although to a slightly lesser extent in the letters of Agnes and Margaret. In the case of Margaret, however, there is a notable contrast between her earlier and later letters.

Syntactically, the development of the pragmatic use of *pray* can be observed in the change of the types of complements that follow the verb. *That*-clauses after *pray* gradually recede and are increasingly replaced by imperatives or complements which may be interpreted as imperatives, i.e. bare infinitives, in the case of the first person subject in the present tense. Although this development progresses to a great extent throughout *The Paston Letters* in general, there are again discrepancies depending upon the author. William I, who is the oldest and the only member born in the fourteenth century, is distinctively conservative, in that he gives only a single instance under the category of "imperatives or bare infinitives". Also fairly conservative are Agnes, Margaret, and Edmond II, although in the case of Margaret there is a gap of usage between her earlier and later letters.

I have further discussed some other features of *pray*, which are not necessarily related to the development of its pragmatic use. Namely, the decline of *that*-clauses can also lead to the development of *to*-infinitives or *for to*-infinitives. The above discussion has revealed that this development is particularly observed outside the context of the first person subject in the present tense and that it is a different path from the development of the pragmatic use of *pray*.

Finally, the above discussion dealt with Rohdenburg's Complexity Principle and investigated how the existence of intervening elements after *pray* can affect the choice of its complements. *The Paston Letters* clearly shows that *that*-clauses, which are supposed to be more explicit than other types of complements, are favoured when some intervening elements are existent. In other words, the presence of intervening elements can delay the decline of *that*-clauses, and, as a result, delay the development of the pragmatic use of *pray* when the subject is the first person, and the development of *to*-infinitives or *for to*-infinitives in all cases.

Notes

1 This research was in part supported by Japan Society for the Promotion of Science Grant-in-Aid for Scientific Research (No. 18652046). An earlier version of this paper was published in Japanese as Iyeiri (2007).
2 Throughout the present paper, the italics in the citations are mine.
3 This is most probably due to the emphasis he placed upon the overall description of the behaviour of *pray*.
4 Examples followed by interrogatives are not available in *The Paston Letters*.
5 Included here are tenseless forms like infinitival and gerundial uses of *pray* as well

as the preterite tense forms. Also, classified here are examples of *pray* preceded by modal auxiliaries (e.g. *I shall pray* ...).

6   Hirayama (2001: 31) states that "The number of the examples [of *pray*] with the first person subject is the largest". Unfortunately, however, he mixes all examples when he analyses the tense of the verb, making the relationship between the subject and the tense invisible.

7   Examples from *The Paston Letters* are cited from Davis (1971).

8   That this tendency is further accelerated by the time of early Modern English is shown by Busse (2002: 205), according to whom the corresponding proportion in Shakespeare's plays is greater than 90 %.

9   Nevalainen and Raumolin-Brunberg (2003) investigate various linguistic developments in the Tudor and Stuart periods and point out that some developments were led by men at the initial stages. The spread of the auxiliary *do* into negative statements was, for example, promoted by men in the sixteenth century according to these authors (p. 126).

10 Hirayama (2001: 36-38) examines the verbs that occur in the complements of *pray* and finds that some particular verbs are repeatedly used. He collects 540 relevant examples of *pray* in the letters of John I, Margaret, John II, and John III, of which 111 display the verb *send* in their complements. Other frequent verbs include: *let, be, remember, take, recommend, weet, vouchsafe, do*, and *make*.

11 Akimoto (2000: 71) refers to another type of ambiguity. He states that *I pray you send* ... may be interpreted as *I pray [you send* ... *]* as well as *I pray you [send* ... *]*. In my view, however, this is not a matter of dispute. The subjective form *ye* and the objective form *you* are usually distinguished in *The Paston Letters*. Thus, the subjective interpretation of *you* is unlikely.

12 This may or may not be an example where *God* is the subject of the verb *make* and where the conjunction *that* is elliptical.

13 Sawada (1997), for instance, discusses how bare infinitives and *(for) to*-infinitives alternated after the causative verb *make* in *Troilus and Criseyde*. Discussions of this kind are abundant.

References

Akimoto, M. (2000) "The Grammaticalization of the Verb *pray*." In Fischer, O. et al. (eds.), *Pathways of Change: Grammaticalization in English*. Amsterdam: John Benjamins, pp. 67-84.

Busse, U. (2002) *Linguistic Variation in the Shakespeare Corpus: Morpho-syntactic Variability of Second Person Pronouns*. Amsterdam: John Benjamins.

Davis, N. (ed.) (1971) *Paston Letters and Papers of the Fifteenth Century*. Part I. Oxford: Clarendon Press.

Hirayama, N. (2001) "The Language of Requests in the *Paston Letters*: The Grammaticalization and Subjectification of X PRAY Y." *Hiroshima Studies in English Language and Literature* 46: 25-43.

Iyeiri, Y. (2003) "'God Forbid!': A Historical Study of the Verb *forbid* in Different Versions of the English Bible." *Journal of English Linguistics* 31: 149-162.

Iyeiri, Y. (2007) "Pasutonke Shokanshu niokeru Doushi *pray* no Youhou nitsuite." (The Verb *pray* in *The Paston Letters*.) In Nakao, Y. et al. (eds.), *Text, Language and Interpretation*. Tokyo: Eihosha, pp. 371-380.

Manabe, K. (1979) *Syntax and Style in Early English: Finite and Non-finite Clauses c900-1600*. Tokyo: Kaibunsha.

Mustanoja, T. F. (1960) *A Middle English Syntax, Part I: Parts of Speech*. Helsinki: Société Néophilologique.

Nevalainen, T. and H. Raumolin-Brunberg (2003) *Historical Sociolinguistics: Language Change in Tudor and Stuart England*. Harlow: Longman.

Rohdenburg, G. (1996) "Cognitive Complexity and Increased Grammatical Explicitness in English." *Cognitive Linguistics* 7: 149-182.

Sawada, M. (1997) "Causative Verbs in Chaucer." *ERA* 15: 1-16.

Traugott, E. C. and R. B. Dasher (2002) *Regularity in Semantic Change*. Cambridge: Cambridge University Press.

Ukaji, M. (1978) *Imperative Sentences in Early Modern English*. Tokyo: Kaitakusha.

A Historical Approach to Variant Word Forms in English

Akiyuki Jimura

1 Introduction

We frequently encounter two different word forms coexisting in Middle English when we study the English language. In addition to the expected Middle English forms, we find the Old English forms which had not yet died out from contemporary usage. Both old and new word forms are sometimes used in a certain manuscript. A scribe may faithfully record older word forms. Some forms may reflect the distinctive dialects of those scribes who have recorded some works. The occurrence of two different forms in the same text sometimes allows us to assume that an author may have used both these forms for the following two reasons. First, he may have at times used both forms of a word unconsciously. Second, he may have consciously chosen both forms for a poetic effect. For example, as Jimura (2002) indicated, Geoffrey Chaucer used the verb 'lipsed' in the "General Prologue" to *The Canterbury Tales* when he wrote, "Somwhat he lipsed, for his wantownesse, / To make his Englissh sweete upon his tonge;" (264-65). According to the *OED*, the form 'lisp' was used before and after Chaucer's lifetime. It appears that Chaucer may have artfully metathesized the two adjacent sounds, /sp/, in 'lisped' to read 'lipsed', thus capturing the Friar's oral affectation designed to attract women. Although we frequently assume that the metathetic forms occurring in different editions of *The Canterbury Tales* and *Troilus and Criseyde* reflect various scribes' dialectal habits, we might also conclude that metathesis reflects Chaucer's creativity. In some instances, he may have chosen to use metathesis to approximate the speech patterns of his characters and narrators. However, Present-day English has a uniform pattern of word forms (except for spellings such as "centre" and "center"), while the coexisting two forms are used flexibly and elaborately in Middle English.

This paper investigates the process of producing a uniform pattern of word forms, dealing with the usages such as "maked" or "made," "ax" or "ask," and "hw-" or "wh-." We are going to discuss the changes of word forms in *Ancrene Wisse*, Chaucer, Langland, and Gower. (The abbreviations of Chaucer's works are from L. Y. Baird-Lange and H. Schnuttgen eds. (1988).)

2 maked or made

First, the word forms in the 13th and 14th century English will be discussed, consulting the four manuscripts of *Ancrene Wisse* in Kubouchi and Ikegami (2003 and 2005). It is obvious that only the Vernon Manuscript shows the medial letter loss.

> A 13v20, V374ra41
> A & *makede* wei to uuel lust . & com þe dede þrefter ...
> C & *makede* wei to uuel lust & / com to dede þer_efter ...
> N & *makede* wei to vuel lust . & / com þe deað þer_efter ...
> V & *made* wei to euel lust . and com þe dede / þerafter ...

The other instances are as follows: A 26v22, V376va08; A 45r09, V379va48; A 59r26, V382rb18; M 220; A 61r03, V382va28; A 82v14, V386rb11; A 82v17, V386rb14; A 82v24, V386rb21.

Now let us turn to the latter half of the fourteenth century English, investigating the instances of Langland, Gower, and Chaucer.

In Langland's *Piers Plowman*, the A, B, and C texts keep the older form: "(y)maked" respectively.

A.2.55 And vnfolde þe feffement þat fals haþ *ymakid*
B.2.73 And vnfoldeþ þe feffement that Fals hath *ymaked*
C.2.75 And vnfoldeth the feffament þat fals hath *ymaked*

We find only one instance of "maked" (5. 680) in Gower's *Confessio Amantis*. This older form rhymes with "naked" in the previous line. The following quotation is from Macaulay (1900).

He fond hem bothe tuo abedde
Al warm, echon with other naked.
And he with craft al redy *maked*
Of stronge chenes hath hem bounde, (5. 678-81)

Then we would like to see Chaucer's English. As some examples of the medial letter loss, the following pairs of forms "maked(e) - made; maked - maad" have been investigated in Table 1. The three forms are illustrated in the quotations following the table.

Table 1. Frequency of "made" and Its Related Words

	CT	BD	HF	Anel	PF	Bo	TC	LGW	ShT	ASTR	Rom
maad	44	0	0	0	0	1	4	3	1	0	17
maade	2	0	0	0	0	0	0	1	0	0	0
made	125	12	13	4	3	5	46	29	10	1	38
maden	9	0	1	0	2	0	1	2	0	0	2
madest	3	0	2	0	1	1	0	2	0	0	0
maked	37	1	1	0	0	23	2	8	1	0	1
makeden	0	0	0	0	0	0	1	0	0	0	0
makedest	0	0	0	0	0	1	0	0	0	0	0
makid	0	0	0	0	0	18	0	0	0	0	2
makyd	0	0	0	0	0	1	0	0	0	0	0

e.g.

> maad: But er that he hadde maad al his array (MilT 3630)
> made: On which he made a-nyghtes melodie (MilT 3214)
> maked: The joye that is maked in the place (KnT 1873)

84 of the total occurrences (125) of "made" precede words beginning with a vowel. 23 of the total occurrences (74) of "maked" and 18 of the total occurrences (20) of "makid" are found in *Boece*. (*Boece* seems not to prefer the form "made" and its related forms.) The word form "maked" might be used, especially when two syllables were necessary in the verse.

Here we have checked the frequency of the different forms in *The Canterbury Tales*: the first shows the word found in Blake's text (BL), the second in Benson's text (BN), and the third in Robinson's text (RB). I should note here that Blake bases his edition on the Hengwrt MS, while Robinson and Benson base theirs on the Ellesmere MS. The number in the round brackets shows the frequency. The first line shows that BL has the medial letter loss, while BN and RB do not. The second line shows that BN and RB have the medial letter loss, while BL does not. The third line shows the other instances.

> maad : make : make (1); maad : maked : maked (1); made : maked : maked (1);
> maked : maad : maad (1) ; maked : made : made (1);
> made : make : made (3); ymaked : ymaad : ymaked (1)

In this way, it would not be so easy to generalize the characteristics of the medial letter loss in Chaucer's several edited texts of *The Canterbury Tales*.

3 ax or ask

While it is a well-known fact that both word forms "ascian" and "acsian" coexisted in Old English, it would be difficult to say that Present-day English "ask" directly comes from the Old English form "ascian," but it would be better to say that Chaucer's use of "ask" is closely connected with Present-day English. In *Ancrene Wisse*, we find the word form "easke" in the three manuscripts in the thirteenth century, while "ask" is used in the Vernon Manuscript. Now we would like to investigate the word forms in Langland, Gower, and Chaucer.

While "ask" is the unmarked form in Langland's *Piers Plowman*, the other forms are used in the following texts: axe (1), axen (2), axide (2) in the A text, axe (2), axed (1), yasked (1) in the B text, and axen (1) in the C text. The A text shows the characteristics of Southern English. Two examples in the B text are used in the rhyming position. The following shows that "axide" is used only in the A text.

A.11.112   And *axide* hire þe heiȝe wey where clergie [dwell]ide,
B.10.160   And *asked* hire þe heighe wey where Clergie dwelte,
C.11.102   And *asked* here þe hey way whare clergie dwelte,

In Gower's *Confessio Amantis*, we find the following examples: aske (1), asken (1), asketh (5), askinge (1): axe (39, including two rhyme words), axed (10, including three rhyme words), axede (2), axen (8), axende (1), axeth (75, including three rhyme words), axinge (9, including two rhyme words), axinges (2, as rhyme words). While all "ask-" forms are used in the medial position of the line, the "ax-" forms are preferred in the rhyming position.

Now let us turn to some general characteristics of metathesis in Chaucer's English and consider the following pairs of words: 'ax' vs.'ask' in Benson's text. According to the *OED*, the forms 'ax' and 'ask' are mixed in fourteenth-century English. While the ratio of frequency between 'ax' (including its derivatives and 'ask' (including its derivatives) in all of Chaucer's works, as in Tables 2 & 3, is 137 to 56, that in *The Canterbury Tales* is 57 to 22. It should be noted that the following word forms: "axest," "axinge," and "axyng(e)" are excluded in Table 2. The frequency of 'ax' and 'ask' in Blake's text is shown under Tables 2 & 3 (Blake, et al. eds.: 1994). When we check the variants of 'ax' and 'ask' respectively, we discover the following data: 'axe' to 'aske' is

28 to 8, 'axed' to 'asked' is 9 to 5, 'axen' to 'asken' is 5 to 4, and 'axeth' to 'asketh' is 10 to 5. Compared with the first type, the latter form, which comes to Present-day English, is not so marked but commonly used in Chaucer's works.

Table 2. Frequency of "ax(e)" or "axen" and Its Derivatives

	CT	BD	HF	Anel	PF	Bo	TC	LGW	ShT	ASTR	Rom
axe	28	3	0	1	1	8	5	2	1	0	2
axed	9	1	1	0	0	2	5	0	1	0	0
axen	6	0	0	0	0	3	7	1	0	0	0
axeth	10	0	0	0	0	4	2	6	2	0	2

Cf. Blake's *The Canterbury Tales*: axe (27); axed (10); axen (7); axeth (11); axeþ (1)

Table 3. Frequency of "ask(e)" or "asken" and Its Derivatives

	CT	BD	HF	Anel	PF	Bo	TC	LGW	ShT	ASTR	Rom
aske	8	1	0	0	0	1	0	1	0	0	12
asked	5	1	0	0	0	0	1	0	0	0	1
asken	4	0	0	0	0	0	1	0	0	0	2
asketh	5	0	0	0	0	1	1	1	0	0	1

Cf. Blake's *The Canterbury Tales*: aske (4); asked (4); asken (2); asketh (2)

As can be seen from the above tables, the Present-day English form 'ask' is more often used in the later works such as *The Canterbury Tales* than in Chaucer's earlier works. Both the Old English and the Present-day English forms are used in the same work, although the latter new forms appear less often than the older forms.

Next, let us turn to the metathetic forms occurring in different editions of *The Canterbury Tales*, *Troilus and Criseyde*, and Dream Poetry, with special attention to the different word forms: "ax" and "ask." The data are based on our book of textual comparison (A. Jimura, Y. Nakao, and M. Matsuo, eds.: 1995, 1999, 2001). The order of word forms in the quotations follows the edition in the round brackets after the title of Chaucer's works. The title of each tale of *The Canterbury Tales* is shown after the number of the frequency.

We have not found any differences between BN and RB as far as the word forms in *The Canterbury Tales* (BL, BN, RB) are concerned. First, there are some instances of *ask* (BL) and *axe* (BN and RB).

> aske axe axe (2): ClT 326, ClT 348;
> asken axen axen (1): ClT 696;
> asketh axeth axeth (1): ClP 25.

It should be noted that this textual difference is seen only in "The Clerk's Prologue and Tale."

Then, we have the opposite word forms, i.e. the instances of "ax-" forms (BL) and "ask-" forms (BN and RB).

> axe aske aske (4): KnT 2422 : KnT 2420, MilT 3551:MilT 3557, MLT 102:MLP 102, Mel 1156
> axed asked asked (2): MilT 3189:MilT3195, MilT 3191:MilT 3197
> axen aske aske (1) Mel 1060
> axen asken asken (3) MLT 101:MLP101, MLT 470, Mel 1091
> axeth asketh asketh (3) KnT 2777, MilT 3539:MilT3545, MLT 878
> axeþ asketh asketh (1) Mel 1083

This textual difference is found in "The Knight's Tale," "The Miller's Tale," "The Man of Law's Tale," and "The Tale of Melibee." The older forms such as "axe" are often used and kept in Blake's text, when comparing the three texts.

We find a following example showing textual difference in *Troilus and Criseyde*(BN, RB, Root Edition(RT), Windeatt Edition(WN)). As for 'asken' and 'axen', we have the following data: axe (4), axed (5), axen (7), axes (1), axeth (2); asked (1), asken (BN, RB, WN) - axen (RT) (1), asketh (1). Except for one instance, almost all of the forms are identical in the four editions, unlike the examples in *The Canterbury Tales*. In short, RT has an older word form.

In Chaucer's dream poetry, there are three instances showing textual difference in *The Parliament of Fowls* (BN, RB, Brewer Edition (BR), Havely

Edition (HV), where BN, RB, and BR have OE forms, HV has a newer word form leading to Present-day English: axe axe axe aske (1) (648); axede axede axede asked (1) (50); axede axede axsede asked (1) (579).

To sum up, we can see that Chaucer used at least two forms of diction in *The Canterbury Tales* and in *Troilus and Criseyde*. In addition to the expected Middle English forms, he used the Old English forms which had not yet died out from his contemporary usage. Furthermore, he used newer forms which are now considered standard in Present-day English. The fact that different editions are based upon particular manuscripts accounts for the textual differences; we can also assume that different manuscripts reflect the distinctive dialects of those scribes who recorded Chaucer's poetry. It should be noted here that there are older forms found in Gower and Chaucer.

4 "hw-" forms or "wh-" forms

When comparing the four manuscripts of *Ancrene Wisse*, we find the word form such as "whom" corresponding to Present-day English in V, while "hw-" forms such as "hwam" are preferred in A, C, and N. Of course, Chaucer used "wh-" forms. According to the *OED*, "hw-" forms had been used until the beginning of the 13th century, while "wh-" forms had taken the place of the older word forms. Here is an instance from *Ancrene Wisse*.

>   A11v17, V37vb04
>   A ...   wið_ute *hwam* we ne mahen ne wel don ne
>   C ...   wið_vte *hwam* / ʒene maʒe wel don ne
>   N ...   / wið_uten *hwam* . we ne muwen ne wel don ne
>   V ...   wiþ_uten *whom* . we ne mouwen / nouʒt wel don . ne

5 Summary

In this paper, we have seen some intermediate states where older and newer word forms are integrated and the latter forms are taking the place of the former, investigating variant word forms in four manuscripts of *Ancrene Wisse*, several editions of Chaucer's works, etc. Some forms may reflect the distinctive dialects of those scribes who have recorded some works. If Chaucer chose the words in order to capture a certain character's oral affectation designed to attract women, it would be possible to say that he might have consciously and linguistically experimented both forms for a poetic effect. Gower made use of the older forms such as "ax" or "maked" as the rhyme words. According to Osgood (1963), Spenser used only one instance of "maked" in order to supply the metrical necessity. We could not find any older forms in Milton's works. We could have undertaken a historical investigation of Present-day word forms such as "ask" or "made" since the Later Middle English period. Today, some historical processes of elision, i.e. the leaving out of a sound in some part of a word, are found in compound words such as "cupboard" or "shepherd" and the dialectal words such as "maa (=make)," where some forms are fixed, while their pronunciations are different from the written forms. It is also a feature of Present-day English, however, that there are some fluctuating words which, having fixed forms, show the loss of a sound in the medial position, while sometimes having a spelling pronunciation. It is true to say that words are like living creatures.

References

Baird-Lange, L. Y. and H. Schnuttgen (eds.) (1988) *A Bibliography of Chaucer 1974-1985*. Cambridge: D. S. Brewer.

Benson, L. D. (ed.) (1987) *The Riverside Chaucer*, 3rd ed. Boston: Houghton Mifflin.

Blake, N. F. (ed.) (1980) *The Canterbury Tales: Edited from the Hengwrt Manuscript*. London: Edward Arnold.

Blake, N., et al. (eds.) (1994) *A New Concordance to The Canterbury Tales Based on Blake's Text Edited from the Hengwrt Manuscript*. Okayama: University Education Press.

Jimura, A., Y. Nakao, and M. Matsuo (eds.) (1995) *A Comprehensive List of Textual*

Comparison between Blake's and Robinson's Editions of The Canterbury Tales. Okayama: University Education Press.

Jimura, A., Y. Nakao, and M. Matsuo (eds.) (1999) *A Comprehensive Textual Comparison of Troilus and Criseyde.* Okayama: University Education Press.

Jimura, A., Y. Nakao, and M. Matsuo (eds.) (2001) *A Comprehensive Textual Comparison of Chaucer's Dream Poetry.* Okayama: University Education Press.

Jimura, A. (2002) "Chaucer no Eigo niokeru Onitenkan," Eigoshi Kenkyukai Kaiho. No.7, pp. 6-10.

Jimura, A. (2003) "A Historical Approach to English: Notes on Word Forms in Chaucer's English," *Studies in Modern English: The Twentieth Anniversary Publication of the Modern English Association.* Eichoshai, pp. 31-44.

Kubouchi, T. and K. Ikegami (eds.) (2003) *The* AW: *A Four-Manuscript Parallel Text. Preface and Parts 1-4* ; (2005) *Parts 5-8 with Wordlists.* Frankfurt am Main: Peter Lang.

Macaulay, G. C. (ed.) (1900) *The English Works of John Gower.* London: OUP.

Oizumi, A. (ed.) (1991) *A Complete Concordance to the Works of Geoffrey Chaucer,* Programmed by K. Miki, 10 vols. Hildesheim, etc.: Olms-Weidmann.

Osgood, C. G. (comp. and ed.) (1963) *A Concordance to the Poems of Edmund Spenser.* Gloucester, Mass.: Peter Smith.

Robinson, F. N. (ed.) (1957) *The Works of Geoffrey Chaucer,* 2nd ed. Boston: Houghton Mifflin.

Root, R. K. (ed.) (1926) *The Book of Troilus and Criseyde by Geoffrey Chaucer.* Princeton: Princeton UP.

Windeatt, B. A. (ed.) (1984) *Troilus and Criseyde: 'The Book of Troilus' by Geoffrey Chaucer.* London: Longman.

Wittig, J. S. (2001) *Piers Plowman: Concordance.* London: The Athlone Press.

Dynamics of Repetition:
Subversion and Resistance in Two Dramas

Sei Kosugi

1 Introduction

This paper analyses the function of repetitions in the texts of two contemporary plays: *The Elephant Man* (first performed in 1997) by Bernard Pomerance and *Think of a Garden* (1991) by John Kneubuhl. In discussing repetitions, I chose the texts relevant to the area of my recent study. One is about the relation between medicine (or psychiatry) and colonialism. The other is from indigenous literature in Oceania. This paper discusses the dynamics of repetition in the two dramas by focusing not only on the repetitions of words or phrases but also on the repetitions of scenes, situations and themes. Gilles Deleuze says in *Difference and Repetition* that repetition is "the historical condition under which something new is effectively produced." Deleuze argues that "[t]he self is ... itself a modification" or "the difference drawn" from repetition.[1] These words of Deleuze have something in common with the postcolonial theory of Homi Bhabha that mimicry is "the representation of a difference." According to Bhabha, "colonial mimicry is the desire for a reformed, recognizable Other, *as a subject of a difference that is almost the same, but not quite.*"[2] The intentional mimicry of the dominant discourse is therefore the means of asserting a difference and of plotting subversion. I would like to discuss the plays by Pomerance and Kneubuhl from this postcolonial viewpoint.

2 *The Elephant Man* : Repetition and Subversion — Nightmare of Dr Treves (or the Empire)

The Elephant Man is set in the London Hospital during the years from 1884 to 1890. The play dramatizes the relationship between a patient of Proteus syndrome called John Merrick and an elite surgeon, Frederick Treves. After the premiere in London, the play succeeded in off-Broadway and Broadway productions and was made into a film by David Lynch. There were several preceding texts such as John Merrick's autobiography[3] and medical notes[4] by Dr Treves. The production of the play was followed by the publication of a novel by Christine Sparks[5] and the Oxford version of the text for children.[6] The story of Merrick (the Elephant man) has been thus reproduced repetitively in various genres. I will not discuss closely the repetitions and differences among those texts since there are some preceding studies.[7]

I just point out here one difference between Pomerance's play and the film. While Dr Treves is described in the film as a humanitarian, conscientious scientist who feels remorse for his own deeds as a doctor, Pomerance poignantly discloses the high-handed attitudes and self-deception of Treves in the first half of the play. The audience keeps its distance from Treves and does not feel sympathy towards him until Treves loses his mental balance in the second half of the play. Pomerance's play is the story of a young elite doctor, who was considered to have a promising future, falls into a nervous breakdown in a metropolitan hospital. The conspiracy of imperialism, science and religion is brilliantly depicted in the play. Treves was expected to be "a credit to medicine, to England, and to Christendom" (Scene 11). The nervous breakdown which Treves experiences is, in a sense, similar to that of Conrad's Kurtz, who falls into insanity as a result of his colonial experience. Why does Treves collapse? What did he see?

This play is full of repetitions. What is emphasized by the repetitions of words, phrases, visual images and scenes is the similarity between the vulgar space of Victorian show business and the London Hospital, which is the central space of imperial science. Wherever he may go, Merrick is destined to be exposed to "the gaze of the curious" (Scene 21). The analogy is clarified through comparison between the scene where the manager Ross shows Merrick to the spectators at the freak show and the scene of a medical congress where Treves presents Merrick's deformity to the audience. Although one of the audience at the medical congress says "It is a disgrace" to let Merrick return to "his exhibition" (Scene 3), Treves' presentation itself is another form of "exhibition." Merrick has been a golden goose for Ross to earn money at the freak show. After he is taken into care at the London hospital, Merrick is used to earn "a lot of contributions" (Scene 19) to the hospital. It is not Merrick alone who is not free. As Merrick has been kept by Ross, the elite doctor Treves, who is employed by Gomm (the administrator of the London Hospital), is firmly bound to the institution (or the empire itself) as "a mainstay" (Scene 17) of the hospital. The mainstay, however, is to fall off the hinges.

Repetition has a subversive power in the text of *The Elephant Man*. To shift a meaning through repetitions is one of the strategies of postcolonial literature. Homi Bhabha expounds in "Of Mimicry and Man" that mimicry produces "its slippage, its excess, its difference," which "rupture" the dominant discourse and pose "an immanent threat to both 'normalized' knowledges and disciplinary powers" (86). The dynamics of a subversive power of repetition can be seen in *The Elephant Man*. When Merrick repeats the words (or grammar) which he learned from Treves, he transforms them by a strange theory of his own to disrupt the dominant discourse of Treves. In Treves' nightmare, Merrick introduces himself, saying "I am with the mutations cross the road" (Scene 17). The word "mutations" here not only refers to his physical deformity but also suggests that 'transformation' or 'to transform something' is Merrick's essential nature. Merrick is the medium to subvert the world of Treves by transforming his grammar and language. We can see an example in the following scene where Treves tries to 'educate' Merrick.

Treves inculcates the social code of 'the normal' into Merrick's mind by making Merrick repeat his words exactly as a school master teaches pupils at British elementary schools. In Scene 8 where Merrick objected to Gomm's having discharged the employee who had came to peek in at Merrick, Treves teaches Merrick how important it is to say "thank you" and to "abide by the rules." Treves also teaches him what is "home."

> Treves: I meant, "Thank you, sir."
> Merrick: "Thank you sir."
> Treves: We always do say please and thank you, don't we?
> Merrick: Yes, sir. Thank you.
> Treves: If we want to properly <u>be like others</u>.
> Merrick: Yes, sir, I want to.
> Treves: Then it is <u>for our own good</u>, is it not?
> Merrick: Yes, sir. Thank you, Mr. Gomm. . . .
> Treves: You are happy here, are you not, John?
> Merrick: Yes.
> Treves: The baths have rid you of the odor, have they not?
> Merrick: First chance I had to bathe regular. Ly.
> Treves: And three meals a day delivered to your room?
> Merrick: Yes, sir.
> Treves: This is your Promised Land, is it not?
>   A roof. Food. Protection. Care. Is it not?
> Merrick: Right, Mr. Treves. . . .
> Treves: You call it, Home. . . . . Say it, John: Home.
> Merrick: Home.
> Treves: No, no, really say it. I have a home. This is my. Go on.
> Merrick: I have a home. This is my home. . . . I have a home. . . .
> Treves: If I abide by the rules, I will be happy.
> Merrick: Yes, sir.

Treves: Don't be shy.
Merrick: If I abide by the rules I will be happy.
Treves: Very good. . . . Why do rules make you happy?
Merrick: I don't know. . . .
Treves: . . . . Rules make us happy because they are <u>for our own good</u>.
. . . Don't be shy, John. You can say it.
Merrick: . . . . They make us happy because they are <u>for our own good</u>.
Treves: Excellent. . . . <u>Mr.Gomm was merciful. You yourself are proof Is it not so?</u> *(Pause.)* <u>Well? Is it not so?</u> (Scene 8, underlines mine)

Treves forces Merrick to agree with him by using tag questions which presupposes the answer. He makes Merrick repeat his words to learn the rules to become "like others."

However, in Scene 16 where Merrick is dissatisfied with having been forbidden to see Mrs.Kendall, Merrick imitates and transforms the words he learned from Treves (underlined part). This provokes Treves to anger and causes him to reveal his real thoughts unintentionally (double-underlined part). Although Treves tries to make Merrick repeat his words, Merrick no longer obeys him (wavy-lined part). The last words of Merrick are the repetition (with the subject changed) of what Treves said at the end of the previous quotation from Scene 8 (underlined part). The position of Treves and Merrick is completely reversed here and Treves in confusion is now at a loss for an answer. His confusion can be seen in the grammatical disorder of the dashed-lined part. The strangely off-the-point response of Merrick disturbs the rational thinking of Treves. Moreover, Merrick's repeated short remarks ("Oh") of surprise or conviction serve also as an expression of irony or silent criticism, which provokes Treves quite effectively.

Treves: There are still standards we abide by.
Merrick: <u>They make us happy because they are for our own good.</u>
Treves: Well. Not always.

Merrick: Oh.

Treves: Look, if you are angry, just say so.

Merrick: Whose standards are they?

Treves: I am not in the mood for this chipping away at the edges, John.

Merrick: That do not always make us happy because they are not always for our own good?

Merrick: Did you see her? Naked?

Treves: When I was operating. Of course —

Merrick: Oh.

Treves: Oh what?

Merrick: Is it okay to see them naked if you cut them up afterwards?

Treves: Science is a different thing. . . . I mean, it is not, well, love, you know.

Merrick: Is that why you're looking for an anesthetic. . . . Because you don't love them.

Treves: Love's got nothing to do with surgery.

Merrick: Do you lose many patients?

Treves: I — some.

Merrick: Oh.

Treves: Oh what? What does it matter? If I love, if any surgeon loves her or any patient or not, what does it matter? And what conceivable difference to you?

Merrick: Because it is your standards we abide by.

Treves: For God's sakes. If you are angry, just say it. . . . Say it: I am angry. . . .

Merrick: I believe in heaven.

Treves: And it is not okay. If they undress if you cut them up. As you put it. Make me sound like Jack the, Jack the Ripper.

Merrick: No. You worry about anesthetics.
Treves: Are you having me on?
Merrick: <u>You are merciful. I myself am proof. Is it not so?</u> (*Pause.*) <u>Well? Is it not so?</u>
Treves: Well. . . . perhaps I was wrong. . . . I seem to. Lose my head . . . . I do not know — what is in me these days.

(Scene 16, underlines mine)

The discourse of Dr Treves and Bishop How who try to 'educate' Merrick echoes the discourse of a psychiatrist who 'normalizes' a patient and that of a missionary who converts the colonial pagan. The bishop goes all out for saving Merrick's soul and Treves tries to let Merrick lead a 'normal' and 'human' life. The double-underlined parts of the quotation from Scene 8 ("be like others" "for our own good") are the expressions repeated in the play. These two phrases and the words "fit in," which Gomm uses in the play, are the terms often seen in the discourse of a psychiatrist.

Gomm: [W]hat do you plan for Merrick?
Treves: Normality as far as is possible.
Gomm: So he will be like us? Ah. (*Smiles.*)
Treves: Is something wrong, Mr. Gomm? With us?   (Scene 7)

Although Treves feels uneasy at the sight of Gomm's ironical smile, he does not understand the problem of becoming "normal" or of becoming "like us" at this point. When he understands it, Treves suffers a nervous breakdown. What he saw is the "deformity" of the world we call 'normal,' that is, the sense of values of the empire represented by the British middle and upper class. It is the "deformity" we have inside our own mentality: "Higher up, sir, above this middle class, I confront these same—deformities—bulged out by unlimited resources and the ruthlessness of privilege into the most scandalous dissipation . . . " (Scene 19). Treves found himself having served as "an awfully good gardener" of the empire who "pruned, cropped, pollarded" and "stupefied" the patient (and also himself and his family) to put him or her into the deformed mold. Treves is tormented by the nightmare that he cannot escape from his role.

One of the repetitions visually effective in the play is Merrick's act of putting pieces one by one upon the model of a church to complete it. The stage direction that "Merrick puts another piece on St. Phillip's" is repeated several times in the second half of the play. It is interesting to notice that Merrick's act of building goes synchronously with the mental collapse of Treves. In Scene 19 where Treves completely falls into mental breakdown and his language no longer can be understood by Bishop How nor Gomm, Treves bursts into tears, powerlessly in search of help. On the other side of the stage, Merrick calmly puts the last piece upon his church model, completing it. The satisfactory words of Merrick ("It is done") ironically sounds as if to mean the breakdown of Treves.

> Bishop: . . . I cannot tell what you are saying.
> Treves: Help me. (*Weeps.*)
> Merrick (*rises, puts last piece on St. Phillip's*): It is done.
> *Fadeout.* (Scene 19)

There is synchronic repetition of theme in *The Elephant Man* and in its contemporary texts. David Cooper, the advocator of anti-psychiatry, discusses the relation between colonialism and psychiatry in *The Language of Madness* (1978), which was published one year after the premiere of *The Elephant Man*. Anti-psychiatry, which was started in Britain by R. D. Laing in the 1960s, and the drama of Pomerance share a similar kind of structure of feeling. In the 1960s Michel Foucault changed the notion of madness in Europe and anti-psychiatry gained popularity in Britain while in the United States Ken Kesey published a novel set in a mental hospital, *One Flew Over the Cuckoo's Nest* (1962) and Janet Frame of New Zealand wrote novels which aim to overthrow the power balance between sanity and insanity.[8] The counter-cultural violation of the boundary between 'sanity' and 'insanity' seen from the 1960s to the 1970s also characterizes the play of *The Elephant Man*. Janet Frame's two novels, *Owls Do Cry* (1957) and *Faces in the Water* (1961), and Ken Kesey's *One Flew Over the Cuckoo's Nest* (1962) criticize the inhuman violence of psychosurgery, such as lobotomy, which changes a patient's character. An ethical criticism contained in these works that to change a patient's character is the same as to kill the person has something in common with the observation made by Treves about Merrick's condition. Treves wonders "To become more normal is to die?" when he realizes Merrick's condition gets more serious as he becomes more 'normal.'

3   *Think of a Garden* : **Repetitive Recollection as Resistance**

Think of a Garden, an autobiographic work of American Samoan playwright John Kneubuhl, is the posthumous play which premiered in 1992 several hours after the author's death in the hospital in Pago Pago, the capital of American Samoa. The protagonist and narrator of the play is a 'half-caste' boy David. His great-great-grandfather was a British missionary and consul while his mother is the descendant of Samoan chief and David's father is a successful plantation owner from America. David grows up in three cultures as the Swiss / Welsh / Samoan author Kneubuhl himself has lived in Samoa, Hawai'i and USA.[9] The garden in the title is the garden of the house in Samoa where the narrator spent his boyhood. It is the secret place where David spent his time with the ghost of a Samoan boy called Veni. *Think of a Garden* is the narrator's recollection of his boyhood and of his homeland, which he left.

Here is the outline of the play. It is Christmas in 1929. A barefoot boy, David, is talking in Samoan to his old Samoan nurse Pito in the garden of the Griffith's house in the village of Leone in American Samoa. David (the narrator/writer) as a man in his forties stands at the edge of the stage, looking at the scene of recollection. David's mother Lu'isa, who was born in Upolu island in Western Samoa, boasts her high-born Samoan blood in her maternal lineage. The Griffith family had vast land both in Upolu and in American Samoa before Samoa was divided into east and west. Educated in New Zealand, Lu'isa loves the accent of New Zealand English and married a wealthy American plantation owner Frank. She is considered to be "white" by the Samoans in the village of Leone. On the day of Christmas, they are waiting for the homecoming of Lu'isa's cousin Tamasese. As the leader of the Mau movement (independence movement) in Western Samoa under New Zealand rule, Tamasese had been deported from Samoa and was permitted to return after years of exile. On his arrival in his hometown Apia, however, Tamasese was assassinated, falsely charged with the crime of having agitated a riot. Frank goes to Upolu to find the truth about the death of his wife's cousin. While he stays together with the Samoans who help the escape of the Mau, Frank feels sympathy towards them and calls them "my people" (76). Lu'isa is torn by the conflicting feelings of hate against the New Zealand government who assassinated her cousin and of her attachment for New Zealand where she spent her girlhood. Cursing the whiteness of her skin, Lu'isa slashes her skin with a piece of broken glass. David's friend (the ghost of a Samoan boy) named Veni comes to the garden and makes David virtually experience the death of Tamasese. Lu'isa feels fear and disgrace at the sight of his son dressed in a loincloth, trying to paint his skin brown as if he were possessed by the ghost of the dead Samoan boy. David is sent to a school in New Zealand. The play closes with a scene where David says good-bye to the garden and to Veni.

Repetitions can be seen in the various layers of the play. Historical repetition of the British imperialism is seen in the New Zealand policy towards Samoa. We hear the echo of Gandhi's nonviolent non-cooperative resistance (which was almost contemporary with the Mau movement) in the resistance of the Samoans who remained silent as to the whereabouts of the Mau leaders without protesting, even when "the police got angry and frustrated and set their huts on fire" or "beat the hell out of the younger people" (74). The assassination of Tamasese in the play is the fictional reproduction of a historical incident called 'Black Saturday' of December 1929 when the New Zealand military police fired at a nonviolent demonstration by the Mau. Frank explains why New Zealand became the country which tries to control Samoa: "It's a disease all white men catch when they live away from home. They're afraid you might become their equal" (19-20). This explains the mechanism of the global repetition of 'the history of colonization.'

Everyman's Encyclopaedia epitomizes the ruler's view of the history of New Zealand's governance over Samoa:

> ...the aim of the administration was to improve the standard of living and the social conditions of the natives; hence the encouragement of self government, and the improvement of health and education. <u>For some years there were difficulties with a strong native organisation known as the Mau; but with its disappearance the administration functioned with complete normality and goodwill.</u>[10] (underline mine)

There is a large gap between this official version of history and the history presented by Kneubuhl. By shedding light to the historical moment which has not been represented in Samoan literature, Kneubuhl rewrites the history of Samoa from a Samoan viewpoint in the form of personal narration and recollection of the history of a certain family.

This drama itself is a repetition of the past in that it is the narrator's recollection. Moreover, David's anachronistic mother Luʻisa, who is proud of having the noble blood of a Samoan aristocrat, also repeatedly recollects her past, desperately trying to save the glory of the past from dying away. The following four figures in the drama reflect each other: The ghost of the Samoan boy Veni who is David's friend, the imaginary brown-skin boy who lived in the mind of David's uncle Lilo who committed suicide (the boy resembles David except for the colour of his skin), David as a little boy who lives in the narrator's recollection and the assassinated hero Tamasese.

> Now, years later, remembering that evening, and I keep repeating my goodbyes to <u>that little boy</u> and to his garden. ... "Never be far from me, <u>little one</u>. Lodge yourself in me, somewhere in the words I will seek all my life, and there, cry out your hurt, and cry until the words become <u>a brown and shining young man raising his hands high and calling above the clamoring pain around us, 'Peace! Peace!'</u> and only the blessed silence answers, that bright silence beyond which new mornings dawn for all of us. Go, Precious, go. Stay with me always." (96, underlines mine)

The figure who is addressed here by the narrator as "little one" is David himself as a boy in his own recollection who is going to leave the garden. At the same time, it is Veni to whom David is going to say good-bye. The figure of "a brown and shining young man" is Tamasese. The ghost of the Samoan boy, who cannot speak English, is the Samoan soul of the narrator, who wishes his words never lose a 'brown' accent like the words of Tamasese and of the brown boy in his mind. Unlike his Europeanized mother, David tries to retain his Samoan nature through his conscious act of recollection, although he leaves for New Zealand and later lives in the United States with his father. This drama is a repetitive act of recollection for the narrator (and Kneubuhl) to awake his own Samoan nature inside himself. By repeating the reproduction of the play on the stage, Kneubuhl can also stir up a Samoan soul in the heart of the coming generations.

This play poses a problem how Samoa should retain its own national identity by resisting the globalizing power of dominance like that of the nineteenth century imperial Britain (New Zealand) and the wave of the twentieth century globalization of the United States. Probably, it is the problem of Kneubuhl himself, who was born between a Samoan woman of chiefly genealogy educated in New Zealand (like Lu'isa in the play) and a navy surveyor from America. After Kneubuhl spent his boyhood in Samoa and in Hawai'i, he entered Yale University and worked in Hollywood for twenty years as a script writer of major TV series (*Mission Impossible*, *Star Trek*, etc.). Kneubuhl, who had once blotted out his Polynesian self to fit into American consumerist culture, went back to Samoa in 1968 to work for the reformation of educational institutions in Samoa. At the same time, he wrote plays to awake the racial consciousness in Samoan people. *Think of a Garden* is set in December 1929, which marks the dawn of the national independence movement in Samoa. By reproducing the memory of that occasion through personal recollection of the narrator, Kneubuhl tries to revive the racial pride in native culture and language of Samoa in the present day.

The text of Kneubuhl, however, stands on a precarious platform. The biracial boy David, who has a deep sense of closeness towards his old Samoan nurse and his friend Veni, is not considered to be one of them by the poor Samoans in the village. It is clear from the fact that David has a stone thrown at by a Samoan man (the younger brother of the dead boy Veni). In the eyes of the Samoans, David who is dressed like a Native American and talks to the ghost of Veni is nothing more than a 'white' boy who disturbs the spirit of the dead. Moreover, Frank's sympathy towards the Samoans ("my people") and his act of risking his life to be with them might be considered mere self-satisfaction of his own heroism. Similarly, to what extent can the language of Kneubuhl come close to the voice of the Samoan public? The Samoans in the village of Leone who live in the neighborhood of the Griffith family or the Samoan crowd who support the Mau movement are on the periphery of the play and never speak in their own voice. Likewise, Tamasese, the hero of the independence movement, is dead in the play and does not speak. Nevertheless, he stands out in the play as a symbolic figure. This play by Kneubuhl is an expression of his earnest wish to become 'their voice' while being conscious of his delicate position and thus avoiding the representation.

4 Conclusion

I have discussed the dynamics of repetition in the two dramas from a postcolonial perspective. Repetition has the subversive power to overthrow the Victorian world of 'normality' in *The Elephant Man* by Bernard Pomerance. In this play we saw the similarity of the discourse of colonialism, religion and medicine (or psychiatry). Merrick is educated to fit in the Victorian norm of 'normality.' In the process of his education, however, Treves' words which Merrick imitates with a slight modification cause a crack in the imperial discourse of Treves, only to dismantle and subvert the world which was supposed to be firm and steady. We have also seen the inter-textual relation between Pomerance's play and its contemporary texts of anti-psychiatry and of postcolonial literature which question the notion of madness and pose the problem of medical ethics. John Kneubuhl rewrites the history of Samoa from a Samoan perspective in *Think of a Garden*. The repetitive recollection in this play functions as a means to keep the national identity of Samoa by resisting the global power of the West. The analysis of these two plays confirms the postcolonial theory of Bhabha that mimicry (repetition) is a strategy to assert a difference in an insidious way. Repetition, like mimicry, can make a fatal crack in the dominant discourse by transforming and shifting the meaning in its process.

Notes

* This paper is based on my essay (written in Japanese) which was published in *Language and Repetition* (The Graduate School of Language and Culture, Osaka University, 2002), pp. 25-36.

1. Deleuze (1997) p. 79, 90.
2. Bhabha (1994) p. 86.
3. "The Autobiography of Joseph Carey Merrick" in Howell et al. (eds.), (1980) pp. 223-224.
4. Treves (1923)
5. Sparks (1980)
6. Vicary (1989)

7   Yamada (2001)
8   Kosugi (2001)
9   As for the biographical information of Kneubuhl, please refer to Johnson (1997)
10 *Everyman's Encyclopaedia* (1978) p. 581.

References

Bhabha, H. (1994) "Of Mimicry and Man" in *Location of Culture*. London: Routledge.

Cooper, D. (1978) *The Language of Madness*. London: Penguin.

Deleuze, G. (1997) *Difference and Repetition*. London: Athlone Press.

Everyman's Encyclopaedia (1978), vol. 10. London: Dent & Sons.

Field, M. J. (1991) *Mau : Samoa's Struggle for Freedom*. Auckland : Polynesian Press.

Frame, J. (1996) (1st, 1957) *Owls Do Cry*. New York: George Braziller.

Frame, J. (1994) (1st, 1961) *Faces in the Water*. New York: George Braziller.

Howell, M. and P. Ford (eds.) (1980) *The True History of the Elephant Man*. Harmondsworth: Penguin.

Johnson, J. P. (1997) "Afterword: A Portrait of John Kneubuhl" in *Think of a Garden and Other Plays*. Honolulu: U of Hawai'i Press: pp. 251-266.

Kesey, K. (1962) *One Flew Over the Cuckoo's Nest*. New York: Signet.

Kneubuhl, J. (1997) *Think of a Garden and Other Plays*. Honolulu: U of Hawai'i Press.

Kosugi, S. (2001) "Formation of Postcolonial Subject in New Zealand: In Search of the Edge of the Alphabet" (written in Japanese) in *Theory and Practice of Cultural Studies*. The Graduate School of Language and Culture, Osaka University: pp. 73-86.

Pomerance, B. (1979) *The Elephant Man*. New York: Grove Press.

Sparks, C. (1980) *The Elephant Man: A Novel*. New York: Ballantine Books.

Treves, F. (1923) *The Elephant Man and Other Reminiscences*. London: Cassell.

Yamada, Y. (2001) "The Intellectual who Represented the Elephant Man" (written in Japanese) in *Theory and Practice of Cultural Studies*. The Graduate School of Language and Culture, Osaka University: pp.35-46.

Vicary, T. (1989) *The Elephant Man*. Oxford: Oxford UP.

How does the Computer Look at the Shakespearian Sonnets?
A Quantitative Observation by Means of Quantification of Contingency Table[*]

Junsaku Nakamura

1 Introduction

Multivariate analysis has been used in corpus linguistics and literary criticisms since the mid 1980s. Principal Component Analysis has been used in the works by Burrows and by Tabata to conduct stylistic analyses of authors such as Jane Austen and Charles Dickens (see References), and Principal Factor Analysis has also been used in many works by Biber for variation studies across different registers of both spoken and written English. Another method called Quantification of Contingency Table (QCT hereinafter) has been employed by Nakamura to examine the behaviours of linguistic items such as words, collocations and grammatical tags across the texts of different genres or domains.

Nakamura (2003) and Nakamura and Kasahara (2007) have demonstrated that, of the three methods, QCT seems to be the most suitable for dealing with a frequency matrix of the words or linguistic items used across different types of texts. The problem with QCT, however, is the high demand it places on memory space and the gigantic number of computations involved as a consequence. This is a serious problem if the number of textual categories and the number of linguistic items to be processed become very large. The demand increases according to the power of the increase. If the number of categories becomes 100 times as large, then the demand will be 10,000 times as heavy. The present study, therefore, is an attempt to deal with a large number of textual categories involving a large number of linguistic samples and to see how it works.

For this purpose, Shakespeare's sonnets were chosen. One hundred and fifty-four pieces of sonnets were taken as textual categories and the words used in each of them were treated as linguistic items to be processed. Shakespearian sonnets are chosen as an object to test simply because of their fair number of pieces, i.e., 154, and their more or less similar lengths, with each piece containing more or less an equal number of words, i.e., 115 words or thereabouts.[1] The total number of word types used throughout the Sonnets, a little over 3,000, is also appropriate, not so large nor so small. If successful, QCT would reveal how Shakespeare's sonnets are related to one another on the basis of the words used in them. In other words, the structure of the Sonnets on the basis of the whole vocabulary would be revealed. This is what is attempted in the present study.[2]

2   Data and Method

2.1   Data

To conduct QCT, a contingency table of rows consisting of words used in the Sonnets and columns consisting of 154 sonnets must be created in the beginning. It involves many steps from finding and downloading the texts, editing them, creating an alphabetical frequency list of words for each sonnet, merging 154 frequency lists into an alphabetical frequency list covering all the sonnets, and finally to producing a contingency table of more than 3,000 words across 154 sonnets. Most of these steps plus conducting QCT and visually displaying the results are all taken care of by a suite of the programs called FreqAnalysis Tool Kit written in Visual Basic 6.0 and developed by the present author.

Texts used in the present study come from Project Gutenberg: the Shakespearian Sonnets, etext No. 1105, which is a plain ascii text consisting of 112KB.[3] This is chosen simply because it is very easy to download and handle and it also does not involve the issue of copyright for the purpose of the study like the present.

Downloaded texts were broken down to each piece identified by the file name with the sonnet number as its part and edited according to the following simple rules:

- An apostrophe indicating possession is changed into "$" and is separated from the preceding noun since it is not a part of the meaning of the noun itself.
- An apostrophe indicating contraction is changed into "&." If the contraction is over two words, the part containing "&" is separated from the preceding word.
- An @ is added to the beginning of proper nouns.

Any further annotations such as POS-tagging are not performed here. Consequently the analysis presented below is just based upon graphic words.

From the edited texts, alphabetical frequency lists of words are created piece by piece and then merged, resulting in the total number of 17,783 tokens and the total number of 3,172 types. In the next step, based upon the merged alphabetical frequency list of 3,172 words thus created, a cross table showing the frequencies of all the words across 154 sonnets was created. This comprises the basic data for QCT, but one final adjustment was performed before QCT was applied; the words unique to a particular sonnet were extracted, collapsed together as a group identified by the sonnet number, and reinserted in the beginning of the cross table. This final step was necessary since the words unique to particular sonnets are given the same quantities according to QCT, eventually overlapping one another in the figures showing the results and making it very difficult to see and analyse the results. Collapsing the words unique to particular sonnets into 154 groups reduced the number of rows of the cross table into 1,459 from 3,172. Since it is impossible to show the whole table, its schematic representation is provided here as Table 1.

Table 1. Schematic Representation of the Cross Table Used in the Present Study.

Word	Total	snt001	snt002	snt003	...	snt152	snt153	snt154
snt001	10	10	0	0	...	0	0	0
snt002	16	0	16	0	...	0	0	0
⋮	⋮	⋮	⋮	⋮	...	⋮	⋮	⋮
$	20	0	0	0	...	1	2	1
$s	190	4	3	1	...	0	2	2
&gaisnt	6	0	0	0	...	0	0	0
⋮	⋮	⋮	⋮	⋮	...	⋮	⋮	⋮
a	163	1	1	0	...	1	6	3
abide	2	0	0	0	...	0	0	0
above	4	0	0	0	...	0	0	0
absence	5	0	0	0	...	0	0	0
⋮	⋮	⋮	⋮	⋮	...	⋮	⋮	⋮
youth	16	0	1	0	...	0	0	0
youthful	2	0	0	0	...	0	0	0

2.2 Method

QCT gives several sets of quantities both to categories and samples simultaneously so that the quantities given to categories (called category weights) and the quantities given to samples (called sample scores) can produce the highest correlation coefficient for the first set (first axis in statistical term) and the next highest for the second set and so on. By using those quantities which attain high correlations, you can see the relationships among categories, the relationships among samples, and ultimately the relationship between categories and samples. Calculation of those quantities involves a complicated mathematical matrix operation called eigen analysis, the details of which are not touched upon here but the gist of which is summarised as solving the eigen equation of a coefficient matrix produced from the original contingency table. Data prepared as in Table 1 was processed and the results were plotted and analysed.

3 Results and Discussion

3.1 QCT Summary

QCT gives (N-1) axes (sets) of category weights and sample scores with N being the smaller of either the number of categories or that of samples. Therefore, 153 axes of category weights and sample scores were produced in the present case in a descending order of the correlation coefficients (theoretically calculated by taking square root of eigen values) between category weights and sample scores. Table 2 shows a part of the whole series of eigen values, correlation coefficients, proportions accounted for and cumulative proportions accounted for for all the axes.

Table 2. Part of QCT Summary.

Axis	Eigen Value	Correlation Coefficient	Proportion Accounted for	Cumulative Proportion Accounted for
1	0.33647553	0.580065105	1.144610663	1.144610633
2	0.33091955	0.575250672	1.125710533	2.270321196
3	0.31971751	0.565435685	1.067603843	3.357925039
4	0.30329260	0.550720073	1.031730144	4.389655183
5	0.29051851	0.538997690	0.988275692	5.377930675
⋮	⋮	⋮	⋮	⋮
153	0.09930000	0.315105455	0.337766171	100.000000000

Proportion accounted for is the amount of information in the original frequency matrix explained by the axis in question and is obtained by calculating the relative amount of eigen values. Cumulative proportion accounted for is the amount of information accounted for up to the axis in question. Since as many as 154 sonnets are involved, proportion accounted for of each axis is not so large although correlation coefficient is quite high. Since the first several axes are usually used for the analysis based upon multivariate analysis, the first three axes are taken into consideration below due to a practical reason: since graphic representation can deal with only up to three dimensions, if you want to make the utmost use of the information of the original frequency list, the maximum of three axes is the only inevitable choice.

3.2 Category Weights Given to Sonnets and Sample Scores Given to Words

Table 3 and Table 4 respectively present the category weights given to the sonnets and sample scores given to the words used in them. A set of quantities taken from Axis 1 of both category weights and sample scores produce the highest correlation coefficient in Table 2, and those taken from Axis 2 produce the second highest, and so on. By examining the category weights in Table 3, the relationships among sonnets can be determined; those given closer values are judged to be qualitatively similar in terms of the words used in them while those given distant values are judged to be qualitatively different. In the same way, by looking at the sample scores, the relationships among words can be determined; if the words are given closer values, they are judged to be qualitatively similar in terms of the sonnets in which they are used. In contrast, if they are given distant values, they are judged to be qualitatively different.

Since the results of the multivariate analysis like the present are all given in numerical figures which are very difficult to process for figuring out the tendencies hidden in them, the given results are usually plotted in graphic forms so that the tendencies can be visually grasped. In the present case, the program for plotting the results developed as a part of the suite FreqAnalysis Tool Kit by the author was used.

Table 3. Part of Category Weights Given to Sonnets.

Sonnet	Axis 1	Axis 2	Axis 3
snt001	0.2393932174	0.1192961845	0.0061027757
snt002	0.4249259778	0.1163109403	-0.1026697554
snt003	0.4753361180	0.1340029696	0.2327313354
snt004	0.7880017925	-0.0193372600	-0.3998499345
snt005	0.2212689879	0.3032852724	0.0758541670
snt006	0.6336366067	0.1845903142	-0.4469382288
snt007	0.1488425041	-2.7023440416	12.0977583779
⋮	⋮	⋮	⋮
snt153	-8.6498355635	0.9657494255	0.0519362343
snt154	-7.6690595367	0.3758967289	-0.2786016789

Table 4. Part of Sample Scores Given to Words.

Word	Axis 1	Axis 2	Axis 3
snt001	0.4127006005	0.2073792700	0.0107930500
snt002	0.7325487665	0.2021898521	-0.1815763616
⋮	⋮	⋮	⋮
$	-2.129033995	0.1883615785	-0.1221208677
$s	-0.105659882	0.1738015065	0.0223579683
&gainst	-0.098778577	0.1127836601	-0.0408363222
⋮	⋮	⋮	⋮
a	-0.8352407942	0.0561364450	0.0829802960
abide	-0.2288610647	-0.9010410086	0.5744956009
above	0.1304016582	-0.0811832900	0.0017183180
absence	0.2519094757	0.3222729409	-0.1967232052
⋮	⋮	⋮	⋮
youth	0.2914063993	-0.5108918674	1.2756184012
youthful	-0.1621057485	-0.4534803340	0.7103935468

3.3 Distribution of Sonnets

Fig. 1 below used the quantities given to the sonnets for the first three axes, i.e., Table 3, to show their distributions based upon the use of words. The posi-

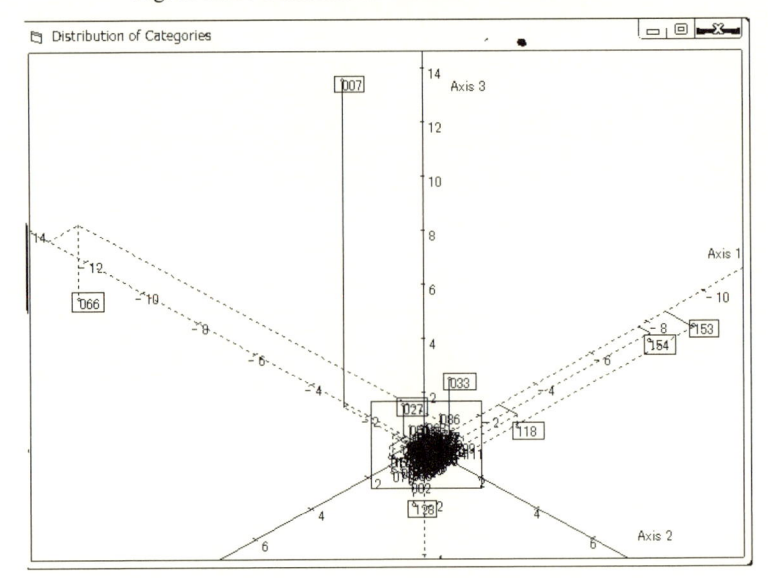

Fig. 1. Three-Dimensional Distribution of the Sonnets.

tions and polarities of three axes were arbitrarily chosen and auxiliary projection lines, solid for positive value and dotted for negative value, were added to show the exact position of each sonnet in a three-dimensional space. The bubbles on the tip of the vertical lines showing the quantities given for Axis 3 indicate the relative amount of the words used in the sonnets. (In the category plot, the bubbles are more or less of the same size since the sonnets consisting of 14 lines end up with 115 words on the average.)

When the results of QCT are plotted, those located on the periphery are supposed to be quite unique in the sense that they tend to use different words from others and those plotted close to the origin of coordinates are supposed to be neutral in that they use the words rather evenly distributed across sonnets. At first glance, there are several sonnets that are found quite far away from the rest of the sonnets. Along Axis 1, two sonnets, Sonnets 153 and 154, are placed far away from the origin in the negative region.[4] Sonnet 118 is also

How does the Computer Look at the Shakespearian Sonnets? **219**

separated from the rest. Along Axis 2, Sonnet 66 is conspicuously separated from the rest again in the negative region. Sonnet 7 is also located away from the origin along Axis 2, but it shows a remarkably high positive value along Axis 3. Sonnets 33 and 27 are also outstanding in the positive region while Sonnets 66 and 128 are conspicuous in the negative region of this axis. Those outliers are found to be somehow different from the others in the ways the words are used although the definite reasons why are not clear at this stage.

Since as many as 154 sonnets are plotted in Fig. 1, the area close to the origin is so densely populated that it is virtually impossible to identify each of them. In order to cope with this problem of overlaps, you can extract and enlarge a part of the figure as in Fig. 2. Those sonnets located close to the origin of the coordinates are the sonnets supposed to be neutral in their ways of using words. But again why they are distributed in the way they are distributed in those figures is not at all clear until you see the distribution of the words.

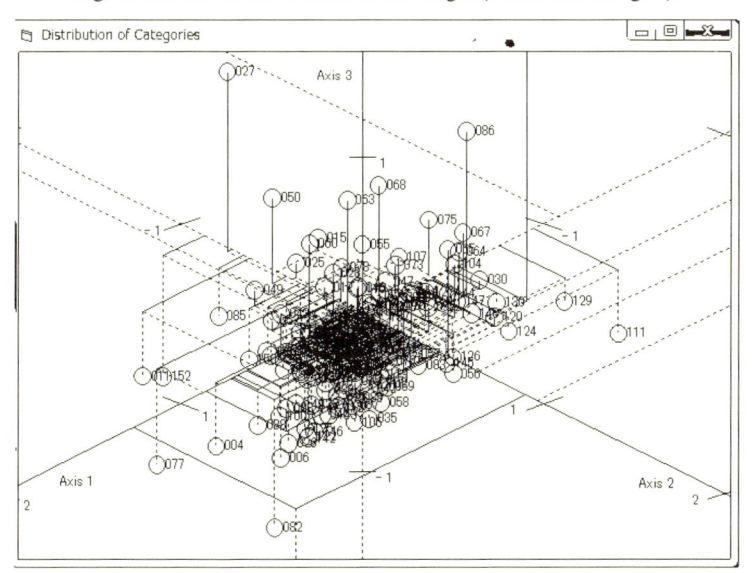

Fig. 2. Sonnets Located Close to the Origin (Extract from Fig. 1).

3.4 Distribution of Words

Numerical values found in Table 4 are used to draw Fig. 3, which shows the overall distribution of the words on the basis of the sonnets in which they occur. Axes are drawn in accordance with the distribution of the sonnets and the bubbles indicate the relative amount of a word in question used in the entire sonnets. The numbers used as labels indicate groups of words unique to particular sonnets identified by them.

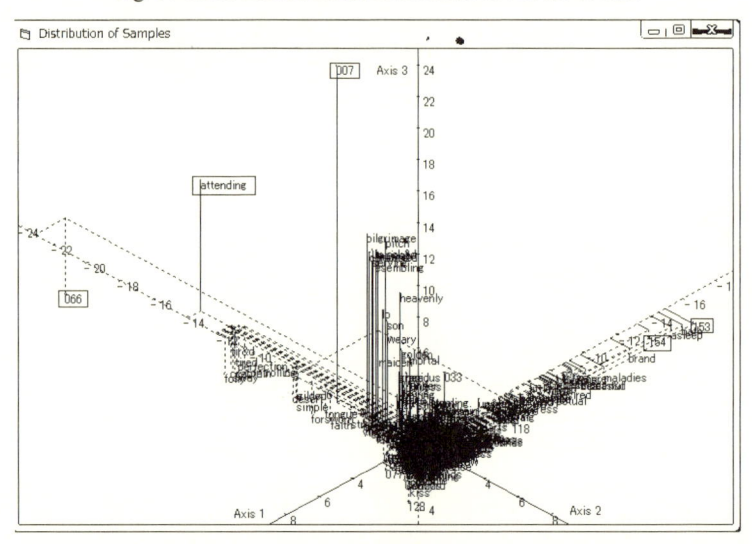

Fig. 3. Three-Dimensional Distribution of All the Words.

Fig. 3 demonstrates what QCT does quite effectively. On the left end of the figure, you can see 066, indicating a group of words unique to Sonnet 66, while 007 placed close to Axis 3 on the top part is Sonnet 7. When you compare those two groups of unique words with the same two sonnets in Fig. 1, their positions are found to correspond to each other. This is also true of the words unique to Sonnets 153 and 154 located in the rightmost area. Thus, the positions of words unique to particular sonnets turn out to indicate the relative positions of the sonnets themselves.

One more thing to be noticed is the word "attending" placed exactly in between the groups of words unique to Sonnet 66 and Sonnet 7. If you draw a line to connect these two sonnets, the word "attending" is found at exactly the mid-point. The word actually occurs twice in the Sonnets, once in Sonnet 66 and once in Sonnet 7, and this fact is clearly reflected in its position. In the same way, positions of all the words depicted in Fig. 3 are supposed to reflect the frequencies of the words used in the sonnets. Thus, the distribution of the Sonnets in Fig. 1 can be explicated by that of the words in Fig. 3 and vice versa; those words located close to a particular sonnet represented by its unique words are the ones characteristically used in that particular sonnet.

As so many overlaps are seen in Fig. 3, a part of the figure can be extracted and enlarged as in Fig. 4, depicting around the negative region along Axis 1 close to Sonnets 154 and 153. The words "bath" and "asleep" are used only in Sonnets 154 and 153 and other words in this figure are used in the sonnets close to the origin and either in Sonnet 153 or in Sonnet 154 or in both of them.

Extracting and enlarging a part of the figure is not the only way to deal with identification of words, but you can also select the words you want according to frequency bands, parts of speech or semantic domains. There are 30 words which occur 100 times or more with the most frequent being "and" occurring 490 times, followed by "the" occurring 436 times and so on. They are picked up in Fig. 5. As you can imagine, most of those words frequently occurring are function words except for the single content word of "love" found in this frequency band, actually occurring 177 times.

Fig. 4. Words in the Negative Region along Axis 1 Close to Sonnets 153 and 154.

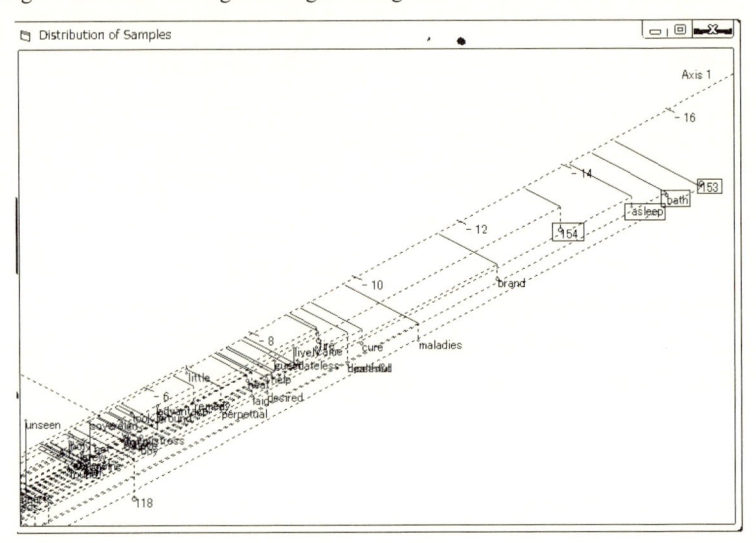

Fig. 5. Distribution of Words Occurring 100 Times or More.

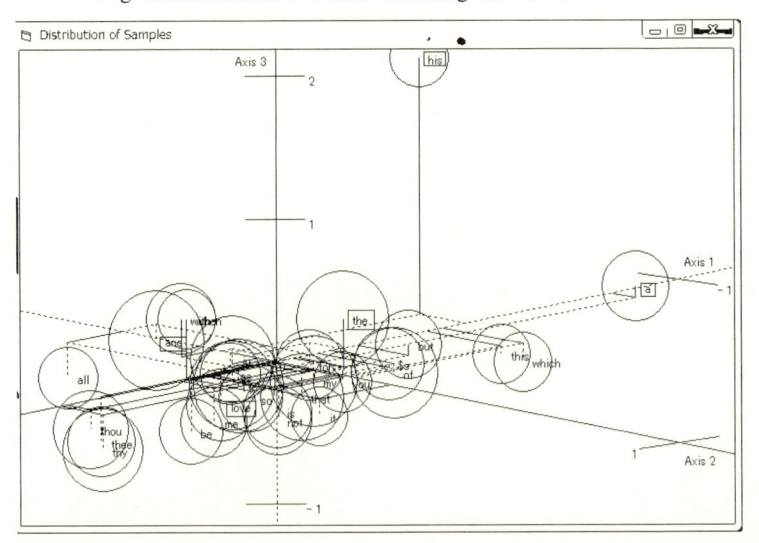

According to QCT, those words used evenly across the sonnets are supposed to be placed close to the origin. As function words are found in all of the sonnets, they all assume the positions close to the origin of the coordinates, revealing the fact that they are evenly used across sonnets. Exceptions to this are "his" located toward Sonnet 7 in which this pronoun occurs seven times and an indefinite article "a" located toward the direction of Sonnets 153 and 154 in which it occurs 6 and 3 times respectively. The most frequent "and" is not closest to the origin but are found toward the negative direction of Axis 2 where Sonnet 66 is located; ten of the 14 lines of Sonnet 66 begin with "and" presumably to induce the effect of adding emotions as the lines progress. Thus the distribution of words reflects the ways in which they are used in the sonnets, enabling to explain the distribution of words with that of sonnets, and vice versa.

4 Conclusion

QCT seems to work effectively to examine the relationships between the sonnets and their uses of words although the words used were simple graphic words, not annotated at all in any sophisticated way. As a result, some of the sonnets have turned out to be quite unique or different in their uses of words; they are placed on the periphery of the distribution when the results were plotted on a three-dimensional space. In contrast, many of the sonnets were located close to the origin of coordinates, indicating they are more or less neutral in their uses of words.

We can explain the relationship between sonnets and their uses of words by looking at the locations of particular words in relation to the unique items belonging to particular sonnets in the graphic representation of word distribution. Closer look at the distribution of words from the viewpoints of frequency, parts of speech or specific semantic domains would contribute to some extent to identify the characteristics of particular sonnets. POS tagging, lemmatisation, or semantic tagging may also contribute to identifying the characteristics of the sonnets in clearer ways.

Needless to say, the tentative results obtained here must be carefully checked and evaluated on the basis of or against the huge amount of qualitative analyses of the Sonnets so far undertaken. Another problem that is to be added is the matter concerning the proportions accounted for. As you notice, they are very low since as many as 153 axes are involved, but the results showed that QCT seemed to work for picking up unique and distinctive sonnets although only three most significant axes were used here. But analysis based upon the rest of axes showing high proportion accounted for is probably needed to examine the structure of the Sonnets in more detail.

The overall results, however, suggest that QCT can deal with quite a number of texts. Although the sonnets contain only a little more than a hundred words, the sizes of the texts do not matter here since, in principle, the number of texts determine the number of axes to be calculated. Therefore, text typology over a huge range of texts on the basis of words or linguistic features they use seems to be plausible.

Notes

* This is a greatly abridged version of the paper presented at the ELR Seminar held in June, 2007 at CARE (Centre for Advanced Research in English), Birmingham University, where the author was staying as a visiting scholar under the overseas research scheme of Ritsumeikan University. The handout covering the details omitted here will be available through the author.

1. This condition of similarity of text sizes is quite important. The present author does not believe in the process of standardising frequencies just by adjusting the observed frequencies proportionally to the text sizes such as is realised by wpm (word per million), since the distribution of types are different when the total numbers of tokens are different. The numbers of tokens of the types are not a linear function proportional to the total numbers of tokens.
2. The present author has had this idea in mind for more than two decades, but the quantification of the sonnets based on the entire vocabulary was impossible at the

time by the personal computer such as PC9801 with a 640 KB main memory with an 8 MHz processor. This situation lasted for quite a long time until recently.
3   http://www.gutenberg.org/dirs/etext97/1ws0710.txt
4   Prof. David Roberts pointed out that these two sonnets have been a topic of discussion as to their dates of composition when the interim report of the present study was presented at University of Central England, July, 2007. Prof. Kate Mcluskie, Director of Shakespeare Institute, University of Birmingham, also agreed that these two sonnets are "unusual" in comparison with the others (personal communication when the author paid the visit to the institute with the interim report of the present study in August, 2007).

References

Biber, D. (1988) *Variation across speech and writing*. Cambridge: Cambridge University Press.

Biber, D. (1989) 'A typology of English texts,' *Linguistics*, 27: 3–43.

Biber, D. (1995) *Dimensions of Register Variation: A Cross-Linguistic Comparison*. Cambridge: Cambridge University Press.

Burrows, J. F. (1987) *Computation into Criticism: A Study of Jane Austen's Novels and an Experiment in Method*. Oxford: Clarendon Press.

Burrows, J. F. (1988) 'Word-Patterns and Story-Shapes: The Statistical Analysis of Narrative Style,' *Literary and Linguistic Computing*, 2: 61–70.

Burrows, J. F. (1992) 'Computers and the Study of Literature.' In C. S. Butler (ed.) *Computers and Written Texts*. Oxford: Blackwell, pp. 167–204.

Nakamura, J. (1993a) 'Quantitative comparison of modals in the Brown and the LOB corpora,' *ICAME Journal*, 17: 29–48.

Nakamura, J. (1993b) 'Statistical Methods and Large Corpora: A New Tool for Describing Text Types.' In M. Baker, G. Francis and E. Tognini-Bonelli (eds.) *Text and Technology: In Honour of John Sinclair*. Amsterdam: John Benjamins, pp. 293–312.

Nakamura, J. (1994) 'Extended Hayashi's Quantification Method Type III and its Application in Corpus Linguistics,' *Journal of Language and Literature, The Faculty of Integrated Arts and Sciences, The University of Tokushima*, 1: 141–192.

Nakamura, J. (1995) 'Text Typology and Corpus: A Critical Review of Biber's Methodology,' *English Corpus Studies*, 2: 75–90.

Nakamura, J. (2002) 'A Galaxy of Words: Structures Based upon Distributions of Verbs, Nouns and Adjectives in the LOB Corpus.' In T. Saito, J. Nakamura and S. Yamazaki (eds.) *English Corpus Linguistics in Japan*. Amsterdam: Rodopi, pp. 19–42.

Nakamura, J. (2003) 'The Structure of the BNC World Edition Based upon the Distribution of –ly Manner Adverbs: Cross-Examination by Means of Principal Component Analysis and Quantification of Contingency Table.' In J. Nakamura and T. Tabata, pp. 1–47.

Nakamura, J. and J. M. Sinclair (1995) 'The World of Woman in the Bank of English: Internal criteria for the classification of corpora,' *Literary and Linguistic Computing*, 10. 2: 99–110.

Nakamura, J. and T. Tabata (2003) A Comparative Study on the Methodologies of Genre and Style Analyses by Means of Multivariate Analyses. Report submitted to the Ministry of Education, Culture, Sports, Science and Technology for Grant-in-Aid for Scientific Research in the Years 2001–2002.

Nakamura, J. and M. Kasahara (2007) 'What's Good and What's Bad in the BNC World Edition? —Cross Examination of Multivariate Analyses Revisited—' Paper presented at ICAME28 held in Stratford-upon-Avon on May 23–27, 2007.

Tabata, T. (1994) 'Dickens's Narrative Style: A Statistical Approach to Chronological Variation,' *RISSH*, 30: 165–182.

Tabata, T. (1995) 'Narrative Style and the Frequencies of Very Common Words: A Corpus-based Approach to Dickens's First-person and Third-person Narratives,' *English Corpus Studies*, 2: 91–109.

Tabata, T. (2002) 'Investigating Stylistic Variation in Dickens through Correspondence Analysis of Word-Class Distribution.' In T. Saito, J. Nakamura and S. Yamasaki (eds.) *English Corpus Linguistics in Japan*. Amsterdam: Rodopi, pp. 165–182.

Tabata, T. (2003) 'Assessing Multivariate Techniques in Studies of Stylistic Variation in Texts: Cross-Examination of Principal Component Analysis and Correspondence Analysis.' In J. Nakamura and T. Tabata, pp. 48–67.

The *Cunningest, Rummest, Superlativest Old Fox:*
A Multivariate Approach to Superlatives in Dickens and Smollett

Tomoji Tabata

> Everything is of the *grandest, greatest, noblest, mightiest, loftiest*; or the *lowest, meanest, obscurest, vilest, and most pitiful.*
>
> (Dickens, "The Poetical Young Gentleman")

1 Introduction

This paper presents a corpus-driven approach to superlatives in Dickens and Smollett. The main focus is on the concomitant variations of frequency among superlatives. By taking a multivariate approach, this study attempts to illustrate how sharply the two authors differ in their uses of superlatives as well as how texts are clustered according to chronology within authorial sets.

While a number of studies describing Dickens' style have noted a tendency for overstatement in his fiction (Brook 1970; Sørensen 1985; Golding 1985; Hori 2004, etc.), surprisingly little attention has been paid to superlatives *per se*. Apart from Dickens studies, however, Biber *et al.* (1999) gives an interesting account of superlatives in four linguistic registers: conversation, fiction, news, and academic prose. According to Biber *et al.* (1999: 521), *–est* superlative adjectives are most frequent in news reportage (c. 1400 times per million words) while "the comparatively low frequency of superlatives in academic writing (c. 800 per million) reflects a general reluctance to make extreme claims", with fiction showing even lower frequency for the word class (c. 700 per million).

Dickens and Smollett contrast in terms of the frequency of superlative adjectives. In Dickens' 23 texts used in the current study, the number of tokens for *-est* superlatives amounts to 4,960, whereas Smollett employs them 634 times in all 7 of his works. In the normalised frequency scale per million words, the frequency in Dickens is nearly twice as high as in Smollett: 1,049 compared to 568. According to a G^2 test, the difference between the two authors is far above statistical significance of $p < 0.0001$ level.

Table 1. *-est* adjectives in Dickens and Smollett

	Tokens	Freq./million
Dickens	4,961	1,049
Smollett	634	568

*G^2(Log-likelihood ratio) for the difference between the authors is 246.9 (based on raw figures). (99.99th percentile; 0.01% level; $p < 0.0001$; critical value = 15.13)

As quoted above, the significantly higher frequency ratio in Dickens might seem due in part to his tendency to use superlatives in succession. Such an excessive repetition of a category is among the stylistic features employed by Dickens, and it is by no means limited to superlatives alone. A variety of alternative parts-of-speech (nouns, verbs, adjectives, and adverbs as well) are often used in concatenation. A simple sum statistic, together with the finding by Biber *et al.* (1999), would surely indicate that Dickens is very fond of superlatives (Brook, 1970: 19). However, the number overshadows a possible variance among superlatives favoured by each author as well as a possible variation within authorial sets. Some types of superlatives are more often used by Smollett than by Dickens. Some occur exclusively in Dickens. There are some types which appear more frequently in early texts than in later works, and so forth. To grasp the overall picture of this variation, it would be useful to employ a multivariate approach as a use of multivariate statistics would provide a graphical representation of the complex interrelationships among variables (words), interrelationships among observations (texts), and underlying associations between words and texts.

2 Multivariate approaches to style/register variation

Various multivariate analyses of texts have been successful in describing linguistic variation over time, variation across registers, variation across oceans, to say nothing of linguistic differences between authors (Brainerd, 1980; Burrows, 1987 & 1996; Biber and Finegan, 1992; Craig, 1999a, b, & c; Hoover, 2003a, b, & c; and Rudman, 2005, to name but a few). My earlier attempt used correspondence analysis to accommodate low frequency variables (words) in profiling authorial/chronological/cross-register variations in Dickens and Smollett (Tabata, 2005). Given the fact that most superlatives tend to be low in frequency, my methodology based on correspondence analysis might be usefully applied to a macroscopic analysis of superlatives.

3 Data

Table 2. Set of twenty-three texts by Dickens and seven texts by Smollett

No.	Author	Texts	Abbr.	Category	Date	Word-tokens
1	Dickens	Sketches by Boz	(SB)	Sketches	1833–6	188,591
2	Dickens	The Pickwick Papers	(PP)	Serial Fiction	1836–7	303,182
3	Dickens	Other Early Papers	(OEP)	Sketches	1837–40	67,149
4	Dickens	Oliver Twist	(OT)	Serial Fiction	1837–9	159,256
5	Dickens	Nicholas Nickleby	(NN)	Serial Fiction	1838–9	325,345
6	Dickens	Master Humphrey's Clock	(MHC)	Miscellany	1840–1	46,085
7	Dickens	The Old Curiosity Shop	(OCS)	Serial Fiction	1840–1	219,558
8	Dickens	Barnaby Rudge	(BR)	Serial Fiction	1841	256,082
9	Dickens	American Notes	(AN)	Sketches	1842	102,068
10	Dickens	Martin Chuzzlewit	(MC)	Serial Fiction	1843–4	339,906
11	Dickens	Pictures from Italy	(PFI)	Sketches	1846	72,636
12	Dickens	Dombey and Son	(DS)	Serial Fiction	1846–8	344,851
13	Dickens	David Copperfield	(DC)	Serial Fiction	1849–50	358,720
14	Dickens	A Child's History of England	(CHE)	History	1851–3	163,188
15	Dickens	Bleak House	(BH)	Serial Fiction	1852–3	357,048
16	Dickens	Hard Times	(HT)	Serial Fiction	1854	104,322
17	Dickens	Little Dorrit	(LD)	Serial Fiction	1855–7	340,657
18	Dickens	Reprinted Pieces	(RPR)	Sketches	1850–6	92,091
19	Dickens	A Tale of Two Cities	(TTC)	Serial Fiction	1559	136,625
20	Dickens	The Uncommercial Traveller	(UT)	Sketches	1860–9	143,148
21	Dickens	The Great Expectations	(GE)	Serial Fiction	1860–1	186,248
22	Dickens	Our Mutual Friend	(OMF)	Serial Fiction	1864–5	328,961
23	Dickens	The Mystery of Edwin Drood	(ED)	Serial Fiction	1870	94,642
				Sum of word-tokens in the set of Dickens texts: 4,730,359		
24	Smollett	Roderick Random	(SRR)	Fiction	1748	192,910
25	Smollett	Peregrine Pickle	(SPP)	Fiction	1751	342,963
26	Smollett	Ferdinand Count Fathom	(FCF)	Fiction	1753	159,088
27	Smollett	Sir Launcelot Greaves	(SLG)	Fiction	1760	89,636
28	Smollett	Travels through France and Italy	(TFL)	Sketches	1766	121,168
29	Smollett	History and Adventures of an Atom	(SAA)	Fiction	1768	59,168
30	Smollett	Humphrey Clinker	(SHC)	Fiction	1771	150,805
				Sum of word-tokens in the set of Smollett texts: 1,115,738		
				TOTAL OF WORD-TOKENS IN THE CORPUS: 5,846,097		

Table 2 shows a list of the texts examined. Dickens' set includes fifteen 'serial fictions', six 'sketches', one 'miscellany', and one 'history', and Smollett's set includes six 'fictions' and one 'sketch'. The total word-tokens in the corpus amount to 5.8 million, with the Dickens component containing 4.7 million word-tokens and the Smollett component totalling 1.1 million word-tokens. The present project was initiated as a study based on a comprehensive collection, not a sample corpus, of texts by the targeted authors, so the imbalance in the number of texts as well as tokens is inevitable. Nevertheless, due attention will be paid in the choice of variables to ensure that a size factor would not come into play in the outcome of analysis.

Table 3. Frequency matrix for 242 types of superlatives across 30 texts: raw frequency scores (*pre-transposed)

Rk.	Types	Sum	SB	PP	OEP	OT	NN	MHC	OCS	BR	AN	MC	PFI	DS	DC	CHE	BH	HT	LD	RPR	TTC	UT	GE	OMF	ED	SRR	SPP	SFCF	SLG	STFI	SAA	SHC
1	most_RBS	4825	257	312	119	110	372	33	125	186	120	222	67	188	207	116	179	50	193	68	57	103	85	135	154	42	529	275	34	29	163	73	158
2	best	2093	55	101	26	53	135	9	67	111	26	136	21	91	147	71	156	36	124	32	40	57	85	135	154	32	87	174	78	30	65	17	60
3	least	1779	51	61	20	27	102	15	49	80	41	128	27	113	114	16	112	22	87	33	20	35	41	76	26	3	73	34	30	4	43	19	66
4	most	567	18	28	18	9	42	2	18	31	17	36	13	26	26	16	35	11	40	12	13	23	19	41	20	14	12	12	4	2	8	4	15
5	greatest	487	20	14	12	9	17	2	13	14	34	15	15	18	15	15	34	10	44	18	12	15	26	20	20	3	53	7	16	2	17	11	24
6	worst	374	13	12	7	13	25	4	16	34	16	20	4	12	18	26	15	4	44	2	13	21	17	26	3	5	24	5	5	4	7	1	9
7	dearest	285	4	5	4	5	4	0	2	0	2	11	0	53	36	1	29	1	27	7	3	4	4	17	49	5	3	3	5	0	3	0	6
8	nearest	198	4	10	0	9	19	0	0	2	2	11	4	9	12	1	9	7	14	2	1	10	10	6	13	3	3	3	3	0	3	1	2
9	slightest	196	24	25	9	8	24	0	2	12	17	14	2	3	3	2	4	7	14	3	2	1	4	2	14	3	0	0	3	0	3	2	4
10	smallest	180	3	15	6	4	25	2	12	13	12	10	6	4	4	0	3	1	13	2	6	2	4	4	14	2	2	4	1	0	2	5	2
11	highest	178	7	9	6	4	7	0	0	12	5	8	0	4	8	2	12	3	11	6	5	2	4	4	14	3	17	1	2	0	0	0	2
12	eldest	172	22	5	6	7	0	0	1	5	0	18	0	7	28	1	8	4	11	6	2	0	5	6	6	0	0	0	1	0	0	1	7
13	youngest	155	20	6	6	2	17	0	6	1	1	49	4	0	8	1	6	1	2	4	5	1	8	10	10	0	2	2	5	0	5	0	4
14	lowest	105	8	3	0	9	2	0	0	3	2	6	4	4	5	5	5	0	4	2	4	1	5	6	10	2	5	3	5	0	5	0	7
15	strongest	84	4	1	2	9	3	0	7	3	2	6	0	4	3	1	5	3	2	4	2	1	2	2	6	0	3	2	2	0	5	1	2
16	deepest	82	4	11	1	1	3	0	2	7	2	11	0	3	5	0	6	1	4	5	1	4	2	6	7	0	0	2	2	0	3	0	4
17	oldest	82	5	4	5	3	4	0	0	3	2	8	0	3	2	4	6	2	4	2	0	5	3	2	14	0	0	0	0	0	0	0	0
18	finest	78	5	2	2	1	8	0	0	3	2	4	0	4	2	4	4	2	4	1	2	0	3	2	2	1	0	1	2	0	8	0	0
19	brightest	66	2	6	2	0	6	2	4	2	2	8	1	4	4	1	0	0	6	3	1	1	0	4	0	1	0	0	0	3	0	0	3
20	earliest	66	2	1	2	0	0	0	0	2	2	6	0	3	6	0	3	2	6	1	1	2	2	10	2	3	0	0	6	0	6	1	0
21	largest	61	1	5	5	0	6	0	5	4	2	2	2	2	2	0	3	0	4	0	1	0	4	0	5	0	0	2	2	0	2	0	3
22	happiest	54	5	4	1	0	4	0	0	1	2	2	2	4	4	0	2	2	1	5	2	1	0	2	2	2	5	6	0	0	0	0	1
23	warmest	53	3	4	1	4	3	0	5	1	0	2	1	0	2	4	0	0	6	0	1	0	0	4	0	0	0	0	0	0	2	1	0
24	strangest	52	2	8	1	1	2	0	0	5	2	6	3	2	4	2	2	0	3	0	0	1	3	0	5	0	0	0	0	0	0	0	0
25	remotest	50	5	3	0	1	3	1	0	2	2	10	1	4	0	0	4	2	0	0	2	0	0	4	0	0	0	0	0	0	2	0	0
26	uppermost	48	0	1	1	1	8	0	2	2	4	8	0	2	6	0	0	0	4	0	2	0	2	0	5	0	0	0	2	0	0	0	0
27	lightest	46	1	3	1	0	0	2	0	2	4	6	0	3	4	0	3	0	6	0	0	4	0	10	2	2	0	0	0	0	2	0	0
28	commonest	44	3	1	0	0	0	0	0	3	0	6	3	0	0	4	8	0	4	0	0	1	2	0	3	1	0	0	0	0	0	0	2
29	faintest	44	0	6	2	2	5	0	0	2	0	4	0	6	0	1	0	0	1	0	0	0	0	0	2	0	0	2	0	0	2	0	0
30	pleasantest	43	0	3	2	0	0	0	4	2	2	2	0	2	2	0	3	0	2	0	0	0	2	0	3	2	0	0	0	0	0	0	3
31	richest	43	2	1	3	0	2	0	1	6	1	2	0	2	3	0	1	0	4	0	0	0	0	2	0	0	2	2	2	0	1	0	0
32	longest	42	2	3	1	0	4	0	2	1	0	2	2	2	0	0	3	0	0	0	0	1	2	2	3	0	0	3	0	0	1	0	0
33	kindest	41	0	2	0	0	2	0	0	6	0	6	0	1	6	0	3	1	3	0	0	0	0	0	2	0	5	0	0	0	0	0	0
34	wildest	40	1	0	0	0	2	0	0	1	0	2	0	0	0	0	3	0	0	0	4	0	0	0	5	0	0	2	0	0	2	0	0
35	hardest	40	1	0	3	0	6	0	0	0	2	2	0	2	0	0	2	4	3	0	0	1	0	0	0	2	1	1	0	0	0	0	2
36	shortest	40	0	3	0	1	4	0	2	6	0	6	3	0	2	2	2	1	0	0	0	0	0	5	0	0	2	2	0	0	0	0	3
37	sweetest	35	1	3	0	0	6	0	0	6	3	4	0	2	3	0	2	0	4	3	0	0	0	2	0	0	0	0	0	0	0	0	0
38	liveliest	34	1	2	1	0	0	0	2	1	1	6	0	0	3	0	3	2	4	0	0	1	3	0	3	1	0	3	0	3	0	0	0
39	fullest	34	2	3	0	0	4	0	0	2	0	4	0	2	0	0	2	0	1	0	0	0	2	0	5	1	2	1	0	0	2	0	1
40	latest	33	0	0	1	0	0	0	0	1	0	2	0	1	2	8	3	0	3	2	0	0	0	0	5	1	0	0	0	0	1	0	0
41	meanest	33	0	0	0	0	0	0	0	0	0	2	0	0	3	0	4	0	1	0	0	0	2	0	2	0	2	2	0	0	0	0	0
42	wisest	31	0	0	0	1	0	0	0	5	0	2	0	2	0	2	3	0	1	0	0	0	0	2	3	0	2	3	0	0	0	0	0
43	goodest	30	2	0	2	0	2	0	0	1	0	6	0	2	3	0	3	0	0	0	0	0	0	2	2	0	2	0	0	0	2	0	0
44	prettiest	29	0	1	0	0	2	0	0	1	0	2	0	3	4	3	3	0	1	0	0	0	0	3	0	1	2	3	0	0	0	0	0
45	tenderest	28	0	1	0	0	2	0	0	0	0	0	0	1	0	0	3	0	1	0	0	0	0	0	2	0	0	0	0	0	0	0	0
46	furthest	27	1	0	0	2	0	0	0	3	0	2	3	1	0	0	2	0	0	0	0	0	0	0	4	0	0	0	0	0	1	0	0
47	purest	27	0	3	1	0	6	0	0	0	2	0	0	0	0	0	2	2	2	0	0	0	0	0	1	0	0	0	0	0	0	0	0
48	darkest	26	2	2	0	0	2	0	2	1	0	2	0	0	0	0	2	0	0	0	0	0	2	0	0	2	0	0	0	0	0	0	0
49	fairest	26	6	4	0	4	2	0	1	0	0	0	0	0	2	2	0	0	2	0	0	0	0	0	1	0	0	0	0	0	0	0	0
50	truest	26	0	0	1	0	0	0	0	0	0	0	0	1	0	2	0	0	0	0	0	0	0	0	1	0	0	0	0	0	0	0	0
...																																
242	weightiest	2	0	0	0	0	0	0	0	0	0	0	0	0	0	0	0	0	0	0	0	0	0	0	0	0	0	0	0	0	0	0	0

The respective frequency of each superlative can be arrayed to form the frequency-profile for the 30 texts (shown in Table 3). The total number of types is 424,[1] but statistical analysis is applied to 242 types which occur in two or more texts, with 182 other types excluded from analysis. This does not mean *hapax legomena* (165 types: *justest, superlativest, unfortunatest, best-temperedest*, etc.) and words occurring in a single text only (17 types: *affablest, cunningest, innocentest*, etc.) do not have stylistic significance, as they certainly do given that most of these 'impromptu' superlatives are uttered by, or refer to, Dickensian comic characters or grotesques as part of their distinctive speech habits indicative of the class to which they belong. The point here is that these words have already been identified. Hence there is no need to employ a multivariate technique to identify where these words occur. Rather, a close examination of concordance lines shows that these words tend to occur in juxtaposition or in concatenation, typically in early Dickens texts. Figure 1 below shows a concatenation of three or more superlatives. Of note is that 17 out of 22 instances are from the first ten years of Dickens' 37 year-long career.

Figure 1. Concordance : Concatenation of three or more superlatives (22 hits)

```
 1    nen was of the very  whitest, finest, and stiffest; his wig of the glossiest,     1836_PP
 2    est; his wig of the  glossiest, blackest, and curliest. His snuff was princes     1836_PP
 3    mail-cart; it's the  neatest, pwettiest, gwacefullest thing that ever wan upon    1836_PP
 4    an, "was one of the  merriest, pleasantest, cleverest fellows, that ever lived    1836_PP
 5    verything is of the  grandest, greatest, noblest, mightiest, loftiest; or the    1837OEP
 6    t, loftiest; or the  lowest, meanest, obscurest, vilest, and most pitiful. He    1837OEP
 7    admiring tone, `the  cunningest, rummest, superlativest old fox -- oh dem! --     1838_NN
 8    t-eyed niece -- the  softest, sweetest, prettiest --' `Alfred!' interposed Mad    1838_NN
 9    th 'em. He was the   cruellest, wickedest, out-and-outerest old flint that eve    1838_NN
10    pole's was the very  snuggest, cosiest, and completest bar, that ever the wit    1841_BR
11    ext minute, was the  mildest, amiablest, forgivingest-spirited, longest-sufferingest1841_BR
12    ing forehead -- the  easiest, freest, happiest man in all the world. Beside hi    1841_BR
13    e back-parlour: the  rosiest, cosiest, merriest, heartiest, best-contented old    1841_BR
14    quite an ogre. The   ugliest, awkwardest frightfullest being, you can imagain    1843_MC
15    e principle, in the  rottenest, craziest, leakingest tub of a wessel that a pl   1843_MC
16       `The worst. The   falsest, craftiest, meanest, cruellest, most sordid, most shameless184
17    t lifted her -- the  lightest, easiest, neatest thing you ever saw -- across t   1843_MC
18    out you; and is the  peaceablest, patientest, best-temperedest soul in the wor   1846bDS
19    ecks of some of the  bravest, wisest, and best in the land. But it never stru   1851CHE
20    ction of it, in the  hardest, barest, and straitest boards, with one dinted or   1855_LD
21    most engaging, the   simplest, truest, kindest, dearest, best fellow that ever   1855_LD
22    or dear, good dear,  truest, kindest, dearest, were the only words she had for   1855_LD
```

4 Correspondence Analysis

Correspondence Analysis (CA) is a dimension-reduction technique, which makes it possible to extract maximum variance from the data set. CA allows examination of the complex interrelationships among row cases (i.e., texts), interrelationships among column variables (i.e., words), and association between the row cases and column variables in multi-dimensional diagrams. It computes the row coordinates (word scores) and column coordinates (text scores) in a way that permutes the original data matrix so that the correlation between the word variables and text profiles are maximized. When the row/column coordinates are projected in scatter diagrams such as those shown in Figures 2 to 7, the relative distance between data points indicates affinity, similarity, association, or otherwise between them.

5 Results

The text-map in Figure 2 shows the two strongest dimensions in the data. Items close to each other are similar to each other over the occurrences of superlatives. Of special interest is that Dickens' texts and Smollett's texts are differentiated along the horizontal axis, a result demonstrating that the two authors have distinctive preferences for the use of superlatives. It is also interesting to note that the early Dickensian texts, such as *Sketches by Boz, Pickwick Papers,* and *Nicholas Nickleby*, are among the closest to Smollett's texts along the horizontal axis. Within the Dickens set, early texts sit on the upper half of the diagram. Later texts, on the other hand, tend to be scattered in the bottom half. The vertical axis can thus be interpreted as representing a contrast between Dickens' early and later works.

Figure 3, the word-map, shows the interrelationships among 242 superlatives. The size (area) of each circle indicates its frequency in the corpus. Items close to each other, again, are similar to each other in their concomitant frequency patterns across 30 texts. Since the text-map and the word-map correspond to each other, it is possible to graphically represent the different preferences for superlatives between Smollett's and Dickens' works. Word entries lying towards the left or the right extremes of Figure 3 have the strongest discriminating power between the two authors.

The Dickens set is more than four times the size of the Smollett set, and the number of types used by Dickens is nearly four times as many as those used by Smollett. Yet, it becomes clear that the size factor does not actually cause nor emphasize the differentiation between the two authors when the number of variables is substantially decreased so that all variables are common to both authors. Despite the reduction of the number of variables to 105 types used by both of the two authors, the configuration of texts is remarkably similar to that based on 242 items (the diagrams are not displayed here due to space limitations[2]).

Figure 2. Correspondence Analysis of superlatives in Dickens & Smollett based on 242 types that appear in two or more texts: Text-map showing interrelationships between 30 texts

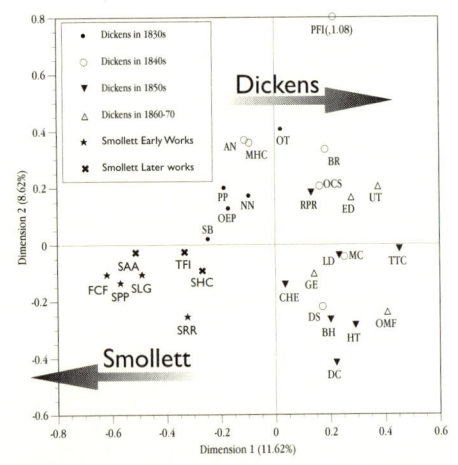

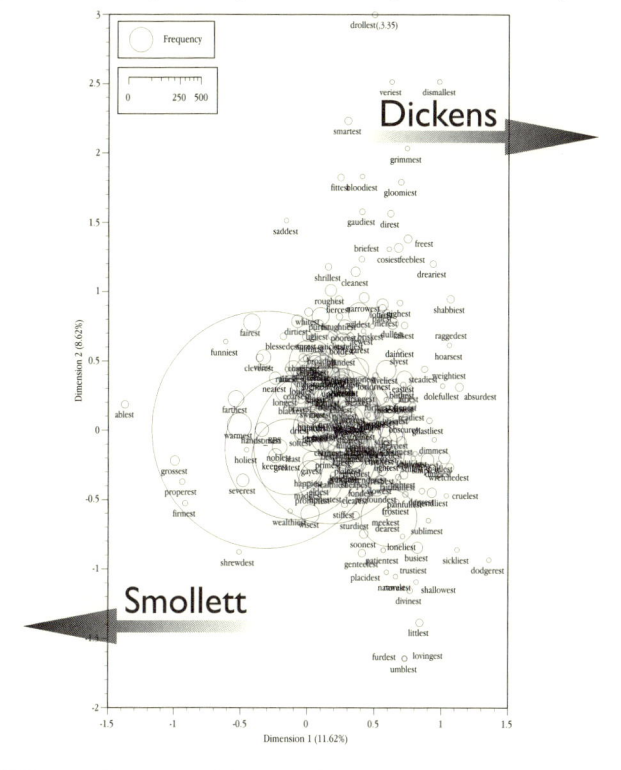

Figure 3. Word-map showing interrelationships between 242 superlatives

The difference between Dickens and Smollett becomes even more striking when the variables include 'periphrastic superlatives', which are made up of *most* + (usually polysyllabic) adjective (of Romance origin) as follows:

> ... and the preparations altogether were on the *most laborious* and *most comprehensive* scale.
> (Dickens, *Sketches by Boz*)

Comparing Table 4 with Table 1 leads us to realise that periphrastic superlatives are substantially more frequent than regular superlatives. Of further interest is that, with periphrastic superlatives included, it is now Smollett who exhibits the higher frequency ratio.

Table 4. Total of superlatives (including periphrastic superlatives)

	Tokens	Freq./million
Dickens	11,136	2,354
Smollett	2,812	2,520

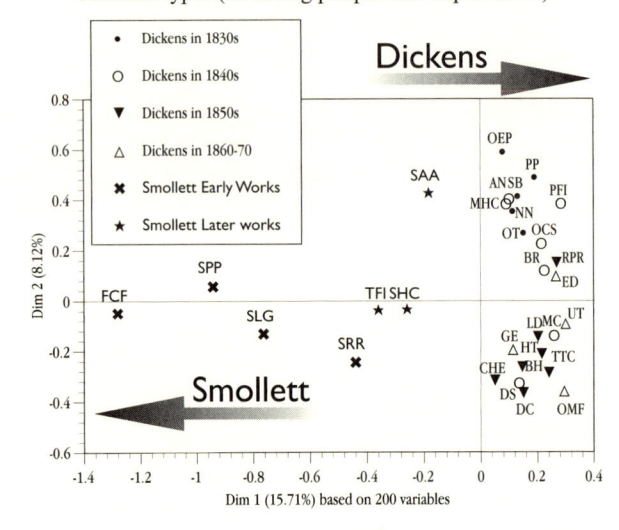

Figure 4. Text-map showing interrelationships among 30 texts based on 200 most common types (including periphrastic superlatives)

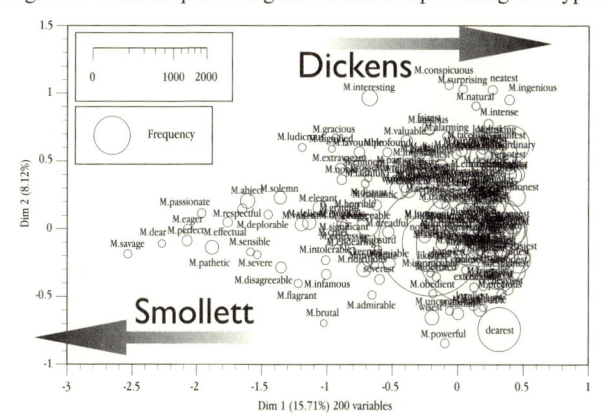

Figure 5. Word-map showing interrelationships among 200 types

Figures 4 and 5 are derived from CA of 200 most common types including periphrastic superlatives. The horizontal axis of Figure 4 demonstrates that the variance within the Smollett set is considerably greater than the variance within the Dickens set. On the other hand, the vertical axis again appears to indicate a variation from early to later Dickens texts. In Figure 5, words beginning with 'M.' are periphrastic superlatives. The prominent feature of the graph in Figure 5 is that the texts by Smollett are more strongly associated with periphrastic superlatives, a feature that betokens Smollett's overall preference for adjectives of Romance origin. This is in contrast to the fact that Dickens employs a considerably larger inventory of regular superlative adjectives. The contrast becomes even more vivid when the number of variables is reduced to the 100 most common types (shown in Figures 6 and 7).

Figure 6. Text-map showing interrelationships among 30 texts based on 100 most common types (including periphrastic superlatives)

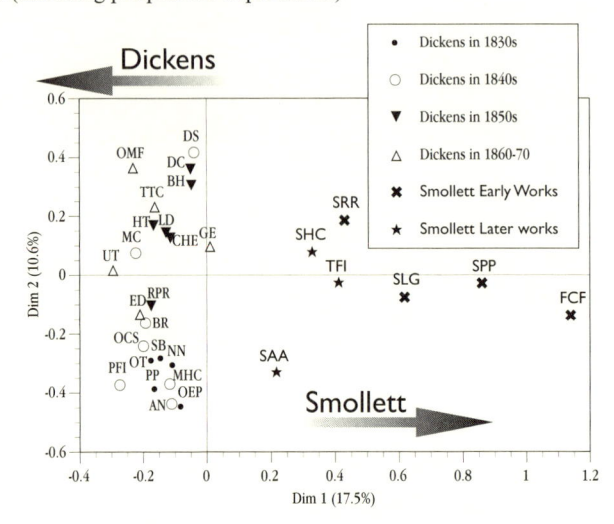

Figure 7. Word-map showing interrelationships among 100 types

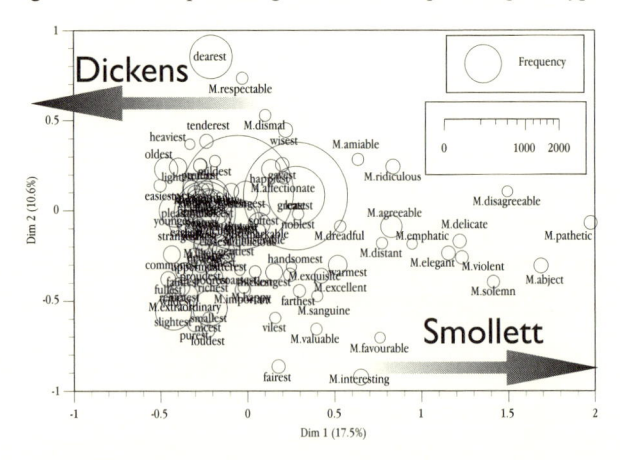

Note that the analyses in Figures 6 and 7 show that the locations of text- and word-entries are reversed along both horizontal and vertical axes. The Dickens

texts sit in the left while the Smollett texts in the right. The Early Dickens texts find themselves in the bottom half while later Dickens works tend to be found in the upper half of the diagram. Of note is the relative positioning of data points. The overall configuration of the texts in Figure 6 is in fact remarkably consistent with Figure 4. This means that the difference between Dickens and Smollett in their uses of superlatives is quite pervasive regardless of the number of variables analysed.

A close examination of outlying words shown in Figure 7 in concordance lines either highlights Smollett's tendency to use superlatives in more or less fixed collocations, or his lack of variety in collocation. Smollett tends to repeat the same collocational frames in a text as the following collocations lines in Figure 8 show:

Figure 8. Fixed collocations

most abject

```
1      had_VBD implored_VBN in_IN the_DT most_RBS abject_JJS manner_NN, after_IN having_VBG bee   1748_SRR
2   mplored_VBN pardon_VB in_IN the_DT most_RBS abject_JJS manner_NN, begging_VBG with_IN man    1751_SPP
3    N an_DT instant_NN, from_IN the_DT most_RBS abject_JJS misery_NN and_CC contempt_NN.        1748_SRR
4     person_NN, who_WP, from_IN the_DT most_RBS abject_JJS misery_NN, had_VBN by_IN his_PP$ i   1751_SPP
5    P was_VBD reduced_VBN to_IN the_DT most_RBS abject_JJS misery_NN, by_IN the_DT death_NN o   1751_SPP
6    N me_PP, I_PP lay_VBD in_IN the_DT most_RBS abject_JJS misery_NN, among_IN straw_NN; and_   1753_FCF
```

most pathetic

```
7    ying_VBG to_IN her_PP in_IN the_DT most_RBS pathetic_JJS manner_NN not_XNOT to_TO go_VB awa  1846b_DS
8     her_PP, therefore_RB, in_IN the_DT most_RBS pathetic_JJS manner_NN, to_TO pardon_VB him_PP, 1751_SPP
9     ess_NN, delivered_VBN in_IN the_DT most_RBS pathetic_JJS manner_NN, made_VBD an_DT impressi 1751_SPP
10    P conjured_VBD him_PP in_IN the_DT most_RBS pathetic_JJS manner_NN, to_TO tell_VB her_PP if 1753_FCF
11    houghts_NNS of_OF parting_NN, a_DT most_RBS pathetic_JJS silence_NN for_IN some_DT time_NN  1751_SPP
12    PP and_CC weeping_VBG in_IN the_DT most_RBS pathetic_JJS silence_NN. Having_VBG performe    1751_SPP
13    N and_CC affection_NN in_IN the_DT most_RBS pathetic_JJS terms_NNS, and_CC begg'd_JJ leave_ 1751_SPP
14    deplorable_JJ case_NN in_IN the_DT most_RBS pathetic_JJS terms_NNS, and_CC intreated_VBD h  1751_SPP
15    ressed_VBD himself_PP in_IN the_DT most_RBS pathetic_JJS terms_NNS, on_IN the_DT untoward_J 1753_FCF
16    y_PP$ love_NN, she_PP in_IN the_DT most_RBS pathetic_JJS terms_NNS recommended_VBD Serafina 1753_FCF
```

most emphatic

```
17    ccordingly_RB preserved_VBD the_DT most_RBS emphatic_JJS silence_NN.    I_PP got_VBD up_RB, 1751_SPP
18    s_NNS to_IN heaven_NN in_IN the_DT most_RBS emphatic_JJS silence_NN; then_RB convey_VB the_ 1762_SLG
19    VBG his_PP$ eyes_NNS, in_IN the_DT most_RBS emphatic_JJS silence_NN  -- ``George_NP (said_  1771_SHC
```

Repeated collocational frames are also found in Dickens, but Dickens is more likely to use them across different texts. Consider the following examples in Figure 9: the concordance lines of the *most solemn* + *NN* framework. *Manner*, again, appears as a favoured head noun for the frame. Given an earlier finding (Tabata, 2005) that Dickens has a much larger inventory of descriptive manner adverbs than Smollett, the relatively lower frequency ratio of *in the most* + *JJ* +*manner* in Dickens could be interpreted as being a trade off by the increased use of descriptive *–ly* manner adverbs. Conversely, in a context where Smollett resorts to descriptive prepositional phrases, Dickens might be more likely to employ *–ly* manner adverbs.

Figure 9. Fixed collocations (cont'd)

```
3127  wick_NP declared_VBD, in_IN the_DT most_RBS solemn_JJS and_CC emphatic_JJS terms_NNS, t    1836_PP
3128  you_PP, by_IN all_DT I_PP hold_VBP most_RBS solemn_JJS and_CC most_RBS sacred_JJS, that    1837b_OT
3129  n_RB and_CC again_RB, in_IN the_DT most_RBS solemn_JJS and_CC fervid_NN manner_NN, that_I  1838_NN
3130  y_PP had_VBD been_VBN of_OF the_DT most_RBS solemn_JJS and_CC tremendous_JJS nature_NN,    1840b_OCS
3131  OF my_PP$ designs_NNS in_IN the_DT most_RBS solemn_JJS and_CC pathetic_JJS vows_NNS.       1748_SRR
3132  uire_NN promised_VBD, in_IN the_DT most_RBS solemn_JJS and_CC fervent_JJS manner_NN, to    1762_SLG
3133  s_VBD proceeding_VBG, with_IN a_DT most_RBS solemn_JJS countenance_NN, to_TO hear_VB the_  1837a_OEP
3134  _DT most_RBS stately_JJS, the_DT most_RBS solemn_JJS, grand_JJS, majestic_JJS, mournful    1846a_PFI
3135  it_PP as_IN constituting_VBG a_DT most_RBS solemn_JJS imprecation_NN.</s> </p> <p> <s>I_   1849_DC
3136  n_WRB he_PP swore_VBD in_IN the_DT most_RBS solemn_JJS manner_NN, that_RB if_IN they_PP w  1751_SPP
3137  conjured_VBN them_PP in_IN the_DT most_RBS solemn_JJS manner_NN to_TO let_VB no_DT impur   1751_SPP
3138  nce_NN, declaring_VBG in_IN the_DT most_RBS solemn_JJS manner_NN, that_IN he_PP had_VBD n  1751_SPP
3139  ord_NN protested_VBD, in_IN the_DT most_RBS solemn_JJS manner_NN, that_IN he_PP still_RB   1751_SPP
3140  _PP had_VBD swore_VBD in_IN the_DT most_RBS solemn_JJS manner_NN, that_IN his_PP$ intenti  1753_FCF
3141  ore_IN entering_VBG into_IN the_DT most_RBS solemn_JJS of_OF covenants_NNS with_IN the_DT  1843_MC
3142  PP had_VBD won_VBN under_IN the_DT most_RBS solemn_JJS professions_NNS of_OF honour_NN an  1753_FCF
3143  PP$ forgiveness_NN, with_IN the_DT most_RBS solemn_JJS promises_NNS of_OF regarding_VBG y  1753_FCF
3144  ssuring_VBG her_PP, with_IN the_DT most_RBS solemn_JJS protestations_NNS of_OF love_NN an  1753_FCF
3145  NN, to_TO whom_WP, after_IN the_DT most_RBS solemn_JJS protestations_NNS of_OF his_PP$ ow  1753_FCF
3146  VBD Mrs_NP Wickam_NP in_IN her_PP$ most_RBS solemn_JJS tones_NNS, ``was_VBD put_VBN upon_  1846b_DS
3147  N; in_IN violation_NN of_OF the_DT most_RBS solemn_JJS treaties_NNS: that_IN he_PP was_VB  1769_SAA
3148  d_VBN to_TO Fathom_NP by_IN the_DT most_RBS solemn_JJS vows_NNS, to_TO witness_VB which_W  1753_FCF
```

6 Final Remarks

This paper has described a multivariate study of superlatives in Dickens and Smollett. What has emerged from this approach might best be summarised by the following four points:

First of all, the two authors differ sharply in their uses of, as well as their repertoire for, superlatives. Dickens has a larger number of tokens of, as well as a larger inventory of, superlative adjectives. Smollett, by contrast, turns more freely to periphrastic superlatives, which reflects his stylistic preference for words of Romance origin.

Second, stylistic change over time is reflected in the distribution of superlatives (though the interrelationships among superlatives associated with the chronological change are yet to be examined in any detail).

Third, Smollett uses superlatives in a more fixed or monotonous fashion, typically sticking to the same collocational frames within a single text. Dickens also favours several types of fixed frames, but his use is not limited to a single text, they are likely to occur across texts.

Fourth, and finally, Dickens coined a large number of 'impromptu' superlatives. Impromptu words tend to occur in succession with other superlatives (juxtaposition or concatenation), and typically in early Dickens works. They are often uttered by, or used to describe, comic characters, to achieve a characterizing effect, to provide an indication of the social backgrounds to which the characters belong.

It is hoped that this multivariate approach might open up an interesting new avenue of investigation to quantitative analysis of superlatives in and across texts.

Notes

1 Superlative adverbs such as *most, best,* and *least* are included
2 The frequency datasheet and the solutions of CA based on 105 superlatives common to both Dickens and Smollett are available from the author upon request.

References

Biber, D. and E. Finegan (1992) 'The Linguistic Evolution of Five Written and Speech-Based English Genres from the 17th to the 20th Centuries,' in M. Rissanen (ed.) *History of Englishes*: *New Methods and Interpretation in Historical Linguistics*. Berlin/New York: Mouton de Gruyter. 668–704.

Biber, D., S. Johansson, G. Leech, S. Conrad and E. Finegan (1999) *Longman Grammar of Spoken and Written English*. Harlow: Pearson Education Ltd.

Brainerd, B. (1980) 'The Chronology of Shakespeare's Plays: A Statistical Study,' *Computers and the Humanities*, 14: 221–230.

Brook, G. L. (1970) *The Language of Dickens*. London: Andre Deutsch.

Burrows, J. F. (1987) *Computation into Criticism*: *A study of Jane Austen's novels and an experiment in method*. Oxford: Clarendon Press.

Burrows, J. F. (1996) 'Tiptoeing into the Infinite: Testing for Evidence of National Differences in the Language of English Narrative', in S. Hockey and N. Ide (eds.) *Research in Humanities Computing 4*. Oxford/New York: Oxford UP. 1–33.

Craig, D. H. (1999a) 'Johnsonian chronology and the styles of *A Tale of a Tub*,' in M. Butler (ed.) *Re-Presenting Ben Jonson: Text Performance, History*. London: Macmillan, 210–232.

Craig, D. H. (1999b) 'Authorial Attribution and Computational Stylistics: If You Can Tell Authors Apart, Have You Learned Anything About Them?' *Literary and Linguistic Computing*, 14: 103–113.

Craig, D. H. (1999c) 'Contrast and Change in the Idiolects of Ben Jonson Characters,' *Computers and the Humanities*, 33. 3: 221–240.

Golding, R. (1985) *Idiolects in Dickens*. New York: St. Martin's Press.

Hoover, D. L. (2003a) 'Frequent Collocations and Authorial Style,' *Literary and Linguistic Computing*, 18: 261–286.

Hoover, D. L. (2003b) 'Multivariate Analysis and the Study of Style Variation,' *Literary and Linguistic Computing*, 18: 341–360.

Hori, M. (2004) *Investigating Dickens' style: A Collocational Analysis*. New York: Palgrave Macmillan.

Rudman, J. (2005) 'The Non-Traditional Case for the Authorship of the Twelve Disputed "Federalist" Papers: A Monument Built on Sand?", *ACH/ALLC 2005 Conference Abstracts*, Humanities Computing and Media Centre, University of Victoria, Canada, 193–196.

Sørensen, K. (1985) *Charles Dickens: Linguistic Innovator*. Aarhus: Aarhus Universitet.

Tabata, T. (2005) 'Profiling stylistic variations in Dickens and Smollett through correspondence analysis of low frequency words', *ACH/ALLC 2005 Conference Abstracts*, Humanities Computing and Media Centre, University of Victoria, Canada, 229–232.

On the Concept of Habitual Style in the BNC

Kaoru Takahashi

1 Introduction

Trudgill (1992) claims that, in terms of sociolinguistics, styles are characterized as varieties of a language which can range on a continuum from very formal to very informal. His notion of style is closely linked to so called factors, which constitute a speech community. Yet the notion of style cannot be limited by formality or informality alone. It may be possible to explore other parameters of style regarding text, linguistic situations and communities. Such an exploration may redefine the notion of style. It is my intention in this thesis to expand the sociolinguistic notion of style by the inclusion of a number of factors in the exploration of style and social contextual variables. In order to achieve this, however, an understanding of the diversity and variety of speaker-hearer communities is indispensable. As Mesthrie (2000:37) points out, traditionally, sociologists study societies in terms of categories like class, ethnicity or region and economic characteristics. Community as typically used in sociology suggests a dimension of shared knowledge, possessions or behaviours. The term speech community came to be used in terms of social organisation, in contrast with community as used in sociology. Yet, speech community is not precise enough to be considered as a technical term. This impression is amplified by the range of definitions of speech community presented by scholars.

1. "Shared language use" (Lyons 1981).

2. "Frequency of interaction by a group of people" (Bloomfiled 1933; Hockett 1958; Gumperz 1962).

3. "Shared rules of speaking and interpretations of speech performance" (Hymes 1972).

4. "Shared attitudes and values regarding language forms and language use" (Labov 1972).

5. "Shared sociocultural understandings and presupposition regarding speech events" (Sherzer 1977).

However, the core meaning of speech community, according to Mesthrie (2000), is that a speech community consists of people who are in habitual contact with each other by means of speech. This involves either a shared language variety or shared ways of interpreting the different language varieties commonly used in the area. This implies a concept which may be associated with the notion of style, habitual. In fact, the concept of speaker's individual habits is discussed by Tannen (1984:1). Tannen claims that many of the basic elements of how people talk, which seem self-evidently appropriate differ from one person to the next and from one group to the next, which largely depends on a speaker's individual habits as well as such differences as gender, ethnicity, class and regional background. Consequently, in this thesis, when I see regularities in a set of data that I claim forms a speech community, I imply that it has been formed by habitual contact. As such, habitual contact is the assumed explanation which allows us to understand the origin of the speech communities identified in this thesis[1].

For the moment, let me highlight an example of the basic elements of how people talk in the light of the construction of sentences. In this respect, I can note the discussion of the habitual sense of the verb by Fraser (1976). Fraser claims that the habitual sense of the verb correlates positively with the *Fred picked up the book* construction. The habitual meaning of the verb phrase can be one semantic variable. If the verb phrase denotes the habitual meaning, then the *Fred picked up the book* construction is preferred to the *Fred picked the book up* construction as follows.

a. *The police are tracking down criminals.*
b. *The police are tracking criminals down.*
c. *The police track down criminals.*
d. *The police track criminals down.*

Fraser (1976:20-1) claims that a. and c. are more natural than b. and d. respectively. In this case, some of particles can take a perfect maker. For example, *up* can take such a marker as *all*, *all the way* or *completely*. This claim is somewhat dubious in that he has no explanation for this observation (Fraser 1976:21). It seems that no study has ever found any support for this claim. Similarly in the case of the semantic variable, Gries (2003:17) suggests that the degree of cognitive entrenchment (or cognitive familiarity) of the referent with the direct object contributes to particle placement. The degree of entrenchment has, been measured by the position of the direct object's referent on entrenchment hierarchy shown in Table 1. On the basis of a corpus analysis and a survey of acceptability judgements by native speakers of British English, Table 1 shows that for frequency counts and acceptability judgements highly entrenched referents of direct objects correlate significantly with *Fred picked the book up* construction while barely entrenched referents of direct objects correlate significantly with *Fred picked up the book* construction. Furthermore, as one attempt, let me focus on the concept of habitual style in the light of sentence usage and later discuss the property of habitual contact. In this respect, the present progressive can be referred to as follows:

> *I'm playing golf regularly these days.*
> *She's not working at the moment.*
> *He's walking to work while his car is being repaired.*

Table 1. A variety of entrenched referents

		Least entrenched		
1.	Abstract entities	inamimate	Abstract	lexical
2.	Sensual entities	▲	▲	
3.	Locations			
4.	Containers			
5.	Concrete objects	animate		
6.	Animate beings (other than humans)			
7.	Kin terms			
8.	Proper names			proper name
9.	3rd person singular pronoun			personal
10.	2nd person singular pronoun	human animate	▼	
11.	1st person singular pronoun	▼	Concrete	
		Most entrenched		

Leech and Svartvik (2002:68) claim that this usage combines the temporary meaning of the progressive with the repetitive meaning of the habitual present. With reference to the present progressive, we can focus on the habitual present, which is used with dynamic verb senses to refer to events that repeatedly occur without limitation on their extension into the past or future. My hypothesis is that when texts comprise the usage of these sentences, the texts assume habitual style. In any case, habitual contact can be seen as one of the cores of the concept in speech community, a core shared by the multiple definitions of speech community given above. In other words, I assume that habitual contact is the key to the use of a range of factors used within a speech community to form meaning.

2 Methodology

Multivariate analysis is a statistical procedure concerned with the analysis of multiple measurements of each individual or object in one or more samples. In linguistics, due to the availability of electronic texts, multivariate analysis promises to allow a computer to do more than just count the frequencies of words or find the functions of specific features in the texts. I am using a multivariate analysis technique in this paper, 'Extended Hayashi's Quantification Type III' (hereafter EHT3).² Focusing on social variables encoded in the BNC, **spolog** is a variable distinguishing Monologue from Dialogue in the spoken texts. **Spolog** 1 is Monologue; **spolog** 2 is Dialogue. Table 2 shows that the number of words in Dialogue is much greater than that of Monologue. Despite the bias in the proportion, it is safe to say that the number of words (almost 100,000) in Monologue is enough to compare it with Dialogue.

Table 2. The varieties of demographic respondent

Interaction type	code	texts	w-units	%	s-units	%
Monologue	spolog1	212	1578614	15.26	94272	9.07
Dialogue	spolog2	698	8763115	84.73	944849	90.92

3 Analysis by a single variable, spolog

The analysis starts with counting the frequencies of POS tags and normalising them to the ratio per sentence and then the normalised frequency table is fed into the statistical procedure. Tables 3 and 4 show salient features with scores resulting from EHT3. Fig 1 is a bar graph of Axis 1.³ The graph shows Dialogue on the positive side and Monologue on the negative side separately.⁴ It is observed that the variable **spolog** tends to distinguish features on the side of Dialogue from those on the side of Monologue. Also, Dialogue has by far more features than Monologue. It follows from this fact that Dialogue is abundant in the usage of verbs. For example, verb groups such as the *do* group, lexical verb group and *have* group, except for VVZ, VVN and VHD are on the positive side, to which Dialogue pertains. However, six verbs in each verb group do not have coherent characteristics. In contrast, VHD, VBG and VBD tend to be more often used in Monologue than Dialogue. In the case of other features, in Dialogue, ITJ, XX0, AVP, PNP, NP0 and PNI are commonly used than in Monologue; in Monologue, PRF, CJT, CRD, UNC, PNX, ZZ0, NN0 and AT0 are more commonly used than in Dialogue.

Table 3. List of domains and features on the positive side along axis 1 in spolog

Tags		
ITJ	Interjection or other isolate	0.531
VDG	The -ing form of the verb DO: doing	0.285
VDB	The finite base form of the verb Do: do	0.271
XX0	The negative particle not or n't	0.211
Categories	spolog2(Dialogue)	0.167
VHN	The past participle form of the verb HAVE: had	0.146
AVP	Adverb particle	0.143
PNP	Personal pronoun	0.134
VBZ	The -s form of the verb BE: is, 's	0.127
VHB	The finite base form of the verb HAVE: have, 've	0.125
NP0	Proper noun	0.120

Table 4. List of domains and features on the negative side along axis 1 in spolog

Tags		
PRF	The preposition of	-0.185
NN2	Plural common noun	-0.170
CJT	The subordinating conjunction that	-0.151
CRD	Cardinal number	-0.148
UNC	Unclassified items	-0.147
VBD	The past tense forms of the verb BE	-0.146
PNX	Reflexive pronoun	-0.146
VHD	The past tense form of the verb HAVE: had, 'd	-0.139
ZZ0	Alphabetical symbols	-0.130
NN0	Common noun, neutral for number	-0.130
VBG	The -ing form of the verb BE: being	-0.124
AT0	Article	-0.109
NN1	Singular common noun	-0.104
EX0	Existential there	-0.097
PRP	Preposition	-0.097
PNQ	Wh-pronoun	-0.095
Categories	spolog1(Monologue)	-0.094

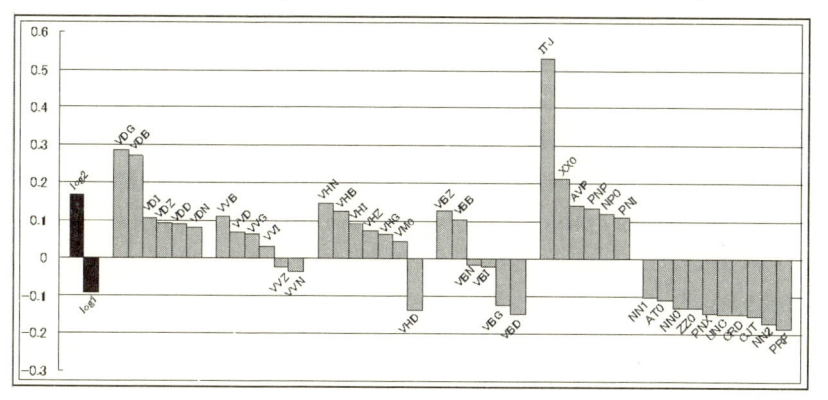

Figure 1. Bar Graph of Categories and Tags on axis 1 of spolog

log1: (**spolog**1: Monologue) log2: (**spolog 2**:Dialogue)

4 Interpretation of spolog dimension

Let me interpret this dimension by taking into account the difference between dialogue and monologue. The most notable difference is that dialogue is the conversation of two or more persons whereas monologue is an extended speech by one person. Dialogue integrates high amounts of information into a text. In contrast, monologue is composed of texts in highly constrained production circumstances. Therefore, it is natural that emotional expression is more used in dialogue than in monologue, as ITJ can be identified as the most salient feature on the side of Dialogue. Negation, XX0, is also the typical marker used in dialogue because as a response to questions, it is thought that negation is often used. On the opposite side, PRF, NN2, and CJT are representative of the negative side concerning Monologue. Common uses of these features on the negative side seem to describe a codified form of texts. Focusing on the features of the side, let me discuss the concept of habitual style. As Tannen (1984:1) claims, many of the basic elements of how people talk, which seem self-evidently appropriate, differ from one person to the next and from one group to the next, which largely depends on a speaker's individual habits as well as such differences as gender, ethnicity, class and regional background. My hypothesis here is that monologue most represents the property of habitual contact, because contact with the person is restricted to himself, when the person behaves habitually without being interfered by any person. Originally, the concept of habitual covers the spoken part, so it may not be acceptable to restrict this concept of style to monologue alone. It is expected that the discussion of habitual will lead me to the interpretation of dialogue. More detailed scrutiny is required in terms of lexis and semantics in Section 6.

5 Analysis by multiple variables, spolog and scgdom

This section deals with the cross-sectional distribution between two variables of the spoken part in the BNC. Subcorpora generated by two variables are analyzed by EHT3, hence the similarity and the dissimilarity in the axes by two variables are made explicit. Although subcorpora have been generated by a single variable, the analyses by two variables, **spolog** and **scgdom**, a classification of domain in context-governed spoken material in the spoken texts, can reveal finer variations of subcorpora. It is hoped, therefore, that I can verify the interpretation of relevant variables given or give more convincing interpretation concerning habitual style. Furthermore, if the analyses do not give us satisfactory results and are left aside, the subcorpora in question are examined in terms of lexis and semantics in Section 6.

As shown in Table 5 when texts of **spolog** are divided by **scgdom**, a classification of domain in context-governed spoken material, it is observed that in Monologue, there are a large number of texts concerning *education/information* and *leisure*, whereas there are relatively few concerning business. However, the bias in this distribution is trivial, so we can discard it. As the result of the same analysis, the distribution of subcorpora is shown in Fig 2 (discard tags plotted in this figure). Along axis 2, the positive side pertains to Dialogue, and the negative side pertains to Monologue in every domain, apart from *Educational*

Table 5. Cross distribution of spolog and scgdom

		spolog1	spolog2	scgdom %
		Monologue	*Dialogue*	
	scgdom %	15.26	84.74	
scgdom1	*Educational/informative*	31.00	25.08	26.60
scgdom2	*Business*	16.45	22.56	20.99
scgdom3	*Public/Institutional*	21.87	28.69	26.93
scgdom4	*Leisure*	30.68	23.68	25.48
	sum %	100.00	100.00	100.00

Figure 2. Distribution of subcorpora by scgdom and spolog

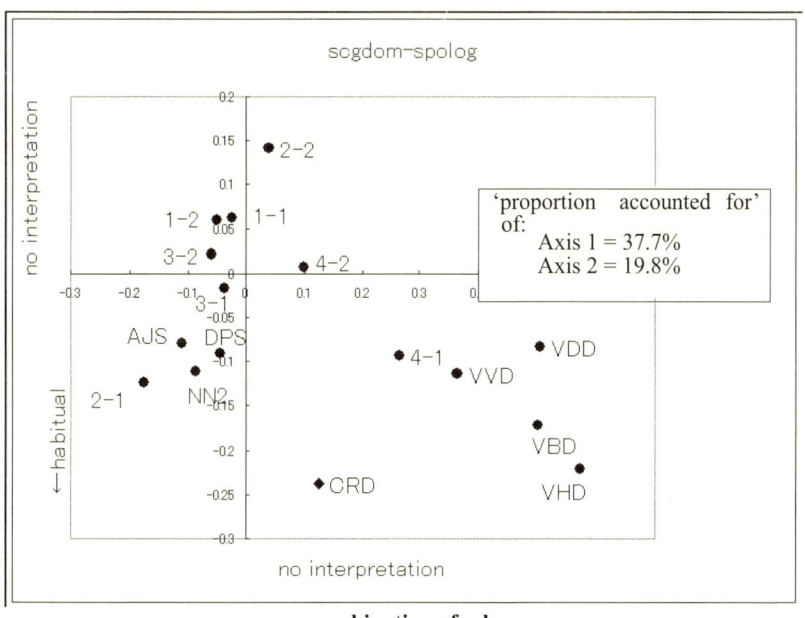

```
scgdom-spolog
```

'proportion accounted for' of:
Axis 1 = 37.7%
Axis 2 = 19.8%

combination of a-b

a=1. *Educational/Informative*   b=1. *Monologue*
   2. *Business*   2. *Dialogue*
   3. *Public/Institutional*
   4. *Leisure*

/Informative. When it comes to axis 1, it is difficult to characterize in the same manner. Therefore, the discussion, in terms of lexis and semantics, is expected to arrive at a conclusion which relates to the property of habitual contact.

6 Analysis and consideration in terms of lexis and semantics

My conclusion so far is that in contrast to dialogue, monologue more represents the property of habitual contact. In the light of tag annotations, ITJ and XX0 are characteristic of Dialogue and, in contrast, NN2 (plural common noun), AJS (superlative adjective), and verb group of the past tense are characteristic of Monologue. In this section, in order to substantiate my claim more convincingly, salient subcorpora generated by **spolog** and **scgdom**, a classification of domain are focused on in the light of relevant lexicon in the same manner as done in the former sections. Focusing on tag annotations in Fig 2, AJS and NN2 are characteristic of the third quadrant to which a subcorpus of *Business* and Monologue (labelled as 2-1) pertains. The past tense of verbs, i.e., VHD, VBD, VDD, VVD is characteristic of the fourth quadrant to which a subcorpus of Leisure and Monologue (labelled as 4-2) pertains. Firstly, let me focus on the subcorpus of Leisure and Monologue. Among features concerning the past tense, VDD is noteworthy. The occurrences of the words tagged as VDD are compared with those in a neutral subcorpus, *Public/Institutional* and Monologue (labelled as 3-1).[5] Tables 6 enumerates words tagged as VVD in both subcorpora in descending order of their ratios as follows, *liked, picked, worked, won, wore, closed, lived, broke, played, sat, got, stopped, called* and *met*. The following words whose ratios amount up to 3.0 are *grew, walked, decided, kept, lost, ended, passed, started, stood, bought, included, enjoyed, used, sent, seemed, left, drew, ran, came, took, stayed, threw, visited* and *held*. Apart from those classified as verbs of attitude such as *liked, enjoyed*, activity verbs such as *picked, worked, wore, closed, broke, played, sat* etc., which are concerned with events occurring in the daily life, are noteworthy. Among them, words with a frequency of more than 100 are *worked, lived, got* and *started*, which are most commonly used in a subcorpus of Leisure and Monologue. Interestingly, regarding the salient word, *worked*, the present form, *work*, tends to be interpreted in a habitual sense (see Quirk et al 1985: 202). In the case of the past tense, the same tendency can be observed as follows:

... *all day Saturday doing the show, and we **worked** all day Sunday clearing the field!*

(F7Y 106 Title: Harlow Study Centre: oral history interview)

The same is true with *lived* as follows:

*Well a lot of those people **lived** round there and they were hovels.*

(FXX 137 Title: Nottingham Oral History Project: interview)

Looking at works categorised as a subcorpus of Leisure and Monologue, most of the texts are from an oral history project or oral history interview.

Table 6. Word tokens and frequencies of VVD in scgdom4-spolog1 and scgdom3-spolog1, along with their ratios

	scgdom4 and spolog 1		scgdom3 and spolog 1		
	Word tokens	Frequencies	Word tokens	Frequencies	Ratio
liked	42	0.001293	2	0.000108	11.972
picked	21	0.000646	1	0.000054	11.963
worked	165	0.005079	8	0.000432	11.757
won	19	0.000585	1	0.000054	10.833
wore	17	0.000523	1	0.000054	9.685
closed	16	0.000492	1	0.000054	9.111
lived	138	0.004248	9	0.000485	8.759
broke	46	0.001416	3	0.000162	8.741
played	29	0.000893	2	0.000108	8.269
sat	28	0.000862	2	0.000108	7.981
got	742	0.022839	69	0.003722	6.136
stopped	21	0.000646	2	0.000108	5.981
called	70	0.002155	7	0.000378	5.701
met	39	0.0012	4	0.000216	5.556

Ratio implies the score when frequency in scgdom4 and spolog 1 is divided by that in scgdom3 and spolog 1.

Therefore, we can take it as a matter of course that the past tense is characteristic of this subcorpus.

In order to find the relationship between this corpus and habitual contact other than habitual sense in verbs *worked* and *lived*, let me once again cite Fraser's (1976) claims that the habitual sense of the verb correlates positively with the *Fred picked up the book* construction. That is, if the verb phrase denotes the habitual meaning, then the *Fred picked up the book* construction is preferred to the *Fred picked the book up* construction. In a subcorpus of Leisure and Monologue, the *Fred picked up the book* construction occurs 13 times as follows:

> FYJ 213 *er er a general labourer actually, but you **picked up** some knowledge, some knowledge* ... (Nottinghamsire Oral History Project: talk)
>
> FYJ 494 *and you **picked up** a couple of guides er, who* ... (Nottinghamsire Oral History Project: talk)

In contrast, *Fred **picked** the book **up*** construction occurs twice, one of which is as follows:

> GYS 445 ... *and er I **picked** him, I **picked** him **up** in the road and you* ... (Oral history project: interview)

The discussion mentioned above alone does not allow me to arrive at the conclusion that a subcorpus of Leisure and Monologue is associated with habitual contact, but it is worthy to have given us a hint that examining the degree of collocation between the verb and the particle in phrasal verbs may lead us to further consideration of habitual contact. Let me move on to the third quadrant of Fig 2, that is, a subcorpus of Business and Monologue. Adjacent features are AJS and NN2.

As Table 7 shows, *largest* is the most distinctive word. Among 11 examples of *largest*, many of them are concerned with trade unions excerpted from the Trade Union Annual Congress. The phrases are: *the **largest** and best training programme of any other union, in Britain's second **largest** union, the **largest*** *unions in Britain, the **largest** section of the union* (2 times), and *the **largest** private sector agreement*. Others are: t*he **largest** majority, the **largest** attack, the **largest** tumour* (2 times) and *the second **largest** ferry port*. The most common word in Table 7 is *worst*, which occurs 17 times in this subcorpus. Judging from these examples, a subcorpus of Business and Monologue, which is representative of habitual style, tends to use more superlative adjectives in the situation to describe the size of the union or the quality of the thing as follows: *the **worst** and most incompetent government, the **worst** of both worlds <pause> a government who wants to attack, the **worst** training, one of the **worst** ministers, which are probably the **worst** cowboy cleaning companies, it's stopping the **worst** of Tory legislation and policies* and so on.

Table 7. Word tokens and frequencies of AJS in scgdom2-spolog1 and scgdom3-spolog1, along with their ratios

Word types	scgdom2 and spolog 1		scgdom3 and spolog 1		Ratio
	Word tokens	Frequencies	Word tokens	Frequencies	
largest	11	0.000735	1	0.000054	13.61111
lowest	8	0.000534	2	0.000108	4.944444
easiest	6	0.000401	2	0.000108	3.712963
strongest	3	0.0002	1	0.000054	3.703704
poorest	2	0.000134	1	0.000054	2.481481
worst	17	0.001135	10	0.000539	2.105751

Ratio implies the score when frequency in scgdom2 and spolog 1 is divided by that in scgdom3 and spolog 1.

According to Beard's (2000, 24) claim, political parties like to stress the importance of their views, so not surprisingly a superlative form appears, which is called **degree**. Therefore, if it is acceptable to regard a subcorpus of Leisure and Monologue as a typical one describing habitual style, degree is one of the characteristics in habitual style. Also note that typical contexts of this subcorpus are concerned with politics, so we can easily identify a group of words that are related in meaning as a result of being connected with a particular context of use, which can be regarded as **coherence**. In this respect, Tables 6 and 7 are noteworthy. The distinctive words tagged as NN2 which occur more than 100 times are: *workers, patients, jobs, conditions, women, issues, members* and *rights*. It is obvious that their coherence is salient in that the contexts are associated with politics. There are other common words excerpted from a certain seminar, one of which is *cells*:

I call this deadwood lying on your spreadsheet, **cells** *that are using up memory,* (HDV 263 Longman Group UK Ltd Lotus 123 seminar, Leisure, Monologue)

In fact, 29 examples out of 30 *cells* are from this seminar. In the case of *systems*, which occur 67 times, the phrases collocating with *systems* are as follows in descending order: *our system* (8 times), *open system* (7 times), *management system* (6 times), *department system* (4 times) and *computer system* (3 times). Sixty-one examples out of 67 *systems* are from a seminar titled Enterprise Two Thousand.

All things considered, it is not difficult to see that the characteristic of Monologue along the dimension describing the extent of the habitual style is largely associated with particular contexts of the monologue, whereby we can identify **lexical cohesion**. What is more, the way to stress the strength of views is different from dialogue in that the superlative form is preferred. Many monologues tend to narrate past events when the past tense can be a salient characteristic of habitual style.

7 Conclusion

In this thesis, given the potential importance of lexis for describing linguistic style, I used lexis for categorization in the study of the spoken part. In fact, this study attempted to detect the typical markers of lexical items describing the extent to which the spoken text is more associated with habitual style, allowing us to discriminate between Monologue and Dialogue. It is natural to expect to apply an identical methodology to other register categories or discourse communities, in the light of other concepts of style. In this respect, the possibility of realising these research questions may be explored by more detailed study in terms of lexis or semantics.

Notes

1. Because only speakers within each BNC file can form a community, there may be a limitation of the use of corpora for identifying speech communities. Multivariate analysis can identify this notion.
2. This type of method is widely known as correspondence analysis. Other kinds of multivariate analyses commonly used are principal component analysis and factor analysis.
3. As a result of calculation, many axes appear. We can tell how powerful an axis is by comparison to others by reference to its ratio of information accounted for, which is called 'proportion accounted for'.
4. Bars are grouped as follows: group of categories or domains, four verb groups and other typical grammatical groups such as nouns, adjectives and so on.
5. I compare the subcorpus of Leisure and Monologue with one located closest to the origin of the coordinates. It is because the one located closest to the origin of coordinates can be regarded as neutral, meaning that it does not have any particular characteristic along the dimension.

References

Beard, A. (2000) *The Language of Politics*. London: Routledge.

Broomfield, L.W. (1933) *Language*. New York: Holt, Rinehart and Winston.

Fraser, B. (1976) The Verb-Particle Combination in English. New York: Academic Press.

Gries, S. Thomas (2003) *Multifactorial Analysis in Corpus Linguistics – A study of Particle Placement*. New York, London: Continuum.

Gumperz, J.J. (1962) "Types of linguistic communities". In *Anthropological Linguistics* 4(1), pp. 28-40.

Hockett, C.A. (1958) *A Course in Modern Linguistics*. New York: Macmillan.

Hymes, D. (1972) "Models of the interaction of language and social life". In Gumperz J.J. and Hymes D (eds.), *Directions in Sociolinguistics: The Ethnography of communication*. New York and Oxford: Basil Blackwell, pp. 35-71.

Labov, W. (1972) *Sociolinguistic Patterns*. Philadelphia: University of Pennsylvania Press.

Leech, G. and Svartvik, J. (2002), *A Communicative Grammar of English*. Edinburgh: Pearson Education.

Lyons, J. (1981) *Language and Linguistics*. Cambridge University Press.

Mesthrie, R., Swann, J., Deumert, A. and Leap, W. (2000), *Introducing Sociolinguistics*. Edinburgh: Edinburgh University Press.

Sherzer, J. (1977) The ethnography of speaking: a critical appraisal. In Saville-Troike, M. (eds.), *Linguistics and Anthropology*. Washington, DC: Georgetown University Press, pp. 43-58.

Tannen, D. (1984) *Coherence in Spoken and Written Discourse*. Ablex Publishing.

Trudgill, P. (1992) *Introducing Language and society*. London: Penguin.

Gentleman in *Oliver Twist*:
A Linguistic Approach to Literature*

Shinichiro Watanabe

1 Introduction

This paper is concerned with the questions of the usage of the naming or appellations of the characters in a novel, and it tries to exemplify the relevance to a literary analysis of the appellations of the main characters in a novel. While there seems to have been little work on the role of the character appellations in literary discussions, this paper tries to show that they may be related to the plots, the narrator's viewpoint, focalization or even the themes of a novel. The character appellations include proper names, pronouns, nicknames and common nouns or super-ordinates and if we analyze these appellations as the story proceeds, or from scene to scene, we may find the usage of these appellations is not merely grammatical or stylistic, but it often has much to do with the literary content.

To prove these points I will first take up the use of the term *gentleman* in Charles Dickens's *Oliver Twist* and try to show that the use of the word *gentleman* reflects the themes of the novel, that is, the contrast between Good and Evil[1]. To be more specific, I will explore the usage of the term *gentleman* in *Oliver Twist* in which this appellation is used to refer to both good and evil characters and I will try to demonstrate that the usage of the term for evil characters is differentiated, if not strictly, from its usage for good characters.

Such differentiation serves to draw an effective contrast between Good and Evil.

I will also discuss the appellations of Nancy, an important character in *Oliver Twist*. Nancy is the one who changes from an evil to a good character. Her moral complexity can be said to be reflected in different ways of naming her, for her moral shift corresponds to the shift in the way she is referred to as the story proceeds. This corresponding shift may well be taken to exemplify the literary significance of the main characters appellations.

2 Themes of the novel

Charles Dickens presents the organizing theme in his preface to the third edition of *Oliver Twist*: "I wished to show, in little Oliver, the principle of Good surviving through every adverse circumstance, and triumphing at last." I take this to mean that the battle between Good and Evil and the eventual triumph of Good are two important themes of the novel.

The themes are closely related to the contrast observed among the main characters, who are either Good or Evil: the main good characters are Oliver, Brownlow, Harry, and Rose, while the main evil characters are Fagin, Sikes, Monks, Noah, and Fagin's young gang such as Jack Dawkins, Charles Bates and Chitling.

Nancy's character is rather complex. She is unique in that she is the only one who shifts from Evil to Good, and this shift is not only of much significance in itself, but also important to the story as a whole as it leads to the triumph of Good. I will discuss the significance of Nancy's moral complexity and shift in character in some detail in section 4.

3 The word *gentleman* and its use in *Oliver Twist*

One of the most frequently repeated words in *Oliver Twist* is *gentleman*, which occurs 336 times in the novel, the second most repeated common noun next to *man*.

The concept of the gentleman in the Victorian period is complex and worth discussing here. The term *gentleman* used to refer to people of a specific social class, but this was no longer the case in the Victorian era. The Victorian usage of the word *gentleman* seems to have become broader in meaning and usage as it was not merely a social or class designation, but it also involved moral qualities. The moral code of the gentleman appeared frequently in the Victorian novels as was the case with Dickens's *Great Expectations* in which the moral qualities of the gentleman are emphasized.

The use of the term *gentleman* in his early novel *Oliver Twist*, however, does not correspond with that in *Great Expectations* and is very peculiar as Dickens often uses the word to refer to those characters who are far from being either morally or socially gentlemen. Consequently, the ironic use, or abuse, of the term is very common in *Oliver Twist*. This is demonstrated with the appellations for Fagin and his gang of young thieves, who are regularly referred to as *gentleman* though one would not normally describe them as such.

The primary aim of this paper is to explore the usage of the word *gentleman* in *Oliver Twist* and to highlight the way the term is used to refer to both good and evil characters. I aim to propose that the usage of *gentleman* for evil characters is differentiated from its usage for good characters in the novel.

3.1 Those referred to as *gentleman* in *Oliver Twist*

Table 1 shows a detailed list of characters that the term *gentleman* refers to and the respective number of times this term occurs in *Oliver Twist*.
There is no doubt that Browlow, the character most commonly referred to as *gentleman*, Losberne, Grimwig and Harry are true gentlemen and these good characters are often referred to as such throughout the novel. The member of the board of the workhouse and the magistrates, though not necessarily morally

Table 1. Who is referred to as *gentleman* in *Oliver Twist*?

Good Characters	Freq.	Evil Characters	Freq.
Browlow	114	Fagin	29
Grimwig	13	the Dodger (Fagin's gang)	15
Losberne	10	Chitling (Fagin's gang)	8
Harry	8	Sikes the murderer	6
Oliver	1	Noah (Fagin's gang)	4
		Bates (Fagin's gang)	3
		Fagin's gang unidentified	3
		Thief	2
Other Characters	Freq.	Other Characters	Freq.
board of workhouse	36	gamekeeper	2
magistrates	21	landlord	2
Bumble	9	apothecary's deputy	1
doctors	6	clergyman	1
singer pianist	3	constable	1
Duff	2	attributive	10
Giles	2	unreferential	24
Total			336

respectable, may be called *gentleman* in the light of their higher social status.[2] On the other hand, there are many characters in *Oliver Twist* who cannot be either morally or socially gentlemen. It may be reasonable to interpret the use of the word in relation to those evil characters as ironic. This ironic use of the word *gentleman* is frequently repeated to refer to members of Fagin's gang of young thieves as Jack Dawkins or the Artful Dodger, Master Bates and Noah, as Table 1 shows. In this way the usage of the term *gentleman* to refer to both good and evil characters in *Oliver Twist* is very peculiar.

3.2 The contrastive use of *gentleman*

The significant usage I wish to emphasize here is that Dickens's use of the word *gentleman* for good characters and his ironical use for evil characters are differentiated by the way the word *gentleman* is combined with its modifiers.

(1) Dickens's collocational differentiation of the term *gentleman*:

The ironic use of the word *gentleman* for evil characters is restricted to descriptive appellations or phrases in which the word is modified by some specific adjectives or some obviously ironical adjectives. Conversely, the use of the word *gentleman* for good characters is not restricted in this way.

The evil characters such as Fagin and his young gang of thieves are never referred to simply as *gentleman* without any modifier attached in the narrative. For instance, Evil Fagin is *the merry old gentleman* or *the playful old gentleman*, and Sikes the murderer is *the worthy gentleman* or *the good gentleman*. All the young thieves are some sort of *young gentleman* as we will see in some detail in section 3.3. Conversely, the use of the word *gentleman* for good characters is different and not restricted in this way. Both Brownlow and Harry are often referred to simply as *the gentleman*. Through his ironical use of such descriptive appellations as *the merry old gentleman* for Fagin, or *the worthy gentleman* for Sikes, Dickens maintains an important theme of the novel by successfully drawing an impressive contrast between Good and Evil.

3.3 The collocation *the young gentleman*

As Table 2 shows, the collocation *young gentleman* occurs 30 times in the text, and refers to such young thieves as Jack Dawkins, Charlie Bates, Chitling or Noah 25 times, and once to the apothecary's deputy, who is hardly worthy of the name *gentleman*. By contrast, Harry, a true young gentleman, is rarely referred to as *young gentleman*; the phrase is used to refer to him only twice or three times if the chapter title is included in the count. Harry is named elsewhere either simply *the gentleman* or *the young man*.

Table 2. *Young gentleman* and its reference as the story proceeds

that young gentleman	Noah
a strange sort of young gentleman (chapter title)	the Dodger
as roystering and swaggering a young gentleman	the Dodger
this strange young gentleman	the Dodger
(7 occurrences of) the young gentleman	the Dodger
the young gentleman with the pipes	one of Fagin's gang
one young gentleman	one of Fagin's gang
that young gentleman	one of Fagin's gang
the young gentleman	the Dodger
the first-named gentleman	the Dodger
that young gentleman	Chitling
this young gentleman	apothcary's deputy
the young gentleman's (nose)	Noah
a young gentleman (chapter title)	Harry
a young gentleman	Harry
the young gentleman	Harry
that young gentleman	Bates
that young gentleman	Bates
a young gentleman in the throng	prisoner A
that young gentleman	prisoner A
that young gentleman	Bates
young gentleman (vocative indirect speech)	Chitling
a young gentleman	Chitling
the young gentleman (in direct speech)	Oliver

Incidentally, the phrase *the young man* occurs 18 times throughout the novel and refers to Harry 15 times. Therefore, this peculiarly restricted use of the collocation *young gentleman* to name those evil characters seems to be characteristic of Dickens's style in *Oliver Twist*. In particular, the peculiarity of his usage of this collocation becomes evident when it is compared with his usage of the phrase *old gentleman*, which is most often used to refer to Brownlow, a true old gentleman.

Furthermore, when the expression *young gentleman* is used to name any of these evil characters, it is often accompanied by some sort of modifier, such as *a strange sort of*, *this strange*, *the first-named* or demonstrative adjectives such as *this* or *that*. The use of these extra modifiers may be said to be markers to indicate that evil characters are being referred to. In this way Dickens appears to make a distinct use of the term *gentleman*, either by using it in complex descriptive appellations for evil characters or by using it simply for good characters.

3.4 Brownlow and Fagin: two old gentlemen

Tables 3 and 4 show the noun phrases in which *gentleman* is used for Brownlow and Fagin.

Table 3. The appellations for Brownlow

the old gentleman	65
the gentleman	37
that gentleman	3
a gentleman	2
a grey-haired gentleman	1
an elderly gentleman	1
the good, kind, old gentleman	1
an absent old gentleman	1
the absent old gentleman	1
gentleman (vocative)	1
this gentleman	1
an impetuous gentleman	1

Table 4. The appellations for Fagin

the old gentleman	12
the merry old gentleman	9
the pleasant old gentleman	1
the playful old gentleman	1
that wary old gentleman	1
a 'espetable old gentleman (in direct speech)	1
the old gentleman referred to	1
the elderly gentleman before mentioned	1
that gentleman	1
the gentleman (in direct speech)	1

The phrase *the old gentleman* occurs 89 times in the text, which includes 65 times for Brownlow and 12 times for Fagin. Brownlow and Fain are the two characters most commonly referred to as *the old gentleman* throughout the novel, though the phrase is used to refer to a few different characters. Brownlow is also named simply *the gentleman* 37 times, and Fagin is named *the merry old gentleman* 9 times. What should first be noted is that Fagin is never referred to simply as *the gentleman* except for one instance, which occurs in

Noah's direct speech. Dickens successfully creates an evil and devilish impression about him through the repeated use of the complex descriptive appellation *the merry old gentleman*, which is peculiar to Fagin.[3]

While such complex descriptive appellations as *the merry old gentleman* or *the playful old gentleman* are used to refer to Fagin, the phrase *the old gentleman* is also used to name him. The same phrase *the old gentleman* is commonly used to name Brownlow, a true gentleman. This fact appears to be a counterexample to the theme I propose in 3.2 above, but in what follows I aim to argue that this is not a counterexample to the claim I make in 3.2. For the purpose of this argument we need to get into a qualitative analysis of Dickens's use of the term *gentleman* for Fagin.

Table 5 shows how Fagin is referred to as *gentleman* as the story progresses. The use of *gentleman* for Fagin is found mainly in the three consecutive chapters 8, 9 and 10. In chapter 8, on his way to London, Oliver meets Jack Dawkins (the Dodger), who says he knows a "'espectable old gentleman" who would provide Oliver with a comfortable place (p. 55). "... Under this impression, he [Oliver] secretly resolved to cultivate the good opinion of 'the old gentleman' as quickly as possible" (p. 55). At the end of this chapter Oliver meets Fagin, who treats him well, giving him food, clothes and shelter. The use of the expression *the merry old gentleman* in reference to Fagin occurs the first time in this chapter. In chapter 9 Fagin is constantly referred to as "the Jew" until, in Oliver's inner speech, *gentleman* is used to refer to Fagin: "Oliver thought the old gentleman must be a decided miser to live in such a dirty place" (p. 61). From this point *the old gentleman* is often used to refer to Fagin. This use either relates to Oliver's inner speech or to Oliver's viewpoint. In the last paragraph of chapter 9, we read Oliver's inner speech again in which the phrase *the old gentleman's* is used to refer to Fagin: "Oliver wondered what picking the old gentleman's pocket in play had to do with his ..." (p. 64).

In this view, the use of *the old gentleman* for Fagin is either related to Oliver's inner speech or to his viewpoint. It is important to note the fact that

Fagin is referred to as *the old gentleman* only when Oliver is around him in

Table 5. Fagin as *gentleman* as the story progresses

Chapter 8	
a 'espetable old gentleman (the Dodger's direct speech)	1
the old gentleman referred to	1
the elderly gentleman before mentioned	1
the old gentleman	1
the merry old gentleman	1
Chapter 9	
the pleasant old gentleman	1
the old gentleman	3
the merry old gentleman	2
the old gentleman	1
the playful old gentleman	1
the old gentleman's	1
Chapter 10	
the old gentleman	1
the old gentleman's	2
the old gentleman	1
Chapter 12	
the merry old gentleman	3
Chapter 13	
the merry old gentleman's	1
the old gentleman's (merry heart)	1
the old gentleman's	1
Chapter 15	
the merry old gentleman	1
Chapter 18	
that gentleman	1
that wary old gentleman	1
Chapter 25	
the merry old gentleman	1
Chapter 42	
the gentleman (speech by Noah)	1

three chapters 8, 9 and 10. After Oliver leaves him in the middle of Chapter 10, Fagin begins to be named *the old man* and no longer *the old gentleman*. All these observations suggest that the narrator's reference to Fagin as *the old gentleman* reflects Oliver's inner consciousness. After Oliver leaves Fagin in the middle of Chapter 10, Fagin is often referred to as *the old man*. *The old man* refers to Fagin 23 times and occurs 25 times in the whole text.

The fact that the same phrase *the old gentleman* is used to refer to both Fagin and Brownlow suggests that there is something common between them; after all, Brownlow and Fagin are both benefactors for Oliver. Oliver once regarded Fagin as such when Fagin provided him with clothes, food and a sleeping place. It may be interesting to note that the use of *the old gentleman* for Fagin is restricted to the scenes where he plays the role of Oliver's benefactor.

4 Nancy's moral shift and referential shift

The most impressive character in *Oliver Twist* is presumably Nancy, a member of Fagin's gang and Sikes's mate.[4] Table 6 shows how Nancy is named as the story progresses from Chapter 9 to Chapter 15. From the outset, Nancy is referred to as *a lady* as in "a couple of young ladies" (in chapter 9). When Nancy appears in the story again in Chapter 13, she is still referred to as *the lady*. Then, Fagin orders her to dress like a woman, and to go out to find Oliver. On the street she is, or pretends to be, *the agonized young woman* in chapter 13 or simply *the young woman*, a phrase repeatedly used in chapter 15. After she catches Oliver and returns to Fagin and Sikes in chapter 16, she begins to lament the course her life has taken and to regret what she has just done. From this point she begins to be named consistently as *the girl*. Except for two occurrences of the phrase *the young lady* in chapter 19, Nancy is always named *the girl* during and after chapter 16. There may seem to be an exception in chapter 39 where "Sikes is waiting for his young lady [Nancy]," but this passage simply implies that in Sikes's consciousness Nancy is still his lady.

Table 6. How Nancy is referred

Chapter 9:	a couple of young ladies
	one of the young ladies
	the two young ladies
Chapter 13:	the lady
	the lady in question
	the young lady's (right hand)
	that young lady
After Nancy went out in search of Oliver, wearing "a clean white apron tied over her gown" and "a straw bonnet": (Nancy in disguise)	
	the agonized young woman
Chapter 15:	At Fagin's den
	the young lady
After Nancy leaves Fagin to find Oliver: (Nancy in disguise)	
	a young woman
	the young woman (5 occurrences)

Throughout the novel the phrase *the girl* occurs 194 times. During and after chapter 16 it refers to Nancy 182 times as Table 7 shows and *the girl* is always used to refer to Nancy, apart from two exceptional occurrences of the phrase *the young lady* in chapter 19 and one occurrence of *his young lady* in chapter 39 seen above.

Table 7. Occurrence frequency of text *the girl* referring to Nancy

Chapter 16	17	Chapter 39	61
Chapter 19	4	Chapter 41	24
Chapter 20	17	Chapter 45	3
Chapter 25	1	Chapter 46	1
Chapter 26	14		

4.1 Nancy's moral complexity and lexical shift

Nancy's moral complexity is reflected in different ways of naming her as the story proceeds.

Figure 1. The shift in Nancy's appellation

young lady	—> (	young woman	) —>	the girl
Nancy the prostitute		Nancy in disguise		Nancy reformed

Nancy's shift from a fallen to a real angel corresponds to the lexical shift from *the young lady* to *the girl* through the intermediate stage of *the young woman*. It may also be interesting to note that of three illustrations of Nancy in the book the first two depict her as a blowzy chubby lady and the last portrays her as a slim angelic girl.

Nancy appears in the novel as a young lady, a lady of sin, and she eventually becomes a girl, a girl reformed with a pure heart who repents for what she has done, though she thinks she is "beyond redemption." The girl sacrifices her life to save little Oliver's life.

Dickens uses the appellation *the girl* to refer to four different characters, and among them is Agnes Fleming, Oliver's dead mother, who is referred to as *the girl* towards the end of the novel. Just as Nancy does, Agnes Fleming also sacrifice her life for a cause, though in her case it is done to hide her father's shame. Dickens's repeated and restricted use of *the girl* may be an attempt to evoke a certain sense of angelic behavior.

5 Concluding remarks

I have tried to show the relevance of the main characters' naming or appellations to the themes of the novel. This paper is an attempt to prove this point by highlighting the use of the term *gentleman* in Charles Dickens's *Oliver Twist*. As I hope to have shown, the contrast between Good and Evil, one theme throughout the novel, is reflected in the distinct ways Dickens adapts the use of the term *the gentleman* to refer to good or evil characters. The different ways of naming Nancy as the story progresses reflect her moral complexity and especially her shift from Evil to Good. The corresponding shift in character and appellation clearly indicates that character appellations are of some importance in an analysis of the theme structure of the novel.

Notes

* The present article is based on the paper "Repetition and the theme of a novel," which I read in the Tenth Conference of the Nordic Association for English Studies held in Bergen, Norway, May 24-26, 2007.

1. Page numbers are based on the Everyman Paperback edition Connor, S. (ed.) (1994) London: J.M. Dent.
2. In particular, *the gentleman in the white waistcoat*, a member of the board at the workhouse who constantly harasses Oliver by saying, "he will be hung" is morally far from being a gentleman. No proper name is given to this character, but the descriptive appellation *the gentleman in the white waistcoat* contributes to hinting at something evil about him.
3. Cf. Paroissien, David (1992) *The Companion to Oliver Twist* Edinburgh: Edinburgh University Press, according to which *the merry old gentleman* referring to Fagin means the devil. The *Oxford English Dictionary* lists the use of *the old gentleman* meaning the devil. Indeed, Fagin is a devilish person. Nancy, for instance, calls him the devil several times. However, as we have seen, the phrase *the old gentleman* used to refer to Fagin should not be interpreted as the devil; otherwise, it leaves the question unresolved of why the same expression is used repeatedly for Brownlow, a truly respectable gentleman. I would rather claim that in Dickens's usage *the young gentleman* means typically a villain in the light of its restricted usage discussed in this paper.
4. I take the following to mean she is seventeen years old: 'I [Nancy] thieved for you [Fagin] when I was a child not half as old as this!' pointing to Oliver. 'I have been in the same trade, and in the same service, for twelve years since' (p. 116).

References

Booth, W. (1961) *The Rhetoric of Fiction*. Chicago: University of Chicago Press.

Dickens, C. *Oliver Twist*. Connor, S. (ed.) (1994) London: J.M. Dent.

Hoey, M. (1991) *Patterns of Lexis in Text*. Oxford: Oxford University Press.

Genette, G. (1972) *Narrative Discourse*. Trans. Jane E. Lewin. Oxford: Blackwell.

Hori, M. (2004) *Investigating Dickens' Style: A Collocational Analysis*. UK: Palgrave Macmillan

Jahn, M. (1999) "More Aspects of Focalization: Refinements and Applications." http://www.uni-koeln.de/~ame02/jahn99b.htm.

Jahn, M. (2003) "Narratology: A Guide to the Theory of Narrative."
http://www.uni-koeln.de/~ame02/pppn.htm.

Paroissien, D. (1986) *Oliver Twist: An Annotated Bibliography*. New York: Garland.

Paroissien, D. (1991) *The Companion to Oliver Twist*. Edinburgh: Edinburgh UP.

Wing, G. (1969) *Charles Dickens*. Edinburgh: Oliver and Boyd.

Translating Julian of Norwich's Politeness into Japanese*

Fumiko Yoshikawa

1 Introduction

This paper treats the expression of Julian of Norwich's attitudes towards God, the Virgin Mary, the church, and to her fellow Christians in terms of politeness, based on Brown & Levinson (1987, first published 1978) and discusses how to translate these attitudes into Japanese. Brown and Levinson (1987: 245) divide world cultures broadly into two categories, 'positive-politeness cultures' and 'negative-politeness cultures', and located both Modern British and Japanese in the latter category. Brown and Levinson also recognized that Japanese culture seems to the British to be more aloof than British culture. Furthermore, they found typical differences depending on social strata within the same culture: the higher strata exhibit clearer recognition of social distance, of rating of imposition, and of relative power values, while the lower strata show less acknowledgement of these three factors.

If we consider the opinions of these earlier studies together with the three major kinds of honorifics in Japanese — that is, Honorific/respectful language, Humble/modest language, and Polite language, we must recognize that we need some strategies for translating Julian's polite expression of her attitude into Japanese. Julian shows such polite attitudes as humility and respect for the church, and empathy with her fellow Christians in both versions of her *Revelations*, and of course demonstrates a clear devotion of the Virgin Mary and adoration of God. Reading her *Revelations* from the viewpoint of politeness strategies could also help us to translate better Julian's writing into Present-day English because the results of research including Brown & Gilman (1989) and papers in Jucker (1995)[1] show that politeness strategies in the Early Modern English period differed in some respects from those employed in Present-day English. This paper particularly addresses techniques to translate her politeness into Japanese, but will also consider the problems in translating polite attitudes from the Late Middle English period into 21st century languages.

2 Brown & Levinson's Theory of Politeness

Brown & Levinson's (1987) theory of 'politeness' is a theory proposing universal strategies to explain and facilitate communication, using the concept of 'face'. It suggests that there are two universal desires, or 'face-wants', in interpersonal communications, and these two 'face-wants' are called 'negative face' and 'positive face'. Negative face is a 'desire to be unimpeded in one's actions' and positive face is a 'desire (in some respects) to be approved of' (1987: 13). They also suggest that 'some acts intrinsically threaten' these desires (Brown & Levinson 1987: 60; hereafter B&L in page references). They are called 'face-threatening acts' (hereafter FTAs). 'Politeness' is defined by the two desires 'positive face' and 'negative face'. Negative politeness is 'redressive action addressed to the addressee's negative face: his want to have his freedom of action unhindered and his attention unimpeded' (B&L 1987: 129), that is, an avoidance of threatening the addressee's negative face. Positive politeness (B&L 1987: 101) is 'redress directed to the addressee's positive face, his perennial desire that his wants (or the actions/acquisitions/values resulting from them) should be thought of as desirable.' Therefore, actual positive politeness strategies are not usually redressive, and in many cases, are positive approaches to the addressee's positive face. What Brown & Levinson (1987: 245) say by comparing British and Japanese, is that the Japanese use many strategies of negative politeness, and that while the British also use negative politeness strategies, they do not use as many as the Japanese, and also use more positive politeness strategies.

Brown & Levinson (1987: 65-68) enumerate FTAs, and say "any rational agent will seek to avoid these face-threatening acts, or will employ certain strategies to minimize the threat." They then illustrate five possible choices of strategies by a speech actor, three of which are of interest here: positive politeness strategies, negative politeness strategies, and off-record strategies (B&L 1987: 69). The five strategies are meta-strategies, and Brown & Levinson enumerate possible sub-strategies of off-record utterances, of positive politeness and of negative politeness. They give examples of fifteen strategies of positive politeness, ten of negative politeness and fifteen of off-record utterances.[2]

Brown & Levinson (1987: 74-78) also suggest a formula to compute 'the seriousness or weightiness of an FTA': $W_x = D(S,H) + P(H,S) + R_x$. The weightiness of an FTA is measured by three values: D, social distance between the speaker (S) and the hearer (H), and P, the power that the hearer has over the speaker, and R_x, the value of imposition of the particular FTA x in that culture. They say that each value is measured 'on a scale of 1 to n, where n is some small number' (1987: 76). Using these strategies, actual analyses have been made by many pragmaticians, but sometimes the relationships of these strategies or sub-strategies are modified. For example, Brown & Gilman (1989), who adapted Brown & Levinson's theory to Shakespeare's four major tragedies, *Hamlet, King Lear, Macbeth* and *Othello*, used modified strategies of negative and positive politeness. Brown & Gilman (1989) say that, in these tragedies, power balance (P) and closeness (D) between two characters are explicit, and that this is the reason they chose these texts to investigate politeness in the Early Modern English period. Regarding Julian's *Revelations*, neither of the constituents (P and D) is as clear as in Shakespeare's tragedies.

Moreover, evidence of the fifth strategy — not doing the FTA — is seldom found in Julian's text, though Brown & Gilman (1989: 169, 170) point out that this strategy can be observed in soliloquies in Elizabethan dramas. Julian's *Revelations* tell us little about the composition and audience of her text, but we may at least assume that it is a text which is intended to be read by someone in the fourteenth century; in other words, that the sentences could be regarded as text utterances and speech acts, and some of her utterances certainly imply her target readers.

Brown and Gilman (1989) gave scores of P and D in those tragedies, and verified whether Shakespeare's tragedies show the same tendency in the relationship between the politeness strategies as shown in Brown & Levinson's theory (1987). In this paper, however, we will simply look at the examples of politeness strategies in *Revelations* but the actual measurement of the values of P, D, and R_x will not be attempted, because we cannot accurately assess their values in *Revelations*. We concentrate our attention on how we can effectively translate some of Julian's politeness strategies into Japanese.

3 Japanese Honorifics

What we have to notice when we translate Julian's politeness into Japanese is that the actual usage of Japanese honorifics is affected by elements other than the three which influence politeness strategies, namely P, D and R. As previously mentioned, Japanese honorifics can be largely divided into three types: Honorific/respectful language, Humble/modest language, and Polite language. When the speaker refers to a socially higher person than himself/herself or his/her in-group as the actor of an act, Honorific/respectful language is used; when the speaker refers to a socially higher person as the receiver or patient of an act, and refers to himself/herself or to his/her in-group as the actor, Humble/modest language is used to express the respect to the patient. Therefore, in the case that the hearer is the patient of an act at the same time and he/she is a socially higher person than the speaker, the speaker humbles himself/herself to the hearer. Polite language is used when people speak politely without having any particular target of respect (Takiura, 2005: 208-56, Tsujimura 1996: 363). These fundamental norms regarding how to choose one of these modes are understandable, and we expect Brown & Levinson's P and D values to be adapted for the judgement on which mode should be used. However, that is the fundamental honorific system in Japanese. Some research in Japanese honorifics including Takiura (2005) mentions that the uses of honorifics are sometimes conventional and at other times the speaker can choose the use of honorifics according to aimed pragmatic effects. The conventional use of honorifics would of course have to be applied to the Japanese translation of *Revelations*. Here is a quotation where such considerations would be needed.

(1) Thus our lady is our <u>moder</u> in whome we are all beclosid and of hir borne in Christe; for she that is moder of our savior is moder of all that shall be savid in our savior. (LT Ch. 57, p. 69, ll. 43-46)[3]

The word 'mother' which is used in this quotation refers to the Virgin Mary and it is a referent showing great respect. However, in the underlined part, she is also mentioned as our mother and in Japanese the use of the honorific forms of mother, *okaasama*, *hahaue*, *hahagimi*, or *gobodou*, is restrained when we refer to our own mother as our in-group even though the Virgin Mary is clearly placed higher than the speaker, Julian. Therefore we will choose the simple expression for mother *haha* in this case. However, in the following sentence Mary is mentioned as Christ's mother, so we can choose honorific forms to say mother *okaasama* or *hahaue*. This is an example of employing or not employing of honorifics. In thinking of the translation devices with her polite attitude, we do not have to think so much about the conventional uses of honorifics, and we should rather think of possible choices in Julian's pragmatic strategies of politeness.

Japanese has a tradition of biblical translation since the sixteenth century. B. H. Chamberlain (1850-1935), who came to Japan in 1873 and taught English until 1911, remarked that, when these translations refer to the Virgin Mary and Jesus at one time, both receive respect and, at the same time, the difference of their status is expressed; that is, the higher status of Jesus than that of the Virgin Mary is expressed by the uses of honorifics (See Takiura, 2005: 14). The following two quotations were originally cited in Chamberlain's *A Handbook of Colloquial Japanese* (London: Trübner & Tokyo: Hakubunsha, 1888/1889):

(2) *Santa Mariya wa   Onshu Zezu Kirisito o   tabitabi idaki-   **mairase rare**-ta.*
St. Mary   Top. Lord Jesus Christ Acc. often   embrace **hum.**   **hon.** pt.
"St. Mary often embraced Lord Jesus Christ."

(3) *Santa Mariya wa   Zezu Kirishito o   idaki   **tatematuri tamau**.*
St.   Mary   Top. Jesus Christ   Acc. embrace **hum.**   **hon.**
"St. Mary embraces Jesus Christ."   (Takiura, 2005: 14)[4]

The words, *mairase* and *tatematuri*, show that Christ is placed higher than Mary. These are nineteenth century translations, so they sound very old to the present-day speakers of Japanese, but Present-day Japanese still has similar functions to distinguish the ranks of referents. To express their different rankings, present-day speakers of Japanese would express the former as (2)' and the latter as (3)' though some present-day speakers might say "*Seibo Mariya wa Shu Ies Kirisuto wo Idaki tatematuri tamau.*", which is historically close to the sentence which Chamberlain cited.

(2)' *Seibo Maria wa   Shu Iesu Kirisuto o   tabitabi daite-   **sashiage mashi**-ta.*
Holy M. M. Top. Lord Jesus Christ   Acc. often   embrace **hum.**   **pol.**   pt.

(3)' *Seibo Maria   wa Shu Iesu Kirisuto o   daite-   **sashiage masu**.*
Holy Mother Mary Top. Lord Jesus Christ   Acc. embrace **hum.**   **pol.**

In *Revelations*, we sometimes see such different rankings within one sentence. Some of the examples are examined in the beginning of the next section.

Takiura (2005: 233-256) illustrates how the application of Japanese honorifics can be explained by using the 'empathy' scales between speaker, hearer, actor of a mentioned action, and patient of the mentioned action. The 'empathy' scale is based on the principle of social distance by Brown & Levinson (1987).

> **Polite**: E (S) > E (H).
> **Honorific/respectful**: E (S) > E (A).
>   Agent = Hearer: E (S) > E (A [H]).
>   Agent ≠ Hearer: E (S) = E (H) > E (A).
> **Humble/modest**: E (S) > E (P).
>   Patient = Hearer: E (S) > E (P [H]).
>   Patient ≠ Hearer: E (S) = E (H) > E (P).
>   E = empathy; A = agent; P = patient (Takiura 2005: 236-242)

Usually a speaker's empathy is greatest for himself/herself, and, when the speaker does not show much empathy with the hearer, Polite Japanese is used. Sometimes speakers do not use Polite language to a hearer because he/she would like to shorten the distance to the hearer. It is a positive politeness strategy.[5] Honorific/respectful language is used when the empathy for the speaker is greater than that for the agent of the act. Humble/modest language is used when the empathy for the speaker is the greater than that of the patient of the act. Honorific language and Humble language are also divided into two cases according to whether the actor/patient is the same person as the hearer. The degrees of empathy for these participants can change from clause to clause even when the referents remain the same. Therefore we have to rate every clause or sentence on the 'empathy' scale. In Japanese, the three types of honorifics are employed in a sentence and the possible combinations depend on the 'empathy' scale between those participants in the clause: speaker, hearer, agent, and patient. The employment of these pragmatic strategies of politeness in Japanese should be fully considered when translating Julian's politeness into Japanese (Takiura 2005: 236-252).

4 Translating Julian's Politeness into Japanese

In Julian's *Revelations* also, sometimes we should differentiate the ranks of referents by using the hierarchy of honorifics. I have given an extract of two parts in *Revelations*: the first, a sequence in which both Jesus and Virgin Mary are mentioned, and the second, in which Jesus and the church are referred to.

(4) and we pray him for his sweete moder love that him bare, and all the helpe we have of her is of his (g)odeness; (LT Ch. 6, p. 6, ll. 36-38)

E (S) ≧ E (H) > E (the Vergin Mary) > E (Christ)

(5) Than was this my desire: that I myte sen in God in what manner that the dome of holy church herin techyth is trew in his syte, and how it longyth to me sothly to knoyn it; wherby thei myte both be savid, so as it wer worshipfull to God and ryte way to me. (LT Ch. 45, p. 48, ll. 14-17)

In quotation (4), child bearing is mentioned as an act, and the speaker, Julian, should be deferential to the actor, the Virgin Mary, and, at the same time, the speaker knows that the Lord Jesus Christ as the patient of the act is higher than her. The empathy for the speaker might be greater than or equal to that for the hearer. The empathy for the agent is less than that for the speaker and hearer and that for the patient is the least.

With regard to the translation of quotation (4), it would be difficult for us to express the difference in ranking between the Virgin Mary and Lord Jesus Christ in Present-day Japanese because the Virgin Mary is also a highly deferential referent for the speaker, and referring to childbearing in the active voice itself sounds impolite even when the Honorific/respectful form *oumininaru* is used as the translation of 'bare'. It would be a possible choice to translate this clause 'that him bare' freely and use indirect expressions such as '*konoyoni ookuri kudasatta*', which means 'to bring him into this world'. This could be one example of *Strategy 9* of off-record strategies: Use metaphor (B&L

1987: 222, 223). This is a conventional off-record strategy of the translator. In many languages including Japanese, mentioning physiological functions is sometimes avoided in formal scenes. In this particular speech act, the value of R_x, which is a culturally defined rating of imposition involved in the FTA, seems to be higher in Japanese than in English.

In quotation (5), the speaker, Julian, is the lowest, and one of the two referents, God, is higher than the other referent, the church. Both God and the church are the objects of respect for Julian, but the deference to the church must be restrained because of its lower position compared to God. In the translation of this passage, it would probably not be possible to use Polite language for the 'dome' or judgement of Holy Church, but only for God.

Julian often uses the phrase 'holy church', which occurs forty-seven times in the Long Text. When the church is referred to, the word is almost always preceded by the deferential adjective 'holy'. Brown & Gilman (1989: 175) score +2 when honorific adjectives are added to titles as address terms. This phrase is not an address term to the church, but the frequent occurrence of this phrase could be taken as an indication of her high esteem for the church, though possibly it was just a set phrase.[6] When she refers to the church using this phrase, she usually states that God wants us to keep the faith of the church, and that her understandings of the revelations she received were consistent with what the church had told her. These speech acts fall under Brown & Levinson's *Strategy 5 of positive strategy: Seek agreement* or *Strategy 6: Avoid disagreement*. In the section explaining *Strategy 5*, Brown & Levinson (1987: 112, 113) introduce two specific means for the speaker (S) to seek agreement with the hearer (H). One is to raise a safe topic and the other is to repeat what the preceding speaker has said in a conversation. Both are strategies to claim a common point of view with the addressee.

(6) the iii is that it nedyth me to wetyn it, as me thynkyth, if I shall levyn here, for knowyng of good and evill, wherby I may be reason and grace

the more depart hem on sundre, and loven goodnes and haten evill as holy church techyth. (LT Ch. 50, p. 54, ll. 7-10)

(7) But we may wele be grace kepe us from the synnes which will ledyn us to endles pay[n]es, as holy church techith us, and eschewen venal, resonable upon our myte; (LT Ch. 52, p. 62, ll. 28-30)

(8) And notwithstonding this rythfull knitting and this endles onyng, yet the redemption and the ageyn byeng of mankynd is nedefull and spedefull in everything, as it is don for the same entent and to the same end that holy church in our feith us techith; (LT Ch. 53, p. 63, l. 42-p. 43, l. 3)

The quotations (6) to (8) are not in a conversation between Julian and the church, but when Julian says 'as Holy Church teaches', we can regard this speech act as a repetition of what the church said. In the sentences including expressions like 'as Holy Church teaches', Julian insists that she received a revelation or understanding which means the same thing as what the church has taught her. When these references to the church are taken as speech acts, the fact that the phrase 'holy church' was repeated so many times in *Revelations* can be construed as a kind of politeness strategy. Her heavy use of this phrase is almost obsessive. Observing the contexts with the phrase 'holy church', we can infer that Julian saw the contents of her writing or understandings of the revelations as FTAs that might cause disagreements with the teachings of the church. In fact, in those days, it was risky for women to write religious works because they might be seen as heresy. It was truly significant for Julian to show that she was standing on the same 'common ground' as the church.

(9) And thow this was swete and delectabil, yet only in the beholdyng of this I cowd nowte be full esyd, and that was for the dome of holy church which I had aforn vnderstond and was continuly in my syte. (LT Ch. 45, p. 48, ll. 4-7)

(10) and the lower dome was lern me aforn in holy church, and therfore I myte in no way levyn the lower dome. (LT Ch. 45, p. 48, ll. 12-14)

Quotation (5) actually follows quotation (10) in the text. Quotations (9) and (10) say that, at first sight, 'the doom of holy church', the judgement of holy church seems to be contradictory to what she was shown by God, but in quotation (5), she is persuaded that they are consistent and she persuades us of their consistency. This is an example of the avoidance of disagreement.

(11) I pray almyty God that this booke com not but to the hands of the[m] that will be his faithfull lovers, and to those that will submitt them to the feith of <u>holy church</u> and obey the holesom vnderstondyng and teching of the men that be of vertuous life, sadde age and profound lernyng; (LT Ch. 86, p. 103, ll. 1-5)

Quotation (11) is from the last chapter of the Long Text. This is a common phrase for mystical treatises, but, from the viewpoint of politeness theory, it can be regarded as an avoidance of disagreement in advance. Alternatively, it is an example of Brown & Levinson's *Strategy 7* of positive politeness to the reader: 'presuppose/raise/assert common ground' (p. 117).

These quotations referring to 'holy church' demonstrate how greatly Julian was concerned about the church. Therefore the translation should reflect her concern while at the same time expressing the differences in ranking between God and the church.

With regard to the power balance (P) and social distance (D) between Julian and the church, we can assert that both P and D are much higher than in typical speaker-hearer relationship conversations, if we take the church to be not only a referent but also a part of the hearers. However, in sentences in which Julian refers to her fellow Christians, the difference between P and D for the speaker and the hearer are smaller. Some sentences referring to her fellow Christians are cited in quotations (12) to (15).

(12) And that I say of me I sey in the person of al myn <u>even cristen</u>, for I am lernyd in the gostly shewing of our lord God that he menyth so; (LT Ch. 8, p. 10, ll. 7-9)

(13) but in general I am in hope, in onehede of charitie with al myn <u>evyn cristen</u>; for in this onehede stond the life of all mankinde that shall be savid; for God is all that is good, on to my sight, and God hat made al that is made, and God lovith al that he hath made, and he that generaly loveith al his <u>evyn cristen</u> for God, he lovith al that is; (LT Ch. 9, p. 10, ll. 27-33)

(14) And thys shewyng I toke singularly to myselfe, but be al the gracious comforte tha[t] folowyth, as ye shal seen, I was leryd to take it to al my <u>even cristen</u>, al in general and nothing in special; (LT Ch. 37, p. 38, ll. 39-42)

(15) And all this leryng in this trew comfort, it is generall to all my <u>even cristen</u> as it is afornseid, and so is Gods will. (LT Ch. 68, p. 84, ll. 1-3)

When Julian refers to her fellow Christians she always uses the word 'Christian' accompanied by the adjective 'even', which means that she feels socially equal to her fellow Christians. Brown & Levinson suggest: 'Use in-group identity markers' as *Strategy 4* of positive politeness and mention that, as a specific means to realize this strategy, a speaker uses address forms like *mate*, *brother* or *sister* to convey in-group membership. As we noted regarding the phrase 'holy church', the phrase 'even Christian' is not an address term either. However, a similar function can be seen in 'even Christian' as in 'holy church'. The use of this phrase expresses that the addressees, here her fellow Christians, belong to the same group, and using this has an effect to redress the threat of an FTA. If you examine quotations (12) to (15), you will find that Julian is trying to say that she is not a person chosen by God, rewarded for her good understanding of God or manifesting a better devotion to God. That her fellow Christians as readers of her work might take her as a selected person by God because she received revelations, must be an FTA for Julian. Even at a negative estimate, to emphasize that she includes herself in the phrase 'even Christian' would redress this threat. From a positive viewpoint, it is an approach to gain the favor of her fellow Christian readers.

Here remember her modest phrases: In the Short Text, 'For I am a woman, leued, febille, & freylle' (Beer 1978: Ch. VI, p. 48, l. 2), and in the Long Text: 'These revelations were shewed to a simple creature that cowde no letter' (Glasscoe 1976: Ch. 2, p. 2, ll. 17, 18). I see a similar effect in her self-abasement in these phrases. She would like to say that she stands on common ground with her fellow Christians. Considering how Julian was concerned with her fellow Christians, we should choose a rather friendly way of speech to her fellow Christians in translating these parts into Japanese.

5 Conclusion

Observing *Revelations* from the viewpoint of politeness theory, it is clear that Julian was alert to the possibility that her sentences could be FTAs for her readers, including priests and lay Christians. Without such an awareness, she would not have used such expressions as we have discussed, although we can not clearly say whether she consciously used politeness strategies. Consciously or unconsciously, it is certain that her text is filled with politeness strategies.

It is a difficult question to answer how much the translator should follow the tradition of biblical translation into Japanese, and how much he/she should focus on making the sentences understandable to our contemporaries. The translator has to make many difficult choices concerning this work. Some translators of *Revelations* might think that a very formal way of speech should be adopted because it is a religious treatise. On the other hand, it can be said that such a way of translation would create an inappropriate distance between Julian and the hearer, which Julian would have tried to avoid. As shown in examples in this paper, one possible choice would be sensitive to the differences of the social power and distance between the writer, reader and the referents, to regard her readers as the writer's in-group, as quite close to the writer, and to translate the text with this consideration in mind.

Notes

*This essay was developed from my paper presented at the Tenth Cardiff Conference on the Theory and Practice of Translation in the Middle Age, Lausanne, 2007. First, I would like to express my gratitude to Prof. M. J. Benson, Prof. J. M. Ronald, Dr. P. Hilliard, Dr. J. Dresvina, and Prof. Dr. T. Kohnen for reading this essay through and making helpful suggestions. I am also grateful for valuable comments from students attending Prof. Ronald's graduate seminar. Last, but most importantly, I would like to express my sincere gratitude and respect for Prof. M. Imai, who was my supervisor and has always encouraged me with my study.

1 See Kopytko (1995) and Nevalainen & Raumolin-Brunberg (1995).
2 See Brown & Levinson (1987: 102, 131, 214) on these substrategies.
3 The excerpts of the Long Text are drawn from Glasscoe (ed.) (1976).
4 Gloss and translation are added by the present author.
5 See Brown & Levinson (1987: 122-24).
6 The *Meddle English Dictionary* takes *holi chirche* as a set phrase under *chirche* (n.) 4a.

References

Austin, J. L. (1975) *How to Do Things with Words*. First published in 1962. Cambridge, MA: Harvard University Press.

Beer, F. (ed.) (1978) *Revelations of Divine Love by Julian of Norwich*. Heidelberg: Carl Winter Universitätsverlag.

Brown, R. and A. Gilman (1989) "Politeness Theory and Shakespeare's Four Major Tragedies." *Language in Society* 18.2: 159-212.

Brown, P. and S. C. Levinson (1987) *Politeness. Some Universals in Language Usage*. First published in 1978. Cambridge: Cambridge University Press.

Colledge, E. and J. Walsh (eds.) (1978) *A Book of Showings to the Anchoress Julian of Norwich*. 2 vols. Toronto: Pontifical Institute of Mediaeval Studies.

Glasscoe, M. (ed.) (1976) *Julian of Norwich. A Revelation of Love*. Exeter: University of Exeter.

Jucker, A. H. (ed.) (1995) *Historical Pragmatics. Pragmatic Developments in the History of English*. Amsterdam: Benjamins.

Kopytko, R. (1995) "Linguistic Politeness Strategies in Shakespeare's Play." In A. H. Jucker. (ed.), *Historical Pragmatics. Pragmatic Developments in the History of English*. Amsterdam: Benjamins, pp. 515-40.

Kurath, H., S. M. Kuhn and J. Reidy (eds.) (1952-2001) *Middle English Dictionary*. Ann Arbor: The University of Michigan Press.

Nevalainen, T. and H. Raumolin-Brunberg (1995) "Constraints on Politeness, The Pragmatics of Address Formulae in Early English Correspondence." In A. H. Jucker. (ed.), pp. 541-601.

Searle, J. R. (1969) *Speech Acts, an Essay in Philosophy of Language*. Cambridge: Cambridge University Press.

Takiura, M. (2005) *Nihon no Keigo-ron,* Politeness-*Riron kara no Saikentou* [Studies of Japanese Honorifics, Review from the Viewpoint of Politeness Theory] Tokyo: Taishukan.

Tsujimura, N. (1996) *An Introduction to Japanese Linguistics*. Oxford: Blackwell.

Mitsunori Imai – Spredte Indtryk af en Japansk Ven

Mogens Magnusson

Forord

Da Professor Shinichiro Watanabe som editor for dette festskrift for mere end et år siden var så venlig at spørge, om jeg ville sende et indlæg, accepterede jeg straks, idet jeg gennem mange år har kendt Professor Mitsunori Imai som en overordentlig trofast og god ven ikke kun af Inger (min afdøde kone) og mig, men tillige af vores familie og af et par af vores venner. Jeg følte mig meget beæret og glad over at få lejlighed til at udtrykke den store hengivenhed, jeg føler for Mitsunori efter nu at have haft fornøjelsen at kende ham og Yasumi i mere end 25 år. Med en deadline mere end 1 år senere forestillede jeg mig, at jeg måtte kunne skrive nogle Haikudigte, der koncist udtrykte mine følelser for min japanske ven. Havde Inger endnu levet, havde hun straks fortalt mig, hvor vanvittig en tanke det var, at jeg skulle kunne skrive Haikudigte. Nu et år senere må jeg erkende, at hun naturligvis, som altid, ville have haft ret. Prosaisk som jeg er, har jeg valgt i stedet for at skrive formbundne digte, at skrive om Mitsunori i form af en statusrapport over oplevelser og indtryk fra min kontakt med ham gennem nu mere end et kvart århundrede. Formen er den, som mange danske naturvidenskabelige forskere (en kategori som jeg har tilhørt i en del af mit lange professionelle liv) i hvert fald i en årrække har brugt, når de har redegjort for deres iagttagelser og overvejelser.

Indledning

Baggrunden for Ingers og efterfølgende også mit bekendtskab og senere venskab med Mitsunori og Yasumi Imai er følgende: I 1973 afholdt The International Union against Tuberculosis and Lung Diseases sin internationale konference i Tokio og umiddelbart efter afholdt "The International Working Group on Mycobacterial Taxonomy" et møde i Hiroshima. Inger og jeg deltog såvel i konferencen i Tokio som i mødet i Hiroshima, hun som passiv jeg som aktiv deltager. En af de japanske deltagere var professorinde Toshiko Nakamura. Hun traf ved flere lejligheder Inger. Mrs. Nakamura var veninde med Yasumi. Da Mitsunori på et tidspunkt i 1978 (jeg ved ikke præcis hvornår) ønsker at prøve at korrespondere på dansk med en dansker, giver Mrs. Nakamura ham Ingers (og dermed også min) adresse, og den 13. januar 1979 skriver Mitsunori sit første brev til Inger og mig. Et brev der, som det vil fremgå af det følgende, efterfølges af talrige.

Materiale og metoder

I et eget (privat) arkiv har jeg opbevaret det meste af korrespondancen mellem Mitsunori og først Inger og efter hendes død, den 17. marts 1991, med mig. I arkivet findes med en enkelt undtagelse ingen kopier af Ingers breve til Mitsunori. Af manuskriptet til to foredrag, som Mitsunori og professor Watanabe var så venlige at sende mig i 2004, fremgår, at japanske sprog- og litteraturforskere i hvert fald i nogle tilfælde bruger optællinger i deres arbejder. Jeg har derfor også i dette indlæg brugt optællinger som led i dokumentationen af mit materiale. En oversigt over omfanget af korrespondancen er vist i Appendikstabellen.

I de første år sker korrespondancen ved udveksling af breve, nogle som luftpostbreve andre som aerogrammer. Fra august 1998 - september 1999 foregår en del af korrespondancen som telefax. Mine kopier af faxerne fra Mitsunori er i dag desværre blevet ulæselige, men der foreligger ufuldstændige notater om teksten i dem. Fra juni 2002 gennemføres hovedparten af korrespondancen som e-mail, omend vi især ved juletid også udveksler breve. Næsten al korrespondancen fra Mitsunori er på letforståeligt og godt dansk. Inger skriver altid på dansk. I enkelte tilfælde beder Mitsunori Inger om at forklare sit ordvalg eller hendes sprogbrug. Den ene gang svarer Inger, at hun skriver dansk uden specielt kendskab til de grammatiske regler for dansk, men at hun om fornødent kan lade Mitsunoris spørgsmål gå videre til vores yngste datter Marianne, der på det tidspunkt studerer dansk på Københavns Universitet. Nogle gange skriver Mitsunori, at han glemmer dansk, når han hverken har læst det eller skrevet det i en periode. Mitsunoris vanskeligheder afspejler sig nu aldrig i hans sprog. Det er meget imponerende.

I 1980 gennemfører Mitsunori et kursus i dansk her i København. I forbindelse hermed møder Inger og jeg ham første gang. Efterfølgende er det gennem årene blevet til mange personlige møder under Mitsunoris ikke helt sjældne besøg i København. Fra Mitsunoris tidligste besøg i vort hjem foreligger der i en velbevaret gæstebog notater om den mad, Inger har serveret for ham. (Inger førte gæstebogen i alle årene fra 1969 til 1990. Det der fik hende til at føre bogen var, at vi havde haft besøg hjemme af nogle amerikanske venner to gange med flere års mellemrum. Efter det andet besøg fortalte de smilende, at Inger havde serveret nøjagtig de samme retter ved begge besøg. Dette havde Inger, som foruden at besidde mange andre gode egenskaber, var en fortrinlig husmoder som kunne lave mange forskellige lækre retter, ikke tænkt over, så hun besluttede, for at forhindre gentagelser af den pinlige hændelse, efter hver gang vi havde haft gæster at notere, hvilke retter måltidet bestod af, hvilken dug og hvilke blomster der var på bordet samt gæsternes placering ved bordet). I appendiks 2 er gengivet, hvad Inger har skrevet i gæstebogen i forbindelse med Mitsunoris besøg i vort hjem. Ud over de ret få besøg Mitsunori har aflagt i vores hjem, er vi mødtes mange gange flere andre steder.

I et andet arkiv opbevarer jeg mere end 100 fotos taget af Mitsunori, af Inger, af min datter Mette, af mig eller i enkelte tilfælde af helt andre under vores sammenkomster (udflugter og museumsbesøg). Vi har sammen været på udflugt til historiske seværdigheder i Danmark (bl.a. Kronborg Slot i Helsingør, se foto nr. 1, Frederiksborg slot i Hillerød, Fanefjord kirke på Møn med seværdige gamle kalkmalerier, Trelleborg nær Slagelse, Blåbæk Mølle, en gammel vandmølle der stadig kan fungere, den 5000 år gamle Øm jættestue, Lejre (se foto nr. 2 og www.megalitgrav.dk) som i Sydsverige, ligesom vi sammen har besøgt flere danske kunstmuseer (Louisiana (flere besøg i selskab med Yasumi), Arken og Sophienholm), Karen Blixen museet (Rungstedlund, to besøg). Ved udflugterne var jeg chauffør, indtil Mette i 2002 overtager rattet, idet jeg på grund af nedsat syn og nedsat reaktionsevne og efter talrige henstillinger herom fra Mettes side opgiver at få mit kørekort forlænget

Foto nr. 1

Foto nr. 2

Allerede på en af vore første udflugter sammenligner Mitsunori Inger med kontroltårnet i lufthavnen. "Kontroltårnet" sikrer, at vi på alle udflugterne, hvor jeg er chauffør, sikkert når vores mål. Da Mette bliver chauffør, og jeg skal fungere som kontroltårn, er ordrerne fra dette (mig) i flere tilfælde misvisende, men Mette sikrer ved helt at se bort fra kontroltårnets (mine) anvisninger, at vi trods det stadig hver gang sikkert og hurtigt når vore mål.

I vore mange udflugter og museumsbesøg er som regel indgået en eller anden form for et fælles måltid. Fælles måltider har vi dog også ofte nydt, uden at de har været forbundet med nogen form for egentlig kulturel aktivitet. Foto nr. tre viser et eksempel på et sådant fælles måltid i dette særlige tilfælde på en økologisk restaurant i København. Ved disse særlige fælles måltider, ofte på udsøgte restauranter, har Mitsunori næsten altid været en yderst generøs vært. Vi har dog også lejlighedsvis mødtes på mere ydmyge steder. Et eksempel er da vi (Professor S. Watanabe, Mitsunori og jeg) i 2004 smagte på det danske øl i restauranten i Københavns Lufthavn på deres vej til eller fra en nordisk kongres.

Foto nr. 3

Resultater

Hvad enten Inger eller jeg varetager korrespondancen fra dansk side, er vi, som det fremgår af appendikstabellen, ikke nær så produktive som Mitsunori. Efter at Inger har modtaget de første håndskrevne breve fra Mitsunori, bliver der en lille pause i korrespondancen. Da Mitsunori genoptager den, forklarer han, at han gerne ville kunne skrive på dansk på maskine, og derfor har han prøvet at købe de særlige danske typer æ, ø og å. De første typer, han får, er imidlertid for store, og da han får nogle andre synes han, at "æ" er for lille. Efter endnu et forsøg får han endelig et sæt typer, han synes, at han kan være bekendt at bruge.

Som det også fremgår af appendikstabellen, sender Mitsunori (i 1982 og 1985) to bånd til båndoptagere og samtidig et par danske tekster, som han beder Inger indtale på bånd, for at han kan høre, hvordan dansk lyder. Da vi får båndene, kan de ikke bruges på vores båndoptager, og vi må derfor købe en ny, inden Inger indtaler teksten og returnerer båndene til Mitsunori, som straks kvitterer for Ingers hjælp og skriver, at han med interesse har hørt hendes "livlige stemme med hemmelighedsfuld lyd". I 1998-99 gennemføres en del af korrespondancen ved udveksling af telefax, en kommunikationsform der jo er meget hurtigere end de gængse luftpostbreve. Faxerne omhandler i de fleste tilfælde hasteansøgninger fra Mitsunori, og han beder om og får sproglig korrektion af den danske tekst i ansøgningerne. En yderligere effektivitetsforøgelse i vores kommunikation sker i 2002, da vi hovedsagelig overgår til brug af e-mail.

Begge parter supplerer den almindelige brevkommunikation ved en årlig udveksling af jule- og nytårshilsner og af kalendere. De japanske altid med overordentlig smukke billeder af japanske haver, blomster, landskaber eller et år med smukke klassiske japanske mønstre. De danske kalendere, vi vælger at sende, er også med landskaber eller seværdigheder, som vi ved, Mitsunori har set under sine besøg eller med gengivelser af ansete danske maleres værker. (Kalender-udvekslingen har med årene haft et så betydeligt omfang, at de japanske kalendere snart må kunne danne grundlag for, at jeg etablerer et tredje eget arkiv: Dette alene med Japanske kalendere. Et sådant tredje arkiv tror jeg, at begge mine døtre vil vide at påskønne, idet det ellers desværre ikke er systematik, der præger de enorme bunker af papirer m.m., jeg har fået samlet i mit lange liv).

Under Mitsunoris efterhånden mange besøg i København har han beriget os med en mangfoldighed af gaver fra Japan. Her vil jeg nu kun nævne en, en smuk Japansk dekoreret tekop af porcelæn. Den har jeg brugt dagligt, lige siden jeg fik den foræret for mere end 20 år siden, så jeg har efterhånden nydt mere end 14.000 kopper te og kaffe af den og dekorationen på den er stadig intakt og lige smuk. Et par enklere gaver, som Inger i sin tid forærer eller hjælper Mitsunori med at købe, er noget dansk lakrids og tre slags dansk ost "Dannebrog", "Castello" og "Sagablue". Mitsunori videregiver lakridsen til deres dengang 9-10 årige søn, der efter at have puttet det i munden råber, at det er djævlens føde. Mere heldigt er det ikke, da Mitsunori forveksler lakrids og chokolade. Inger har givet Mitsunori nogle lakridspastiller med hjem til Japan i en cellofanpose. I den tro, at det er chokolade, som Mitsunori har oplevet, at Inger har brugt til dekoration på en kage, beder han Yasumi om at bruge indholdet af posen som pynt på en kage. Desværre bliver sønnen også i dette tilfælde et ufrivilligt offer for forvekslingen, idet han forventer, at det er chokolade Yasumi har dekoreret sin hjemmelavede kage med.

Så er der lidt mere held med prøverne af dansk ost, idet Mitsunori i et brev skriver, at selv om Yasumi kun kan lide "Castello", sætter alle de tre ovennævnte ostenavne, når han ser dem, mod i ham selv på mange måder.

Fra et af besøgene af Mitsunori og Zenhua Yang hjemme hos os, vil jeg mindes at Zenhua skriver et klassisk kinesisk tegn på en serviet. Efter at Mitsunori har studeret tegnet omhyggeligt, er der ikke enighed om tegnets betydning. Den ene mener, så vidt jeg husker, at det er et digt, den anden at det er en madret. Desværre arkiverede vi aldrig servietten, og ingen i min familie kunne fungere som opmand, så spørgsmålet om tegnets betydning kan aldrig blive endelig afklaret. Med mit totale ukendskab såvel til kinesiske og japanske tegn som til japansk og kinesisk sprog, har jeg aldrig kunnet forstå, at nogen kan tyde meningen såvel af kinesiske som af japanske skrifttegn, uden samtidig at kunne forstå begge talesprog. Medens der er meget mening i kinesiske og japanske skrifttegn, hvis man ellers kender dem eller kan tyde dem, er der jo ingen mening i vore latinske bogstaver, når de står alene (og desværre heller ikke altid, når de står flere sammen i ord eller sætninger). I øvrigt gør det ved mere end en lejlighed indtryk på Mitsunori, at vi i Danmark såvel i private hjem som på enklere kroer spiser fisk med to gafler.

Ud over de ovenfor anførte pudsige indtryk og i kontrast til dem, må jeg nævne det dybe indtryk det har gjort på mig, at Mitsunori og Yasumi såvel ved deres besøg her i 1991 kort efter Ingers død som ved et besøg her for nylig havde blomster med, som de lagde på Ingers grav. Det blev jeg og er jeg stadig dybt rørt over.

Diskussion

Det er tankevækkende, at Mitsunoris interesse i for mere end 25 år siden at lære dansk har bibragt min familie, mine venner og ikke mindst mig selv så mange positive indtryk og uventede oplevelser, indtryk som jeg føler, at jeg slet ikke har ydet retfærdighed gennem dette indlæg.

Konklusion

Jeg må med beklagelse konstatere, at den fremstillingsform, jeg har valgt, er uegnet til mit egentlige formål, idet jeg føler, at fremstillingen desværre er blevet rodet, overfladisk, mangelfuld og usystematisk. Jeg skulle nok alligevel have forsøgt mig med Haikudigte.

Tak

Jeg skylder min datter Marianne stor tak for hendes store og yderst velvillige hjælp ved den endelige udarbejdelse af manuskriptet.

Appendikstabel

Kategori	Antal			
	Fra Mitsunori		Til Mitsunori	
	1979-91	1992-2007	1979-91	1992-2007
Brev	31	22	16	14
Postkort	-	4	-	-
Aerogram	2	-	-	-
Telefax	-	6	-	5
Tape	2	-	2	-
E-mail	-	40	-	27
Telefonopkald	6	8	3	5

Apendiks 2 Uddrag af Ingers gæstebog

Følgende fremgår af notater i den gæstebog Inger førte:

Mitsunori besøger os første gang herhjemme den 15. august 1980. Inger serverer franskbrød med champignon og creme fraiche, stegt rødspætte, rødgrød med mandler og piskefløde. I September 1981 spiser vi stegte sild, forloren hare og kanelæbler. I samme forbindelse står "etruskerne". Den 27. november samme år er vi sammen med Mitsunori og Zenhua Yang, Chengdu, Sichuan, Peoples Republic of China først på udflugt til Kullen, Sverige. Senere samme dag serverer Inger hjemme hos os orientalsk mørbrad med krydderier, marengsbund med sveskegrød og flødeskum. Juledag (25. december) er Mitsunori, Zenhua Yang sammen med noget af vores familie gæster i vort hjem og Inger serverer stor julefrokost: glarmestersild, sennepssild, karrysild, sildesalat med ymerpeberrod, leverpostej, sylte, spegepølse med løgfedt, grape- reje - og banansalat, rejesalat med asparges, gulerodssalat, laks, skinke med brunkål og endelig ostebrød. 24. april 1983 holder vi afskedsparty for professor Imai. Foruden M. Imai og Zenhua Yang er gæsterne vore og Imais venner Jytte og Niels Kruse, min svoger og svigerinde (Peter og Jenny) og vores datter Mette. Inger serverer laksørred med kolde asparges og champion, oksefilet med ostesovs, grøn salat, franske ærter og nye kartofler, lagkage med abrikoser, is, chokolade pyntet med mandariner. Drikkevarer: hvidvin til fisken, rødvin til oksekødet og portvin eller sherry til desserten.

Tekster til fotos

#1. Mitsunori, Inger, Mette og Mogens pænt på række foran tårnet på Kronborg Slot, juli 1987.

#2. Mitsunori på vej ned i Øm Jættestue (5000 år gammel) ved Lejre, oktober 1995.

#3. Mitsunori, Mette, Mogens, Peter og Jenny (min svoger og svigerinde) på restauration Cap Horn, Nyhavn, maj 1991.

II

Paston Letters and Papers における否定接続詞 ne

宇賀治　正朋

1

　本論文は，一般に The Paston Letters の名で呼ばれる，15 世紀イングランドの Paston 家一族が 4 代にわたって発信および受信した書簡ならびに関連書類にみられる英語の否定構造に関する研究の一部で，否定接続詞 ne の統語法を扱う。書簡ならびに関連書類は現在次の題名で出版されている。

　　Norman Davis (ed.), *Paston Letters and Papers of the Fifteenth Century*, 2 parts. Oxford: The Clarendon Press, 1971(part I), 1976(part II)

第 1 巻は Paston 家一族が家族のものに宛てて発信した書簡と関連書類合計 421 通（1425-1503）を，世代・兄弟・姉妹・夫妻の順序で発信者ごとに，判明可能な限り日付の年月日順に収録し，第 2 巻は一族が家族構成員以外から受信した書簡 445 通（1425-not after 1520）と関連する文書類 64 点（1426-1510）の合計 509 点を，第 1 巻と同じ記載順で構成員ごとに，同じく年月日順に収める。第 1，第 2 巻を通して総計 930 点には通し番号が付けられ，各書簡・関連文書の本文に 5 行刻みで行数字が付されている。第 2 巻が収録する書簡および関連書類の中には，当時の下記の国王 3 人と王妃 1 人が書いた書簡および認可書 (grant, licence)12 通が含まれている（括弧内は書簡，認可書の番号と作成年）：Henry VI (458:1450; 890:1460),

Edward IV (640:1461; 686:1464; 750:1468; 757:1469; 763:1469; 896:1466; 897:1466), Henry VII (804:1486; 839:1500), Elizabeth (Woodville), Queen of Edward IV (927:1467). 本論文は例文その他のデータを Davis 編の上記エディション（以下 *PL*）に拠っており，各引用例文の末尾には当該書簡，書類の作成年，番号，行数字がこの順で付記されている。

　なお，既刊の 2 巻のほかに第 3 巻も刊行が予定されているが，こちらは 2007 年末現在未刊である。第 3 巻には書簡の発信人，受信者，書簡類に言及されている出来事等についての注のほか，言語論，第 1, 2 巻で収録対象外とされた関連文書，グロッサリ，索引が収録されることになっている。また，上記エディション 2 巻は 2004 年に，若干の誤植と編集上の誤記を訂正し，それ以外はなんらの変更を加えずに，同じく Davis 編として The Early English Text Society 叢書に組み入れられ，別途出版された (Part I:S.S. 20; Part II:S.S. 21)。

2

　本論に入る前に，以下に引用する例文の書き手，書かれた時期を知るための手掛かりとして，書簡集に発信人，受信人として登場する一族 4 代の家族構成員の各生・没年と家族関係を，書簡集第 1 巻の冒頭に述べられている Davis 執筆の Introduction に即して略述し，併せて当人が発信，受信した書簡数をこの順で付記する。さらに，引用例文の書き手を同定するために便宜として，発信書簡数に続けて括弧内に当該数の書簡の最初と最後のものの番号を付記した。例えば 2 代目当主 John Paston I については 44(35-78) + 267 とあるが，これは彼が 44 通の書簡を発信し，それらの番号は 35 から 78 までであること，それとは別に 267 通を受信していることを示す。

表1

第1世代
William Paston I (1378-1444) Norfolk 州 Paston 村の Clement Paston (d.1419) の息子。Agnes Berry と結婚 (1420)。 12(1-12) + 12
Agnes Paston (-1479) 22(13-34) + 3

第2世代 (William と Agnes 夫妻の子供)
John Paston I (1421-66) Margaret Mautby と結婚 (c1440)。 44(35-78) + 267
Edmond I (142(5-49) 2(79-80) + 2
William II (1436-96) 33(81-113) + 2
Clement (1442-not later than 1479) 7(114-120) + 0
Elizabeth (1429-88) 3(121-123) + 30
Margaret Paston (-1484) 107(124-230) + 30

第3世代 (John I と Margaret 夫妻の子供)
John II (1442-79) 86(231-316) + 47
John III (1444-1504) Margery Brews と結婚 (1477)。 77(317-393) + 70
Edmond II (-not later than 1504) 8(394-401) + 1
Walter (after 1455-c1479) 4(402-405) + 0
William III (c1459-became insane probably 1503) 9(406-414) + 6
Margery Paston (-1495) 6(415-420) + 1

第4世代 (John III と Margery 夫妻の子供)
William IV (c1479-1554) 1(421) + 5

3

3.1

英語の最も古い否定辞は ne であり，ne は否定副詞のほか，否定接続詞としても用いられた。OE からの次の引用文を見られたい。

(1) *Ne* meaht ðu nu giet þinre wyrde nauht oðwitan *ne* þin lif no getælan, *ne* eart þu no eallunga to nauhte gedon swa swa þu wenst. (c888 Alfred *Boethius* 23. 2-4) (Sedgefield (1968))[1]

'And yet you cannot reproach your fate in any point, nor blame your life in any way, nor are you made utterly undone as you think.'

(1) では ne が 3 回生起する。そのうち最初の ne は副詞，他の 2 つは接続詞として機能している。

　OE 以後の副詞 ne の史的変化については，これまで OED 以外にも Jespersen (1917) を始めとして Jack (1978a, 1978b, 1978c), LaBrum (1982), Iyeiri (2001), Mazzon (2004), Haeberli and Ingham (2007) など研究は多い。大抵は ne 単独のほか，より多く not との共起形 ne...not を考察の対象とした。それらが明らかにしたところよれば，副詞 ne は個別作家，作品による違いはあるものの，おおよそ，OE 以降しだいに衰退し，1300 年頃からは退潮が著しく，ME 末期までに実質的に消失した。消失後は，既に 14 世紀前半から通用が始まっていた not が代わって英語の代表的否定辞となった。一方，副詞と区別しての接続詞 ne は，OED, Jack (1978b) を別とすればこれまで研究対象とされることは少なく，発達の詳細も明らかでない。比較的少数の従来の研究が明らかにしたところによれば，接続詞 ne は副詞 ne に比して生命が長く，ME を越えて ModE 初期まで存続したが，遅くとも 17 世紀末までには廃用に帰した。廃用後は，それ以前 14 世紀前半に出現した nor が，より古い neither とならんで英語の唯一の否定接続詞となった。

　このような ne の史的変化過程の中にあって，本論文は *PL* における否定辞 ne の統語法の解明を目的とするが，いちおう副詞 ne (=not) と接続詞 ne (=nor) を分けて別々に考察する。否定副詞 ne については既に宇賀治 (2006) で論じた。本稿はその続編を意図し，以下に否定接続詞 ne の統語法を記述する。

3.2

　PL には，書簡，文書の (ほぼ) 全文がラテン語で書かれているものを除いて，第 1, 2 巻合わせて 237 個の ne の用例が見られる。[2] このうち副詞 ne は 25 個，接続詞 ne は 212 個であり，接続詞 ne が圧倒的に多い。上述の OE 以来の副詞，接続詞 ne の発達の史的展開に沿った頻度である。下記表 2 は，Paston 家一族各構成員，および第 2 巻に登場し，一族に書簡，文書

を寄せた発信人別による副詞，接続詞 ne の使用頻度である。配列順は，一族では表 1 の順と同じ，一族以外では発信者の書簡，文書の番号順で，同一人による書簡，文書が複数ある場合には最初のものの番号順に従った。一族以外の発信人氏名の後の括弧内数字は当人が発信した書簡，文書数を指す。Paston 家一族以外の発信者で副詞 ne を使用せず，かつ接続詞 ne の頻度が 3 未満である者の氏名は多数にのぼるので表から除外し，彼ら全体の接続詞 ne の使用合計数のみ記載した。表 2 には，ほかに，対比のため，接続詞 ne の交替形で，やがてその後継語となる nor の PL における使用人別頻度を添付した。PL における nor の生起総数は 536(異つづり形 ner, nere, nerre, nore を含む) である。

表 2

	副詞 ne	接続詞 ne	nor
Paston 家一族			
William Paston I	3	28	0
Agnes	0	0	5
John Paston I	8	40	31
Edmond I	0	0	0
William II	0	1	19
Clement	0	0	6
Elizabeth	0	3	0
Margaret	0	17	110
John II	0	3	89
John III	0	0	73
Edmond II	0	0	1
Walter	0	0	0
William III	1	0	4
Margery	0	0	4
William IV	0	0	0
計	12	92	342

	副詞 ne	接続詞 ne	nor
Paston 家一族以外			
James Gresham (20)	2	9	3
Elizabeth Clere (4)	0	5	0
Thomas Denys (9)	1	8	3
Sir John Fastolf (31)	0	6	3
King Henry VI (2)	1	0	0
William Cotyng (3)	1	1	0
William Worcester (22)	0	41	1
The Earl of Warwick (2)	1	0	0
Thomas Howes (8)	0	15	1
Friar John Brackley (14)	0	5	0
John Felbrigg (1)	1	0	0
The Fourth Duke of Norfolk (4)	1	1	1
Piers (2)	1	0	0
John Pympe (3)	1	3	1
Margaret Richmond (2)	1	0	0
Memorandum on Oxnead (1)	1	0	0
Sir Walter Blount (1)	1	0	0
Others	0	26	181
計	13	120	194
総計	25	212	536

表2から次の3つの事実が明らかとなる。

  (2) Paston 家一族では，発信書簡数の少ない Agnes, Edmond 1 世, Clement の 3 人 (それぞれ 22, 2, 7) を除けば，第 1 世代，第 2 世代の各全員と，第 3 世代の長子 John 2 世までは接続詞 ne を使用するが，次の John 3 世以降の家族構成員は誰も使用しない。即ち，一族では，世代，出生順が下がるにつれて否定接続詞 ne の使用が減少する。第 2 世代で John1 世に次ぐ高頻度の Margaret は同世代最後に順序付けられているが，彼女は John1 世の妻であるので，家族関係からは John1 世の直後に順序付けられる。ne の nor に対する相対的頻度 (%) は John では 56.3, Margaret では 13.4 である。

  (3) 逆に，第 3 世代第 2 子の John 3 世以降では，発信書簡数が少ない Walter と William 4 世 (それぞれ 4 と 1) を除けば，全員が nor を使用する。この事実は前項 (2) と合わせて，一族 4 代の推移過程で，否定接続詞に関し，OE 以来の ne から新しい nor への移行が進行していることを示す。

  (4) Paston 家一族以外でも，強い傾向として，一族へ書簡，関連文書を発信した人々の発信年が下がるにつれて接続詞 ne の使用頻度は下がる。

接続詞 ne の機能は，先行否定辞と相関して 2 つ (以上) の，典型的には等位の構成素を否定的に接続することである．以下，接続詞 ne の統語法を，いかなる先行否定副詞と ne が相関するかの観点から概観する．

3.3　ne_ad…ne_conj

最初に取り上げるのは，接続詞 ne が副詞 ne に後続し，この ne と相関しながら第 2 の構成素を導く構造である．相関否定接続構造の中では最も古く，PL の中にも生起する．

> (5) Wherefore we pray, wil, and charge you and euerysche of you, that ye *ne* vexce, trouble, manase, *ne* greve the forseid persones, *nor* eny of them, for the kepyng of the seide manere contrary to the Kynge our Sovereynge Lordes lawyes, (1469 *PL* 909.10-13)

(5) には 3 個の否定辞が見られる．最初の ne は副詞，2 番目の ne は接続詞，3 番目は新しい否定接続詞 nor である．上記 OE からの引用文 (1) にみられる否定構造とまったく同じ型で，いわば (1) をそのまま引き継いだ構造である．唯一の違いは，3 番目の否定辞が (1) では古来の ne であったものが，(5) では新しい nor に置き換えられていることである．PL ではそもそも否定副詞 ne の生起数が僅か 25 に減少しているので，副詞 ne で始まるこの型の否定構造の生起数も少なく，(5) を含めて 4 を数えるだけである．PL における否定副詞 ne の生起に見られる統語上，使用域 (register) 上の制約的特徴は宇賀治 (2006) で指摘されているが，(5) もこの特徴を具現したもので，Norfolk 公がケースター城の明け渡しについて発した声明 (Statement by the Duke of Norfolk on the Surrender of Caister) 中に見られるものである．他の 3 例は下記の (6), (7), (8) である．

> (6) And where þe seyd Walter þe tyme of þe seyd trespas and of þe seyd bylles makyng *ne* longe tofore, *ne* neuer aftyr biforn þe seyd comyng of þe seyd Duc of Norffolk to Norwich, *ne* no tyme hangyng þe seyd sute, *ne* þe tyme of makyng of þe seyd arbitrement and ordinaunce, (1426-7 *PL* 5.121-124)

(7) And not with-stondyng þe seyd trepas and greuaunce by þe seyd / Walter doon to þe seyd William, ne þat þe seyd William *ne* is not satis/fied of þe seyd cxx li. *ne* no peny þer-of, and hath absteyned hym of al / maner of execucion, sewyng of godes or catelles þat by force of þe seyd / processe or ony othyr he myght have had ageyn þe seyd Walter or hese / borwes, (1426-7 *PL* 5.133-138)

(8) Ryht so forgotyn ye have yowr pore Pympe, That wrytith, sendith, and wisshith alday yowr wele More than his owne; but ye *ne* here, *ne* see, *Ne* sey, *ne* send, and evyr I write and sele In prose and ryme as well as hit will be. (1477 *PL* 776. 7-11)

(6) と (7) は *PL* に登場する Paston 家一族第 1 世代の当主 William 1 世の個所に纏められている書簡類中の一つからのものである。全体 182 行に及ぶこの長い文書は仲裁者宛覚書 (Memorandum to Arbitrators) と題され, 筆者は William 1 世本人ではなく, *PL* の編者 Davis の注記によれば「同定不能の助手の筆跡」(unidentified clerk's hand) とされる。仲裁者とは, William I が巻き込まれたある訴訟事件の際の仲裁者をいう。この覚書は, 否定構造に関して多重否定が特別に多く, この点で第 2 巻に収録されている William Worcester が Winchester の司教 William Wainfleet および司教の召使に宛てた文書 (それぞれ 912(1470) と 913(1470)) とともに *PL* 中際立っている。(6) では 2 組の相関否定表現 ne...ne が生起し, 両方とも 'neither...nor' を意味する。同様に (7) では 134 行目の þat 節内の ne...ne が相関否定表現である。(8) は John Pympe が Paston 2 世に宛てた書簡中の韻文部分に見られるもので, ここでは 4 つの各構成素の前に ne が配置され, ne A, ne B, ne C, ne D という構造になっている。発信人の John Pympe は Kent 州の旧家の一員という。

3.4 neither...ne

接続詞 ne は否定副詞 neither と相関共起することがある。

(9) Alle þe seyd lerned men telle me trewely þer is *nother* perill *ne* doute in þe takyng doun of þe instrument and þe bille to no creature, which

jnstrument and bille I send yow a-geyn by þe berare of this, which I prey yow to kepe as pryué as ye may. (1426 *PL* 4.49-52)

(10) and as for the remenant, I trow it shall abyde tyll ye come hom because I can *nother* be purveyd of joystys *ne* of bord not yettte. (1452 *PL* 150.8-9)

neither は OED によれば 1200 年頃に出現した。従って neither...ne は ne...ne よりも新しい。これ以外の相違点は，neither...ne のほうが ne...ne よりも接続する 2 つの構成素間の相関性が強いことであろう。これは neither の語源に由来する。Hoad(1986) によれば，neither は副詞として 'not either' を意味し，OE nawðer, naðer に遡り，これは nāhwæðer (<nā 'no' + hwæðer 'whether') の縮約形である。つまり，neither は語源に由来する意味の一部として本来「2 者のうちのどちらか 1 つ」を含み，相手方があることを含意している。品詞に関しては，OED も副詞が neither の最初の用法であったとしている。

neither...ne が 3 つの構成素を接続する例が見られる。下記 (11) は ne が最後の構成素の前にだけ配置される構造 *neither* A, B, *ne* C，(12) は ne が 2, 3 番目各構成素の前に等分に配置される構造 *neither* A *ne* B *ne* C である。

(11) I pray you socour my wif, for she is wedow yet for me and shal be til more is done, sith I se that *neythre* plee, trety, *ne* werre may make my peas; (1461 *PL* 626.36-38)

(12) by the concideracion that the said Ser Thomas wold neuer apere in his persone ne by his atturney at no sessions of oir determyner holden in the said counté to answer *neyther* to the billes *ne* inditementz forsaid *ne* to non of thaym, (1451 *PL* 881.34-37)

neither...ne は，ne がやがて新しく 14 世紀前半に登場する否定接続詞 nor に換えられて neithr...nor となるが，PL にはまだ上例 (9), (10), (11), (12) を含めて 31 例見出される。使用者の内訳は次表の通り。表は neither...nor の使用者分布も含む。ただし，Paston 家一族で neither...ne, neither...nor のどちらも使用しない者は表から省かれている。一族以外については使用者名は明記されず，全体の頻度のみ示されている。

表3

Paston 家一族	neither...ne	neither...nor
William Paston I	5	0
Agnes	0	1
John I	2	4
William II	0	2
Clement	0	1
Margaret	5	18
John II	0	11
John III	0	15
計	12	52
Paston 家一族以外	19	27
総計	31	79

表3から次が明らかとなる。

(13) Paston 家一族では，第2世代まで neither...ne を使用するが，第3世代以降は誰も使用しない。他方，neither...nor については，第1世代の Agnes から使用が始まり，以降世代が下るにつれて使用頻度が漸増する。この事実は，一族において，世代の推移とともに古い neither...ne から新しい neither...nor への移行が進行していることを示す。生起数も，neither...ne の12に対して neither...nor は52である。

(14) Paston 家一族以外でも新しい neither...nor が優勢である。生起総数だけであるが，neither...ne の19に対して neither...nor は27である。

3.5 NOT...ne

ne, neither 以外の否定副詞で PL 当時すでに通用していたものの大抵は接続詞 ne と共起する。この類の否定副詞の代表は not で，この類をここでは仮に NOT と表記する。頻度はこの構造が最大である。1, 2 の例示にとどめる。

(15) and I pray you thynk *not* in me that I wyll supporte hym *ne* fauour hym in no lewdnesse, (1465 *PL* 179.24-25)

(16) As for yowr sone, ye knowe well he *neuer* stode yow *ne* me in profite, ese, or help to valew of on grote, sauyng at Calcot Hall whane he and hes brothir kept it on day ageyns Debenham, (1465 *PL* 73.18-21)

(15) では not は主節動詞 thynk の直後へ繰上げられているが、論理的には従属節の最初の動詞 wyll と supporte の間に位置すべきものである。この位置にあって not は後続の ne と相関する。いわゆる否定辞繰上げ (Neg Raising) の一例と解される。

3.6　[Neg]…ne

これまでに取り上げた相関否定接続構造では、最初の否定辞である副詞 ne, neither, not, never などは明示的に表現されていた。ところがこの否定副詞が表現されておらず、にもかかわらず意味上その存在を仮定せざるをえない構造もある。本節ではこの構造を考察する。暗示されている否定辞を仮に [Neg] と表記しておく。引用例文中でも暗示的否定辞が仮定される個所に [Neg] を当てておく。

(17) and the rigth of these bothe patentis hath be putte in juges and lerned men, affor hom [Neg] the seyd Ser Philipp *ne* his conceyll cowd <u>neuer</u> prove hes tytill lawfull be his seyd patentis; (1455 *PL* 51.11-14)

(18) [Neg] My maystyr yowr broþyr J. P., *ne* ye, *ne* Maystyr T. Howys, *ne* I may <u>not</u> esily be brokyd in the jugys conscyens, &c. (1460 *PL* 705.88-90)

[Neg] は nor, neither(*conj.*) との相関構造においても生起する。

(19) Ye must spek wyth your mastyr and comon some remedye hastyly, or be God I enswyr yow whyll owyr Dwk is thus cherysheid wyth the Kyng [Neg] ye <u>nor</u> I shall <u>not</u> haue a man vnbetyn or slayn in thys contré, <u>nor</u> ouyr-sylfe <u>nowthyr</u>, as well ye as I, quod iuratum est onys ayen. (1470 *PL* 339.68-72)

(20) What schal be do ther I wot not yet, for as for any jndytementes that we schuld labor a-yenst them, it is but wast werk, for [Neg] the scheryf *ner* the jurrours wol no thyng do a-yenst them. (1465 *PL* 189.81-83)

(21) wherfore [Neg] þe seyd William *nothyr* hese frendes *ne* hese seruauntz in hys companye at here fredam sithen þe seyd parlement at Leycestre durst not, ne yet ne dar not, rydyn ne goo abowte swyche occupacion as he arn vsed and disposed, to here grete and importable drede and vexacion in here spirites and gret harme and damage and losse of here pouere goodes. (1426-7 PL 5.146-151)

表層上ゼロである [Neg] で始まるこの否定構造の特色として2点が指摘できる。第1点は，この構造で，[Neg] と相関する接続詞 ne, nor, neither の後に別の否定辞が極めて高い頻度で生じていることである。即ち，極めて高い確率で多重否定が生じることである。上掲例 (17)-(21) のすべてにおいても多重否定が生じており，余剰的否定辞には下線が施されている。観察した当該例 33 個のうち，31 までが多重否定を含む。あたかも [Neg] の存在が多重否定が生じるための必要条件であるかのごとくである。理由は，多分，最初の否定辞の明示的不在を後で否定辞の多重使用によって補っているのであろう。統語分野における一種の代償強化 (compensatory strengthening) である。多重否定を含まない珍しい例を1個挙げておく。

(22) My Lord Bedford wylle was made yn so bryeff and generall termys that yn-to thys day by the space of xx yeer can neuere hafe ende, but allwey new to constrew and oppynable; so a generallté [Neg] shall *ne* may be so gode as a particuler declaracion. (Probably 1456 *PL* 537.13-16)

第2点は，素朴な疑問である。[Neg] A, ne B (ne C, ne D) と一般表示できるこの構造では，最初の構成素 A を修飾する否定辞は表層上伏せられ，2番目の構成素から明示されているにもかかわらず，このままの形で広く通用しているが，一体，読者または聴者の側で意味解釈上なんの支障もないのか，ということである。確かな答は本稿の論者には不明であるが，当面の答として，英語の等位接続構造の特性がこの構造を可能にしている，ということが考えられる。英語に限らず，普遍的，通言語的特徴であるの

かもしれない。上例 (11) で neither A, B, ne C の構造がみられたが、ここでは ne は最後の構成素 C の前にだけ配置されていて、2 番目の構成素 B の前は空 (くう) である。にもかかわらず、英語の母語話者なら誰でも迷うことなく B の前にも ne を補って正しく意味解釈する。そのほか (5) でも肯定形等位接続構造 '…we pray, wil, and charge you and eueryshe of you' がみられた。ここでは 3 つの動詞句が等位接続され、最後の構成素の前にだけ and が表出され、等位項がここで終わることを標示しているが、英語の母語話者なら間違いなく and が先行の構成素にも等しく適用することを言語知識として知っている。(8) の '…wrytith, sendith, and wisshith alday yowr wele' も同じ。(16) では 'in profite, ese, or help' という 3 つの構成素が or という離接的 (disjunctive) 接続詞で接続されているが、or は最後の構成素の前にだけ配置されている。ここでも英語の母語話者なら誰でも or が先行する各構成素にも等しく適用することを知っている。一般に、構造 A, B, C, and D があれば、すべての母語話者は瞬時的に D の前の等位接続詞 and は B, C にも等しく適用するものと判断して、A, and B, and C, and D を意味するものと正しく解釈する。同様に A, B, C, or D に対しても、or は B, C にも等しく適用するものとして B, C にも配分し、A, or B, or C, or D を意味するものと正しく解釈する。同じ判断が [Neg] A, ne B (ne C, ne D) の場合にも働いているものと解したい。この事実は、接続詞 ne が and, or と統語上同列の等位接続詞であることの最も確かな証拠である。

4　結論

1　OE 以来の否定接続詞 ne は PL ではまだ頻度がかなり高く、生起総数は 212 にのぼる。ただし、Paston 家一族では世代、出生順が下がるにつれて否定接続詞 ne の使用は減少する。

2　否定接続詞 ne は相関する先行否定副詞として ne, neither, not その他と共起する。これらのうち最も古い ne との共起形 ne…ne は PL では、副詞 ne の生起数が僅少であることもあって、わずか 4 例に過ぎない。

3 ne...ne の第 1 要素の副詞 ne はやがて 14 世紀前半に現れた副詞 neither に置き換えられて neither...ne となるが，neither...ne は *PL* でも既に使用が始まっており，ne...ne よりも頻度は高く，総数 31 個の用例が見られる。

4 neither...ne の ne は 14 世紀前半に出現した nor に置き換えられて neither...nor になるが，古い neither...ne から新しい neither...nor への移行は，Paston 家一族 4 世代の推移の過程でも早く第 1 世代から始まって着実に進行し，一族内での最終的生起数は neither...ne の 12 に対し，neither...nor は 52 であって，neither...nor が遥かに優勢である。

5 相関否定接続構造の第 1 要素である副詞が表層上明示されていない [Neg] A ne B (ne C ne D) は，極めて高い頻度で多重否定を招来する。

6 接続詞 ne は and, or と統語上同列の等位接続詞である。

注

1 作品名 *Boethius* の後の数字は Sedgefield 版のページ，行数を表す。
2 ne に関する資料提供を茨城女子短期大学準教授内桶真二氏に負う。同氏に深謝する。

参考文献

Haeberli, Eric and Richard Ingham (2007 "The Position of Negation and Adverbs in Early Middle English," *Lingua* 117:1-25.

Hoad, T. F. (ed.) (1986) *The Concise Oxford Dictionary of English Etymology*, The Clarendon Press, Oxford.

Iyeiri, Yoko (2001) *Negative Constructions in Middle English*, Kyushu University Press, Fukuoka.

Jack, George B. (1978a) "Negative Concord in Early Middle English," *Studia Neophilologica* 50:29-39.

Jack, George B. (1978b) "Negative Adverbs in Early Middle English," *English Studies*, 59:295-309.

Jack, George B. (1978c) "Negation in Later Middle English," *Archivum Linguisticum*, New Series 9:58-72.

Jespersen, Otto (1917) *Negation in English and Other Languages*, Det. Kgl. Danske Videnskabernes Selskab. Historisk-filologiske Meddelelser. 1, 5.

LaBrum, Rebecca Wheelock (1982) *Conditions on Double Negation in the History of English with Comparison to Similar Developments of German*, Ph. D. Dissertation, Stanford University.

Mazzon, Gabriella (2004) *A Hisory of English Negation*, Pearson Longman, Harlow, England,

Sedgefield, Walter John (ed.) (1968) *King Alfred's Old English Version of Boethius De Consolatione Philosophiae*, Wissenschaftliche Buchgesellschaft, Darmstadt.

宇賀治正朋 (2006) "*Paston Letters and Papers* における否定構造" 田島松二 (編)『ことばの楽しみ―東西の文化を超えて』南雲堂, pp. 29-45.

BNC の自然会話資料
― 乳幼児とテープレコーダの「いる」日常 ―*

内田　充美

1　はじめに

　総語数約1億語の The British National Corpus World Edition（以下 BNC）には，全体の約1割にあたる合計約1,000万語の話し言葉（Spoken）資料が収録されている。これらは900個あまりのファイルに分けて収められているが，[1]そのうちのおよそ4割，ファイル数にして2割弱にあたる153ファイルが，いわゆる人口統計的情報を含んだ自然会話資料（Demographic / Conversation）で，約420万語を成している。それ以外の資料は文脈指定（Context-governed）と分類され，放送や会議，講義などの記録もこの中に含まれている。[2]

　自然会話資料は，124人のボランティアが日常生活の中でテープレコーダを持ち歩き，ふだんの会話を録音することによって収集されたものである (Burnard, 2000)。1億語規模の BNC の中で，もっとも自然で，インフォーマルな言語資料を成すと言える。この特性を生かして，Mair (2006) は，現代英語の変化を捉えようとする試みの中で，インターネットのウェブ上に存在する言語資料に次いで最も変化が進んでいるはずのものとして，この自然会話資料を利用している。

　自然会話資料を構成するファイルには，人口統計的情報として，記録者および話者の年齢，性別，社会階級，母語，教育レベル，地域方言の項目が用意されている。空欄のままのもの，情報が不十分なものも少なくない

が，不完全とはいえ，大規模コーパスに付与されたこのような情報は貴重である。年齢，性別，社会階級などの情報は，社会言語学的観点からの変異研究に役立つであろうことが直接意図されており (Aston & Burnard, 1998:112)，年齢情報は，変化研究において "apparent-time" 分析を可能にするという点でも有用である (Mair, 2006: 114 などを参照)。

本稿では，BNC の自然会話資料の特徴を，語彙の面から探り，そこを糸口にして，資料に収められた人々の日常生活の一端を垣間見る。それを通して，興味深い一面であると同時に研究目的と方法によっては留意を要するであろう特徴として，乳幼児および録音機器の存在とその影響について考察する。

2 付与された情報の問題点

この節では，比較的明らかな問題点について概観する。

2.1 人口統計的情報の空欄（年齢・性別）

前節で触れたように，人口統計的情報には記載もれが少なくない。Hoffmann (1997) によると，話者 1,442 名中，年齢不明の話者が 423 人（総ターン数 526,113 のうち 95,324, 総語数 4,206,058 語のうち 572,600 語にあたる），性別不明の話者が 373 人（ターン数 88,830, 語数 511,952 語）に上る。中には半数を超える話者の年齢，あるいは性別が不明というファイルもある。[3] 年齢・性別両方の情報が揃っているのは，1,018 名（ターン数 430,789, 語数 3,633,458）であり，これは，語数に基づいた計算では，全自然会話資料のうちの 86.4%にあたる。つまり 15 %弱の資料については話者の年齢または性別，あるいはその両方が不明となっていることになる。

2.2 場面情報

自然会話資料は，テープを預けられたボランティアごとにひとつのファイルが対応している。ファイルの大きさはさまざまである。短いものでは，9 ターンの場面ひとつのみから成るもの (KPS) から，長いものでは，16,097 ターン，13 時間以上に相当する会話をおさめたファイル (KBW) まである。また，それぞれのファイルに収録されている場面の長さに規準はなく，その結果ひとつのファイルに収められている場面の数は 1 個から 228 個と多様である (Lee, 2003 を参照)。(1) は短い「会話」1 場面の全文である。

(1) Hey!
What have you got?
<pause dur=7> Stop playing with that phone again!
You're a pain you! <voice quality: laughing> You do it every time <end of voice quality>!
Aye!
They do, when I'm trying to do summat.　　　　　　(KDF)

上の例が示すように，書き起こされた自然会話資料を分析する際には，話者たちが何をしているのかという場面情報が必要と感じられることが多い。BNC では，場面情報 (Setting Information) の中の activity という項目がこれにあたる。しかし，Unspecified と記されていることが多いばかりでなく，たとえ情報が与えられている場合でも，talking, chatting といったあいまいなものも多く，何よりも個々の会話の区切り (場面) ごとには付与されていないため，資料の性質を知るためのヒントとしてはあまり役立たない。

3　話し言葉資料全体との比較：語彙面での特徴

本節では，添付されている情報からでは直接読み取れない，BNC 自然会話資料の性質について，語彙面からのアプローチを試みる。BNC の話

し言葉資料全体と，自然会話資料で特徴的に異なった頻度を示す語彙については，Leech et al. (2001a, b) に詳しいが，ここでは，Davies による VIEW/BNC を利用した語彙別頻度傾向の観察を通して，BNC 自然会話資料の特徴をさらに明らかにする。

VIEW/BNC では，2 つの言語資料のグループを指定して，それらのグループ間で著しく異なる頻度を示す語彙を知ることができる。[4] 包含関係にある資料グループを比較することも可能である。話し言葉資料全体と，自然会話資料とを比較して得られた結果のうち顕著な相違のある語彙を，以下，名詞・動詞の順で検討する。

3.1 特徴的名詞語彙：*mummy, daddy* から探る乳幼児の存在

話し言葉資料全体における生起状況と比較した場合に，目立って高頻度を示す名詞の上位 10 語を次に示す。カッコ内は，話し言葉全体における頻度を 1 とした場合の，自然会話資料での頻度比率である。

(2) 1. mummy (158.83)[5]　2. daddy (87.51)　3. darling (52.25)
　　 4. shit (40.34)　　　　5. nan (30.76)　　6. bastard (30.60)
　　 7. toast (28.03)　　　　8. aunty (25.76)　9. grandma (24.95)
　　10. mum (24.13)

目立つのは，*mummy, daddy, nan, aunty, grandma, mum* といった家族を指す語・呼称である。

一般に幼児語とみなされている *mummy, daddy* の生起例の文脈を実際に読むと，その話者は幼児だけではないことがわかる。自然会話資料中に 2,716 件ある *mummy, daddy* の生起例について，話し手の年齢層による内訳と各年齢層ごとの生起頻度（百万語あたり）を図 1, 2 に示す。

BNC の標準的な年齢区分 (0-14, 15-24, 25-34, 35-44, 45-59, 60$^+$) に加え，0-14 歳についてはファイル情報を参照する手作業によって，より精密に 5 歳ごとの区切りとした。4 歳までの発話者の使用頻度が高い点は予測通りと言ってよい。この年齢層では 1 ターンあたりの語数が少ないことも頻度

を押し上げている。ここでむしろ注目すべきは，25歳以上の発話者が全生起例のおよそ41%に上る1,114例を発していることであろう。

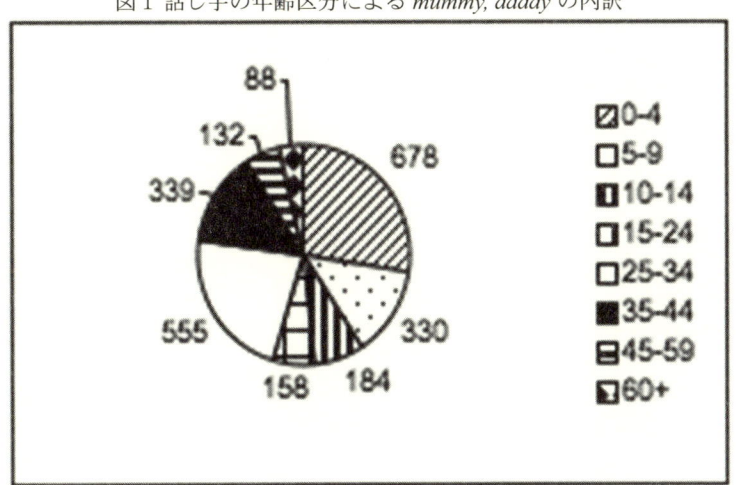

図1 話し手の年齢区分による *mummy, daddy* の内訳

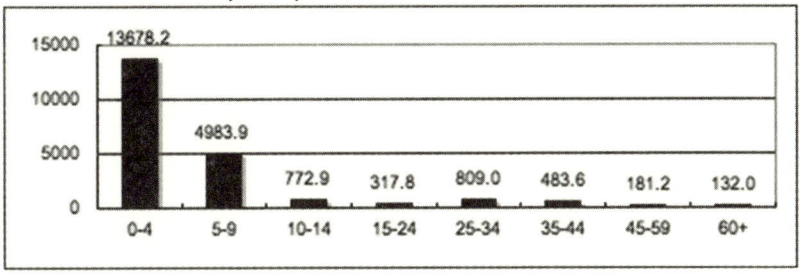

図2 *mummy, daddy* の年齢層別使用頻度（百万語あたり）

　これらのほとんどは，乳幼児がその場にいる時に発話されたものである。話者IDを付与された4歳までの乳幼児の発話資料が含まれているファイルは26個であるが，ただ泣くだけ，そこにいるだけで発話をしない乳幼児が少なくともこれ以外の3ファイルに存在しており，さらに，発話があってもIDを与えられていない乳幼児もいる。最初に述べたように，ひ

とつのファイルには複数の会話場面が収められており，すべての場面にそれらの乳幼児が同席しているわけではないが，上記の 29 ファイルを合わせると自然会話資料全体の 2 割以上，95 万語を超えるという事実は注目に値する。[6]

乳幼児の存在は，さまざまな形でその場にいる大人の会話スタイルに影響を与える。したがって，たとえ，BNC 検索時に 0-14 歳の話者による発話を分析対象から外したとしても，乳幼児の存在による影響は排除しきれない。特に 25-34 歳，35-44 歳の女性話者のグループに注意が必要であることが，図 3 の頻度分布から示唆される。

図 3 は，25-34 歳，35-44 歳の女性話者による *mummy, daddy* の使用頻度が顕著に高いことを示しているが，同時に，資料として収められた個々の場面において，この年齢層の女性の会話スタイルが影響を受けているであろうことも示唆している。

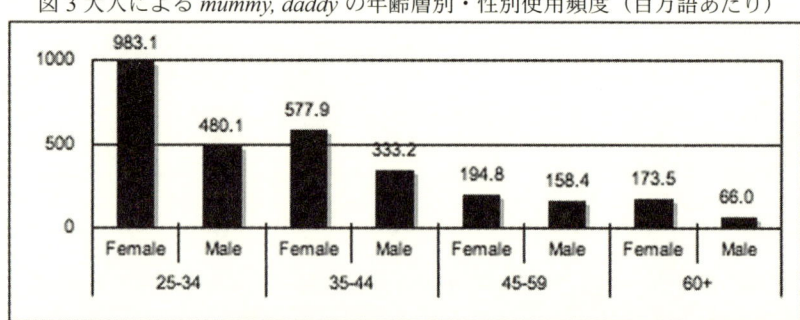

図 3 大人による *mummy, daddy* の年齢層別・性別使用頻度（百万語あたり）

年齢	Female	Male
25-34	983.1	480.1
35-44	577.9	333.2
45-59	194.8	158.4
60+	173.5	66.0

次の例で，None と記された話者はファイル情報に話者として記載されていない幼児である。前後の文脈から判断すると，Elaine (28 歳) と Kevin (29 歳) がその両親，Audrey (61 歳) が祖母にあたる。

(3) None A biscuit.
  Audrey Eh!
    It's a nice a perm that Elaine.
  None <voice quality: whining> A, a biscuit <end of voice quality>.

BNCの自然会話資料　　　　　　　　　　**323**

  Audrey I've got none!
  None I want a biscuit.
  Elaine Do you think I'd come home with packets of biscuits for you?
  None < −|− > No! < −|− >
  Elaine < −|− > Say mummy < −|− > I like your hair.
  None <voice quality: whining> A biscuit <end of voice quality>.
  Elaine < −|− > Say that. < −|− >
  Audrey < −|− > Were they < −|− > nice people?
  Kevin Say mummy, I like your < −|− > hair. < −|− >
  Elaine < −|− > Great!
      < −|− > It's just like a proper salon, but talk about professional!
  Kevin < −|− > My mother goes. < −|− >
  None < −|− > <voice quality: whining> Biscuit <end of voice quality>.
      < −|− >   (KBC)

　この例が表しているように，乳幼児が同席している場合，子どもと大人の間のやりとりが，大人同士の会話と並行して進行することが特徴的である。乳幼児の言動によって大人の会話が分断されることは誰もが経験で知っている通りである。このような場面を書き起こした会話資料を分析するにあたっては，文脈への格段の注意が要求される。また，量的な観察を行う場合には，乳幼児の存在という場面の偏りを考慮に入れて，その影響に注意する必要がある場合もあるだろう。

3.2　特徴的動詞語彙：*taping*, *tape* を手がかりに探るテープレコーダの存在

　自然会話資料で目立った高頻度を示す動詞の上位10語を示す。カッコ内は，話し言葉全体での頻度を1とした場合の，自然会話資料での頻度比率を表す。

(4) 1. in (38.59)[7]　　2. taping (38.02)　　3. kiss (29.47)
　　4. tastes (23.68)　　5. tape (23.39)　　6. shaved (17.40)
　　7. lick (16.89)　　8. bugger (16.17)　　9. mate (15.96)
　　10. swapped (14.12)

ここでは，BNC自然会話資料に特徴的な語彙として，*taping, tape* に注目する。

前述したように，BNCの自然会話資料はボランティアがテープレコーダに記録したものである。すなわち，そこに収められた会話の場面には，いつもテープレコーダが存在するわけである。非日常的な存在であるだけに，話題の的になるのも自然の成り行きと言えよう。これら目立った頻度を示す動詞 *taping, tape* を手がかりにすると，研究プロジェクトの実際の様子をうかがい知ることができるような場面にたどり着く。次の例での *they* (5, 6, 8), *she* (7), *this man* (9) は調査者を指している（以下，イタリックは内田）。

(5) Alan　*They* want to know what spoken English is like　(KB0)
(6) Joyce　It's a survey, erm market research < −|− > thing < −|− > (...)
　　Joyce　we'll tape you know, *they*'re going, *they* want the English language
　　　　　<pause>
　　　　　(...)
　　Joyce　< −|− > Yes so you're < −|− > taped, *they* want the English language *they* want all < −|− > different er < −|− >
　　　　　(KB2)

(6)の中略部分では，謝礼として商品券25ポンド分がもらえること，依頼があったのが前の週で，この日にテープの回収が行われる予定であることが述べられている。

プロジェクトそのものの性質については，市場調査と認識している人(6, 7)，辞書改訂のために協力していると思っている人(8)，よくわからない

がおもしろそうだし報酬もあるからと割り切る人 (9) と，受けとめ方はさまざまである。

(7) Evelyn　　I mean <pause> for this market research one, we ought to finish this tonight because if *she* comes tomorrow
　　Arthur　　Which one?
　　Evelyn　　This tape that's in <pause> this erm <pause> <"music playing"> <pause> this market research tape.　　　　　　　　　　　　　　　　　　　　(KBB)
(8) Ann　　　(. . .) it's for a dictionary and *they* want <pause> new words that are commonly used <pause> and *they* don't want <pause> and all old words that never get used it'll be dropped in the next < −|− > edition of the dictionary. < −|− >　　　　　　　　　　　　　　　　　　　　(KB7)
(9) Dorothy　And <pause> <voice quality: laughing> *this man* came to the door <end of voice quality>, and *he* went to get the hold– <pause> belt, that should just have a tape recorder on conversation just throughout the week <pause> so it's getting all sorts of rubbish going in there, < −|− > <voice quality: laughing> <unclear> <end of voice quality>　< −|− > (. . .)
　　Dorothy　and it's all do with erm <pause> you know <unclear> people and the erm <pause> wives and <pause> < −|− > language of the nineties. < −|− > (. . .)
　　Dorothy　< −|− > I'll do anything for money and chocolate! < −|− >　　　　　　　　　　　　　　　　　　　　(KBW)

また人口統計的にバランスのとれた資料収集のために，調査者 (*a lady*) が苦労している様子もうかがえる。[8]

(10) Carl <pause> No there was a lady came round the other day, you know asking for erm <pause> volunteers to erm <pause> tape, you know, recording conversations between people and yourselves and the family, you know? (...)
Carl Well you obviously, she was looking for a spec–a gentleman within a certain age range.   (KBG)

　以上に例示したように，特徴あるキーワードに着目することによって，プロジェクトそのものについての背景的事実を知ることができる点は興味深い。しかし，録音機器の存在が言語資料の文脈にさまざまな影響を与えていることもまた事実であり，無視できない問題をはらむ可能性もある。[9]

　ひとつには，人々がテープレコーダに文字通り話しかけている場合があることに注意が必要であろう。たとえば間投詞の区分で頻度比較を行った場合に，*hello* や *bye-bye* は，自然会話資料での頻度が高い語彙として分類される。[10] しかし，この中には，(11)〜(13) のように，機械に向かって発せられたものが含まれていることには気づきにくい。

(11) Emma < –|– > Gonna switch it off?
　　　　　< –|– > Cheerio then < –|– > darling! < –|– >
　　　　　　　　　　　　　　　　　　　　　　　　　(KCE)
(12) Jean   Hello Dot!
　　 Dorothy Hello!
　　　　　　<pause> We're here again!   (KBW)
(13) Helen   It only picks
　　 Clare   Hello! <pause>
　　 Helen   Stop it.   (KCD)

　また，より面倒な問題としては，すでに上で言及したように，録音行為にまつわるトピックが通常より多いこと，それに伴う語彙の偏りが予測される。

　さらに，規範意識の問題がある。次の (14), (15) に例示するように，「録音しているのだから言葉遣いに気をつけなければならない」という主旨の

発言が少なからず見られる。また，録音されているから話せないということが明示的に述べられる場面 (16, 17) もある。

(14) Angela   All the neighbours was looking at I.
              I thought <unclear> bloody hell.
     Ben   Bloody hell.
     Angela   Oops.
              We'll scrub that off the tape.   (KB6)
(15) Terry   Mom, you have to speak English.
              No, I told you yesterday
     Mother   I can't hear
     Terry   Well you have to speak English
     Mother   Why is that?
     Terry   Cos thing
     Mother   What thing?
     Terry   This
     Mother   Oh you mean you are taping me   (KR2)
(16) PS000   Are you ready to tell me now?
     Orgady   No, because the tape recorder will hear me say it.
              <pause>   (KPW)
(17) Maggie   I reckon people's conversations ought to be bleeding
              private not on bloody < −|− > tape <unclear> <
              −|− >   (KBE)

自然会話であるとはいえ，テープレコーダという存在があるために，トピックやスタイルの点で一定の制約がかかってくることは常に避けられない事実である。たとえば，スウェアワードの頻度を比較するような場合に，特定の属性によって分けた話者グループ間で差が確認されたとしても，録音されていることを知っている話者と知らずに話している話者が混在している場合には，その評価が困難になる。

4 まとめ

BNC の話し言葉資料は，その規模の大きさと，注意深いサンプリング方針，使用インターフェイスと参考資料が充実している点で，非常にすぐれた特長を持つ。話し言葉約 1,000 万語，うち自然会話約 420 万語という資料規模をもってすれば，2.1 で述べたような問題点があるとしても，話者のさまざまな属性によって構築したサブコーパスを用いた調査研究が可能である (Mair 2006, Uchida 2006)。

しかし，研究目的と方法によっては，3.1 と 3.2 で考察したような資料の特徴が影響を及ぼす可能性を考慮に入れておく必要がある。日常生活には子どもがいて，とりわけ乳幼児の言動は大人のそれとは大きく異なる。大人はそれを時にいなし，時に面と向かい，場合によってはあしらいながら自身の会話を進める。現実問題として，そういう場面に居合わせることが多いのは 25-34 歳の女性であるかもしれない。しかし，乳幼児が同席した時の会話が，25-34 歳の女性を特徴づける会話スタイルや語彙を示すものだというような分析結果を導き出すことは，どのような枠組みであれ言語研究の目指すところではないであろう。また，資料収集の方法を知り，資料の中に展開されている場面を想像すれば，テープレコーダという特殊な「参加者」が常に存在し，静かに影響力を発揮していることに気づく。

本論では，大規模コーパス資料の調査分析にあたって，ともすれば忘れがちな，そこに描き取られた生活と人々に向けるまなざしに立ち返り，BNC の自然会話資料に見られる特徴を，語彙分布傾向を手がかりにして議論した。

注

* 本研究は平成 19-20 年度科学研究費補助金（基盤研究 C, 課題番号 19529428）のもとに行われた。また，2005 年 4 月より 2006 年 3 月までウェリントンのヴィクトリア大学で行った在外研究の成果から派生したものである。一連の研究のきっかけになる重要な助言と援助をくださった同大学 G. Kennedy 教授とチューリヒ大学（当時）の S. Hoffmann 博士に心より感謝する。柳朋宏氏には原稿段階で目を通していただき，貴重なコメントをいただいた。

1 Leech et al. (2001) では 915, Lee (2002) では 909。誤差 6 ファイルのうち 4 件については，重複を解消したためと Lee (2002) にある。
2 "Demographic (Dem)", "Context-governed (cg)" は BNC 情報中 "Domain" 項目での用語，"Conversation" は "Genre" 項目での用語。BNC におけるジャンル，ドメインなどの類似概念についての問題点は Lee (2001) が詳細に論じている。
3 半数を超える数の話者の年齢がわからないファイル：KB4 (4/6), KST(7/8), KBU (8/9), KC4 (9/10), KC5 (7/10), KCD (5/8), KCK (7/9), KCS (5/9), KDB (7/11), KDG (8/11), KDP (9/10), KDW (17/26), KDY (7/9), KE0 (9/10), KE1 (8/10), KNS (5/6), KNT (3/5), KP2 (5/9), KP3 (6/10), KPB (3/4), KPK (7/10), KPM (8/9), KPV (6/10), KST (7/8), KSV (8/9)。半数を超える話者の性別が不明のファイル：KBU (8/9), KC4 (9/10), KC5 (7/10), KCD (5/8), KCK (7/9), KCS (5/9), KDB (7/11), KDG (8/11), KDP (9/10), KDW (17/26), KE0 (9/10), KE1 (8/10), KNS (5/6), KNT (3/5), KNU (2/3), KPB (3/4), KPK (7/10), KPM (8/9), KST (7/8), KSV (8/9)。ただし，カッコ内の数字は，不詳者数/話者数を表す。
4 レンマ化は行われない。
5 *mummy* という形式のほかに，*mammy* が 3 件，*mommy* が 5 件資料中に収められているが，それら計 8 件は，少数であるためここでの調査対象から除外した。
6 KB3, KB6, KB7, KB8, KBG, KBH, KBV, KBW, KC1, KCA, KCM, KCU, KCX, KD1, KD3, KD4, KD6, KDE, KDF, KDJ, KDN, KP7, KP8, KPC, KR0, KR2。これに加えて，KB9, KBC, KDG には明らかに乳幼児がいる。29 ファイルの合計語数は 957,514 語 (Hoffmann, 1997 および Lee, 2003 を元に算出)。
7 第 1 位の *in* は，*isn't it* の縮約形 *innit* の be 動詞部分である。
8 KBF ファイルには話者情報を収集している場面が収められている。
9 会話相手に録音していることを知らせずに収集されている例も数多い。このことは，*are you taping me? / I'm taping you* という表現が多数見られることにも現れており，次のように，こっそり録音したことが話題になっているケースもある：
... like that, no one knew, I was driving the car and I recorded everything that was in the car all night <laugh> no one knew until the end of the night, I got the tape home, I go this is gonna be interesting <laugh> (KC2)
Burnard (2000) によると，"as unobtrusively as possible" に録音すること，会話参加者が録音の事実を知らなかった場合には事後に承諾を得る，了承が得られない部分は録音資料を消去するという手順が標準的なものとして意図されている。
10 *bye-bye* の自然会話資料での生起頻度比率は，話し言葉全体での頻度を 1 とした場合 18.94, *hallo* は 5.83, *hello* は 3.79 である。

参考文献

Aston, G. and L. Burnard (1998) *The BNC Handbook: Exploring the British National Corpus With SARA*. Edinburgh: Edinburgh University Press.

Burnard, L. (ed.) (2000) *Reference Guide for the British National Corpus (World Edition)* [オンライン資料]. URL: http://www.natcorp.ox.ac.uk/docs/userManual/

Davies, M. *Variation in English Words and Phrases (VIEW/BNC)* [オンライン資料]. URL: http://corpus.byu.edu/bnc/

Hoffmann, S. (1997) *Speakerinfo.txt*. [オンライン資料]. URL: ftp://escorp.unizh.ch/pub/bncstuff/databases/

Lee, D. (2001) "Genres, Registers, Text Types, Domains, and Styles: Clarifying the Concepts and Navigating a Path through the BNC Jungle." *Language Learning and Technology* 5 (3): 37-72.

Lee, D. (2002) *Notes to Accompany the BNC World Edition (Bibliographical) Index*. [オンライン資料]. URL: http://clix.to/davidlee00

Lee, D. (2003) *The BNC Index*. [オンライン資料]. URL: http://clix.to/davidlee00

Leech, G., P. Rayson, A. Wilson (2001a) *Word Frequencies in Written and Spoken English: Based on the British National Corpus*. London: Longman.

Leech, G., P. Rayson, A. Wilson (2001b) *Companion Website for* Word Frequencies in Written and Spoken English: based on the British National Corpus. [オンライン資料]. URL: http://ucrel.lancs.ac.uk/bncfreq

Mair, C. (2006) *Twentieth Century English: History, Variation and Standardization*. Cambridge: Cambridge University Press.

Uchida, M. (2006) "Gender Preferential Variations in the BNC and Descriptions in Dictionaries." In The JACET Society of English Lexicography (ed.) *English Lexicography in Japan*. Tokyo: Taishukan. pp. 222-234.

1600年代イギリス文学作品における
過去形と現在完了形の交替
─ 散文と演劇を比較して ─

大津　智彦

1　導入

　筆者は大津 (2007) において，19世紀イギリス文学作品における過去形と現在完了形の交替に関する調査を行った。そのなかで，過去形から現在完了形への移行は，(i) 19世紀後半になるほど進んでいること，(ii) 構文の違いによって移行の程度に差が生じていたこと，(iii) 書き言葉と話し言葉を比較すると書き言葉において現在完了形の頻度がより高かったことなどを明らかにした。そして，なかでも現在完了形の史的発展に大きな意味を持つものとして (iii) に着目し，書き言葉において現在完了形がより広く浸透していることから，現在完了形の発達は書き言葉から始まったという推論を立てた。本稿は，Visser (1966:751) によって機能上，過去形と現在完了形の区別がなされるようになったとされるシェークスピア以降の時代，つまり1600年代を対象として，書き言葉・話し言葉における過去形と現在完了形の交替を調査し，この推論を検証することを主な目的としている。

2 コーパスの検索

2.1 コーパス

コーパスとして用いたのは，書き言葉には Project Gutenberg からダウンロードした，付録に記載の散文 10 作品，話し言葉には Chadwyck-Healey Literature Collections に所収の，同じく付録に記載した散文劇 40 作品である。

1600 年代におけるこのふたつのジャンルのテキストは書き言葉・話し言葉としてどのような位置にあるか，前回の調査と同じく Biber and Finegan (1992) を用いて確認してみる。同論文は書き言葉と話し言葉の区別に関わるものとして下記の三つの Dimension を設け，各 Dimension について 17 世紀から 20 世紀までの文学作品などの量的分析を行っている。

　　Dimension A – Informational versus Involved Production
　　Dimension B – Elaborated versus Situation-Dependent Reference
　　Dimension C – Abstract Style

各 Dimension の内容を簡単に説明すると，Dimension A は情報内容の密度や正確性の高い情報伝達と情緒的で相互作用を主とする情報交換との比較を表す。Dimension B では明示性とその場の状況への依存度の高低を見る。Dimension C は抽象性，専門性，形式度の高い文体か否かを示す。言語的特徴としては，例えばあるジャンルのテキストが書き言葉の性質を示す場合，Dimension A では名詞，前置詞句，多音節の単語などの頻度，Dimension B では関係代名詞節，pied-piping 構文，名詞化変形などの頻度，Dimension C では受動構文，合接詞（conjuncts），副詞節などの頻度が高い。逆に，話し言葉の性質を示す場合，Dimension A では接続詞 *that* の省略，縮約形，現在形の動詞などの頻度，Dimension B では時や場所を示す副詞類，その他副詞句などの頻度が高く，Dimension C では語彙項目の種類の多様性を持つ。

これら三つの Dimension で見た場合，1600 年代の散文（essays）はどの Dimension においても，もうひとつの書き言葉のジャンルとして採用されて

いる fiction と比較して年代を問わず同等以上に書き言葉としての高い数値を示す。[1] また，1600年代の散文演劇に関しては，やはりどの Dimension においても，もうひとつの話し言葉のジャンルとして採用されている dialogue in fiction と同程度の話し言葉寄りの数値を示す。特に Dimension B と C においては，現代の対面型の会話（London-Lund Corpus）と変わらない数値を示し，現実の会話に酷似していることがわかる。以上の理由により，1600年代の散文および散文演劇をそれぞれ書き言葉・話し言葉の代表として用いるものとする。

2.2　対象とする構文

前回の調査，大津（2007）においては，過去形と現在完了形が特に意味の変化がなく交替でき，両者が変異形をなしていると解釈できる場合のみを対象とすることから，現在とのつながり（present relevance）を持つ標識となる ever を含む文または節を検索した。今回は，下の例文にあるように，ever に加えて同じく present relevance を表す always を含む文または節を検索し，両者における現在完了形の発達の進度の違いを比較，検証する。[2]

(1) Perjured knaves, knights of the post, liars, crackers, bad husbands, &c. keep their several stations; they do still, and always did in every commonwealth. (W: Burton 1621)[3]

(2) I have always thought the actions of men the best interpreters of their thoughts. (W: Locke 1660)

(3) I always held it better to vse sharpe Counsell then smooth flattery. (S: Mabbe 1631)

(4) Poor little Rogue, she has always been very dutiful to me. (S: Dilke 1696)

コーパスの検索においては上記50作品について，コンコーダンサーで ever および always（両者とも異綴りを含む）を持つすべての文を抽出し，

さらにその中から手作業で過去形，現在完了形の文のみを拾い出した。ただし，過去形の文を選ぶ際には，現在完了形との交替の可能性がある必要がある。*ever* および *always* を持つといっても，現在とのつながり (present relevance) のない，全く過去の出来事を表現する場合もあり得る。ある文が現在とのつながりを念頭において書かれているかどうかはその筆者の視点によるもので，外部からは窺い知るのが困難な面があるが，今回も前回の調査と同じく，過去形の文については，筆者の視点をできる限り汲み取れるよう文脈をよく吟味し，過去を話題にしていると思われる場合は対象からはずした。[4] しかし，実際は判断に窮するというケースはまれで，例えば次の (5) は関係詞節の動詞が過去形であるから *ever* を含む節も過去の話であると容易に判断できるので対象外となる。

    (5) ... those that were great politiques indeed ever ascribed their successes to their felicity and not to their skill or virtue. (W: Bacon 1605)

次の (6) では過去形が用いられているが，明らかに現在の筆者の嗜好を語っているものであり対象となる。

    (6) If my testimony were aught worth, I could say as much of myself; no man ever took more delight in springs, woods, groves, gardens, walks, fishponds, rivers, &c. (W: Burton 1621)

逆に，(7) のように現在完了形を使ってはいるが本来過去に属していると解釈すべき用例があり，対象からは外した。

    (7) I may not deny but that there is some profitable meditation, contemplation, and kind of solitariness to be embraced, which the fathers so highly commended, ... as many of those old monks used it, to divine contemplations ... Or to the bettering of their knowledge, as Democritus, Cleanthes, and those excellent philosophers have ever done, to sequester themselves from the tumultuous world. (W: Burton 1621)

Democritus や Cleanthes は古代ギリシャの哲学者であり，文脈上も現在とのつながり（present relevance）を認め難い。

3 分析

3.1 全体像

まず *ever* もしくは *always* を含む文または節の全体像から考察していく。表1から見て取れるのは，1600年代において，現在完了形は演劇（話し言葉）よりも散文（書き言葉）において圧倒的に頻度が高いということである（8%対49%）。また，同様の傾向は表2の *always* を含む文または節においても見られる。ここでも散文における現在完了形の比率は86％，演劇における同比率は48％とやはり散文における現在完了形の浸透度の方が圧倒的に高い。大津（2007）で行った調査において，19世紀の文学作品の「語り」の部分（書き言葉）における現在完了形の比率は64％,「会話」の部分（話し言葉）の同比率は39％であったことから，現在完了形の浸透は書き言葉から始まったという推論を立てたが，機能上，過去形と現在完了形の区別がなされるようになったとされる1600年代において表1や表2のような結果が見られるということは，現在完了形は書き言葉から広がったとする推論を裏付けるものである。

現在完了形が書き言葉から広がったとすればその理由としてまずラテン語の影響が考えられる。Elsness (1997: pp. 244-5) によると，ラテン語が英語の現在完了形の出現に与えた影響に関して，Benveniste (1971) を引用して，迂言的完了形（*have* + 過去分詞形）はゲルマン語の初期から確立しているもので，ラテン語がその源であるのではなく，ゲルマン語で独自に発達したものとしているという。一方，Traugott (1972) では英語の完了形の出現がラテン語の影響によるものであることは否定しているものの，英語の迂言的完了形がラテン語の同じ構文によって強化された可能性は高いとしているという。今回の調査結果で書き言葉において現在完了形がより発達しているのは，Traugott (1972) が述べているようにラテン語による強化という作用が働いたためであると十分考えることができるのではないだろうか。

表 1　everを含む文または節

	過去形 (a)	現在完了形 (b)	合計 (c)	比率 (%) (b)/(c)
散文	46	45	91	49
演劇	276	24	300	8
合計	322	69	391	—

$\chi^2 = $　82.2097; p<0.01

表 2　alwaysを含む文または節

	過去形 (a)	現在完了形 (b)	合計 (c)	比率 (%) (b)/(c)
散文	2	12	14	86
演劇	22	20	42	48
合計	24	32	56	—

$\chi^2 = $　6.22222; p<0.01 (Fisher's exact test)

3.2　要因別分析

全体像を見たので，次は過去形と現在完了形の交替に関して1600年代に観察される特徴について種々の観点から詳細に分析していきたい。

3.2.1　副詞による偏り

表1から，1600年代演劇において everを含む文または節では現在完了形が使用される頻度は過去形に比べ非常に低いことが分かるが，表1から窺えない事実として，現在完了形の数が少数の作品に偏っていることがある。具体的には，24例中，過半数以上の14例までが3つの作品（Mabbe 1631）5例，（Carlell 1639）4例，（Farquhar 1699）5例から抽出したものである（因みに検索した演劇は40作品）。ところが興味深いことに，表2が示すように alwaysを含む文または節では，演劇のなかで現在完了形が使用される頻度は過去形とほぼ同等で高い比率を見せているのだが，everの場合と違い作品による偏りがなく現在完了形の20例は17の異なる作品から抽出したものである。語彙内に音声変化が浸透していく様子を表す理論として lexical diffusionがあるが，everと alwaysの作品による偏りに関する

違いはこの lexical diffusion を応用することによって説明することができる。つまり，*ever* を含む文や節において現在完了形の頻度が低いのは，その形式を使う頻度が各作家ごとにまんべんなく低いのではなく，少数の作家に偏っているためであることを示し，*always* を含む文や節のように現在完了形の頻度がある程度以上に高いということは多数の作家の間に広まっているためであるという言語変化のモデルが想定できる。

ever と *always* はともに Jespersen (1909-49: IV 64) や Elsness (1997: 298) によって過去形と共起しやすいとされ，その理由はこれらの副詞自体が現在とのつながり（present relevance）を表すのに十分な役割を果たしているためであるという。今回そのような副詞においても現在完了形の浸透度に差が生じていたことが分かったが，この差を意味的に説明することは困難である。例文を見ると *ever* は "at any time" や "at all times"，*always* は "at all times" といった意味で用いられているが，どちらかの方が現在とのつながりをより強く表していると判断することはできない。他に理由を考えるとすれば両者の頻度の違いがある。表1，2から分かるように *ever* の用例の総数は391例であるのに対し，*always* は56例である。Bybee (2005) によると統語においても頻度の高い用例の方がより保守的な構造を維持する傾向があるとされるが，このケースにあてはめると *ever* は過去形と共起する頻度の高さから *always* などよりも現在完了形への移行が遅れたと考えられる。

次の例は上記の事情を一つの文の中に体現したものとして興味深い。

(8) I did ever thinke thou wudst come to some good, for thou hast beene always an honest Trojan. (S: Chamberlain 1640)

3.2.2 構文別分析

筆者は大津(2007)において，19世紀の文学作品に見られる3種類の注目すべき構文を取り上げ，過去・現在完了形の交替に関してそれぞれの構文が見せる特徴を分析した。ここでは紙幅の関係上，そのうち19世紀に

おいて現在完了形への移行が顕著であった1種類の構文について2世紀遡った時点の姿を観察したい。

3.2.2.1 *Did you ever . . . ?* と *Have you ever . . . ?*

大津 (2007) で19世紀のイギリス英語を対象とした際，口語に特徴的に見られるこのふたつの構文を取り上げて，*Have you ever . . . ?* の比率が口語全体の現在完了形の比率と比較して高いことから，この構文のように口語においてさえ過去形から現在完了形への移行が少なからず進行しているケースがあったとした。また，19世紀に *Did you ever . . . ?* の形式で見つかった用例の半数は相手の答えを期待しない修辞疑問文であり，19世紀にはこの形式の固定化・イディオム化が相当進んでおり，このようにイディオム化した用法が ever を含む文で過去形の使用が多い印象を与えている可能性を指摘した。

まずは後者の観点から1600年代における *Did you ever . . . ?* を調べてみよう。表3は *Did you ever . . . ?* が純粋に返答を求める疑問文である場合と返答を特に求めない修辞疑問文である場合との比率を時代別に示したものである。1600年代演劇の方が修辞疑問文の比率が低いが，1800年代小説との間に統計学的な有意性はない。しかし，表には現れていないが興味深い事実として，1600年代演劇で返答を求める純粋な疑問文と解釈される場合でも，*Did you ever* のあとに11例中6例までが see もしくは hear があとに続くことを述べておかなければならない。因みに修辞疑問文と解釈された3例すべてにおいて see もしくは hear があとに続く。このあたりの事情には頻度が関わっているものと思われる。つまり，*Did you ever . . . ?* は基本的に経験を問う疑問文であるが，そういった場合，「見聞きしたことがあるかどうか」を問題にすることが多く，see や hear が頻回に用いられることになる。そして頻度の高い形式は保守的になる傾向があるので現在完了形への移行に抵抗を示し，*Did you ever . . . ?* の形を保持するが，頻度が高ければ決まり文句として固定化・イディオム化しやすい。下の例文 (9) は返答があるので疑問文，(10) は返答がないので修辞疑問文と

して処理したが，両者の境界は曖昧である。*see* や *hear* を伴う疑問文の修辞疑問文への転用は容易であったと思われる。[6]

(9) Boob.: Did you ever hear such pure Compliments?
Rash.: Never in all my days. (S: Crowne 1675)

(10) Peg.: O dear, Aunt! did you ever hear the like?
Aunt.: Believe him not, he's a lying, flattering London varlet.– he'll spirit thee away beyond Sea. (S: Ravenscroft 1681)

表3　時代別に見た疑問文もしくは修辞疑問文としての *Did you ever ... ?*

	疑問文 (a)	修辞疑問文 (b)	(b)/(a)+(b)
1600年代演劇	11	3	21%
1800年代小説（会話部分）	14	14	50%

次に表4は *Did you ever ... ?* と *Have you ever ... ?* の比率を時代別に示したものである。時代の違いによる統計学上の有意さは表面的には認められない。しかし，1600年代演劇における *Have you ever ... ?* の4例をよく見ると，すべてFarquhar (1699) からのものであり，特定の作家に偏っている。またそれが1600年代最後の年の作品であることを考え合わせると，1600年代においては *Have you ever ... ?* も他の *ever* を含む文または節と同じように口語では珍しく，その発達は1700年代以降であったことがわかる。[7,8]

表4　*Did you ever ... ?* と *Have you ever ... ?* の時代別比率

	Did you ever ... ? (a)	*Have you ever ... ?* (b)	(b)/(a)+(b)
1600年代演劇	11	4	27%
1800年代小説（会話部分）	14	12	46%

4 まとめ

　以上，1600年代のイギリス文学作品（散文，演劇）をコーパスとして用いて，過去形と現在完了形の交替について調査を行った。その結果，まず第一に，19世紀に認められた書き言葉における現在完了形のより高い頻度は，過去形と現在完了形が今日のように使い分けられるようになったとされる1600年代当初から確認できた。前回の調査で立てた現在完了形の発達は書き言葉から始まったとする推論が強く裏づけられたことになる。第二にわかったことは，今回，*ever* もしくは *always* を含む文と節を調査対象としたが，随伴する副詞によって現在完了形への移行度が大きく異なることである。これは両者の意味の違いによる差であるとの説明はつけがたく，頻度の違いに着目した。つまり，*always* よりも頻度が数倍高い *ever* を含む文または節では，頻度の高さから従来の形式，すなわち過去形を保持する傾向があったのではないかと見た。第三には，1600年代の *Did you ever…？* を1800年代のそれと比較するとイディオム化（修辞疑問文）において統計的な有意差はなかった。しかし，この構文では1600年代から主節動詞が *see* や *hear* である例文が多く，そういったケースが後にイディオム化して修辞疑問文として用いられるようになったと思われる。

注

1. Biber and Finegan (1992) の p. 696 にある figure 2 では Essays (17c) の平均値が誤ってプロットされており，p. 692 の figure の平均値が正しいものと思われる。
2. *always* を選択したのは次のふたりの研究者のコメントによる。
   Poutsma (1926: 262)：

   > Also *always*, *ever* and *never* may denote a length of time beginning at some indefinite moment in the past and extending to the moment of speaking. The normal tense to be used in connexion with these adverbs, when employed in this application, would, accordingly, be the perfect. There is, however, a distinct tendency to use the preterite instead, which it is difficult to account for.

   Elsness (1997: 24)：

Adverbs of the set *never*, *ever*, *always* also combine freely with either the present perfect or the preterite. It is noteworthy that in such combinations the preterite as well as the present perfect may express reference to time-up-to-zero.

3 　出典は書き言葉（W）・話し言葉（S）の区別，著者名，出版年の順に記す。
4 　例えコンピューターコーパスを使った研究であっても，フィロロジーのようにテキストを深く読むという作業が必要な場合があり，今回の調査ではその作業が欠かせない要素となっていると考える。
5 　lexical diffusion の統語への応用に関しては Ogura (1993) および Tottie (1991) を参照。
6 　これは大津 (2007) を執筆した時点では気付かなかったことだが，改めて確認すると表 3 の 1800 年代小説（会話部分）の修辞疑問文 14 例のうち 13 例までが *see* または *hear* を含む。
7 　因みに *Have you ever ... ?* 4 例のうちそれに続く動詞は *discovered, been, seen, received* の 4 つである。
8 　これは推論ではあるが，*Have you ever ... ?* の発達は *Did you ever ... ?* のイディオム化と関連していると考えることができる。つまり，表 3 で見たように，（統計学的な有意差はないものの）1800 年代の方が *Did you ever ... ?* のイディオム化が進んでおり，現在とのつながりを表すための構文の必要性が高かったため *Have you ever ... ?* が広がる余地があったが，1600 年代ではそれほど *Did you ever ... ?* のイディオム化が進んでいなかったため *Have you ever ... ?* が用いられる機会も少なかったとも見ることができるのである。但し，*Did you ever ... ?* のイディオム化が先か，*Have you ever ... ?* の浸透が先かは難しい問題である。

参考文献

Benveniste, E. (1971) *Problems in General Linguistics*. Translated by M. E. Meek. Coral Gables, Florida: University of Miami Press.

Biber, D. and E. Finegan (1992) "The Linguistic Evolution of Five Written and Speech-Based English Genres from the 17th to the 20th Centuries." in Rissanen, M., O. Ihalainen, T. Nevalainen, and I. Taavitsainen (eds.), *History of Englishes, New Methods and Interpretations in Historical Linguistics*. Berlin: Mouton de Gruyter, pp. 688-704.

Bybee, J (2005) "From Usage to Grammar: The Mind's Response to Repetion." Paper downloaded from http://www.unm.edu/~jbybee/Bybee%20plenary.pdf.

Bybee, Joan, and Sandra A. Thompson (1997) "Three Frequency Effects in Syntax." Berkeley Linguistics Society 23, pp. 378-88.

Chambers, J.K. (2002) "*Patterns of Variation Including Change.*" in J.K. Chambers, Peter Trudgill, & Natalie Schilling-Estes (eds), *The Handbook of Language Variation and Change* . Oxford, England: Blackwell, pp 358-361.

Denison, D. (2003) "Log(ist)ic and Simplistic S-curves" in Hickey R. (ed.), *Motives for Language Change*. Cambridge: Cambridge University Press, pp. 54-70.

Elsness, J. (1997) *The Perfect and the Preterite in Contemporary and Earlier English*. Berlin: Mouton de Gruyter.

Jespersen (1909-49) *A Modern English Grammar on Historical Principles*, Part IV. London: George Allen & Unwin Ltd..

Ogura, M. (1993) "The Development of Periphrastic *do* in English: a Case of Lexical Diffusion in Syntax." *Diachronica* X, pp. 51-85.

Otsu, N. (2007) "On the Alternation between Preterite and Present Perfect in Nineteenth-Century English Literature, with Special Reference to a Sentence or a Clause Containing *ever.*" *English Corpus Studies*, No. 14, pp. 1-16.

Tottie, G. (1991) "Lexical Diffusion in Syntactic Change: Frequency as a Determinant of Linguistic Conservatism in the Development of Negation in English." in Kastovsky, D. (ed.), *Historical English Syntax,* Berlin: Mouton de Gruyter, pp. 439-67.

Traugott, E. C. (1972) *A History of English Syntax: A Transformational Approach to the History of English Sentence Structure*. New York: Holt, Rinehart & Winston.

Visser, F. Th. (1966) *An Historical Syntax of the English Language*, Vol. II. Leiden: E. J. Brill.

Appendix

散文作品（初版年順）

Bacon, F. *The Advancement of Learning* 1605

Burton, R. *The Anatomy of Melancholy* 1621

Bacon, F. *The New Atlantis* 1627

Browne, T. *Religio Medici, Hydriotaphia, and the Letter to a Friend* 1643, 1680, 1690

Hobbes, T. *Leviathan* 1651

Walton, I. *The Complete Angler* 1653

Locke, J. *An Essay Concerning Humane Understanding, Volumes I & II* 1660-1662

Boyle, R. *Experiments and Considerations Touching Colours* 1664

Digly, K. *The Closet of Sir Kenelm Digby Knight Opened* 1669

演劇作品（初版年順）

Marston, J. *The Dutch Courtezan* 1605

Anonymous *Everie Woman in her Humor* 1609

Chapman, G. *May-Day* 1611

Jonson, B. *Every Man In His Humor* 1616

Anonymous *Two Wise Men & All the Rest Fooles* 1619

Shakespeare, W. *The Merry Wiues of Windsor* 1623

Anonymous *Wine, Beere, and Ale* 1629

Mabbe, J. *The Spanish Bawd* 1631

Brome, R. *The Northern Lasse* 1632

Rowley, W.M.T. *A Match at Mid-Night* 1633

Anonymous *The King and Queenes Entertainment at Richmond* 1636

Heywood, T. *The Wise-Woman of Hogsdon* 1638

Killigrew, H. *The Conspiracy* 1638

Carlell. L. *Arviragvs and Philicia* 1639

Chamberlain, R. *The Swaggering Damsel* 1640

Jonson B. *Bartholmew Fayre* 1640

Quarles, F. *The Virgin Widow* 1649

Cowley, A. *The Guardian* 1650

Tatham, J. *The Rump* 1660

Flecknoe, R. *The Damoiselles a la Mode* 1667

Cavendish, M. *The Convent of Pleasure* 1668

Caryll, J. *Sir Salomon* 1671

Lacy, J. *The Dumb Lady* 1672

Dryden, J. *Marriage A-la-Mode* 1673

Crowne, J. *The Countrey Wit* 1675

Wycherley, W. *The Country Wife* 1675

Etherege, G. *The Man of Mode* 1676

Betterton, T. *The Counterfeit Bridegroom* 1677

Leanerd, J. *The Country Innocence* 1677

Howard, E. *The Man of Newmarket* 1678

Ravenscroft, E. *The London Cuckolds* 1681

Behn, A. *The False Count* 1682

Otway, T. *The Atheist* 1684

Boyle, R. *Mr Anthony* 1690

D'Urfey, T. *Love for Money* 1691

Mountfort, W. *Greenwich-Park* 1691

Congreve, W. *The Old Batchelour* 1693

Dilke, T. *The Lover's Luck* 1696

Vanbrugh, J. *The Relapse* 1697

Farquhar, G. *Love and a Bottle* 1699

キャクストン訳『イソップ』における軽動詞表現
― 中仏語による原典との比較 ―

尾崎 久男

1 序論

　イギリス最初の活版印刷家であり翻訳家でもあったウィリアム・キャクストン (William Caxton; 1422?-1491) は当時のヨーロッパで流行していた数々の作品を自ら英訳して出版した。彼の活字印刷本は英語の標準化に多大な影響を及ぼしたが，筆者は軽動詞表現 (*don, yeven, haven, maken, taken* ＋動作名詞) の通時的考察という観点から，数年来，彼の翻訳作品における当該表現のデータ構築を目標としてきた。また，同時に彼の翻訳技法にも注目すべく，『きつね物語』(*The History of Reynard the Fox*) の場合は中蘭語版 (*Van den Vos Reynaerde*)，『パリスとヴィエンナ』(*Paris and Vienne*) の場合は中仏語版 (*Paris et Vienne*) というように，原典とキャクストンによる翻訳を比較検討して翻訳借用 (loan translation) の可能性も探索してきた。そこで，次なる対象作品として，本論では『イソップ』(*Aesop*) を選択する。なお，夥しい数の使用例のうち，今回は提示するものを *yeven, maken, taken* ＋動作名詞に限定した。本論に入る前に，B. Perry (1965; ix-xix) 等に従って『イソップ』からキャクストン訳に至るまでの過程を概観してみたい (なお，『イソップ』の伝承と変容については，随時，小堀桂一郎 (2001) を参照したが，文庫本ながらも詳細に記述されている)。

　アイソーポス (Αισωπος) は紀元前 6 世紀頃に活躍したギリシア人だが，現代日本では習慣的にイソップという名前で慣れ親しまれている。古くは，

1593年に宣教師たちによって天草で邦訳されたキリシタン版ローマ字綴り口語体による活字本『イソポのハブラス』、また1639年および1659年の漢字平仮名交り文語体による『伊曾保物語』が刊行された頃にはイソポあるいはイソホ等と呼ばれていた。イソップの名前は古代西欧の文献においてもしばしば引用されているが (例えば、アリストパネース ($Αριστοφανης$)) の『鳥』($Ορνιθες$) や『蜂』($Σφηκες$) 等)、彼が物語ったと伝えられる寓話は紀元前3世紀頃に散文で編集されて以来、次々に増補されて現在の形を取ることになる。したがって、『イソップ』は、これまで誰もが耳目に触れた経験を持つ『アンデルセン』や『グリム』とはまったく性格を異にするものである。ディオゲネース・ラーエルティオス ($Διογενης\ Λαερτιος$) は『ギリシア哲学者列伝』(Vitae philosophorum) という著作の中で、『文体論』($Περι\ ερμηνειας$) で有名なデーメートリオス ($Δημητριος\ Φαληρευς$; 前350?-280) が『イソップ』を撰したと記述しているが、残念ながらこれは現存していない。しかしながら、「デーメートリオス集」を基にして紀元後1世紀にはバブリウス・ヴァレリウス (Babrius Valerius) が希語韻文に、パエドルス・ガイウス (Phaedrus Gaius) が羅語韻文に移し、さらに4世紀になるとアヴィアーヌス (Avianus) がバブリウスの希語韻文を羅語の詩形に翻案した。17世紀のフランス詩人ラ・フォンテーヌ (Jean de la Fontaine) も1668年に出版された『寓話』(Fables) の序文で、以下のように述べている：

> La Fontaine, *Fables*
>
> Socrate n'est pas le seul qui ait considéré comme sœurs la poésie et nos fables. **Phèdre a témoigné qu'il était de sentiment; et par l'excellence de son ouvrage, nous pouvons juger de celui du prince des philosophes. Après Phèdre, Avienus a traité le même sujet.** Enfin les Modernes les ont suivis: nous en avons des exemples, non seulement chez les étrangers, mais chez nous. （強調は筆者による）

9～10世紀の間に成立した「ロムルス集」(*Romulus*) は中世で最も流行した『イソップ』だが、これは「パエドルス集」を羅語によって散文化したものである。他方、ルネサンスも盛りの14世紀、ビザンチンのコンスタ

ンチノープルにマクシムス・プラヌーデス (Maximus Planudes) という修道士がいた。彼が「バブリウス集」を希語散文に訳したと伝えられているが，残念ながら実際に「マクシムス・プラヌーデス集」が現存している訳ではない。また，『イソップ』には『イソップの生涯』(Vita Esopi) というイソップ伝の一種が併載されることが多いが，これはマクシムス・プラヌーデスの構想に基づいている。実際に彼が『イソップの生涯』を書いたという証拠はないが，次に見られる通り，近世ではしばしば誤解されていたようである：

『イソポのハブラス』
イソポが生涯の物語略。
これをマシモ・プラヌーデといふ人ゲレゴの言葉よりラチンに翻訳せられしものなり。（強調は筆者による）

1474年に「マクシムス・プラヌーデス集」はイタリア人レヌティウス (Renutius) によって羅語散文に翻訳され，同じくイタリア人アントニウス・ザラトゥスによって印刷され「レヌティウス集」(これは別名「レミキウス集」(*Remicius*) とも呼ばれる) として世に上梓された (『イソップの生涯』を含む)。それから数年後 (1477-78年)，ドイツのウルム (Ulm) で『イソップ』が出版されたが，翻訳者はその名をハインリヒ・シュタインヘーヴェル (Heinrich Steinhöwel; 1412-82) といい，出版者はヨーハン・ツァイナー (Johan Zainer) といった。「シュタインヘーヴェル集」は「デーメートリオス集」以来の集大成だが，これには羅語のテキストに独語訳が添えられていた。「シュタインヘーヴェル集」を基にして，後述のジュリアン・マショ (Julien Macho) による仏語訳 (1480)，トゥッポによる伊語訳 (1485)，エンリケ公子による西語訳 (1496)，さらに『阿呆船』(*Das Narrenschiff*) で有名なセバスティアン・ブラント (Sebastian Brant; 1457?-1521) による独語版が続いた。

O. Walshe (1962: 345-47) によれば，シュタインヘーヴェルはドイツ南部，バイエルン州南西部のシュヴァーベン地方出身の医者であった。彼はウィーンやハイデルベルクで学び，イタリアのパドヴァで医学の学位を取得した。

彼はまた文人としても優れていて,『ティルスのアポロニウス』(*Apollonius of Tyre*) の翻訳を手始めに,特に伊文学に精通していたため,ボッカッチョ (Giovanni Boccaccio; 1313-1375) の『デカメロン』(*Decameron*) や『グリセルディス』(*Griseldis*) 等の独語訳を残した。しかしながら,彼の名声が最高潮に達するのは,やはりボッカッチョの『名婦伝』(*De claris mulieribus*),そして『イソップ』の翻訳である。「シュタインヘーヴェル集」は瞬く間に西欧社会に広まってゆき,フランスではリヨン (Lyon) にあるアウグスティノ会の修道士ジュリアン・マショが,その序文にもある通り,羅語を仏語に翻訳した (Et esté a translaté de latin en françoys par reverend docteur en theologie frere des Augustins de Lyon)。神学博士でもあった彼は『聖書』に関する著作や「聖人伝」等をいくつか残しているが,『イソップ』の翻訳を手掛けたのは少々奇異に感じられる:*Les livres de l'Ancien Testament, histoirés en françois*; *L'exposicion et la vraye declaracion de la Bible tant du Viel que du Novel Testament*; *Le Nouveau Testament*; *La légende des saints nouveaux*; *L'Ésope* (仏語版と言えば,マリ・ド・フランス (Marie de France) による韻文訳も有名だが,彼女の作品は「シュタインヘーヴェル集」を基にしていない。ちなみに,彼女が『寓話』(*Fables*) の跋文で「私はフランス出身のマリ」(***Marie** ai num, si sui **de France***) と自称しているため,今日ではマリ・ド・フランスと呼ばれている)。マショが「シュタインヘーヴェル集」の羅語を翻訳した仏語版からキャクストンによる英語訳 (1484),そして蘭語訳 (1490) が生まれた。

マショ訳は 1480 年に初版が刊行されて以来,数回にわたって版を重ねたが,代表的な写本として以下のものが現存する (P. Ruelle 1982: XIV-XVI):A. Lyon, Nicolas Philippe et Marc Reinhard, 26 août 1480 (Tours, Bibliothèque municipale, IV, AF, 3266 (Rés 7598), B. Lyon, Mathieu Hucz (= Husz) et Jean Schabeller, 15 mai 1484 (Paris, Bibl. nat., Rés Yb. 98), C. Lyon, Jean Numeister et Mathieu Husz, vers 1485 (Milan, Biblioteca Nazionale Braidense, AO, XVI. 36), D. Lyon, Mathieu Husz, 9 avril 1486 (= 1487 nouveau style) (Vienne, Bibl. nat. 10-G-1), E. Lyon, Michel Topié et Jacques Heremberck, vers 1489 [1480?] (Londres, Brit. Mus., G 7806), F. Lyon, Pierre Mareschal et Barnabé Chaussard, vers 1498 [1499?] (Londres, Brit. Mus., IB. 41979), G. Lyon, Pierre Mareschal et Barnabé Chaussard, 8 novembre 1499 (Paris, Bibl. nat., Rés. Yb. 430)。

R. Lenaghan (1967: 237) によれば，キャクストンは主に上記Aの初版を使用したが，それ以降の版も随時参照したということである。キャクストンによる英語訳『イソップ』も「シュタインヘーヴェル集」の流れを汲むマショ訳の忠実な翻訳であるため，同様に以下の7部から構成されている (Lenaghan 1967: 5-8)：*Life of Aesop*（『イソップの生涯』），Romulus Collection（「ロムルス集」），Fifth Book（「選外寓話集」），Ribuccio's Fables（「レミキウス集」(抄)），Fables of Avianus（「アヴィアーヌス集」(抄)），*Disciplina Clericalis* of Petrus Alphonsus（「アルフォンスス集」(抄)），*Facetiae* of Poggio Bracciolini（「ポッジョ笑話集」(抄))。ただし，「ポッジョ笑話集」については，第7話の途中から原典の仏語とキャクストンによる英語訳が一致しない。

2　キャクストン訳『イソップ』における *yeven, maken, taken* ＋動作名詞

キャクストン訳『イソップ』における *yeven, maken, taken* の頻度数は以下の通りである：*Yeven* (145: *gaf(e), gaue(st), geuen, gyue(n), gyuest, gyueth, gyuyng(e), yeue(n)*)，*Maken* (309: *maad(e), made(st), make(n), maked, makest, maketh, makyng(e)*)，*Taken* (293: *take(n), takest, taketh, tok(e), tokest, took(e), takyng(e)*)。これらのうち，*maken* の使役用法などを除外してゆき，今回の調査対象である軽動詞用法に限定すると，それぞれ以下の通りである：***Yeven* 53 例，*Maken* 155 例，*Taken* 52 例**。頻度から言えば，*maken* が最も頻繁に動作名詞を伴うことになり，*yeven, taken* と続く。

以下にそれぞれの動詞＋動作名詞の例をアルファベット順に列挙するが，＊は中英語と中仏語において同様あるいは類似の表現が使われていることを示す (なお，中英語の引用例の左側にある <000/00> という数字は Lenaghan による校訂本のページと行を示す)。

2.1 *Yeven* ＋動作名詞

Yeven と共に用いられる動作名詞は，以下の通りである：*ayde, ansuere, audyence, counceylle, credence, doctryne, ensample, enseygnement, force, glorye, grace, help, helthe, Ioye, Iugement, lernynge, leue, mercye, remedy, sentence, socour, solas, solucion, stroke, worde, worship, yefte* (以上 27 種類).

> **Yeven ansuere* (古英語 giefan/sellan andsware を参照)**: <054/21> wherfore he demaunded of the peple tyme & space for to **gyue** herupon an **ansuere** / (484 Et Xantus ceste chose ignoroyt et, pour ce, leur demanda temps pour leur **donner responce**,)

> **Yeven credence***: <060/32> THe kynge Lycurius byleuynge and **gyuyng credence** to the accusacion maade ageynste Esope was gretely wrothe / (567 Le roy Licurius, **adjoustant foy** a l'accusation contre Esope,)

> **Yeven ensample***: <114/08> Thus this fable sheweth to vs / that the fader ought to teche and **gyue** good **ensample** to his children (1204 le pere doit **donner** doctrine et bon **exemple** a son enfant)

> **Yeven enseygnement**: <055/25> wherfor yf ye wil / that I **gyue** yow good **enseygnment** of that that ye demaunde & aske I requyre you that ye do make me free (502 Et, pour ce, se vous voulés que je vous **enseigne** ce que demandés,)

> **Yeven remedy**: <179/30> I am a maystresse in medecyn / and canne **gyue remedy** to al manere of sekenes (2125 Je suis la maistresse de medicine et sçay **guerir** de toutes maladies)

> **Yeven solucion***: <039/01> but I haue a seruaunt here whiche shal enforme & **gyue** the **solucion** of thy question (197 mais j'ay ung serviteur qui te saura informer et **donner solucion** de ta question)

> **Yeven stroke**: <137/29> the Mule **gaf** hym suche a **stroke** with his foote before his forhede / that almost the brayne ranne oute of his hede / (1478 le mullet luy **bailla** si grant **cop** du pié ou front que il luy rompit toute la cervelle.)

Yeven yefte*: <029/07> And also she **gaf** to hym the **yefte** of speche for to speke dyuerse fables and Inuencions / (30 Et la deesse de Hospitalité a luy s'apparut et lui **donna** sapience et habilité et le **don** de langue)

2.2 *Maken* ＋動作名詞

Maken と共に用いられる動作名詞は，以下の通りである：*accusacion, answere, auauntynge, auowe, bargayne, bataill, berd, boost, byrthe, chere, commaundement, couenaunce (couenaunt), crye, debate, distinction, dylygence, effors, ende, enquest, enterpryse, estymacion, extyme, fart, feest, gladness, Ioye, Iustyce, lesynge, maryage, menace, mencyon, noyse, obeyssaunce, oblygacion, ordenaunce, orysons, oultrages, paction, pees, playnte, plee, prayer, proclamacion, promesse, prouysyon, pylgremage, question, request, rumour, signe, solucion, sorowe, sowne, stryf, testament, theftys, token, trayson, vyage, watche, way, weddynge, werre, wounde* (以上 64 種類)．

> **Maken answere***: <038/15> a child of the kechyn shold haue**made** as good an **answere** / (194 car ung enfant de cuisine eust bien **fait** telle **responce** >>.)
>
> **Maken byrthe**: <221/04> And whanne the Cowe sawe that she hadde **maade** suche a **byrthe** / (2682 Et, quant la vache vit qu'elle avoit **vellé** si terrible beste,)
>
> **Maken commaundement***: <224/13> yet they haue **made commaundement** that none be so hardy to vexe ne lette in no wyse ony other / (2730 si ont **fait commandement** qu'i ne soyt nulz si hardy qui doyve nuyre a aultruy,)
>
> **Maken crye/proclamacion**: <056/06> And anon he that **made** there the **cryes** and **proclamacions** wente in to al the places where suche cryes were done / (509 Et, adonques, le crieur va **crier** :)
>
> **Maken distinction***: <094/06> For yf thow **makest distinction** of the tyme thow shalt wel accord the scryptures / (980 car, si tu **fais distinction** du temps, tu accorderas les Escriptures.)

Maken ende: <205/04> And anon after the kynge awoke the fabulatour / and sayd to hym in this manere I pray the that thow wylt **make an ende** of thy fable / (2479 le roy l'esveilla et luy dist : << Je te prie que tu me **fines** ta fable. >>) **Maken lesynge**: <065/33> the kynge thenne seyd to hym / Esope I had neuer byleuyd that thow sholdest haue **maade** soo grete a **lesynge** before me / (638 Esope, je n'eusse jamais cuidé que tu m'eusses ainsi **menti**,)

Maken maryage*: <217/19> Renommee / and that he was Indygent or fawtyf of that thynge / wherfore **maryage** is **made** / (2631 et qu'il estoit indigent de celle chose pour quoy l'on **fait** le **mariage**.)

Maken menace*: <099/21> SOmme **maken** grete **menaces** / whiche haue no myghte / (1035 Aulcuns **font** grans **menasses** qui ont grant paour.)

Maken mencyon*: <029/01> This History **maketh mencyon** how the goddesse of hospitalite gaf speche of his tonge to esope / (28 La seconde histoire **fait mencion** comment la deesse de Hospitalité donna le don de langue a Esope)

Maken obeyssaunce*: <090/20> And after they approched to theyr kynge for to **make obeyssaunce** vnto hym / (935 Et puis aprés se approucherent de leur roy pour luy **faire obeissance**.)

Maken question*: <066/25> of Babyloyne / And one of them sayd to the kynge / Syre we must yet **make** to hym another **question** / (650 Et l'ung des nobles dist au roy : << Sire, il fault **faire** une aultre **question**,)

Maken request*: <090/15> they alle to gyder of one assente & of one wylle **maade** a **request** to Iupiter that he wold gyue them a kynge / (933 et toutes d'ung accord et union, **firent requeste** a Jupiter que il leur donnast ung roy.)

Maken solucion*: <038/14> what **solucion** hast thow **made** / what is that cometh of dyuyne prouydence / (194 Quelle **solucion** as tu **faicte** que cecy vient de la divine Providence ?)

Maken trayson*: <092/04> Ne that by ony yeftes none **maketh** some

trayson ageynst his mayster or lord (953 ne par dons ne **face traison** a son seigneur et maistre.)

2.3 Taken ＋動作名詞

Taken と共に用いられる動作名詞は，以下の通りである：*aduys, afflyction, consolacion, courage, debate, disporte, doctryne, enherytaunce, ensample, gladnesse, glorye, hede, Ioye, labour, leue, melancolye, payne, playsyr, recreacion, reioysshynge, solas, sorowe, stryfe, thought, vengeaunce, way*（以上 26 種類）．

> **Taken consolacion/disporte***: <219/14> And for to haue **take** somme **disporte** and **consolacion** he prayd to hym ... (2659 et, pour **avoir** aulcuns **soulas** et **consolacion**, il pria a celuy ...)
>
> **Taken debate/stryfe***: <156/18> HE is not wyse / whiche for to haue vanyte and his plesyr **taketh debate** or **stryf** / (1780 Celluy n'est pas saige qui pour avoyr vanité et son plaisir **prent noise** et **debat**,)
>
> **Taken ensample***: <131/11> And therfore he is wel happy that **taketh ensample** by the dommage of other / (1413 Et, pour ce, cellui est bien eureux qui **prent exemple** au dommaige d'aultruy,)
>
> **Taken hede (古英語 niman ware を参照)**: <050/06> Madame yf it please yow / ye shal **take hede** to this mete that the dogges or cattes ete it not / (430 << Ma dame, se il vous plaist, **gardés** les viandes que je metz icy, que les chiens ne les mengent,)
>
> **Taken labour/payne***: <215/10> For he hath **taken** to moche **payne** and **labour** for to haue it made vp myn owne werke / (2597 car je ne luy sçay ne gré ne grace de ce qu'il a **prins** tant de **paine** de faire mes besoignes et ne vueil plus qu'il s'en mesle,)
>
> **Taken leue* (古英語 niman leafe を参照)**: <147/37> And whanne he had sayd these wordes / he departed fro the lyon and **toke** his **leue** / (1636 Et, quant il eut dit ces parolles, il **print congié** du lyon et s'en alla,)

Taken recreacion*: <201/36> And on a day at euen when he was wery and had trauaylled sore / for to **take** his **recreacion** (2435 Et, ung jour au vespre, ainsi qu'il estoyt lassé et travaillé de labourer, pour **avoyr recreacion**,) **Taken vengeaunce***: <125/13> I am not come hyther to **take vengeaunce** on them whiche haue had pyte and myserycorde of me / (1350 Je ne suys pas venue pour **avoyr vengence** de ceulx qui ont eu pitié et misericorde de moy)

3 結論

　これまでの調査結果を踏まえた上で，今回キャクストン訳『イソップ』において yeven, maken, taken という軽動詞が動作名詞を従える表現を中仏語による原典と比較調査してみると，以下の諸事実が明らかになった：
1. 紙面の都合で例文は大幅にカットしたが，『きつね物語』/『パリスとヴィエンナ』でも『イソップ』でも用いられている軽動詞表現が数多く見られた。換言すれば，それらの表現がすでにキャクストンの英語の中で確立した語法になっていたということになろう。
2. 仏語との対応を見ると，原典においてはまったく別の表現や単純動詞が使用されているにもかかわらず，キャクストンの英語において軽動詞表現を使って翻訳されている箇所がしばしばあった。例えば，*maken byrthe : veller, maken crye : crier, maken ende : finir* 等である。
3. 軽動詞・動作名詞ともに英仏で同様の対応が見られる場合 (例えば，*yeven solucion : donner solucion, maken mencyon : faire mension, taken ensample : prendre exemple* 等)，それらの言回しが仏語に起源を持つ翻訳借用である可能性が高くなろう。
4. 動作名詞が仏語起源であっても，共起する動詞は必ずしも英仏で一致 (*yeven = donner, maken = faire, taken = prendre*) しないため，動詞の選択に関しては英語の嗜好によると考えられよう (例えば，*maken promesse : avoir promys, maken prouysyon : avoir provision, taken recreacion : avoir recreacion* 等)。

　翻訳借用という言語現象を研究するには，自ずと膨大なデータの比較分析

が不可欠になってくる。今後もキャクストンの言語データ収集の充実を図るべく，原典と翻訳のパラレル・テキストを用いて諸作品を調査してゆきたい。

注

本稿は平成 19 年度文部科学省科学研究費補助金 (基盤研究 (C)) による研究の一部をなすものである

参考文献

A. 一次資料

Duff, J. & A. Duff., ed (1982) *Minor Latin Poets*. Vol. 2. *Loeb Classical Library* 434. Cambridge, MA: Harvard UP.

Lenaghan, R., ed (1967) *Caxton's Aesop*. Cambridge, MA: Harvard UP.

Perry, B., ed (1965) *Babrius and Phaedrus. Loeb Classical Library* 436. Cambridge, MA: Harvard UP.

Ruelle, P., ed (1982) *Recueil général des Isopets*. Vol. 3: *L'Esope de Julien Macho*. Paris: Société des anciens textes français.

新村出・柊源一 校注 (1993) 『吉利支丹文学集２』 東洋文庫 570. 東京: 平凡社.

B. 二次資料

Blake, N (1969) *Caxton and His World*. London: Andre Deutsch.

Orr, J (1962) *Old French and Modern English Idiom*. Oxford: Blackwell.

Prins, A (1952) *French Influence in English Phrase*. Leiden: Universitaire Pers.

Walshe, O (1962) *Medieval German Literature: A Survey*. London: Routledge.

小堀桂一郎 (2001) 『イソップ寓話：その伝承と変容』 講談社学術文庫 1495. 東京: 講談社.

中世文学とテクスト校訂
― 『梟とナイティンゲール』二つのテクスト校訂 ―

菊 池 清 明

序

　1838年の J. Stevenson による校訂本以来，Neil Cartlidge によって 2001 年に出版されたものに至るまで，『梟とナイティンゲール』 The Owl and the Nightingale については，刊本で 11 種類，さらにファクシミリ，翻訳，コンコーダンスなどを含めれば優に三十以上をこえる研究書が何年か置きに出版され続けている。十三世紀後半に書かれたとされる所謂問答詩の一つに過ぎない本作品がこれほど間断なく研究の対象とされ続けている背景をわれわれは知る必要がある。その理由はいくつかある。一つには，この時代に英語で書かれた宗教的または訓戒的な文学作品以外で現存する文献としては，ブリテン王の先祖となったブルート王の伝説をはじめ，アーサー王やウェールズ地方の伝説を集めたラヤモンの『ブルート』 Brut を除けば，本作品が唯一のものであるということ。また本作品が古英語から中英語の転換期における韻文の言語研究に関する数少ない資料のうちでも最も重要なものであるという点があげられる。
　韻律法について言えば，本作品で使用されたラテン詩の四音歩格から発達した八音節の対句詩形は，クレティエン・デ・トロワが宮廷風物語で用いた詩形であり，後にチョーサーが，『公爵夫人の書』 The Book of the Duchess や『名声の館』 The House of Fame を書いた時や『薔薇物語』を英訳するときに用いたものである。『梟とナイティンゲール』の詩人が見事に駆使

したこの詩形を目にすれば，この詩形がいきなり十四世紀にチョーサーによって洗練，完成されて突如英文学に出現したのではないことがわかる。年代記と宮廷風物語にこの詩形が用いられていたフランスでの文学事情を踏まえた上で，『梟とナイティンゲール』の詩人が，チョーサーよりもおおよそ100年以上も前にこの詩形を英語に取り入れ成功したのである。つまり，チョーサーと比べても，この詩人が逸早くフランス風の脚韻形式を取り入れイギリスにおける韻律法の確立に資するところ少なくなかったことを理解するのである。

　英文学史上における本作品の価値は重要である。本作品は，1066年のノルマン征服から1200年ごろに至る時代の英文学とフランス文学，そしてアングロ・ノルマンと称するフランス語の一地方方言で書かれたアングロ・ノルマン文学の様々な諸相を包摂しており，イギリス文学史上はじめて古英語の束縛を脱し，中世的さらには近代的な特質さえも示している。こうした事柄や本作品の言語表現や文体がそれ以降の英文学に及ぼした影響の大きさを考慮すれば，この作品の刊本や関係書が出版され続けられている理由も容易に理解できよう。因みに，W.P.Kerが名著 *Medieval English Literature* でこの作品を "a kind of good-humoured ironical satire which is very like Chaucer's own. This is the most *modern* in tone of all the thirteenth-century poems", あるいは "the most miraculous piece of writing"[1]といった言葉で評価したことも十分頷ける。いわば古英語と中英語の両者にまたがり，しかも両者の言語の特質を示しながら，同時に時代を超えた特質をもつ本作品は，中世はもとより，広く英語・英文学を研究する者にとってこの上なく重要な一書である。本作品は，今後も韻律，写本間の異文比較，さらには最新の批評理論さえも取り込んだ様々な視点からの検証作業を必要とし，そして編者の言語観・文学観が新たに盛り込まれた作品解題とともに刊本にされ，われわれに絶えず提供される運命にあるといってよい。

　本論では，先ず校訂の歴史や校訂本と人との関わりを概観した後，Neil CartlidgeとE.G.Stanleyの校訂本をその校訂方法に注目しながら比較検討し，新しい校訂の仕方を検証し，見解を述べてみたい。

I

　これまでの中世英語英文学研究の発展と隆盛には,『オックスフォード英語辞典』 The Oxford English Dictionary(OED) は必須の辞典であったし, 1864 年に創設された初期英語文献協会 Early English Text Society(EETS) は不可欠な組織であった。これらのどちらかが欠けても中世研究は到底成り立たなかった。また中世文学への評価というものがある時期を境にして大きく変わったのも, EETS の存在と 1884 年の第 1 分冊の出版から 1928 年の最終冊まで 44 年かけて完成した OED の編纂によるといってよい。OED 編纂にあたって用例探索に欠かせない古英語・中英語の引用に値するテクストの提供を目的として, Frederic James Furnivall が中心になり, Richard Morris や Walter W. Skeat といった現代の英語英文学研究の礎を築いたフィロロジストらの助力を得て設立されたこの協会は, 中世文学作品を校訂し, 今日までその校訂本を出版し続けることになる。主だった中世テクストが優れた編者の監修のもと古英語・中英語の重要な写本を正確に活字化し, 詳細な注解と作品解題を付して刊行されたのである。とりわけ, 1864 年, 当協会の第 1 集, 第一巻として, Richard Morris の校訂により,『真珠』 Pearl,『純潔』 Cleanness,『忍耐』 Patience の 3 篇を収めた Early English Alliterative Poems(O.S.1), また同年その第 4 巻として,『ガウェイン卿と緑の騎士』 Sir Gawayne and the Green Knight (O.S.4) が刊行されたことは,『ガウェイン卿と緑の騎士』の名付け親であった Sir Frederic Madden といった限られた人たちを除けばこれらの作品が当時その存在さえも全く知られていなかったことと, とくに後者の作品が中世ロマンスの傑作と後に評価されるようになったことを併せて考えれば, その意義は限りなく深い。

　さらに Skeat 校訂による『農夫ピアズの夢』 Piers Plowman (O.S. 17, 28, 38, 54, 67, 81), Henry Sweet の『牧人の心得』 Pastoral Care (O.S.45, 50) といった初期に刊行された中世刊本テクストは, 当時のフィロロジィストたちに大きな関心を呼び起こし, 彼らの英語・英文学史研究の質を高めるのに大いに貢献した。1864 年から 2001 年までの Original Series で 317 巻,

1867年から1935年までのExtra Seriesで126巻，そして1970年から1990年までのSupplementary Seriesによる12巻を含めると，総数455巻を本協会は世に送っている。中世英語英文学研究のみならず中世に関する研究全般において研究者がこれらの校訂テクストにいかに恩恵を蒙っているかは，これまで出版されてきた中世研究書の末尾に付された参考文献に基本資料として列記されているこれら校訂本の数をみれば即座に得心がいくであろう。

　文学に関して言えば，上述したようにJohn Gower, William Langland, *Gawain*-poetといった中世の詩人たちが一躍脚光を浴び，広く一般の人たちにその存在と価値が認められた時期もOED編纂の始まりとEETSの創設時期とほぼ重なる。アングロ・サクソン時代から15世紀までの作者不詳の叙事詩，説教詩，宗教詩，教訓詩，謎詩，聖者伝，動物寓意詩，ロマンス，問答詩，宗教劇，抒情詩，さらには数十行にみたない小作品に至るまで，こうした作品が現存し，われわれが現在そうした作品を容易に利用できるのもOEDの編纂事業とEETSによる校訂テクストという作業があったからに他ならない。この二つの事業と作業がなければ，これらの作品の多くは第一次世界大戦とその後に続く大戦の戦禍や火災を被り，＜失われた文学＞の墓標に名を刻まれ，われわれにその存在さえ知られることなく消失する運命にあったことは想像に難くない。とりわけ，存命中から今日まで名声を保持し続けているGeoffrey Chaucerにしても，EETS創設に関わった同じメンバーにより1868年に設立されたChaucer Societyなしには，現代におけるその評価の高まりばかりか，今日のChaucer研究の隆盛はなかったといえよう。つまり，中世に書かれたほとんどの作品は，これら二つの協会またはOEDと何らかの関わりを持つことによってその存在と価値が広く認められるようになったのである。そういう意味で，中世の作品は，ほとんど近代以降においてその評価が確定されたといってよい。しかし，現在もなお，中世文学のテクストが校訂され刊行され続けていることと，以前に校訂されたものでも学術的に不満足なものは改訂もしくは修正され再刊されるとなると，先に下された評価が覆されることもありうる。

　また，中世文学のテクスト校訂となれば，校訂者には当然中世テクスト

に関わる広範囲な分野への類まれな能力が求められることになる。中世イギリスにおけるラテン語・フランス語・英語という多言語併用の複雑な言語環境と修辞法への該博な知識は勿論のこと，汎ヨーロッパ性に根ざした複合的な文学伝統への識見，さらには写本筆写からヨーロッパ全体の社会思潮と社会状況にまで通じた卓識，そしてそれらの要素を睥睨しつつ共時的かつ通時的な視点に立ちその時代に即した価値観や文化観を再構築する知性など，包括的な学識が校訂作業の前提となる。中世テクストの校訂には，そうした十全な学殖の上に，根気と忍耐力も求められるが，これまでの校訂者の経歴が示すとおり，校訂本が評価されればこの上なく報われる作業でもある。その反面，あるテクストの校訂本の出版によって，それまでの校訂本が使用されなくなることもあれば，作品そのものの評価が大きく変わることもあろうし，またそのことにより校訂者を取り巻く人間関係が少なからずきしむこともあるであろう。評価された校訂本により研究者としての地位を確固たるものにする人もあれば，当然逆のこともありうるであろう。校訂本を出版することは，研究者にとってある意味で学者生命を賭する危うい作業といえる。

II

そこで校訂本と人との係わり合いを概観してみる。Skeat による校訂本,*The Complete Works of Geoffrey Chaucer*, 6 Vols. with Supplement. (Oxford, 1894-97) は『カンタベリー物語』の決定版として長く受け入れられた。従って，Skeat が 1878 年にケンブリッジで最初の Elrington and Bosworth Professor of Anglo-Saxon に任命されたのも，English Dialect Society の設立や語源辞典の編纂などによる功績もあろうが，やはり『農夫ピアズの夢』の EETS 版 (1867-84) と Parallel Texts(1866-86) や『アングロ・サクソン福音書』*Anglo-Saxon Gospels* (1871-87)，そして後の Chaucer 全集といった一連の校訂作業において彼が披露した言語・文学にたいする上に述べたような博学多識かつ厳密な学風によるところが大であったといえよう。しかし，F.N.Robinson 校訂による *The Poetical Works of Chaucer*(Oxford, 1933)，そ

して1957年にその第2版が出版されるや，Skeat版はこの校訂本に取って代わられ，図書館の片隅で埃をかぶったまま，ほとんど研究者に用いられることはなくなってしまう。Robinson版も，1987年にLarry Dean Bensonを主幹として，テクスト，グロッサリー，註解，参考文献，そして固有名詞索引などが大幅に修正・加筆され再編された，*The Riverside Chaucer,* 3rd ed., based on *The Works of Geoffrey Chaucer*, edited by F.N.Robinson(Boston: Houghton Mifflin Company) が出版されると同じ運命を辿ることになる。

　J.R.R.Tolkienも，彼が中世研究者として広く認められたのは，『ガウェイン卿と緑の騎士』の校訂本を1925年にE.V.Gordonと一緒に出版したことにあった。その校訂本は，1967年にNorman Davisによって改訂が加えられ，現在においても，初版以来，本作品の最良の校訂本として使用され続けている。当代きっての写本研究の第一人者であるオックスフォード大学のRalph Hanna教授は，作品にまつわる独自の諸情報と詳細な注釈・グロッサリーを備えた最初の本格的なcritical editionであるこの改訂版を「理想の校訂本」と絶賛する。勿論，二人には他にも多くの業績はあり，この功によるばかりではないが，Skeatよろしく，Tolkienも，『ガウェイン卿と緑の騎士』の校訂本を上梓した1925年にオックスフォードからRawlinson and Bosworth Professor of Anglo-Saxonの肩書きを得る。そして，彼は1945年には，1885年のその創設をもって，オックスフォード大学英文学部(Faculty of English Langugae and Literarture)の設立とすることもできる由緒ある教授職，Merton Professorship of English Language and Literatureに就任する。弟子であるDavisも，1959年に恩師Tolkienと同じこのProfessorshipを得る。ただ，この改訂本の成功は，Gordon夫人とTolkienの了承を得たDavisの如才ない周囲への顧慮があったことを見逃してはならない。オックスフォード大学のSt. Crossにある英文科図書館のSenior Common Roomの廊下にかかる歴代英文学部教授の写真のコーナーには二人が並び，二階に上がれば，Tolkienの立派な胸像まである。かくも，校訂本の出版とは，かの国においては研究者としての地位を決定する重要な業績である。しかも，その裏には様々な人間模様が織りなされているのである。

III

 1960 年に Eric Gerald Stanley により, Old & Middle English Texts の一書として出版されたものと, 2001 年に Exeter Medieval English Texts and Studies シリーズの一書として Neil Cartlidge により出版された二冊[2]のうち, 特に後者の出版の経緯やその反響, また校訂本を取り巻く社会的環境と両書の校訂方法の違いに注目しながらこれまでとは幾分違った批評をしてみたい。2001 年に出版された Neil Cartlidge による本校訂がこれまでの刊本の中でどのように位置付けされるのかを探るために, 主要な刊本と写本を概説しておく。本作品を研究する場合, 必ず手許に置いておかなければならない刊本は, 少なくとも 4 冊ある。現在においてもその価値を失わないで利用されている, 1922 年の J.W.H.Atkins による現代語訳, 解説と詳細な注解を付したもの, EETS より 1935 年に刊行された H.G.Grattan と G.F.H.Sykes によるもの, また E.G.Stanley によって 1960 年に校訂されたものと, N.R.Ker が 1963 年に EETS からファクシミリ版として出版した 4 冊である。[3]

 現存する写本は二種残っている。これまでの校訂者によって, それぞれC写本, J写本とよばれる, 古写本の収集家であった Sir Robert Bruce Cotton によって寄贈された大英博物館蔵の MS Cotton Caligura A.ix とボードリ図書館に架蔵されているオックスフォード大学, Jesus College 所有の MS29(II) の二つである。これら二つの写本には, 多くの共通した作品, 例えば, ともに Chardi 作とされるフランス語の聖者伝二作とフランス語の韻文問答詩 Petit Plet, それに英語による宗教抒情詩の小作品がみられる。また, C写本にはアングロ・ノルマン語による散文年代記『イギリス王伝』*Li Rei de Engleterre* や歴史叙事詩ラヤモンの『ブルート』, 一方J写本には修道女や隠遁者として生きる女性の励ましのために書かれた托鉢修道士 Thomas of Hales 作の Love-song(Luue-Ron) や英語による 18 編の宗教抒情詩, この世の人生の儚さ虚しさを主題とした瞑想詩 Poema Morale, 外典の一書である「トビトの書」についての Guillaume le Clerc の *Tobie* といった作品が含まれる。こうした事実から, Cartlidge は, 二つの写本は宗教教

団で作成されたが，必ずしもそうした施設でのみ使用されたわけではなく，家族や平信徒の教育や娯楽のための雑録集として編纂された可能性もあると述べている。さらに，彼は，写本に含まれる作品の多様性と特質から，重要な点を指摘する。本作品は，英文学史上創作において不毛，貧困だった時代に書かれた特殊な作品と評価されてきたが，実際には，十二，三世紀は極めて文学活動隆盛の時期であり，また英文学の発達におけるアングロ・ノルマン語とアングロ・ラテン語の役割の重要性を強調している。

　Stanley によって，1960 年に出版された本作品の校訂本は，その長い歳月に何種類かの校訂本が出版されながらも，以来ほぼそのままの形で 40 年にわたって，OED や言語に関する先行研究が豊富に提供する資料への精確な学識と手堅い判断に基づく最良の校訂本としての評価を受け続けてきた。そして，Skeat や Tolkien のように，Stanley もすぐれた校訂本の出版というその功績により 1962 年にはロンドン大学のリーダーそして教授，1977 年にはオックスフォードで Rawlinson and Bosworth Professor of Anglo-Saxon の地位につくのである。ところで，Stanley は，1849 年に創刊された歴史ある学術誌 Notes and Queries の共編者としても長く務め，退職した今も多くの研究誌に精力的に寄稿し続け，アングロ・サクソン研究界の重鎮として現役で活躍している人物である。そして，Cartlidge の恩師の一人でもある。

　一方，Cartlidge の新しい校訂本は，*Medium Ævum* (LXXI.2, pp.328-29)，*Journal of English and Germanic Philology*(April,2004,pp.261-63)，そして *Notes and Queries* (March' 2003,pp.89-90) といった主だった国際研究誌において歓呼の声とともに迎えられた。[4] にもかかわらず，必ずしもよい運にめぐりあえず，すぐれた校訂本を出した者に相応しい処遇を得ていないように思われる。Cartlidge はその 'Acknowledgements' で，恩師に 3 行ほどの感謝を綴って，"…very grateful to him for his extraordinary generosity with his books, notes and time, and his conviviality during my time in Oxford." と述べ，共に酒を酌み交わすその交誼は人も羨むほどの深いものがある。なのに，何故，Cartlidge は，Davis が Gordon 夫人と Tolkien の了承を得て『ガウェイン卿と緑の騎士』の改訂版を出版したように，恩師である Stanley

の許可の下，Stanley の名を残しながらその改訂版としなかったのか。

IV

その理由を考える前に，Stanley 版と Cartlidge 版の校訂本の内容をここであらためて比較してみよう。Stanley 版と比較して，Cartlidge 版での「詩人，製作年代，そして制作場所」に関する見解に格別新しいものは見出せない。むしろ，Stanley が指摘したこれらの点について，Cartlidge は明言する確固たる証拠がないと断言をさけ，様々な可能性を提示するにとどまっている。一見して消極的とも思えるこうした Cartlidge の姿勢は，実は恩師 Stanley を含むこれまでの研究者たちへの批判と不信感の表れであり，Cartlidge の厳正なアカデミズムといってよい。Stevenson による 1838 年の校訂本以来，本校訂に至るまでの 11 種類の刊本の中で，Cartlidge の校訂本における最もすぐれた点は，本作品の解釈・批評に見られるそのアプローチにある。

従来の解釈への Cartlidge の批評は明快であり，説得力がある。封建社会の聖職者階級と貴族階級，聖と俗，哲学と芸術，あるいは伝統的な自国文化とフランス文化，説教法における対立や教訓詩と宮廷風恋愛詩，さらにはヘンリー二世とトマス・ベケット，リチャード一世と異父兄弟のジェフリーといった，特定の機関，階級，文化あるいは歴史上の人物における様々な対照を表象するという解釈については，研究者たちの本作品の制作年代，著者，社会環境についての疑わしい先入観に依存するものであり，特定の箇所に適用した場合には魅力的であるが，全体としてはこの詩の持つ広やかな響きからすれば，この作品が特定の問題のためにのみ構想されたことを証明することはできないと Cartlidge は否定的な見解をとる。人間の論争好きという厳粛な内容を戯画化した滑稽な風刺として読む Kathryn Hume，さらには James Murphy や Nancy M.Reale による中世の雄弁術と弁証法の教授テクスト，はたまた社会，哲学，神学についての論争詩といったこれまでの本作品への様々な解釈を検証した上で，Cartlidge は従来の解釈とは違った観点から全く新しい光をこの作品に投げかける。

Cartlidge は，詩の全篇に，女性論，聖職禄への不満，聖フランシスの宗教観，ラテラノ公会議などへの言及から当時の社会的，政治的，哲学的そして神学的な問題まで多くの議論や表象がみられるが，論争の中心になっているのは，こうした真面目な問題ではなく，二羽の鳥であり，それぞれの鳥の特質であるという。二羽の鳥の自然界あるいは日常生活でのこの上なく魅力的な細密画は，当時のゴシック調の文学様式として理解される。しかも，問答の堂々巡り，主題・視点の一貫性のなさ，結末の保留といった欲求不満はすべて綿密に練られた結果であり，それこそが＜ゴシック的感性＞を表現するものに他ならないと分析し，美術歴史家 Arnold Hauser による "Gothic Style" の定義が本作品の解釈と批評に見事に展開される。異なる視座を楽しむ態度，いかなる議論も可能だとする事実の強調，そして真面目さと不真面目さの混交といった特質は，現代の審美的価値観や関心と同質のものであり，また共鳴する特質であるという，従来全く指摘されることのなかった本作品の本質を衝いた斬新な解釈を提示する。こうした Cartlidge の射程の広い解釈の背後には，写本作成の場所，社会状況，作品の主題・ジャンル・筆写・編集，そして中世ヨーロッパ全体の文化的伝統から作品の評価を試みる＜マニュスクリプト・コンテクスト＞，換言すれば，＜学際的なアプローチ＞の実践がある。Cartlidge による校訂本はその成果であり，Stanley 版には見られなかった視点であり，収穫であった。

　勿論，Cartlidge 版においても，Stanley 版と同様，*OED* やこれまでの言語研究の成果が集約され作品の言語特徴も詳細に記述されている。Cartlidge は，現存する 2 つの写本の形態上，統語上の特徴を綿密に分析して，英語史上における本作品の位置づけから，語彙への鋭い指摘にいたるまで，Stanley 先生の薫陶よろしきをえて，Stanley 版に劣らず新しいかつ興味深い情報を提供している。特に，形態上・統語上の特徴からいって古英語の傾向が強いが，古英語の屈折体系のくずれが進んでいること，文法上の性も見られるがすでに自然の性に一致していること，古英語の等位構文が現代英語の when...then といった構文にかわりつつあったこと，未来時制は wille と schal の助動詞によって通常あらわされ叙法の意味を失っていること，さらに不変化詞 þe や a(n) がすでに一般化していること，与格と属格

中世文学とテクスト校訂　　　**367**

は通常前置詞構文に取って代わられつつあったことなど，本作品の言語特徴を詳細に分析している。

　それでもなお両者には画然とした相違がみられる。Cartlidge が新しい校訂本で披瀝してくれた姿勢は，主として *OED*，*MED*，そして言語研究に依拠した言語事実を重視し，言語を中心とする情報に基づくこれまでの校訂方法への批評であり，同時に言語のみならず文化，社会，政治，経済，宗教，考古学，美術，さらには最新の文学批評理論といった様々な分野を複合させた広角な視点からテクストを読み解くという，学際性に基づく今後の校訂への在り方にたいする期待と願望といってよい。そうしてみると，新しい校訂の仕方を念頭においた構想では，これまでの校訂本の一部改訂というようなものでは済まされなかったであろう。Davis による『ガウェイン卿と緑の騎士』の改訂版の場合のように，Stanley から許しを得て改訂するということもありえなかったのであろう。Cartlidge には，改訂版ではなく，校訂にたいする自分の考えを反映する新たな校訂本を出すという以外，選択肢は残されていなかったのである。

　本書の出版は，*OED* や *MED* といった辞書や言語に関する先行研究が提供する言語事実のみに偏りすぎた従来の校訂の仕方から，複合的な視点を通した様々な分野や要素への考察という学際的な方法への転換をわれわれに強く印象付け，提示してくれたといってよいだろう。中世文学の大きな遺産に対して Cartlidge が示したこれまでとは違った新しい校訂の方法と仕方により，われわれは長く看過してきた本作品の重要な要素を見出す機会を得ることができた。例えば，本作品に対する，Cartlidge のこれまでにない言語文化的な視点からの考察により，人間性への関心や日常生活への緻密な観察，そして現実世界への肯定，さらには自己意識・認識の表現，ユーモアなどを積極的に読み取り，同時に本作品を「問答詩」という狭隘なジャンルから解放し，英文学史上，古英語から中英語への転換期における実に貴重な文学作品として取り扱うことが可能となったことは，大きな成果といえよう。ただ，本作品の評価というものは，そうしたものに止まらないように思えてならない。弟子である Cartlidge が学恩ある師 Stanley の存命中に新たに校訂本を世に問い，恩師の説や考えに疑問符を与えて課

題を提示したことには，大きな勇気と覚悟を要したであろうことは，状況を自分に置き換えなくても容易に想像がつくことである。若い研究者であるCartlidgeがとった，そのこころの持ち方と行動は，本校訂本の出版と共に忘れてはならないし，讃えられなければならない点であろう。

　2001年，Cartlidgeから贈られた新しい校訂本を手にし，そこで展開される恩師への彼の率直な意見や修正を読んだ時の感銘は深いものがあった。本校訂本の質の高さばかりか，Cartidgeの，これぞオックスフォードの開かれた知の伝統，学問の自由と，阿諛追従することのないその姿勢に心の中で快哉を叫んだのだ。先に示した本版への主だった書評を読んでも，本校訂本への評価は高い。にもかかわらず，Cartlidgeのその後の経歴は，果たしてそれに見合ったものかと訝しがる人も多いと思う。Cartlidgeが本校訂で果たした大きな功績は，これまでの校訂本の歴史を一瞥しただけでも明らかである。今回の出版は，校訂本の歴史ばかりか，これまでの中世英語英文学研究全体から見ても深い意味合いをもつ。その事実が，近い将来に理解されることを確信するとともに，彼が彼に相応しい地位と環境の中で活躍することが望まれてならない。

注

本稿は，2007年『英語青年』「二十一世紀の洋書棚」コーナーに連載したうちの一稿，「中世文学の遺産とその評価」（第153巻/第8号，33-35頁）に大幅に加筆し書き改めたものである。

1　W.P.Ker, *Medieval English Literature* (1912; rpt. Oxford: Oxford University Press, 1948), p.64 と p.134.
2　本書の詳細な内容については、次の書評を参照のこと。菊池清明、Neil Cartlidge (ed.), *The Owl and the Nightingale* (Exeter: University of Exeter Press,2001):『英文学研究』（日本英文学会編）第80巻/第1号,76頁-82頁
3　ここに挙げた校訂版は以下の通り。J.W.H.Atkins(ed), *The Owl and the Nightingale* (1922; reissued New York: Russel & Russel, 1971), J.H.G. Grattan and G.F.H. Sykes(eds.), *The Owl and the Nightingale*,EETS ES(London, 1935), N.R.Ker(ed.), *The Owl and the Nightingale*: Facsimile of the Jesus and Cotton Manuscripts, EETS OS 251(London, 1963), Eric Gerald Stanley(ed.), *The Owl and the Nightingale*, 2nd ed.(1960; rpt. Manchester: Manchester University Press, 1970).

4 *Medium Ævum* (LXXI.2, pp.328-29) ; Reviewer:Marilyn Corrie, London University, *Journal of English and Germanic Philology* (April, 2004, pp.261-63); Reviewer: Janet Schrunk Ericksen, University of Minnesota, *Notes and Queries* (March, 2003, pp.89-90); Reviewer: Claire Fennell, Trieste University.
他にも、*The Medieval Review* (July, 2003) ; Reviewer: James Morey, Emory University. などがあり、Morey は、本版を excellent new edition と絶賛している。
*Neil Cartlidge には、他に *Medieval Marriage: Literary Approaches, 1100-1300* (Woodridge: Boydell and Brewer, 1997) などの著作がある。

参考文献

Carpenter, Humphrey (1977) *Tolkien: A Biography*. New York: Ballantine Book.

Carpenter, Humphrey and Christopher Tolkien(eds.)(1981) *The Letters of J.R.R.Tolkien*. London: George Allen & Unwin.

Cartlidge, Neil (ed.) (2000) *The Owl and the Nightingale: Text and Translation*. Exeter: University of Exeter Press.

Cooper, Helen (2000) "Welcome to the House of Fame; 600 years dead: Chaucer's deserved Reputation as "the Father of English poetry"" based on a lecture given in Oxford on October 25, on the 600th anniversary of Chaucer's, *The Times Literary Supplement*, pp.3-4, October27.

Lucy, John A. (1987) *Language Diversity and Thought: A Reformulation of the Linguistic Relativity Hypothesis*. Cambridge: Cambridge University Press.

Mate, Mavis (1999) *Women in Medieval English Society*. Cambridge: University Press.

Muscantine, Charles (1957) *Chaucer and the French Tradition: A Study in Style and Meaning*. California: University of California Press.

Patterson, Lee (1987) *Negotiating the Past: The Historical Understanding of Medieval Literature*. Madison: University of Wisconsin Press.

Spiegel, Gabrielle (1990) "History, historicism, and the social logic of the text in the Middle Ages," *Speculum*, 65, pp.59-86.

Tolkien, J.R.R. (1934) "Chaucer as a Philologist: *The Reeve's Tale*," *Transactions of the Philological Society*. London, pp.1-70.

Turville-Petre, Thorlac (1996) *England the Nation: Language, Literature, and National Identity 1290-1340*. Clarendon Press: Oxford.

West Saxon Gospels マルコ伝翻訳者の統語上の一特徴
— 等位主節における VO/OV の選択に関して —

小塚　良孝

1　序

1.1　研究の目的

　古英語では，and などの等位接続詞に導かれた主節 (以下「等位主節」) において，従属節と同様に，定形動詞が節の末尾または後方に置かれる傾向がある。この古英語の特徴については特に Mitchell (1964, 1985) により現在では広く認知されているが，更に踏み込んで，等位主節の中でもどのような場合に動詞後置が起きやすいのかという点に関しては研究がまだ少なく，十分に明らかになっていない。[1] 本稿では，古英語訳福音書 *West Saxon Gospels* (以下 *WSG*) のマルコ伝を資料とし，考察対象を定形動詞と名詞目的語の語順に限定して，この問題を論じる。
　WSG における動詞の目的語の位置に関する研究には，既に Kojima (1996) がある。この論文は，主語，動詞，目的語を含む主節の語順を網羅的に調査し，[2] その三要素がどのようなパタンで，どの程度現れるかを詳細に示している。しかしながら，上記の問題については論じられてはいない。
　本稿で特に論じられるのは，マルコ伝では VO/OV の選択が語彙やコロケーションにより左右される部分があった，という点である。[3]

1.2 資料

WSG については Skeat (ed. 1871) 所収の Corpus 写本 (Cambridge, Corpus Christi College 140) のテキストを調査に用いた。また，比較するラテン語聖書としては Weber *et al.* (eds. 1994) を参照した。*WSG* のラテン語原典のテキストは不明であるが，Liuzza (2000: 1-49) の詳細な分析によれば，Weber *et al.* (eds. 1994) のような現代の *Vulgate* と，想定される *WSG* のラテン語原典の間には，大きな相違はなかったと推定される。従って，比較対象として Weber 版 *Vulgate* を使用することに大きな問題はないと思われる。[4]

2 分析

2.1 用例の概要

本節では，*WSG* のマルコ伝の等位主節に現れる定形動詞と名詞目的語の語順を分析する。分析対象とする用例は次の三つの条件の下で収集された。(1) 主語が明示された節，省略された節のいずれも扱う。[5] (2) 単一他動詞 (monotransitive verb) 構文だけでなく，二重他動詞 (ditransitive verb) 構文も用例に含め，後者については，二つの目的語はそれぞれ別の用例として扱う。(3) 分析対象は平叙文に限定し，その内，倒置，再叙 (resumption)，話題化が関わる場合，目的語が関係節を取る場合については用例から除外する。以上の条件で得られた 111 例が本節で扱う用例である。

表 1 に示したように，この 111 例の殆どは and で導かれた節であり，用例全体における VO:OV の比率はおよそ 3:2 である。

表 1　等位接続詞の種類と語順

	VO	OV
and	62	44
ac	3	1
ne		1
計	65	46

以下では，この用例を Vulgate の対応箇所との関係，目的語の重さと語順との関係，目的語となる名詞の種類と語順の関係の三つの観点から分析する。

2.2 Vulgate との比較

表 2 は WSG の用例と Vulgate におけるその対応箇所の語順の比較を示したものである。

表 2　WSG と Vulgate の統語構造の比較

		Vulgate			計
		VO	OV	その他	
WSG	VO	54	2	9	65
	OV	30	10	6	46

表注: Vulgate の VO/OV の分類については，動詞の定形，非定形の区別は無視した。従って，例えば，Mk 15:36 et **implens spongiam** aceto [WSG 7 **fylde áne spingan** mid ecede] は VO に含まれている。

表 2 に示したように，WSG には OV の用例が 46 例あるが，その内 Vulgate の対応箇所でも OV となっているのは僅かに 10 例で，大半は以下のように Vulgate の構造を変えて OV にしている。

<Vulgate VO → WSG OV>

(1) et **convocant totam cohortem** (Mk 15:16)
  → 7 hi to-somne **eall werod clypedon**;

(2) qui **sciens versutiam** eorum ait illis (Mk 12:15)
  → Þa cwæð he 7 **heora lot-wrenc-ceaste wiste**.

<Vulgate その他→ WSG OV>

(3) et **relicto patre suo Zebedaeo** in navi cum mercennariis (Mk 1:20)
  → 7 hi **heora fæder zebedeo** on scipe **forleton**. mid hyrlingum.

従って，WSG の OV 語順の使用は基本的にはラテン語の構造に影響されたものではないと言える。

2.3 目的語の重さと語順

VO/OV の分布を目的語の重さ (=目的語を構成する語数) に基づいてまとめると表 3 のようになる。

表 3 目的語の重さ (=構成語数) と語順

	VO	OV
3 語以上	16	2
2 語	38	30
1 語	11	14
計	65	46

表 3 から，他の古英語期の散文と同様に，[6] *WSG* マルコ伝でも目的語が軽いほど OV の比率が高くなることが指摘される。つまり，目的語が三語以上から構成されている場合には圧倒的に VO が選択されるが (VO:OV=16:2),[7] 構成要素が二語以下になると VO/OV の比率は同等 (VO:OV=49:44) になる。[8]

2.4 名詞の種類と語順

以上の *Vulgate* との比較と目的語の重さによる分析からは，OV の使用に関してラテン語の影響は少ないこと，目的語が軽い場合には OV 率が顕著に高くなることが確認された。視点を変えて，個々の目的語の名詞に着目すると，より具体的なマルコ伝翻訳者の VO/OV 選択に関する特徴や翻訳の癖が認められる。

マルコ伝の用例には，語順が OV に偏る名詞が幾つか見られる。最も顕著なのは，身体または身体の一部を表す名詞で，11 例全てが動詞の前に置かれている (cneow 'knee' 1 例, eare 'ear' 1 例, finger 1 例, hand 4 例, heafod 'head' 2 例, lic 'body' 1 例, tunge 'tongue' 1 例)。それ以外で用例中に複数見られ，その全てが動詞の前に置かれていた名詞には，anweald 'authority, power' (2 例), deofolseocnes 'demonic possession' (2 例), sæd 'seed' (2 例), man (2 例), god (2 例) がある。これら OV に偏

る名詞は，OV の全用例 46 例の半数近く (21 例) を占める。以下では，OV 偏向名詞の用例を詳しく分析し，そこから窺がうことのできるマルコ伝訳者の特徴を幾つか指摘する。

2.4.1 身体名詞

以下の (4)〜(13) は，身体または身体の一部を表す名詞が目的語となっている 11 例と *Vulgate* におけるその対応箇所である (*Vulgate* は *WSG* の用例中のボールド体部分に対応する箇所のみ提示されている)。

(4) Soðlice se hælend him ge-miltsode. **7 his hand aþenode** 7 hine æthrinende 7 þus cwæð; [*Vulgate* extendit manum suam] (Mk 1:41)

(5) He þa eallum út adrifenum. nam petrum 7 þæs mædenes modor. 7 þa ðe mid him wæron ⋯ **7 hire hand nam** 7 cwæð. [*Vulgate* et tenens manum puellae] (Mk 5:40-41)

(6) And he hine þa on cwerterne beheafdode. **7 his heafod on disce brohte** 7 hit sealde þam mædene. [*Vulgate* et adtulit caput eius in disco] (Mk 6:27-28)

(7) Ða his cnihtas þ ge-hyrdon hi cómon **7 his lic namon.** 7 hine on byrgene ledon; [*Vulgate* et tulerunt corpus eius] (Mk 6:29)

(8) Ða nam he hine onsundran of þære menigu. **7 his fingras on his earan dyde 7 spætende his tungan onhrán;** [*Vulgate* misit digitos suos in auriculas et expuens tetigit linguam eius] (Mk 7:33 (2 例))

(9) 7 spætte on his eagan. **7 his hand onasette** 7 hine axode hwæþer he aht gesawe; [*Vulgate* inpositis manibus suis] (Mk 8:23)

(10) **7 hi hyra handa on hine wurpon.** 7 namon hine; [*Vulgate* at illi manus iniecerunt in eum] (Mk 14:46)

(11) Soðlice án of þam þe ðar embe-uton stodon his swurde abræd 7 sloh þæs sacerdes þeow. **7 his eare of acearf;** [*Vulgate* et amputavit illi auriculam] (Mk 14:47)

(12) 7 beoton hine on þheafod mid hreode. 7 spætton hi*m* on. **7 heora cneow bigdon.** 7 hine ge-eaðmeddon; [*Vulgate* et ponentes genua] (Mk 15:19)

(13) And þa ðe forð-stopon hine gremedon **7 hyra heafod cwehton.** 7 ðus cwædon; [*Vulgate* moventes capita sua] (Mk 15:29)

これら 11 例について注目されるのはその翻訳法である。WSG では，11例中 7 例が「and ＋人称代名詞属格＋身体名詞＋定形動詞」という同一の構造を成し，それ以外の 4 例もこの形式に主語や前置詞句など若干の要素が加わっただけの類似した統語形式となっているが，*Vulgate* の対応箇所はこのように均質なものではない。動詞の形態 (定形・非定形)，人称代名詞属格の有無，目的語と動詞の語順について様々である。例えば，Mk 8:23 (用例 9) では，絶対奪格 (ablative absolute) が OV に訳されている(*Vulgate* inpositis manibus suis → *WSG* 7 his hand onasette)。このように，マルコ伝の翻訳者は上記の身体名詞 11 例においては，多様なラテン語の構造を「and ＋人称代名詞属格＋身体名詞＋定形動詞」という単一構造に基本的には訳している。これはマルコ伝訳者の翻訳上の常套パタンの一つであったと考えられる。

2.4.2 anweald/deofolseocnes/god/man/sæd

以下の (14)～(18) は，身体名詞以外で OV に偏った anweald, deofolseocnes, god, man, sæd の全用例とその *Vulgate* における対応箇所である (*Vulgate* は WSG の用例中のボールド体部分に対応する箇所のみ提示されている)。

<anweald>
(14) a. 7 **hi*m* anweald sealde** untru*m*nessa to hælanne. 7 deofol-seocnessa út to adrifanne. [*Vulgate* dedit illis potestatem] (Mk 3:15)

b. 7 **hi*m* anweald sealde** unclænra gasta. [*Vulgate* dabat illis potestatem] (Mk 6:7)

West Saxon Gospels マルコ伝翻訳者の統語上の一特徴　　　377

<deofolseocnes>[9]
(15) a. 7 on deofla ealdre he **deoful-seocnessa ut adrifð**. [*Vulgate* eicit daemonia] (Mk 3:22)

　　b. 7 hi **manega deofol-seocnessa út-adrifon**. [*Vulgate* daemonia multa eiciebant] (Mk 6:13)

<god>
(16) a. Ða het he sittan þa menegu ofer þa eorþan; And nam þa seofon hlafas 7 **gode þancode**. 7 hi bræc [*Vulgate* gratias agens] (Mk 8:6)

　　b. 7 onfeng calice. 7 **gode þancas dyde** 7 sealde hi*m*. [*Vulgate* gratias agens] (Mk 14:23)

<man>
(17) a. 7 ealle þas yfelu of þa*m* innoðe cumað 7 **þone man besmitað**; [*Vulgate* communicant hominem] (Mk 7:23)

　　b. And hi ut eodon. 7 flugon fra*m* þære byrgene. 7 wæron áfærede for þære gesyhðe þe hi gesawon. 7 **hig nanon men naht ne sædon**. [*Vulgate* nemini quicquam dixerunt] (Mk 16:8)

<sæd>
(18) a. And þa nam se oðer hi. 7 wearð dead. **ne sé sæd ne læfde**; Gelice se þridda [*Vulgate* nec iste reliquit semen] (Mk 12:21)

　　b. 7 ealle seofon hi hæfdon 7 **sæd ne læfdon**; [*Vulgate* non reliquerunt semen] (Mk 12:22)

以上の用例において注目されるのは，anweald (用例 14)，deofolseocnes (用例 15)，god (用例 16)，sæd (用例 18) の用例である。それぞれの例において，目的語だけでなく動詞も共通ないし類似している (anweald syllan, deofolseocnessa ut adrifan, gode þancian/þancas don, sæd læfan)。これらの同一または類似コロケーションの用例でラテン語の対応箇所も OV となっているのは deofolseocnes の一例 (15b) のみである。

翻訳法という点で興味深いのは，god の二例 (Mk 8:6 gode þancode, Mk 14:23 gode þancas dyde) である。この二例の *Vulgate* 対応表現は共に gratias agens「感謝して」という分詞構文であり，gode に対応する表現は含まれていない。つまり，この二例の gode は翻訳者によって付け加えられたのだが，その追加要素の gode が二例とも動詞の前に置かれている。この翻訳手法から，gode þancode/gode þancas dyde が翻訳者にとって定形的な表現であった

ことが示唆される。ここで注目されるのは gode þancode が古英詩では定形句として度々用いられていることである。筆者の調査では,*Andreas* (1011b gode þancade), *Beowulf* (227b gode þancedon, 625b gode þancode, 1397b gode þancode, 1626b gode þancodon), *Christ* (1255b gode þonciað), *Daniel* (86b gode þancode), *Elene* (961b gode þancode, 1138b gode þancode) に見られる。[10] こうしたことから,一つの可能性として,マルコ伝の訳者にこの韻文定形句の知識があり,それが訳文に幾らか影響を与えたことが考えられる。[11]

3 結語

以上,*WSG* のマルコ伝を資料として,等位主節における名詞目的語と定形動詞の語順の選択要因について考察してきた。*Vulgate* との比較と目的語の重さに着目した分析からは,OV の使用に関しラテン語原典の影響は僅かであること,目的語が軽い (2 語以下) 場合には OV 率が顕著に高まることが示された。更に,個々の目的語の名詞に着目するとより具体的な特徴が明らかとなった。すなわち,OV に偏る名詞があり,その用例では,節全体が同一または類似の統語形式を有していたり,目的語と共起する動詞も同一または類似していることが指摘された。こうした OV 偏向名詞は,OV の用例の半数近くに見られた。以上の語彙に着目した分析からは,マルコ伝訳者については,OV/VO の選択はある程度,語彙またはコロケーションと関連性があることが示唆された。

今後は資料を拡大し,ここで観察され,推定されたことがどの程度一般性を持つかを調査する必要がある。また,コロケーションや語彙と語順に強い結びつきが認められるとすれば,その原因や源泉はどこにあるのかについての調査も今後進める必要がある。

注

1 この点を論じた最近の研究に Ohkado (2005: 235-48) がある。この論文はÆlfric's *Catholic Homilies* (first series) における等位主節の動詞後置の要因を考察

し，等位接続詞の意味，交差配列 (chiasmus) の使用，情報構造の三点が関係するものと論じている。
2　明らかに非文法的な場合や，目的語が関係節を含む場合は考察対象から除外されている。
3　WSG の各福音書の翻訳者は同一人物でなかった可能性がある。この点についての詳細は，Liuzza (2000)，Kozuka (2006) を参照されたい。
4　本稿の WSG, *Vulgate* の引用中のボールド体は全て筆者によるものである。用例では，マルコ伝を Mk と略記する。
5　Kojima (1996) では主語が省略された節は用例に含まれていない。
6　例えば，Kohonen (1978) ではÆlfric's *Catholic Homilies*，Suzuki (2006) では *Apollonius of Tyre* などについて同様の傾向が指摘されている。
7　三語以上の目的語で OV となっている二例は Mk 1:20 (7 hi **heora fæder zebedeo** on scipe forleton. mid hyrlingu*m* [*Vulgate* et relicto patre suo Zebedaeo in navi cum mercennariis]) と Mk 7:7 (7 **manna láre 7 bebodu** lærað [*Vulgate* docentes doctrinas praecepta hominum]) である。
8　主語のタイプによる VO/OV の分布は以下の通りである。

<主語と語順の関係>

	VO	OV
名詞	4	2
代名詞	29	15
主語なし	32	29
計	65	46

9　このコロケーションの用例はマルコ伝にもう一例ある (Mk 1:34 7 manega deofolseocnyssa he ut adraf [*Vulgate* et daemonia multa eiciebat])。しかし，その例では deofolseocnes が話題化の位置に置かれているので，用例には含まれていない。
10　*A Microfiche Concordance to Old English* と *The Dictionary of Old English Corpus in Electronic Form* を利用して行った調査の結果である。定形句 gode þancode に関しては，Ogura (2003) や Orchard (2003) にも言及がある。
11　この点については，2007 年 9 月 7 日に名古屋大学にて開催された The Society of Historical English Language and Linguistics (SHELL) のシンポジウム " Old English Versions of the Gospels – A Dialectal-Synchronic Comparison " (司会 小倉美知子先生) にて口頭発表 (" An Aspect of OV order in the *West Saxon Gospels* with Special Reference to the Collocation V+*God/Gode*") を行った。詳細は Kozuka (forthcoming) を参照されたい。

参考文献

The Dictionary of Old English Corpus in Electronic Form. TEI-P3 Conformant Version (for 3.5 inch floppies). 1998 Release. Dictionary of Old English Project. Toronto: University of Toronto.

Healey, A. diPaolo and R. L.Venezky (comp. 1980) *A Microfiche Concordance to Old English.* Toronto: University of Toronto.

Kohonen, V. (1978) *On the Development of English Word Order in Religious Prose around 1000 and 1200 A.D.: A Quantitative Study of Word Order in Context.* Åbo: Åbo Akademi.

Kojima, K. (1996) "Element Order Patterns in Independent Clauses in the West-Saxon Gospels: An Exhaustive Analysis (III)" *Gakujutsu Kenkyu (English Language and Literature)* 45: pp.1-14. School of Education, Waseda University.

Kozuka, Y. (2006) *A Linguistic Study of the Authorship of the West Saxon Gospels.* Osaka: Osaka University Press.

Kozuka, Y. (forthcoming) "An Aspect of OV Order in the *West Saxon Gospels* with Special Reference to the Collocation ' Verb+*God/Gode.* '"

Liuzza, R. M. (2000) *The Old English Version of the Gospels. Vol. II. Notes and Glossary.* EETS. O.S. 314.

Mitchell, B. (1964) "Syntax and Word-Order in the *Peterborough Chronicle* 1122-1154." *Neuphilologische Mitteilungen* 65: pp.113-44.

Mitchell, B. (1985) *Old English Syntax.* 2 vols. Oxford: Clarendon Press.

Ogura, M. (2003) "Words of Emotion in Old and Middle English Psalms and Alliterative Poems." *Jimbun Kenkyu* (Chiba University) 32: pp.393-427.

Ohkado, M. (2005) *Clause Structure in Old English.* Nagoya: Manahouse.

Orchard, A. (2003) *A Critical Companion to Beowulf.* Cambridge: D. S. Brewer.

Skeat, W. W. (ed. 1871, rpt. 1970) *The Gospel according to Saint Mark in Anglo-Saxon and Northumbrian Versions, Synoptically Arranged, with Collations Exhibiting All the Readings of All the MSS.* Cambridge: Cambridge University Press. (rpt. Darmstadt: Wissenschaftliche Buchgesellschaft)

Suzuki, H. (2006) *Word Order Variation and Determinants in Old English.* Nagoya: Manahouse.

Weber, R. *et al.* (eds. 1994) *Biblia Sacra iuxta Vulgatam Versionem* (Vierte, verbesserte Auflage). Stuttgart: Deutsche Bibelgesellschaft.

ガウェイン詩群における「人物」を表す絶対形容詞*

田島　松二

1　はじめに

　中英語頭韻詩の文体的特徴としてしばしば言及されるものに形容詞の名詞的用法，つまり絶対形容詞がある。次の (1) – (4) に例示するイタリック体の形容詞を指し，英語で 'adjectives as nouns/substantives' とか，'absolute adjectives' あるいは 'substantival adjectives' などと呼ばれる統語法のことである。

    (1) *Gawain* 672 Al þat seȝ þat *semly* syked in hert.
            'All who saw that <u>seemly (one)</u> sighed in their hearts'
    (2) *Pearl* 421 '*Blysful*', quod I, 'may þis be trwe?
            '<u>Blissful (one)</u>', said I, 'can this be true?'
    (3) *Gawain* 424 Þat þe *scharp* of þe schalk schyndered þe bones.
            So that the <u>sharp (blade)</u> of the man shattered the bones'
    (4) *Patience* 298 Þurȝ mony a regioun ful roȝe, þruȝ *ronk* of his wylle
            'Through many a rough region, in the <u>pride</u> of his will'

上例 (1) では「立派な」という意味の *semly*, (2) では「至福の」という意味の *blysful* という形容詞の表す属性によって特徴づけられた人物を指す。つまり，前者は騎士 Sir Gawain を指し，後者は詩人の亡き娘 Pearl に対する呼びかけ語として使われている。(3) では「鋭い」を意味する形容詞 *scharp* が「剣」という具体的な事物を，(4) では「誇り高い」を意味する形容詞 *ronk* が「思い上がり」という抽象概念を表す名詞として使われている。このように形容詞が定冠詞 the や指示詞 that 等を伴って，あるいは単独で，「人物」や「事物」，または「抽象概念」を指示する名詞として使われる用法は OE 以来見られるものである。が，形容詞の屈折語尾が消失するとともに，韻文，特に頭韻詩を除くと減少してゆき，14 世紀以降は one または man/woman/lady/thing などの名詞を伴う構造が増大する。[1] 今日では，定冠詞を伴い，複数の普通名詞に相当し，総括的に人を表す *the rich* = 'rich people' のような用法や，定冠詞を伴い，抽象名詞的な意味を表す *the beautiful* = 'beauty', *the true* = 'truth' といった文語的な用法を除けば極めて限定されている。

　このような名詞的用法の形容詞，つまり絶対形容詞が中英語頭韻詩に多いことを系統立てて指摘したのは Koziol (1932, pp. 35–38) であるが，ほぼ同時期により詳細な研究を行ったのは Oakden (1930–35) である。[2] その Oakden (1935, pp. 394–99) は，14, 15 世紀の作と考えられるほとんど全ての頭韻詩を調査し，収集した多くの用例を「具体的事物 (the concrete)」，「人物 (the personal)」，「抽象概念 (the abstract)」という 3 つのタイプに分類・提示している。[3] その中で，中英語頭韻詩では「人物」を指すタイプが極めて広範囲に用いられていること，「具体的事物」と「抽象概念」を指すタイプはそれほど多くないこと，などが指摘されている。そして，いずれのタイプもガウェイン詩群 (*Gawain*-poems) に顕著な特徴であることが強調されている。

　ところで，その Oakden の豊富な収集例を検討してみると，用例の誤読に加え，見落とされた例も決して少なくない。今日利用できるような種々の刊本テキストもなければ，MED (1952–2001) も存在しなかった時代の研究の所産であり，そもそもこの用法だけを調査対象とした訳でもないこ

とを考えると，やむを得ない点もあろう。大著ゆえの瑕疵とでも言うべきものかもしれない。しかし，この Oakden の見解と収集例が十分な検証も行われないまま，優に半世紀以上たった今日でも，多くの中英語関係，とりわけ頭韻詩関連の研究書，論文，刊本等で，ほとんどそのまま受け入れられ，独り歩きしている現実を考えると，このまま看過するわけにはゆかないのではないか。[4] 然るに，その後，この用法を本格的に論じたものといえば，頭韻詩 Morte Arthure を，「人物」を表す形容詞に限って調査したわが国の鈴木榮一氏の研究 (Suzuki 1965) ぐらいである。筆者は，現在，この絶対形容詞が中英語頭韻詩で実際にどの程度見られるものなのか，そしてどのような特徴を有するものなのか，さらには脚韻詩には見られないものなのか，といった点などに関して広範囲にわたる調査を行っている。紙数の関係で，今回は 14 世紀後半のガウェイン詩群（Pearl, Patience, Cleanness, Sir Gawain and the Green Knight）だけを取り上げ，それも「事物」，「人物」，「抽象概念」のうち，最も一般的な「人物」を指すタイプに限定して，その使用状況を報告したいと思う。[5] というのは，この詩群こそ，Oakden が多岐にわたる用例を最も多く記録し，且つ，この文体的特徴を最も代表している作品群であると考えていることと，近年の刊本もこぞってこの詩群の注目すべき統語法と考えているからである。[6]

2 「人物（または動物）」を表す絶対形容詞

形容詞の名詞的用法で，圧倒的に多いのが「人物」（または「動物」）を指すタイプである。ガウェイン詩群全体では 70 の異なる形容詞（以下，70 種類と表記）が 152 回使用されている。それらを，Oakden に倣って以下に作品別に列挙する。該当する形容詞をアルファベット順に並べ，出現箇所（行数）を示す。参考までに，Oakden が記録している例も，一部の不適切なものを除いて種類数と用例数を [ ] 内に示す。[7] 当該形容詞と構造をなす冠詞や指示詞も示すが，冠詞等を伴っておらず，単独で用いられているものもある。行数の前のアスタリスク (*) は Oakden が記録していない用例である。また，用例の後の (voc.) は当該形容詞が呼格用法 (vocative)

であることを示す。

Pearl (1,212 ll.) : 21 種類, 26 例 [Oakden : 12 種類, 19 例]

*1063 þe *Almyȝty* 'the Almighty': 279 my blysfol *best*e 'my happy best one'; *421 *blysful* (voc.) 'blissful one'; *1100 my *blysful*; *755 *bryȝt* 'fair one' (voc.) ; *775 So mony a *comly* on-vnder cambe 'So many a lovely one under comb'; *777 alle þo *dere* 'all those worthy ones'; 368 my dere *endorde* (voc.) 'my dear adored one'; 195 þat *frech* as flor-de-lys 'that one fresh as a fleur-de-lis'; 1155 my *frely* 'my fair one'; 189 þat gracios *gay* 'that fair lovely one'; 433 þat *gaye* 'that beautiful one'; 602 þat *gentyl* 'that gentle one'; *669 Þe *gyltyf* 'a guilty one'; *668 þe *gyltleȝ* 'a guiltless one'; *799 Þat gloryous *gyltleȝ*; 909 *hynde* (voc.) 'gracious one'; *418 Hys *lef* 'his beloved one'; 398 þat *lufsoum* of lyth and lere 'that one lovely of limb and face'; *721 hys *mylde* 'his gentle ones'; *689 þys *ryȝtwys* 'this righteous man'; 166, 965 þat *schene* 'that fair one'; 240 þat *swete* 'that sweet one'; 325 my *swete* (voc.); 47 þat *worþyly* 'that precious one'.

Cleanness (1,812 ll.) : 37 種類, 53 例 [Oakden : 2 種類, 2 例]

*130 þe *best* 'the noblest ones'; *276 þe *biggest* 'the most prominent one'; *811 Þe *bolde* 'the most prominent one'; *88 *bonde* 'bondmen'; *470 þe *bryȝt* 'the fair one'; *1097 þat *cortayse* 'the courteous one'; *1394 *dere* 'noblemen'; *1399 þe *dere* 'the great one'; *1306 all þe *doȝtyest* and *derrest* in armes 'all the boldest and bravest ones in arms'; *1167 þe *faythful* 'the faithful people'; *1168 þe *falce* 'the false people'; *88 *fre* 'freemen'; *275 fre 'a noble one'; 929 þat *fre* 'the noble one'; *1180 þe *gentylest* 'noblest ones'; 1216 alle hise *gentyle* 'all his nobles'; 1363 all þe *gete* 'all the great men'; *796 þe *ȝep* 'the alert man'; *1653 þe *hyȝest* 'the Highest'; *491 *jumpred* 'jumbled ones'; *1093 *lodly* 'loathsome people'; 977 *þo *luly-whit* 'those lily-white ones'; *279 þe *maȝty* 'the mighty ones'; 776 þy *meke* 'thy humble one'; *1359 þe *nice* 'the wanton man'; *1226 his *noble* 'his nobles'; *615 þi *pouere* 'thy poor one'; *1300 þe *pruddest* 'the proudest ones'; *567 alle *quykeȝ* 'all living creatures'; *1208 *Ryche* 'noblemen'; *1321 Þat *ryche* 'that noble man'; *1572 þe *rychest* 'the worthiest one'; *716 *sakleȝ* 'innocent ones'; *870 þo *semly* 'those fair ones'; *1055 þat *semly* 'that seemly one'; *716 *synful* 'sinful ones'; *311, *362 (þe) *tame* '(the) tame animals'; *751 þretty *þryuande* 'thirty worthy ones'; *1639 þe þryd *þryuenest* 'the third most worthy one'; *763 ten *trysty* 'ten true men'; *702 two *true* 'two virtuous men'; *718 þe *wykked* 'wicked people'; *311 *wylde* 'wild animals'; *362, *387, *503, *529, *1674 þe *wylde* '(the) wild animals'; *1319 þe *wyse* 'a wise man'; *1741 þat *wyse* 'that wise man'; *718 þe *worþy* 'worthy people'.

Patience (531 ll.) : 4 種類, 4 例 [Oakden : 1 種類, 1 例]

175 þe *gulty* 'the guilty one'; *502 þo *redles* 'those desperate ones'; *169 þe *spakest* 'the wisest one'; 163 þo *wery* 'those men'.

Sir Gawain (2,530 ll.) : 33 種類, 69 例 [Oakden : 22 種類, 33 例]

972, *1317 þe *alder* 'the elder one'; 948 an *auncian* 'an old woman'; *550, *1325 þe *best* 'the best knights'; *986, *1645 þe *best* 'the best one'; 21 *bolde* 'bold men',; *351 mony so *bolde* 'many so bold men'; 1489 þe *clere* 'the fair lady'; *81 þe *comlokest* 'the fairest lady'; 674 þat *comly* 'that fair knight'; 1755 þat *comly* 'that fair lady'; 2411 þat *cortays* 'that gracious lady'; *445, *483 (þe) *derrest* '(the) noblest ones'; 678 ȝonder *dere* 'that noble knight'; 928 þe *dere* 'the noble knight; *1492 my *dere* (voc.) 'my dear lady'; *1798 *dere* (voc.) 'good sir'; *2334 þat *doȝty* 'that brave man'; 1585 þe *felle* 'the wild beast'; 1545 my *fre* (voc.) 'my noble lady'; 1549, 1783 þat *fre* 'that noble lady'; 970 þat *gay* 'that fair lady'; *1213 *gay* (voc.) 'fair lady'; 1822 my *gay* (voc.) 'my fair lady'; *2023 Þe *gayest* 'the fairest knight'; 2035 þat *gay* 'that fair knight'; 542 þat *jentyle* 'that gentle knight'; 464 þat *grene* 'the green man'; 2490 þe *grete* 'the great one'; 951, *1317 þe *ȝonge* 'the young one'; 827, 1104 þe *hende* 'the noble man; *896 as *hende* 'like a gentleman, politely' [MED]; 946 þat *hende* 'that noble lady'; 1252, 2330 *hende* (voc.) 'good sir'; 1813 *hende* of hyȝe honours (voc.) 'noble knight of high honour'; *542 Mony *ioylez* 'many joyless ones'; *973 Þe *loueloker* 'the lovelier one'; 1814 þat *lufsum* vnder lyne 'that lovely lady under linen'; 555 mony oþer *menskful* 'many other noble knights'; 1268 þe *menskful* 'the noble lady'; 1750 þat *noble* 'that noble knight'; 66, 362 *riche* 'nobles'; *1130 þe *rychest* 'the nobles'; 2177 his *riche* 'his noble steed'; *83 a *semloker* 'a lovelier lady'; 672 þe *semly* 'that fair knight'; *1659 þat *stalworth* 'that stalwart knight'; *1567 þe *styffest* 'the strongest ones'; 214 þe *sturne* 'the grim knight'; *1108 *Swete* (voc.) 'good sir'; 1222 þat *swete* 'that fair lady'; *1713 þre *þro* 'three fierce hounds'; *1150, *2003 þe *wylde* 'the wild creatures'; *1167 What *wylde* 'whatever wild beast'; *1586, *1900 þe *wylde* 'the wild beast'; *1905 þis *wyly* 'the wily beast'; 1988 þat *wlonk* 'that noble knight'; 1276 *worþy* '(voc.) 'noble lady'; 1508 þat *worþy* 'that noble lady'.

以上がガウェイン詩群全体で確認された絶対形容詞とその出現箇所である。各作品の行数の違いを考慮しても，*Pearl, Cleanness, Sir Gawain* の3作品における種類，用例数の多さは際だっているが，*Patience* では極めて稀な用法であることがわかる。また，一見，*Cleanness* が形容詞の種類の多さを誇るが，頭韻語より日常語が多いことが目をひく。そして *Pearl* や *Sir Gawain* には後述するように，頭韻詩特有の語彙が目立つように思われる。

「事物」や「抽象概念」と異なり，この「人物（または動物）」を表す絶対形容詞については，Oakden も 'reasonably complete' (p. 398) と自負するほど多数の用例を収集している。そしてガウェイン詩群がこの種の絶対形容詞を広範囲に使っていることを特記している。その点に関しては Oakden の指摘通りである。他の頭韻詩と比較しても，絶対形容詞の種類と用例数の多さは突出している。しかし，肝心のガウェイン詩群に限っても，形容詞の種類，出現箇所の両方に関して，実に多数の漏れ（上記引用例中，*を付したもの）を指摘できる。Oakden が挙げる形容詞はごく少数の不適切な例を除いて 29 種類，つまり *auncian, best, bolde, clere, comly, cortays, dere, endorde, felle, fre, frech, gay, gentyle/jentyle, grene, grete, ʒong, hende, lufsum, meke, menskful, noble, riche, schene, semly, sturne, swete, wery, wlonk, worþy(ly)* であるが，全く挙げていない形容詞は 41 種類にものぼ

る。即ち，*alder, Almiȝty, biggest, blysful, bonde, bryȝt, doȝty, falce, faythful, gyltyf/gulty, gyltleȝ, ȝep, hyȝest, jumpred, joylez, lef, lodly, loeloker, luly-whit, maȝty, mylde, nice, pouere, pruddest, quikeȝ, redles, ryȝtwys, sakleȝ, synful, spakest, stalworth, styffest, tame, þryuande/þryuenest, þro, trysty, true, wykked, wylde, wyly, wyse* である。むしろ見落されている形容詞の方がはるかに多い。にもかかわらず，絶対形容詞がガウェイン詩群に特に多いという Oakden の指摘自体は首肯できるものである。以下，ガウェイン詩群の用例を少し詳しく見てみよう。

2.1

Oakden (p. 398) に倣って，絶対形容詞が単数を指示する場合と複数を指示する場合に分けて考えてみたい。全 152 例のうち，単数を表すのが 101 例，複数が 51 例で，単数用法が全体の約 3 分の 2（約 66 ％）を占める。この点は，複数用法が一般的な今日の用法と大きく異なるところである。まず単数用法から見てゆく。

2.1.1

名詞的に用いられた形容詞は，単数で，特定の人物（または動物）を指示する場合が最も多く，全 70 種類，計 152 例のうち，47 種類 90 例（59.2 ％）を数える。そして þat（33 例），þe（30 例）を伴う場合が最も多く，時どき代名詞の所有格（13 例）を，そして稀に þis（2 例），ȝonder（1 例）を伴う。決定詞を伴わず，全くの単独で起こる場合も時折（11 例）ある。用例の一部はすでに冒頭の (1) と (2) に示している。この「人」を指示する絶対形容詞の用法で注目される点は，*Pearl* と *Sir Gawain and the Green Knight* の 2 作品で特定の人物を指示する形容詞の種類が極めて豊富なことである。具体的に見てみよう。（以下の例文中，φ は形容詞が冠詞等を伴っておらず，単独で用いられていることを示す。）

Sir Gawain and the Green Knight の中で，騎士ガウェイン卿は種々の名

詞による指示のほかに，(9) に示すように，

(9) þat comly, φ/ʒonder/þe dere, þat doʒty, þat/þe gay(est), þat ientil, φ/þe/þat hende, þat noble, þat semly, þat stalworth, φswete, þat wlonke

と，11通りの形容詞を使って指示されている。[9] 14世紀には，「男性」を指す名詞としては，man, knight, lord, king といった日常語のほかに，伝統的な頭韻語 burn(e), freke, gome, hathel, lede, renk(e), schalk, segge, tulk, wyʒe があったが，それらに加えて，これだけの形容詞が名詞として用いられ，頭韻の要請に応えていたのである。[10]

ガウェイン詩群において，「男性」を指示する形容詞以上に，重要な役割を果たしたと思われるのが，「女性」を指示する形容詞群である。例えば，Sir Gawain and the Green Knight の中で，ガウェイン卿が逗留した城の主 Bercilak の妻は

(10) þe clere, þat comly, þat cortays, my dere, my/þat fre, þat/φ/my gaye, þe ʒonge, þe loueloker, þat lufsum, þe menskful, þat swete, φ/þat worþy

と，12通りに形容される。[11] 更に，Pearl では，娘 Pearl が

(11) #my blysfol beste, φ/my blysful, φbryʒt, #my dere endorde, þat frech, my frely, #þat gracios gaye, þat gentyl, φhende, þat lufsoun, þat schene, þat/my swete, þat worþyly

と，実に13通りの絶対形容詞で指示されている。[12] そのうち3例（#印を付した例）は，もうひとつの限定形容詞に修飾された形式を取っている。[13]

Sir Gawain and the Green Knight や Pearl で，とりわけ女性（婦人や乙女）を指示する絶対形容詞が特に目立つのは，女性を指す伝統的な名詞（lady, wommon, may(den), burde や，OF 由来の dame, damsel）が少なかったことによる。[14] 換言すれば，頭韻の要請に応えるだけの同義語がなかったために，新たな同義語創出の手段として絶対形容詞が多用されたことによると考えられる。中英語ロマンスに数多く登場する騎士や女性を描写するためには，個々人のある資質を強調する意味もあったであろうが，それ以

上に頭韻を維持する有力な手段として、多数の同義語が必要だったのである。因みに、ガウェイン詩群中、*Patience* と *Cleanness* という説教詩では「人物」を描写する名詞のヴァリエーションは豊かであるが、*Patience* には絶対形容詞自体の用例がほとんどなく、*Cleanness* でも貴族等を指す複数用法が主である。

ガウェイン詩群の用法でもう一つ目立つ点は、形容詞が呼びかけ語 (vocative) として使用されることが多いことである。この用法は *Pearl* と *Sir Gawain and the Green Knight* だけに見られ、(12) に示すように、代名詞の所有格を伴う例が 7 例、単独の例が 10 例起こる。例えば、絶対形容詞を多用する頭韻詩 *Morte Arthure* などと比べても際だっている。[15] この呼格用法の絶対形容詞が多いこともガウェイン詩群の特徴のひとつと言えるかもしれない。

(12) *Pearl* 279 my blysfol *beste*, 1100 my *blysful*, 325 my *swete*, 368 my dere *endorde*; *Gawain* 1492 my *dere*, 1545 my *fre*, 1822 my *gay* // *Pearl* 421 *Blysful*, 755 *bryʒt*, 909 *hynde*; *Gawain* 1798 *dere*, 1213 *gay*, 1252/1813/2330 *hende*, 1108 *Swete*, 1276 *worþy*

これまで見てきた例はすべて単数・特定の「人物」を指す例であったが、特定の「動物」を指す例もごく稀に見られる。(13) に示すように、4 種類の形容詞が 5 回使われている。順に、鳩を指す *bryʒt*、猪を指す *wylde*、狐を指す *wylde* と *wyly*、馬を指す *riche* である。

(13) *Cleanness* 470 þat *bryʒt* ; *Gawain* 1586 þe *wylde* ; *Gawain* 1900 þe *wylde*, *Gawain* 1905 þis *wyly* ; *Gawain* 2177 his *riche*

以上はいずれも、名詞的用法の形容詞が単数・特定の人物（または動物）を指示する用例であった。一方、単数・不特定の人物（または動物）を指示することもある。しかし、この用法は稀で、全 70 種類の形容詞 152 例のうち、10 種類の形容詞が 11 回（全用例の 7.2%）用いられているだけである。the を伴う例がやや多く（5 例）、不定冠詞 a と共起する例が 3 例である。ほかに what を伴う例が 1 例、単独用法も 2 例ある。the の例は 2 例のみ示し、他はすべて挙げる。

(14) *Pearl* 669 Þe *gyltyf*, *Cleanness* 1319 as þe *wyse*; *Pearl* 775 So mony a *comly* on-vunder cambe; *Gawain* 83 A *semloker*; *Gawain* 948 an *auncian*, *Gawain* 1167 What *wylde*; *Cleanness* 275 for *fre* , *Gawain* 896 As *hende*

2.1.2

　形容詞が þe や þo (= 'those'), mony (= 'many') や数詞を伴ったり，あるいは単独で，複数の人物（または動物）を指示することがある。単数の場合同様，特定の人物（または動物）を指すこともあれば，不特定の人物（または動物）を指すこともある。ただし，複数の意味の絶対形容詞は単数の例と比べて，はるかに少ない。ガウェイン詩群では全 70 種類，152 例のうち，35 種類，52 例（約 34 %）が複数の意味で用いられている。þe を伴う例が 22 例と最も多く，指示詞の複数形は þo が 5 例見られるだけである。ここでも形容詞を単独で用いる例が 13 例と目立つ。

　複数の意味を表す形容詞の名詞的用法を扱う場合，Oakden (p. 398) も，*the rich* = 'rich people' のように，形容詞が示す人々を総括的に表現する形式[16]と単数・特定の人物を指示する用法の延長線上にある複数用法とを区別する必要があると述べているが，判断が難しい例もある。ここでは文脈上，特定の人物を指すか不特定の人物を指すかを目安として，分類してみると，複数・特定の人物（または動物）を指す例が全 52 例中 42 例とほぼ 8 割に達する。「the ＋形容詞」が概して，総括的，集合的な意味で使われる今日の英語と大きく違う点である。

　Oakden (p. 398) は，このような複数形容詞に関しては代表的な例を挙げるだけである。つまり，頭韻詩全体から 9 種類の形容詞について 12 例（ガウェイン詩群からは 4 種類の形容詞 5 例）を記録している。そして，このタイプは mony を伴うことが多く，ガウェイン詩群では形容詞の単独用法が好まれると述べている。実際には，ガウェイン詩群だけでも，Oakden の挙げる全用例の 3 倍以上，具体的には 30 種類の形容詞が 42 例確認でき

る。その 42 例中，mony を伴う例は僅かに 3 例，ガウェイン詩群で好まれるという単独用法も 6 例しかなく，必ずしも Oakden の説明通りではない。(15) に例を少し示す。

(15) *Cleanness* 1306 alle þe *doȝtyest and derrest*; *Cleanness* 870 þo *semly*; *Pearl* 721 hys *mylde*; *Cleanness* 751 þretty þryuande; *Gawain* 542 Mony *joyleȝ*; *Cleanness* 1093 *lodly*

また Oakden (p. 398) は，複数・特定の動物を指す例も 2 例挙げているが，ガウェイン詩群からの例は挙げていない。そのガウェイン詩群では 3 種類の形容詞が 8 回使用されている。

(16) *Cleannes* 362 þe *tame*; *Cleannes* 387 þe *wylde* of þe wode (also in *Cleanness* 362, 503, 529; *Gawain* 1150, 2003); *Gawain* 1713 þre þro

複数・不特定の人物（または動物）を指示することは，単数・不特定の場合同様，ごく稀である（9 種類の形容詞 10 例で，全用例の 6.6 %）。そのうち，今日でも使われる，人を表す複数普通名詞に相当する形式「the + 形容詞」は僅かに 3 例で，いずれも説教詩 *Cleanness* にしか見られない。

(17) 718 þe *wykked* and þe *worþy* schal on wrake suffer 'wicked people and worthy people must suffer one punishment', 1674 þe *wylde* 'wild animals'

ほかには，all を伴う例が 1 例，単独の形容詞が 6 例ある。

(18) *Cleanness* 567 alle *quykeȝ*; *Cleanness* 1208 *Ryche*, 716 *synful* and *sakleȝ*, 311 for *wylde* and for *tame*; *Gawain* 21 *Bolde*

2.2

最後に，これまで観察した「人物（稀に動物）」を指示する絶対形容詞を，頭韻・非頭韻の割合で見てみると，全 152 例のうち，130 例 (85.5 %) が頭韻の位置に起こる。非頭韻の位置に起こる形容詞は 22 例，そのうち

9例は厳密な意味では頭韻詩とはいえない *Pearl* に見られる。*Pearl* の用例を除外し，*Cleanness, Patience, Sir Gawain and the Green Knight* だけで考えると127例中114例，約90％が頭韻の位置に起こる。非頭韻の位置に起こるのは，best, tame, wylde, noble, grete などごく僅かである。いずれも日常語であり，頭韻詩特有の語彙ではない。逆に言えば，形容詞の名詞的用法が頭韻上の有力な手段であったことを裏付けている。なお，one, man, lady 等を伴わないことで，絶対形容詞は韻律上の要請にも応えていることは言うまでもない。

3　おわりに

　以上，中英語頭韻詩の中でも，とりわけガウェイン詩群の文体的特徴と目される形容詞の名詞的用法，つまり絶対形容詞の使用状況を，それも最も一般的な「人物」を表す形容詞に限って観察した。他の頭韻詩あるいは脚韻詩との更なる比較が必要であることは言を俟たないが，現時点でも Oakden ほか諸家の指摘通り，ガウェイン詩群に目立つ文体であることは確認できたと思う。そして，ガウェイン詩群では単数・特定の人物を指す例が大半を占めること，呼びかけ語の例が多いこと，などを明らかにした。加えて，Oakden の収集例に数多くの見落としや不適切なものが含まれていること，また Oakden の見解がいくつかの点で必ずしも適切でないことも明らかにできたと思う。

　ガウェイン詩群，とりわけ *Pearl* と *Sir Gawain and the Green Knight* に絶対形容詞が多いのは，特定の人物，中でも騎士や女性に関する形容詞が多種多様なことによる。同じように騎士，貴族，婦人に関する描写も多く，行数的にも遙かに長大な頭韻ロマンス *Morte Arthure* もこの絶対形容詞を多用しているが，それと比べても，形容詞の種類の多さ，頻度は際だっている。ガウェイン詩群においては，この絶対形容詞が頭韻を維持するために必要な種々の同義語，とりわけ女性を意味する語彙の不足を補う重要な手段であったことは間違いないように思われる。

注

*小論は旧稿（田島 2003）の一部に加筆修正をほどこしたものである。せっかくの今井光規教授の記念論文集に中英語ロマンスに関する論文を考えていたが，間に合わなかった。いつの日か埋め合わせをしたいと思っている。

1 Brunner (1973 [1960], pp. 454–59), Mustanoja (1960, pp. 663–64), 中尾 (1972, p. 235) 等参照
2 もっとも，この用法自体の指摘はもっとずっと早く，1865 年刊の G. G. Perry (ed.), *Morte Arthure* (EETS OS 8), p. xiii に，注目すべき特徴として挙げられている。20 世紀に入ると *Sir Gawain and the Green Knight* の形容詞を詳述した Schmittbetz (1909) もこの用法を論じている。
3 用例収集の基準が示されていないので，Oakden がどのようなものまでを名詞的用法と見なしているのか不明であるが，引用例から判断して，種類，状態，性質などを表す，いわゆる記述形容詞（Descriptive Adjectives）だけを収集しているようである（p. 185 参照）。起源的には形容詞であった数量，色彩等を表す形容詞，前置詞＋形容詞からなる成句（e.g. *on high, in derne, in hiȝe and in loȝe, in hot and colde, at þe laste*, etc.），同格用法（e.g. Alexander *the great*）の形容詞等は除外されている。
4 Clark (1950), Benson (1965, pp. 129–30), Mustanoja (1960, p. 645), Suzuki (1965), Anderson (1969, p. 66), 中尾 (1972, pp. 235–36), Trigg (1990, p. 43) ほか。ただし，*Sir Gawain and the Green Knight* の文体を論じた Borroff (1962) にはこの絶対形容詞に関する直接の言及はない。
5 「事物」と「抽象概念」については，田島（2003, pp. 66–69 & 79–81）参照。
6 Tolkien-Gordon-Davis (1967, p. 144), Silverstein (1984, p. 29), Andrew & Waldron (1987 & 1996, p. 46) など。
7 Oakden が挙げる例のうち，誤読例は別として，*Pearl* に 5 回起こる *innocent* も，小論では MED に従って名詞と解し，統計から除外した。
8 Oakden (1935, pp. 396-98) 及び田島 (2003, p. 73) 参照。
9 この中には，1813 *hende of hyȝe honours* 'noble knight of high honour' といった頭韻語句も含まれている。
10 このような絶対形容詞の文体的効果については，Krishna（1976, p. 30）参照。
11 この中には，*Gawain* 1814 *þat lufsum* under lyne 'that lovely one under linen, i.e. that lovely lady' といった頭韻語句も含まれている。なお，Benson (1965, p. 38) は 14 種類の形容詞を挙げているが，1 例は誤読であり，もう一例は形容詞ではなく，不定代名詞の例である。
12 この中には *Pearl* 195 *þat frech* as flor-de-lys 'that one fresh as fleur-de-lis', 398 *þat lufsoun* of luth and lere 'that one lovely of limb and face', 166 *þat schene* an-vnder shore 'that fair one on the shore' といった頭韻語句も含まれている。
13 「女性」を指す例ではないが，もう 1 例キリストを指す類似の例がある。*Pearl* 799 *þat gloryous gyltleȝ* 'That glorious innocent (one), i. e. Christ'

14 この点については，Benson (1965, pp. 129–31) 及び Turville-Petre (1977, p. 81) 参照。
15 田島 (2003, p. 76) 参照。
16 Oakden (1935, p. 398) はこれを 'vague inclusive plurals' と呼んでいる。

参考文献

Primary Sources:

Gordon. E. V. (ed.)(1953) *Pearl*. Oxford: Clarendon.

Anderson, J. J. (ed.)(1969) *Patience*. Manchester: Manchester University Press.

Anderson, J. J. (ed.)(1977) *Cleanness*. Manchester: Manchester University Press.

Tolkien, J. R. R. and E. V. Gordon (eds.)(1967) *Sir Gawain and the Green Knight*, 2nd edn., rev. N. Davis. Oxford: Clarendon.

Secondary Sources:

Andrew, M. and R. Waldron (eds.) (1987 & 1996) *The Poems of the Pearl Manuscript*. Exeter: University of Exeter Press.

Benson, L. D. (1965) *Art and Tradition in 'Sir Gawain and the Green Knight'*. New Brunswick, NJ: Rutgers University Press.

Borroff, Marie (1962) *'Sir Gawain and the Green Knight': A Stylistic and Metrical Study*. New Haven, CT: Yale University Press.

Brunner, K. (1960-62) *Die englische Sprache; Ihre geschichtliche Entwicklung*. Tübingen: Max Niemeyer. （松浪有ほか共訳／ブルンナー『英語発達史』大修館書店，1973）

Clark, J. W. (1950) "'The *Gawain*-Poet' and the Substantival Adjective". *JEGP* 49, 60–66.

Koziol, H. (1932) *Grundzüge der Syntax der mittelenglischen Stabreimdichtungen*. Wien und Leipzig: Wilhelm Braumüller.

Krishna, Valerie (ed.) (1976) *The Alliterative Morte Arthure*. New York: Burt Frnklin.

MED = *Middle English Dictionary*, ed. H. S. Kurath, M. Kuhn and R. E. Lewis. Ann Arbor, MI: The University of Michigan Press, 1952–2001.

Mustanoja, T. F. (1960) *A Middle English Syntax*. Part I. Helsinki: Société Néophilologique.

Oakden, J. P. (1930–35) *Alliterative Poetry in Middle English*. 2 vols. Manchester: Manchester University Press; repr. in one volume, Hamden, CN: Archon Books, 1968.

Perry, G. G. (ed.) (1865) *Morte Arthure or The Death of Arthur*. (EETS OS 8.) London: Oxford University Press.

Peterson, Clifford (ed.) (1977) *Saint Erkenwald*. Philadelphia: University of Pennsylvania Press,

Schmittbetz, K. R. (1909) "Das Adjektiv in *Sir Gawain and the Green Knight*". *Anglia* 32, 395–83.

Silverstein, T. (ed.) (1984) *Sir Gawain and the Green Knight*. Chicago: The University of Chicago Press.

Suzuki, E. (1965) "The Substantival Adjective in *Morte Arthure*".『東北学院大学論集』48, 1–17.

Trigg, S. (ed.) (1990) *Wynnere and Wastoure*. (EETS OS 297.) Oxford: Oxford University Press.

Turville-Petre, T. (1977) *The Alliterative Revival*. Cambridge: D. S. Brewer.

田島松二 (2003)「中英語頭韻詩における絶対形容詞—ガウェイン詩群を中心に」『英語英文学論叢』(九州大学) 第 53 集, pp. 63–84.

中尾俊夫 (1972)『英語史 II』(英語学大系 9) 大修館書店.

Caxton の翻訳技法としての Word Pairs
— *Paris and Vienne* —

谷　明信

1　はじめに

　Time and tide や *war and peace* のような word pairs (以下 WP) が，西欧中世で重要な修辞技法であり，中世の英語作品でも頻出することはよく知られている。このため，中世文学の批評家たちは，この修辞技法に注目し議論を行ってきた。
　本研究では，Caxton が中フランス語の原典から英語に翻訳し，1485 年に出版した *Paris and Vienne* (以下 *Paris*) を対象に，原典と比較して，2 語から構成される WP を考察する。

1.1　Word Pairs の先行研究

　Caxton が WP を多く用いたことは周知の事実で，Bennett (1947: 210) は，"The practice of using pairs of synonymous words was especially cultivated by Caxton" とまで述べている。よって，Caxton の WP については，多くの先行研究が存在する。特に重要なものとして，WP の構成要素間の意味関係の解明に意を尽くした Leisi (1947)，Caxton の WP のために一章を割いた Mueller (1984) がある。また，特に *Paris* を扱った尾崎 (2006) がある。しかしながら，翻訳原典を参照した研究が望まれるところである。

Caxton のほぼ全ての著作が翻訳であることを考えると，原典との比較対照を行ったうえで，WP を考察する必要があることは明らかである。このような考察として，*Caxton's Aesop* の翻訳のあとがきに載せた伊藤 (1995) があるが，残念ながら 2 ページ足らずに簡単に記述されているに過ぎない。また，この点を重要視して，逆に翻訳原典の影響がないと考えられるテキスト部分 (*Caxton's Own Prose*) の WP を意味論的に考察した Nakao & Matsutani (1996) は興味深いと言えよう。したがって，原典との比較という観点から Caxton の WP を見直すことは必要で，Caxton の翻訳技法を考える上でも重要である。実際，この問題は 1 世紀以上前に Emerson (1893) が指摘しているが，その後の研究で十分に行われたとは言いがたい。

　翻訳技法としての中英語の WP を考察した先行研究は，Chaucer の翻訳を考察した Geissman(1952) や Chaucer の *Boece* を考察した Machan (1985)，John Trevisa のラテン語からの翻訳である *Polychronicon* に現れる WP を原典と対照研究した Waldron (2001) がある。Waldron は Trevisa が WP を利用した理由のひとつとして，原典の語の意味範囲を包含しようとする意図があったと主張する。また，Chaucer の *Melibee* を調査した Bornstein (1978) は，Chaucer が大陸の "style clergial" を模倣しながらも，独自の文体を創出するため，原典に更に WP を追加したことを実例で示した。しかしながら，*Paris* は，その内容・ジャンルにおいて，Chaucer の散文作品や *Polychronicon* と大きく異なり，散文ロマンスである。したがって，Chaucer などの作品との比較の資料としても，*Paris* の WP の翻訳技法としての研究は必要かつ有用と言える。

1.2　Middle English と Middle French の使用テキスト

　本研究は *Paris* の Caxton の英語のテキストとして，Leach (1957) を利用した。

　Paris の Middle French (以下 MF) 原典の写本には Version I と Version II が存在し，Caxton のテキストにより近いのは Version II である (Leach, 1957: iv-xvi)。Version I の諸写本は，Kaltenbacher (1904) が校訂しており，

Version II 中で Caxton のテキストに最も近い現存する MF 写本である B.N. Fr. 20044 は Babbi (1992) が校訂している。実際に 2 つの MF 校訂本を Caxton の校訂本と比較した結果，Babbi のテキストの方が対応関係が強いので，これを MF テキストとして用いた。

Babbi のテキストは，Caxton と表現が一部で異なったり，パッセージの対応が見られない箇所もあるが，大筋 Caxton のテキストに対応する。本研究は，Babbi と Leach の校訂本を電子化し，更にパラレルテキスト化し，これに基づいて調査を行った。[1]

2 翻訳技法としての WP

WP の原典と翻訳の対応関係については，1) retention, 2) addition, 3) reduction, 4) deletion の 4 パターンが考えられる。個々の用例を検討する前に，Paris の MF 原典と ME 翻訳に生起する WP にどのような傾向があるのかを考察する。

Chaucer の *The Tale of Melibee* を考察した Bornstein (1978) は，*Melibee* ではすべてのパターンが見られるが，addition が顕著に見られると論じている。

この点，*Paris* はどうであろうか。MF と Caxton の両テキストの全語数中の WP の頻度を計算し比較すれば，全体的な傾向が見て取れる。このため，電子化したパラレルテキストを用いて，両テキストでの生起数を数え，1000 語あたりで標準化した頻度を表 1 に示す：

表 1：WP の数と 1000 語あたりの頻度

	# of WP	Freq per 1000 wds	Total wds
Paris-Caxton	508	16.27	31214
Paris-MF	289	10.29	28092

Caxton のテキストのほうが少し長いが，WP の数は原典に比べて 2 倍近い。1000 語あたりの頻度は，Caxton のテキストは原典の 1.5 倍である。このことから，Caxton が翻訳の際に，WP を追加した用例が圧倒的に多いこ

とは明らかである。

2.1 Caxton による WP の追加と保持

次に，より詳細に検討する。まず，Caxton の *Paris* に生起した WP と，それに対応する MF の表現を比較した結果を，下に表 2 として挙げる：

表 2: Caxton の WP と MF 原典の表現の対応関係

MF	Caxton	retention of MF element	#		
Correspondence			453		
single wd	WP	yes	99	21.85%	← Caxton's addition
single wd	WP	no	148	32.67%	
WP	WP	1 wd	55	12.14%	←partial correspondence
WP	WP	2 wd	48	10.60%	←total correspondence
WP	WP	no	96	21.19%	
3WP	WP	1 wd	2	0.44%	
3WP	WP	no	4	0.88%	
Others	WP	no	1	0.22%	
Non-Correspondence					
	WP		55		

まず，Caxton の *Paris* に生起する WP 全 508 例中，453 例は何らかの対応関係があり，テキスト上に対応関係が見られないものの Caxton では WP となっている用例が 55 例見られた。このようにテキストに対応関係がない部分で Caxton のテキストに生起する WP の例としては，次のようなものがある：[2]

(1) where as the kynge was & the other grete <u>lordes & knyghtes</u> 17/17-18

(2) thre knyghtes moche <u>stronge and puyssaunte</u> 18/26-27

これら対応関係がないものについては慎重に取り扱う必要がある。既に述べたように，Babbi (1995) の底本である写本 B.N. Fr. 20044 は，現存する MF 写本中 Caxton の英語のテキストに最も類似しているものとは言え，Caxton がその翻訳に直接利用したものではないからである。

対応関係がある用例中，MF の単一語を保持して Caxton が WP として翻訳した例で，元々の MF の語が WP の構成要素として保持されているものが 99 例，一方 MF の単一語が構成要素として保持されていない用例が 148 例ある。すなわち，Caxton による WP の追加の用例が計 247 例ある。これらは，対応関係のある WP 中で，54.52%と約半数を占める。次の例では Caxton の WP において MF の単一語が構成要素として保持されている：

(3) & took acqueyntaunce & amytye 49/32 < Et print grant amitié

(4) & shal to you obeye and serue 29/22 < et vous vueil servir

また，MF の単一語を構成要素として保持せず WP として翻訳された例は，次のようなものがある：

(5) Moder how is it that ye haue not kepte my chambre cloos and shytte
　　　　　　　　　　　　　　　　　　　　　　　　　　　　　　　　25/25-26
　　< Ma dame, comment avez tenuz mes choses et ma chambre fermee?

(6) Ryght dere & honourable syr and fader playse it you to wete that...
　　　　　　　　　　　　　　　　　　　　　　　　　　　　　　　　45/17-8
　　< Chier Pere, vueillés scavoir que...

上記の例から，MF の語を保持していない場合も，原典と意味の対応関係がないのではなく，MF 原典の語を意味的に相当する WP で訳していることが理解できる。

一方，MF 原典の WP が Caxton でも WP に訳されている例が全 199 例で，対応関係のある WP 中 43.93%である。ただし，このうち，構成要素2 語ともが完全に対応する例は 48 例，10.60%である：

(7) Also dere syr and fader I praye you & supplye that . . . 45/30
  < Et auxi, cher seigneur et pere, vous prie et supplie que . . .

(8) vyenne hath had so moche Ioye and so grete playsyr 48/24
  < vienne a eu si grant plaisir et grant joye

次に，もとの MF の WP の構成要素の一語が Caxton の WP において保持されている例は 55 例，全体の 12.14%を占める：

(9) many fayre scaffoldes for the ladyes and damoyselles to be sette on
  13/5-6
  < les chauffaus en quoy estoient toultes les dames et damoiselles

(10) the noblesse of the barons & knyghtes soo wel horsed and armed
  15/9-10
  < la noblesse des barons et chevaliers si bien armés et abillez

前者では，初期中英語の *Ancrene Riwle* で既に使用例が見られる *dame* を用いず，本来語の *lady* を用いている。また，後者の例の後半で，Caxton は *horsed* という語を導入し，元の WP の意味を変容させている。

さらに，MF の WP の構成要素を保持しないものの，Caxton でも WP に訳されている例は 96 例，21.19%になる：

(11) hath eten nothyng but brede and water onely 54/4
  < ne menge ne ne boyt si non du pain et de l'eaue

(12) for thynobedyence that ye doo to your fader and to your moder 55/8-9
  < pour la vengence de vostre pere et de vostre mere

(13) and prayed our lord bothe nyght & day 1/18-9
  < et pryoient nuyt et jour nostre Seigneur

これらの例から明らかなように，MF の WP の構成要素を保持しない場合も，それに意味的に相当する語で訳している。これら以外は MF の triplet を WP で訳した例などであるが，対応関係のある中では少数である。

2.2 Caxton による WP の簡略化と削除

Caxton が WP を追加するのが一般的な傾向であることは既に見た。しかし，Caxton が MF の *Paris* に現れる WP を 1 語に簡略化したり，あるいは全く削除する例も見られる。表 3 はそのような例をまとめたものである：

表 3：Caxton による WP の簡略化と削除

MF	Caxton	retention	#	Total
Correspondence				
WP	single wd	yes	31	70
WP	single wd	no	39	
Non-Correspondence				
WP	none		20	20
				90

まず，MF と対応があり，MF の WP が Caxton で単一語として訳された用例は 70 例で，一方，対応する表現が見当たらない削除例が 20 例である。後者に関しては，Caxton が意識的に削除したものか，あるいは，Caxton が使った MF テキストと我々のテキストの違いによるものなのか，にわかには同定し難い。

次に，MF の WP の構成要素の 1 語を用いて Caxton が訳している用例は 31 例である：

(14) I am moche sorouful and heuy of my cruel aduenture 45/18-9
 < moult triste suis et doulant de ma cruelle adventure et affliction

(15) none my3t make the pees betwyxte theym 10/35
 < nul n'y povoyt mectre remede ne paix

このような例のほかに，1 語の対応ながら，副詞形成接尾辞がフランス語の -*ment* から英語の -*ly* に変えられた例で，もし *humbly* の後に *and* を用いていれば WP になったであろう例として，次の例がある：

(16) humbly with grete shamefastnes 29/9
 < moult humblement et toult vergoigneulx

これらに加え，MF の構成要素を含まない用例が 39 例である：

(17) ye wote neuer to whom to gyue thankynges of so moche honour

18/33-34

< vous ne scavez a qui vous devés rendre graces ne mercy de tant de honneur

(18) After . . . paris kyssed vyenne 39/31 < puis le va baisier et embrasser

(19) wythoute yssue 1/17 < sans avoir filz ne fille

最初の 2 例は MF の WP 構成要素を含まないものの，英語の相当する語を充てている。第 2 例目では，MF では kiss に相当する同義語が存在するのに対して，英語では同義語が存在しないために，1 語で訳している。最後の例は，MF の表現の意を汲んで一語で言い直したものである。

2.3 Caxton による WP の改変

前のセクションで見てきたように，Caxton による WP の追加と保持と簡略化と削除の割合は次のようになる：

追加：保持：簡略化：削除＝ 247 (99+148)：199 (55+48+96)：70(31+39) : 20

これから明らかなように追加 (addition) が圧倒的に多いことが分かる。さらに，MF 原典に対応箇所がなく，Caxton では WP となっている例が 55 例にのぼり，このような例が，追加の度合いを強めていることは明らかである。これらの結果，セクション 2 の初めで指摘したように，Caxton での 1000 語あたりの WP の頻度は，MF 原典での約 1.5 倍になるのである。

3 Caxton の WP 追加の特徴 － 語源からの考察

Bornstein (1978) によれば，Chaucer は WP の追加などを通じて，"style clergial"（Burnley (1986) によれば正しくは curial style）という同時代の大陸の散文で用いられていた文体を，*Melibee* において洗練させた。中世

の修辞学で知られた WP の使用を，Chaucer と同じ目的で Caxton が用いたことは推測できるが，Chaucer と同じような反応をしたのであろうか。Chaucer の散文の WP においては，OF 系の構成要素が圧倒的に多い (cf. 谷 (forthcoming))。この点を確かめるため，また，Caxton の WP の翻訳方法を確認するために，本セクションでは，Caxton の WP を語源構成の観点から考察する。

3.1 対応関係があるものの，MF の構成要素を保持していない場合

既に見たように，対応関係があるものの MF の構成要素を保持しない場合，MF の構成要素をそれに相当する別の語で訳出していることを見た。より詳細に確認するため，1) MF の単一語が Caxton で対応なく WP として翻訳されている場合，2) MF の WP をその構成要素を保持せず Caxton で WP として翻訳している場合に分け，それぞれの語源構成を調査する。

それぞれを語源構成別で分けた結果を表 4，表 5 にまとめた。

表 4 : MF single wd → Caxton - WP
MF 構成語の保持のない用例の語源

OE	OE	57	38.51%
OE	OF	40	27.03%
OF	OE	31	20.95%
OF	OF	19	12.84%
Others		1	0.68 %
Total		148	

MF の WP の構成要素が保持されない場合は，表 4 と表 5 の結果から明らかなように，頻度順では OE+OE > OE+OF > OF+OE > OF+OF となる。その割合に違いはあるものの，どちらの場合も OE+OE の WP が圧倒的に使用されている。

表 5：MF WP → Caxton - WP
MF 構成語の保持のない用例の語源

OE	OE	60	60.61%
OE	OF	18	18.18%
OF	OE	13	13.13%
OF	OF	6	6.06%
Others		2	2.02%
Total		99	

3.2 MF と対応関係がない場合

MF のテキストに対応箇所がなく，Caxton が WP に翻訳している用例を，同じように語源別で分類し，その結果を表 6 にまとめた：

表 6：MF 対応箇所なく、Caxton で
WP の用例の語源

OE	OE	17	30.90%
OE	OF	14	25.45%
OF	OE	13	23.63%
OF	OF	11	20%
Total		55	

この場合も，セクション 3.1 の場合と同じように，語源別の割合の順は，

OE+OE > OE+OF > OF+OE > OF+OF となる。

しかし，MF と対応関係がある場合との違いは，OF+OF の割合が高いことである。既に指摘したが，対応箇所がない理由は，Caxton が使った MF テキストと我々が使用した B.N. Fr. 20044 とが異なっているからである。ただ，このような OF+OF の WP の割合の高さは，Caxton が使用した MF テキストに，WP に対応する単一語あるいは WP が存在していたのではないかと推測させる。このことは次のセクションで見る，MF の WP の構成要素を保持している場合の OF+OF の WP の割合の高さを勘案しての結果である。

3.3 MFの構成要素を保持している場合

次に，MFの単一語がそのまま保持され，CaxtonでWPとして訳されている用例を，語源構成から分類した結果を表7にまとめた。表7の結果から，MFの単一語をCaxtonのWPにおいて構成要素として保持される用例での語源構成を頻度順に並べると，OF+OF > OF+OE > OE+OFとなる。また，それぞれの語源構成のWPの数は，OF+OF ≒ (OF+OE) + (OE+OF)となる。すなわち，MFの語が1語保持される場合，もう一方の構成要素にOE系かOF系の語をCaxtonが結合させる可能性は，ほぼ五分五分となる。

表7 : MF single wd → Caxton - WP
MF構成語の保持のある用例の語源

OE	OF	19	19.79%
OF	OE	29	30.21%
OF	OF	47	48.96%
Others		1	1.04%
Total		96	

表7と表4表5を比較すると，CaxtonにおいてMF構成要素の保持される場合とされない場合では，WPの語源構成が全く異なることは明らかである。つまり，MF構成要素を保持しないCaxtonの用例ではOF+OFのWPの割合が10%でしかなく，MF構成要素を保持する場合のOF+OFのWPの割合は48.96%にも達するのである。

さらに，MFの単一語をCaxtonのWPで構成要素として使用するOF+OFのWP中，第一構成要素がMFの単一語に対応する例は28例，一方，第二構成要素がMFの単一語に対応する例は19例である。よって，目の前にある翻訳原典テキストに存在するMFの構成要素の後に，何か別のOF系の語を第二構成要素としてCaxtonが追加しWPを創出して文体を考え，翻訳していた傾向が強いことが分かる。

4　翻訳された WP の意味関係

次に Caxton がどのような意味関係の WP を創出したのかを検討するため，MF テキストの単一語を構成要素として Caxton が保持して WP に翻訳している用例を調査した。

WP の構成要素間の意味関係を，Kosenniemi (1968) は次のように分類する：1) nearly-synonymous, 2) associated with contiguity of meaning (=metonymic), 3) complementary or antonymous, 4) enumerative。この分類に基づいて，当該の WP を分類した結果を表 8 にまとめた。

表 8：構成語間の意味関係

Semantic Relations	
synonymous	79
metonymic	16
antonymous	0
enumerative	0
others	3
Total	98

この表の結果から明らかなのは，Caxton は同意的な WP を用いるのが最も通常であり，それに続いて metonymic な WP が多く，反意的あるいは列挙的な WP は *Paris* においては見られないことである。[3] なお，Koskenniemi の分類に収まらない 3 例は others として分類した。

以下，それぞれの意味関係の WP を検討する。

1) Synonymous な WP

　(19) how she was <u>pure and clene</u> of hyr body 41/11-2 < pure

　(20) she had not so <u>good vysage ne chere</u> as she had thenne 48/1-2

　　　　　　　　　　　　　　　　　　　　　　　　　< bonne chiere

　(21) he dyd doo sette these thre <u>Ioyaulx or Iewels</u> in the baners 13/26-7

　　　　　　　　　　　　　　　　　　　　　　　　　< joyaulx

2) Metonymic な WP

(22) & shal to you <u>obeye and serue</u> in al thynges 29/22 < servir

(23) knyghtes <u>wel armed & wel horsed</u> 15/6 < bien armez

1) の synonymous な WP については，(19) はヒロイン Vienne の描写で，彼女の *pure* さを強調するために同義の語を重ね WP としたと考えられる。なお，同じ WP がさらに 2 度使用され，それに対応する MF は *necte* と *necte et pure* である。(20) では，*chere* という語が多義であったため（*MED* は 7 つの意義が挙げている），比較的意義が単純な *visage* を重ねて，*chere* の意義を限定した可能性がある。(21) は同一語の異綴り語を含み，当時まだ固定化していなかった綴り字をより容易に理解できるよう，異綴り語を列挙した可能性がある。次に 2) の換喩的な WP については，(22)(23) とも，*serue* と *armed* と意味的に近接した *obeye* と *horsed* を用いたと考えられる。これらの用例は，Caxton の翻訳により，意味が変容しているが，より具体的なイメージを与えると考えられる。

次に意味関係を others とした用例 3 例は次のものである：

(24) to gyue to hym … <u>Ioye & excellence</u> 18/36-7 < joy exellenté

(25) vylayne & vassal that thou arte 32/26 < villain vassal

(26) parys answerd <u>humbly and wyth grete reuerence</u> 27/30-1

< a humble reverence

最初の 2 例は，MF で名詞と修飾する形容詞という構成の名詞句を分解して，両構成要素を名詞として並列させて WP とし，最後の例では，前置詞句中の名詞句を分解し，形容詞を副詞として，その構成要素を除いた前置詞句を *and* で並列させて WP を創出している。これらの構成要素の意味関係は，もともと修飾関係により成立していた意味関係を，*and* による並置で compositionality により再現した。

5 結論

　Caxton の *Paris* に生起する WP を，原典と対照して，翻訳技法という観点から考察した。まず，原典と比較しての WP の追加と保持と簡略化と削除の割合を示すと，追加：保持：簡略化：削除＝ 247：199：70：20 である。つまり，原典と比べると，Caxton は WP の簡略化や削減も行ったものの，追加の方が圧倒的多数である。また，このように追加された WP の構成要素間の意味関係は，同義的なものが圧倒的多数である。よって，MF 原典の単一語を WP にしたからと言って，翻訳テキストで意味的に違いは出ない。Caxton が WP を追加する際に，用例 (24)(25) で見たような MF の形容詞と名詞を分解して WP として創作したような手の込んだ例も少数はあるものの，通常 WP を作る手法は，翻訳原典にある語に別の語を後続させ *and* で結ぶもので，automatic と言っても過言ではない。従って，Trevisa の如く，原典の語の意味をカバーするためのような細やかな翻訳はしていないと言ってよかろう。

　次に，MF の単一語を Caxton が WP の構成要素として保持するかしないかで，創出される WP の語源構成が異なることも確認した。まず，MF 原典の単一語を保持しない場合は，OE+OE から成る WP の割合が高く，OF ＋ OF から成る WP の割合が低い。一方，MF 原典の元の語を保持して WP の構成要素とする場合は，OF+OF から成る WP の割合が高いことが分かった。つまり，Caxton は WP を用いるという当時の文体の流行に敏感で WP を用い，また，できるだけ OF 系の語を用いようとした。OF 系の語が翻訳原典にあった場合はそれに刺激され，もう一つの構成要素を OF とすることでより洗練された WP を創出したが，原典の語を保持しない場合，つまり原典の語に依らずに Caxton 自身が WP を創出した場合は，OF+OF の WP よりも素朴な OE 系の語を構成要素とする WP であることが多かったのである。

注

1 電子テキスト化とパラレルテキスト化は，それぞれ元関西外国語大学の西村公正氏と大阪大学の尾崎久男氏の尽力であることをここに記し，謝辞とする。
2 Leach(1952) のテキストのページ/行数で行い，当該の WP に下線を付す。
3 反意的および列挙的な意味関係の WP は *Paris* では生起せず，従来等閑視されてきたが，これらの意味関係の WP も重要である。これらの研究については，Imai (1997), Imai (2005), Imai (2007) を参照のこと。

参考文献

Babbi, Anna Maria (1992) *Paris et Vienne. Romanzo Cavalleresco del XV Secolo*. Milan: Franco Angeli.

Bennett, H. S. (1947) *Chaucer and the Fifteenth Century*. Oxford: Clarendon P.

Bornstein, Diane (1978) "Chaucer's *Tale of Melibee* as an Example of the Style Clergial." *Chaucer Review* 12, pp.236-54.

Burnley, J.D. (1986) "Curial Prose in England." *Speculum* 61, pp. 593-614.

Emerson, Oliver Farrer (1893) "Prof. Earle's Doctrine of Bilingualism." *Modern Language Notes*, Vol. 8, No. 7, pp. 202-206.

Geissman, Erwin William (1952) "The Style and Technique of Chaucer's Translations from French." PhD. Dissertation submitted to Yale U.

Imai, Mitsunori (1997) "Merism in *Havelok the Dane*.". In M. Imai (ed.) *Computer-Assisted Study of Early Modern English*. Osaka U.

Imai, Mitsunori (2005) "Catalogue and Repetition in *The Squyr of Lowe Degre*." In J. Fisiak & H. Kang (eds.) *Recent Trends in Medieval English Language and Literature in Honour of Young-Bae Park* Vol.1 Seoul: Thaehaksa, pp.133-46.

Imai, Mitsunori (2007) "Enumeration in Middle English Metrical Romance." In Tanaka, Kenji, Michiyasu Shishido, and Shigeo Uematsu (eds.) *22 Essays in English Studies: Language, Literature, and Education*. Tokyo: Shohakusha, pp.3-21.

Kaltenbacher, Robert (1904) "Der altfranzoesische Roman Paris et Vienne." *Romanisch Forschungen*, xv, pp.321-688z

Koskenniemi, Inna (1968) *Repetitive Word Pairs in Old and Early Middle English Prose*. Turku: Turun Yliopisto.

Leach, MacEdward (ed.) (1957) *Paris and Vienne*. EETS. OS.234.

Leisi, Ernst (1947) *Die tautologische Wortpaare in Caxton's "Eneydos."* Zürich and New York: Hafner

Machan, Tim William (1985) *Techniques of Translation: Chaucer's Boece.* Norman, Okla: Pilgrim Books.

Mueller, Janel M. (1984) *The Native Tongue and the Word: Developments in English Prose Style, 1380-1580.* Chicago & London: U of Chicago P.

Nakao, Yoshiyuki & Midori Matsutani (1996) "Descriptive Notes on Paired Words in the Language of Caxton's Own Prose." *Bulletin of the Faculty of Education*, Yamaguchi University 46 (1), pp.83-111.

Waldron, Ronald (2001) "Doublets in the Translation Techniques of John Trevisa." In Christian J. Kay and Louise M. Sylvester (eds.), *Lexis and Texts in Early English: Studies Presented to Jane Roberts.* Amsterdam: Rodopi, pp.269-292.

伊藤正義訳 (1995)『ウイリアム・キャクストン:イソップ寓話集』東京: 岩波ブックサービスセンター.

尾崎久男 (2006)「キャクストン訳『パリスとヴィエンナ』に見られる慣用対句 — and/or/ne で結ばれた同義反復表現を中心に—」『ことばと反復 3』(言語文化共同研究プロジェクト 2005) pp.23-30.

谷明信 (Forthcoming)「Chaucer の散文作品におけるワードペア使用」

Chaucer の言語とメトニミー
― *Troilus and Criseyde* の場合 ―

中尾　佳行

1　はじめに

　近年著しく発達してきた認知言語学は，従来文学的な技巧として捉えられていたメタファー (metaphor) とメトニミー (metonymy) を，日常言語の創出にも本質的に関与する人間の根源的な推論システムとして位置付けた。言う迄もないが，メタファーは類似性による意味創出の原理，メトニミーは近接性（全体と部分，器と中身，原因と結果の関係等）によるものである。Lakoff and Johnson (1980: 39) は，これら二つは我々の言語のみならず，思考，態度，行動をも規定する，と述べている。文学作品（特に詩）においては従来メタファーが中心的に扱われてきたが，メトニミーに対しても等分の評価を促しことは注目に値する。メトニミーを意識して文学作品を読み返してみると，今まで意識しなかった要素が意識され，それらが強く因果関係をなしてリンクするように思える。Chaucer の *Troilus and Criseyde* はまさにそのような作品である。本作品は，包囲されたトロイが起点となり，住人である主人公，その主人公が住む家，そして彼・彼女が活動する部屋，更には彼らの心の中，とまるで中国のからくり箱のように，器と中身の関係がベースとなって展開している。Troilus と Criseyde を結び付けようとする Pandarus は，器の中に納めようとする仕掛け人で，また二人の愛の破綻は，この器からの脱却である。このような器（囲い）の設定は，人物の視点を規定し，それはまた言語の意味の一つの層を生み

出してもいる。本論は，*Troilus and Criseyde* において，メトニミーがどのように作用し，作品の言語をいかに意味深いものにしているか，その一端を捉えてみたい。

2 先行研究

Chaucer におけるメトニミーの重要性は，早くは Brewer (1974) によって指摘された。Jakobson (1960) による人間の根源的な推論システムとしてのメタファーとメトニミーに注目し，Chaucer 研究で等閑視されてきたメトニミーに光を当てた研究である。The Clerk's Tale に繰り返し出る形容詞 sad を取り上げ，この語のコロケーションとその語の中の意味関係に着目している。*Troilus and Criseyde* は考察の対象とはなっていない。地村 (1987) は，*Troilus and Criseyde* の「場所」を表わす語を物語の流れに沿って取り上げている。主人公の愛の進展と関連付け，その文脈的な意味を記述しているが，メトニミーの効果には触れていない。Holley (1990) は，Chaucer の物語が人物の視力の制限を伴って，つまり一定の枠組み（frame）を介して展開していることを検証した。'optical' な観点（目の動き，認知の動き）からの考察で，*Troilus and Criseyde* では，囲われ狭められた空間が人物の目の動きを規定することを論じている。これは器と中身，原因・結果の関係というメトニミーの思考に深く係わるもので，極めて示唆性に富むものである。しかし Holley は，当該観点の背後にあると考えられるメトニミーの効力には言及していない。中尾 (2004) は，Chaucer の曖昧性に貢献する意味創出の重要な原理として，メトニミーを取り上げた。しかしそれは言語の意味記述に留まった。メトニミーの観点から，テクストのマクロ構造，ミクロ構造，そして言語特性の細部に至るまで，今尚再検討の余地があるように思える。

3 方法論 ——メトニミーの叙述と二重プリズム構造——

　Lakoff and Johnson (1980: 39) が言うように，メトニミーは我々の言語だけでなく，思考，態度，行動を背後で深く規定するものである。本論はこの考え方を援用し，メトニミーの作用をまず作品の全体像に及ぶと考えられるマクロ構造，即ち，テーマ，プロット，人物造型の観点から考察する。次いでテクストのミクロ構造，特に首尾一貫性 (coherence) の観点から，そして最後に言語構造（統語，語，音）の観点から考察する。説明の都合上分けて記述し，オーヴァーラップする場合はそれぞれの観点を明示して記述したい。

　メトニミーは，中尾 (2004) が提案した曖昧性を記述する枠組み，二重プリズム構造に位置付けると，「第一プリズム」である作家の視点を色付けるものである。言論の自由が十分に保障されていない時代において，しかも宮廷人を前に，Chaucer はメッセージをいつも露骨に示せるわけではない。人物，語り手，更には作品の全体を統治する作者の立場を介して語っている。この「第一プリズム」は「現象」を自分の視点から，あるいは「第二プリズム」である読者の反応を想定しながら，認識し，「表現」を通して「第二プリズム」に提示する。この読者は人物に，語り手に，あるいは作者に対して反応する。中尾 (2004) は，柔軟に複数の読者間を動くことができる読者を，視点の転換装置，'I' として原理的に設定した。この 'I' を動かしながら，読みを生成するのである。

　メトニミーは，*Troilus and Criseyde* においては，人物が「現象」を見る枠を定め，また逆に彼・彼女がその枠から脱却するとどうなるかを，方向付けている。また同時的にその枠の外から批判的に見る視点も許していて，その枠をどのように作用させるかは，最終的には「第二プリズム」の読者に委ねられている。

　以下では「第一プリズム」と「第二プリズム」を対峙させながら，メトニミーの効用を捉えてみたい。

4 メトニミーとテクストのマクロ構造

メトニミーは，*Troilus and Criseyde* のマクロ構造，即ち，テーマ，プロット，人物造型の基盤を作り上げている。第一プリズムの作家は作品を構想し，第二プリズムの読者は彼の表現を通して，メッセジを読み解いていく。メトニミーは，第一プリズムと第二プリズムを繋ぐ強力な推論法である。

4.1 テーマ

本作品のテーマは愛であると言っても異論はなかろう。しかし，愛は，宮廷恋愛，宗教的な愛，そして生身の人間の自然愛，と綾をなして微妙に重なり合う。宮廷恋愛は，Lewis (1936) が言ったように，愛の宗教，秘密，不倫，そして礼節という基本特徴を持つ。この概念はメトニミーの器，狭められた器の形成に貢献している。愛の宗教は，愛している相手を変えないという愛の束縛があり，また秘密，不倫——本作品では王子で独身の騎士 Troilus と寡婦で宮廷貴婦人の Criseyde の恋——は，恋の展開に密室性が伴う。つまり二人は秘密の箱の中での愛を貫こうとしているわけである。Troilus は Criseyde への愛を貫くとしても，彼女はこの世の肉を持った生身の存在である。生身の人間が動くのは古今東西変わらぬ事実である。この箱は絶えずそれを破ろうとする力に曝されているのである。Criseyde がトロイの囲い（箱）から出てギリシャ陣営に行くと，狭い箱から開放されたように，生身の人間の愛，愛の流動性が顕現する。また物語の最後でキリスト教的な愛，変わらないものへの愛の重要性が示されるが，それはこの世においてではなく，Troilus がこの世の囲い（箱）を脱却した死後の世界での認識である ('And dampned al oure werk that foloweth so / The blynde lust, the which that may nat laste,' Tr 5.1823-4)。[1]

4.2 プロット

　本作品のプロットは，囲いの中とそれからの脱却のドラマである。この物語は，第1巻において，トロイがギリシャ軍に包囲されている状況で始まる ('Assegeden' Tr 1.60)。この囲いがその後の登場人物の行動を強く縛ってしまう。彼らはこの囲いの中を行ったり来たりするわけであるが，Pandarus は Troilus と Criseyde の愛を具現するために，企画・立案・実行する創造者の役割を担う ('For everi wight that hath an hous to founde ... sende his hertes line out fro withinne' Tr 1.1065-8)。第2巻において，彼の計画通り二人の愛は徐々に進展し，第3巻においては大きく加速する。二人の愛を実行する場所は，決まって家の中，更に言えば，ベッドルームの中である。家，部屋，窓，床の開き戸等，建物及びその一部を表わす語が続く (狭められた器のイメージは巻を通して現れている ――'in his chambre' Tr. 1.547, 'muwe' Tr 1.381, 'closet' Tr 2. 599, 'a litel wyndow in a stewe' Tr 3.601, 'this secre trappe-dore' Tr 3.759, 'out of the chaumbre' Tr 4. 1701, etc.)。第3巻において愛はクライマックスに達するが，それは最も狭い場所，ベッドの上で行われる ('And with that word he gan undon a trappe, / And Troilus he brought in by the lappe.' Tr 3.741-2; 'But certeyn, at the laste, / For this or that, he into bed hym caste,' Tr 3.1096-7)。第4巻では Criseyde と捕虜の交換が決められ，第5巻ではトロイの囲いを出て彼女はギリシャ陣営に送られる。彼女はギリシャの武将，Diomede の執拗な求愛に屈する。彼女は狭い囲いの中から開放され，この世の中で流れに逆らわないで生き続ける。Troilus は彼女の裏切りを知った後でも愛し続け，ひたすら恋敵を打とうと戦う。しかし，願いかなわず Achilles に殺されてしまう。彼は死後この世の呪縛から開放され，第8天界 ('the eighthe spere' Tr 5.1809) に登る。そこから地上を見て流動的なものにとらわれ迷う人間の無知を笑う。Criseyde が水平移動で囲いを越え，この世に留まるとすると，Troilus は垂直移動でこの世の囲いを越え，天上に向かうのである。しかし，Troilus の天上への上昇は，真に心を向けるべき（キリスト教の）神に比し，第8天界に段階付けられている (Cf. Dante, *Divinia Comedia: Paradiso*)。詩人は，

神をどんな境界によっても囲まれない，その囲いの外（'uncircumsript, and al maist circumscrive' Tr 5.1865）に位置付けている。かくしてプロットは，囲いの中に入っているものが，更に小さな囲いの中に入り，最小の囲いでのクラマックスを契機に，囲いから開放されていくように展開している。器とその中身のメトニミーが持続的・発展的に作用し，expanded metonymy とでも称せる効果を挙げている。

4.3 人物造型

登場人物は，囲いの中に閉じ込められた形で動いていく。囲いの中に閉じ込められると，視野も狭められてくる。ここには器と中身，原因・結果のメトニミーが作用している。テーマで述べたように，宮廷恋愛は秘密や秘め事が伴い，またプロットで述べたように，クライマックスに至っては最も狭いところ，ベッドで達成される。しかしそのクライマックスがいかに脆いものであるかはすぐにも知らされる。囲いはその中に住む者の視点を決定付けていく。Troilus は寺院で Criseyde を見たことで，彼女に一目ぼれし（'His eye percede, and so depe it wente, / Til on Criseyde it smot, and ther it stente.' Tr 1.272-3），彼女が神か人間かわからなくなる（'But wheither goddesse or womman, iwis, / She be, I not, which that ye do me serve; ' Tr 1.425-6）。神を祭る寺院において，生身の人間を神のように捉えようとすることはアイロニカルである。彼は愛を徐々に深め，哲学的とも言える段階に達するが，生身の人間である動くものを動かないように信じ込むのには無理がある。このことに気付くのは，彼が死後この地上のしがらみを越え，第8天界に昇ってからのことである。Pandarus は，Troilus と Criseyde の 'go-between' として精力的に動くが，それは彼が作る囲いの中での達成であり，安定である。プロットで述べたように，二人の愛は彼の企画通りに，彼の家の中で，寝室の中で，ベッドの上で実現する。二人の関係が彼の囲いの中に納まらないと，彼は沈黙するしかないのである（'As stille as ston; a word ne kowde he seye.' Tr 5.1729）。Criseyde はトロイの囲いの中では，宮廷貴婦人としての威厳を示し，優しさを示し，Troilus に対し誠実に

振舞うが，彼女がトロイの囲いを出ることになると，同時に彼女の動きも大きくなる。囲いの中の制約から解き放たれるのである ('For bothe Troilus and Troie town / Shal knotteles thorughout hire herte slide;' Tr 5.768-9)。

以上，*Troilus and Criseyde* のマクロ構造において，囲いと中身というメトニミーが強く作用し，囲い故の束縛とそれからの脱却が第一プリズムの思考・態度を決定付けていることを考察した。

5　メトニミーとテクストのミクロ構造

文を超えた範囲ではあるが，テクスト全体までは射程に入れていない比較的小さい談話構造をミクロ構造と呼ぶことにする。パラグラフ（連）とパラグラフ（連），文と文の意味的な関連性，即ち，首尾一貫性 (coherence) を問題にしてみたい。ここでは *Troilus and Criseyde* の中で最も重要な転換点，囲いから出た Criseyde がどのように振舞うかに注目してみよう。第5巻，Criseyde が Diomede の求愛を受け入れる直前の場面で，語り手はこの行為に係わる3人物の性格を集約している。

> This Diomede, as bokes us declare,
> Was in his nedes prest and corageous,
> With sterne vois and myghty lymes square,
> Hardy, testif, strong, and chivalrous
> 　　　　. . .
> Criseyde mene was of hire stature;
> Therto of shap, of face, and ek of cheere,
> Ther myghte ben no fairer creature.
> 　　　　. . .
> And, save hire browes joyneden yfeere,
> Ther nas no lak, in aught I kan espien.
> 　　　　. .
> She sobre was, ek symple, and wys withal,
> The best ynorisshed ek that myghte be,
> And goodly of hire speche in general,
> Charitable, estatlich, lusty, fre;
> Ne nevere mo ne lakked hire pite;

> Tendre-herted, slydynge of corage;
> But trewely, I kan nat telle hire age.
>
> And Troilus wel woxen was in highte,
> And complet formed by proporcioun
> So wel that kynde it nought amenden myghte;
> Yong, fressh, strong, and hardy as lyoun;
> Trewe as stiel in ech condicioun;
> Oon of the beste entecched creature
> That is or shal whil that the world may dure.
>
> . . .
>
> His herte ay with the first and with the beste
> Stood paregal, to durre don that hym leste.　Tr 5.799-840

　原典，*Il Filostrato* ではこのような挿入はなく，Cressida がストレートに Diomeda に屈するように書かれている (*Filostrato* 6.8.6-8)。しかし，Chaucer の場合 Criseyde が Diomede を受け入れる一連の行為はこの引用の後，Tr 5.841 から徐々に始まっていく。彼女はトロイの囲いの外に出てはいるが，語り手は Criseyde の裏切り行為に対し一種の間（ま）を与えている。この間（ま）は近接性の作用（Diomede の求愛——＞ Criseyde の受け入れ）を抑制している。これは類似性に依拠するメタファーと連動してもいる。Criseyde が Diomede に屈するには，寄せ付けまいとする空間的な距離があり，それは（屈する迄の）時間的な距離でもあり，またそれは彼女の彼に対する心理的な距離でもある。ここには彼女の裏切りをストレートに言いたくない第一プリズム，詩人の深い同情があるようにみえる。一見脱線ともみえる Chaucer の挿入は，出来事の流れに密接に係わり，深い心理的な陰影を醸し出しているように思える。

　連と連の関係を見てみよう。最初の 1 連が Diomede に，次の 3 連が Criseyde に，そして最後の 2 連が Troilus に当てられている。Schaar (1967) が指摘するように，Criseyde は恋のライバル，Diomede と Troilus の間に，両者の引き合いの間に入れられている。この順序は牽引関係を写すメタファーであり，また彼女がいずれに強く引かれるかは，メトニミーの作用の強弱でもある。

この連の中身を見てみよう。それぞれの人物において，外面描写 (effictio) と内面描写 (notatio) が併置され，性格を特徴付けている。この外面描写と内面描写は，相互に予測的である。外にあるものが内側に，内側にあるものが外に，というのは中世の性格描写のスキーマである。外面と内面の包含関係はメトニミー，肉体的意味と心理的意味の類似関係はメタファーである。ここでの性格付けは，因果関係をなして以後の行動を導く——Diomede の執拗な Criseyde への求愛，彼女の眼前のものを無碍に否定できない哀れみの心，彼女の移ろい，Troilus の変わらない彼女への愛，それ故の悲劇的な死。彼女は，捕虜交換で送られたギリシャ陣営において，Troilus（精神的存在）と Diomede（肉体的存在）の間で牽引関係に置かれる。この牽引関係はメトニミーの発展的使用である。

6 メトニミーと言語構造

6.1 統語法

Jakobson (1960) は，統合軸 (syntagm) は近接性が作用し，系列軸 (paradigm) は類似性が作用することを指摘している。統語法は近接性によって関係付けられている。Criseyde はトロイの囲いから出ていくことで，彼女の心の動きが一層活発になる。Diomede の執拗な求愛を Criseyde は遂に受け入れる。彼女は自然の流れに逆らわない形で対応していく (Tr 5.1051-85)。自分の名誉の喪失を憂い，他にどうしようもないことから，せめて Diomede に忠義を尽くそう，と前向きに考える。そして泣くことで，罪の浄化を行い，以後自己回復する。Troilus を哀れんだり，距離を置いたり，自分の罪を責めたり，また言い訳したりして，最終的には，運命の流れと一体になる，解脱の状態に身を置く。下記の引用は彼女の独白の最終部である。

> And certes yow ne haten shal I nevere;
> And frendes love, that shal ye han of me,
> And my good word, al sholde I lyven evere.
> And trewely I wolde sory be
> For to seen yow in adversitee;

> And gilteles, I woot wel, I yow leve.
> But al shal passe; and thus take I my leve." Tr 5.1079-85

gilteles は，文頭位置に置かれ，それが関係すると思われる代名詞 I または yow から引き離されている。両者をどのように関係付けるかは，読者に委ねられている。「あなたは罪を犯していないのに，私はあなたとお別れです」，あるいは「あなたとお別れするけど，私は悪くはない」，更には「このようにお別れするけれど，あなたは悪くはない，でも私も悪くはない」。転換装置の読者 'I' は，視点を動かしながら二様，三様に近接関係の可能性を探っていく。このような Criseyde の流動的な統語法は，既に 'Tendre-herted, slydynge of corage;' (Tr 5.825) にも見てきている。語り手は二つの句の間に接続詞を入れてはいない。どのように近接関係を作るかは，読者の再建に委ねられている。「心が柔らかいが故に，心が移ろう」あるいは「心は柔らかく優しいが，心変わりしてしまう」。

このような流動的な統語法は，第二プリズムに働きかけるメトニミーの創造的な使用である。

6.2 語

箱と中身の拡充的な使用（トロイの囲い，Pandarus の家，彼の家の寝室，ベッド等）は，メトニミーに依拠した語と語のネットワークである。これについては 4．2 のプロットで示した。本節では言説への視点の介入，それ故の意味付け，そして語の中の意味関係に焦点を置いて考察したい。

Criseyde はトロイの囲いの中，彼女の家にいて，彼女の家の窓枠越しに，Troilus の凱旋を目にする。

> So lik a man of armes and a knyght
> He was to seen, fulfiled of heigh prowesse,
> For bothe he hadde a body and a myght
> To don that thing, as wel as hardynesse;
> And ek to seen hym in his gere hym dresse,
> So fressh, so yong, so weldy semed he,
> It was an heven upon hym for to see. Tr 2. 631-7

語り手の言説だが，近代小説家が好んで用いた自由間接話法に似ている。²
ここには Criseyde 個人の視点が深く介入している。Troilus の軍人としての
勇ましさ，溌剌とした姿，精力みなぎった男っぽさが彼女の目に飛び込ん
でくる。Troilus 同様生身の人間を動かすのは目である。Holley (1990: 76)
を参照すると，Criseyde は眼前の光景を窓枠という限られた範囲の中での
み見ており，遠くまで見通す眼力には欠けている。つまりこれから先二人
の関係がどのようになるかは皆目見当もつかないのである。彼女は第5巻
で Troilus との約束（一旦ギリシャ側に行って，その後トロイに帰ってく
るという約束）が果たせず，未来が読めなかったと述懐する。'Prudence'
(Tr 5.744) の欠如を認識する。読者が彼女の視点，女性としての視点を押
し進めてみると，語は微妙な意味の広がりをみせる。thing (Tr 2.634) は何
でも含む上位語であるが，その中身は何であろうか。fressh (Tr. 2.636) や
weldy (Tr 2.636) が彼女の評価だとすると，どのような行為を想定してい
るのだろうか (OED s.v. wieldly 'capable of wielding one's body or limbs')。
これらの語は一種の double entendre で性的な意味を伏せているようにも
読み取れる。'It was an heven upon hym for to see.' (Tr 2.637) の heven はど
のような意味であろうか。語り手が喜びを表わす時の定型句 (Cf. Tr 2.826,
Tr 3.1742) なのか，それとも Criseyde が Troilus を見て，エクスタシーに
至ることを示しているのだろうか (MED s.v. heven は 1b (b) a supremely
blissful experience で引用している)。heven は *Troilus and Criseyde* におい
て繰り返し現れ，話者の視点に応じて意味が推移している (Tr 3.8, Tr 3.618,
Tr 3.1745, Tr 4.1396, Tr 5.1819, Tr 5.1825, Tr 5.1844)。世俗的な「エクスタ
シー」は，宗教的な「天上の至福」(Tr 5.1844) とは好対照をなしている。

　トロイの囲いの外に出た Criseyde は，6．1 で述べたように，囲いの
中で束縛されるのではなく，心は滑るように動いていく。'Tendre-herted,
slydynge of corage;' (Tr 5.825)。この corage を，MED は 1. (a) The heart as
the seat of emotions, affection, attitudes, and volition; heart, spirit; disposition,
temperament の意味で捉え，引用している。諸々の感情が宿る器として捉
えているが，近接性を作用させて器の中身に焦点を当てることも可能で

ある。MED 2 (a) Inclination, desire; (b) sexual desire あるいは 3. (a) Valor, courage がそれである。語り手は，ここでは作者の意図と言ってもよいかもしれないが，Criseyde の後の行動を想定して，背後にこれらの意味を伏せた可能性がある。読者 'I' はここでも Criseyde の視点を想定しながら，意味の間を動くのである。

以上のように，語り手の言語に人物の視点が入り，その視点にかざして語の意味付けが行われている。thing, weldy あるいは corage は，包含関係ないし因果関係に依拠して新たな意味を生成している。言語は誰の目にも同じではなく，固有の視点が設定され，その視点を通して語が意味付けられ，そして語の中の意味関係（近接関係）が活性化する。ここでもメトニミーが積極的に用いられている。

6.3 音

ここでは Leech (1969) が言う脚韻の 'chiming' 効果に注目してみよう。響きあう 2 語には，器と中身，あるいは原因と結果の因果関係が読み取れる。*Troilus and Criseyde* に反復する脚韻，Troie-joie（31 回）は，そのようなメトニミー効果を端的に示すものである。但し，この関連性はトロイの囲いの中では肯定的・積極的な価値を持つが，Criseyde がトロイの囲いを出て，ギリシャ陣営に行ってからは，否定的ないしアイロニカルな陰影を深めている。第 2 巻の Troilus の凱旋場面では，Troie-joie の脚韻は肯定的に響いている (Tr 2.643-4)。しかし，Criseyde がトロイの囲いから出て，二人の愛が破綻する段階では，否定的に響いている (Tr 5.729-31)。この脚韻ペアについては，既に Masui (1964: 270-1, 278-80) の研究があり，'Thus, Troy is, by the principle of proximity, equated with joy.' と指摘している。Masui はトロイと喜びを等価（類似性）に捉えているが，私はメトニミーの観点から見直してみた。

メトニミーの効果のある他の脚韻ペアには，trouthe (untrouthe も含む) – routhe（17 回），sterve – serve（12 回），そして place – grace（16 回）がある。いずれも肯定的・否定的場面にまたがって使用されている。特に

place – grace は，場所と中身を直接的に示すもので，メトニミーの効果が明白である。第3巻において，トロイの囲いの中，誰も見ていない密室でいよいよ Troilus と Criseyde は愛のクライマックスを遂げようとしている (Tr 3. 921-4)。他方，Criseyde はギリシャ陣営に捕虜交換で行ってしまい，Troilus は空しく彼女と過ごした場所とそこでの彼女の優しさを思い出すばかりである (Tr 5.580-1)。(脚韻ペアの 'chiming' 効果については，中尾 (2004) の第 13 章を参照のこと。)

7　おわりに

以上，メトニミーの観点から，*Troilus and Criseyde* のテクストのマクロ構造，ミクロ構造，そして言語表現を見直してみた。メトニミーの推論特徴，器と中身，また原因・結果の関係付けが，第一プリズムである作家の思考・態度から言語の細部に至るまでを強く方向付け，それは第二プリズムである読者に対して表現を読み解く大きな基盤となることを検証した。この度の研究はメトニミーが作用していると考えられるサンプルを示したに過ぎない。また今までの研究を単に再解釈したところもある。今後の研究に待たれるのは，メトニミーの観点からの新しい言語事実の発掘であり，体系的・網羅的な研究の推進である。これは将来の課題である。

注

1　Chaucer テクストからの引用及び作品の略記は Benson (1987) による。
2　Leech and Short (1981: 324) を参照。

参考文献

Benson, L. D. (ed.) (1987) *Riverside Chaucer. Third Edition Based on The Works of Geoffrey Chaucer Edited by F. N. Robinson.* Boston: Houghton Mifflin Company.

Brewer, D. S. (1974) "Some Metonymic Relationships in Chaucer's Poetry." *POETICA* 1: 1-20.

Griffin, N. E. and A. B. Myrick. (eds. & trs.) (1978) *The Filostrato of Giovanni Boccaccio.* New York: Octagon Books.

Holley, L. T. (1990) *Chaucer's Measuring Eye.* Houston, Texas: Rice University Press.

Jakobson, R. (1960) "Closing Statement: Linguistics and Poetics." In T. A. Sebeok (ed.), *Style in Language.* Cambridge, Massachusetts: The M.I.T. Press, pp. 350-7.

地村彰之. (1987)「Chaucer の館の表現」「白羊宮叢書」編集委員会編『人の家・神の家』京都 : あぽろん社, pp. 5-43.

Lakoff, G. and M. Johnson. (1980) *Metaphors We Live By.* Chicago and London: The Univesity of Chicago Press.

Leech, G. and M. Short. (1981) *Style in Fiction.* London: Longman.

Masui, M. (1964) *The Structure of Chaucer's Rime Words — An Exploration into the Poetic Language of Chaucer.* Tokyo: Kenkyusha.

中尾佳行. (2004)『Chaucer の曖昧性の構造』東京 : 松柏社.

Schaar, C. (1967) *The Golden Mirror.* Lund: C.W.K. GLEERUP.

Sinclair, John D. (ed.) (1975) *The Divine Comedy of Dante Alighieri (1: Inferno, 2: Purgatorio, 3: Paradiso).* London, Oxford, New York: Oxford University Press.

PPCME2, PPCEME に見る強意副詞*

西村 秀夫

1 はじめに

　本稿では，一般に Helsinki Corpus (HC) の拡大版と位置づけられることの多い Penn-Helsinki Parsed Corpus of Middle English 2nd edition (PPCME2), Penn-Helsinki Parsed Corpus of Early Modern English (PPCEME) における強意副詞 full, right, very の出現状況を報告する。調査対象は後期中英語期以降 (1350-) のファイルである。[1] HC を対象に同様の調査を行った西村 (1994) では，強意副詞のような周辺的な文法現象を扱う場合，HC の語数（約 157 万語）では必ずしも十分ではないことを指摘したが，約 3 倍の規模に拡大した PPCME2, PPCEME ではどのような結果が得られるのか興味あるところである。

2 HC 以後の通時的英語コーパス

　1991 年の公開当初，HC の編者たちは 5 年をめどに拡大改訂版を出すとしていたが，[2] 結局今日に至るまで彼ら自身の手になる改訂版が編纂されることはなかった。しかしながら HC を補完する動きのひとつとして，HC のファイルを元に語数を拡大し，品詞標識・構文解析を施したコーパスの編纂が進められてきている。その概要を，塚本 (2006: 177) が掲げる表に一部修正を加えて以下に示す。

表 1　品詞標識・構文解析コーパス

コーパス名	概略
The York-Helsinki Parsed Corpus of Old English Poetry (York Poetry)	Helsinki Corpus 古英語時代の詩の一部 71,490 語
The York-Toronto-Helsinki Parsed Corpus of Old English Prose (YCOE)	古英語散文約 150 万語
The Brooklyn-Geneva-Amsterdam-Helsinki Parsed Corpus of Old English (Brooklyn Corpus)	Helsinki Corpus 古英語時代の散文の一部 106,210 語
The first edition of the Penn-Helsinki Parsed Corpus of Middle English (PPCME1)	中英語時代散文 510,000 語
The second edition of the Penn-Helsinki Parsed Corpus of Middle English (PPCME2)	Helsinki Corpus 中英語時代の散文を中心に 120 万語弱
The Penn-Helsinki Parsed Corpus of Early Modern English (PPCEME)	初期近代英語時代の約 180 万語
The Penn Parsed Corpus of Modern British English (1700-1914)	1700 年から 1914 年までの 200 万語（編纂中）
The Parsed Corpus of Early English Correspondence (PCEEC)	220 万語私信（2006 年公開）

　これらのうち，YCOE（150 万語），PPCME2（120 万語），PPCEME（180 万語）を合わせると約 450 万語で，HC 本体の約 3 倍の規模となることから「現行版 HC が抱える語数（規模）の問題はかなり解消される」（齊藤他編 (2005: 169)）と期待は大きいのであるが，それぞれのコーパスがどのようなものか十分理解されているとは言えないのが実情ではないか。

3　PPCME2, PPCEME の概要

3.1　PPCME2

　PPCME2 は散文テキストによるコーパス編纂を基本方針とするため，HC に含まれていた韻文テキストは The Ormulum (M1) を除いてすべて削除されている。また散文テキストでも，HC が設定するテキストタイプで言えば，Law, Document, Preface/Epilogue, Proceeding, Letter に含まれるテキストがすべて省かれている。このため，HC の基本的なフォーマットを踏襲

するPPCMEと関連付けた通時的研究が困難になってしまった。同じHCの拡大版と言っても，PPCME2とPPCMEはまったく異質なコーパスと考えるべきである。

PPCME2で新たに加えられたテキストは，Ancrene Wisseに取って代わるAncrene Riwle (M1 63,790語 Religious treatise), Kentish Homilies (M1 4,048語 Homily), Mirror of Edmund (Vernon MS)(M3 12,843語 Religious treatise), Mirror of Edmund (Thornton MS) (M4 13,949語 Religious treatise), Richard Rolle's Epistles (M4 17,960語 Religious treatise)の5テキストで，計112,590語である。

HCからそのまま引き継がれたファイルの一部は50,000語を越えるサイズにまで拡張されている。塚本(2006: 181)によれば，HCの元ファイルの5倍以上になっているのが14テキスト，そのうちの2テキストは10倍を超えるサイズになっている。筆者の調査によれば，HCとPPCME2に共通する49テキストの語数はHCが331,600語，PPCME2が1,043,375語となり，増加率は約315%である。

3.2 PPCME

PPCMEの特徴については，齊藤(2006b: 7)が次のように簡潔にまとめている。

> 周知のように，The Penn-Helsinki Parsed Corpus of Early Modern English (PPCME) は，Pennsylvania大学のチームがHelsinki CorpusのEModEの部分（約60万語）を3倍（約180万語）に拡張したもので，このPPCMEは(1) Helsinki, (2) Penn1, (3) Penn2の3つのsubcorpus（各約60万語）より構成されている。(1)はHelsinki CorpusのEModEの部分を使い，(2)と(3)はPennsylvania大学側がHelsinki Corpusを補足した部分であり，原則的にはHelsinki Corpusと同じ資料から未採録部分を採り，不足分は新たな資料から補足している。時代区分やテキストジャンルもHelsinki Corpusをそのまま踏襲している。

それぞれのsubcorpusについて，時代区分ごとの総語数を表2に掲げる（マニュアルの誤りは修正済み）。

表2　PPCEME の語数[3]

	HC	Penn1	Penn2	Total
E1	195,546	195,226	185,423	576,195
E2	197,742	223,064	230,234	651,040
E3	179,477	197,908	189,394	566,779
Total	572,765	616,198	605,051	1,794,014

4　PPCME2, PPCEME に見る full, right, very

西村 (1994) の元になった，HC の M3 以降における full, right, very の出現状況を表3に示す。

表3　HC における full, right, very（用例数と 10,000 語あたりの生起率，以下同）

	full			right			very		
	+Adj	+Adv	計	+Adj	+Adv	計	+Adj	+Adv	計
M3	153	101	254	51	23	74	1	0	1
	8.30	5.48	13.78	2.77	1.25	4.02	0.05	0.00	0.05
M4	104	98	202	118	70	188	20	1	21
	4.86	4.58	9.44	5.52	3.27	8.79	0.94	0.05	0.99
E1	7	7	14	44	18	62	127	33	160
	0.36	0.36	0.72	2.25	0.92	3.17	6.49	1.69	8.18
E2	0	1	1	13	0	13	177	80	257
	0.00	0.05	0.05	0.66	0.00	0.66	8.95	4.05	13.00
E3	0	0	0	8	1	9	291	125	416
	0.00	0.00	0.00	0.45	0.06	0.50	16.21	6.96	23.18

この結果から，西村 (1994: 9) では，1) 強意副詞の出現率が全般に低いこと，2) M4 で full が減少傾向にあるのに対し，right が勢力を伸ばし，また very の例がわずかながら見られ始めたこと，3) E1 で full が激減，right も減少傾向にあるのに対し，very の頻度が急増したこと，4) very の増加，

その反動として full, right の衰退が E2 以降いっそう顕著になったことを指摘し，Mustanoja (1960) の "*Full* is still quite common in the 16th century... (320)" および "In the 15th century *very* is not uncommon as an intensifying adverb of degree. (372)" という主張に疑問を投げかけた。

4.1　HC と PPCME2 の比較

PPCME2 全テキストを検索した結果は表 4 の通りであった。表からは M4 での full の減少，right と very の増加を読み取ることができる。これは HC の検索結果と同様である。

表 4　PPCME2 全テキストにおける full, right, very

	full			right			very		
	+Adj	+Adv	計	+Adj	+Adv	計	+Adj	+Adv	計
M3	243	140	383	60	46	106	9	0	9
	6.03	3.47	9.50	1.49	1.14	2.63	0.22	0.00	0.22
M4	178	175	353	105	62	167	15	0	15
	4.44	4.37	8.81	2.62	1.55	4.17	0.37	0.00	0.37

HC と PPCME2 の比較を容易にするため，時代区分ごとに結果を再編集したものを次に掲げる。

表 5　HC と PPCME2 全テキストの比較 (M3)

	full			right			very		
	+Adj	+Adv	計	+Adj	+Adv	計	+Adj	+Adv	計
HC	153	101	254	51	23	74	1	0	1
	8.30	5.48	13.78	2.77	1.25	4.02	0.05	0.00	0.05
PPCME2	243	140	383	60	46	106	9	0	9
	6.03	3.47	9.50	1.49	1.14	2.63	0.22	0.00	0.22

表6　HC と PPCME2 全テキストの比較 (M4)

	full			right			very		
	+Adj	+Adv	計	+Adj	+Adv	計	+Adj	+Adv	計
HC	104	98	202	118	70	188	20	1	21
	4.86	4.58	9.44	5.52	3.27	8.79	0.94	0.05	0.99
PPCME2	178	175	353	105	62	167	15	0	15
	4.44	4.37	8.81	2.62	1.55	4.17	0.37	0.00	0.37

M3, M4 を通じて，PPCME2 における full と right の出現率が HC に比べて低いことが指摘できる。これは full の出現する比率が圧倒的に高い韻文のテキスト，(1)(2) に示すような，right を用いた定型表現（書き出し，結び）が出現する比率の高い書簡のテキストが PPCME2 ですべて省かれたことに原因がある。

 (1) Thankyng with all our soules your most soueraign excellence and noble grace of þe *right* gentell, *right* graciouse, and *right* confortable lettres...　(CMOFFIC3)

 (2) *Ryght* worshipfull husbond, I recomaund me to yow...　(CMPRIV)

次に very に目を向ける。M3 における very はまだ文法化が進んでおらず，純然たる強意副詞とは言えないのであるが，後の時代との比較のため，形容詞の前位置に現れたものをカウントした。その例を以下に示す。

 (3) thanne is thilke the *verray* parfit blisfulnesse that parfitly maketh a man suffisaunt...　(CMBOETH)

 (4) þanne he schal be knowe a *verrey* myʒtful God　(cmaelr3)

M3 で PPCME2 における very の頻度が HC に比べて高いのは語数拡大の結果と考えられるのに対し，M4 では PPCME2 における very の頻度が HC に比べて低くなっている。これは一見奇妙なことであるが，実は書簡のテキストが省かれたことに原因がある。

M4 の書簡のテキストにおける very の特徴は，他のテキストでは強意副詞として定着した full, right としか共起しない語との共起例が見られることである。[6] その例を (5)(6) に示す。

(5) but trwly sche was *very besy* to make hyre redy　　(CMPRIV)
(6) ffor it is to me *veray grete* comfforth þat ye so be　　(CMPRIV)

このように very が多様なコロケーションのパターンを示すということは，書簡のテキストにおいて very の文法化の度合いが進んでいたことを示すものであるが，書簡を省いてしまった PPCME2 ではそれが見えにくくなっている。以下に，HC と PPCME2 の M4 において very と共起する語のリストを示す。(7) でイタリック体表示の語は書簡のテキストに出現するもの，(8) で網掛け表示の語は HC と共通する語である。

(7) HC: true (4 exs.) red (4 exs.) grand just prone soothfast wise; *busy faithful glad good great heavy sore* (adv.)
(8) PPCME2: true (3 exs.) contemplative false grand just painful prone pure right soothfast sorry wholesome wise

4.2　HC と PPCEME の比較

次に PPCEME のすべてのテキストを検索した結果を表 7 に示す。出現頻度が 10 に満たない E2 の full, E3 の full, right を除くと，どの sub-corpus でもほぼ同様の結果が現れている。PPCEME を用いて目的語付き動名詞構文の発達を調査した齊藤 (2006b: 8-9) は，「動名詞構文のように頻度の高い文法項目の調査では，苦労して語数の多い PPCEME 全体を検索する必要がなく，約 60 万語の subcorpora のどれか 1 つを検索すれば十分であることが証明されたと言えよう」と述べているが，同じことは，頻度数が少ない強意副詞の調査にも当てはまる。

・E1

表7　PPCEME における full, right, very

	full			right			very		
	+Adj	+Adv	計	+Adj	+Adv	計	+Adj	+Adv	計
HC	7 0.36	7 0.36	14 0.72	44 2.25	18 0.92	62 3.17	127 6.49	33 1.69	160 8.18
Penn1	4 0.20	14 0.72	18 0.92	34 1.74	14 0.72	48 2.46	111 5.69	34 1.74	145 7.43
Penn2	7 0.38	9 0.49	16 0.86	61 3.29	20 1.08	81 4.37	94 5.07	28 1.51	122 6.58
Total	18 0.31	30 0.52	48 0.83	139 2.41	52 0.90	191 3.31	332 5.76	95 1.65	427 7.41

・E2

	full			right			very		
	+Adj	+Adv	計	+Adj	+Adv	計	+Adj	+Adv	計
HC	0 0.00	1 0.05	1 0.05	13 0.66	0 0.00	13 0.66	177 8.95	80 4.05	257 13.00
Penn1	2 0.09	0 0.00	2 0.09	11 0.49	2 0.09	13 0.58	195 8.74	79 3.54	274 12.28
Penn2	1 0.04	3 0.13	4 0.17	17 0.74	3 0.13	20 0.87	178 7.73	65 2.82	243 10.55
Total	3 0.05	4 0.06	7 0.11	41 0.63	5 0.08	46 0.71	550 8.45	224 3.44	774 11.89

・E3

	full			right			very		
	+Adj	+Adv	計	+Adj	+Adv	計	+Adj	+Adv	計
HC	0	0	0	8	1	9	291	125	416
	0.00	0.00	0.00	0.45	0.06	0.50	16.21	6.96	23.18
Penn1	2	0	2	0	0	0	334	123	457
	0.10	0.00	0.10	0.00	0.00	0.00	16.88	6.22	23.09
Penn2	0	0	0	4	2	6	312	113	425
	0.00	0.00	0.00	0.21	0.11	0.32	16.47	5.97	22.43
Total	2	0	2	12	3	15	937	361	1,298
	0.04	0.00	0.04	0.21	0.05	0.26	16.53	6.37	22.90

5 まとめ

本稿では PPCME2 の M3 以降のテキストおよび PPCEME のすべてのテキストを対象に，強意副詞 full, right, very の出現状況を調査し，HC を対象に同様の調査を行った西村 (1994) で得られた結果と比較した。その要点をまとめると次のようになる。

・PPCME2 においても，M4 で full の減少，right と very の増加が見られた。しかし，PPCME2 では韻文のテキスト，書簡のテキストが省かれたため，full と right の出現率が HC に比べて低くなっている。また，HC の書簡のテキストでは顕著であった very の文法化の進行の様子が PPCME2 では見えにくくなっている。

・PPCEME では，どの時代区分についても，Penn1, Penn2 の subcorpus において HC と同様の結果が得られた。

以上のことから，HC の中英語部分と PPPCME2 は別コーパスと考えるべきであること，したがって，PPCME2 と PPCEME とはまったく性格を

異にするコーパスであり，両者を関連付けた通時的な研究は困難であることが指摘できる。また HC で得られた結果と PPCEME で得られた結果が同様であったことは，齊藤 (2006a: 149) が指摘するように,「小規模」が問題視されがちな HC の有効性を示すものであると言えよう。

6 残された問題

本稿を準備する中で遭遇しながら，まだ十分検討できていない問題として次の 2 点を指摘しておく。

・HC が意図していたサンプルの均衡性を度外視して語数を拡大した PPCME2 はどのような史的研究に適しているのか。もちろん，品詞標識や構文解析を施したファイルが文法研究に有効であることは確かである。しかし，プレーンテキストのファイルはどうか。HC では可能であったテキストタイプの多様性を考慮したきめの細かい言語研究が，PPCME2 では難しくなっているので，PPCME2 ならではの言語研究の可能性を模索しなければならないのではないか。

・PPCEME の検索結果について齊藤 (2006b: 9) はコーパスの「代表性 (representativeness) の問題に関連して,「全く違う資料を使っていれば，違った結果が出る可能性があるのではないかと提起し，さらに「この疑問の検証は，全く別の資料を使った EModE の汎用コーパスができるまで待たなければならないわけであると述べている。しかし，この問題は PPCEME で語数に不足が生じた際に補足のために用いられたテキストや Corpus of Early English Correspondence (CEEC) などの特定ジャンルのコーパスを調査することで，ある程度の見当をつけることができると考えている。これについては稿を改めて論じたい。

注

*本稿は，2006 年 9 月 23 日（土）に京都大学で開催された英語史研究会第 16 回大会において発表した内容の一部である。

1 HCの中英語期以降のテキストは，M1 (1150-1250), M2 (1250-1350), M3 (1350-1420), M4 (1420-1500), E1 (1500-1570), E2 (1570-1640), E3 (1640-1710) の7つの時期に区分される。
2 たとえば，Kytö and Rissanen (1993: 3) は次のように述べている。

It is our intention to expand and improve the corpus in the future by adding new samples and dropping less suitable ones — the time for a new issue might be, for instance, five years after the publication of the present version.

3 表2におけるHCの語数はPPCEMEのマニュアルに基づいたもので，HCのマニュアルに記された語数と微妙に異なる。
4 西村 (1994: 13) 参照。
5 HCのファイルはすべて大文字で，PPCME2およびPPCEMEのファイルはすべて小文字で表記される。
6 Nishimura (2002: 190) 参照。

参考文献

Kytö, Merja (1996³) *Manual to the Diachronic Part of the Helsinki Corpus of English Texts*. Helsinki: Department of English, University of Helsinki.

Kytö, Merja and Matti Rissanen (1993) "General introduction," Matti Rissanen, Merja Kytö and Minna Palander-Collin (eds.) *Early English in the Computer Age*. Berlin and New York: Mouton de Gruyter, 1-17.

Mustanoja, Tauno F. (1960) *A Middle English Syntax, Part I: Parts of Speech*. Helsinki: Société Néophilologique.

西村秀夫 (1994)「Helsinki Corpus に見る強意副詞」『英語コーパス研究』1: 7-18.

Nishimura, Hideo (2002) "Degree Adverbs in the Corpus of Early English Correspondence Sampler", Toshio Saito, Junsaku Nakamura and Shunji Yamazaki (eds.) *EnglishCorpus Linguistics in Japan*. Amsterdam: Rodopi. 183-93.

齊藤俊雄 (2006a)「初期近代英語における目的語付き動名詞構文の発達―The Penn-Helsinki Parsed Corpus of Early Modern English を検索して―」田島松二編『ことばの楽しみ―東西の文化を越えて』南雲堂．138-51.

齊藤俊雄 (2006b)「The Penn-Helsinki Parsed Corpus of Early Modern English を検索して」『英語史研究会会報（研究ノート）』7-12.

齊藤俊雄・中村純作・赤野一郎（編）(2005)『英語コーパス言語学―基礎と実践―』（改訂新版）研究社．

塚本聡 (2006)「英語史研究における構文解析コーパス」『英語コーパス研究』13: 177-90.

Dafydd ap Gwilym の詩注解

吉岡　治郎

　今回注解を試みるのは Dafydd ap Gwilym の詩である。彼は中世ウェールズの最も優れた詩人，あるいは多分ウェールズの全時代を通じての最大の詩人であると目されている。日本の英文学関係の多くの人達に彼の名前が知られたのは *The New Pelican Guide to English Literature* 1. *Medieval Literature Part One: The European Inheritance* の中の Patrick Sims-Williams による 'Dafydd ap Gwilym and Celtic Literature' を通じてであろう。そこには May, Summer, the Mist, Disillusionment の四篇の詩の訳が含まれており，今回の注解ではこの中の May を取り上げて注解を試みる。Sims-Williams の文は碩学の筆になるものであり，簡潔ではあるが種々示唆に富む。Sims-Williams はその後もケルト学の幅広い分野で立派な仕事を成し遂げてきておられ，一番新しい単著は *Ancient Celtic Place-Names in Europe and Asia Minor* (2006) であろう。

Dafydd ap Gwilym の生年・没年など
Dafydd ap Gwilym の生年・没年ははっきりしない。1315/20-1350/70 となっておりかなりの幅がある (Companion)。cf. Chaucer (?1340-1400), Langland (c1330-c1400), Wycliffe (?1320-84), Petrarca (1304-74), Boccaccio (1313-75). Chaucer より少し前の時代の詩人である。同時代のウェールズの著名な詩人としては Iolo Goch (c1325-c1398) がおり，彼は Dafydd ap Gwilym を悼む詩を書いている。

出自

Brogynin 生まれ，これは Llandbarn Fawr 教区内にある，Aberystwyth (= the mouth of the River Ystwyth, であるが，歴史地図で古い時代を見ると，Aberystwyth でなく Llandbarn の地名が記載されている）の北数マイルのところ。Strata Florida の修道院の境内［現在は廃墟］に埋葬されたと言われている（異説もあるようであるが，ここでは詳説は避ける）。

cf. Llandbarn Fawr = the Principal Church of (St.) Padarn [llan = church; badarn = lenited form of 'Padarn'; fawr = lenited form of 'mawr' = big]

Dafydd was born into one of the most influential families of *uchelwyr* in south Wales. [uchelwyr = pl. of 'uchelwr' = nobleman, gentleman, landed proprietor, etc. 他言語に訳せいない語であるとのこと］uncle（伯父か叔父か分からない）である Llywelyn ap Gwilym (d.1346?) は Newcastle Emlyn Constable（中世君主国の高官）であり，非常に豊かな学識の所有者であり，Dafydd ap Gwilym に大きな影響を与えたと言われている。この uncle は有名な the Black Prince (the Hundred Years's War [1337-1453] の初期に活躍した「黒太子」[1330-76]) に忠誠を誓った一人とされている。

テキスト

Parry, Thomas (1904-85): *Gwaith Dafydd ap Gwilym* [Work of Dafydd ap Gwilym] (1952,63). これは現在までの決定版である。Parry が多くの写本の調査をし，厳密な基準を設定して，以前 Dafydd ap Gwilym の作とされていた作品から 100 位の作品を排除した，残りの作品は 150 篇あまりである。非常に有名な詩人であったので，彼の影響の下に詩作した他の詩人達の作品が彼の作品とされていた。

　この注解に当たっては，*Geiriadur Prifysgol Cymru* (The Dictionary of the Welsh Language) ［1950-2002, 最初の部分の改訂中であり，2007 年 10 月現在第 8 分冊 Arffedogaeth-Atchwelaf まできている］に引用されている場合は引用と付記した（注解中では *G.P.C.* と略記）。この辞書の編纂の当初は Dafydd ap Gwilym の詩の引用は Ifor Williams and T.Roberts,eds., *Cywyddau Dafydd ap Gwilym a'i Gygoeswyr* (1935) を使用しており，その

略記号は DGG である。筆者の調べた限りでは，この辞書の p.341 までは DGG からの引用であり，p.342 から Thomas Parry の書からの引用であり，その略記号は GDG である（もちろんこれはこの辞書の元版に関することである）。古い時期のウェールズ語を読むに当たっては必須の書である D.Simon Evans の *A Grammar of Middle Welsh* も絶えず参照したが，その略記号は *GMW* とした。

翻訳

Thomas Parry が Dafydd ap Gwilym の作と認定した作品の全訳は以下の2書のみ，Loomis,Richard: *Dafydd ap Gwilym : the Poems, Translation and Commentary* (1982); Thomas,Gwyn: *Dafydd ap Gwilym, His Poems* (2001)

選訳

Bromwich, Rachel: *Dafydd ap Gwilym, A Selection of Poems* (1982)
(56篇の詩の原文と対称ペイジの英語訳，内容についての詳しい注解付きであり，今回の注解に当たり大いに参考にさせて頂いた)
Clancy,J.P.: *Medieval Welsh Lyric* (1965)
一部分の詩の翻訳は多くのウェールズ語の詩の翻訳書に含まれている。

MIS MAI

  Duw gwyddiad mai da y gweddai
  Dechreuad mwyn dyfiad Mai.
  Difeth irgyrs a dyfai
  Dyw Calan mis mwynlan Mai.
5 Digrinflaen goed a'm oedai,
  Duw mawr a roes doe y Mai.
  Dillyn beirdd ni'm rhydwyllai,
  Da fyd ym oedd dyfod Mai.

 今回の注解で扱う本詩 Mis Mai (= May Month) と，Yr Haf (= The Summer) は Dafydd ap Gwilym の全ての詩の中にあってただ二篇の monorhyme の詩であるとされている。すなわち本詩にあっては，一行おきに出てく

る行末の Mai と imperfect 3 人称単数の語尾 -ai（中世ウェールズ語の通常の語尾は-ei, cf. *GMW* p.114）が脚韻になっており，詩全体を通じてそれが踏襲されている。また Dafydd ap Gwilym の詩は *Cynghanedd* という頭韻，語中韻などを使った複雑な韻律法に基づいて作詩されている。*Cynghanedd* の複雑な韻律について英語で読むことのできる一番詳しい説明は，Eurys I.Rowlands, ed. *Poems of Cywyddwyr* (1976) の Introduction xxvii-xlix にある。この *Cynghanedd* の一端については，前述の Sims-Williams による *Dafydd ap Gwilym and Celtic Literature*, pp.303-4 を参照されたい。この複雑な韻律に加えて，monorhyme で全体を見事に纏めているので，Sims-Williams はこの Mis Mai と Yr Haf の両詩を virtuoso poems（名人芸の，洗練極まりない詩 p.303）と称揚している。現代英語訳では，ウェールズ語原文に合わせて，一行置きに行末に May がくるようにした苦労のうかがわれる翻訳がいくつかあるが，日本語による試訳ではそのような試みは当然不可能でもあり，また筆者の力を遥かに超えてもいるので，以前の試訳の場合と同じく内容をほぼ伝えるだけのものでしかない。mis = month; Mai = May で，Mis Mai = Month of May, ウェールズ語では名詞が並列されている場合には後ろの名詞が前の名詞を修飾する。Mai が「夏の月」であることは，以前に注解を加えた Mis Mai a Mis Ionawr (= May and January) の 1.2 Fis Mai haf (= Month of May of summer→Summer's May Month) とあるのでも分かる。Dafydd ap Gwilym の詩には夏を称える詩が多くあり，緑鮮やかな五月が夏の象徴としてしばしば姿を現わす; Duw = God; gwyddiad = imperf. 3 sg. of 'gwn,gwybod' = know,be aware of,perceive, see (cf. *GMW* p.122); mai = that it is（この mai の用法については，*GMW* p.144 参照）; da = good, suitable, well; y = preverbal ptcle.; gweddai = imperf. 3 sg. of 'gweddaf' = become, suit, be fit; dechreuad = beginning, start 引用初例; mwyn = tender, mild, gentle であるが，同じ綴りの別語 mwyn = benefit, treasure, wealth があり，この後の方の語の意味が反映していると指摘している学者もいる。mwyn は青葉の柔らかさとその豊穣さを併せ示していることになる; dyfiad = lenited form of 'tyfiad' = growth, vegetation（現存ケルト諸語にあっては，語頭子音が色々な条件の下で音変化を起こし，これを lenition と言う。そ

の lenition を起こした形を以下 lenited form と呼び，lenition を起こす前の形を提示する）引用初例; difeth = without fail, unfailing 引用; irgyris はこのままの形では G.P.C. に意味の記述はなく irgyrs という形が上げてあり ir + cors を見よとある，ir (= green, verdant) + cors (= reed, grass, stem) の意味となる; a = preverbal ptcle. （動詞の前に置かれる preverbal ptcle. の種類・用法は多岐にわたるので，ここでは詳しくは述べない); dyfai = lenited form of 'tyfai' = imperf.3 sg. of 'tyfaf' = grow; dyw = day; Calan = calends, the first day of the month, 五月一日は古い時期のウェールズでは伝統的に夏の始まりの日であった。中世にはブリテン全土で May-day には種々の儀礼，しきたりによる行事が執り行われた; mis 前出; mwynlan = gentle and pleasant 引用初例; digrinflaen もこのままの形では G.P.C. にはなく，digrin があり，di + crin となっている，di (= un,dis,etc.) + crin (= withered) + blaen (= tip, end) → unwithered tips; goed = lenited form of 'coed' = wood; a = preverbal ptcle.; 'm = me; oedai = imperf.3 sg.of 'oedaf' = delay, postpone, keep 引用; Duw 前出; mawr = great; a = preverbal ptcle.; roes = lenited form of 'rhoes' = imperf.3 sg. of 'rhoddaf' = give; doe = yesterday; y = to; dyllyn = thing of beauty, precious thing, jewel; beirdd = pl. of 'bardd' = bard, poet (英語の bard はケルト語よりの借用語), dyllyn beirdd については，五月に対する greetings であり，詩人にあってはずっと決まりのテーマであったとの指摘あり; ni = not; 'm = me; rhydwyllai については，この語の動詞形と目される rhydwyllaf は G.P.C. には見当たらないが，rhydwyll という形が収録されており，その意味は wily, deceitful とあり，語源として rhy (= intensive の意味) + twyll (= deceit, deception) とある，それで rhydwyllaf (= deceive, cheat) の imperf. 3 sg. か; da 前出; fyd = lenited form of 'byd' = life; ym = to me; oedd = imperf. 3 sg. of 'bot' = be; dyfod = come (の verbal noun), この 1.8 は，動詞の時制が oedd (= was) が yw (= is) に変化するだけで，他は同じで 1.50 に再度現われる。

「五月」

　　神は見そなわしぬ，五月の初めが柔らかな草木の成長にふさわしい時節であることを。尽きることなき青々とした若芽がおだやかな楽しき五月の

一日に芽をふきぬ。色褪せぬ木々の梢が我を引き止めぬ。昨日偉大なる神は五月を我等に与えし。詩人達の宝玉は我を偽ることはなかりき。五月の到来は我にとり祝福でありし。

　1.3 の difeth は注の中でも述べたように，without fail, unfailing の意味であり，Bromwich は without fail の意味に取っているが，他の訳者達のように unfailing の意味に取り訳した。

　1.5 の digrinflaen は注の中でも触れたように，unwithered の意味で訳したが，Sims-Williams のみが untrembling と訳している。-crin- に似た綴りの cryn (=trembling) があり，その語と誤解したのか不明である。意味の上から untrembling でなければならぬ理由も筆者には思い浮かばない。他の訳者はすべて unwithered としている。

　　　　　　　　Harddwas teg a'm anrhegai,
　　　10　Hylaw wr mawr hael yw'r Mai.
　　　　　　　　Anfones ym iawn fwnai,
　　　　　　　　Glas defyll glan mwyngyll Mai.
　　　　　　　　Ffloringod brig ni'm digiai,
　　　　　　　　Fflwr-dy-lis gyfoeth mis Mai.
　　　15　Diongl rhag brad y'm cadwai,
　　　　　　　　Dan esgyll dail mentyll Mai.
　　　　　　　　Llawn wyf o ddig na thrigai
　　　　　　　　(Beth yw i mi?) byth y Mai.

harddwas はこのままの形では *G.P.C.* に収録されていないが，hardd (= handsome) + gwas (= boy, young man); teg = beautiful, fair; 'm = me; anrhegai = imperf. 3 sg. of 'anrhegaf' = reward, bestow 引用; hylaw = generous 引用; wr = lenited form of 'gwr' = man であり，非常に多出の語。ラテン語の vir, ゴート語の wair の他，印欧語族のいくつもの語派共通の著名な語; mawr は 1.6 にも前出の語であるが，意味範囲の広い語であり，ここでは noble の意味か，現代英語訳では nobleman, lord, prince など; hael = generous, open-handed; yw = pres. 3 sg. of 'bot' = be; 'r = y (= the); Mai この Mai が

Dafydd ap Gwilym の詩注解

G.P.C. に引用されている; anfones = pret. 3 sg. of 'anfonaf' = send, dispatch; ym = to me, cf l.8; iawn = true, right, genuine; fwnai = lenited form of 'mwnai' = currency, money, wealth, Bromwich の注に, The fourteenth century saw a spread and increase of a money economy in Wales, gradually replacing barter. とあり; glas は色彩語として英語より意味の幅が広いので有名な語であるが, ここでは green, verdant の意味; defyll = lenited form of 'tefyll' = pl. of 'tafell' = slice, piece; glan=pure, clean, fair; mwyngyll = mwyn (= tender, amiable) + cyll (= pl. of 'collen' = hazel); ffloringod = pl.of 'ffloring '= florin, two-shilling piece 引用; brig=tree-tops, topmost branches; ni = not, cf. l.7; 'm = me; digiai = imperf. 3 sg.of 'digiaf' = vex, harass, offend; flwr-dy-lis = fleur-de-lis 引用初例; gyfoeth = lenited form of 'cyfoeth' = wealth, riches, この語と同じ語が1.46にあり, *G.P.C.* はそちらを引用, この ll.13-14 については, Bromwich の詳しい注があり参考になるので引用しておく. "The young leaves are compared to golden florins. The florin was first minted in Florence in 1252 and it bore on its obverse the fleur-de-lis, which was the heraldic device of the city of Florence (as well as of the kings of France), and this device was retained on all florins subsequently minted in other European countries. The only florin to be minted in England was the gold florin of Edward III, valued at 6 shillings, which was minted only between January and August 1344, and subsequently withdrawn from circulation as a base coin, because its gold value fell short of its nominal value. It was replaced by the gold noble, worth 6s 8p." この後他の学者の説に対する批判があり, 次の文に連なる. "I would myself regard the pejorative comparison of the gold coin with the fresh leaves of May as but one facet of the constant *leitmotif* underlying Dafydd's poetry: the exaltation of nature's riches are preferable to all human artefacts."; diongl = not angular, smooth, soft, easy 引用初例; rhag = against; brad = treachery, betrayal; y = preverbal ptcle.; 'me = me; cadwai = imperf. 3 sg. of 'cadwaf' = defend, guard; dan = beneath; esgyll = pl. of 'asgell' = wing; dail = leaves; mentyll = pl. of 'mantell' = mantle, cloak, robe; llawn = filled with; wyf = pres. 1 sg. of 'bot' = be; o = of, from; ddig = lenited form of 'dig' = anger, grief 引用; na = not; thrigai = lenited form of 'trigai' = imperf. 3 sg. of 'trigaf' = stay, dwell; beth = what, cf. *GMW* p.76; yw = pres. 3 sg. of 'bot' = be; i (= y) = to, for; mi = me, この 'Beth ym i mi' については Bromwich の注記があり，lit. 'What is it to me' とあり，the poet contemplates the impermanence of his own life and of all human mortality. と記しているが，Bromwich が 16-17 としているのは誤記であり，l.18 である，指している内容は l.17 に対してのこと。

　　　端正なるいい顔立ちの若者が，我に贈り物をせり，五月は物惜しみせぬ気前よき高貴の生まれの者。彼は真正の財貨を我に与えし，五月の柔らかな綺麗なハシバミの緑の葉を。木々の梢のフロリン貨，五月の富の百合の花は，我を失望せしめることはなかりき。彼は五月のマントの木の葉の翼の下で，欺瞞から我を守りき。この五月が永遠には止どまらぬ故（我にとりこれはなんということか），我が胸は悲しみに満てり。

l.12 に出てくる collen(=hazel) ［ハシバミ］は色々な国の伝承に姿を現わす語であり，もちろんケルトの伝承にも現われ，オガム文字の樹木のリストにも含まれている。情報豊かであり，また楽しい書である加藤憲一『英米文学植物民俗誌』pp.248-251 を参照されたい，ケルトについての言及もある。また同じく情報に富む Alwyn Rees and Brynley Rees, *Celtic Heritage* p.161,311 参照，ここでは hazel-nut が扱われている。collen は本詩以外の Dafydd ap Gwilym の詩のあちこちに見出だされる。

　　　　　Dofais ferch a'm anerchai,
20　　　Dyn gwiwryw mwyn dan gor Mai.
　　　　　Tadamaeth beirdd heirdd, a'm hurddai,
　　　　　Serchogion mwynion, yw Mai.
　　　　　Mab bedydd Dofydd difai,
　　　　　Mygrlas, mawr yw urddas Mai.
25　　　O'r nef y doeth a'm coethai
　　　　　I'r byd, fy mywyd yw Mai.

dofais = pret. 3 sg. of 'dofaf' = tame, bring under the yoke, restrain 引用; ferch = lenited form of 'merch' = girl, lass; a = rel. pron.; 'm = me; anerchai =

imperf. 3 sg. of 'anerchaf' = greet, address; dyn = woman, maiden; gwiwryw = noble, dignified, splendid, Bromwich の seemly は少しずれるかと思えるが splendid の意訳か, Thomas は noble, Loomis は well-born, Sims-Williams の訳では脱落か意図的に省いたか; mwyn = tender, gentle, cf. 1.2; dan = beneath, cf. 1.16; gor = lenited form of 'cor' = choir; tadmaeth = fig. use of 'foster-father' 引用; beirdd, 1.7 に前出; heirdd = pl. of 'hardd' = splendid, fine, 1.32 を引用, 中世ウェールズ語の形容詞に複数形を持つ語が多いことについては, *GMW* p.35 参照; a = rel. pron.; 'm = me; hurddaf = imperf. 3 sg. of 'urddaf' (Sandhi h のついた形, *GMW* p.23 参照) = honour, dignify; serchogion = pl. of 'serchog' = sweetheart, lover; mwynion = pl. of 'mwyn'; yw, cf. 1.10,18; mab = son, child, Dafydd ap Gwilym の ap はこの語の古形である map の語頭音脱落からの語である; bedydd = baptism で mab bedydd = god-child; Dofydd = the Lord, God 引用; difai = perfect, complete; mygrlas = mygr (= beautiful, fair, 1.42 で引用) + glas (= green, covered with green grass, clothed with verdure or foliage); mawr, cf. 1.6,10; yw 多出; urddas = dignity, honour, cf. 1.21 'hurddai'; o'r = from the; nef = heaven; doeth = pret. 3 sg. of 'deuaf, dyfod' = come; a = rel. pron. 関係詞節が表現されている先行詞なしに (without expressed antecedent) 使用されることについては, *GMW* p.72 参照, それでここでは he who の意味になる; 'm = me; coethai = imperf. 3 sg. of 'coethaf' = refine, purify, fashion skillfully 引用初例; i'r = to the; byd = world, earth, 1.8 の fyd と同じ語であるが, ここでは別の意味; fy = my; mywyd = lenited form of 'bywyd' = life, existence; yw 多出.

　　　　我を迎えくれし乙女を, 我が支配の下に置きぬ, 五月の聖歌隊の下, 気
　　　　高く優しき乙女なりし。立派な詩人達の, 優しき恋人達の里親, 我を礼遇
　　　　せしは五月なり。完璧なる主の名付け子, 麗しき緑に覆われる五月は気品
　　　　に満つ。我を清めし者は天よりこの世に来たりぬ。我が命五月なり。

1.20 の 'cor' について, cor を forest trees のメタファーとして使用するのは, 他に Mis Mai a Mis Ionawr (= May and January) や Y Llwyn Celyn (= The Holly Grove) などの詩にその例がある。

        Neud glas gofron, llon llatai,
        Neud hir dydd mewn irwydd Mai.
        Neud golas, nid ymgelai,
30   Bronnydd a brig manwydd Mai.
        Neud ber nos, nid bwrn siwrnai,
        Neud heirdd gweilch a mwyeilch Mai.
        Neud llon eos lle trosai,
        Neud llafar man adar Mai.
35   Neud esgud nwyf a'm dysgai,
        Nid mawr ogoniant ond Mai.

neud = affirmative ptcle. その用法については，*GMW* pp.169-170 参照。このスタンザにあっては，1〜3,1 行おいて，5〜9 行が，この同じ neud で始まる; glas = green, 1.12 に前出; gofron = gently-rising hill, slope, hillock 引用初例; llon = merry, cheerful, glad 引用; llatai = love-messenger, Dafydd ap Gwilym の詩にはよく出てくる語であり，彼の詩の一つのキーワードにもなっており，自然，動物など色々なものが love-messenger になりうる; hir = long; dydd = day, time of daylight; mewn = in; irwydd = green trees, trees in foliage; golas = green, verdant 引用; nid(=ni の母音の前の形)=not; ymgelai = imperf. 3 sg. of 'ymgelaf' = ym (= reflexive) + celaf (= hide, conceal) であり，文字通りには they didn't hide themselves であるが，Bromwich,Thomas などの訳では現在で訳されている。韻律の関係で原文では imperfect が使用されているが，この辺りの前後関係から現在でなければおかしいので，そのように訳したのかと推測する; bronnydd = pl. of 'bron' = hill-side, slope, breast (of hill); a = and; brig, 1.13 に前出; manwydd = small trees, shrubs, bushes 引用; ber (*G.P.C.*) byr = brief, short; nid, 1.29 に前出; bwrn = burden, nuisance; siwrnai = journey; heirdd = pl. of 'hairdd' = fine, splendid 引用, cf. 1.21; gweilch = pl. of 'gwalch' = hawk, falcon; a = and; mwyeilch = pl. of 'mwyalch' = blackbird; llon,1.27 に前出，引用はこの箇所; eos = nightingale; lle = where; trosai = imperf. 3 sg. of 'trosaf' = go, move, be restless, Thomas の訳 fusses, Bromwich の訳 warble は最後の意味の意

訳か，Sims-Williams は dwelt, Loomis は tarried; llafar = loquacious, loud, talkative; man = small, little; adar = birds; esgud = quick, swift, lively; nwyf = vivacity, vigour, energy; a = preverbal ptcle.; 'm = me; dysgai = imperf. 3 sg. of 'dysgaf' = teach, instruct; nid = not; mawr 多出; ogoniant = lenited form of 'gogoniant' = glory, fame, majesty; ond = with the exception of.

　　　丘辺は緑なり，恋の使者は楽しげなり。五月の豊かな緑の木々にあっては，日は長し。その身を隠さぬが故，五月の丘辺と繁みの頂きは鮮やかな緑なり。夜は短く，旅も苦にならぬ。鷹とツグミは五月には見事である。サヨナキドリは囀り嬉しげであり，小鳥達は五月には鳴きざわめく。五月の教えてくれしは溌剌たる元気，五月にのみ大いなる栄光存す。

　　　　　Paun asgellas dinastai,
　　　　　Pa un o'r mil? Penna'r Mai.
　　　　　Pwy o ddail a'i hadeilai
　　40　Yn oed y mis onid Mai?
　　　　　Magwyr laswyrdd a'i magai,
　　　　　Mygr irgyll man defyll Mai.
　　　　　Pyllog, gorau pe pallai,
　　　　　Y gaeaf, mwynaf yw Mai.

paun = peacock, fig. use 引用，この paun については Bromwich の注記があり，The personification of May changes abruptly from that of a *gwr mawr hael* (l.10) to that of peacock; 'it' refers to the luxurious growth of verdure and trees; the underlying thought is probably of a peacock's tail castellated or spread out to display its rich colouring.; asgellas = asgell (= wing) + glas (= green) か，このままの形では *G.P.C.* になし，意味は green wing; dinastai = pl. of 'dinasty' = house in a town or city, town-house, mansion 本例のみ引用; pa un = which one; o'r = of the; mil = a thousand, a great number; penna' (= pennaf) = superl. of 'pen' = chief, supreme, great; 'r = the; pwy = who; o = from, out of; ddail = lenited form of 'dail' = leaves, cf. l.16 の 'dail'; a'i = a (= preverbal ptcle.) + i (= it); hadeilai = h (sandi h) + adeilai = imperf. 3 sg. of 'adeiliaf' = build, construct; yn = in, within; oed = time, space of time; y = the;

onid は通常は if ～not, unless, except (before a vb) であり，l.36 に出てくる ond とは用法のずれがあるが，ここでは音節を一つ増やすために onid を使用した，意味は ond と同じ with the exception of のままで; magwyr = stone wall, fortification, bulwark, etc. 引用; laswyrdd = lenited form of 'glaswyrdd' = dark green, green であるが，*G.P.C.* の初出例が 1460-90 となっているのは何故か，100 年以上も前のこの例を見落としたのであろう，この magwyr laswyrdd についても，Bromwich の注記があり，'green battlements'; cf. the *bwlch dail* 'battlements of leaves', of no.25 (GDG 63), 16. The forest is a fortified defence to the poet's imagined secret retreat. と参考になる見解を述べている; a'i = a (= preverbal ptcle.) + i (= it), cf. l.39; magai = imperf. 3 sg. of 'magaf' = rear, foster; mygr = beautiful, fair, shining 引用; irgyll = ir (= green, verdant) + cyll (= pl. of 'collen' = hazel), 'ir' は l.3 の 'irgyrs' の前半部に，'cyll' は l.12 の 'mwyngyll' の後半部に前出; man = fine, elegant, cf. l.34; defyll = lenited form of 'tefyll' = pl. of 'tafell' = slice, piece; pyllog = full of hollows, full of holes, full of pools or ditches 引用初例; gorau = superl. of 'da' = good →best; pe = if; pallai = imperf. 3 sg. of 'pallaf' = fail, die, be destroyed; y = the; gaeaf = winter; mwynaf = superl. of 'mwyn' = tender, mild, gentle, pleasant 引用, cf. l.2 他; yw 多出。

> 邸宅の緑の羽を持てる数多くの孔雀のいずれよりも，最高であるのは五月。五月を除き，誰が一月の間に木の葉でそのようなものを築くことが出来たのか。それは緑の砦を築ついた，緑鮮やかなる五月のハシバミの新鮮なる葉でもって。冬は水溜まりでいっぱいになる，来ぬのが最上である。一番優しいのは五月である。

l.42 の tafell は文字通りには piece, slice の意味であり，Thomas は piece を，Loomis は slice を使用して訳している。一方 Bromwich は leaves と，Sims-Williams は little-leaved と訳している。slice とか piece を使用すると，「ハシバミ」の実の方に連想が傾くのではないか，「ハシバミ」の実は綺麗な茶色であり，実が成るのが八月であるのは，ハシバミの実の別名の filbert（英語）が St. Philibert からであり，St. Philibert's Day（8月22日）の頃に熟することから来ているのも分かる。ここでは Bromwich に従い「葉」

ということにした。Sims-Williams の little-leaved の little は原文の意味の slice, piece を意識したのかも知れないが、「ハシバミ」の葉が小さいといえるのであろうか。

1.43 の pyllog を Loomis が 'mantled' としているのは、pyll (= mantle) から来た誤解であろう、「冬」ということで 'mantle' と勘違いしたのか。

    45   Deryw'r gwanwyn, ni'm dorai,
           Eurgoeth mwyn aur gywoeth Mai;
           Dechrau haf llathr a'i sathrai,
           Deigr a'i mag, diagr yw Mai.
           Deilgyll gwyrddrisg a'm gwisgai,
    50   Da fyd ym yw dyfod Mai.
           Duw ddoeth gadarn a farnai
           A Mair i gynnal y Mai.

deryw = pres. 3 sg. of 'darfyddaf, darfod', with perfective meaning (*GMW* P.145) = come to an end, cease, die; gwanwyn = spring; ni'm = not me; dorai = imperf. 3 sg. of 'doraf' = matter, be of importance 引用; eurgoeth = eur(= gold) + coeth (= pure, refined, fine); mwyn = ore, mineral; aur = gold, made of gold, golden; gywoeth = lenited form of 'cywoeth' = (*G.P.C.*)cyfoeth,cywoeth = wealth, riches 引用; dechrau = beginning, commencement, cf. l.2 の dechreuad; haf = summer; llathr = bright, brilliant; a = preverbal ptcle.; i = it; sathrai = imperf. 3 sg. of 'sathraf' = trample on,step on; deigr = tear; a'i, cf. l.47; mag = pres. 3 sg. of 'magaf' = rear, foster, nurture; diagr = fair, beautiful; deilgyll = pl. of 'deilgoll' = leafy hazel 引用，Dafydd ap Gwilym の詩からの 2 例のみ引用; gwyrddrisg = having green bark 本例のみ引用; a'm = a (= preverbal ptcle.) +'m(= me); gwisgai = imperf.3 sg.of 'gwisgaf' = dress,clothe; da = good; fyd = lenited form of 'byd' = life; ym = to me; yw 多出; dyfod = coming, 前述のように1.8 とほとんど同じ; Duw = God 多出; ddoeth = lenited form of 'doeth' = wise, prudent; gadarn = lenited form of 'cadarn' = strong, powerful; a = preverbal ptcle.; farnai = lenited form of 'barnai' = imperf. 3 sg. of 'barnaf'

= judge, sentence; a = with; Mair = Mary; i = to; gynnal = lenited form of 'cynnal' = keep, observe.

  春は終わりぬ，されどそれにより煩わされることはなかりき，五月の金色の富は純粋なる金。涙の育てしものを夏の輝かしき到来が散り散りにせり，麗しきは五月。緑の樹皮のハシバミの葉が我を装いし。五月の到来は我にとり祝福である。偉大にして賢明なる神が，マリア様と共に五月を祝うことを定め賜いぬ。

 1.48 の deigr a'i mag については，Bromwich の次のような注記あり。Alternatively 'tears nurture it' or 'it'(May's departure) has fostered tears. *Deigr* 'tears' are presumably raindrops; in fact the April showers which traditionally precede the beginning of May. この注記はまた，Chaucer の *The Canterbury Tales* の General Prologue の冒頭の部分を想起せしめる。以前の *POD* の記述の March, associated with cold winds; April, noted for alterations of sunshine and showers; May, associated with greenery. また，March winds and April showers bring forth May flowers. も参考になる。日本語の芭蕉の日光での「あらたふと青葉若葉の日の光」や「目に青葉，山ほととぎす，初鰹」の連想も出てくる。

 Dafydd ap Gwilym については語るべきことは多々ある，例えば，彼の詩の多様性，自然（動物，植物，自然物など）に対するきめの細かな観察とそれらの精妙な描写，ウェールズの詩の伝統から彼が受け継いできたこと，またウェールズの詩に新たに彼が付け加え寄与したこと，他の国の文学から彼が受けた影響（特に Ovidius からの）などなどである。彼の詩の持つ多様性については，具体的に紹介してゆくことが出来ればと思っている。

注

文中に Companion と記したのは次の書である。
Stephens, M. ed.; *The New Companion to the Literature of Wales* (1998) の Dafydd ap Gwilym の項。本書は *The Oxford Companion to the Literature of Wales* (1986) の全面改訂版であり，出版元も University of Wales Press に変更になった。400 項目増，150 ペイジ増（1 page に入る量も増えていると思われる）であるし，簡潔要領を得た説明は見事であり，ウェールズ文学に興味のある方には必須の文献である。旧版 Oxford 版を使用しておられる方も，今後この新版を使用されるべきである。

Jarman,A.O.H. and Hughes,G.R.(eds.) : *A Guide to Welsh Literature* Vol.2 (1979,1984), Chapter V Dafydd ap Gwilym (by Bromwich) も専門家による全般的な記述であり参考になる。

Dafydd ap Gwilym に関連の研究書についても，一流の学者達による優れた諸著があるが，将来紹介する機会があることを期待している。

芸術作品の擁護
──『ベーオウルフ』「グレンデルのヘオロット襲撃」の文章構造と詩人の技法 ──[1]

渡辺 秀樹

1 最近の古英詩 *Beowulf* への関心の高まり

　最近この古英詩が急速に一般人に知られるようになった。まずノーベル賞受賞詩人 Seamus Heaney がこの詩の現代英語訳を出版したことがある。ヒーニーは 1999 年に英国で現代英語訳を出してから，2000 年には米国で原文との平行訳を出し，これらは両方ともベスト・セラーになった。次いで J. R. R. Tolkien 原作『指輪物語』の映画化がファンタジーブームに乗って行われて，中世時代や騎士と龍の話への関心が高まった。OED には 152 個の用例がトルキーンから取られているが，ほとんど全部が『指輪物語』からで，見出し語 orc では語義 2 番にトルキーンからの引用 12 例が並んでいる。OED を見ればこの戦争好きの醜い怪物族の名前は，本来水に住む怪物を漠然と意味していたこと，*Beowulf* に出て来る怪物の名前 orcneas と関係していることがわかる。トルキーンはこのように古英語や古北欧語の単語を自分の小説にたくさん取り入れているので，『指輪物語』愛読者の中には当然『ベーオウルフ』に興味を持つ人が出てくるわけである。2007 年にはロバート・ゼメキス監督の映画 *Beowulf* が公開された。日本でもテレビのスポットコマーシャルが流されて，有名女優アンジェリーナ・ジョリーがグレンデルの妖艶な母を演じる事もあり，興行的には成功したようだ。が，その内容は原作とはかなり隔たっており，フロスガール

王は自殺,ベーオウルフは故国イエーアトには戻らずデンマークの王となり,この二人は共にグレンデルの母と交わって息子をもうけ,それがおのおのグレンデルと火竜であり,数十年後にデンマークに厄災をもたらすという筋であった。

　英語学研究者,中世英語研究者ではない『指輪物語』の一般ファンの人々は,トルキーンが『ベーオウルフ』学者であることを知ると,その古英詩を現代英語訳で読むこともあるだろう。日本人のファンならば日本語訳で読み,怪物グレンデルや火龍との戦いを中心とする英雄物語であることを知って,彼らが好きなファンタジーの典型作品(英雄が悪に支配される未知の国を訪れ,龍に代表される悪を退治して,国を救い美女を手に入れる)として理解するのではないか。数年前にはなかったような『ベーオウルフ』関連サイトが次々にインターネット上に現われて活況を呈している。我々研究者に向けた有益な学問的サイトも多いが,噴飯もののホームページも目に付く。勿論『ベーオウルフ』は専門研究者だけの作品ではないし,古典作品の現代での受容,映画化やドラマ化で筋の変形や新解釈を伴うことは常識である。そのような広範な受容と批評をうけること自体が,原作の懐の深さ,様々の解釈を許す傑作である事を証明してもいるだろう。

　しかし,四半世紀に渡って古英詩の文体論や解釈に関わってきた者から見れば,昨今の中世・ファンタジーブームの過熱がとうとう英語で書かれた最古の作品に及び,皆が寄って集って「『ベーオウルフ』をいじる」ことを始めたと思えるのである。実際にその映画 Beowulf に出演した役者たちが「学生の頃に読まされて全くつまらなかった」とか「原作は読んだ事がないし,演じるに当たって脚本の方が大事だから,読まない」などと発言し,監督や脚本家が「原作の筋は入り組んで面白みに欠けるので,原文に書かれていないが読み取る事が可能な事柄を出してひとつの国の話に再構成した」という趣旨を述べているのを読んで,落胆したのであった。[2]

　本詩の評価は時代と共に変遷してきた。異教とキリスト教の要素が混交している為に,19世紀半ばまでは「継ぎ接ぎ」作品として主として歴史的興味から見られていたものが,立派な校訂版が出されるに連れてその

「グレンデルのヘオロット襲撃」の文章構造と技法　　**457**

　テーマへの理解が深まり，1936 年にはトルキーンが講演で（後にモノグラフとして出版），この叙事詩の「深い主題と統一された芸術性」を主張した。主筋を中断する挿話の頻出も，かつては継ぎ接ぎ製作過程を示すものとして貶められていたものが，今の有力な議論では物語の大小円環構造中に全て仕組まれたもの，逆に芸術性を高める要素として理解されている。筆者が感銘を受けるのは，特に予弁によるサスペンスであって，これは対照法・ヴァリエーション（同一物の言い換え）・繰り返しのレトリックを意識的に用いた文体が醸し出す効果であると考える。その文体上の技巧が明白に，典型的に現れているのが，所謂「グレンデルのヘオロット襲撃」と呼ばれる本詩 702 行後半からの一節である。筆者は本詩を再読，再々読するたびに，この一節についてはいつもそれまで気付かなかった文体技法を新たに見つけ，この英雄詩に対する敬意と愛着が増すのである。

　以下はその時の感銘と発見の興奮とを次の 2 種類の人々に伝える事を目的とする。まず『ベーオウルフ』に興味はあるが古英語を学んだ事のない人に対して，原詩を 1 行ごとに区切って，語形や語義から作詩上の技法や詩全体のテーマを含めて解説する，そして若い古英語研究者でこの詩を講義や演習で一度は読んだ事のある人に対しては，「古典を読む」ということは「ゆっくり細かく読むこと」であって，「繰り返し読むこと」によって常に新しい意味が見出されることを示したい。実際，この有名な一節のテーマと文体技巧について書かれた論文で，以下に示すような内容と語彙の対照表現や繰り返しにおける相補表現法を全て指摘しているものはない。今回本稿を執筆中に新たに気付いた点もある。

　現代英語訳を 2 種，20 世紀初頭に出た Francis Gummer 訳，世紀末に出た Seamus Heaney 訳を引用したが，ここで解説する原詩の構造や配語法が英語を母国語とする研究者・翻訳家に理解されているかどうかを検証，詩人の技巧や意図が理解されている場合，それが如何様に現代語に移行・訳出されているか，またはいないかを確認し，今後の現代英語訳や日本語訳が目指すべき文体上の要件を示す為である。

2 「グレンデルのヘオロット襲撃」の原文と現代英語訳の例

Grendel's Approach to Heorot in *Beowulf* Wrenn's Edition (702b-730)

　　　　　　　　　　　　Com on wanre niht　　702
scriðan sceadu-genga; sceotend swæfon,
þa þæt horn-reced healdan scoldon,
ealle buton anum. þæt wæs yldum cuþ,　　705
þæt hie ne moste, þa Metod nolde,
se syn-scaþa under sceadu bregdan,
ac he wæccende wraþum on andan
bad bolgen-mod beadwa geþinges.
　　Ða com of more under mist-hleoþum　　710　　Fitt XI.
Grendel gongan, Godes yrre bær;
mynte se man-scaða manna cynnes
sumne besyrwan in sele þam hean.
Wod under wolcnum, to þæs þe he win-reced,
gold-sele gumena gearwost wisse,　　715
fættum fahne. Ne wæs þæt forma sið
þæt he Hroþgares ham gesohte.
Næfre he on aldor-dagum ær ne siþðan
heardran hæle heal-ðegnas fand.
Com þa to recede rinc siðian　　720
dreamum bedæled. Duru sona onarn
fyr-bendum fæst, syþðan he hire folmum gehran:
onbræd þa bealo-hydig, ða he gebolgen wæs,
recedes muþan. Raþe æfter þon
on fagne flor feond treddode,　　725

eode yrre-mod ; him of eagum stod
ligge gelicost leoht unfæger.

Geseah he in recede rinca manige,
swefan sibbe-gedriht samod ætgædere,
mago-rinca heap. Ða his mod ahlog.   730

Francis Gummer's Translation (1909)

Thro' wan night striding,
came the walker-in-shadow. Warriors slept
whose hest was to guard the gabled hall , –
all save one. 'Twas widely known
that against God's will the ghostly ravager
him could not hurl to haunts of darkness;

wakeful, ready, with warrior's wrath ,
bold he bided the battle's issue.
THEN from the moorland, by misty crags,   XI.
with God's wrath laden, Grendel came.
The monster was minded of mankind now
sundry to seize in the stately house .

Under welkin he walked, till the wine-palace there ,
gold-hall of men , he gladly discerned,
flashing with fretwork. Not first time, this,
that he the home of Hrothgar sought,–
yet ne'er in his life-day, late or early,
such hardy heroes, such hall-thanes, found!
To the house the warrior walked apace,
parted from peace; the portal opened,
though with forged bolts fast, when his fists had struck it,

and baleful he burst in his blatant rage ,
the house 's mouth. All hastily, then,
o'er fair-paved floor the fiend trod on,
ireful he strode; there streamed from his eyes
fearful flashes, like flame to see.
He spied in hall the hero-band,
kin and clansmen clustered asleep,
hardy liegemen. Then laughed his heart;

Seamus Heaney's Translation (1999/2000)

       Then out of the night
came the shadow-stalker, stealthy and swift;
the hall-guards were slack, asleep at their post,
all except one; it was widely understood
that as long as God disallowed it,
the fiend could not bear them to his shadow-bourne.
One man, however, was in fighting mood ,
awake and on edge , spoiling for action.
  In off the moors, down through the mist bands
God-cursed Grendel came greedily loping.
The bane of the race of men roamed forth,
hunting for a prey in the high hall .
Under the cloud-murk he moved towards it
until it shone above him, a sheer keep
of fortified gold. Nor was that the first time
he had scouted the grounds of Hrothgar's dwelling —
although never in his life, before or since,
did he find harder fortune or hall-defenders.
Spurned and joyless, he journeyed on ahead

and arrived at the bawn . The iron-braced door
turned on its hinge when his hands touched it.
Then his rage boiled over , he ripped open
the mouth of the building, maddening for blood,
pacing the length of patterned floor
with his loathsome tread, while a baleful light,
flame more than light, flared from his eyes.
He saw many men in the mansion , sleeping,
a ranked company of kinsmen and warriors
quartered together.And his glee was demonic

3 「グレンデルのヘオロット襲撃」部分の精読

　前節に印刷した *Beowulf* 702b-30 行は，"Grendel's Approach to Heorot" と呼ばれるこの詩の中でも特に有名な一節である。Fitt X から XI にかけての部分，ベーオウルフ一行を歓待するフロスガール王の館ヘオロットでの宴会がはねて，王はベオウルフとその手下のイエーアタスの武士 14 人にこの館の警護を託す。夜が深まり寝ずの番をすべきイエーアタス人は，首領ベーオウルフを除いて皆寝込んでいる。その館へ向かって，沼地を抜けて陰のように，怪物グレンデルが近づいて来る。

　以下，古英語テキストを読みながら，解説を加える。

○ Com on wanre niht/ scriðan sceadu-genga;
wanre は形容詞「暗い」の *wan* の与格で，動詞 *scriðan* は後で詳論するが「くねって進む」の意。最後に来る主語 *sceadu-genga* は shadow-goer，つまり「陰を歩む者」である。「暗い夜に身をくねらせて進み来るは陰を歩む者」

○ sceotend swæfon,/ þa þæt horn-reced healdan scoldon,/ ealle buton anum.
sceotend は動詞 *sceotan* に現在分詞と同じ語尾をつけて作られた動作主名詞で「投げつける者，弓を射る者」よって「戦士」。*Swæfon* は動詞 *swefan*

「眠る」の過去複数形，次の þa は副詞ではなく関係代名詞の複数で先行詞は sceotend, þæt horn-reced (ここでは中性) は horn「鹿の角で飾られた」reced「館」であるから Heorot のこと。heorot (m) は現代英語の hart に当たり，「牡鹿」の意。healdan scoldon の healdan は現代英語の hold で，「保つ，守る」，scoldon は現代の should よりも意味が強く，合わせて「守る義務を負った」の意，ealle buton anum は all but one「一人を除いて全員」，つまりベーオウルフだけが起きているわけである。「武士たちは眠っていた，この鹿角で飾られた館ヘオロットを守護すべきであるのに，ベーオウルフだけを除いて皆が」

○þæt wæs yldum cuþ,/ þæt hie ne moste, þa Metod nolde,/se syn-scaþa under sceadu bregdan,/

この þæt–þæt は correlative construction 相関構造といい，現代英語では it-that の仮主語構文に相当する。yldum は判りづらいが ieldo, 現代英語の old に当たる名詞形与格，"to old age, old people" のこと，cuþ は cunnan の過去分詞で形容詞の known で「人々に知られていた」。その「知られている」内容が2番目の þæt 以下である。hie「彼らを」は後ろの他動詞 bregdan「傷つける」の目的語でベーオウルフと部下たちを指す。ne moste は motan の過去単数形で否定，「出来なかった」，その主語は冠詞 se の付いている名詞句 se syn-scaþa「罪深い殺戮者」。「人々に知られていた，その罪深い殺戮者は，神が望まぬならば，陰に隠れて彼らを蹂躙することはできないことを」

○ ac he wæccende wraþum on andan/ bad bolgen-mod beadwa geþinges./

初めの逆接接続詞 ac は先行する文の内容に対して逆接となるのではなく，単に否定 ne moste による否定の環境を肯定に変えるもの。he は目覚めているベーオウルフを指し，wæccende は wæccan の現在分詞。wæccan は現代英語では wake と watch の二重語に発達した。wake には James Joyce の Finegan's Wake のように寝ずに起きている通夜の意味があり，watch にも「見る」ではなくて「起きていて見張る，寝ずの番をする」の意がある。wraþum は今の wrath「怒り」の与格で「怒りを持って，怒って」の意，名詞 anda も「怒り」で on andan "in anger" という前置詞句の副詞は

「グレンデルのヘオロット襲撃」の文章構造と技法　　**463**

予格の副詞 *wraþum* と平行構造をなす。*bad* は *bidan*「待つ」の過去単数形，*bolgen-mod* は「怒りの気持ちで」という主格補語の形容詞，*beadwa* は「戦い」の意味の名詞 *beadu/-o* の所有格で次の *geþinges* にかかり，こちらは「結果，成り行き」の意の名詞 *geþing* の所有格で，*bidan*「待つ」の目的語である。この一節では「怒り」という名詞・形容詞が繰り返されている。「彼は大変に怒って戦いの結果を待ちながら，眠らずに見張っていた」

○Ða com of more under mist-hleoþum/ Grendel gongan, Godes yrre bær;/
2度目の *com* プラス現在分詞の構文。*mist-hleoþum* は *mist-hlið* "misty slope" の意で，動詞 *gongan* は今の *go* であるが，意味は単に「行く」ではなく「歩いて行く」。*gongan* vs. *ridan* は歩きか馬か，現代英語ならば *walk or ride* でさしずめ徒歩か車かという対比。*Godes yrre bær*，*bær* は *beran*「携える，持つ」の意の動詞過去単数形。*mist-hleoþum* は大抵の訳では「霧に隠れて」として *hleoþum* が無視されているが，現代英語の "under the wall"「壁際で，壁の内側で」というような用法を考慮すれば，グレンデルの棲む沼地の岸・断崖を示しているととれる。「そして沼地から，霧深い崖から，グレンデルは歩み進む，神の怒りを負って」

○ mynte se man-scaða manna cynnes/ sumne besyrwan in sele þam hean./
mynte は *myntan* の過去単数形で syncope を起こしている短い形で「意図する，狙う」。*man-scaða* は「人間の殺戮者」ではなく，*man* は長母音で「罪深い」。後ろの *manna cynnes* が所有格で前にかかる。*mynte* の目的語が不定詞 *besyrwan* で，この動詞に目的語，対格の *sumne* が前置されて付いている。*sele* は「館，建物」，*hean* は高い現代の *high* に当たる *heah* の対格形だが，別の形容詞 *hean*「惨めな」と同形になった言葉遊び，paronomagia 掛詞とされている。「その邪悪な，人間の殺戮者は考えた，あの高殿の中で（惨めな建物に変えて），誰かを罠にかけてやろうと」

○ Wod under wolcnum, to þæs þe he win-reced,/ gold-sele gumena gearwost wisse,/ fættum fahne.
初めの過去形動詞 *wod* は現代英語の *wade* に相当。後ろで動詞をまとめて再考するが，水の中などを歩くこと。*under wolcnum*「雲の下を」，*wolcen*

はドイツ語で Wolken, 現代英語では welkin。to þæs þe は関係詞で,「そこへ向かって」。win-reced は「ワインを飲む館」, gearwost は形容詞・副詞 gearwe「用意が出来ている」の最上級,「一番良く知っている」の意, 12年間も沼地から通って殺戮を繰り返してきたので当の館を知り抜いていること。fættum は金属の飾り板のことで, 与格, fahne は「飾られた」の意味の fah の対格。gold-sele gumena は「人々が黄金を分け与えられる広間」ととれば win-reced と同様, 館の機能を示し,「人々の黄金で飾られた館」ととれば, fættum fahne がその館の様相を再叙していることになる。「雲の下を渡り進む, 彼グレンデルが, 人々が酒を飲み交わす館, 人々の黄金で飾られた広間がそこにあるとよく知っているところへ向かって」

○ Ne wæs þæt forma sið/ þæt he Hroþgares ham gesohte./
forma sið は「初めての旅」, ここも þæt-þæt の相関構造。ヘオロットは Hroþgares ham「フロスガールの家」と説明されて, gesohte の目的語になっている。「彼, グレンデルがフロスガールの家を探すのは, これが初めてではなかった」 つまりこれは直前の,「よく知っていた」の言い換え, または理由。

○ Næfre he on aldor-dagum ær ne siþðan/ heardran hæle heal-ðegnas fand./
aldor-dagum は "days of life", ær ne siþðan は "before nor after"「後にも先にもない」, heardran は形容詞 heard "hard" の比較級で構造上 hæle と heal-ðegnas の両方にかかる。hæle は hælo (f)「運命」の対格単数, heal-ðegnas は hall-thane「館(警護)の武士」, 最後の過去単数形の動詞 fand, findan の過去形, の目的語。「彼グレンデルは, 後にも先にも生きている間に, これより辛い運命にも, 強い館警護の武士にも, 会ったことがなかった」

○ Com þa to recede rinc siðian/ dreamum bedæled.
ここで3度目の com プラス現在分詞が出る。グレンデルはこの時点で館に着いた。rinc は主語で「武士, 戦士」, dreamum bedæled では, bedæled は bedælan「奪う」の過去分詞, 奪われたものは dreamum「喜びを」と複数与格で表す。「そしてとうとう館に来たのだった, その戦士は, 喜びを奪われながら, 旅をして」

○ Duru sona onarn/ fyr-bendum fæst, syþðan he hire folmum gehran:/
sona は soon, onarn は on-irnan の過去単数形で, irnan は rinnan = run, 語幹の母音が前後に入れ替わる metathesis「音位転換」の例。Wrenn の校訂本のグロッサリーでは "rush open" という語義が与えられている。直訳すると "ran on" となる。日本語でも, 刀が鞘から自然に抜けることを「鞘走る」と言う。OED の run の語義 2. a. "To go about freely, without being restrained or checked in any way." が参考になる。現代英語の run に "to open" の意味は記載されていない。fyr-bendum fæst は「火で鍛えられた留め金でしっかりと固定されていたのに」, という逆接の読みをしたい。hire は duru (f. ol.) の言い換えで目的語, folmum は folm "hand" の与格で具格。gehran は gehrinan「触れる」の単数過去形。「ヘオロットの扉はすぐに開いた, 火で鍛えられた留め金で補強されていたにもかかわらず, 彼グレンデルが手で触ったとたんに」 先にあげた Gummer 訳では "the portal opened,/ though with forged bolts fast, when his fists had struck it,/ and baleful he burst in his blatant rage,/ the house's mouth." と逆接の意味で形容詞 fyr-bendum fæst が訳出されているのは Fred C. Robinson (1985) における逆説の読みの主張を先取りしたような慧眼と言える。
○ onbræd þa bealo-hydig, ða he gebolgen wæs,/ recedes muþan.
onbræd は onbregdan "to pull open" の過去単数形でその目的語は終わりの recedes muþan「館の口」つまり扉, bealo-hydig は「戦いを心に思った」という形容詞で, 省略された主語にかかる主格補語でグレンデルの心の状態を示す。gebolgen wæs は「怒って」, これは 709 行目の bolgen-mod と呼応して, これから格闘することになる両者の怒りを反響させている。「それから戦いを思うこの怪物は, 怒りに駆られて, 館の扉を押し開けた」
○ Raþe æfter þon/ on fagne flor feond treddode,/ eode yrre-mod;
Raþe は副詞で「すぐに」, on fagne flor の fagne は 716 行の fættum fahne と同じ語で形容詞 fag の変化形ととれば「飾られた床」の意となるが, fæge "doomed, accursed" の対格変化形ととれば「呪われた床, 死の運命にある床」となる。両義を掛けてあるとすれば 713 行後半 in sele þam hean と同じ状況となる。主語は feond "fiend", eode は gan の過去形。現代英語でも

go は過去形が語源の異なる動詞に由来して *went* となるが，古英語の時から defective verb「欠損動詞」であった。*treddode* は現代英語 *tred* の過去形。「その後すぐに，模様のある床の上を（死の運命の床の上を），その敵は歩んでいった，怒りながら進んでいった」

◯ him of eagum stod/ ligge gelicost leoht unfæger./
of eagum は「両目から」，*stod* は *standan* の過去単数形，主語は終わりの名詞句 *leoht unfæger*，直訳すると「美しくない光」であるが，ここは litotes「緩叙法」で，"not bad" が "good" となるように「醜い」の意。OED の見出し語 *unfair* を見ると語義 1. b. に "wicked, evil, bad" があり，初例が 14 世紀の頭韻詩になっているが，*Beowulf* のこの行も "wicked" に取れる筈。*ligge gelicost* は「炎によく似ている」。*Gelicost* はしばしば半行単位での直喩表現で用いられる。ベーオウルフ一行がイエーアトからデネに向かう舟は *fugle gelicost*「まるで海鳥のように」と喩えられている (218)。「彼の両目からは，まるで炎のような，邪悪な光が立っていた」この光が立つという主語・動詞の collocation は，他の自然現象と共に覚えるべきで，英語では霧も雲も臭気も煙も立つというが，日本語でも同様，靄，霧，霞，雲，煙が立つと言うのは面白い一致である。「噂が立つ」と言うのに「音が立つ」と自動詞形ではもはや言わない。しかし「音を立てるな」とは言う。古英語も音や噂を主語に述語 *standan* を使う。

◯ Geseah he in recede rinca manige,/ swefan sibbe-gedriht samod ætgædere,/ mago-rinca heap.
geseah は *geseon* の過去単数形，*rinca manige* は「多くの武士達」，グレンデル自身が 3 つ目の *com* プラス現在分詞の構文で *rinc* と呼ばれていた。*swefan* は「眠る」の不定形 infinitive で意味上の主語は前の *rinca manige* と，その variation の *sibbe-gedriht*「同族の人の一群」。*samod ætgædere* は「皆一緒に」の決り文句，*mago-rinca heap* はベオウルフ達を指す 3 つ目の variation で「若い戦士の群れ」。「彼は見た，館の中に武士がたくさんいるのを，同族の群が一緒に眠っているのを，若い戦士の群れを」

◯þa his mod ahlog;
ahlog は *ahleahhan* の過去単数形，*a-* は意味を強める接頭辞。*hleahhan* は

今の *laugh*。「その時彼の心が笑った」表情は獰猛でありながら，心中でしめたと会心の笑みを漏らした，という心理描写で，近代的感覚。

4 文体上の技巧：語句の対応と対照・平行構造と繰り返し・サスペンスの醸成

(1) 動詞 *com* の3度繰り返し（下線部）

以上のような内容がわかったところで，描写の技法について考えてみたい。まずレトリックの大きな構造として動詞 *com* の3度の繰り返しはすぐに気付くところだ。本節冒頭，第1の *com* にはグレンデルの襲撃の時が示されている。*Com on wanre niht scriðan sceadu-genga*「暗い夜にからだをくねらせながら，やって来たのは，陰の中を歩むものであった」主語の *sceadu-genga* は倒置語順で最後に置かれ，まるでグレンデルの姿が闇に紛れて見えないように文中でもなかなか現われない。次の710行目の *com* には，*Ða com of more under mist-hleoþum Grendel gongan, Godes yrre bær* と，グレンデルという固有名詞と共に *of more* "out of moor"「沼地からやって来た」と出発点が示されている。先に見たようにグレンデルはアベル殺しのカインの裔で神の怒りを負っている。さらに10行後，720行に3度目の *com* が目的地とともに出て，ここでとうとうグレンデルはヘオロットに到着する。*Com þa to recede rinc siðian dreamum bedæled*.「そしてやって来た，この館に，戦士は旅をして，喜びを奪われて」2番目の *com* 以下で神の怒りを負ってという表現があるが，ここではそれを喜びを奪われてとヴァリエーションで言い換えている。

過去単数形の動詞 *com* に付く現在分詞がグレンデルの移動の様子を示すのであるが，その現在分詞も *scriðan*「身をくねらせて進む」，*gongan*「歩いて進む」，*siðian*「旅をする」と皆異なり，多面的な描写になっている。このように *com* と現在分詞からなる構文で，グレンデルが真夜中に沼地を抜け出して，陰のように朧に，蛇のようにくねりながら，この19行の間に，ある程度の距離を歩いて目的地のヘオロットに到着した様子が，その到着の描写を故意に遅らせてサスペンスを醸し出す。まるで初めの *com*

が青の警告ランプで敵の出発を告げ，近づいて来て黄色に変わり，ドアのすぐ表に怪物が到着した時，赤の警告ランプが点灯するかのように，事の緊急さと緊張感を増す描写がされている。この3度の *cuman* の繰り返しは古くから知られている。そのサスペンス構造に初めて言及したのは Alain Renoir, (1962) "Point of View and Design for Terror in *Beowulf*" で，闇の中から次第に明らかにされてゆくグレンデルの描写を cinematograph という語を使ってカメラのクローズアップに喩えた。

(2) *under* 句の3度の繰り返し（波線下線部）
2番目の *com* プラス現在分詞の構文には前置詞 *under* が導く句が起きているが，この文の前後にもそれを挟んで *under* が導く句が起きている。これらは shadow, mist, clouds と皆，グレンデルの陰の存在を印象付けるような，ものを隠すイメージの名詞を別語で繰り返しているのだ。過去形動詞 *com* 構文もそうであるが，この3度の繰り返しが意図的であることは，同じように敵対者が近づいて来る描写で，同一動詞を3度繰り返すパターンが *Beowulf* が収められている写本に断片が残された *Judith* という詩にも見えることから明らか（***Judith* (200b-229a):** Stopon cynerofe/ secgas ond gesiðas, bæron sigeþufas,/ foron to gefeohte forð on gerihte,/ hæleð under helmum, of ðære haligan byrig/ on ðæt dægred sylf. Dynedan scildas,/ hlude hlummon. Þæs se hlanca gefeah/ wulf in walde, ond se wanna hrefn,/wælgifre fugel. Wistan begen/ þæt him ða þeodguman þohton tilian/ fylle on fægum; ac him fleah on last/ earn ætes georn, urigfeðera,/ salowigpada sang hildeleoð,/ hyrnednebba. Stopon heaðorincas,/ beornas to beadowe, bordum beðeahte,/ hwealfum lindum, þa ðe hwile ær/ eldeodigra edwit þoledon,/ hæðenra hosp. Him þæt hearde wearð/ æt ðam æscplegan eallum forgolden,/ Assyrium, syððan Ebreas/ under guðfanum gegan hæfdon/ to ðam fyrdwicum. Hie ða fromlice/ leton forð fleogan flana scuras,/ hildenædran, of hornbogan,/ stælas stedehearde; styrmdon hlude/ grame guðfrecan, garas sendon/ in heardra gemang. Hæleð wæron yrre,/ landbuende, laðum cynne,/ stopon styrnmode, stercedferhðe,/ wrehton unsofte ealdgeniðlan/ medowerige;）3度の繰り返しのパターンは聖書にも

頻繁に見られる。例えば、旧約聖書『サミュエル記』上の 3:4-14 では 3 度名前を呼ばれて Eli という名前の司祭が、それが神のお召しであることに気付くこと、『イザヤ書』6:3 では holy, holy, holy is the Lord of hosts. という形容詞の強調、『エレミア』22:29 の O, earth, earth, earth、新約聖書『ヨハネ伝』21:15-17 の、イエスのシモン・ペテロよ、汝、我を愛するかという 3 度の問いなど。語句に限らずテーマ・モチーフにも見られることは、例えば Sir Gawain & the Green Knight の 3 度の狩の場面でもわかるだろう。

『ベーオウルフ』のこの一節では、com プラス現在分詞の構文と under の前置詞句が入れ子細工のように組み合わさって、同じパターンを繰り返しながら怪物の移動の時・起点・到着点を分け示し、scriðan, gongan, siðian と動詞でも移動の様相を分け示し、shadow, mist, clouds の類語で陰の存在を多面的に描写する。

(3) グレンデルの歩みを示すさらなる動詞のヴァリエーション（二重下線部分）

これら scriðan, gongan, siðian の他にも wadan と treddian が怪物の歩みを表している。グレンデルの歩行を表す動詞を OED ではどのように扱っているか。初めの scriðan は Beowulf 中に 3 度しか使われておらず、初めが複数形（163 行）でグレンデルに眷族、仲間がいることを匂わせる。2 番目がこの一節で使われるのであり、3 個目は物語後半の火を吐く龍の動きを描写している。この動詞はゲルマン語の古い段階では、爬虫類の地面を擦る音や細長い身をくねらせる動きを表したようで、古北欧語や古英語では、蛇、龍、舟、魚の鮭 (leax) などに共通して使われていることから、その古い意味が明らかだ。古英語では星や太陽などの天体の動き、1 日や年月、機織の横糸を縦糸に通す船形の shuttle（ひ）と呼ばれる道具もこの動詞の主語になる。つまり周期運動や繰り返しの含意もありえるのだ。とすれば身体をくねらせる爬虫類、つまり蛇・龍としてのグレンデルの歩行様態とともに、この怪物が 12 年間繰り返し繰り返し沼地とヘオロットを往復したことまで含意しうるが、深読みかも知れぬ。OED では語義 1 に Beowulf の第 1 の使用例が引用されており、定義の後半、"to glide, creep, wander" などがここの解釈には適当である。注目すべきは第 2 例のラヤモンで軍隊の動きがこの動詞で示されている（「彼はスコットランド人の大群を引き連れてこの国になだれ込んだ」）。近づく戦闘を予期させる動詞である。

　次の wod under wolcnum 雲の下を歩み行くだが，OED の見出し語 wade の語義 1 で，「何かの中を通って進む」の意味であるとしているので，霧や靄，雲の中を通って隠れて進むグレンデルにぴったりの動詞である。語義 3 番の b. を見ると，wade through blood, slaughter と死体の間を縫って歩く，行くところを死体と血だらけにして去る，という比喩的な読み込みも，ここの初例が 1400 年頃であるから，後智恵のある我々としてはできるわけだ。そこまで故意に比喩に取らなくても，グレンデルは沼地に住む怪物であるから，常に水の中を歩いているということで，wade は scriðan とともにグレンデルの本質的動きを表す動詞であると言える。

(4) 怒りを意味する語の繰り返しパターン（囲み部分）
　ほとんど注目されてこなかったもう一つの平行性には，待ち受けるベーオウルフも，殺戮を始めようとするグレンデルも，グレンデルをカインの末裔として呪う神も，この場面に関わる 3 者が皆怒っているという一致がある。印刷した古英語テキストと現代英語訳では枠で囲ってその対応を示した。その繰り返しのパターンは，wraþ-anda-bolgen-yrre-bolgen-yrre と続き，これを意図的同意語の繰り返しと見て，現代英語訳で再現しようとしている訳者がいる（Roy Michael Liuzza 訳を見られたし。彼は 6 個の怒りを意味する語のうち，初めの二つを訳文では出さず，bolgen-yrre-bolgen-yrre の 2 語の繰り返しを rage と anger に対応させて訳出しているのである。Liuzza は他の語についても詩人による意図的な繰り返しであると判断すると，同じ表現で繰り返し訳出している）。

(5) ヘオロットを指示する名詞表現のヴァリエーション（網掛け・囲み部分）
　ヘオロットはこの一節において複合語及び名詞句で 7 度（i-vii）言及さ

れるが，この言い換えを注意を払って見てみれば，頭韻のための音合わせや間に合わせの言い換えではなく，順番に，その外観 (i)「角もて飾られた館」，(ii)「高く聳える館」，機能 (iii)「酒を飲み交わす館」，所有者 (iv)「フロスガール王の家」とヘオロットを多面的に，しかも情報として重複することなく提示していることがわかる。グレンデルが襲うのは，角もて飾られた館であるが，ベーオウルフに敗れて朝には自らのもぎ取られた腕が晒される事になる運命への隠れた予弁 (i), そして館を守るべき戦士らは酒に酔って眠り込んでいる事 (iii), これから対決・格闘するのは外国人のベーオウルフと同じく侵入者のグレンデルであるが，当の館はデネのフロスガール王の家であって，本来はデネの戦士が守るべきである事への皮肉 (iv), そして最も重要な呼称が慧眼の研究者によって指摘されて以来既に定説となっているが，2番目の *sele þam hean* であり，形容詞 *heah*「高い」の対格形と「惨めな」の意味の形容詞 *hean* を掛けることにより (punning), グレンデルの殺戮で「豪奢な」館が「惨めな」館に変貌することを，グレンデルの移動中の描写に予見的に入れ込んでいる。そしてGrendel が館に到着して殺戮がいざ始まるとなると *reced* (v, vi, viii)「館」という simplex しか用いられなくなり，館の様子や価値から格闘者の描写に重きが移行していることからも，優れた作品に表れる繰り返しが単なる繰り返しではなく，意味を付与され，恐怖描写を目的とする全体構造の有機的部分をなすことがわかるのである。

(6) 掛詞による曖昧性と予弁の繰り返し

『ベーオウルフ』に掛詞の技法が用いられていることを認めるならば，この一節での使用こそ恐怖感の醸成に最も効果的に用いられているのではないか。713 行では "mynte se man-scaða manna cynnes/ sumne besyrwan in sele þam hean." と，グレンデルが向かう *sele*「館」ヘオロットが「豪華な高殿」であっても，グレンデルの殺戮によって悲惨の館に変貌していることが述べられているが，この怪物が到着して足を踏み入れた時の描写 725 行では "Raþe æfter þon/ on fagne flor feond treddode,/ eode yrre-mod" と *on fagne flor* の *fagne* がやはり *fag*「飾られた」か *fæge*「死す運命の，呪われ

た」のどちらか迷うところとなっている。そして「呪われた床，死の運命にある床」という句が，「ヘオロットを警護する武士がグレンデルに殺される」の意味から転じ，今や「この殺戮者は，自らが死ぬ事になる床へと足を踏み入れた」との予弁の意味を響かせて，ベーオウルフとの対決へ続くことになる。

(7) 闇の中で心が笑う

「心が笑った」は，『ツロのアポロニアス』に見える表現 "þa gefeol hyre mod on his lufe." 「その時彼の心は恋に落ちた」とも通じる（cf. *Apollonius of Tyre* (Goolden p. 26, l. 22) Latin counterpart: incidit in amorem.）。グレンデルは表情で笑っているのではなく，顔は獰猛でなくてはならない。顔がどうであるかを詩人はわざと描写していないのであって，ヘオロットの闇の中で人々に見えるのはグレンデルの猛獣のような光る両目だけである。逆にグレンデルには眠っているイエーアトの戦士が見えた。『ベーオウルフ』の詩人は，グレンデルの外面描写は出来る限りせずに不可知の存在に留めている。物語の中でも，その全身をくまなく見たのはベーオウルフだけであり，デネの人々はベーオウルフにもぎ取られてヘオロットの入り口に高く掲げられたグレンデルの腕や，グレンデルの母との戦いの後で，切り取られてヘオロットに持ち帰られたグレンデルの頭だけしか見ていない。実際，この後に続くベーオウルフとグレンデルの格闘の描写では，暗闇の中の大音響とグレンデルの叫び声がデネの人々を恐怖に陥れたことが述べられて，何も見えない闇の中の音に焦点が当たっている。

ヒーニー訳では "his glee was demonic" と訳しているが，これは掛け言葉である。glee とはグリー・クラブ男声合唱のグリーで「大喜び・はしゃぎ」の意味と，スコットランド方言で「横目で見る，狙いを定める」の両義である。ヒーニーの描き出すグレンデルは，獲物を定めるグレンデルの目付きはまこと悪鬼のようであり，彼の心はこれからの殺戮にはしゃいでいたとでもなるであろうが，これを訳し過ぎと考える人々がいる。一方上で述べたように，予弁のサスペンスが *in sele þam hean* と *on fagne flor* の掛詞によって助長されているとするならば，そしてその事を詩人が直感で

嗅ぎ取り，自らも同じ節で掛詞を使ってグレンデルの描写を行ったとすれば，天与の詩才と褒むべきである。[3]

注

1　本稿は2003年10月に日本中世英語英文学会主催研究助成セミナー（於福岡女子大学）で筆者が行った「*OED*の利用方法と古英詩の精読」における口頭発表原稿を基にして，時間が足りずに十分行えなかった*Beowulf*の「グレンデルのヘオロット襲撃」部分の精読を拡大し，その後に気付いた事柄を含めて改訂したものである。今井光規教授は2003〜4年度に日本中世英語英文学会の会長を務められ，筆者は当時評議員であった。そのセミナーの*Beowulf*に関する解説は大阪大学言語文化研究科における1998年度の大学院演習「*Beowulf*講読」に基づいている。この時期に今井教授は大阪大学言語文化部の評議員であられ，後に部長を務められた。こうした経緯から筆者はこの精読の試みを本記念論文集に捧げるものである。

2　劇場で販売のパンフレットには，予想された日本中世英語英文学会員の*Beowulf*専門研究者による文章はなく，2007年夏出版の苅部恒徳・小山良一編『古英語叙事詩「ベーオウルフ」対訳版』（研究社）から当詩の1251-59行（グレンデルの母が復讐を決意する部分）が転載されていたのみ。解説は法政大学教授，翻訳家の金原瑞人氏が書き，ゼメキス監督のインタヴューの内容で，映画の筋は原作とは異なってデンマーク1国の話に組み換えられたことが述べられてはいる。

3　渡部眞一郎先生を初めとして本記念論文集の編集に当たられた諸先生方に感謝致します。

参考文献

Brodeur, A. (1953) 'Design for Terror in the Purging of Heorot' *Journal of English and Germanic Philology* 53: 503-13.

Greenfield, S. B. (tr.) (1982) *A Readable Beowulf*. Southern Illinois University Press.

Kermode, F. (2000) Review. "*Beowulf: A New Translation* by Seamus Heaney, *Beowulf: A New Verse Translation* by R. M. Liuzza," *The New York Review of Books* July 20: 18-21.

Orchard, A. (1995) *Pride and Prodigies: Studies in Monsters in the Beowulf-Manuscript*. Cambridge: D. S. Brewer.

Orchard, A. (2003) *A Critical Companion to Beowulf*. Cambridge: D. S. Brewer.

Renoir, A. (1962) "Point of View and Design for Terror in *Beowulf*," *Neuphilologische Mitteilungen* 63: 154-67.

Renoir, A. (1982) "Introduction" to *A Readable Beowulf*. Southern Illinois University Press. pp. 1-26.

Watanabe, H. (1988) 'Monsters Creep?: the Meaning of the Verb *scriðan* in *Beowulf*,' *Studies in Language and Culture* 14: 107-20. Osaka University.

Watanabe, H. (2000) "Quotations from *Beowulf* and Other Old English Poems in *the Oxford English Dictionary*," *Lexicographica* Series Maior, 103: 263-9. Tübingen: Max Niemeyer.

Watanabe, H. (2005) *Metaphorical and Formulaic Expressions in Old English Reconsidered*. Tokyo: Eihosha.

Watanabe, H. (2006) "Beowulfiana in Japan: A Brief Survey of the Past 75 Years with Special Focus on the Japanese Translations and Interpretive Studies," *Studies in Medieval English Language and Literature*. 21: 1-10.

苅部恒徳・小山良一編 (2007)『古英語叙事詩「ベーオウルフ」対訳版』研究社.

渡辺秀樹 (2002)「シェイマス・ヒーニー訳『ベーオウルフ』の評価」『言語文化研究』28: 367-77. 大阪大学言語文化部

渡辺秀樹 (2003)「古英詩『ベーオウルフ』の日本語訳」『言語文化研究』29: 435-54. 大阪大学言語文化部

『ユリシーズ』第 8 挿話を読む ― 不完全なる完全

今井　安美

はじめに

　『ユリシーズ』の第 8 挿話は，第 4・第 5・第 6，そして第 13 挿話の後半と同様に，ブルームの内的独白によって彼の人物像を読者に伝える挿話である。特にこの第 8 挿話はこの作品の中でも夫として困難な立場に置かれているブルームと，それを直視しょうとしない彼の態度を，広告という独特の表現方法を用いて描き，この作品の中心となるテーマを読者に伝え考えさせるという点で重要な役割を持つ挿話と言えよう。
　グレアム・レモン菓子店の看板の下を，友人ディグナムの葬儀に参列して喪服姿のままのブルームが通り過ぎていく。彼はこの日あと数時間も経たないうちに，妻モリーが自分の家で自分以外の男と逢い引きすることになっているという，深刻な家庭の問題をかかえているのだ。彼はそのことを考えまいとしながらもみじめな思い，緊張と心の昂り，それでいてまだ些かの余裕のある複雑な心境で，周りのことや目に入ってくる様々な広告に注意を向け，心の中でじつに饒舌にしゃべっている。
　第 8 挿話は広告の挿話と言えよう。広告取りブルームの目に次から次へと広告が飛び込んできて彼の関心を引いている。それらの広告の中で，ブルームの心の問題に深く関わっている特に二つの広告業社，すなわちヒーリー社とプラムツリー社の広告を取り上げ，ブルームがいかに社会人とし

て家庭人として不安定で不完全な状態であるかを，彼が大切に持ち歩くレモン石けんを絡めて考えてみたいと思う。

1　ブルームの仕事

　通りでブルームは5人のサンドイッチマンに行き会う。文房具製造販売業ヒーリー社の広告である。彼はこの広告を評価せず，「『フリーマンズ・ジャーナル』紙の第一面の死亡記事欄の下に出ているプラムツリー社の広告のようだ」と批判している (8. 138–39)。実はブルームは以前このヒーリーの会社に雇われていて，吸い取り紙の販売や集金周りの仕事をしていたことがあるのだ。彼はかつてヒーリーにいくつかの広告のアイデアを提案したのに却下されたと回想している (8. 131–37)。[1]

　このようにブルームが否定的な評価をしているヒーリー社とは実際はどのような会社だったのだろうか。私はたまたま2004年にブルームズ・デイ100年祭のダブリンで買い求めた *A Bloomsday Postcard* という本の中にヒーリー社の名前を見つけた。1904年当時のこの会社は，絵はがきなどの印刷や出版業で大いに名をはせた会社だったようだ。絵はがきは数多く出回り，切手付きで2ペンス以下で手に入り，人々は盛んに利用したそうである。

　エドワード7世統治下のダブリンでは郵便制度が驚くほど進んでいて，1日に5回（日曜日は1回）の集配が行われていたらしい。『ノーラ』の著者ブレンダ・マドックスも，ジョイスとノーラの関係が急速に進んだのは，この優秀な郵便制度に負うところが大きいと言っている。恋人たちはこの制度を利用して，夜のデートの約束を当日の朝したり，キャンセルする場合は昼前に投函したとある。[2]

　『ユリシーズ』の挿話の多くにも，当時の絵はがきの普及振りがしのばれる言及がなされている。たとえば第4挿話では，朝の8時過ぎにブルームの家の玄関先にはもう郵便物が届いている様子が描かれているし (4. 243)，第13挿話にも，夜9時の配達をしている郵便配達人の姿をブルームが目撃するところが描かれている (13. 1170)，といった具合である。

『ユリシーズ』第8挿話を読む　　**477**

　ではなぜその名だたるヒーリー社をブルームは良く思っていないのだろうか。印刷出版業といえば，作者であるジョイスは『ユリシーズ』を執筆するまでに，『ダブリンの市民』などの出版をめぐって，印刷出版業者たちと揉め事を繰り返してきたという苦い経験があるので，彼らに対して良い感じを持っていないということは容易に想像がつく。ブルームとこの会社の関係は，彼の回想を通してみるとその深層に横たわっているものが見えてくる。

　ブルームがヒーリー社に就職したのはモリーと結婚した 1888 年のこと。6 年間勤めて今から 10 年前に辞めたと言っている (8. 158–59)。その年 1894 年とは息子ルーディを生後 11 日目で亡くした年である。そしてそれ以来彼ら夫婦の関係は変わってしまったのだ (8. 610)。彼はヒーリー社を自分から辞めたと言っているが，第 18 挿話のモリーの回想から，私たちは彼が辞めたのではなく，どうやら辞めさせられたのだということを知らされる。

　それどころか色々な挿話で言及されている彼のこれまでの職歴を拾ってみると，ヒーリー社の次は同じく印刷出版業のトム社で，その後は家畜業の管理者カフのもとで働いていた。そしてさらにはドリミーの保険会社でも働いていたようである。これらの職歴に加えてブルームは，彼自身とモリーの回想や，口さがないサイモンたちの会話から，ヒーリー社を首になった後，古着の売買にも手を出していたようである (8. 349–52; 11. 476; 18. 561-67)。カフの職場ではその頑固さゆえに首になり，モリーは取りなしに行かされのだが無駄だったと回想している (18. 510)。

　またブルームには会話の相手に対して "…don't you see？" (7. 976–77; 12. 465) とか，"That's well known. Did you not know that?" (12. 888) とかいう口癖があるようで，第１２挿話の「市民」も，カフのところで働いていた当時のブルームの様子を "Mister Knowall" (12. 838) と揶揄しているように，「知ったかぶり」をしては雇い主の機嫌を損ねてきたのだろう。

　今携わっている『フリーマンズ・ジャーナル』社の仕事にしても，広告取りといってもフリーの身分で，他者の目に映るブルームの姿が描かれた第 7 挿話で見た限りでは，順調にいっているとは言えない様子である。酒

やお茶の販売業者アレキサンダー・キーズとの新聞広告の契約更新の件で，新聞社側とキーズ側の板挟みになってブルームは困っている。

このキーズという名前を，ブルームはこれから行こうとしている国立図書館にある『キルケニー・ピープル』紙に出ているハウス・オブ・キーズのキーズに掛けて，その紋章の二つの鍵をその広告の図案に用いようと考えているようだが，皮肉なことにこの日自分の家の鍵を持っていないブルームが，自分の家の悩み事を解決する「鍵」も見つけられない状態でこの仕事に携わっているのだから，契約の行く末が案じられるというものである。そして案の定，この問題は第8挿話はおろか，この日の終わりになっても解決することはないのだ。

このように仕事面では，過去においても現在も，incomplete で不安定な状態のブルームは，5人のサンドイッチマンを見て，つらい家庭の問題まで掘り起こされてしまって，その不満をこの広告を貶すことで発散させているのである。

2　ブルームの家庭

第8挿話の広告，「もしもご家庭にプラムツリー社の "potted meat" がなかったら。不完全。あってこそ至福の家」，

> What is home without
> Plumtree's Potted Meat?
> 　　Incomplete.
> With it an abode of bliss. (5. 144–47)

この広告をブルームが初めて目にしたのは第5挿話で，マッコイに出会ったときであった。気の進まない会話に『フリーマンズ・ジャーナル』紙の第一面を開いてみたとき，死亡欄の下に見たのだ (5. 143–47)。ところで，この広告もそしてそれが新聞の死亡欄の下にあったというのも実はフィクションで，ジョイスが創り出したものである。しかし平型の陶製の容器に詰められた肉（以後は「陶器詰め肉」）を製造するプラムツリー社は1904年に存在していて，ジョイスはそれを巧みに広告文に用いているのである。

ヒーリー社と同様に，このプラムツリー社の広告をよく思っていなかったブルームは，再び第8挿話でも思い出し，「なんと馬鹿げた広告」(8. 743)と全く評価していない。なぜなのか。そして彼の家にはこの陶器詰め肉はあるのだろうか。この答えを出す前に，広告の挿話とも言える第8挿話におけるジョイスの技法について考えてみたい。
　そもそも広告の目的は商品を買って貰うことにあるのだから，普通商品や製造元あるいは売り手の名前を明記し，買い手に印象づけ，認識させ，覚えて貰わなければならない。広告取りのブルームを感心させた，リフィー川に止めている船の上に取り付けられた広告，

　　　Kino's
　　　 11/-
　　　Trousers (8. 90–92)

一目でわかる「キノ商店の11シリングのズボン」の広告である。
　しかしながらこれとは違って，はじめはわざと商品名を伏せたり他の表現を使うことによって，買い手の好奇心をあおり注意を引きつけて，その商品を認識させる広告方法がある。ジョイスはこの方法を巧みに利用して，ブルームにある人物の名前を代名詞や服装などによるエピセットを用いさせることで，その人物をより鮮明に買い手ならぬ読者に伝えている。ブルームが会うのを避けて，名前を口にしようとはせず，代名詞などでしか呼ばないその人物とは，他ならぬ妻の姦通相手であるボイランその人なのである。
　いくつか例を挙げてみよう。まずブルームがどんな場所でも広告に利用できると考える場面で，性病を治す医者の広告のことを思い出した直後，「もしボイランが性病にかかっていて，モリーがうつされたら」と考えてしまうところ，

　　　If he....?
　　　O!
　　　Eh?
　　　No...... No.

> No, no. I don't believe it. <u>He</u> wouldn't surely?
> No, no. (8. 102–107)　（下線は筆者）

ブルームの意識の中に第8挿話ではここで初めて登場するボイランは，このように代名詞 he で表現されている。

　次は町を行くブルームがふと2週間ほど前の夜のことを思い出しているくだり，

> The full moon was the night we were Sunday fortnight... （中略）Walking down by the Tolka. （中略）She was humming. The young May moon she's beaming, love. <u>He</u> other side of her. Elbow, arm. <u>He</u>. Glowworm's la-amp is gleaming, love. Touch. Fingers. Asking. Answer. Yes.
> Stop. Stop. If it was it was. Must. (8. 587–92)　（下線は筆者）

その満月の夜，ブルームとモリーと「代名詞の君」の3人は，モリーを真ん中に，トルカ川のほとりを散歩していたのだ。そしてその時ブルームの傍らで，モリーと彼（すなわちボイラン）の仲は，愛のデュエットで交感しながら急速に接近したのである。ブルームはそのことを必死に忘れようとしている。

　そして最後は昼食をとりに入ったデイヴィー・バーンの店でのこと。ブルームが食べ物のことにあれこれ思いをめぐらせていたときに，牡蠣が精力増強剤になるということから，またまたボイランのことを思い出している。

> Fizz and Red bank oysters. Effect on the sexual. Aphrodis. <u>He</u> was in the Red Bank this morning. Was <u>he</u> oysters old fish at table perhaps <u>he</u> young flesh in bed... (8. 865–67)　（下線は筆者）

牡蠣を食べてさぞかし精力が付いたのだろうとブルームの想像するボイランは，ここでも代名詞扱いとなっている。

　さらにもうひとつ興味深いのは，上の引用文で見られるように，ジョイスは単に代名詞を使うだけではなく，ハリー・ブラマイアーズが "powerful Joycean economy"[4]，そしてアーウィン・スタインバーグが "condensation"[5]，

と呼ぶ，広告にふさわしい無駄のない切りつめた表現方法をこの挿話のあちこちで用いている。この手法についてはまた後で触れたいと思う。

　先程のプラムツリー社の広告の問いかけに話を戻そう。「なければ不完全，あってこそ至福の家庭」という陶器詰め肉はブルームの家にはあるのだろうか。その答えは "Yes" であり，同時に "No" でもある。"Yes" である理由は，第 17 挿話の教理問答 (catechism) の形式で書かれた挿話の中で得られる。スティーヴンをつれてエクルス通りの家に帰ってきたブルームは，台所の食器戸棚を開けて，真ん中の段にプラムツリー社の空っぽの容器を見つける (17. 296–307)。これは第 10 挿話でボイランが訪問に先駆けて，果物やポートワインと共にモリーのもとに届けさせるあの陶器詰め肉で，ブルームが外を歩き回っている間にボイランとモリーによってベッドの中で食べられて，その食べかすが寝る前にブルームによってベッドから取り除かれることになる肉の入っていた器なのだ (17. 2122–25)。こういう訳でブルームの家にはプラムツリー社の陶器詰め肉は存在し，一時的にせよ「complete な至福の家」になるのである。

　しかしながらブルーム自身にとっては事情が異なる。第 8 挿話のブルームは，プラムツリー社の陶器詰め肉が，この様な形で自分の家に持ち込まれることになるとはまだ知るよしもなく，ブルームが後に台所で目にすることになるのは，ただの空っぽの容器で，彼はその中身を食べるはずもなく，さらには空いた器が一つしかないということは，もともと彼の家には陶器詰め肉がなかったということになるので，ブルームにとっての答えは "No" であり，彼の家は「至福のない incomplete な家庭」なのである。

　ところで "to pot one's meat" とは，"copulate" を意味するあからさまなスラングだそうなので[6]，ボイランは実際に陶器詰め肉を食べるだけではなく，ブルームの妻まで「食べて」しまうということになり，もう 10 年以上もの間妻とは incomplete な形の夫婦の関係しか持っていない (17. 2282–84) ブルームが貶し，第 17 挿話で最悪の広告の例として挙げている (17. 596–99) この広告は，まさに妻を寝取られ，幸せな家庭を持たない，不安定な状態のブルームを象徴する広告と言えよう。

空腹を覚えたブルームが昼食をとろうと最初に入ったバートンの店で，彼に吐き気を催させ，そこから逃げ出させた「肉を食する」人間達が，ホメロスの『オデュッセイアー』の食人種「ライストリュゴネス族」に対応するものと捉えられているが，それに加えてまるで巨人のような存在感を持ってブルームを脅かしているボイランこそ，ペネロペイアの求婚者に対応する存在でありながら，同時に「食人種」にも対応しているのであろう。[7]

　こういうわけでブルームは，「食人種」の群れるその店にもしかしたらあの「食人種」ボイランもいるのではないかと思ったのに姿を見かけず，"Not here. Don't see <u>him</u>."(8. 695)（下線は筆者）と言っているのだろう。バートンの店を出て「道徳的な」デイヴィー・バーンの店に入り，もともと「獣や鳥の内臓を好んで食する」(4. 1-2) ブルームではあるが，この挿話では「食人種」と一線を画すためか，チーズのサンドイッチを食べているのだ。

　昼食を終えたブルームは，「まず図書館へ行かなければ」(8. 1167) と思うのだが，次の瞬間とうとうボイランに遭遇してしまう。第6挿話で墓地に向かう馬車の中からレッド・バンク牡蠣料理店の入り口付近にいた彼を見かけて，同乗の他の三人が彼に挨拶を送る傍らで，爪を見るふりをしてやり過ごして以来，この日二度目の出会いである。図書館を目前にしたこの場面でも，もう既に読者にははっきりと認識されているボイランを，ブルームは依然として名前ではなく，「麦わら帽子に，黄褐色の靴に，折り返しの付いたズボン」(8. 1168) というエピセットで認知している。

　今回は対決は避けられない。しかしブルームのとっさに取った行動は，ボイランを避けて向きを変え，行き先を急きょ変更して，彼に背を向けて歩きながら何かを探すふりをする，というよりは本当に何かを探している。

　　　I am looking for <u>that</u>. Yes <u>that</u>. Try all pockets. Handker.
　　Freeman. Where did I? Ah, yes. Trousers. Potato. Purse. Where?
　　　Hurry. Walk quietly. Moment more. My heart.
　　　His hand looking for the where did I put found in his hip pocket soap lotion have to call tepid paper stuck. Ah <u>soap</u> there I yes. Gate
　　　Safe! (8. 1188-93)　　（下線は筆者）

悪戦苦闘の末，最後にズボンの後ろのポケットから彼が取り出したのは，ジャガイモのお守り[8]ではなく，新聞紙がくっついた石けんであった。これを手にして「助かった！」とブルームは無事に博物館の入り口にたどり着くことができたのである。

3　ブルームのお守り

"Incomplete" の動く広告塔のようなブルームが，この挿話のおわりで今見たように，危機一髪のところで「食人種」ボイランから逃れる様子は，まさに先程触れたジョイスの効果的な圧縮された文体で描写されている。ここではブルーム自身が語り手と渾然一体となって，彼の動転した心と体の動きを私たちに伝えている。そして彼が最後にポケットから探し出して手にしたこの石けんは，やはり代名詞で表されている。しかしながら，ただ一度だけ "Boyl" (8. 130) と途中までは出かかるものの，それっきり挿話の終わりまでブルームによって名前で呼ばれることのないボイランとは違って，彼が探していたのは石けんであったということを，私たちは最後には明確に知らされるのである。この彼の窮地を救う働きをする，新聞紙の張り付いた石けんが，なぜ彼にとってそれほど大切な物なのだろう。ブルームが登場する『ユリシーズ』の大部分の挿話に現れる，このレモン石けんを初めから順を追って見てみよう。

　この石けんをブルームは，第5挿話でモリーのためにオレンジフラワー水入りのローションを注文しにスウィニーの店に立ち寄ったとき，その香りに惹かれて自分のために4ペンスで手に入れた物であった (5. 509–12)。キリスト教絵画の世界では，柑橘類は結婚の祝いを象徴し，特にレモンは「貞節」を表す[9]そうだが，その香りはブルームにその名もシトロンという友人達に囲まれた，モリーとの幸せだった結婚生活の日々を思い出させるようだ。

　スウィニーの店を出たブルームは，この石けんを手に，『フリーマンズ・ジャーナル』紙を小脇にはさんで歩いていたが，その後出会ったバンタム・ライオンズにあげようとしたけれども受け取られなかったその新聞紙を

きちんとたたみ直し，その中に石けんを包み込んだ (5. 543–44)。

　第5挿話と第6挿話の間で風呂に入ったと思われるブルームは，その濡れた石けんを新聞紙に包んでズボンの後ろポケットに入れていたのを，第6挿話の馬車の中で思い出し，どこか他の場所に移さなければと考えている (6. 21–23)。墓地に着くと彼はその新聞紙がくっついた石けんを，素早くハンカチを入れる内ポケットに移しかえた (6. 494–96)。

　第7挿話で，"ONLY ONCE MORE THAT SOAP" (7. 221) というタイトルを付けて貰った石けんを，ブルームはハンカチ入れのポケットだと滑り落ちてはいけないと思い，もう一度ズボンの後ろポケットに入れ直した (7. 226–29)。同じく第7挿話では，モリーが男たちの間で，"Dublin's prime favourite" (7. 610) と石けんの広告のキャッチフレーズで皮肉たっぷりに呼ばれている。またしばしば指摘されるように，モリーという名前はギリシャ神話の魔法の薬草モリュ (moly) を連想させるものでもある。[10]

　従って第8挿話の終わりで，ボイランからブルームを護ることになる，『フリーマンズ・ジャーナル』紙の切れ端がペタッと張り付いたレモン石けんは，その新聞社の広告取りのブルームが，合体しているかのようにモリーにしがみついた姿を象徴するものであり，彼女との昔の幸せな生活への彼の執着心を表したものであると思われる。だからブルームは他でもないこの石けんを探し出し，安堵の吐息をもらしたのだろう。

4　ブルームの流れ

　第8挿話が暗い前途をはらんでいるのに，グレアム・レモン菓子店のパイナップル・ロックやレモン飴などという，なにか明るい出だしで始まったのだが，ブルームの心にも常に明るさと暗さが混在している。夫婦間にそれほど差し迫った危機が訪れようとしているというのに，それを阻止し，家庭を護ろうとする様子もなく，心の底ではむしろそれを楽しんでいる節さえ見られる。彼にとって一番大切なのは，モリーとのホース岬での甘いキスの思い出なのである。一時的にせよ他の男に自分の家庭を明け渡し，そこを complete な至福の場所にされてしまえば，ブルームは性にお

ける三角関係から余分なはみ出し物となり，自らを慰めるより他にすべはない。[11]

「ヘンリー・フラワー」という偽名を使って，偽の新聞広告を出しマーサという文通相手を見つけても，それ以上どうするわけでもなく，未来のない中途半端な関係なのだ。仕事の面では既に見てきたように，地に足の付いた状態は望めない。そしてどうにかうまくボイランとの邂逅をかわしたかに思われた第8挿話の最後の場面でも，やはりブルームは incomplete な結果しか得られなかったのである。なぜならば当初の行き先は図書館であって博物館ではなかったのだし，やっと探し出した石けんは，スウィニーの店にモリーのローションをその日取りに行かなかったため，その代金と共にまだ未払いで，完全には彼の物とは言えなかったのだから。

ところで第15挿話の中の幻想的な場面で，「ブルームと私は似合いのカップル」(15.338) と言っていた，あのブルームの大切なレモン石けんはどうなったのだろう。1日の彼の行動の総復習の挿話である第17挿話に，再びそして最後となる石けんの姿が見られる。台所でブルームは流れる水で，風呂で使って少しは減ったけれどもまだ新聞紙が張り付いた，あのバリントン社の代金未払いでレモンの香りのする石けんを使って，自分の汚れた手を洗っている (17.229–34)。

流れる水。この日第8挿話のブルームは，空飛ぶカモメにえさを買って投げ与えた後で，リフィー川[12]の流れる水を見ながら，人生の流れについて考えていた。

> How can you own water really? It's always flowing in a stream, never the same, which in the stream of life we trace. Because life is a stream. (8.93–95)

流れ行く水を止めることはできない。行く水は決して同じではない。命の流れも同様である。人は生まれて死んでいく。ディグナムが死に，ブルームの気遣うピュアフォイ夫人が長い苦しみの末に子どもを産むように。世代から世代へと人の命が流れる水のように引き継がれていくのだ。

時の流れも引き留められるものではない。手に水を溜めておけないように。

> Can't bring back time. Like holding water in your hand. (8. 610-11)

たとえプラムツリー社の陶器詰め肉の空いた容器しかない incomplete な家庭でも，ブルームの人生はこのまま流れていくしかないであろう。この人生を達観したブルームの姿にこそ，ジョイスが『ユリシーズ』で描きたかった，彼にとって唯一無二のヒーロー[13]である，不完全でありながら完全な，そしてオールラウンドな，ギリシャの英雄オデュッセウスの姿を，私たちは早くもこの第 8 挿話で見るのである。

注

本論は 2007 年 6 月 16 日（Bloom's day）に青山学院大学で開催された日本ジェイムズ・ジョイス協会第 19 回大会におけるシンポジウム「『ユリシーズ』第 8 挿話」で行った口頭発表に加筆・修正したものである。

1. 使用テキストは James Joyce.(1986) *Ulysses*. Penguin's Student's Edition。本文中の引用箇所の挿話番号と行数は括弧内に記す。翻訳は基本的には，丸谷才一，永川玲二，高松雄一訳『ユリシーズ』（河出書房 1996）に依拠しているが，引用者による拙訳を含んでいる。
2. 『ノーラ』, pp. 50-51.
3. Gifford, p. 87.
4. Blamires, p. 72.
5. Steinberg, p. 82.
6. Gifford, p. 87.
7. Ellmann は「ブレイゼスってヘアリーな野郎だぜ」というノーズィ・フリンの台詞について次のように言っている。この "hairy" は "clever"「油断のならないという意味だがこれはライストリュゴネス人にふさわしい形容詞であり，彼らの性行為は女性の肉を食べるという一種の原始的な食人行為なのだ」。*Ulysses on the Liffey*, p. 78.（邦訳『リフィー河畔のユリシーズ』p. 118）。
   　Mark Osteen も，モリーのもとに向かうボイランが歯と歯の間にくわえたカーネーションの語源はラテン語の "carnis" で，これは "flesh" すなわち「人の肉」を意味すると，ボイランの肉食性に言及している。"Female Property: Women and Gift Exchange in *Ulysses*", p. 34.
8. Gifford, p. 71. ユダヤ人（ブルームの父方）にとって，命の継続のお守りであるジャガイモは，アイルランド人にとっても命を守る大切な糧である。このお守りは息子のいないブルームにとっては無用の物だが，母親から貰った形見として身につけている。
9. 宮下喜久朗, p. 164.

10 この "absolutely pure" な石けんの広告のキャッチフレーズ ("Dublin's favourite" soap) が，1904 年 9 月 11 日付けのフリーマンズ・ジャーナル紙に出ていたということ，および，モリーの名前と moly の関連への言及は Osteen, p. 35.
11 Herring, p. 83.
12 Liffey はアイルランド語では "life"（命）を意味する。
13 Budgen, pp. 15-18.

参考文献

Benstock, B. (1989) *Critical Essays on James Joyce's Ulysses*. Boston: C. K. Hall & Co.

Blamires, H. (1996) *The New Bloomsday Book: A Guide through Ulysses*. 3rd Edition. London: Routledge.

Budgen, F. (1972) *James Joyce and the Making of Ulysses*. Oxford University Press.

Dent, R. W. (1994) *Colloquial Language in* Ulysses: *A Reference Tool*. London and Toronto: Associated University Presses.

Ellmann, R. (1983) *James Joyce*. New and Revised Edition. Oxford University Press.

Ellmann, R. (1972) *Ulysses on the Liffey*. Oxford University Press.（和田旦・加藤弘和訳（『リフィー湖畔のユリシーズ』国文社 1985）

Gifford, D.and R. J. Seidman (1988) *Ulysses Annotated: Notes for James Joyce's Ulysses*. Revised and Expanded Edition. Berkley: University of California Press.

Herring, P. F. (1974) "Lotuseaters." In C. Heart and D. Hayman (eds.), *James Joyce's Ulysses: Critical Essays*. University of California Press. pp.71-89.

ジェイムズ・ジョイス研究会訳 (1997)『ジェイムズ・ジョイス事典』松柏社（A. N. Fargnoli and M. P. Gillespie, *James Joyce A to Z*, 1995）

Kershner, R. B. (ed.) (1996) *Joyce and Popular Culture*. University of Florida.

宮下規久朗 (2007)『食べる西洋美術史：「最後の晩餐」から読む』光文社新書.

Murphy, N. (2004) *A Bloomsday Postcard*. Dublin: The Lilliput Press.

Osteen, M. (1997) "Female Property: Women and Gift Exchange in *Ulysses*." In J. W. Wawrzycka and M. G.. Corcoran (eds.), *Gender in Joyce*. University Press of Florida. pp. 29-46.

Steinberg, E. R. (1972) "Characteristic Sentence Patterns in Proteus and Lestrygonians." In F. Senn (ed.), *New Light on JOYCE from the Dublin Symposium*. Indiana University Press. pp. 79-98.

丹治愛監訳 (2001)『ノーラ』集英社. (Maddox, B. *Nora*, 1988)
Tymoczko, M. (1994) *The Irish Ulysses*. University of California Press.

メタファーに見る感情のプロトタイプ特性

大森 文子

1 はじめに

　Lakoffを中心とする概念メタファー理論研究の枠組において，感情のメタファーに関してはKövecses (1986, 1990, 2000) が精力的に研究を行なっている。感情に関する彼の一連の研究の発端となったのは，1986年に発表した怒りの概念に関するLakoffとの共同研究で，＜怒り＞と＜容器内の熱湯＞という概念領域の間の写像関係に関するその詳細な研究はLakoff (1987) でも詳しく紹介されている。感情一般については，それを特徴づけるさまざまなメタファーと感情のプロトタイプについての考察がKövecses (1990, 2000) によりなされている。

　本稿は，感情のプロトタイプ特性の解明を試みるものである。第2節ではKövecsesの見解の妥当性について考察し，3つの疑問を提示する。第3節では1つ目と2つ目の疑問，第4節では3つ目の疑問について，その解決を試みる。British National Corpus World Edition（以下BNCと略記）から抽出したメタファー用例の分析を通して，感情のプロトタイプの性質について考察し，プロトタイプから見た個別感情の位置づけを明確化する。

2　Kövecses (1990) の見解

Kövecses は，感情領域を理解するための最も強力なメタファーは＜容器＞（CONTAINER）のメタファーであるとし，[1] 感情のプロトタイプについて，＜容器＞のメタファーを用いた説明を試みる (1990, Ch.11)。

【図1】容器内の液体の熱力学的変化と感情生成の対応関係 (Kövecses 1990, 183 を改訂)

容器内の液体の熱力学的変化（根源領域）	⇒	感情の発生から消滅まで（目標領域）
容器内の液体は温度が低く静かである	→	感情の欠如
外界のできごとが容器内に熱と振動をもたらす	→	感情の存在
水面が上昇，液温が上昇，容器内の振動が激化	→	感情の激しさが増加する
熱により蒸気が発生し，圧力が増加する	→	感情的圧迫が増加する
加圧には限界があり，限界を超えると爆発する	→	感情の激しさは無限に増加することはなく，限界を超えると制御不能な反応を引き起こす
一定量の対抗力の適用により爆発は妨げられる	→	感情を制御する試みがなされる
圧力に対抗するにはかなりの抵抗力が必要	→	感情は制御困難である
圧力が抵抗力より強くなれば爆発する	→	感情の制御力を失えば制御不能の反応を引き起こす
容器は機能不全となり，破片が空中に飛び散り，中身が飛び出し，周囲の人や物に損害を与える	→	自分にも他者にも害を及ぼす
圧力は解消される	→	感情は解消される

【図1】は，プロトタイプ的感情が心の中に生じてから消えるまでのプロセスと容器の熱力学的変化のプロセスとの対応関係についての Kövecses の議論を図の形に表示しなおしたものである。Kövecses は上記の＜容器＞のメタファーを用いた感情概念の特徴づけに基づき，感情のプロトタイプを表示する5つの段階からなる認知モデルを提示する。すなわち，〔0．感情的平静の状態〕→〔1．原因〕→〔2．感情の存在〕→〔3．制御の試み〕→〔4．制御不能状態〕→〔5．行動〕→〔0．感情的平静の状態〕という円環構造をなすモデルである。そして，この感情のプロトタイプに最も近い感情は怒りであり，怒りには感情のプロトタイプと同様の5つの段階があると主張する (ibid.)。

確かに人間の感情は，ときに理性では手に負えないほど激しくなる。Kövecses のモデルは，制御不可能な感情の激しさという側面を明示している。しかし，＜容器＞のメタファーは，はたして感情全般を理解する認知的方策として十分な説明力をもつのだろうか。Kövecses のモデルに対するこの疑問は，具体的に述べると，以下の3つの疑問となる。

〔疑問1〕 感情の制御不能状態を特徴づける写像元として＜容器内の液体の加熱＞は他のいずれの概念よりも適切と言えるか。

〔疑問2〕 感情の激化を特徴づける写像元として＜液体の温度の上昇＞は適切か。

〔疑問3〕 ＜怒り＞は感情のプロトタイプに最も近いとする位置づけにはどの程度の妥当性があるのか。

　まず〔疑問1〕について。容器に液体を入れ，それを加熱するという概念は，人間が炊事の際に鍋ややかんを用いて行う日常的活動の観点から容易に理解できる概念である。炊事などにおける容器内の水温の上昇は，人為的な操作の帰結であり，火災などの特殊な場合を除き，通常は人間の力で制御可能である（鍋の中の水温は，コンロの火力を調節することで，その上昇の速度を緩めたり上昇を止めたりすることができる）。感情の制御不能状態を理解するための認知的方策としては，＜容器内の液体の加熱＞ではなく人間の制御が全く不可能な何らかの別の要素を写像元として設定する方が効果的ではないだろうか。

　〔疑問2〕について。Kövecses のモデルでは，＜平静であった心にある感情が生まれる＞という変化をもたらす要因は，根源領域における＜容器内の液体の温度を上昇させる熱源＞という概念を通して理解され，＜感情が次第に激しさを増し，制御不能になる＞という変化は＜容器内の液体の温度が上昇し，液体の分子運動が活発になる＞という変化を通して理解される。このモデルは，ある感情を経験したときに体温が上昇し，血流が活発になり，毛細血管の拡張によって顔色が赤らみ頬の辺りが熱くなるという，私たち人間の実際の生理的反応と強く結びついている。人間は自らの身体を容器として理解しているという Lakoff (1987) のイメージスキーマの概念を援用すると，＜容器内の液体の温度の上昇＞を感情の激化を特徴づける写像元とする見解は，一見，説得力があるように感じられる。

　しかし，感情はすべて＜熱＞や＜温度の上昇＞と関連づけられるものと言えるのか。ある感情を経験したときに，私たちはその経験を「熱さ」ではなく「寒さ」と関連づけることはないのか。日本語では「冷え冷えとした心境」「心が寒い」「心が凍りつく」「ぞっとする」というような言い回

しが容易に思い浮かぶ。＜低温＞や＜温度の下降＞と結びつく感情は確かに存在するように思えるが，そうだとしたら，それらはプロトタイプから外れる例外的な感情と結論づけるべきなのだろうか。

〔疑問3〕は，上の2つの疑問から導き出される。確かに Kövecses のモデルは＜怒り＞の生成プロセスについてのわれわれの直観に適合する。怒りに伴う人間の身体的経験は，身体という容器に満ちる血液がかっと熱くなり，頭から蒸気が噴出するかのような感覚として特徴づけることができる。しかし，このことから，感情のプロトタイプに最も近い感情が＜怒り＞だという結論を引き出すべきであろうか。むしろ，Kövecses のプロトタイプモデルは，＜怒り＞という特定の感情を念頭において作り出されたものだと言うことはできないか。〔疑問1〕〔疑問2〕に関する綿密な考察により，＜容器内の液体の加熱とそれに伴う液温の上昇＞以外の写像元が設定されうるとしたら，＜怒り＞以外の何らかの個別感情をプロトタイプに近いものとして位置づける可能性も出てくるのではないだろうか。

3　コーパスを用いた感情概念の調査

3.1　直観とコーパスデータ

上記の疑問は，従来の認知言語学の枠組を用いたメタファー研究一般の方法論と深い関わりがある。Deignan (2005) は，認知的メタファー論者が伝統的に，研究者自身の内省的言語経験に基づく直観により生み出されたデータを用いて議論することを指摘し (p.110)，研究者が直観に基づいて作り出した表現例とコーパス内で頻度の高い表現には食い違いがあることを，コーパス検索結果を用いて実証している (pp. 95-96)。[2]

Deignan の指摘は，概念のプロトタイプについての研究にとっても重要な知見となりうる。ひとつのカテゴリーのプロトタイプ特性を考察する際に，そのカテゴリーを指す語と，プロトタイプ特性の候補となる性質を表す語の共起の頻度を有益な尺度として用いることができるからである。以下では，感情のプロトタイプがどのような性質をもち，プロトタイプに近

い個別感情とはどのようなものなのか，BNCのコーパスデータに基づいて分析する。

3.2 感情の制御不可能性を表すメタファー表現

感情を目標領域とするメタファーの主要な根源領域の一つに＜自然現象＞ (NATURAL PHENOMENA) がある（大森（2007a, b））。筆者は，英語には "flood of joy" のように根源領域 (NATURAL PHENOMENA) と目標領域 (EMOTION) の両方の要素を具現化する表現様式（以下 "N of E" 型と略記）が豊富に見られることに着目し，「前置詞 of ＋ 感情を表す語」（例："of joy," "of sorrow"）をキーワードとして BNC を検索し，感情用語全般にわたり，"N of E" 型メタファーの豊富な表現例を抽出した。＜感情＞一般 (EMOTION) を表す "N of E" 型メタファーを調査すべく "of emotion," "of emotions," "of feeling," "of feelings" をキーワードとして検索した結果を【表1】に記す（データの詳細は大森（2007b）を参照）。

【表1】＜感情＞ (EMOTION) を目標領域とするメタファー

SD＼TD	"emotion(s)"	"feeling(s)"	件数計	例（一部）
AIR	7	2	9	"crosswinds of emotion," "outbursts of feelings"
WATER	45	31	76	"wave of emotion," "surge of emotion," "current of feeling"
FIRE	6	1	7	"flash of emotion," "inflamed rush of feeling"
EARTH	2	8	10	"volcano of emotion," "depths of feeling"

この調査では，＜自然現象＞の下位領域として四大元素 (AIR, WATER, FIRE, EARTH) の4領域を設定し，メタファー表現例をこの4領域に分類した。その結果，メタファー用例計102例のうち，＜水＞の領域に属する表現が76例あり，突出して多いことがわかった。これらの表現例には，海に関連するもの，河川に関連するものなど，さまざまな水の形態を表すものがある。上記の76例を水の形態によりさらに細かく分類すると【表2】のようになる。

【表2】＜感情＞を表すメタファーの根源領域となる＜水＞の形態

水の形態	"of emotion(s)" と共起する水関連語	"of feeling(s)" と共起する水関連語	件数
海	ebb and flow, maelstrom, sea, surge (3), surges, swirl, tidal wave, tide (4), upsurge, up-surging, vortex (2), wave (6), waves (3), welter (2), whirlpool	groundswell, maelstrom, surges, tide (3), tides, upsurge (2), wave (4), waves, waves and currents, whirlpools	45
河川	rush (5), torrent (2), torrents (2)	current (3), currents (2), flood, flow, rush (2), stream, torrent, undercurrent	21
水源（泉）	outpouring (2), spring, welling-up, wells	outpouring	6
容器内の水	cocktail, tubs	boiling tumult	3
その他	−	drop	1

【表2】では，メタファー表現として用いられている水の形態を5種類に分け，用例件数の多いものから順に並べて表示している。件数が少なくなるにつれて水の形態の規模が小さくなることがわかる。規模が大きい水の形態が媒体として選ばれる傾向が強いというこの事実こそが，「感情の制御不可能性」を描写しようとするメタファー話者の動機づけを反映している。水は，その形態の規模が大きくなればなるほど，人間の制御能力を超える。自然界で最も規模の大きい海に関連する表現例45件のほとんどは，大波，津波，潮汐，渦など，人間の力をはるかに超える莫大なエネルギーを伴う海水の運動を字義通りの意味として持つものである。河川の流れも，ときに人間の制御を超え，氾濫を起こし人間の生活に甚大な損害を及ぼすことがある。その激しい流れを指す語も，海に関する表現に次いで，感情の制御不可能性を描写する表現として多く用いられている。これらのメタファー表現はしばしば，(1)のように，その莫大なエネルギーに抵抗し制御しようとする人間の努力，あるいは(2)や(3)のように力及ばず制御に失敗するさまを表す表現と共起する。一方，＜容器内で沸騰する水＞を写像元とする用例は1件しかなく，感情の制御不可能性を特徴づけるモデルとしては＜自然界の大規模な水の流動＞が選ばれる傾向がはるかに強い。[3]

(1) She stopped again, *struggling with the torrent* of emotions she'd unleashed. (JY3 2752)

(2) I want my home, she thought, and was appalled by her childishness; but the *tide* of emotion was *irresistible, surging through her like great waves*. (F99 2651)

(3) He ran a hand through his hair, *unable to deal with the sudden wave* of emotion the conversation had brought with it. (JYB 3423)

3.3 温度のメタファーと感情

　感情を「温度を持つもの」ととらえる認識は，どのような表現に具現化されるのだろうか。一般的な感情を表す "emotion(s)" あるいは "feeling(s)" が形容詞 "cold" あるいは "hot" と共起する例を検索すると，感情を＜冷たい＞とする認識が反映された例は，"cold feeling" が 13 例，"cold feelings" が 1 例，計 14 例見られた。一方感情を＜熱い＞とする認識が反映された例は "hot emotion" が 1 例，"hot feeling" が 1 例で，形容詞 "boiling" との共起関係を調べても，"boiling emotions" が 1 例のみであった。＜熱い＞という捉え方よりも＜冷たい＞という捉え方を表す例の方が多いことがわかる。ただし，比較的高い温度を表す "warm" が前置する例を調べると，"warm feeling(s)" が 18 例，"warm" と "feeling(s)" の間に他の語句が入る場合が 12 例あるので，感情の温度を低いとする捉え方が典型的だと言うことはできない。しかし，この調査からは，少なくとも＜容器の中で沸騰する液体＞のメタファーが感情のプロトタイプを表示するモデルだという結論は導き出せない。また，"warm" に形容される感情は，"warm feeling of happiness" (FPM 1582), "warm, satisfying feelings" (ALH 1595), "warm, friendly feeling" (HP6 1215) などが表すようにポジティブな感情である。これらの調査結果は，＜怒り＞が感情のプロトタイプに最も近いという Kövecses の見解を支持するものではない。

　人間が＜感情＞を＜冷たい＞ものと捉えるとき，それは具体的にどのような感情なのだろうか。"cold feeling(s)" が用いられた用例群には，(4) のように "dread" と共起し，その感情が＜恐怖＞であることを明示する例がある。

(4) Memories of blood-red wine and cruelly glinting shards of glass came back to haunt her. It had been wickedly symbolic, stage-managed to stir in her a *cold feeling of dread*. (HA6 1921-22)

そこで "cold" をキーワードとして検索し，具体的な感情名詞との共起関係を調べると，"fear"（31 例），"terror"（7 例）"horror"（6 例）のように＜恐怖＞に関連する語との共起が見られる。[4] (5) では＜冷たい恐怖＞は体内を駆け巡るもの，(6) では病的なもの，(7) では血を凍らせるものという認識が見られる。[5]

(5) As he dressed for dinner in his room, Dorian remembered what he had seen and *cold fear* ran through him like a knife. (GUS 943)

(6) If you let it, fear will hurl you into a sick, *cold terror*. (G35 641)

(7) And it came to him, with a *cold steely horror* chilling the bloodstream as if from a lethal injection.... (AT4 1693)

注目すべきことに，"cold" をキーワードとした検索では，＜怒り＞を表す名詞との共起例も見られる。"fury" 15 件，"anger" 15 件，"rage" 5 件がヒットした。[6] (8) は近づいてきた男の表情をつぶさに見ることで，男の感情が単なる嘲りや怒りを越えたものであることを感じ取った Fran という女性の認識を表すもので，男の激怒が氷のような冷たさをもつものとして捉えられている。(9) は 2 人の男が一騎打ちをする場面で，相手から挑発の言葉を受けた男が覚えた，感覚を研ぎ澄ませ，時間の流れも緩やかなものに感じさせる怒りが，冷たいものとして表現されている。(10) に描かれた男の怒りは，発する言葉のアクセントが不明瞭になるほど激しいものであるが，拳銃を発砲するには至っていない，というものである。これらの＜冷たい怒り＞はいずれも，怒りの程度は甚だしく高く，しかも怒鳴り声や暴力などの手荒い表出行為を伴わないようなものとして表現されている。これらの例は，Kövecses が感情のプロトタイプに最も近いと位置づけた＜怒り＞そのものが，＜高温＞ではなく＜低温＞のものとして認識される場合があり，＜感情の激化＞を特徴づけるモデルとして＜液体の温度の上昇＞が万能ではないことを示している。

(8) Now that he had moved nearer Fran could see that there was a muscle ticking along the hard line of his jaw and that his eyes were glittering with something more than mere mockery, and she went cold. He wasn't just angry, he was furious, a *cold, icy fury*, which made answering shivers trickle along her spine. (JXV 615-16)

(9) 'Are you frightened, Englishman?' the Lieutenant laughed. Sharpe felt the anger then; the *cold anger* that seemed to slow the passage of time itself and make everything appear so very distinctly. (CMP 1605-06)

(10) His *cold rage* thickened his accent, but the revolver in his hand remained steady. (CKE 243)

4 感情のプロトタイプ特性

上記の考察により，感情の制御不可能性を特徴づける写像元として，＜自然界に存在する大規模な形態の水＞が典型的な写像元となること，激化した感情の＜温度＞は必ずしも＜高温＞とは限らず，＜低温＞という認識のしかたもあることが明らかになった。本節では，感情のプロトタイプに近い個別感情にはどのようなものがあるのかを考察する。

3.2節の【表1】に示したように，"N of E" 型メタファーの根源領域は，＜水＞が圧倒的に多く，次いで＜地＞，＜大気＞，＜火＞の順であった。大森 (2007a, b) ではさまざまな個別感情を表す "N of E" 型メタファーについてBNCの検索結果に基づき考察したが，その中から，ここでは9つの感情に注目する。それぞれの根源領域を四大元素ごとに下位分類し，その写像の傾向について一般的な感情と比較した結果を【表3】に示す。各感情で最も多く用いられた根源領域については，メタファー全用例中の割合をパーセント表示している。さらに，各感情で用いられた根源領域の割合をグラフ化し，＜感情＞一般で最も多く用いられている＜水＞の領域を基準として，＜水＞由来の用例の割合の多い順に並べて図示したものが【図2】である。

【表3】＜感情＞一般と9つの個別感情領域への写像の傾向の比較

目標領域	"of E" 検索合計	メタファー 件数合計	根源領域						
			WATER		AIR	FIRE		EARTH	
EMOTION	1,003	102	76	(74.5%)	9	7		10	
PLEASURE	937	75	46	(61.3%)	9	17		3	
SADNESS	325	27	15	(55.5%)	7	1		4	
ANGER	542	117	47	(40.2%)	28	40		2	
HOPE	503	125	4		4	116	(92.8%)	1	
DESPAIR	264	39	4		6	1		28	(71.8%)
DESIRE	304	35	22	(62.8%)	4	7		2	
RELIEF	708	39	28	(71.8%)	3	4		4	
ANXIETY	431	18	13	(72.2%)	3	1		1	
FEAR	401	40	22	(55.0%)	13	5		0	

【図2】 "N of E" 型メタファーにおいて用いられる根源領域の割合の比較

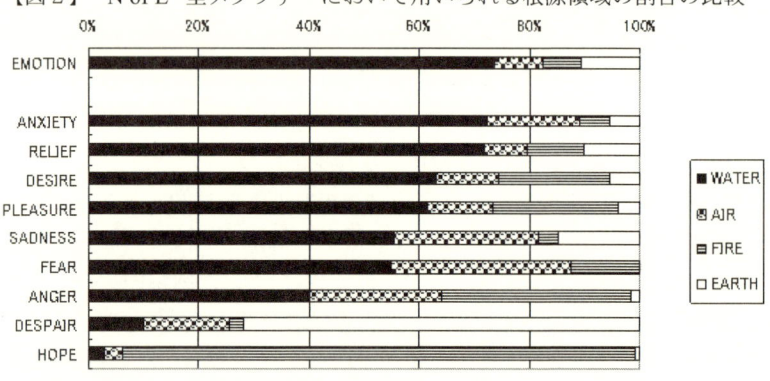

　＜感情＞一般では＜水＞を根源領域とする例が70%以上を占める。個別感情では，＜水＞を根源領域とする例が70%以上のものに＜不安＞と＜安堵＞, 60%以上のものに＜欲望＞と＜喜び＞があり，これらが＜感情＞のプロトタイプに近いものとして位置づけられることがわかる。次いで50%以上のものには＜悲しみ＞と＜恐怖＞がある。3.3節で＜恐怖＞を＜低温＞と結びつける認識の存在について考察したが，＜低温＞と結びつくこの感情も，決して＜感情＞のプロトタイプから大きく外れるものではないことがわかる。一方＜怒り＞は，＜水＞を根源領域とする例は40%強しかなく，感情のプロトタイプからは多少外れる。＜絶望＞と＜希望＞はプロトタイプから大きく外れ，＜水＞に由来する例は非常に少ない。

ここで注目すべきことは＜欲望＞と＜希望＞の関係である。一般的にDESIREとHOPEは類義関係にあるとされるが，【図2】を観察すると，この2つの感情の性質は全く異なることがわかる。それぞれ頻度の高い根源領域は，＜欲望＞には＜水＞，＜希望＞には＜火＞である。前者は感情のプロトタイプ特性をもち，後者はもたない。＜欲望＞に類似する概念はむしろ＜喜び＞であり，両者に用いられる根源領域の割合は驚くほど似ている。

プロトタイプに近いものとして位置づけられる感情が＜水＞を写像元とするメタファーで表現される場合，媒体となる水の形態はどのようなものがあるか。"of anxiety," "of relief," "of desire," "of pleasure" をキーワードとした検索結果から＜水＞を写像元とする "N of E" 型メタファー表現を抽出し，水の形態により表現例を分類すると【表4】のようになる。

【表4】プロトタイプに近い個別感情を表すメタファーの根源領域となる＜水＞の形態

水の形態	各キーワードと共起する水関連語			
	"of anxiety" と共起	"of relief" と共起	"of desire" と共起	"of pleasure" と共起
海	surge (2), upsurge, waves (2)	surge (9), surges, tide (2), wave (5), waves	sea, surge (3), tidal wave, tide, wave (3), waves (3), whirlpool	sea, surge (4), tide (2), wave (4), waves (4), whirlpool
河川	flood, current, rush, undercurrent (3)	flood (2), flow, rush (3), wash	flood, floods, flow, river, rivers, rush	flood (2), rills, stream
湖・池	ripples	ripple, ripples	−	ripple, ripples
水源（泉）	−	gush	swell	springs, spurt (5)
容器内の水	−	−	water bottles	−
その他	dollop	−	infusion	trickles

3.2節で＜感情＞一般への写像元となる＜水＞の形態の傾向を調査した（【表2】参照）が，その結果と同様，個別感情においても，海や河川のように，規模が大きく，自然界で人間の制御の及ばない莫大なエネルギーを伴う水の流動を表す語が媒体として用いられる頻度が高いことがわかる。これらの検索データの分析により，感情のプロトタイプに近いものとして位置づけられる4つの感情領域，すなわち＜不安＞と，＜不安＞から突然開放されたことに起因する＜安堵＞，＜欲望＞と，＜欲望＞が成就されたことに起因する＜喜び＞は，それぞれ，活発で制御の困難な典型的情動と

して特徴づけることができる。

注

　本論文の提出後，本研究に基づき加筆修正を施した論文が *Metaphor and Symbol* 23 巻 2 号（2008）に掲載されているので参照されたい。

1　＜容器＞のメタファーを具現化した感情に関する表現として Kövecses (1990, Ch.9) が挙げる例には，"She was *filled* with emotion," "I feel *empty*," "He *poured out* his feelings to her," "He *bottled up* his emotions" などがある。なお，Kövecses (1990) が挙げる感情を理解するためのメタファーの根源領域には，＜容器＞の他に，＜自然エネルギー＞，＜敵対者＞，＜物体＞，＜貴重品＞，＜壊れ物＞，＜生物＞などがあるが，彼は，＜容器＞以外の根源領域によるメタファー群はそれらを総合することで＜容器＞のメタファーの説明力と同様の説明力が得られると主張し，＜容器＞のメタファーの説明力を高く評価する。

2　Deignan は Yu (1995) の研究を取り上げ，Yu が挙げた＜怒りは火である＞ (ANGER IS HEAT) というメタファーを具現化する用例 7 つについて，Bank of English のサブコーパスを検索して調査を行い，2 例（"These are *inflammatory* remarks," "After the argument, Dave was *smoldering* for days." ）については，そこで述べられている火の関連語が怒りの意味で用いられる例がコーパス内でも豊富に見つかるが，他の 5 例（"She was doing a slow *burn*," "He was breathing *fire*," "Your insincere apology has added *fuel to the fire*," "Boy, am I *burned up*," "*Smoke* was pouring out of his ears."）における火の関連語が怒りのメタファー表現となる例はコーパスでは稀であるか，あるいは皆無であることを指摘している。

3　水以外の領域においても，強風 ("crosswinds," "flurry," "storm") や火山岩の噴出に関連する表現 ("volcano," "eruption") など，人間が制御不可能な自然現象を表す語句を用いた感情メタファーの例が見られることも注目に値する（大森（2007b）参照）。

4　他に "cold chill of fear" (JXV 1633), "icy fear" (CDA 2522, 他 3 例) のような例も見られた。

5　(5) には＜恐怖＞を刃物に喩える "like a knife" という表現が見られる。(7) では "cold steely" が "horror" を形容するが，"cold steel" とは刀剣類を表す（*OED* "steel" 3.b. 参照）。他に "cold knives of fear" (JXV 2837) という例もある。＜冷たい＞と認識される恐怖感と＜刃物＞の連想関係は，刺されたときの出血とそれに伴う体温低下という概念に基づいて成立しているものと考えられる。

6　比較のために "hot" をキーワードとし，＜怒り＞を表す名詞との共起関係を調べると，"rage" との共起例が 7 件，"anger" との共起例が 6 件であった。＜熱さ＞と＜怒り＞を結びつける認識と比べ，＜冷たさ＞と＜怒り＞を結びつける認識が決して例外的なものではないことがわかる。

参考文献

Cruse, D.A. (1986) *Lexical Semantics*. Cambridge: Cambridge University Press.

Deignan, Alice (2005) *Metaphor and Corpus Linguistics*. Amsterdam: John Benjamins.

Kövecses, Zoltán (1986) *Metaphors of Anger, Pride, and Love*. Amsterdam: John Benjamins.

Kövecses, Zoltán (1990) *Emotion Concepts*. New York: Springer-Verlag.

Kövecses, Zoltán (2000) *Metaphor and Emotion*. Cambridge: Cambridge University Press.

Kövecses, Zoltán (2005) *Metaphor in Culture: Universality and Variation*. Cambridge: Cambridge University Press.

Lakoff, George (1987) *Women, Fire, and Dangerous Things: What Categories Reveal about the Mind*. Chicago: The University of Chicago Press.

Lakoff, George and Mark Johnson (1980) *Metaphors We Live By*. Chicago: The University of Chicago Press.

Lakoff, George and Mark Johnson (1999) *Philosophy in the Flesh*. New York: Basic Books.

大森文子 (2007a)「自然現象と感情のメタファー写像:"a flood of joy"型の表現をめぐって」『言語と文化の展望』639-655. 英宝社.

大森文子 (2007b)「感情に関するメタファーと写像の特性:"a flood of joy"型の表現をめぐって (2)」『文化とレトリック (言語文化共同研究プロジェクト 2006)』5-19. 大阪大学大学院言語文化研究科.

Stefanowitsch, Anatol and Stefan Th. Gries (eds.) (2006) *Corpus-Based Approaches to Metaphor and Metonymy*. Berlin: Mouton de Gruyter.

Yu, Ning (1995) "Metaphorical Expressions of Anger and Happiness in English and Chinese," *Metaphor and Symbolic Activity*, 10, 59-92.

語彙概念構造の潜在項と多義性
―「つく」と「つける」を中心に―[†]

板東　美智子

1　はじめに

　動詞が多義的に解釈される要因の一つに，その動詞と共起する名詞句がその多義派生に意味的影響を与えるという場合がある。例えば，英語の他動詞 *bake* は共起する目的語によって，(1a) 状態変化と (1b) 創造の二通りに解釈される。

(1)　a. John baked the potato.
　　　b. John baked the cake.　　　　　　　(Pustejovsky, 1995: 122)

日本語の場合も，(2a,b,c) のように共起する名詞句によって，自動詞「つく」は，「付く」，「着く」，「就く」と書き分けられるような多義性がある。

(2)　a. 雨の日に外を歩くとはねがあがってズボンにしみが付くから嫌いです。
　　　b. 同記者はモスクワからブカレストに着いた。
　　　c. ぼくは，将来，コンピュータ関係の仕事に就きたいと思っている。
　　　　　　　　　　　　　　　　　　　　　　（日本語動詞の結合価）

他動詞「つける」の場合も「付ける」，「着ける」，「就ける」の多義性がある。

(3) a. ボタンを付ける。
    b. 船を着ける。　　　　　　　　　　　　　　　　　　（広辞苑）
    c. 局長の地位に就ける。　　　　　　　　　　　　　　（広辞苑）

本論は，日本語の自動詞「つく」と他動詞「つける」を取り上げ，それらが名詞句とどのように組み合わされて多義が派生されるのかを考察する。まず，国広 (1999) の現象素の考え方を参考に，その共通の意味情報を仮定し，それを，語彙概念構造 (Lexical Conceptual Structure, 以下，LCS) で記述する。特に，統語構造には現れていない LCS の潜在項の存在を仮定し，その存在が多義派生に関係することを指摘する。次に，LCS のどの項がどのような名詞句の意味情報と結び付けられて多義が派生されるのかを考察する。その記述には，動詞の LCS と，Pustejovsky(1995) で提唱された特質構造 (Qualia Structure, 以下，QS) との組み合わせを用いることとする。

2　動詞の語彙概念構造と名詞の特質構造

2.1　動詞の語彙概念構造 (LCS)

動詞の意味的特徴を記述するについては，影山・由本（1997）の達成動詞の LCS を応用する。なお，(4) の CAUSE の下位事象は到達動詞の LCS である。

(4) 達成動詞 (accomplishment verbs):
　　[$_{\text{EVENT}}$ [ ]x ACT ON-[ ]y] CAUSE [$_{\text{EVENT}}$ BECOME [$_{\text{STATE}}$ [ ]y BE AT-[ ]z]]
　　（下線部は任意の要素を示す）　　　　　　　　　（影山・由本, 1997: 6）

(4) の LCS にある，[ ]x, [ ]y, [ ]z が動詞の項 (argument) である。しかし，これらの項がいつも全て統語構造に結び付けられるとは限らない。中には，潜在項 (implicit argument) として，LCS に留まる項もある。潜在項については，Pinker (1991) の説明を (5) に引用しておく。

(5) ...*John was hit.* Despite the absence of a *by*-phrase, the agent role in short passives is a well defined "implicit argument". For example,

the sentence *The ship was sunk* entails that there was some agent or force that sunk the ship; in the unaccusative counterpart *The ship sank*, no such implication exists. ... Moreover, purposive adjuncts, which require agentive events to control them, can occur with short passives: *The ship was sunk to collect the insurance* (cf. **The ship sank to collect the insurance*, ...) ...　　　　　　　　　　　　　　(Pinker, 1991: 90)

潜在項とは，統語構造上には項として現れていなくても，意味的には含意されるような要素をさす．以下では，このような潜在項が動詞の多義派生に一役買っていることを指摘したい．

2.2　名詞の特質構造 (QS)

　主語や目的語名詞句の意味情報を形式的に記述するにあたっては，Pustejovsky (1995) で提唱された特質構造 (QS) の形式を援用したい．例えば，印刷物の「本」という名詞は，印刷物という「もの」とその中の「情報」の二つの意味がある．この多義をドット・オブジェクトと呼び，(7) のように表す．

　　(6) ... nominals such as *book* are a sort of container, which are further specified as a relation between a physical object and the textual information contained within it. ... Assume that book is a species of "printed material," associated with the type print_matter. Then the lexical conceptual paradigm (lcp) for this dot object is given in (7) below.
　　　　　　　　　　　　　　　　　(Pustejovsky 1995: 118-119, 150)

　　(7) print-matter_lcp = {physobj・info, physobj, info}
　　　　　　　　　　　　　　　　　　(Pustejovsky 1995: 151)

このドット・オブジェクトの「本」の意味情報を Pustejovsky(1995: 101) は (8) のような QS で形式化している．

(8)
$$\begin{bmatrix} \text{book} \\ \text{ARGST} = \begin{bmatrix} \text{ARG1} = x\text{: information} \\ \text{ARG2} = y\text{: phys\_obj} \end{bmatrix} \\ \text{QUALIA} = \begin{bmatrix} \text{information} \cdot \text{phys\_obj\_lcp} \\ \text{FORMAL} = \text{hold}(y, x) \\ \text{TELIC} = \text{read}(e, w, x \cdot y) \\ \text{ARENT} = \text{write}(e', v, x \cdot y) \end{bmatrix} \end{bmatrix}.$$

QSのなかの，FORMAL（形式役割）は本の外的な性質を表し，TELIC（目的役割）は本の本来的な機能や目的を表す。AGENT（主体役割）は本の成り立ちや出処を表す。QSには他にCONST（構成役割）があり，そこでは，内的な構成や性質を表す。以下では，「つく／つける」と共起する名詞句の記述にQSを用いるが，常に，全ての役割を表すのではなく，当該の多義派生に関連する役割のみを書いておくこととする。

3 「つく」と「つける」のLCS

「つく／つける」が名詞句と組み合わされて多義が派生される仕組みを考察するにあたって，まず，動詞がもっている意味情報を観察し，その特徴をLCSを用いて記述してみよう。

3.1 「つく」と「つける」の多義の関連性

3.1.1 辞書による多義の漢字の書き分け

実際に，辞書で「つく」と「つける」は一つの見出し語のなかで，どのような漢字で書き分けられているのであろうか。以下の四冊の辞典を調べてみた。

(9) 岩波古語辞典：
「つき」（四段）→「付き」「着き」「就き」,
「つけ」（下二）（つき（付）の他動詞形）→「付け」「着け」「就け」
(10) 広辞苑：
「つく」（自五）→「付く」「附く」「着く」「就く」「即く」,
「つける」（他下一）→「付ける」「附ける」「着ける」「就ける」「即ける」
(11) 新明解国語辞典：
「つく」（自五）→「付く」「着く」「就く」「憑く」「漬く」,
「つける」（他下一）→「付ける」（「身に着ける」「ガスを点ける」とも書く）
(12) 日本国語大辞典：
「つく」（自カ五（四））→「付」「着」「就」「即」「憑」,
「つける」（他カ下一）→「付」「着」「就」「即」

四冊に共通する多義は,「付」,「着」,「就」として書き分けられている。従って，以下の議論においてもこの三つの多義を考察していくこととする。

3.1.2 国広 (1999) の多義間の関連性を体系化した研究から

具体的に「つく」と「つける」の LCS を考察する前に，国広 (1999) による，類義語「とまる（止・泊・留）」の多義配列法を参考にしてみよう。国広は 11 種類の用法をもつ「とまる」を (13) のような単一の現象素に基づいた一個の多義語とみなしている。

(13) 「とまる」の現象素：

⎯⎯⎯→　●　- - - →
　　　　停止点

（国広, 1999: 6, 一部改変）

(13) の図には三つの型の視野が考えられている。まず，I. 移動から停止点までに視野をおいた表現が「電車が駅にとまった」であり，II. 停止点に重

点をおいた表現が「船が港にとまっている」である。最後に，III. 停止点からそれ以後に視野をおいた表現が「ホテルにとまる」となる。以上が線的な進行を表す例であるが，次に，各視野ごとに...（略）...「進行―運動―状態」の順に配列していくと，「とまる」の多義の体系が表示される（国広, 1999: 4-7）。本稿でも，国広の現象素の考え方を基本的に応用するが，国広ではその現象素をどのように決定したのかが具体的に示されていない。そこで以下では，様々な例文を観察しながら，より具体的に動詞の項の数や含意を調べて，多義派生の基となる動詞の中核的な意味的情報を仮定し，それをLCSで表記してみることとする。[1]

3.1.3 「つく」の多義の関連性

他動詞「つける」は自動詞「つく」からの転換であるので，まずは，自動詞「つく」と共起する要素，＜人／もの＞と＜具体的／抽象的場所＞との関連性を(2)の一部を再掲した(14)の例でみてみよう。

(14) a. ズボンにしみが付く。
b. 同記者がブカレストに着く。
c. 僕は（将来）コンピュータ関係の仕事に就く。

(14a)は，＜もの＞が着点についたことに焦点があり，含意としてその結果状態は存続している。(14b)は，＜人＞が出発点からある着点に移動してきたことが含意され，その＜具体的場所＞についたことに焦点が当たっている。ずっとその場所にいるという結果残存の含意はない。(14c)では，物理的移動はなく，＜人＞が＜抽象的場所＞につくことに焦点が当たっている。ここでは移動や結果残存の含意はない。以上の様子を(15)の表にまとめておく。

(15)

焦点の位置	移動あり 人／ものが	移動あり 具体的場所に	移動なし 人／ものが	移動なし 抽象的場所に
移動		↓		
着点	（ズボンに）しみが付く	（同記者が）ブカレストに着く		（僕は）コンピュータ関係の仕事に就く
結果状態	↓			

3.2　影山 (1996) の -e- 使役化接辞―使役主の取り付け―

次に，他動詞「つける」の意味的特徴を観察してみよう。「つける (tuk-e-ru)」は自動詞「つく (tuk-u)」に使役化接辞-e- を付加して転換されたものである。また，影山 (1996) によると，-e-他動詞は主語を「動作主」に特定し，(故意であれ不注意であれ) 事態の発生を直接的にコントロールするという特徴がある。

(16)　a. {大工さんが／*彼の持ち家願望が}家を建てた。
　　　b. {子供が／*電車の振動が}石を並べた。（影山（一部抜粋），1996: 196）

(16) と同じテストを「つける (tuk-e-ru)」で試してみる。

(17)　a. {お母さんが／*針と糸が}シャツにボタンを付けた。
　　　b. {キャプテンが／*強風が}ボートを岸に着けた。
　　　c. {部長が／*営業成績が}鈴木さんを課長に就けた。

結果は，「付ける」，「着ける」，「就ける」の全てにおいて，(16) と同様，＜人＞が事態の発生を直接的にコントロールする場合に限るようである。そこで，他動詞「つける」の使役の LCS を影山 (1996) から引用して (18) とする。

(18)　-e-他動詞：x CONTROL [EVENT ...]　　　　　　（影山, 1996: 197）

(18) の x は＜動作主＞であり，下位事象には「つく」の事態が入ることになる。

3.3 「つく」／「つける」の中核的 LCS

それでは，他動詞「つける」の下位事象にはいる「つく」がとる項の特徴はどのようなものか観察してみよう。

3.3.1 自動詞「つく」の項構造について

自動詞「つく」は，深層構造で内項をもつ非対格自動詞か，あるいは，外項をもつ非能格自動詞かをみてみよう。使役接辞 -e- を付加できるということから，外項位置が空いていて内項位置が満たされている非対格自動詞であることは容易に予測できる。実際，自動詞文 (19) を，事態を直接的にコントロールする＜人＞を主語にした他動詞文に転換してみると，全て可能である。

(19)　a. シャツにボタンが付いた。→ お母さんがシャツにボタンを付けた。
　　　b. ボートが岸に着いた。→ キャプテンがボートを岸に着けた。
　　　c. 赤子が次の王位に就いた。→ 女王が赤子を次の王位に就けた。

ここで，(19a,b,c) の自動詞「つく」の項構造を (20) とする。

(20) 非対格自動詞「つく」の項構造：＜ ＿ ＜ y ＞＞

一方，同じ自動詞でも，主語が＜人＞である「同記者がブカレストに着いた」のような例文では，非対格自動詞文に特徴的である非意図的解釈をするのは無理である。そこで，「つく」の非能格自動詞の可能性も考えてみることにする。非能格自動詞はすでに外項が満たされているため使役主は取り付けられない。従って，その他動詞形「つける」は派生されないはずである（影山，1996: 204）。

(21)　a. 太郎は（そのバスケットの試合で）マンツーマンで先頭のプレーヤーに付いた。→＊監督が太郎をマンツーマンで先頭のプレーヤーに付けた。
　　　b. 同記者がようやくブカレストに着いた。→＊局長が同記者をようやくブカレストに着けた。
　　　c. 太郎は進んでその任に就いた。→＊社長が太郎を進んでその任に就けた。

(cf.「社長が本人の許可なく勝手に太郎をその任に就けた」のような非対格的解釈の場合は可)

予測どおり，(21) の自動詞文から，意図的 < 人 > を主語にした他動詞文を派生できない。この結果から，「つく」には (22) の項構造の可能性もあることになる。

(22) 非能格自動詞「つく」の項構造: $< x < \_\_ >>$

「つく」は共起する名詞句によって非対格にも非能格にもなることがわかった。しかし，典型的な非能格自動詞，例えば，「歩く」,「走る」,「泳ぐ」，などは意図性のほかに未完了の特徴を備えている (「一時間走った／*一時間で走った」)。ところが，「つく」は (15) の表でみたように，いずれの語義においても着点を明示するか含意する完了の自動詞である。そこで，意図的な外項と完了の事態の両方を兼ね備えた項構造として，(22) に代わって，(23) のような一種の再帰的他動詞構造を仮定する。

(23) 再帰的他動詞構造の「つく」: $< x_i < y_i >>$

以上より，自動詞「つく」の項構造を (24) とし他動詞「つける」を (25) とする。

(24) 「つく」: $< x_i < y_i >> (x = y) / < \_\_ < y >>$
(25) 「つける」: $< x_i < y_j >> (x \neq y)$

3.3.2 「つく」の中核的 LCS の潜在項について

これまで「つく」と「つける」がもつ統語構造に反映される項構造をみてきたが，LCS には 2 節で紹介した潜在項が存在する場合がある。自動詞「つく」についてその潜在項の有無を調べてみよう。「つく」と共起する意味的要素には，< 対象 > あるいは < 動作主 >，そして，< 具体的／抽象的場所 > がある。まず,「付く」の場合を観察してみよう。

(26) a. 非対格「付く」の＜動作主＞の存在：ボタンが丁寧に付いている。
b. 非対格「付く」の＜場所＞の存在：ボタンが上の方に付いている。
c. 非能格「付く」の＜対象＞の存在：太郎がマンツーマンで先頭のプレーヤーに付いた。
d. 非能格「付く」の＜場所＞は必須：*太郎が付いた。

「付く」の自動詞文 (26a) に行為を修飾する「丁寧に」との共起が可能であることから，統語構造上には現れていなくても意味的には＜動作主＞が含意されていることが示唆される。同じ自動詞文の (26b) は場所を修飾する「上の方に」という修飾語句との共起も可能である。従って，どこにボタンを付けるかが明示されていなくても，＜場所＞の含意あることがわかる。(26c) は意図的＜動作主＞が主語になっている自動詞文であるが，その「太郎」が先頭のプレーヤーに付けた＜対象＞は「自分自身」である。つまり，「太郎は自分自身をマンツーマンで先頭のプレーヤーに付けた」という意味である。そして，表面上，この再帰目的語が省略されて自動詞文となったと考えられる。従って，ここでは再帰目的語の含意を仮定できるだろう。また，同じ意図的＜動作主＞主語の (26d) の＜場所＞の要素は統語上でも必須の項であるようだ。次に，「着く」の場合を観察してみる。

(27) a. 非対格「着く」の＜動作主＞の存在：*荷物がひとりでに着いた。
b. 非対格「着く」の＜場所＞の存在：荷物が間違って着いている。
c. 非能格「着く」の＜対象＞の存在：同記者がブカレストに着いた。
d. 非能格「着く」の＜場所＞は必須：?同記者が着いた。

「ひとりでに」は「ドアがひとりでに開いた」のように，非対格自動詞文では共起可能である。しかし，(27a) の場合は非文法的になっている。このことから，「着く」は非対格自動詞として用いられていてもその文には荷物を送った＜動作主＞が含意されていると考えられる。また，(27b) を「間違った目的地に」という意味で「間違って」で修飾することができる。「着く」の場合にも潜在的に＜場所＞が含意されているのであろう。(27c) についても，「同記者がようやく自分自身をブカレストに着けた」という他

動詞文に言い換えることができる。この再帰目的語が省略されて自動詞化したと仮定する。(27d) の文は，会話において「ここに」か，または，その会話で了解された場所を指すときにのみ可能であるが，それ以外は＜場所＞の省略は不可である。従って，「着く」の場合も，＜場所＞は統語的にも必須の項である。最後に，「就く」の場合を観察してみよう。

(28) a. 非対格「就く」の＜動作主＞の存在：*赤ちゃんがひとりでに次の王位に就いた。
b. 非対格「就く」の＜場所＞は必須：*赤ちゃんが就いた。
c. 非能格「就く」の＜対象＞の存在：太郎はようやく希望の職に就いた。
d. 非能格「就く」の＜場所＞は必須：*鈴木さんが（ようやく）就いた。

(28a) の結果より，非対格自動詞の場合の「就く」においても＜動作主＞の存在が含意されている。また，(28b, d) より，「就く」は非対格自動詞の場合も再帰的な場合も＜場所＞の項は必須要素である。(28c) も「太郎は自分自身をようやく希望の職に就けた」のような文の再帰目的語の省略と考えておく。以上，(26), (27), (28) の観察から，非対格自動詞「つく」と，再帰的他動詞から派生した非能格自動詞の「つく」の意味構造には，統語構造上には現れていなくても，＜動作主＞，＜対象＞，＜場所＞の項があると仮定する。

3.3.3 「つく」／「つける」の中核的 LCS について

以上，潜在項も含めた「つく」と「つける」がもつ項構造を観察した。次は，「付」「着」「就」という漢字で書き分けられるようなそれぞれの特有の意味的違いについてみてみよう。特有の意味とは，その漢字について我々がもつ最も典型的な意味であり，それが定項としてレキシコンに記載されていると仮定する。自動詞「つく」を「付く」と表した場合の典型的な意味とは，「二つのものが離れない状態になる」ことである。それを，*ADHERED* で表しておく。「着く」と書いた場合の典型的な解釈は「ある人やものが他のところまで及び至る」ということである。それを *ARRIVED* と表しておく。そして，「就く」と書いた場合は「ある人がある地位にその

身をおく」というのが基本的な解釈であろう。それを *INDUCTED* と表しておく。以上のそれぞれの定項を (29) にまとめる。

(29) a. 「付く」:... BE *ADHERED* [±LOCATION AT ...]
b. 「着く」:... BE *ARRIVED* [+ LOCATION AT ...]
c. 「就く」:... BE *INDUCTED* [− LOCATION AT ...]

3.3.4 「つく」／「つける」の中核的 LCS

「つく」と「つける」について，以上観察した項構造とそれぞれの定項をまとめると (30) のようになる。

(30) [EVENT x_i CONTROL [EVENT BECOME [STATE y_j BE *ADHERED* [±LOC AT z]/ $y_{i/j}$ BE *ARRIVED* [+ LOC AT z]/ y_i BE *INDUCTED* [− LOC AT z]]]]

(x: 動作主, y: 対象, z: 場所)

(30) は,「つく」／「つける」が表しえる出来事の範囲全てをカバーする LCS である。これを「つく」／「つける」の中核的 LCS と呼んでおく。選択肢のなかの *ADHERED* が選ばれたとき，移動した＜対象＞に焦点があり，*ARRIVED* のとき，移動後の＜具体的場所＞に焦点がある。*INDUCTED* のとき，＜抽象的場所＞に焦点がある。x≠y のときは他動詞「つける」か，または，動作主が含意された自動詞「付く」,「着く」の文と結び付く。x＝y のとき，再帰的意味の「着く」,「就く」と結び付く。次節では，自動詞「つく」を例に，この中核的 LCS が名詞の意味情報とどのように組み合わされて多義的になっているかを考察する。

4 「名詞句＋つく」動詞句の多義派生を例に

最も単純な例で多義派生を考察するために，(2) の例文を (2)' のように単純化した。括弧内は省略可能な語句である。

(2)' a. (ズボンに) しみが付く
b. 同記者がブカレストに着く
c. ぼくは (将来，コンピュータ関係の) 仕事に就く

まず，(2a)' の例を取り上げてみる。(2a)' では，＜対象＞に焦点があり，その項は統語構造に結び付く。＜動作主＞と＜場所＞の項は潜在項としてLCSに留まることが可能である。では，y項が「しみ」の場合の典型的な意味的特徴を表わしてみよう。「しみ」というのは，水たまりの泥はねであったり，インクを落としたりしてできるので，その外的な属性と成り立ちは明らかである。従って，形式役割と主体役割を書いておく。また，意図された目的をもった人工物でないので目的役割はもたない。以上から「しみ」の特質構造を (31) と書いておく。

(31)
$$\boxed{1}\begin{bmatrix}しみ\\ 形式役割＝自然の液体(\boxed{1})／人工の液体(\boxed{1})\\ 主体役割＝[\ ]x が \boxed{1} [\ ]y を \boxed{2} [衣服や皮膚など]z に密着させる\end{bmatrix}$$

中核的 LCS(30) の y 項に (31) の「しみ」が組み合わされた場合，(31) QS の主体役割の属性「〜に密着させる」が (30) の *ADHERED* と合致する。また，形式役割の属性は人工物または自然物なので動作主と対象は同一人物ではない。つまり，x≠y となり，使役（x CONTROL）の意味は LCS に留まる。結果，(32) の「しみが付く」の動詞句が生成される。

(32) 「しみが付く」の概念構造：
[$_{\text{EVENT}}$ x_i CONTROL [$_{\text{EVENT}}$ BECOME [$_{\text{STATE}}$ $\boxed{1}$ BE *ADHERED* [$_{\pm\text{LOC}}$ AT $\boxed{2}$]]]]

次に，(2b)' の例を考えてみよう。「同記者」というのは，個体であって，通常は形式役割に外的な属性だけを書いておけばよい。その個体の所属先などが問題になる文脈では構成役割 (part_of(x, y)) が必要であるが，今回は関係しないので省略しておく。

(33)
$$\boxed{1}\begin{bmatrix}同記者\\ 形式役割＝人(\boxed{1})\end{bmatrix}$$

「ブカレスト」というのは具体的な場所を指す地名である。従って，通常，この場合も外的な属性だけを示す形式役割だけになろう。

(34)
$\boxed{2}\begin{bmatrix} ブカレスト \\ 形式役割＝具体的場所 (\boxed{2}) \end{bmatrix}$

(34)の具体的場所$\boxed{2}$は，中核的 LCS(30) の [+ LOCATION AT z] と合致してその位置に挿入されると，自動的に ARRIVED の定項が選択される。同時に，BE ARRIVED の項 $y_{x/j}$ は，ここに「人」または「もの」(＜対象＞)が入るが，形式役割に「人」の属性をもつ(33)の「人」が組み合わされると，動作主 x と同定されて，x＝y となる。(35)は中核的 LCS の変項 x, y, z にそれぞれ，(33)，(34)が挿入された概念構造である。

(35) 「同記者がブカレスト着く」の概念構造：
[EVENT $\boxed{1}$ CONTROL [EVENT BECOME [STATE $\boxed{1}$ BE ARRIVED [+ LOC AT $\boxed{2}$]]]]

最後に，(2c)' の例を考えてみる。まず，「ぼく」という名詞であるが，性別や年齢が関係する文脈であれば詳しい形式役割 (male(x) など) が必要であるが，この例文では「人」であることだけが関連しているため，(33)と同じ QS である。

(36)
$\boxed{1}\begin{bmatrix} ぼく \\ 形式役割＝人 (\boxed{1}) \end{bmatrix}$

「仕事」については，その名詞そのものは「抽象的場所」であり，本来的に意図された目的をもつため，ここでは，形式役割と目的役割が必要である。

(37)
$$\boxed{2}\begin{bmatrix}仕事\\形式役割＝抽象的場所\ (\boxed{2})\\目的役割＝\boxed{1}[\ ]x_i\ が生計のために\ \boxed{1}[その身]y_i\ を\ [\boxed{2}]z\ におく\end{bmatrix}$$

(37) の形式役割の属性が抽象的場所なので，(30) の LCS の [− LOCATION AT z] と合致し，自動的に，BE *INDUCTED* が選択される．また，BE *INDUCTED* の項 y は CONTROL の第一項 x と同定されるため，ここに「ぼく」の QS が挿入されると自動的に x＝y となり，再帰的な解釈が可能になる．(30) の LCS に (36) の $\boxed{1}$ と (37) の $\boxed{2}$ の名詞（句）が組み合わされた概念構造が (38) である．

(38) 「ぼくは（将来コンピュータ関係の）仕事に就く」の概念構造：
[EVENT $\boxed{1}$ CONTROL [EVENT BECOME [STATE $\boxed{1}$ BE *INDUCTED* [− LOC AT $\boxed{2}$]]]]

5　おわりに

自動詞「つく」と他動詞「つける」の多義性（「付く」「着く」「就く」／「付ける」「着ける」「就ける」）は主語，または，目的語名詞句との組み合わせによって生成されている．その多義派生の要因として，「つく」／「つける」には，それが表しうる出来事の範囲全てが記載されているような共通の意味基盤があると仮定した（中核的 LCS）．特に，その中核的 LCS には統語構造に反映される項の他に反映されないような潜在項も全て記載されているとし，QS を用いてある名詞句の意味的属性が中核的 LCS のどの定項と合致するか，そして，その名詞句が LCS のどの項と置き換わるかによって多義派生の仕組みを考察し記述した．

注

† 本稿は言語処理学会第 13 回年次大会 (NLP2007) ワークショップテーマセッション 2(1)：「語の意味」と言語学・言語処理 (2007 年 3 月 22 日龍谷大学) で口頭発表

した内容に加筆・訂正をしたものです．本発表に際して，有益なご助言を頂いたOWL(Otsu Workshop of Linguistics) 研究会の皆様に心より感謝申し上げます．

1　Pustejovsky(1995), 小野 (2005) では，中核的意味情報を仮定せず，動詞の QS の一部の属性が無指定のまま残っている（不完全指定）とし，それを補部名詞の語彙情報によって補完する意味生成のプロセスによって多義が生成されるとしている．

参考文献

影山太郎 (1996)『動詞意味論』くろしお出版.

影山太郎・由本陽子 (1997) 中右実 (編)『日英語比較選書 8: 語形成と概念構造』研究社出版.

国広哲弥 (1999)「日本語動詞の多義体系 (3)」『神奈川大学言語研究』神奈川大学言語研究センター No. 22: 1-12.

小野尚之 (2005)『生成語彙意味論』くろしお出版.

Pinker, S. (1989) *Learnability and Cognition*. Mass: MIT Press.

Pustejovsky, J. (1995) *The Generative Lexicon*. Mass: MIT Press.

辞書・その他

『岩波古語辞典』補訂版 (1974) 大野晋・佐竹昭広・前田金五郎（編）岩波書店.

『広辞苑』第五版 (1998) 新村出（編）岩波書店.

『日本国語大辞典』第十三巻 (1975) 日本大辞典刊行会（編）小学館.

『日本語動詞の結合価』(2003) 付属 CD-ROM. 荻野孝野・小林正博（編）日本システムアプリケーション（監修）三省堂.

『新明解国語辞典』第五版 (1972) 金田一京助他（編）三省堂.

デジタル時代における言語研究

細谷　行輝

　様々な分野にて，アナログからデジタルへの移行が喧伝される昨今，旧来の「象牙の塔」にもデジタルの波が押し寄せている。本来，二進法の物差しでオンかオフか，一かゼロか，といった切り方をするデジタル的思考が，文系の物の考え方には馴染まないとして，なかなか文系に浸透して来なかった背景には，デジタルの本質ならびにその応用の可能性が，文系の多くの研究者の目には，実体として映らなかったことがあろう。

　デジタルの本質は，その「共有」と「再利用」にある。一度作成されたデータは，無限の複製が簡単に実現する特性に鑑み，独りが占有するのではなく，共有して初めて最大の効果が得られるのであるが，言語研究を含む従来の文系研究においては，その質の如何は別として，オリジナリティーが求められ，ある意味で「共有」とは相容れない分野であった。従って，理工系とは異なり，先人の成果を後輩が継承することも，本質的に難しいとされてきた。しかしながら，オリジナリティーとは言っても，当然のことながら真にオリジナルな部分は少なく，その他は，何らかの意味において，先人の成果の賜物である。ただ，先人の成果の受容の方法が，文系の個々人の感性により，多様でありうる点，理工系とは大きく異なっていると言えよう。

　こうした姿勢に基づく言語研究が，自己満足ではなく，他者の評価を受け，他者の思考を何らかの意味において刺激する客観性を有するには，科学的なアプローチが緊要と思われる。すなわち，文系といえども，自己のオリジナルな主張を客観的に受け入れてもらうためには，その主張を裏付

ける根拠を，極力，客観的，科学的に提示する必要があるが，オリジナリティーを標榜するあまり，文系研究者は，従来，この種の努力を怠ってきたのではあるまいか。とするならば，今，文系研究，とりわけ言語研究に，客観性，科学性を導入するには，どういう方法があろうか。筆者は，日本の生んだ優れた言語学者，関口存男（せきぐちつぎお）の意味理論，「意味形態論」を長年研究してきたので，意味論の分野について，以下に論じたいと思う。

　関口存男の意味形態論は，「語感」を真正面から取り扱っているという意味においても特異な意味理論である。従来，「語感」は，主観的として，言語研究の世界では継子扱いされてきた感がある。研究の対象は客観的なものでなければならない，というのが，伝統文法，従来の形式文法の一見正当な理屈である。しかしながら，「語感」にも客観的な側面があること，この点について従来の文法はあまりにも鈍感であった。言語習得の要諦は，詮ずる所，語彙の習得や文法の把捉の重要性はいわずもがな，なによりもまずネイティブの客観的語感を如何に習得するか，にかかっている。たとえば，外国人が，日本語助詞，「は」と「が」の語法上の相違について，100人のネイティブに尋ねた場合，たとえ客観的な説明が不可であっても，感性として，ネイティブの語感を根拠に，この場合は「が」正しい，といった主張をするネイティブが8割程度存在するならば，ここには通底する客観的な語感が存在すると考え，客観的である以上は，言語研究の対象とすることが可能となろう。その他，這般の事情は，ネイティブの語感を有する翻訳者の翻訳結果と，辞書を片手に悪戦苦闘する翻訳結果とを比較すれば一目瞭然であろう。

　意味形態論は，まさしくこの種の客観的な語感を研究対象としており，こうした意味理論を形成するに至った根本的な言語観として，関口は，「意味の世界」と，これに対立する「言語の世界」（意味の世界とは直接の関係を持たない）とを峻別する。本来，「言語の世界」が，「意味の世界」に従うべきところ，「言語の世界」特有の自由気儘な性質により，逆に「言語の世界」が「意味の世界」を規定し始めたために生じて来る第三の世界，これがすなわち「意味形態の世界」であって，意味と言語の間に想定される

「中間の世界」である。「故に意味形態は，意味そのものでもなければ，形態そのものでもない。意味の形態であり，形態の意味です。」(関口存男，ドイツ語学講話，三修社，1975，S.7)

　こうした「中間の世界」を想定しない文法を，素朴文法として関口は斥けるのであるが，斥ける根拠として，無論，意味形態論的観点が導入される。たとえば，ドイツ語 Entwicklung (「発展」) という名詞について，これが可算名詞か不可算名詞か，という問いは無意味である。Entwicklung (「発展」) それ自身は，可算名詞でも不可算名詞でもない。そうではなくて，Entwicklung (「発展」) を可算名詞として取り扱う思惟形式，あるいは，不可算名詞として取り扱う思惟形式が人間の頭脳に存するのみであって，この取り扱いの形式，思惟形式がとりもなおさず意味形態である。つまり，語や意味に固定した考え方が存在するのではなく，あくまでも，中間の世界，意味形態の世界に依拠して，可算名詞にも不可算名詞にもなりうるのである。無論，こうした考え方は独り関口に留まらず，ドイツにおけるヴァレンツ理論の領袖である，M.D. Stepanowa/G.Helbig にも次のように記されている。

> Wortarten ergeben sich nicht mehr unmittelbar und direkt aus der Sachbedeutung der Wörter, sondern aus der verallgemeinerten Bedeutung, wie sie im Prozeß des menschlichen Denkens entsteht. Demnach wären Substantive("Dingwörter") nicht mehr einfach Wörter, die Dinge bezeichnen, sondern Wörter, die vom Denken als "Dinge" oder "Größe" gefaßt und abgebildet werden, Adjektive nicht mehr einfach Wörter, die Eigenschaften bezeichnen, sondern Wörter, die bestimmte Sachverhalte als Eigenschaften fassen bzw. darstellen usw. (Wortarten und das Problem der Valenz in der deutschen Gegenwartssprache. S.45)

> 品詞はもはや語義から直接的に生まれるものではなく，人間の思考過程において成立する一般化された意味から生ずる。これに従えば，名詞(「物」語)は，もはや単に物を表す語ではなく，人間の思考により「物」としてあるいは「一定の大きさ」として捉えられ

写像される語となる．形容詞ももはや単に性質を表す語ではなく，一定の事実関係を性質として捉えないし描写する語となる．

すなわち，名詞に留まらず，言語というものは，考え方，思惟形式，「意味形態」の観点から眺められてはじめて，有意味となる．かつて哲学の世界で，とある対象が，「物」か「事」か，どちらに分類されるべきか，紛糾したことがあるが，これはそもそも観点が間違っていよう．問題の対象そのものは，「物」でもなければ「事」でもない．そうではなくて，問題の対象を物として考える思惟形式，事として考える思惟形式が存するのみである．この意味において，言語を考察するにあたっては，

対象 ⟹ 認識 ⟹ 表現

なる関係を常に意識し，「対象」がどのような「認識」形態，思惟形式に嵌っているか，つまり，最終的な「表現」に至るまでの過程，とくに中間の世界を措定する必要があろう．「Entwicklung」（発展）という語そのものは，可算名詞でも不可算名詞でもない．「対象 ⟹ 認識 ⟹ 表現」という過程の中で可算名詞の「認識形態」（すなわち，「意味形態」）に嵌れば，たとえば，Da habe ich Entwicklungen gemacht.（様々な発展を見た）のように，複数形の表現も可能となる．この種の過程を見ずして意味を云々することぐらい不毛なことはなかろう．

さて，すべての文法，哲学は，こうした意味形態の観点から見直されなければならない，とするのが関口の大胆にして挑戦的な姿勢であるが，こうした結論に至った背景には，言葉に対する関口の超人的な感性と努力があったものと思われる．具体的に関口は，万巻の書を読み，言語研究に有用な様々な言語現象を多角的に捉えてその解明を試みているが，その際，膨大な文例を書き留めている．この文例集は，"Sekiguchi-Collectanea" と呼ばれ，A4判にて88巻，総ページ数24,502ページに及ぶ（なお，この文例集は，関口の長男，関口存哉氏のご好意により，大阪大学にも寄贈されており，筆者は，この文例集をデジタル化して，インターネット上に公開しているので，ご関心の向きは http://www.mle.cmc.osaka-u.ac.jp/hosoya/

にアクセスされたい)。この文例集にて関口が特筆している言語現象は，後輩研究者にも極めて有用と思われるので，目次のみではあるが，これを以下に記載する。

分類番号	分類題目	総頁数	評価
01	名詞 Substantiv	134	B
02	名詞の型 Substantivtypen	233	A1〜A2
03	性と数 Genus und Numerus	645	B〜A2
04	格支配 Rektion	304	A1
05	一格 Nominativ	60	A2〜B
06	二格 Genitiv	366	A1
07	三格 Dativ	205	A2〜B
08	四格 Akkusativ	202	A2〜B
09	Apposition	77	A2
10	不定冠詞 unbestimmter Artikel	306	A1
11	定冠詞 bestimmter Artikel	435	A1
12	物主形容詞 Possesivpronomen	134	A1
13	形容詞 Adjektiv	403	A1
14	形容詞（形態）Adjektiv:Formen	421	A1
15	名詞化 Nominalisierung	165	A2
16	比較 Komparation	477	A1
17	関係代名詞 Relativpronomen	415	A1
18	人代名詞 Personalpronomen	289	A1
19	副詞 Adverb	374	A1〜A2
20	noch,nun,nur,schon,so,und,wieder	379	A1〜A2
21	eben,einmal,erst,gar,immer,ja,je	165	A2
22	denn,doch,aber,auch,da,das	276	A1〜A2
23	間投詞 Interjektion	160	A1
24	接続詞（一般）Konjunktion,allg.	443	A1

分類番号	分類題目	総頁数	評価
25	接続詞（各論）Konjunktionen	680	A2
26	助詞 Hilfswörter	24	A2
27	指示詞 Demonstrativ	659	A1
28	前置詞（一般）Präposition, allg.	205	A1
29	前置詞 Präpositionen	1073	A1
30	数詞 Numerale	336	A1
31	定形 Verbum finitum	327	A1〜A2
32	不定形 Verbum infinitum	611	A1
33	時称（一般）Tempus, allg.	123	A1〜A2
34	時称（各論）Tempora	369	A1
35	述語（主）Prädikat-I	546	A1
36	述語（副）Prädikat-II	128	A2
37	自動と他動 intransitiv und transitiv	91	A2
38	動詞の語形 Verbformen	189	A2
39	疑問文 Fragesatz	272	A1
40	否定 Negation	476	A2
41	再帰動詞 reflexives Verb	259	A2
42	分離動詞 trennbares Verb	134	A2
43	非人称 Impersonalia	276	A1
44	分詞 Partizip	206	A1〜A2
45	受動 Passiv	200	A2
46	助動詞（一般）Hilfsverb, allg.	214	A2
47	助動詞（各論）Hilfsverben	482	A1
48	接続法 Konjunktiv	607	A1
49	迂言動詞 Verba periphrastica: Funktionsverbgefüge	256	A1
50	命令形 Imperativ	100	A2

分類番号	分類題目	総頁数	評価
51	認容文章 Konzessivsatz	172	A2
52	結果挙述 Resultativ,Effektiv	105	A2
53	Aktionsart	252	A1～A2
54	修辞 Rhetorik	382	A2
55	文肢 Satzglied	205	A1
56	文章論一般 Syntax,allg.	210	A2
57	語順 Wortstellung	301	A1
58	主観的 subjektiv	68	A1
59	句読点 Interpunktion	25	B
60	連語 Wörter in Paaren	143	A1
61	省略 Auslassung	267	A1
62	挿入句 Einshub	63	A2
63	発音 Aussprache	213	B
64	英語 Englisch	26	C
65	羅 Latein	151	C
66	雑 Verschiedenes	299	A2
67	σ φ ο δ ρ α Elativität	107	A1
68	合成語 Zusa　　ensetzung	148	A2
69	an	383	A1
70	auf,aus	547	A1
71	B-D	244	A1～A2
72	E-L	236	A1～A2
73	M-T	402	A1～A2
74	U	208	A1
75	von,vor	316	A1～A2
76	W-Z	294	A1
77	A	366	A1

分類番号	分類題目	総頁数	評価
78	B-S	385	A1
79	U-Z	408	A1
80	in	479	A1
81	結果の in "in" des Ergebnisses	76	A1
82	前置の in "in" der Voranstellung	51	A1
83	従事方面の in "in" der Beschäftigung	53	A1
84	特殊前置詞 spezielle Präpositionen	328	A1
85	語形 Wortform	325	B
86	語形 (m)Wortform:m	164	B
87	雑 (1)Verschiedenes-I	29	C
88	雑 (2)Verschiedenes-II	12	A1

　言語研究にとって，生きた文例は不可欠の命脈であるが，関口は微に入り細に入り，意味形態を意識しつつ，重要な例文（約10種の言語からの出典）を書きとめ，上記，24,502ページにも及ぶ文例集となったのである。この目次を見ても分かるように，前置詞には，1073ページと最多のページが割かれているが，これには，前置詞の種類が豊富という理由以外に，意味形態的理由が存在する。前置詞は，冠詞同様，それ自身，意味らしき意味を有せず，意味形態のみを有する。すなわち，文脈，前後関係，シンタクス的制約等により発動される意味用法が前置詞の意味として結実するのである。従って，前置詞や冠詞の研究には，多くの生きた文例が不可欠であり，文例集でも比重が重いのは当然である。前置詞のほか，関口は，冠詞についても多くの記述をものしており，この文例集をもとに，彼の畢生の作とも言うべき「冠詞」（三修社，定冠詞篇：1088頁，不定冠詞篇：616頁，無冠詞篇:656頁）が1960年に上梓された。この「冠詞」は，B5判で，合計2300ページを超える大作であるが，量よりも質について注目すべきであろう。すなわち，「冠詞」の副題に，「意味形態的背景より見た

るドイツ語冠詞の研究」ともあるように，この冠詞論は，従来の冠詞論のような，「形式」を中核に据えた研究ではなく，「意味形態」を背景にした，世界で最も詳しい冠詞論ということができよう。たとえば，語形を持たない無冠詞形について，656 ページも記述した冠詞論がこれまでに存在したであろうか。関口の冠詞は，ドイツ語冠詞について書かれたものではあるが，英語，フランス語，ギリシャ語，ラテン語等々，多様な言語から，多様にして有用，実証的な例文が数多く引用されている。英語界にて，冠詞を論じる著作も多々見られるが，関口のこの「冠詞」に見られる，文例・データを徹底的に重視する言語学的方法論に触れたならば，英語冠詞の記述にも大きな変化がもたらされるものと筆者は確信する。

具体的に英独の両言語を比較すると，英語定冠詞の説明として，

> Unique "The"（唯一 the）：太陽・月・地球などわれわれが経験によって唯一の物と考えている存在物を表す名詞につける定冠詞

との概説が「英語冠詞活用辞典」（金口儀明，大修館，1979 年）に見られるが，この概説が不十分なことは言うまでもなかろう。宇宙には，太陽も月も無数に存在するのであるから，唯一の物と考えるのはそもそも事実に反する。ただし，言語が事実の反映ではなく，認識形態，意味形態の反映と考えるならば，「唯一の物と考えた場合には定冠詞を付する」という説明となり，事実ではなく考え方の問題となる。考え方の問題ならば，「あの銀河系には，一風変わった太陽がある」と表現したい場合，無論，不定冠詞を用いて，紹介導入・説明することになる。つまり，考え方，意味形態に依存して冠詞の用法も異なってくる。

そもそも「定冠詞」の本質は，関口の「冠詞」（定冠詞篇）において，

> 定冠詞の機能は，その次に置かれた名詞の表示する概念が，何等かの意味において既知と前提されてよろしいということを暗示するにある

と規定されている。そしてこの「何等かの意味において既知」という観点を深く掘り下げることにより，定冠詞の意味用法が詳述されているが，英

語の Unique "The"（唯一 the）に関連する機能として,「通念の定冠詞」なる意味形態を創出している。通念とは，一概に取り扱われた概念であり，たとえば「太陽」にもいろいろな「太陽」があって，本来，一概に「太陽」とは言えないが，これを一概に「太陽」という場合には,「太陽に二つはない」との含みがあり，この含みが通念である。事実の如何に拘わらず，一概に取り扱う思惟形式,「通念」なる意味形態に当て嵌めるならば，人間の頭上に存在する，人間にとって説明を要さずして既知存在である太陽を意味することができるのである。

　関口は，万巻の書を読み，多角的な文例を自ら収集し，膨大な文例集を作成して，意味形態的分析研究の要としたのであるが，コーパス・データベースからの生きた有用な文例が利活用可能な現在，ネイティブの語感を客観的に分析する意味形態論が，デジタル時代の言語研究に大きな一石を投ずることを期待してやまない。

エッダ神話詩動詞出現形と作品形式との関係

堀井 祐介

1 はじめに

　本稿では，北欧神話分析の第一次資料の一つである「エッダ詩集（神話詩）」14 作品の動詞について分析し，14 作品の形式によるグループ分類と使用されている動詞出現形 (Entry) との関係について考察する。分析対象とする 14 作品で用いられている動詞総数は，4,097 個である。

<表1>

名称（略語）	動詞数	名称（略語）	動詞数
Völuspá(VSP)	312	Hávamál(HAV)	1056
Vafþrúðnismál(VM)	260	Grímnismál(GRM)	325
Skírnismál(SKM)	221	Hárbarðslióð(HRBL)	271
Hymiskviða(HYM)	174	Lokasenna(LS)	413
Þrymskviða(TRK)	168	Alvíssmál(ALV)	164
Baldrs draumar(BDR)	92	Rígsþúla(RT)	275
Hyndlulióð(HDL)	236	Grottasöngr(GRT)	130

2 エッダ詩集とは

　「エッダ詩集」とは，古西ノルド語で書かれている北欧神話分析の第一次資料とされる韻文作品群である。「エッダ詩集」という名称は，類似の形式，内容をもつ韻文作品に対して用いられる総称であり，個々の作品

の作者は特定されていない。この「エッダ」という名称は，中世北欧を代表する文人であるスノッリ・ストゥルルソンが1220年頃に書いた古西ノルド語韻文入門書『エッダ』から来ている。「エッダ詩集」の作品は主に『王の写本』Codex Regius (GKS 2365 4to) に見られる。この『王の写本』は，17世紀にアイスランドの司教ブリュンヨールヴル・スヴェインソン (Brynjólfur Sveinsson) がアイスランドで発見し，それをデンマーク王フレデリク三世 (Frederik III, 1609-70) に献上したものである。献上の際，スヴェインソンはこの写本を12世紀にアイスランドの有名な賢者セイムンドゥルの作品で，スノッリの『エッダ』に先行する作品であると考えたため，献上する際に 'Edda Sæmundi multiscii 1643' と書いた。そのため『王の写本』はセイムンドのエッダ (Sæmundar-Edda) または古エッダと呼ばれるようになった。しかし「エッダ詩集」に見られる作品はセイムンドゥルの時代よりはるか以前から存在しており，様々な年代にわたって作られているため，『王の写本』がセイムンドゥルの作品であるとは現在では考えられていない。[1]「エッダ詩集」はその内容によって神話詩と英雄詩に分けられる。本稿ではそのうちの神話詩14作品を分析対象とする。

3　分析対象作品紹介

分析対象とする個々の作品について少し紹介しておく。[2]作品名の後に，（　）内に略語とその作品の主たる表現形式（語り，対話，物語）分類を示す。

  Völuspá(VSP)　　　　　＜語り＞
   巫女が世界の創世から滅亡までを語る。
  Hávamál(HAV)　　　　　＜語り＞
   オージン (Óðinn) の格言集およびルーン，呪文について。
  Vafþrúðnismál(VM)　　　　＜対話＞
   オージンが巨人のヴァフスルーズニル (Vafþrúðnir) のもとを訪れ，そこでお互いに世界についての知識を披瀝し，勝負する。バルドル (Baldr) の火葬の際の知識でオージンが勝つ。

Grímnismál(GRM)　　　＜語り＞

オージンとその妻フリッグ (Frigg) がそれぞれのひいきの英雄を自慢し、その後オージンがグリームニル (Grímnir) と名乗り、今は王となっている自分が庇護している英雄のもとを訪ねる。しかし、王はオージンの正体を知らずに縛り上げてしまう。その後、グリームニルが神話的内容を語り始め、王はそれがオージンと気付くが、既に時遅く自らの剣の上に倒れて死んでしまう。

Skírnismál(SKM)　　　＜対話＞

フレイ (Freyr) がオージンの高御座から世界を見渡して、巨人の娘ゲルズ (Gerðr) に恋をしてしまう。そこでフレイの召使のスキールニル (Skírnir) がフレイに代わって求婚に出向き、神々の力を誇示しながら、フレイの求婚を受け入れるように説得する。フレイはその見返りとしてスキールニルに自らの最大の武器である剣を与える。

Hárbarðslióð(HRBL)　　　＜対話＞

ソール (Þórr) が遠征からの帰りに川に差しかかると、そこには渡し守がいてハールバルズ (Hárbarðr) と名乗る。ハールバルズはソールを渡すことを拒む。ソールとハールバルズはお互いの武勇伝、恋の話を披瀝しあう。ハールバルズとは実はオージンの変装した姿である。

Hymiskviða(HYM)　　　＜物語＞

ソールが神々の宴会で使う大きな醸造用の釜を巨人ヒュミル (Hymir) のところに借りに出向く。ソールはそこでミズガルズ蛇をつりあげようとする。最後に、ソールがヒュミルを殺して釜を奪うことになる。

Lokasenna(LS)　　　＜対話＞

神々の宴会の席にロキ (Loki) がやって来て、その場にいる神々の行ないを神々にふさわしくないと罵る。最後にロキは捕まえられて縛り上げられる。

Þrymskviða(TRK)　　　＜物語＞

ソールがハンマーミョッルニル (Miöllnir) を巨人スリュム (Þrymr) に盗まれる。巨人は女神フレイヤ (Freyja) を花嫁に要求する。そこでソールが花嫁に化けて巨人の館に出向き、ハンマーを取り戻す。

Alvíssmál(ALV)　　　＜対話＞

ソールが侏儒アルヴィース (Alvíss) にいろいろと物の呼び方を尋ね，アルヴィースがそれに答える。最後にアルヴィースは太陽光に捕まえられて石になってしまう。

Baldrs draumar(BDR) 　　　　　　＜語り＞

バルドルの不吉な夢を解き明かすためにオージンが地下の国へ出向く。そこで，巫女がバルドルの死について語る。

Rígsþula(RT) 　　　　　　＜物語＞

リーグ (Rígr) と名乗ってヘイムダッル (Heimdallr) が旅をし，立ち寄った先で奴隷，自由農民，王侯の祖先が誕生する。

Hyndlulióð(HDL) 　　　　　　＜語り＞

フレイヤが猪オッタル (Óttar) に乗って女巨人ヒュンドラ (Hyndla) のもとを訪ねる。ヒュンドラはフレイヤの愛人オッタルの家系について語る。

Grottasöngr(GRT) 　　　　　　＜語り＞

グロッティ(Grotti) は夢の臼で，デンマーク王フロージ (Fróði) が持っていた。この臼は富と平和，死と滅亡をひくことができた。王は2人の女巨人フェニャ(Fenia) とメニャ(Menia) に黄金をひかせていた。彼女たちは歌いながらひいていた。王は彼女たちを休ませなかった。彼女たちは怒って，滅亡をひき，最後に臼は壊れる。

これら14作品について，形式による分類をまとめると以下のようになる。

＜表2＞

作品分類	作品略
語り	VSP, HAV, GRM, BDR, HDL, GRT
対話	VM, SKM, HRBL, LS, ALV
物語	HYM, TRK, RT

4 データ分析方法紹介

<データベース画面>[3]

```
ALLEDDA
WORD    bl~ess          ENTRY   bl%asa              PLACE   VSP 46.5.VG
  COMBI         x                   ADVERB  h%att           AUX_MAIN  m
  PHRASE        x
  MEANING       吹く                                M_CATEGORY  1
  FORM:         pres            TENSE   pres        MOOD        ind
  REF_FORM      x               ENCLITIC  x         METER       x
SUBJECT   Heimdallr                                 S_GRM       x
  S_REAL        ヘイムダッル
  S_TYPE    n       S_CATEGORY  gma    S_PERSON  3  S_NUMBER  s
COMPLEMENT    x
  C_REAL        x
  C_TYPE        x               C_CATEGORY  x
OBJECT    horn
  O_REAL    角笛                                    O_TYPE    o
  O_CAT     ong             O_PERSON  3     O_NUMBER  s     O_CASE  ag
TEXT_2    at en<o> galla
TEXT_1    Giallarhorni;
TEXT      h%att *bl~ess Heimdallr,
TEXT1     horn er %a lopti,
TEXT2     m~elir %O¥dinn

レコード: 14  4    1001   ▶ ▶I ▶*  / 15426
```

　本稿では堀井（１９９８）で作成した，Word, Entry, Form, Tense, Meaning など 38 フィールドからなるデータベース（レコード総数 15,426）を用いて分析を行った。このデータベースは，北欧神話研究第一次資料である「エッダ詩集（神話詩）」，「エッダ詩集（英雄詩）」，「ギュルヴィの惑わし」，「ユングリンガ・サガ」の動詞を網羅したものである。以前の研究では，神々，英雄，巨人その他に特徴的な動詞について分析を行ったが，本稿では，このデータベースのフィールドのうち Form（出現形）に注目し，動詞出現形と形式から見た作品区分に関係があるのかについて考えてみたい。

5 数値データ分析

「エッダ詩集（神話詩）」14作品に用いられている動詞のFormデータ一覧は以下の通りである。Formについて，inf（不定詞形），pres（現在形），pret（過去形），pres.p（現在分詞形），past.pp（過去分詞形受身），past.ps（過去分詞形完了），imp（命令形），conj1（接続法現在形），conj2（接続法過去形）の9つに分類した。

<表3>

	動詞総数	inf 個数	%	pres 個数	%	pret 個数	%	pres.p 個数	%	past.ps 個数	%
14作品全体	4097	646	15.77%	1641	40.05%	1051	25.65%	35	0.85%	121	2.95%
VSP	312	43	13.78%	130	41.67%	109	34.94%	4	1.28%	13	4.17%
HAV	1056	179	16.95%	581	55.02%	85	8.05%	18	1.70%	30	2.84%
VM	260	26	10.00%	113	43.46%	55	21.15%	0	0.00%	5	1.92%
GRM	325	41	12.62%	150	46.15%	88	27.08%	1	0.31%	12	3.69%
SKM	221	49	22.17%	88	39.82%	33	14.93%	0	0.00%	4	1.81%
HRBL	271	58	21.40%	86	31.73%	79	29.15%	0	0.00%	5	1.85%
HYM	174	26	14.94%	32	18.39%	91	52.30%	2	1.15%	6	3.45%
LS	413	63	15.25%	148	35.84%	112	27.12%	1	0.24%	18	4.36%
TRK	168	28	16.67%	41	24.40%	67	39.88%	2	1.19%	6	3.57%
ALV	164	17	10.37%	103	62.80%	4	2.44%	2	1.22%	5	3.05%
BDR	92	17	18.48%	35	38.04%	23	25.00%	1	1.09%	2	2.17%
RT	275	57	20.73%	10	3.64%	191	69.45%	1	0.36%	2	0.73%
HDL	236	25	10.59%	93	39.41%	68	28.81%	2	0.85%	5	2.12%
GRT	130	17	13.08%	31	23.85%	46	35.38%	1	0.77%	8	6.15%

	動詞総数	pastpp 個数	%	imp 個数	%	conj1 個数	%	conj2 個数	%
14作品全体	4097	139	3.39%	139	3.39%	238	5.81%	87	2.12%
VSP	312	11	3.53%	0	0.00%	1	0.32%	1	0.32%
HAV	1056	29	2.75%	17	1.61%	105	9.94%	12	1.14%
VM	260	9	3.46%	20	7.69%	28	10.77%	4	1.54%
GRM	325	16	4.92%	3	0.92%	9	2.77%	5	1.54%
SKM	221	6	2.71%	13	5.88%	26	11.76%	2	0.90%
HRBL	271	1	0.37%	10	3.69%	12	4.43%	20	7.38%
HYM	174	2	1.15%	5	2.87%	3	1.72%	7	4.02%
LS	413	13	3.15%	25	6.05%	15	3.63%	18	4.36%
TRK	168	3	1.79%	11	6.55%	3	1.79%	7	4.17%
ALV	164	5	3.05%	13	7.93%	15	9.15%	0	0.00%
BDR	92	6	6.52%	6	6.52%	1	1.09%	1	1.09%
RT	275	11	4.00%	0	0.00%	1	0.36%	2	0.73%
HDL	236	18	7.63%	11	4.66%	12	5.08%	2	0.85%
GRT	130	9	6.92%	5	3.85%	7	5.38%	6	4.62%

エッダ神話詩動詞出現形と作品形式との関係　　　535

　これらのうち，pres.p，past.pp，past.ps，imp，conj1，conj2 については，＜表3＞からもわかるように作品によっては出現数が0または1というものがあり，数値データから特徴を見出すことが困難と考えられるため本稿では，inf，pres，pret の3つの出現形について分析，考察を行うものとする。そこで，Form の数値データ（inf，pres，pret）を，上記作品紹介で分類したグループごとに並べ替えると以下のようになる。

<表4>

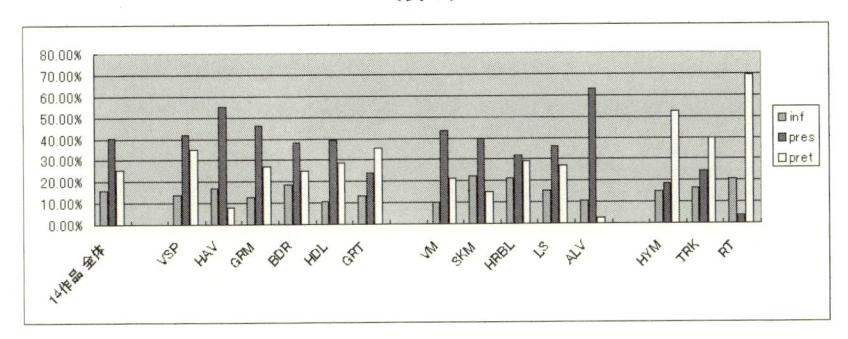

<表5>

		inf			pres			pret			動詞総数
		個数	%	順位	個数	%	順位	個数	%	順位	
	14作品全体	646	15.77%		1641	40.05%		1051	25.65%		4097
語り	VSP	43	13.78%	9	130	41.67%	5	109	34.94%	5	312
語り	HAV	179	16.95%	5	581	55.02%	2	85	8.05%	13	1056
語り	GRM	41	12.62%	11	150	46.15%	3	88	27.08%	9	325
語り	BDR	17	18.48%	4	35	38.04%	8	23	25.00%	10	92
語り	HDL	25	10.59%	12	93	39.41%	7	68	28.81%	7	236
語り	GRT	17	13.08%	10	31	23.85%	12	46	35.38%	4	130
対話	VM	26	10.00%	14	113	43.46%	4	55	21.15%	11	260
対話	SKM	49	22.17%	1	88	39.82%	6	33	14.93%	12	221
対話	HRBL	58	21.40%	2	86	31.73%	10	79	29.15%	6	271
対話	LS	63	15.25%	7	148	35.84%	9	112	27.12%	8	413
対話	ALV	17	10.37%	13	103	62.80%	1	4	2.44%	14	164
物語	HYM	26	14.94%	8	32	18.39%	13	91	52.30%	2	174
物語	TRK	28	16.67%	6	41	24.40%	11	67	39.88%	3	168
物語	RT	57	20.73%	3	10	3.64%	14	191	69.45%	1	275

5.1 出現形別分析

　infについて見てみると，1位のSKM(22.17%)から14位のVM(10.00%)までの比較的狭い範囲(12.17ポイント)に収まっており，infの出現比率は作品間で大きな差が無いことがわかる。一方presは1位のALV(62.80%)から14位のRT(3.64%)との間には非常に大きな差(59.16ポイント)がある。RTを特殊例と考えても，13位のHYM(18.39%)との間でさえ44.41ポイントもの差になる。またpretについても1位のRT(69.45%)と14位のALV(2.44%)との間には67.01ポイントという大きな差がある。こちらについてもRTとALVを特殊例と考えても2位のHYM(52.30%)と13位のHAV(8.05%)との間には44.25ポイントもの差がある。ただ，pres, pretについては，HAV, ALV, HYM, RTを特殊例として除いて考えると，上下の差はpresで3位のGRM(46.15%)，12位のGRT(23.85%)の間の22.3ポイント，pretでは，3位のTRK(39.88%)，12位のSKM(14.93%)の間の24.95ポイントとなる。ちなみに，RTの数値はpres, pretの両方で平均値より標準偏差2個分の外側に位置し，HAV, ALV, HYMの数値もそれぞれ平均値よりpres, pretの両方で平均値より標準偏差1個分の外側に位置している。なお，inf, pres, pretそれぞれの相関を調べてみると以下のようになり，presとpretの間には強い相関関係があることがわかる。

<表6>

inf/pres

	inf	pres
inf	1	
pres	-0.42642	1

<表7>

pres/pret

	pres	pret
pres	1	
pret	-0.93766	1

<表8>

inf/pret

	inf	pret
inf	1	
pret	-0.259022	1

5.2　作品グループ別分析

上記＜表5＞を見ると，「物語」グループとされる HYM，TRK，RT では pret が高く，pres が低いことがわかる。pret の順位で見ても，上記3作品が上位3位までを占めている。一方，pres についてはその逆で下位4位までにこの3作品が入っている。これら3つの「物語」形式作品では，いわゆる地の文と呼ばれる部分で「した」と訳される表現が多いことは作品を読めばわかるが，そのことが動詞出現形に過去形が多いことからも確認できる。しかし，「物語」以外の「語り」，「対話」についてはグループとして inf，pres，pret 出現比率で際立った特長は見られない。「語り」，「対話」における pres，pret の比率には，一部の作品 (HAV，ALV) を除いて特に大きな差異は見られない。

＜表9＞

inf		pres		pret	
		RT	3.64%	ALV	2.44%
				HAV	8.05%
VM	10.00%	HYM	18.39%	SKM	14.93%
ALV	10.37%				
HDL	10.59%	GRT	23.85%	VM	21.15%
GRM	12.62%	TRK	24.40%	BDR	25.00%
GRT	13.08%			GRM	27.08%
VSP	13.78%	HRBL	31.73%	LS	27.12%
HYM	14.94%	LS	35.84%	HDL	28.81%
LS	15.25%	BDR	38.04%	HRBL	29.15%
TRK	16.67%	HDL	39.41%		
HAV	16.95%	SKM	39.82%	VSP	34.94%
BDR	18.48%			GRT	35.38%
		VSP	41.67%	TRK	39.88%
		VM	43.46%		
RT	20.73%	GRM	46.15%		
HRBL	21.40%				
SKM	22.17%	HAV	55.02%	HYM	52.30%
		ALV	62.80%	RT	69.45%

<表10>

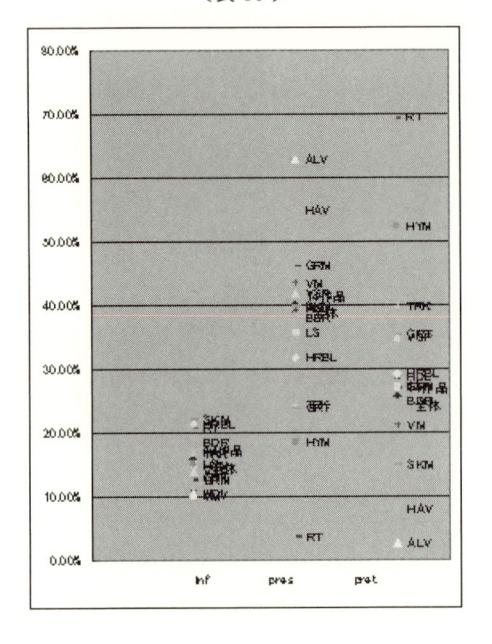

5.3 個別作品分析

　＜表9＞、＜表10＞からわかるように、数値データが突出している個別の作品について調べてみると、HAV, ALV, HYM, RT については、その属しているグループ内だけでなく、全体との比較においても pres または pret の比率が非常に高くなっている。HYM, RT については既にグループ別の分析のところで触れた。HAV は全部で164節からなる作品であり、格言詩、忠告詩、ルーンを含む呪文が全体の9割以上の148節となっており、残りの16節がオージンの女巨人とのかかわりについてのエピソードとなっている。[4] 格言、忠告、呪文は、時代、時間に関係なく適用可能なものであり、pret の出現比率が低いことは当然と考えられる。ALV は先にも述べたが、ソールと侏儒アルヴィースとの対話形式でいろいろなものの呼び方が紹介される作品であり、対話の行われている時間に「そう呼ばれて

いる」という表現が多用されているため，pret が少ないものと思われる。

6 まとめ

今回は，「エッダ詩集（神話詩）」動詞データベースの Form（出現形）に注目し，個別作品形式と出現形における inf, pres, pret 比率の関係について考えてみた。pres と pret の相関関係が高いことが確認でき，「物語」形式の 3 作品 (HYM，TRK，RT) での pret 出現率が他に比べて高いこともわかった。しかし，inf の比率，「語り」，「対話」形式作品グループにおいては，それぞれ際立った特徴は見出せなかった。また，個別の作品については，HAV，ALV については他の作品に比べて pres の比率が高く，pret の比率が低いことがはっきりとわかった。これらのことから，作品の形式（「語り」，「対話」，「物語」）と動詞の出現形との関係は一部には見られるものの，全般的に当てはまる規則はないことが明らかになったと思われる。動詞の出現形については，むしろ，HAV，ALV に見られるように個々の作品の内容により規定される部分が多いのではないだろうか。本稿では十分明らかにすることは出来なかったが，今後，動詞データベースの修正，改良と共に，個々の作品の内容，動詞の用いられている場面などを考慮し，一部統計的手法も取り入れる形で，動詞出現形をはじめとするデータベースフィールド毎の分析を進めていき，動詞の形態からわかる動詞用法の特徴を明らかにしていきたい。

注

1　Kulturhistorisk Leksikon for nordisk middelalder fra vikingetid til reformationstid III, p.480, Jónas 1988, pp.25-33
2　谷口 1973，松谷 1986 より
3　WORD(Word): 単語（分析対象の動詞），ENTRY(Entry): 見出し語（WORD を辞書でひく場合の形），PLACE(Place): WORD のテキストでの出現場所，COMB(Comb): WORD と他の動詞との結びつき，ADVERB(Adverb): 副詞，PHRASE(Phrase): WORD が文法上の目的語や，複合語などと結びついて一つの意味を作っている場合のセットフレーズ，MEANING(Meaning): WORD の意味，M_CATEGORY(M_Cat): WORD の意味のカテゴリー，FORM(Form): WORD

のテキスト中での出現形，TENSE(Tense): WORD の時制，MOOD(Mood): WORD の法，REF_ FORM(Reflex): WORD が形態上再帰形の場合の分類，AUX_ MAIN(A/M): WORD が助動詞なのか本動詞なのか，ENCLITIC(Enclitic): WORD の接辞，METER(Meter): 韻律，SUBJECT(Subject): 主語（意味上の主語），S_REAL(S_Real): 主語の実体，S_TYPE(S_Type): 主語のタイプ，S_CATEGORY(S_Cat): 主語のカテゴリー，S_PERSON(S_Person): 主語の人称（文法上），S_NUMBER(S_Num): 主語の数（文法上），S_GRM(S_Grm): WORD が意味上の主語を主格でとらない場合，COMPLEMENT(Complement): 補語，C_REAL(C_Real): 補語の実体，C_TYPE(C_Type): 補語のタイプ，C_CATEGORY(C_Cat): 補語のカテゴリー，OBJECT(Object): 目的語（Phrase における目的語，文法上の目的語），O_REAL(O_Real): 目的語の実体，O_TYPE(O_Type): 目的語のタイプ，O_CATEGORY(O_Cat): 目的語のカテゴリー，O_PERSON(O_Person): 目的語の人称，O_NUMBER(O_Num): 目的語の数，O_CASE(O_Case): 目的語の格，TEXT_2(Text-2): WORD が出現するテキスト（2行前），TEXT_1(Text-1): WORD が出現するテキスト（1行前），TEXT(Text): WORD が出現するテキスト，TEXT1(Text+1): WORD が出現するテキスト（1行後），TEXT2(Text+2): WORD が出現するテキスト（2行後）

4　Evans 1986 p.8.

参考文献

Evans, David A. H. (ed.) (1986) *Hávamál*. London: Viking Society for Northern Research.

Helgason, Jón (udg.) (1971) *Eddadigte I. Völuspá, Hávamál*. København: Ejnar Munksgaard.

Helgason, Jón (udg.) (1971) *Eddadigte II. Gudedigte*. København: Ejnar Munksgaard.

Jacobsen, Lis; Danstrup, John (ed.) *Kulturhistorisk Leksikon for nordisk middelalder fra vikingetid til reformationstid I-XXII*. København: Rosenkilde og Bagger.

Kristjánsson, Jónas (author); Foote, Peter (tr.) (1988) *Eddas and Sagas.Icelandic Medieval Literature*. Reykjavík: Hið íslenska bókmenntafélag.

菅原邦城 (1984) 『北欧神話』. 東京. 東京書籍.

シーグルズル・ノルダル著 菅原邦城訳 (1993) 『巫女の予言. エッダ詩校訂本』. 東京. 東海大学出版会.

谷口幸男訳 (1973) 『エッダ－古代北欧歌謡集』. 東京. 新潮社.

堀井祐介 (1998) 「神々の動詞, 英雄の動詞 －北欧神話データベースの分析－」

松谷健二訳 (1986) 『エッダ／グレティルのサガ』. 中世文学集 III. 東京. 筑摩書房.

日本の友人今井光規氏の折々の印象

モーンス・マグヌッソン
堀井　祐介訳

1　はじめに

　一年以上も前にこの記念論文集の編者である渡部眞一郎教授から非常に鄭重な寄稿の依頼を受けたとき，私はすぐに快諾した。というのは，今井教授と私は，亡き妻インガーと私だけでなく，私たちの家族，友人たちにとっても心から信頼している良き友人として，長年にわたる親交があるからである。25年以上にわたって光規とその妻安美と友人であり続けられた幸せを感じた上で，私が光規に対して抱いている大いなる好意を表現できる機会を得たことは，非常に光栄であり，感謝に堪えない。一年以上先の締切に向けて，私は日本の友人への気持ちを簡潔に表す俳句を作ろうと考えた。もしインガーが生きていたら，俳句を作るなどということが如何に愚かな考えであるか，即座に指摘してくれたであろう。あれから一年後の今，ごく当然のように，またいつものことながら，私は彼女の考えが今回も正しかったことを認めざるを得ない。俳句を作ることは諦めて，面白くない形ではあるが，型にはまった文章で光規のことを，今や半世紀以上にわたる交流の経験と印象に基づいて報告書の形で書くことにした。この形式は，多くのデンマークの自然科学研究者（私の長い人生の一部が属していたカテゴリー）が，観察や考察を記述するときに，昔から使ってきたものである。

1.1　序説

　インガーと私が今井光規・安美夫妻と知り合い，その後友人となった経緯は以下の通りである。1973 年，結核および結核撲滅国際連合の国際学会総会が東京で開催され，それに続く形で，放線菌分類学会の国際ワーキンググループの会合が広島で開催された。私は学会の会員として，そしてインガーは随員として，東京での総会と広島での会合に参加した。日本人参加者の一人に中村敏子教授夫人がいた。彼女はたびたびインガーと話す機会があり，中村夫人の友人が安美だったのである。正確な時期は覚えていないが，光規が 1978 年のある時期にデンマーク人とデンマーク語で文通したいと希望したとき，中村夫人がインガー（と私）の住所を教え，1979 年 1 月 13 日に光規が初めてインガーと私に手紙を送ってきた。この一通の手紙が，この後述べるように，その後の数多くの手紙につながるものとなった。

2　資料と調査方法

　私の書庫に，最初は光規とインガーとの間で，そして 1991 年 3 月 17 日にインガーが亡くなってからは，私との間で取り交わした手紙が保管されている。その書庫には，一部の例外を除いて，インガーから光規への手紙のコピーは無い。光規と渡部教授が 2004 年に私に送ってくれた二編の研究発表の原稿を見ると，言語と文学のこれら二人の日本人研究者が論文の中で部分的に統計の手法を取り入れていることが分かる。そこで私も，この原稿を書くに当たって手紙の集計を基にすることにしたいと思う。3 人が係わった文通の数は付録に示した通りである。
　最初の数年間，文通は，ときには航空便，ときには航空書簡の交換であった。1998 年 8 月から 1999 年 9 月の間は，一部はファックスで行われた。私の手許に残る光規からのファックスは残念ながら，今では劣化して読めなくなってしまっている。しかし，完全ではないが，そこに書かれていることについてのメモは残っている。2002 年 6 月から，ほとんどの文

通がメールとなった。しかし，とくにクリスマス時期には手紙の交換もある。光規からの通信のほぼ全てが，わかりやすい，きれいなデンマーク語で書かれている。インガーは，いつもデンマーク語で書いていた。ときおり，光規がインガーに自分の語彙選択や彼女の語法について説明を求めることもあった。あるときインガーは，自分は文法を意識してデンマーク語を書いているのではないと答え，当時コペンハーゲン大学でデンマーク語を学んでいた一番下の娘マリアンネに光規からの質問を回わさなければならないこともあった。光規はときどき一定期間デンマーク語を読んだり書いたりしないとデンマーク語を忘れると嘆いていた。しかし，光規のデンマーク語で意味が分かりにくいと感じることは一度もなかった。それには非常に感心させられた。

　1980年，光規は当地コペンハーゲンでデンマーク語の夏季コースを受講することになった。インガーと私はそのとき初めて光規と会った。その後，年を重ねるとともに，光規がたびたびコペンハーゲンを訪問するようになり，文通ではなく直接会う機会が増えた。

　光規が初めて私たちの家を訪問したとき以来，インガーが出した食事のことが詳しく記述されているゲストブックが残っている。インガーは1969年から1990年までのゲストブックを保存していた。なぜゲストブックを保存するようになったかというと，あるアメリカ人の友人がかなりの期間を隔てて二度私たちの家を訪問したことがあるのだが，二度目の訪問の後，彼らはインガーが前回と全く同じ料理を出したと微笑みながら語ったことがあるからである。他の数多くの能力に加えて，数多くのおいしい料理を作れる優れた主婦であるインガーは，そんなことは夢にも考えなかった。だから，彼女は二度とそのようなヘマを繰り返さないようにゲストを迎えるたびに，どんな料理を作ったか，どんなテーブルクロス，どんな花を用意したか，ゲストの座った場所はどうだったか，などを詳細にゲストブックに書き記すことにしたのである。付録2に光規が私たちの家を訪問した際にインガーがゲストブックに何を記したかを再掲している。光規は私たちの家をたびたび訪問したが，私たちは他のいろいろな場所でも何度も会っている。

私はもう一つ別の場所に私たちが一緒に遠足や美術館巡りに出かけたときに撮った写真を100枚以上も保存している。それらの写真には，光規，インガー，私の娘メッテ，私，そしてときには，その他の人も写っている。私たちは一緒にデンマークの史跡や文化財を見て歩いた。たとえば，ヘルシングェアのクロンボー城（写真1参照），ヒラロズのフレデリクスボー城，ムン島のファネフィヨルド教会の見事な古い壁画，スレーエルサ近郊のトレレボー，ブロベックムッラ（今でも動いている風車），南スウェーデンのようなライアの5000年前のウムの石造古墳（写真2参照，www.megalitgrav.dk）など。私たちは一緒に多くのデンマークの美術館も訪れた。ルイシアナ（安美と一緒に何度も）アーケン，ソフィエホルム，カーレン・ブリクセン美術館（ルングステッドルンド，2回）などである。遠足では，2002年にメッテが私からハンドルを奪うまで，運転手はいつも私だった。というのは，私の視力と反応力が低下し，メッテが何度も運転をやめるように忠告してくれたため，その年ついに，私は免許の更新をあきらめたのだった。
　最初の遠足のときからすでに，光規はインガーを空港の管制塔にたとえていた。管制塔は，私が運転手を務めていたころの遠足では，いつも確実に目的地に着くよう誘導してくれていた。メッテが運転手になり，私が管制塔へ配置換えになってからは，管制塔はしばしば間違った指示を出した。しかし，メッテはきちんと管制塔からの指示を無視し，私たちはいつも確実に，しかも早く目的地に到着した。
　私たちはたびたび遠足や美術館巡りに出かけたが，そのような折には，たいてい何らかの形で一緒に食事をとった。こんなときの食事は，正式な文化活動の形になっているとは言えなかったとしても，いつも楽しいものだった。写真3はコペンハーゲンのエコロジーレストランでのそのような食事の一コマである。
　私たちはしばしばすばらしいレストランで食事をとった。光規がホスト役をつとめたこともたびたびあったが，そのようなときに彼は非常に気品のある振る舞いをした。しかし私たちはときには，もっと慎ましやかな場所で会うこともあった。例えば，渡部教授と光規が，北欧での学術会議出

席の途中で立ち寄ったコペンハーゲン空港では，空港内のレストランで三人が落ち合い，デンマークビールを堪能した。

3　調査結果

　インガーと私はデンマーク側から文通を続けていたが，付録表でわかるように，私たちは光規の勤勉さには及ばなかった。インガーが最初の手書きの手紙を光規からもらった後，しばらく文通は途絶えた。光規が再開したとき，彼はタイプライターでデンマーク語を打ちたいと考え，デンマーク文字æ, ø, åが打てる特別の機種を買った。しかし彼が購入した最初の機種では，後に購入した機種に比べてæの文字が小さすぎるように思えた。しばらく試行錯誤の後，彼はようやく満足できる機種を手に入れた。

　付録表にあるように，光規は1982年と1985年にカセットテープを2巻と何冊かのデンマーク語のテキストを送ってきて，デンマーク語の発音がどのように聞こえるかを確認するために，インガーにテープに吹き込むように依頼した。テープを受け取ったとき，私たちの持っていた機械では使えなかったため，私たちは新しい機械を購入し，インガーがテキストを吹き込み，光規に返した。光規はすぐに受け取ったことを返信して来た。テープに録音されたデンマーク語の神秘的な発音を彼女の生の声で聴けて大変興味深かったと書いていた。

　1998年から99年にかけては，文通の一部はファックスで行われた。ファックスは通常の航空便よりも非常に早いコミュニケーションの手段であった。ファックスはたいていの場合，光規からの急ぎの依頼であった。彼が自分で書いたデンマーク語の文章のネイティブ・チェックの依頼だった。2002年になると，主にメールでやり取りするようになり，私たちのコミュニケーションはさらに便利になった。

　毎年クリスマス，新年の挨拶，カレンダー交換などの際には，通常の手紙によるやりとりが続いている。日本のカレンダーには，いつも日本の庭，花，風景，またある年には伝統的な日本の模様の非常にきれいな写真がついていた。私たちが選んで送ったデンマークのカレンダーには，光規が訪

問したときに目にした風物，私たちが知っている風景や名所，またはデンマークの高名な画家の複製画などの写真がついていた。長年にわたるカレンダーの交換で，私の手許にある日本のカレンダーは，それだけでまもなく第三の置き場所を用意しなければならないほどの量となった。このような第三の書庫は，私の二人の娘たちがきっとありがたく思うことだろう。というのは，これら以外では，残念ながら，私が長い人生で集めてきた非常に多くの紙の束などは体系的に整理されていないからである。

　これまでの光規の多くのコペンハーゲン訪問の積み重ねで，私たちは多くの日本からの贈り物を貰った。ここでは，その中の一つにだけに言及したいと思う。それは，美しい日本の装飾がついた磁器のティーカップである。私はそれを20年以上前に貰ってから今日まで毎日使っている。今では，14,000回以上の紅茶，コーヒーをこのカップで飲んだことになる。このカップについている飾りは今でもきれいなままである。インガーがかつて光規にプレゼントしたり，買い物の際にアドバイスを与えたものの中に，デンマークのラクリスと3種類のデンマークチーズ（ダンネブロ，カステロ，サガブルー）がある。光規はそのラクリスを当時9才か10才だった彼の息子に与えたが，その子はそれを口に入れた途端に，悪魔の食べ物だと叫んだ。光規がラクリスとチョコレートを間違えたのは幸運とは言えなかった。インガーは光規にセロファンで包んだラクリス飴を日本に持って帰らせた。光規はインガーがケーキのデコレーションにチョコレートとして使ったのはこれだと思い込んで，袋の中身をケーキの飾りに使うように安美に頼んだ。何も知らない息子は，気の毒なことに，再びこの誤解の被害者となった。デンマークチーズについてはもう少しましな話がある。というのは，光規が手紙に書いてきたことだが，デンマークチーズのうち安美が好んだのはカステロだけだったが，光規には上に述べた三つのチーズはどれもすべて味はもとより名前の由来に至るまで，あらゆる面で食指を刺激するものだったようである。

　光規とゼンフア・ヤンという私の教え子の中国人が私たちの家を訪問したときの思い出は，ヤンがナプキンに中国の古い文字を書いたときのことである。光規はその文字の意味を一生懸命に考えたのだが，二人の間で結

局意見は一致しなかった。私の覚えている限り，一方は詩だといい，もう一方は料理の名前だろうといった。残念ながら，私たちはそのナプキンを書庫には残していない。仮に残っていたとしても，私たちは中国語の文字も日本語の文字についても，また中国語も日本語についてもまったく知識が無いため，わが家の誰も審判役は出来ない。したがって，そのとき書かれた漢字の謎は決して明らかにされることはないのである。中国語や日本語の文字にはいろいろな意味があるのだろうが，私たちのラテンアルファベットには（残念ながら，たとえそれらが集まって語や文となっていても）それ単独では意味を持たない。

さらに，私たちがデンマークでは自宅や質素な飲み屋ででも，魚を食べるのにフォークを2本使うことに光規は，一度ならず驚いた。

これまでに述べた楽しい話の他に，私が非常に感動した話をしなければならない。それは，インガーが亡くなった直後に光規と安美が訪問してくれたときと，最近改めて訪問してくれたときに，インガーのお墓に花を手向けてくれたことである。そのことに私は感激し，今でも心に残っている。

3.1 考察

光規が25年以上にわたりデンマーク語学習に関心を持ち続けたことにより，私だけでなく，私の家族，私の友人たちにも，非常に多くの好印象と予期せぬ体験や，私がこの原稿を通してだけでは決して表現できない感銘を与えてくれたことには感慨深いものがある。

4 結論

私は，残念ながら，自分が選んだこの表現方法が本論の目的にはふさわしくなかったことを認めなければならない。なぜなら，この表現方法はまとまりが無く，表面的で不完全であり，体系的でないと感じているからである。やはり俳句で表現すればよかった。

謝辞

この原稿を最終的な形に仕上げる際に，最大限の優しさでもって手伝ってくれたわが娘マリアンネに謝意を表したい。

付録表

カテゴリー	回数			
	光規から		光規へ	
	1979-91	1992-2007	1979-91	1992-2007
手紙	31	22	16	14
葉書	-	4	-	-
航空書簡	2	-	-	-
ファックス	-	6	-	5
カセットテープ	2	-	2	-
E メール	-	40	-	27
電話	6	8	3	5

付録2　インガーのゲストブックからの抜粋

以下の文は，インガーのゲストブックに記されていたものである：

光規は，1980年の8月15日にわが家に初めて訪ねてきた。インガーは，フランスパン，マッシュルームとクレーム・フレッシュ，鰈のソテー，アーモンドとホイップクリームの入った煮果物を出した。1981年9月には，ニシンのソテー，ミートローフ，シナモンリンゴを食べた。このなかに，「エトルリア」もある。同じ年の11月27日，中華人民共和国のゼンフア・ヤン，チェング・ドゥと一緒に初めてスウェーデンのクッレンに行った。同じ日，インガーは自宅で，メレンゲの上に乗った東洋風の香辛料のかかったヒレ肉煮プルーン，ホイップクリームを出した。クリスマスの日（12月25日），光規とゼンフア・ヤンは他の客と一緒にわが家を訪問，インガーは，盛大なクリスマスランチを出した：光りニシン，マスタードニシン，カレーニシン，白チーズとニシンのサラダ，レバーペースト，ピクルス，ニンニク油サラミ，グレープ，エビ，バナナのサラダ，アスパラガス入りエビサラダ，にんじんサラダ，サーモン，ブラウンキャベツ添えハム，チーズパン。1983年4月24日，私たちは今井教授とお別れパーティーをした。今井光規，ゼンフア・ヤンの他に，今井と私たちの共通の友人ユッテ＆ニー

ルス・クルーセ，私の義理の弟と妹（ペータとイェニー），私たちの娘メッテが同席。インガーは，冷やしたアスパラガスとマッシュルームを添えた鱒，チーズソースのサーロインステーキ，グリーンサラダ，フランス豆，新じゃが，アプリコットののったラウケーア，アイスクリーム，チョコレートのかかったアーモンドを出した。飲み物は，魚料理には白ワイン，牛肉には赤ワイン，デザートにはポートワインまたはシェリー酒であった。

写真説明

写真は本文参照。

#1. 1987年7月。光規，インガー，メッテ，モーンスがクロンボー城の前できちんと整列。

#2. 1995年10月。ライア近くの5000年前のウムの石造古墳に入っていくところ。

#3. 1991年5月。光規，メッテ，モーンス，ペータ，イェニー（私の義理の弟と妹）がニューハウンのキャップホーンレストランにて。

今井光規教授略歴

今井光規（いまい・みつのり）

1938 年 12 月 4 日，岡山県生まれ。

学歴

1957 年 3 月	岡山県立西大寺高等学校卒業
1957 年 4 月	神戸大学文学部文学科入学
1962 年 3 月	神戸大学文学部文学科英米文学専攻卒業
1968 年 3 月	大阪大学大学院文学研究科博士課程英語学専攻単位取得退学

学位等

1965 年 3 月	文学修士［大阪大学］
2005 年 6 月	博士（比較社会文化）［九州大学］

職歴等

1966 年 4 月	大阪経済大学助手
1968 年 4 月	大阪経済大学講師
1969 年 3 月	広島大学教養部講師
1970 年 10 月	広島大学教養部助教授
1974 年 6 月	広島大学総合科学部助教授
1982-1983 年	コペンハーゲン大学留学
1985 年 10 月	大阪大学言語文化部助教授

1986-1987 年	アメリカ合衆国アラバマ州立大学ハンツヴィル校客員助教授
1988 年 5 月	大阪大学言語文化部教授
1989 年 4 月	大阪大学大学院言語文化研究科担当（応用言語技術）
1989 年 4 月	大阪大学大学院文学研究科担当
1994 年 4 月	大阪大学評議員
1995 年 4 月	大阪大学大学院言語文化研究科応用言語技術講座兼任教授
1997 年 4 月	大阪大学言語文化部長
2002 年 3 月	大阪大学定年退職
2002 年 4 月	大阪大学名誉教授
2002 年 4 月	摂南大学国際言語文化学部教授
2003 年 4 月	摂南大学国際言語文化学部長
2005 年 4 月	摂南大学外国語学部長
2007 年 10 月	摂南大学学長

非常勤講師歴

神戸大学文学部，広島女学院大学文学部，安田女子大学文学部，神戸松蔭女子大学文学部，京都大学総合人間学部，大阪教育大学大学院，龍谷大学大学院，岡山大学教育学部，熊本大学文学部等において非常勤講師（集中講義を含む）を務める。

学会活動

西日本言語学会，広島大学英文学会，日本英文学会（大会準備委員会委員 1997-1999 年度），日本英語学会（評議員 1995-2006 年度），近代英語協会，日本文体論学会，英語コーパス学会（運営委員 1993 年-；会長 2001-2003 年度），日本中世英語英文学会（評議員 1994-2004 年度；編集委員 1995-1998 年度；西支部長 1995-1996 年度；副会長 2001-2002 年度；会長 2003-2004 年度），Nordic Association for English Studies, International Association of University Professors of English などに所属。

今井光規教授研究業績
（2008 年 9 月 30 日現在）

編著書

1988	*A Concordance to Middle English Metrical Romance*, Vol. I. The Matter of England. Vol. II. The Breton Lays. Frankfurt am Main: Peter Lang.（共編）
2000	*Reading the Ancrene Riwle: Proceedings of the International Symposium Held on 25 January, 1997 at Osaka University.* Faculty of Language and Culture, Osaka University.（共編）
2008	『ことばの響き ― 英語フィロロジーと言語学 ―』（三浦常司教授記念論文集）(*Words at Heart: Papers in Linguistics and English Philology*) 開文社出版（共編著）
近刊	『イギリス・フランスの中世ロマンス ― 語学的研究と文学的研究の壁を越えて』音羽書房鶴見書店（共著）

論文

1965	「*Beowulf* に見られる Nominal Compounds について」*Osaka Literary Review* (大阪大学大学院英文学談話会) 3, pp. 1-15.
1968	"Subjunctive Mood in Thomas Nashe" 大阪経大学会『大阪経大論集』63, pp. 117-51.
1968	「Thomas Deloney に於ける接続法」*Cassiopeia* 1, pp. 19-27.
1969	「must と have to 及びそれらの否定形について」*Cassiopeia* 2, pp. 36-41.

1969	「Thomas Nashe に於ける動詞副詞結合覚え書き」(1) *Cassiopeia* 3, pp. 1-7.
1970	「Thomas Nashe に於ける動詞副詞結合覚え書き」(2) *Cassiopeia* 4, pp. 27-32.
1971	「Thomas Nashe に於ける動詞副詞結合覚え書き」(3) *Cassiopeia* 5, pp. 21-27.
1979	「１７世紀の英語散文の統語法と文体」 広島大学総合科学部『言語文化研究』4, pp. 55-77.
1980	「「接続詞＋分詞」型構文再考」『毛利可信教授退官記念論文集』(柴原出版) pp. 55-70.
1980	"'Conjunction + Participle' Reconsidered" 大学英語教育学会『紀要』11, pp. 21-34.
1984	「*Havelok the Dane*: 写本と版本」広島大学総合科学部『言語文化研究』9, pp. 103-123.
1984	「デンマーク語の呼応について ― 英語との比較 ―」 西日本言語学会 *NIDABA* 13, pp. 1-6.
1985	「*Havelok the Dane* における thorn と th について」 西日本言語学会 *NIDABA* 14, pp. 21-25.
1986	「中世英国のオルフェウス物語について」広島女学院大学『英文学会会報』30, pp. 31-40.
1988	「中英語韻文ロマンスのコンコーダンス編纂について」 大阪大学言語文化部『言語文化研究』14, pp. 33-53. (共著)
1989	"Rhyme Indices to *King Horn*" 大阪大学言語文化部『言語文化研究』15, pp. 127-146. (共著)
1990	"A Rhyme Index to *Sir Launfal*" 大阪大学言語文化部『言語文化研究』16. pp. 253-267. (共著)
1992	「中英語韻文ロマンスのコンコーダンス編纂計画とその現状」英潮社『英語英文学研究とコンピュータ』pp. 249-272. (共著)

1993	「パソコンを使って用例カードを作る：エリザベス朝英語散文の分詞の研究に向けて」『近代英語の諸相』英潮社 pp. 224-234.
1995	"Textual Transmission of *Sir Orfeo*" 大阪大学言語文化部『言語文化研究』pp. 77-96.
1996	「ME ロマンスのメリズム ― *Havelok the Dane* の場合 ―」『言語と文化の諸相』英宝社 pp. 3-14.
1996	"Merisms in *Havelok the Dane*," *Proceedings from the Sixth Nordic Conference for English Studies, Tromsø, May 25-28, 1995*, University of Tromsø. Vol. 2, pp. 327-336.
1997	「コーパス言語学」『言語文化学概論』大阪大学出版会 pp. 165-174.
2002	「『アセルストン』の決まり文句」大阪大学言語文化部『言語文化研究』28, pp. 1-18.
2002	「中世英国韻文ロマンスにおける反復」『大阪大学言語文化共同研究プロジェクト 2001』pp. 1-11.
2003	"Syntax and Style in some Middle English metrical romances with special reference to the displacement of syntactic components," *Proceedings from the 8th Nordic Conference on English Studies* (Gothenburg Studies in English 84) (Göteborg: Acta Universitatis Gothoburgensis), pp. 47-58.
2004	"Repetition in Middle English Metrical Romances" in Risto Hiltunen and Shinichiro Watanabe (eds.), *Approaches to Style and Discourse in English* (Suita: Osaka University Press), pp. 27-50.
2005	「中世英国韻文ロマンスにおける反復について」*Studies in Medieval English Language and Literature* 20, pp. 1-16.
2005	"Catalogue and Repetition in *The Squyr of Lowe Degre*" in J. Fijiak (ed.), *Recent Trends in Medieval English Language and Literature in Honour of Youg-Bae Park* (Seoul), 1, pp. 133-46.

2005	"Syntax and Style in Middle English Metrical Romances"（博士学位論文, 九州大学）未出版
2006	「中世英国韻文ロマンスにおける事物列挙」 田島松二編『ことばの楽しみ ― 東西の文化を越えて』南雲堂, pp. 77-90.
2007	"Enumeration in Middle English Metrical Romance" in Tanaka, Shishido, and Uematsu (eds.), *22 Essays in English Studies: Language, Literature, and Education.* Tokyo: Shohakusha, pp. 3-17.
2008	"How a line begins in Middle English metrical romances"『ことばの響き ― 英語フィロロジーと言語学 ― 』（三浦常司教授記念論文集） 開文社出版, pp. 137-154.
2008	"Food and Feasts in Middle English Romance," *Setsunan Journal of English Education* 2, pp. 53-69.
2008	「『マディソン郡の橋』と中世ロマンス」 田島松二・末松信子編『英語史研究ノート』開文社出版, pp. 29-34.

翻訳

1976	I. A. ゴードン著『英語散文の発達』研究社（共訳）
1981	ボー/ ケイブル著『英語史』研究社（共訳）
1981	M. ボウルトン著『小説とは何か－英米作家を中心に－』英宝社（共訳）
1983	『中世英国ロマンス集』第1集 篠崎書林（共訳）
1985	「K・ケスター：「ハヴェロック物語論」」 広島大学英文学会『英語英文学研究』29, pp. 59-69. (A Japanese translation, with a brief introduction, of "Oplysninger om Havelok-Sagnet" in Kristian Køster's *Sagnet om Havelok Danske* (Copenhagen, 1868)
1986	『中世英国ロマンス集』第2集 篠崎書林（共訳）
1993	『中世英国ロマンス集』第3集 篠崎書林（共訳）
2001	『中世英国ロマンス集』第4集 篠崎書林（共訳）

書評

1989   "W. R. J. Barron: *English Medieval Romance*" 日本英文学会『英文学研究』66, 1, pp. 116-120.

1990   "Kinshiro Oshitari *et al*.: *Philologia Anglica: Essays Presented to Professor Yoshio Terasawa on the Occasion of His Sixtieth Birthday*," *Studies in English Literature* (English Number) 日本英文学会, pp. 169-177（共著）

教科書編纂

1978   Marjorie Boulton: *The Anatomy of Language* 成美堂（原著 Routledge & Kegan Paul, 1959）（共編注）

1978   Charles Barber: *The Story of English* 英宝社（原著 Pan Books, 1964, 1972）（共編注）

1978   *E. M. Forster on Music, Painting, and Literature* あぽろん社（共編注）

1983   Marjorie Boulton: *The Anatomy of Literary Studies* 英宝社（原著 Routledge & Kegan Paul, 1980）（共編注）

1989   Philip S. Jennings: *Medieval Legends* 英宝社（原著 St. Martin's Press, New York, 1983）（共編注）

科学研究費研究成果報告書

1990 年 3 月   『コンピュータによる中世英国韻文ロマンスのコンコーダンス編纂』（一般研究 (C) 研究成果報告書）大阪大学言語文化部（共著）（研究分担者）

1992 年 3 月   『コンピュータによる中世英国韻文ロマンスのコンコーダンス編纂』（一般研究 (C) 研究成果報告書）大阪大学言語文化部（共著）（研究分担者）

1994 年 3 月	『コンピュータによる中世英国韻文ロマンスのコンコーダンス編纂』（一般研究 (C) 研究成果報告書）大阪大学言語文化部（共著）（研究分担者）
1993 年 3 月	『コンピュータによる初期近代英語の分詞構文の研究』（平成 3～4 年度一般研究 (C) 研究成果報告書）大阪大学言語文化部（研究代表者）
1995 年 3 月	『コンピュータによる初期近代英語の分詞構文の研究』（平成 5～6 年度一般研究 (C) 研究成果報告書）大阪大学言語文化部（研究代表者）
1997 年 3 月	"Computer-Assisted Study of Early Modern English"（平成 8 年度大学間協力研究研究成果報告書）Osaka University（共著）（研究代表者）
2000 年 3 月	"Computer-Assisted Study of Early Modern English"（平成 9～11 年度科学研究費補助金，大学間協力研究研究成果報告書）Osaka University（共著）（研究代表者）
2001 年 3 月	『中世英国韻文ロマンスの表現特性』（平成 9～12 年度基盤研究 (C)(2) 研究成果報告書）大阪大学言語文化部（研究代表者）
2005 年 3 月	『コンピュータを利用した英語文体論の通史的総合研究』（平成 13～16 年度基盤研究 (B)(2) 研究成果報告書）大阪大学言語文化部（研究分担者）
2007 年 3 月	『中世英国韻文ロマンスの表現特性』（平成 15～18 年度基盤研究 (C) 研究成果報告書）摂南大学外国語学部（研究代表者）
2009 年 3 月 予定	『中世英国韻文ロマンスの表現特性』（平成 19～20 年度基盤研究 (C) 研究成果報告書）摂南大学外国語学部（研究代表者）

コンコーダンス編纂（プリントアウト版）

1986年3月 *Osaka University Concordances to Middle English Metrical Romances*, Vols. 1-4. 大阪大学言語文化部（共編）

1986年8月 *Osaka University Concordances to Middle English Metrical Romances*, Vols. 5-11. 大阪大学言語文化部（共編）

1988年3月 *Osaka University Concordances to Middle English Metrical Romances*, Vols. 12-19. 大阪大学言語文化部（共編）

1990年3月 *Osaka University Concordances to Middle English Metrical Romances*, Vols. 20-29. 大阪大学言語文化部（共編）

1991年3月 *Osaka University Concordances to Middle English Metrical Romances*, Vols. 30-36. 大阪大学言語文化部（共編）

1994年3月 *Osaka University Concordances to Middle English Metrical Romances*, Vols. 37-40. 大阪大学言語文化部（共編）

口頭発表・講演等

1978年5月 「１７世紀の英語散文の統語法と文体」日本英文学会第５０回大会（西南大学）シンポジウム

1985年5月 「中世英国のオルフェウス物語について」広島女学院大学英文学会講演会

1988年11月 「MEロマンスの対照表現について」日本英語学会第6回大会（青山学院大学）シンポジウム

1990年5月 「パソコンを使って用例カードを作る」近代英語協会第7回大会（就実女子大学）シンポジウム

1994年5月 「中世英国ロマンス：「ブレトン・レイ」の世界」日本英語学会第６６回大会（熊本大学）シンポジウム（司会）

1995年5月 "Merisms in *Havelok the Dane*", The Sixth Nordic Conference for English Studies, University of Tromsø, Norway.

1995年6月 「コーパス言語学の現状と可能性」日本中世英語英文学会西支部例会（帝塚山大学短期大学部）（講演）

1998年1月	「コーパス言語学の現状と課題」名古屋大学文学部（大学院高度化推進）（講演）
1998年1月	「大阪大学言語文化部および大学院言語文化研究科の現状と課題」（九州大学言語文化部会議室）（講演）
2001年5月	"Syntax and Style in Some Middle English Metrical Romances, with Special Reference to the Displacement of Syntactic Components," The Eighth Nordic Conference for English Studies (University of Göteborg, Sweden)
2004年5月	"How a Line Begins in Middle English Metrical Romances," Ninth Nordic Conference for English Studies (University of Aarhus, Denmark)
2004年11月	「コーパス言語学とは何か ── その意義と利用法」（安田女子大学英語英米文学科）（講演）
2006年3月	"Enumeration in Middle English Metrical Romances," Romance in Medieval England 10th Biennial Conference (University of York, UK)
2006年5月	「中世ロマンス─文学的研究と語学的研究の壁を越えて」日本英文学会第78回大会（中京大学）第5部門シンポジウム（司会）
2007年5月	"Food and Feasts in Middle English Romance," Tenth Nordic Conference for English Studies (University of Bergen, Norway)

その他

1982年	「ロマンスを求めて」 広島大学『学内通信』220, pp. 8-9.
1988年	「遥かなるテネシー川のほとり ── アラバマ大学体験雑録」大阪大学『言文だより』5, pp. 33-36.
1993年	"Osaka-Copenhagen Exchange Agreement Now in Effect" 大阪大学『言文だより』(*Newsletter*) 10, pp. 6-8.

1995 年	「NAES 学会のこと」菊池清明・市川雅雄・田尻雅士編 *SENTENTIAE*（『水鳥喜喬教授還暦記念論文集』）北斗書房 pp. 81-87.
1998 年	「はじめに」,「沿革と理念・目的」,「課題と展望」『現状と課題』大阪大学言語文化部, pp. 1-2, 160-166.
1999 年	「外国語教育とインターネット」大阪大学情報処理教育センター『廣報』16, pp. 4-8.
1999 年	「言語文化部の現状と課題」『大阪大学言語文化部２５年・大学院言語文化研究科 10 年「歩み」』大阪大学言語文化部 pp. 1, 71-74.
1999 年	「『ハヴェロック』― 中英語ロマンスに見るイギリスとデンマーク」（大阪大学コペンハーゲン間学術交流協定締結記念シンポジウム）大阪大学言語文化部・大学院言語文化研究科『言文だより』16, pp. 10-11.
2001 年	「外部評価報告書」名古屋大学言語文化部・大学院国際言語文化研究科 自己評価・外部評価報告書『未来へのプロフィール』3, pp. 115-121.（外部評価委員会委員長として）
2001 年	「私のＣＡＬＬ英語授業 ― 去年と今年」大阪大学サイバーメディアセンター『サイバーメディア・フォーラム』2, pp. 47-49.

あとがき

　本書は長年日本における英語史・英語学の分野で貢献された今井光規教授の古希をお祝いする論文集です。デンマーク，フィンランド，スェーデンの北欧3カ国，スコットランド，ウェールズ，韓国の世界的に著名な学者9名と日本中世英語英文学会や英語コーパス学会等において第一線で活躍されている25名による英語史研究・英語コーパス研究の分野を中心とする最新の研究成果を収めた論文集となっています。

　今井先生は北欧と日本の交流にも貢献されています。今井先生は若い頃からデンマークをこよなく愛され，今までに20回以上もデンマークを訪問しておられます。デンマーク語にも精通されていますが，これは独学だけでなく，ご寄稿者のマグヌッソン博士の亡くなられた奥様から長い間デンマーク語の個人教授を受けて本格的に勉強されました。その一途な気持ちというのは今井先生を思う時に，一番強く感じます。今井先生はいろんな役職を担われてきましたが，いつも一途に，そして誠実に任務に取り組まれました。それは生来の人柄の良さというもので，今井先生のように優れた学者でありながら，ひじょうに尊敬できる人物というのはそんなに多くはいないのではないでしょうか。今井先生の古希をお祝いする論文集に日本だけでなく，北欧を中心にいろんな国の多くの方々から寄稿していただき，さらにデンマーク大使から序文をいただきましたことは，この記念論文集を企画した者として最上の喜びであり，今井先生の偉大さを改めて知った思いがいたします。

　この記念論文集の刊行は，TEX/LATEX の組版を担当していただいた大阪大学のサイバーメディアセンターの山本厚子さんの献身的な協力に負うと

ころがひじょうに大きく，心より感謝いたしたいと思います。また，マグヌッソン博士のデンマーク語によるご寄稿を日本語に翻訳していただいた堀井祐介教授のご尽力に対して感謝申し上げます。最後に，この企画をご快諾くださった松柏社の森信久社長にも心よりお礼申し上げます。

平成 21 年 3 月 10 日

　　　　　　　　　　　　　　　　　　編集者　渡部眞一郎　細谷行輝

CONTRIBUTORS 執筆者一覧（執筆順）

Contributors from abroad:

Karin Aijmer
Professor Emerita, University of Gothenburg, Sweden

Graham D. Caie
Professor of English Language and Vice-Principal, University of Glasgow, UK

Dorrit Einersen
Associate Professor of English, University of Copenhagen, Denmark

Risto Hiltunen
Professor of English, University of Turku, Finland

Maldwyn Mills
Professor Emeritus, University of Wales, Aberystwyth, UK

Young-Bae Park
Professor of English, Kookmin University, Korea

Päivi Pietilä
Professor of English, University of Turku, Finland

Matti Rissanen
Professor Emeritus, University of Helsinki, Finland

Arne Zettersten
Professor Emeritus, University of Copenhagen, Denmark

Mogens Magnusson
Former Head, Tuberculin Department, Statens Seruminstitut, Denmark

Contributors from Japan:

家入葉子　(Yoko Iyeiri)
京都大学大学院文学研究科准教授 (Associate Professor at the Graduate School of Letters, Kyoto University)

地村彰之　(Akiyuki Jimura)
広島大学大学院文学研究科教授 (Professor at the Graduate School of Letters, Hiroshima University)

小杉世　(Sei Kosugi)
大阪大学大学院言語文化研究科准教授 (Associate Professor at the Graduate School of Language and Culture, Osaka University)

中村純作　(Junsaku Nakamura)
立命館大学大学院言語教育情報研究科教授 (Professor at the Graduate School of Language Education and Information Science, Ritsumeikan University)

田畑智司　(Tomoji Tabata)
大阪大学大学院言語文化研究科准教授 (Associate Professor at the Graduate School of Language and Culture, Osaka University)

高橋薫　(Kaoru Takahashi)
豊田工業高等専門学校一般学科教授 (Professor at General Department, Toyota National College of Technology)

渡部眞一郎　(Shinichiro Watanabe)
大阪大学大学院言語文化研究科教授 (Professor at the Graduate School of Language and Culture, Osaka University)

吉川史子　(Fumiko Yoshikawa)
広島修道大学商学部准教授 (Associate Professor at the Faculty of Commercial Sciences, Hiroshima Shudo University)

宇賀治正朋　(Masatomo Ukaji)
東京学芸大学名誉教授 (Professor Emeritus, Tokyo Gakugei University)

内田充美　(Mitsumi Uchida)
大阪府立大学人間社会学部准教授 (Associate Professor at the School of Humanities and Social Sciences, Osaka Prefecture University)

大津智彦　(Norihiko Otsu)
大阪大学大学院言語文化研究科准教授 (Associate Professor at the Graduate School of Language and Culture, Osaka University)

尾崎久男　(Hisao Osaki)
大阪大学大学院言語文化研究科准教授 (Associate Professor at the Graduate School of Language and Culture, Osaka University)

菊池清明　(Kiyoaki Kikuchi)
立教大学文学部教授 (Professor at the School of Literature, Rikkyo University)

小塚良孝　(Yoshitaka Kozuka)
愛知教育大学教育学部講師 (Lecturer at the Faculty of Education, Aichi University of Education)

田島松二　(Matsuji Tajima)
九州大学名誉教授 (Professor Emeritus, Kyushu University)

谷 明信　(Akinobu Tani)
兵庫教育大学大学院学校教育研究科准教授 (Associate Professor at the Graduate School of Education, Hyogo University of Teacher Education)

中尾佳行　(Yoshiyuki Nakao)
広島大学大学院教育学研究科教授 (Professor at the Graduate School of Education, Hiroshima University)

西村秀夫　(Hideo Nishimura)
姫路獨協大学外国語学部教授 (Professor at the Faculty of Foreign Studies, Himeji Dokkyo University)

吉岡治郎　(Jiro Yoshioka)
神戸海星女子学院大学名誉教授 (Professor Emeritus, Kobe Kaisei College)

渡辺秀樹　　(Hideki Watanabe)
大阪大学大学院言語文化研究科教授 (Professor at the Graduate School of Language and Culture, Osaka University)

今井安美　　(Yasumi Imai)
龍谷大学非常勤講師 (Part-time Lecturer, Ryukoku University)

大森文子　　(Ayako Omori)
大阪大学大学院言語文化研究科准教授 (Associate Professor at the Graduate School of Language and Culture, Osaka University)

板東美智子　　(Michiko Bando)
滋賀大学教育学部准教授 (Associate Professor at the Faculty of Education, Shiga University)

細谷行輝　　(Yukiteru Hosoya)
大阪大学サイバーメディアセンター教授 (Professor at Cyber Media Center, Osaka University)

堀井祐介　　(Yusuke Horii)
金沢大学大学教育開発・支援センター教授 (Professor at Research Center for Higher Education, Kanazawa University)

English Philology and Corpus Studies:
A Festschrift in Honour of Mitsunori Imai
to Celebrate His Seventieth Birthday

英語フィロロジーとコーパス研究

今井光規教授古希記念論文集

編者　渡部眞一郎／細谷行輝

Copyright © 2009 by Shinichiro Watanabe and Yukiteru Hosoya

2009年 6月1日　初版発行

発行者　森 信久
発行所　株式会社 松柏社
〒102-0072　東京都千代田区飯田橋1-6-1
TEL. 03-3230-4813（代表）　FAX. 03-3230-4857

装幀　熊澤正人＋熊谷美智子（パワーハウス）
印刷・製本　モリモト印刷株式会社

ISBN978-4-7754-0157-6
定価はカバーに表示してあります。
本書を無断で複写・複製することを固く禁じます。
落丁・乱丁本は送料小社負担にてお取り替えいたしますので、ご返送ください。

Printed in Japan